CITYGUIDE
ATLANTA

FODOR'S TRAVEL PUBLICATIONS

NEW YORK • TORONTO • LONDON • SYDNEY • AUCKLAND

WWW.FODORS.COM

A   B   C   D

1

Rydal
Halls Station
Waleska
CHEROKEE
COUNTY
Keithsburg
White
Cement
PINE LOG
MOUNTAIN
WILDLIFE
MANAGEMENT
AREA
Cassville
McCallie
Oakland
Heights
Canton
Buffington
Etowah R.
Kingston
Sutallee

2

Laffingal
Etowah R.
BARTOW
COUNTY
Cherokee
Hickory
Flat
Euharlee
Cartersville
Allatoona Dam
LAKE
ALLATOONA
MANAGED
HUNTING
AREA
Cherokee
Mill
Holly Springs
RED TOP
MOUNTAIN
STATE PARK
Eutaw
Mounds
Lake
Allatoona
Andersonville
Stilesboro
Emerson
Allatoona
Payne
Oak Grove
Little R.
Woodstock
Taylorsville

3

POLK
COUNTY
N
Acworth
Black Wells
Noonday
Huntsville
Kennesaw
Sandy
Plains
Roxana
Braswell
PICKETT'S
MILL STATE
HISTORIC SITE
Red Rock
KENNESAW MTN.
NATIONAL
BATTLEFIELD
Westoak
Mount Bethel
Due West
Marietta
Chattahoochee
Plantation

4

Hamlin
McPherson
Lost
Mountain
COBB
COUNTY
Fair
Oaks
PAULDING
COUNTY
Dallas
Macland
Smyrna
Vinings
Hiram
Powder
Springs
Gilmore
Nickajack
Mableton
Nebo
Clarkdale
Sweetwater Cr.

5

New Georgia
Brownsville
Austell
Oakdale
Lithia
Springs
DOUGLAS
Douglasville
Beulah
Six Flags
Adamsville
Temple
Villa
Rica
Winston
Midway
SWEETWATER
CREEK
STATE PARK
Stratford
Fort
McPherson

6

COUNTY
Chapel Hill
Ben Hill
CARROLL
COUNTY
Bill Arp
College
Park
Sand Hill
Phillips Mill
Campbellton
Tell
Fairplay
FULTON
COUNTY
Hulett
McWorter
Union City
Stonewall
Riverdale
Hannah
Rico
Fairburn

7

Cross Plains
Palmetto
Kenwood
Clem
Banning Mills
Lees Mill
Wansley
Roscoe
Tyrone
Smiths
Crossroad
Whitesburg
COWETA
COUNTY
McCollum
Major
Fayetteville

8

Sargent
Arnco Mills
Gloverton
Madras
Thomas
Crossroad
Fischer's
Crossroad
Shake Rag
Harp
Welcome
White Oak
Longstreet
Peachtree
City
FAYETTE
COUNTY
Newnan
Handy
East Newnan
Powers
Crossroads
Stephens
Crossroad
Oaklawn
Sharpsburg
Raymond
Gordon
Turin
Senoia
Starrs Mill

E F G H

Ball Ground • | Hightower • | • Matt | 19 400 | • Chestatee | Gainesville •
Gober • | | • Heardville | • Coal Mountain | 306 |
| | Ducktown • | | Chicopee • | 13 | 985
Orange • | 372 | 20 | Lake | Oakwood • | | 1
20 • | | Drew • Cumming • | 19 | Sidney Lanier | HALL
White City • | Free Home • | | | | COUNTY

Batesville • | FORSYTH | Flowery Branch • | Chestnut Mountain • | 53
• Birmingham | COUNTY | 20 | Buford Dam | 13 | 2
140 | • Big Creek | 141 | Sugar Hill | Rest Haven • | Roberts Cross Road •
Arnold • | | | Buford • | | 85
• Crabapple | | Level Creek • | Carrolls Crossing • |
Mountain Park | 400 | | 985 |
Alpharetta • | 19 | FULTON | Suwanee • | Hog Mountain • | BARROW COUNTY
Roswell • | 141 | COUNTY | 13 | 20 | Auburn • | 3
Chattahoochee National Recreation Area | | Duluth • | 23 | 8 | Dacula •
9 | | Berkeley Lake • | 316 | 29 | Apalachee R.
Sandy Springs • | Dunwoody • | Norcross • | Murphyville • | Lawrenceville • | Harbin •
| | Bethesda • | GWINNETT COUNTY | Alcovy R. |
285 | Doraville • | 85 | 29 8 | Grayson • | Bold Springs • | 4
19 | Cross Keys • | Mercer University | Lilburn • | 124 | 20 | 78
Chamblee • | Atlanta Baptist College | Five Forks • | Snellville • | Loganville •
Buckhead • | Oglethorpe University | Tucker • | 78 | Split Silk • | 81 | Between •
| | STONE MOUNTAIN | Centerville • | Lenora • | Youth •
85 | Scottsdale • | Stone Mountain • | MEMORIAL PARK | Caleb • | WALTON COUNTY | 138 | 5
78 8 | Emory University | 285 | DEKALB COUNTY | Bermuda • | • Norris Lake | Walnut Grove •
State Capitol | Decatur • | Redan • | Rock Chapel • | 138 |
Atlanta | 20 | 155 | 273 12 | Lake Capri • | 20 |
75 85 | Panthersville • | Wesley Chapel • | Collinsville • | Yellow R. | • Hi Roc Shores
75 | Hapeville • | Snapfinger • | Pine Mountain • | Milstead • | Georgetown • | 81 | 6
Henrico • | Panola • | ARCADIA MOUNTAIN PARK | Conyers • | Dialtown •
Hartsfield International Airport | Forest Park • | Scarborough Cross Roads • | South R. | ROCKDALE COUNTY | • Oxford
Lake City • | | Swan Lake • | 162 | Covington • | 278 12
Morrow • | | 155 | Pace • | Porterdale •
CLAYTON COUNTY | 675 | Stockbridge • | Whitehouse • | NEWTON COUNTY | Starrsville • | 7
Jonesboro • | 75 | 23 | Indian Cr. | Kelleytown • | Oak Hill • | 81
54 | 138 | 42 | HENRY COUNTY | 20 | Snapping Shoals • | 36
Bonanza • | Flippen • | 155 | Leadmore • | Yellow R. | Alcovy R.
Lovejoy • | Blacksville • | McDonough • | Ola • | 81 | Stewart •
| 19 | 81 | 23 | • Fincherville | Alcovy Shores •
Inman • | 41 3 | Greenwood • | 42 | Worthville • | Jackson Lake | 8
Woolsey • | Hampton • | 75 | Locust Grove • | BUTTS COUNTY
SPALDING COUNTY | Sunnyside • | Luella • | 155 | 23 42 | • Stark
Lowery | | | Jenkinsburg • | Lloyd Shoals Dam

A B C D

1

Pleasant Rd.
Reinhardt College Pkwy.
Fincher Dr.
Fincher Rd.
Friendship Rd.
Ammons Rd.
Land Rd.
Burris Crossroads
Hornage Rd.
Hornage Rd.

Reinhardt College

Lower Burris Rd.
Smith Rd.
Lower Bethany Rd.
Long Rd.
Cherokee County Airport

Waleska

140

2

Cable Rd.
John Cline Ln.
Sardis Cr.
Sardis Rd.
Worley Rd.
Fate Conn Rd.
Heard Rd.
Bishop Rd.
24

Little Refuge Rd.
108
Darby Rd.

Ball Ground Hwy.

Fincher Rd.
Sam Nelson Rd.
Puckett Cr. Rd.
Lower Burris Rd.
Keithsburg

Amos Rd.

CHEROKEE
COUNTY
Honeydew Dr.
140
Pea Ridge
Waleska Rd.
Vanover Rd.
575

3

Rampley Tr.
North Canton
Elmwood St.
713
20

Canton

Riverstone Pkwy.

Etowah R.
BOILING PARK
Main St.
CANTON COUNTRY CLUB
19
Cumming Hwy.
20
BUF

4

U.S. ARMY CORPS OF ENGINEERS
Marietta Rd.
17
140
Eppers on

Boat Ramp
Knox Hwy.
20
Knox Hwy.
16
Scott Rd.
Avery Rd.

Brick Mill Rd.

5

Boat Ramp
FIELDS LANDING PARK
BARNETT PARK
Butterworth Rd.
205
Univeter Rd.
575
Univeter
Univeter Rd.
Hickory Flat Hwy.

Fields Landing
Bells Ferry Rd.
ASKEW PARK
14
Gray Rd.
Shiloh Rd.

Allatoona Lake
Ridge Rd.
Keeter Rd.
Main St.
Stringer Rd.

6

Sixes
Holly St.
Holly Springs
Hickory St.
Hickory Rd.
HICKORY ROAD PARK

Steel Bridge Dr.
Bells Ferry Rd.
Cherokee
Sixes Rd.
Marble Quarry Rd.
Canton Hwy.
754
Main St.
Old Magnolia Wy.
Morgan Rd.
Hickory Flat Rd.
Ranchwood Ter.
E Cherokee Dr.
Waters Rd.

Little River Landing

U.S. ARMY CORPS OF ENGINEERS
11
Lebanon
Toonigh Rd.
Blalock Rd.
Holly Springs Rd S

7

EAGLE WATCH GOLF COURSE
Rope Mill Rd.
Andersonville
Mill Creek Rd.
Tripp Rd.
Arnold Mill Rd.

Rose Creek Dr.
575
Canton Rd.

Putnam Ferry Rd.
P. Eagle Dr.
Lake Pkwy.
Putnam Ford Rd.
Arnold Mill Rd.
Arnold Mill Rd.
Barnes Rd.
SETTING D CREEK GOL

8

Bascomb Carmel Rd.
8
W Mill St.
Woodstock
Dupree Rd.
Trickum Rd.
Ragsdale Rd.
Wylie Bridge Rd.

Bells Ferry Rd.
Alabama Rd.
7
754
92
Alabama Rd.

STREETFINDER

NORTHWEST SUBURBS: CHEROKEE COUNTY

A · B · C · D

1
2
3
4
5
6
7
8

Old Federal Rd.
Nicholson Rd.
Westray Rd.
Elmo Rd.
Mockingbird Rd.
Concord Rd.
Mount Tabor Rd.
Whitmre Rd.
Matt Hwy.
Hightower
Bannister Rd.
N. Wallace Rd.
Riley Rd.
Oak Grove
Oa
Matt
Matt Hwy. (369)
(369)
WallaceTatum Rd.
Wright Bridge Rd.
Burnt Bridge Rd.
Dr. Bramblett Rd.
John Burrus Rd.
H. Martin Dr.
Matt Hwy
Pooles Mill Rd.
Hurt
Bridge Rd.
Hendricks Rd.
Heardville Cir.
Heardville
Pisgah Rd.
Holbrook Rd.
Karr Rd.
Gravitt Rd.
Frix Rd.
Pleasant Grove Rd.
McCoy Cir.
Twin Lakes Rd.
Spot Rd.
Mountain Rd.
Franklin Goldmine Rd.
Heardville Rd.
Sewell Rd.
Watson Rd.
Aaron Sosobee Rd.
FORSYTH COUNTY
Bettis Tribble Gap Rd.
Dunn Rd.
Dahlonega Hwy.
Ducktown
Canton Hwy.
Friendship Cir.
(20)
Sawnee Dr.
Pirkle Woods
County Line Rd.
Howard Rd.
Hyde Rd.
Post Rd.
Aaron Sosobee Rd.
Bethelview Rd.
Chamblee Gap Rd.
Greenacres Dr.
Pine Lake Dr.
Canton Rd.
(9)
Pilgrim Mill Rd.
Drew
Drew Rd.
Drew Campground Rd.
Kelly Mill Rd.
Kelly Mill Rd.
Cumming
(20)
Bald
Ridge
Turnel
MIDWAY PARK
Atlanta Rd.
Mary Alice
Bentley Rd.
Pittman Rd.
Mountain Hollow
Old Buford Rd.
Campground Rd.
Bethelview Rd.
Castleberry
Hutchison Rd.
Buford
POLO FIELDS COUNTRY CLUB
Piney Grove Rd.
Sanders Rd.
14
Nuckols
Longstreet Lively Rd.
Wilts Rd.
Post Rd.
Majors Rd.
Turner MacDonald Pkwy.
Haw Creek Rd.
Buford Hwy.
Rogers Rd.
Castleberry Rd.
Atlanta Hwy.
Pedley Rd.
(9)
13
Daves Creek Rd.
Trammel Rd.
Hamby Rd.
Brannigan Rd.
(141)
Old Atlanta Rd.
Daves Creek Dr.
Francis Cir.
Mullinax Rd.
Fowler Rd.
Francis Rd.
Windy Hill Dr.
Majors Rd.
Gilbert Rd.
Alpharetta Rd.
Shiloh Rd.
(19)
(400)
Peachtree Pkwy.
Trammel Rd.
UnionHill Rd.
James Hill Rd.
McFarland Rd.
Stoney Point Rd.
Clements Rd.
Sharon Rd.
Nichols Dr.
(9)
Tidwell Rd.
Union Hill Rd.
Shiloh Rd.
Big Creek
Hemrick Rd.
Nichols Rd.
James Burgess
Bethany Rd.
12
Turner McDonald Pkwy.
Bagley Rd.
Caney Rd.
Mathis Airport Rd.
Old Atlanta Rd.
Settles Rd.
Morris Rd.
Webb
McGinnis Ferry Rd.
Old Alpharetta Rd.
Mathis Air Park
Southers Cir.
Windward Union Hill Rd.
Windward Pkwy.
McGinnis Ferry Rd.
Brookwood
Brookwood Rd.
Laurel Springs Rd.
11
Lake Windward
Douglas Rd.
Jones Bridge Rd.
Peachtree Pkwy.
Webb Bridge Rd.
FULTON COUNTY
(141)

15

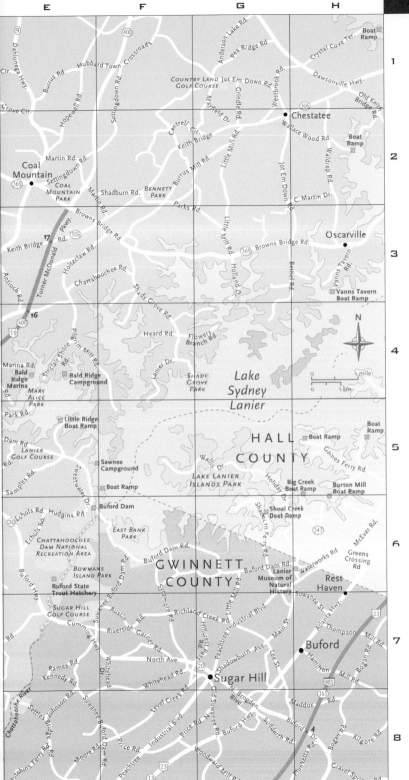

NORTHEAST SUBURBS: FORSYTH COUNTY AND LAKE LANIER

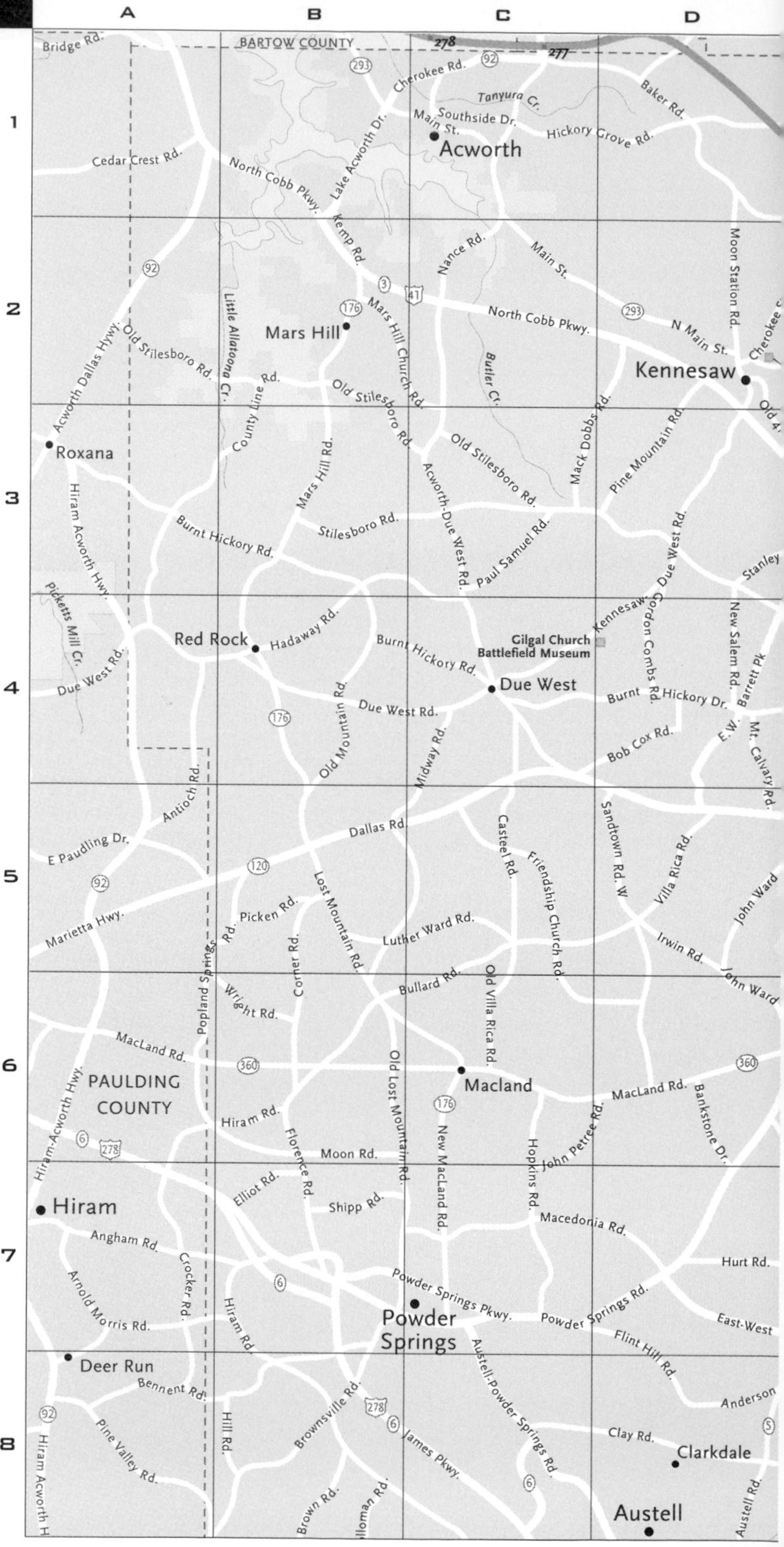

A
B
C
D
1
2
3
4
5
6
7
8
BARTOW COUNTY
Bridge Rd.
278
277
293
92
Cherokee Rd.
Tanyura Cr.
Baker Rd.
Southside Dr.
Main St.
Hickory Grove Rd.
Acworth
Cedar Crest Rd.
North Cobb Pkwy.
Lake Acworth Dr.
Kemp Rd.
Nance Rd.
Main St.
Moon Station Rd.
3
41
176
Mars Hill Church Rd.
North Cobb Pkwy.
N Main St.
Cherokee
Mars Hill
Little Allatoona Cr.
Acworth Dallas Hwy.
Old Stilesboro Rd.
County Line Rd.
Old Stilesboro Rd.
Butler Ct.
Kennesaw
Mack Dobbs Rd.
Pine Mountain Rd.
Roxana
Mars Hill Rd.
Acworth-Due West Rd.
Old Stilesboro Rd.
Hiram Acworth Hwy.
Burnt Hickory Rd.
Stilesboro Rd.
Paul Samuel Rd.
Due West Rd.
Stanley
Picketts Mill Cr.
Red Rock
Hadaway Rd.
Burnt Hickory Rd.
Gilgal Church
Battlefield Museum
Kennesaw
Gordon Combs Rd.
New Salem Rd.
Barrett Pk
Due West Rd.
Old Mountain Rd.
Due West Rd.
Due West
Burnt Hickory Dr.
Midway Rd.
Bob Cox Rd.
E.W.
Mt. Calvary Rd.
Antioch Rd.
Sandtown Rd. W
Casteel Rd.
Friendship Church Rd.
Villa Rica Rd.
Dallas Rd.
E Paulding Dr.
120
John Ward
Marietta Hwy.
Lost Mountain Rd.
Picken Rd.
Popland Springs Rd.
Luther Ward Rd.
Irwin Rd.
John Ward
Corner Rd.
Bullard Rd.
Old Villa Rica Rd.
Wright Rd.
MacLand Rd.
360
Old Lost Mountain Rd.
PAULDING
COUNTY
Macland
MacLand Rd.
Bankstone Dr.
Hiram-Acworth Hwy.
Hiram Rd.
Florence Rd.
New MacLand Rd.
John Petree Rd.
Hopkins Rd.
6
Moon Rd.
Elliot Rd.
Hiram
Shipp Rd.
Macedonia Rd.
Angham Rd.
Hurt Rd.
Arnold Morris Rd.
Crocker Rd.
Hiram Rd.
Powder Springs Pkwy.
Powder
Springs
Powder Springs Rd.
East-West
Flint Hill Rd.
Deer Run
Austell-Powder Springs Rd.
Bennent Rd.
Anderson
Hill Rd.
Brownsville Rd.
James Pkwy.
Clay Rd.
Clarkdale
Pine Valley Rd.
Hiram Acworth H
Brown Rd.
Austell
Austell Rd.
5

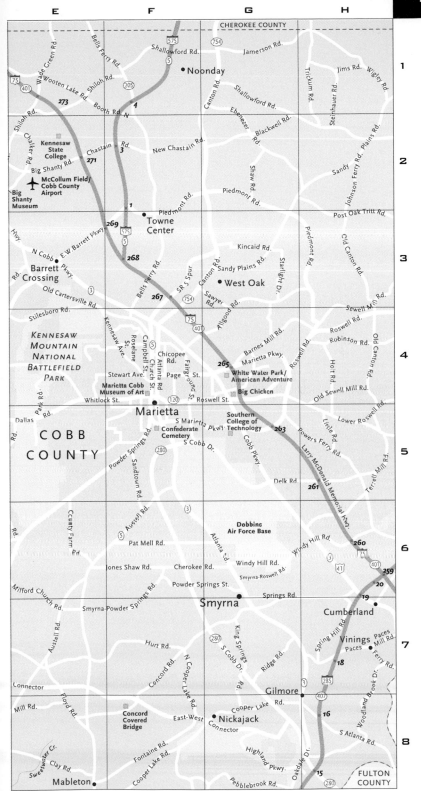

4

CHEROKEE COUNTY

575

754

Shallowford Rd.

5

Jamerson Rd.

• Noonday

Jims Rd.

Wigley Rd.

1

75

401

Wade Green Rd.

Bells Ferry Rd.

Wooten Lake Rd.

Shiloh Rd.

205

Booth Rd.

N

273

4

Shallowford Rd.

Canton Rd.

Trickum Rd.

Steinhauer Rd.

Shiloh Rd.

Chalker Rd.

Kennesaw State College

Big Shanty Rd.

Chastain Rd.

3

271

New Chastain Rd.

Ebenezer

Blackwell Rd.

Shaw Rd.

Johnson Ferry Rd.

Sandy Plains Rd.

2

McCollum Field/ Cobb County Airport

Big Shanty Museum

1

Piedmont Rd.

Piedmont Rd.

Post Oak Tritt Rd.

Hwy.

269

575

5

Towne Center

Piedmont Rd.

Kincaid Rd.

Piedmont Rd.

Old Canton Rd.

3

Barrett Crossing

E.W. Barrett Pkwy.

N Cobb Pkwy.

268

Bells Ferry Rd.

267

SR S. Spur

Canton Rd.

Sandy Plains Rd.

• West Oak

Starlight Dr.

754

Sawyer Rd.

Sewell Mill Rd.

Old Cartersville Rd.

3

Stilesboro Rd.

75

401

Allgood Rd.

Roswell Rd.

Robinson Rd.

Old Canton Rd.

4

KENNESAW MOUNTAIN NATIONAL BATTLEFIELD PARK

Kennesaw Ave.

Roselane St.

Campbell St.

Church St.

5

Atlanta Rd.

Chicopee Rd.

Page St.

Fairground St.

265

Barnes Mill Rd.

Marietta Pkwy.

Roswell Rd.

Hot Rd.

Old Sewell Mill Rd.

Park Rd.

Stewart Ave.

Marietta Cobb Museum of Art

Whitlock St.

120

Roswell St.

White Water Park/ American Adventure

Big Chicken

Dallas Rd.

Marietta

S Marietta Pkwy.

Confederate Cemetery

Southern College of Technology

263

Lower Roswell Rd.

Little Rd.

5

COBB COUNTY

Powder Springs Rd.

Sandtown Rd.

280

S Cobb Dr.

Cobb Pkwy.

Powers Ferry Rd.

Terrell Mill Rd.

Rd.

261

Delk Rd.

Larry McDonald Memorial Hwy.

County Farm Rd.

Austell Rd.

3

Dobbins Air Force Base

Windy Hill Rd.

260

75

6

Rd.

5

Pat Mell Rd.

Atlanta Rd.

Windy Hill Rd.

411

401

259

Jones Shaw Rd.

Cherokee Rd.

Smyrna-Roswell Rd.

20

Milford Church Rd.

Powder Springs Rd.

Powder Springs St.

Springs Rd.

19

Cumberland

Austell Rd.

Smyrna-Powder Springs Rd.

Smyrna

Spring Hill Rd.

Vinings

Paces Mill Rd.

7

Hurt Rd.

280

N Cooper Lake Rd.

King Springs Rd.

S Cobb Dr.

Ridge Rd.

18

Paces Ferry Rd.

Connector

Concord Rd.

285

Mill Rd.

Floyd Rd.

Concord Covered Bridge

East-West Connector

407

Gilmore •

3

16

Woodland Brook Dr.

• Nickajack

Cooper Lake Rd.

S Atlanta Rd.

8

Sweetwater Cr.

Clay Rd.

Fontaine Rd.

Cooper Lake Rd.

Highland Pkwy.

Oakdale Dr.

15

280

FULTON COUNTY

• Mableton

Pebblebrook Rd.

CENTRAL COBB COUNTY, KENNESAW, AND MARIETTA

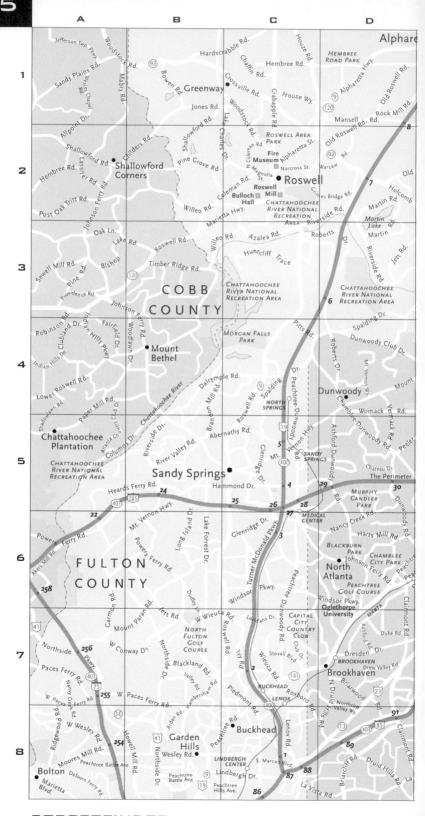

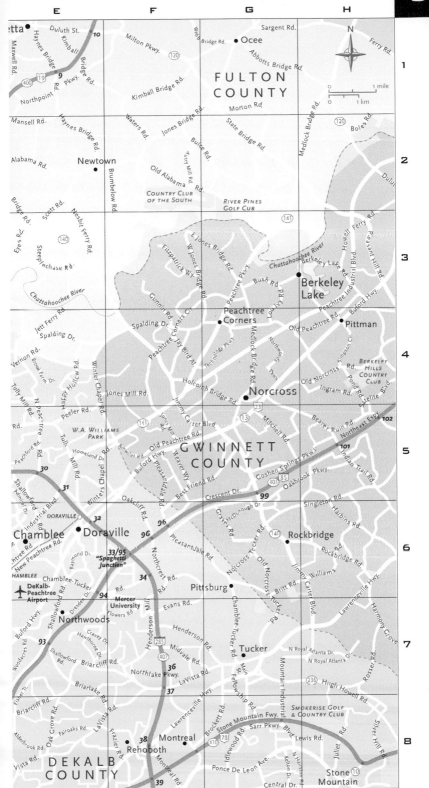

NORTHERN FULTON AND DEKALB COUNTIES

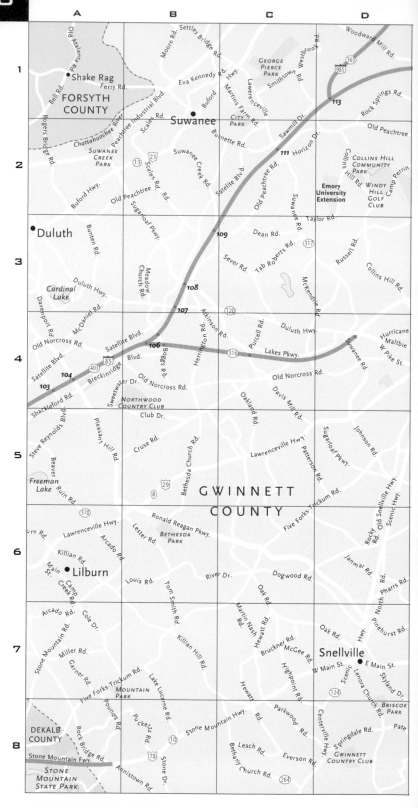

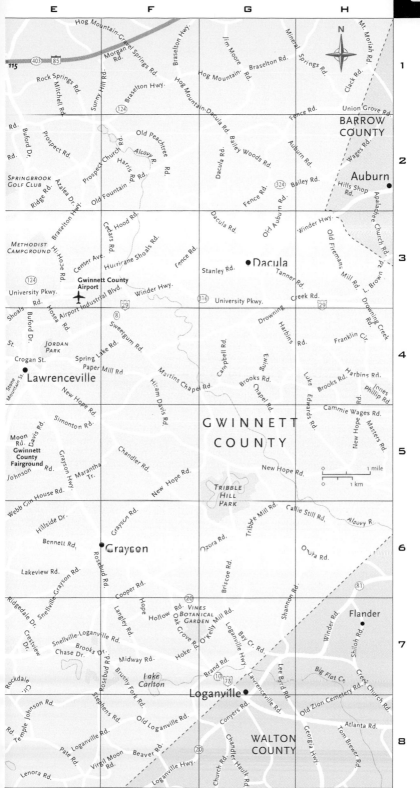

NORTHEAST SUBURBS: GWINNETT COUNTY

A   B   C   D

1

6

Austell Powder Springs Rd.

Austell

Austell Rd.

Old Alabama Rd.

Old Powder Springs Rd.

Dodgen Rd.

78 / 78

8 Bankhead Hwy.

Buckner Rd.

COBB

James Pkwy.

S Gordon Rd.

Cardell Rd.

Factory Shoals Rd.

Mableton Pkwy.

Allen

Queens Mill Rd.

COUNTY

78 8 5

Thorton Rd.

Hillcrest Dr.

139

Lithia Springs

6

Skyview Dr.

N Blairs Bridge Rd.

2

Sweetwater Rd. S

20 402

Blairs Bridge Rd.

44

Six Flags Dr.

Hartman Rd.

46

47

✈ Fulton County Airport/ Brown Field

41

Lee Rd.

Factory Shoals Rd.

Six Flags Rd.

Bob White Rd.

Six Flags Over Georgia

70

49

20 402

Adam

Mount Vernon Rd.

SWEETWATER CREEK STATE PARK

Rockhouse Rd.

Thorton Rd.

Riverside Pkwy.

Fulton Industrial Blvd.

Bakers Ferry Rd.

3

DOUGLAS COUNTY

Great Southwest Pkwy.

Cascade Rd.

TRAMMELL CROW PARK

Boulder Park Dr.

Cascade Knolls

Danforth Rd.

4

92

Riverside Pkwy.

70

Fulton Pkwy.

Camp Creek Pkwy.

166

Wallace Rd.

SANDTOWN PARK

New Hope Rd.

Campbellton Rd.

Nisby Lake Rd.

County Line Rd.

Kimberly Rd.

166

92

Fairburn Rd.

Butner Rd.

Ben H

166

Campbellton Rd.

6

Chattahoochee River

Ebb Duncan Memorial Hwy.

154

Cascade Palmetto Hwy.

Stonewall Tell Rd.

Enon Rd.

FULTON COUN

5

Stubbs Rd. W.

Miles Union Rd.

Camp Creek Pkwy.

Welcome All Rd.

Butner Rd.

Butner Rd.

Pittman Rd.

Tharton Rd.

Old Fairburn Rd.

LAKESIDE GOLF CLUB

6

Cambellton Hwy.

92

Demooney Rd.

Stonewall Rd.

Derreck Rd.

Scarborough Rd.

WELCOME ALL PARK

Welcome All Rd.

Bethlehem Rd.

Hall Rd.

7

Clark Rd.

N

Jones Rd.

Thompson Rd.

McClure Rd.

Fairburn Hwy.

Koweta Rd.

Wexford Rd.

South Fulton Pkwy.

High Point Rd.

Tell Rd.

Roosevelt Hwy.

29

14

Mallory Rd.

8

Short Rd.

South Fulton Pkwy.

Cedar Grove Rd.

White Mill Rd.

Dodson Rd.

Jonesboro Rd.

Flat Shoals Rd.

Union City

14

Rivertown Rd.

Bishop Rd.

Rivertown Rd.

J. Rivers Rd.

Virlyn Smith Rd.

Broad St.

29

138

64

Fairburn

Fayetteville Rd.

○ 1 mile
○ 1 km

STREETFINDER

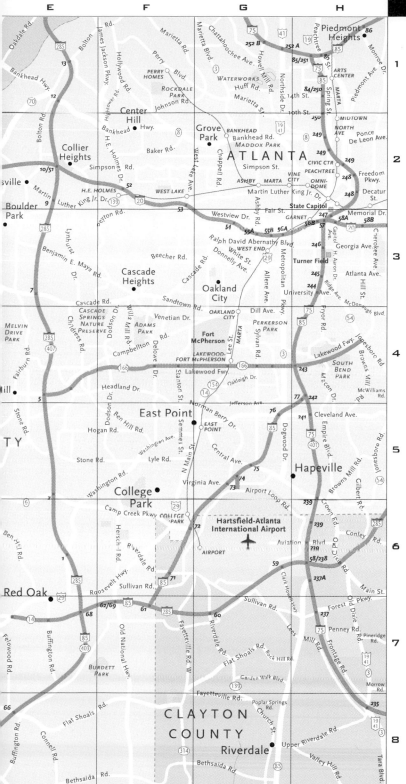

ATLANTA AND SOUTH-CENTRAL FULTON COUNTY

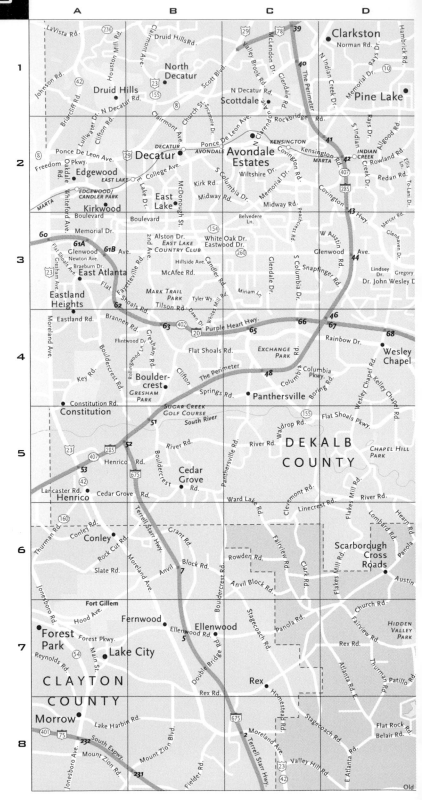

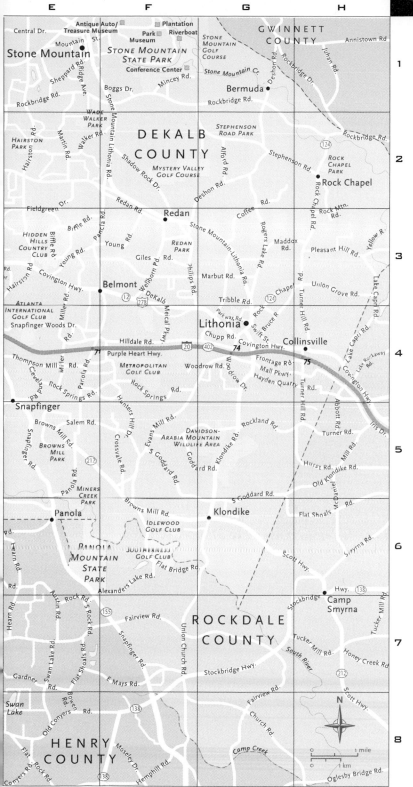

EAST SUBURBS: DEKALB COUNTY

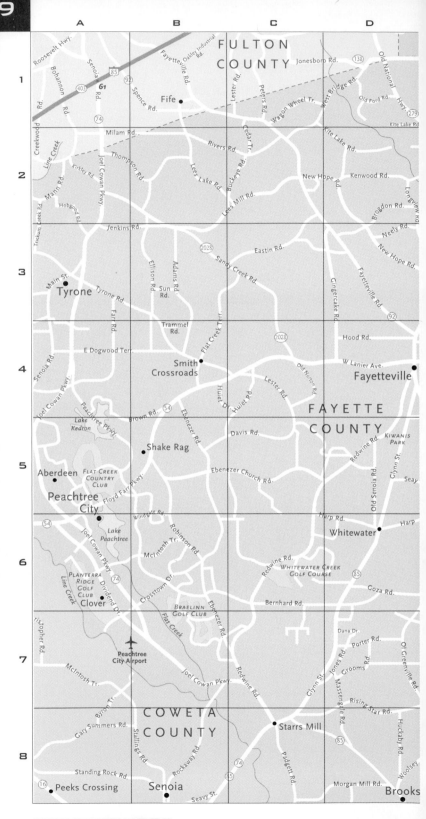

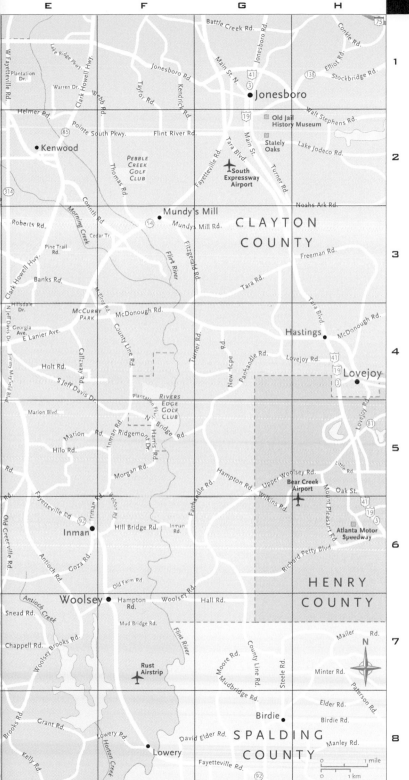

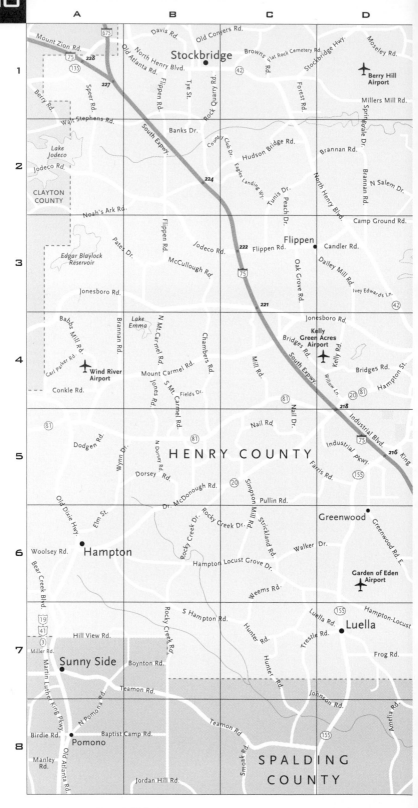

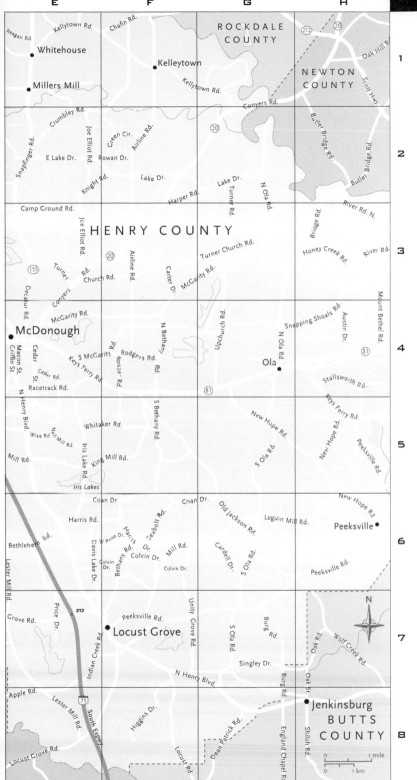

SOUTHWEST SUBURBS: HENRY COUNTY

A B C D

1

2

3

4

5

6

7

8

Randall Mill Rd.
Beechwood Dr.
Castlegate Dr.
W Paces Ferry Rd.
Northside Dr.
Valley Rd.
Blackland Rd.
Powers Ferry Rd.
Old Ivy Rd.
Stratford Rd.
Wieuca Rd.
Peachtree-Dunwoody Rd.
Phipps Blvd.
Tuxedo Rd.
Knollwood Dr.
Woodhaven Rd.
Buckhead Loop
BUCKHEAD
Ivy Rd.
Lenox Rd.
Northside Pkwy.
Howell Mill Rd.
Moores Mill Rd.
Wood Valley
Chateau Dr.
Marne Dr.
Arden Rd.
Habersham Rd.
Roswell Rd.
Lakeland Dr.
Andrews Dr.
W Paces Ferry Rd.
Peachtree Rd.
E Paces Ferry Rd.
Peachtree Dr.
Dale
Greenview Ave.
Burke Rd.
Piedmont Rd.
Mitchell
Moores Rd.
Rockingham Dr.
Castlewood Dr.
Northside Dr.
Argonne Rd.
Normandy Dr.
Pharr Rd.
Delmo
Rumso
Pharr Rd.
GARDEN HILLS
Lenox Rd.
Harris Mathis Pkwy.
Wesley Rd.
Battle Ave.
Manor Ridge Dr.
Battle Ave.
Woodland Dr.
Devonwood Dr.
Wesley Rd. E
Lindberg Dr.
Acton Ave.
Brookwood Dr.
Sharondale Dr.
Sidney Marcus
Canterbury Rd.
Creek Pkwy
Northcliffe Dr.
Woodley Dr.
Longwood Dr.
Woodward Wy.
Peachtree St.
Peachtree
ATLANTA MEMORIAL PARK
Cheshire Bridge
Collier Rd.
Howell Mill Rd.
De Seaboard Ave.
Mantissa St.
Claremont Ave.
Harper Wy.
Collier Rd.
28th St.
Brighton Rd.
Camden Rd.
Armor Dr.
Ottley Dr.
ANSLEY GOLF COURSE
Wimbledon Rd.
Rock Spring Rd.
Wellbourne Dr.
Wildwood
Chattahoochee Ave.
Ellsworth Industrial Dr.
De Chattahoochee Ave.
Bellmeade Ave.
Holmes St.
Antone St.
Mott Forrest St.
Hascall Rd.
Robin
Montgomery Ferry Dr.
Monroe Dr.
Morningside
Sherwood Rd.
Pelham Rd.
Huff Rd.
Fairmont Ave.
Atlanta Water Works
Deering Rd.
Trabert Ave.
Bishop St.
Mecaslin St.
Maddox Dr.
Peachtree Cir.
Barksdal
Cumberland Rd.
Yorkshire Rd.
Hill Pine Dr.
Northview Ave.
Church St.
Niles Ave.
Marietta St.
Howell Mill Rd.
Northside Dr.
16th St.
14th St.
Holy St.
Fowler St.
I-85
Woodruff Arts Center
PIEDMONT PARK
Botanical Gardens
Courtenay Dr.
Amsterdam Ave.
Monroe Dr.
Los Angeles Ave.
Park Dr.
Center St.
McMillan St.
11th St.
Ethel St.
Calhoun St.
10th St.
14th St.
MIDTOWN
10th St.
Piedmont Ave.
Peachtree St.
W Peachtree St.
Spring St.
13th St.
Cooledge Ave.
Virginia Ave.
Herndon St.
Jefferson St.
Fulton County Jail
8th St.
Hemphill Ave.
Georgia Institute of Technology
North Expwy.
North Ave.
Peachtree St.
W Peachtree St. W
Spring St.
Juniper St.
Piedmont Ave.
Myrtle St.
8th St.
6th St.
4th St.
Argonne Ave.
Monroe Dr.
Ponce De Leon Ave.
Adair Ave.
Greenwood
St. Charles
Ponce De
Bankhead
Ave.
Jefferson St.
Oliver St.
Ashby St.
James P. Brawley Dr.
Paines Ave.
Pelham St.
Bankhead
Tech Pkwy.
B Lambert St.
Grant Field
North Ave.
Coca-Cola World HQ
Ponce De Leon St.
North Ave.
Bedford St.
Linden Ave.
Angier Ave.
Glen Iris Dr.
City Hall East
Boulevard
MADDOX PARK
Tazor St.
North Ave.
Kennedy St.
Northside Dr.
Gray St.
Pine St.
Hunnicutt St.
Mills St.
EXIT 249B
EXIT 249C
EXIT 249D
SciTrek Museum
Proctor St.
Simpson St.
Jones St.
Ave.
Marietta St.
EXIT 249A
Ralph McGill Blvd.
Freedom Pkwy.
Highland
Lake Ave.
SPRINGVALE Park
Mason Turner Rd.
St. Peters St.
Old Est.
Thurmond St.
Sunset Ave.
Spencer St.
Magnolia St.
Georgia World Congress Center
International Philips
Techwood
Blvd.
Courtland St.
248C
Irwin
Auburn St.
248B
Edgewood Ave.
DeKalb Ave.
Wylie St.
Martin Luther King Jr. Dr.
Morris Brown University
Clark-Atlanta University
Beckwith St.
Parsons St.
Georgia Dome
OMNI DOME GEORGIA WORLD CONGRESS CTR
Mitchell St.
DOWNTOWN
Edgewood Ave.
Georgia State University
Martin Luther
ATLANTA
Fair St.
Westview Dr.
Abernathy Fwy.
Morehouse University
Ashby St.
Lee St.
Fair St.
Spelman College
Northside Dr.
Walker St.
Peters St.
Whitehall St.
Garrett St.
Memorial Dr.
State Capitol
Martin Luther
Memorial Dr.
Woodward Ave.
OAKLAND CEMETERY
Carroll St.
Fulton Ter.
Kirkwood Ave.
Estoria St.
Fulton Ter.
54
55A
Morehouse School of Medicine
55B
Abernathy Fwy.
WEST END
Atwood St.
Peeples St.
Ralph David Abernathy Blvd.
Windsor St.
McDaniel St.
WEST END
Glen Iris St.
Oglethorpe Ave.
246
245
Turner Field
56A
56B
Fulton St.
57/247
57A
58A
Glenwood Ave.
Fulton St.
Georgia Ave.
58B
Abernathy Fwy.
GRANT PARK
Cyclorama
Hansell St.
Berne St.
Glenwood Memorial
59B
59A
Capitol Ave.
Fraser St.

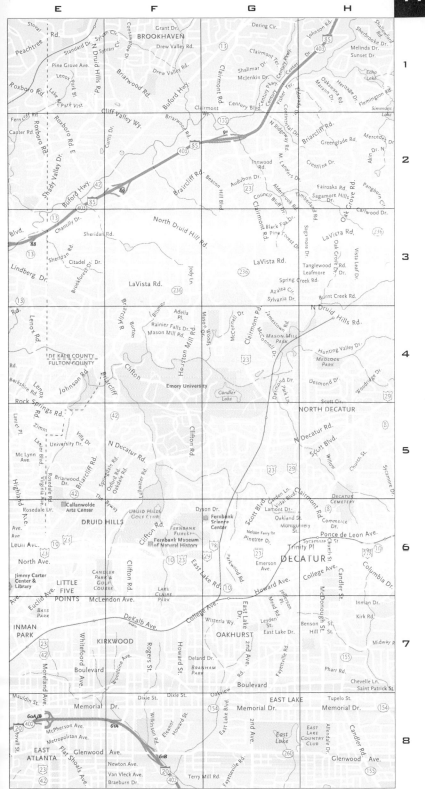

CENTRAL ATLANTA, BUCKHEAD, DECATUR OVERVIEW

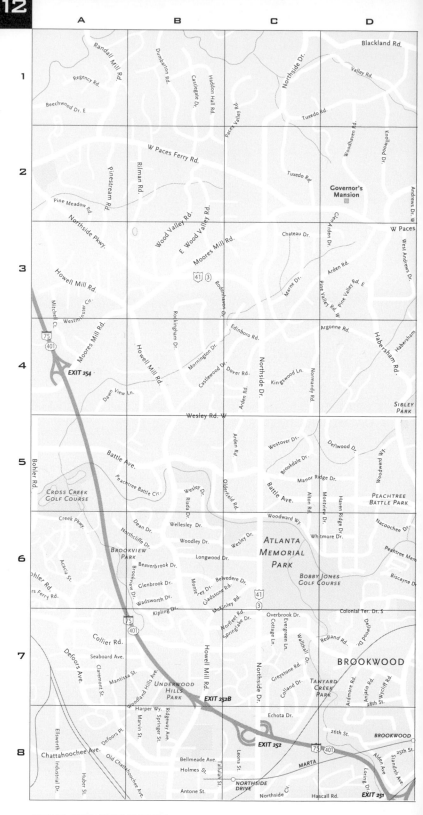

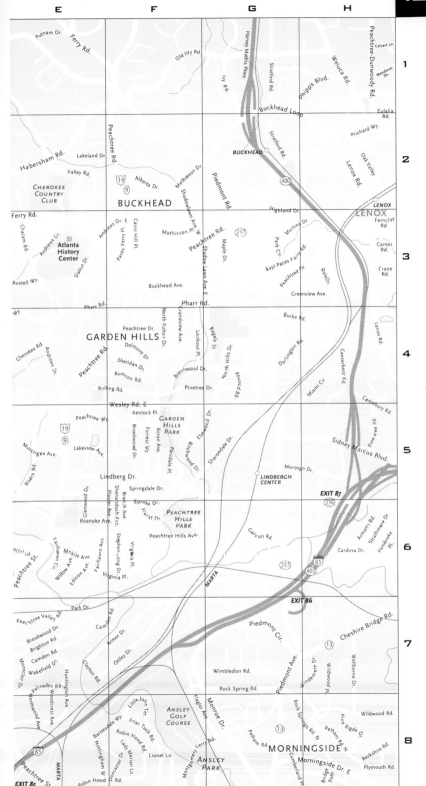

BUCKHEAD, BROOKWOOD, MORNINGSIDE

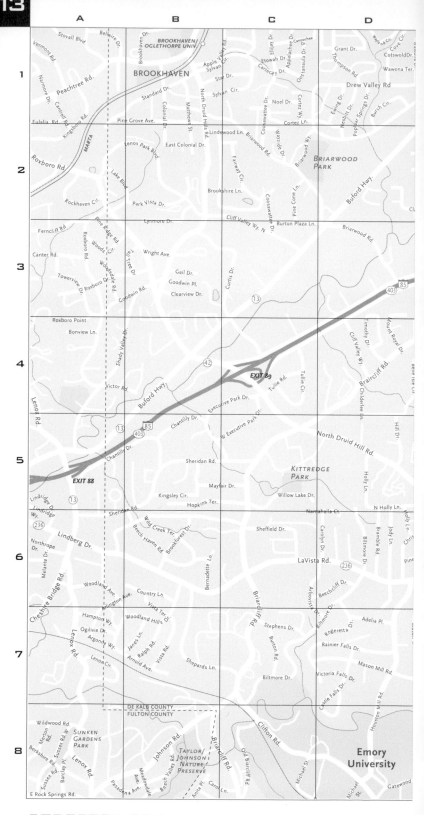

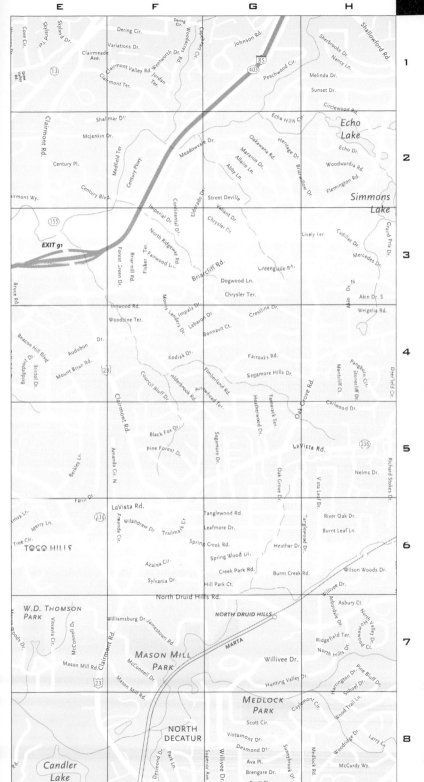

A   B   C   D

1
2
3
4
5
6
7
8

Rock Springs Rd. E.
Valley Rd.
Poplar Crove Dr.
Hills Dr.
Dantzler Dr.
Uppergate
Lanier Pl.
Cumberland Rd.
Reeder Clr.
Zimmer Dr
Mark rue Dr.
Villa Dr.
42
Emory Rd.
Harvard Rd.
Fraternity Dr.
Clifton Rd.
Avalon Pl.
Lanier Blvd.
University Dr.
Cornell Rd.
Asbury Cir.

Mc Lynn Ave.
Amsterdam Ave.
Rosewood Dr.
Lanier Blvd.
L.A. Ave.
Virgina Ave.
North Decatur Rd.
Hancock Dr.
Normandy Dr.
Chalmette Dr.
Briarwood Dr.
Briarcliff Rd.
The Byway
Springdale Rd.
Briardale Ln.
Oxford Rd.
Oakdale Rd.
Emory Rd.
Lullwater Rd.
Clifton Rd. E.
Emory Dr.
Rosedale Rd.

VIRGINIA
HIGHLAND
Rosedale Dr.
Callanwolde
Arts Center
42
DRUID HILLS
LULLWATER
CONSERVATION
PARK
DRUID
HILLS
GOLF
CLUB
Dyson
Fernbank
Science
Center
FERNBANK
FOREST

Highland
View
Drewry St.
Briarcliff Pl.
St. Louis Pl.
St. Charles Pl.
Frederica St.
Ponce De Leon Ave.
10 23
Ponce De Leon Dr. S
Clifton Rd.
Fernbank Museum
of Natural History
Ponce De Leon Ave. S.
DELLWOOD
PARK
N Ponce De Leon Ave.

Blue Ridge Ave.
North Ave.
Linwood Ave.
Seminole Ave.
23
Fairview Rd.
10
East Lake
Ponce De Leon Ave.

LITTLE
FIVE
POINTS
Jimmy Carter
Center &
Library
Colquitt Ave.
Druid Pl.
Candler St.
Candler St.
Sterling St.
Benning Pl.
Candler Park Dr.
CANDLER
PARK
Miller Ave.
CANDLER
PARK &
GOLF
COURSE
Terrace Ave.
Page Ave.
Muriel Ave.
Harriet Ave.
Clifton Rd.
Hardendorf Ave.
Harold Ave.
Marlbrook Dr.
Leonardo Ave.
LAKE
CLAIRE
PARK
Lakeside Dr.
Claire Dr.
Tuxedo Ave.
Palifox Dr.
McLendon
Dekabb Pl.

Washita Ave.
Euclid Ave.
BASS
PARK
Austin
Ave.
Alta Ave.
INMAN
PARK
Hurt St.
DeKalb Ave.
Euclid Ter.
Candler St.
Josephine St.
Elmira St.
Candler St.
Ferguson St.
Iverson St.
Candler Park Dr.
McLendon Ave.
Mell Ave.
Glendale Ave.
DeKalb Ave.
Nelms Ave.
Connecticut Ave.
Indiana Ave.
Matthews Ave.
Gordon Ave.
W College Ave.
Fowler St.
MARTA
EDGEWOOD/
CANDLER PARK
La France St.
Mason Ave.
Flora Ave.
Marion Pl.
Caroline St.
23
42
INMAN PARK/
REYNOLDSTOWN
Moreland Ave.
Wirewood Dr.
Finley St.
Hardee St.
Sanderson St.
Whiteford Ave.
Chipley St.
1st Foote St.
Haydee Cir.
Rogers St.
Clay St.
Warren St.
Emery Pl.
Trotti St.
BRANHAM
PARK
Howard St.
Kirkwood Rd.
Norwood Ave.

Wetherby St.
Walthall St.
Wylie St.
Colmer Ave.
Ericson St.
Leslie St.
Montgomery St.
Hutchinson St.
Meridian St.
Woodbine Ave.
Boulevard
WESLEY
CONN
PARK
Stanwood Ave.
Wyman St.
Clifton St.
Clay St.
Bixby St.
Warren St.
Deahorn St.
Howard St.

Mauldin St.
Cummings St.
Stovall St.
Mortimer Ave.
Battlefield Ave.
Paxon St.
Vaughn St.
Memorial Dr.
Dixie St.
Dixie St.
Dixie St.
Palatka St.
Douglas St.

EXIT 60A/B
20 402
Stovall St.
Glenwood Pl.
Faith Ave.
Sanders Ave.
Lytle Ave.
Hemlock Ave.
Portland Ave.
Moreland Ave.
Brownwood Ave.
McPherson Ave.
Hass Ave.
Patterson Ave.
Metropolitan Ave.
Flat Shoals Ave.
Monument Ave.
E Side Ave.
Marbut Ave.
Blake Ave.
Pasley Ave.
McWilliams St.
Maynard Ter.
EXIT 61A
Glencoe Ln.
DeKalb
MEMORIAL
PARK
Warren St.
Wilkinson Rd.
Liberty Ave.
Lincoln Ave.
Eleanor St.
Overland Ter.
Eastport Ter.
Fairway Hill Dr.
Glencove Ave.

Glenwood Ave.
May Ave.
Gresham Ave.
Stokeswood Ave.
Van Epps Ave.
Newton Ave.
Van Epps Ave.
Van Vleck Ave.
Blake Ave.
E Side Ave.
Pasley Ave.
Maynard Ter.
May Ave.
Ora Ave.
Clifton Wy.
EAST
ATLANTA
EXIT 61B
20 402
Pennington Pl.
Lomita Rd.
Terry
Berne St.
Mercer St.
Pendleton St.
Pickens St.
23
42
Braeburn Dr.
Braeburn Cir.

DE KALB COUNTY
FULTON COUNTY

STREETFINDER

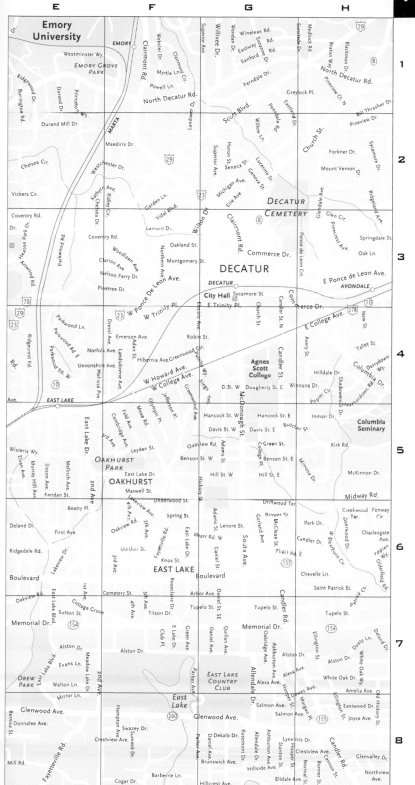

DECATUR, DRUID HILLS, VIRGINIA-HIGHLAND

A B C D

1

Ellsworth Industrial Dr.
Fairmont St.
Fairmont Ave.
English St.
Boyd Ave.
Culpepper Ave.
Morris St.
Forrest St.
Berkeley Ave.
Hawthorne St.
Hascall Rd.
Deering Rd.
Trabert Ave.
Bishop St.
Northside Dr.
Howell Mill Rd.

Atlanta Water Works

EXIT 251

Huff Rd.

16th St.
15th St.
Barnes St.
Holy St.
Francis St.
Fowler St.

2

Rice St.
Church St.
Niles Ave.
Tilden St.
Carr St.
Baylor St.
Warfield St.
Longley Ave.
Reynolds St.
Herndon St.
Marietta St. W
14th St.
11th St.
11th St.
Brady Ave.
Hemphill Ave.
Hampton St.
Center St.
Ethel St.
Calhoun St.
Atlantic Dr.
State St.
Westshire Pl.

14th St.
HOME PARK

10th St.

**Alexand
Memori
Coliseu**

3

Marietta Blvd.
Herndon St.
Hornady St.
Glass St.
Jefferson St.
Jefferson St.
Lindsay St.
Oliver St.
English Ave.
James P Brawley Dr.
Ashby St.
8th St.
Bankhead Ave.
Marietta St.
Tech Parkway
9th St.
Curran St.
McMillan St.
8th St.
6th St.
Fesrt St.
Hemphill Ave.
State St.
Atlantic Dr.
Plum St.
Flower St.
6th
5th
4th St.
Bobby Dodd Wy.

Fulton County Jail

Georgia Institute of Technology

BANKHEAD
Bankhead Ave.

4

MADDOX PARK
Finley St.
Pelham St.
Poland St.
Norfolk St.
North Ave.
Cairo St.
Tazor St.
Neal St.
Temple St.
Proctor St.
Oliver St.
Lindsay St.
Ashby St.
Jett St.
Painrs Ave.
English Ave.
Griffen St.
Sunset St.
Elm St.
Lambert St.
Pelham St.
Davighey St.
North Ave.
Meldrum St.
Kennedy St.
Travis St.
Julian St.
Vine St.
Walnut St.
Jett St.
Davis St.
Strong St.
Emmi St.
Gray St.
John St.
Western Ave.
Jones Ave.
Northside Dr.
North Ave.
Coca-Cola World HQ
Venable St.
Luckie St.
Marietta St.
Lovejoy St.
Hunnicutt St.
Mills St.

5

Mobil St.
Troy St.
Burbank Dr.
Arcadia Cir.
Washington Heights Ter.
Mason Turner St.
Ashby Cir.
Westmoor Dr.
Michigan Ave.
Bronx St.
WASHINGTON PARK
Desoto St.
Simpson St.
KENNEDY PARK
Sciple Ter.
Newport St.
Thurmond St.
James P Brawley Dr.
Washington Dr.
Pascal Blvd.
Play Ln.
Griffen St.
Sunset St.
Elm St.
Thurmond St.
Spencer St.
Foundry St.
Magnolia St.
Western Ave.
Jones Ave.
West Jones Conn Ave.
Simpson St.
Baker St.
Magnum St.
Georgia World Congress Center
International Blvd.
Technwood Dr.
Wall St.
Georgia Dome
Philips Stadium

6

Sharon St.
Fenwood St.
Holderness St.
Rosser St.
1st St.
Ollie St.
Fountain St.
White House St.
Parsons Pl.
Peeples St.
Beckwith St.
Parsons Pl.
Camilla St.
Fair St.
Lawton St.
Frank St.
Abbott St.
Washington St.
Abbott St.
Parsons St.
Beckwith St.
Parsons St.
Milton St.
Walnut St.
Pine St.
Lawshe St.
J.P. Brawley Dr.
Roach St.
Fair St.
Larkin St.
Walker St.
Peters St.
Forsyth St.
Elliot St.
Chapel St.
Haynes St.
Markham St.
Spring St.
Trinity
Garnett St.

MARTA
ASHBY
VINE CITY
Rhodes St.
Carters St.
Morris Brown University
Herndon Home
Northside Dr.
Mitchell St.
OMNI DOME/ GEORGIA WORLD CONGRESS CTR
MARTA
Alabama
Martin Luther King Jr. Dr.
Clark-Atlanta University

7

Westview Dr.
Lawton St.
W. Dragan Pl.
Sells Ave.
Ashby St.
Abbott St.
Wellborn St.
Lee Street
West End Ave.
Westview Ave.
Morehouse University
Spelman College
Greensferry St.
Norcross Ave.
Whitehall St.
GARNETT
Peachtree St.
Pryor St.
Formwalt St.
Central Ave.
Gannett St.
Memorial Dr.
EXIT 57
EXIT 54
20
Abernathy Fwy.
Greenwhich St.
EXIT 55A
Park St.
Morehouse School of Medicine
19
EXIT 55B
Fulton St.
20
402

8

Hopkins St.
Atwood St.
Lucile Ave.
Oak St.
West End Pl.
Peeples St.
Oak St.
Dunn St.
Atwood St.
Ralph David Abernathy Blvd.
Wren's Nest
WEST END
Queen St.
White St.
Oglethorpe Ave.
Gordon Pl.
York Ave.
Azalia
WEST END
Evans St.
Whitehall St.
MARTA
EXIT 55B
3
Wells St.
McDaniel St.
Glen St.
Shelton Ave.
Metropolitan Pkwy.
Sandtown St.
PHOENIX PARK
Richardson St.
Windsor St.
Crumley St.
EXIT 246
R.D. Abernathy Blvd.
Smith St.
Bass St.
Stephens St.
Stephens St.

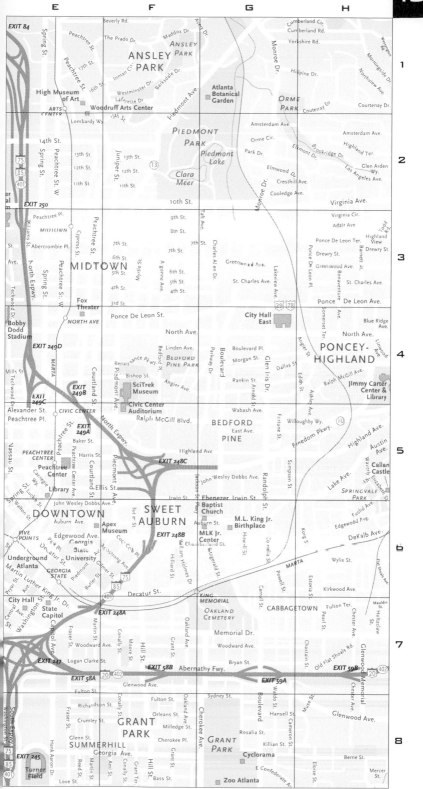

DOWNTOWN, MIDTOWN, ANSLEY PARK

The Sourcebook
For Your City

MANY MAPS • WHERE & HOW

FIND IT ALL • NIGHT & DAY

ANTIQUES TO ZIPPERS

BARGAINS • BAUBLES • KITES

ELEGANT EDIBLES • ETHNIC EATS

STEAK HOUSES • FISH HOUSES

BISTROS • TRATTORIAS

CLASSICAL • JAZZ • CABARET

COMEDY • THEATER • DANCE

BARS • CLUBS • BLUES

COOL TOURS

HOUSECLEANING • CATERING

LOST & FOUND • THE CABLE GUY

GET A LAWYER • GET A DENTIST

GET A NEW PET • GET A VET

MUSEUMS • GALLERIES

PARKS • GARDENS • RINKS

AQUARIUMS TO ZOOS

BASEBALL TO ROCK CLIMBING

FESTIVALS • EVENTS

DAY SPAS • DAY TRIPS

HOTELS • HOT LINES

PASSPORT PIX • TRAVEL INFO

HELICOPTER TOURS

DINERS • DELIS • PIZZERIAS

BRASSERIES • CAFÉS

BOOTS • BOOKS • BUTTONS

BICYCLES • SKATES

SUITS • SHOES • HATS

RENT A TUX • RENT A COSTUME

BAKERIES • SPICE SHOPS

SOUP TO NUTS

Fodor's

CITYGUIDE
ATLANTA

SERIES CREATED BY MARILYN APPLEBERG

FODOR'S TRAVEL PUBLICATIONS

NEW YORK • TORONTO • LONDON • SYDNEY • AUCKLAND

WWW.FODORS.COM

FODOR'S CITYGUIDE ATLANTA

EDITOR
Constance Jones

EDITORIAL CONTRIBUTORS
Stephen Brewer, Ren Davis, Vicky Forrest, Jane Garvey, Hollis Gillespie, Michael Hagaerty, Lynne McGill, Jill Sabulis, Joe Silva, Jamie Vacca

EDITORIAL PRODUCTION
Stacey Kulig

MAPS
David Lindroth Inc., *cartographer*; Bob Blake, *map editor*

DESIGN
Fabrizio La Rocca, *creative director*; Allison Saltzman, *text design*; Tigist Getachew, *cover design*; Jolie Novak, *picture editor*

PRODUCTION/MANUFACTURING
Robert Shields

COVER PHOTOGRAPH
Chuck Pefley

Series created by Marilyn Appleberg

COPYRIGHT

First Edition

ISBN 0–679–00510–2

ISSN 1528–9249

SPECIAL SALES

CONTENTS

METROPOLITAN LIFE

On a bad day in a big city, the little things that go with living shoulder-to-shoulder with a few million people wear us all down. But the special pleasures of urban life have a way of keeping us around town—and thankful, even, for every second of stress. The field of daffodils in the park on a fine spring day. The perfect little black dress that you find for half price. The markets—so fabulously well stocked that you can cook any recipe without resorting to mail-order catalogs. The way you can sometimes turn a corner and discover a whole new world, so foreign you can hardly believe you're only a few miles from home. The never-ending wealth of possibilities and opportunities.

If you know where to find it all, the city cannot defeat you. With knowledge comes power. That's why Fodor's has prepared this book. It will put phone numbers at your fingertips. It'll take you to new places and remind you of those you've forgotten. It's the ultimate urban companion—and, we hope, your **new best friend in the city.**

It's the **citywise shopaholic,** who always knows where to find something, no matter how obscure. We've made a concerted effort to bring hundreds of great shops to your attention, so that you'll never be at a loss, whether you need a special birthday present for a great friend or some wild fabrics to make Halloween costumes for your kids.

It's the **restaurant know-it-all,** who's full of ideas for every occasion—you know, the one who would never send you to Café de la Snub, because she knows it's always overbooked, the food is boring, and the staff is rude. In this book we'll steer you around the corner, to a perfect little place with five tables, a fireplace, and a chef on his way up.

It's a **hip barfly buddy,** who can give you advice when you need a charming nook, not too noisy, to take a friend after work. Among the dozens of bars and nightspots in this book, you're bound to find something that fits your mood.

It's the **sagest arts maven you know,** the one who always has the scoop on what's on that's worthwhile on any given night. In these pages, you'll find dozens of concert venues and arts organizations.

It's also the **city whiz,** who knows how to get you where you're going, wherever you are.

It's the **best map guide** on the shelves, and it puts **all the city in your briefcase** or on your bookshelf.

Stick with us. We lay out all the options for your leisure time—and gently nudge you away from the duds—so that you can truly enjoy metropolitan living.

YOUR GUIDES

No one person can know it all. To help get you on track around the city, we've hand-picked a stellar group of local experts to share their wisdom.

Author of our parks, gardens, and sports chapter, **Ren Davis** is a native Atlantan and contributor to publications from the *Atlanta Journal–Constitution* to the *Atlanta Homes and Lifestyles Magazine.* He is co-author with his wife, Helen, of *Atlanta Walks: A Comprehensive Guide to Walking, Running, and Bicycling the Area's Scenic and Historic Locales* (Peachtree, 1993, 1995, 1998) and *Georgia Walks: Discovery Hikes Through Georgia's Natural and Human History,* (Peachtree, 2000). A firm believer in the great outdoors, Ren has conducted guided walking tours around Atlanta for a wide variety of groups.

For many years **Victoria Forrest,** our women's clothing shopping maven, has been a journalist in Atlanta, writing for *Creative Loafing, The Marietta Daily Journal, Women of Atlanta, The Piedmont Review,* and *Travel Holiday,* to name just a few publications. For a time she published her own monthly magazine, *Forrest Seen and Heard,* which covered everything from entertainment to travel. Vicky is also active in Atlanta radio and television production.

Author of our restaurants, arts and nightlife, hotels, and city sources chapters, **Jane Garvey** has lived in Georgia for 40 years and in Atlanta for more than 30 of those years. She has been a college professor and a real estate broker, and since 1990 has been a full-time writer. Covering food and wine, art, travel, and Southern culture and history, Jane is a regular contributor to the *Atlanta Journal–Constitution,* the *Atlanta Wine Report,* *Where Atlanta* magazine, and the Atlanta edition of *Museums & Galleries* magazine.

Hollis Gillespie, our "Places to Explore" expert, was born in Southern California but moved to Atlanta in 1989, almost immediately swapping her Valley Girl accent for a Southern drawl. Today she pens a weekly humor column for the *Atlanta Press* and is also a regular contributor to *Atlanta Magazine.*

One of fewer and fewer native Atlantans, our shopping writer **Michael Hagearty** has been writing and editing for local publications since 1997. He currently splits his time evenly between sitting in traffic and rooting for the Braves.

Atlanta native and shopping writer **Lynn McGill** lives in Roswell, Georgia. She marvels that Roswell, which used to be a day trip from Atlanta, is now described by realtors as "close in." A writer and magazine journalist for 25 years, she currently serves as *Traditional Home* magazine's regional editor and writes on art, architecture, antiques, interior design, and home improvement. Hesitating to use the term "obsessive," Lynn prefers to call herself a "serious" shopper.

Jill Sabulis is the *Atlanta Journal–Constitution's* Personal Shopper columnist. Her weekly columns cover shopping in metropolitan Atlanta stores and on the Internet. She has been a newspaper and magazine editor and reporter for the past 19 years. A Buckhead resident, she had the delectable task of researching for us the best places to shop for food.

Joe Silva, who checked out stores that sell all things wheeled, electronic, and musical, is a contributor to the *Atlanta Press*. He also freelances for various print and on-line periodicals and is at work on his first book, for Simon & Schuster. He gulped approximately one half-gallon of Cuban café con leche while producing his contributions to the shopping chapter.

Shopping writer **Jamie Vacca** is an associate editor at *Atlanta Magazine*. Hailing from North Carolina, she has lived in Atlanta since 1995.

It goes without saying that our contributors have chosen all establishments strictly on their own merits—no establishment has paid to be included in this book.

HOW TO USE THIS BOOK

The first thing you need to know is that everything in this book is **arranged by category and alphabetically** within each category.

Now, before you go any farther, check out the **city maps** at the front of the book. Each map has a number, in a black box at the top of the page, and grid coordinates along the top and side margins. Listings throughout the CITYGUIDE are keyed to one of these maps. Look for the map number in a small black box preceding each establishment name. The grid code follows in italics. For establishments with more than one location, additional map numbers and grid codes appear at the end of the listing. To locate a museum that's identified in the text as , turn to Map 7 and locate the address within the e-6 grid square. To locate restaurants nearby, simply skim the text in the restaurant chapter for listings identified as being on Map 7.

Throughout the guide, we name the neighborhood or town in which each sight, restaurant, shop, or other destination is located, as well as the MARTA stop, if there's one within walking distance. We also give you complete opening hours and admission fees for sights, and reservations, credit card, closing hours, and price information for restaurants.

At the end of the book, in addition to an **alphabetical index,** you'll find **directories of shops and restaurants by neighborhood.**

Chapter 7, City Sources, lists essential information and resources for residents—everything from vet and lawyer-referral services to caterers worth calling.

We've worked hard to make sure that all of the information we give you is accurate at press time. Still, time brings changes, so always confirm information when it matters—especially if you're making a detour.

Feel free to drop us a line. Were the restaurants we recommended as described? Did you find a wonderful shop you'd like to share? If you have complaints, we'll look into them and revise our entries in the next edition when the facts warrant. So send us your feedback. Either E-mail us at editors@fodors.com (specifying Fodor's CITYGUIDE Atlanta on the subject line), or write to the Fodor's CITYGUIDE Atlanta editor at Fodor's, 280 Park Avenue, New York, NY 10017. We look forward to hearing from you.

Karen Cure
Editorial Director

chapter 1

RESTAURANTS

N o one need ever go hungry in Atlanta, nor fail to satisfy a taste for both the noble and the humble in the culinary arts. Dining in this city can take you from the simple glories of homestyle country fare to sophisticated dishes by internationally renowned chefs. Ethnic communities have added their own special grace, allowing the hungry patron to sample everything from Indian vegetarian dishes to South African sosaties. An inland city once starved for good seafood, Atlanta's now blessed with fine seafood restaurants that bring to their patrons both the familiar catfish and the exotic mahi mahi.

NO-SMOKING

No metropolitan Atlanta jurisdiction to date has enacted a restaurant-focused no-smoking ordinance. In lieu of no-smoking laws, restaurants are free to establish their own policies, and most have well-separated no-smoking sections; some restaurants are entirely no-smoking, putting the offending puffers out on patios to smoke.

RESERVATIONS

Atlantans have gotten a reputation for making reservations all over town, then not keeping them. To combat such bad manners, many restaurants may ask for your contact telephone number so they may confirm your reservation a day ahead. Still others fend off the misbehavior by not taking reservations at all, leaving patrons to wait in line for a table; in some busy places, especially those at shopping malls, the host may hand you a beeper and page you when your table is ready. Another scheduling device that's surfaced recently is "call-ahead" seating—you call ahead to inquire about table availability and indicate that you'll be arriving with a party in tow at a given hour. It's almost like a reservation, except it's not guaranteed.

TIPPING

How much you leave is up to you, but 15%–20% is customary and that's how much will be added to the bill automatically for large parties (six or more). In very fine restaurants, if the sommelier or maître d' has taken special care to enhance your evening, an appropriate tip—15% of the value of the selected bottle for the sommelier, for instance—would be well received.

PRICE CATEGORIES

Pricing is estimated by number of dollar signs, ranging from $ ($20 or less for appetizer, entrée and dessert, on average) to $$$$ (more than $40 for appetizer, entrée and dessert, not including beverage, tax, or gratuity).

CATEGORY	COST*
$$$$	over $40
$$$	$30–$40
$$	$20–$30
$	under $20

*per person for a three-course meal, excluding drinks, service, and 7% sales tax.

restaurants by cuisine

AMERICAN

14　a-3

AMERICAN ROADHOUSE

A great place to take the family, kids in tow, for plenty of hearty, no frills, down-home food cooked the right way, the Roadhouse fills up quickly for all meals—especially for brunch on weekends. So get there early or plan to eat late. Breakfasts are stellar, with plenty of eggs, grits, pancakes, and all the trimmings, while great meat loaf and mashed potatoes and roast chicken basted with Georgia's own Red Brick Ale are favorites on the lunch and dinner menus. *842 N. Highland Ave., Virginia-Highland, 404/872–2822. AE, D, DC, MC, V. $*

5　f-8

BLUE RIBBON GRILL

Crowds line up here for chalkboard specials, which include a fresh soup (such as black bean or broccoli cheese), special vegetables, and, if you're lucky, fresh Georgia trout. On the regular menu, the hungry hordes favor the homemade meat loaf, grilled salmon, and the fabulous blue cheese burger (or any of the burgers, really). The salads are good, too, and the wine list is decent for this kind of casual spot. *4006 LaVista Rd., Northlake, 770/491–1570. AE, DC, MC, V. Closed Sun. $*

10 b-2
BUCKHEAD BREWERY & GRILL

Gleaming copper brew tanks shine through the big windows of this new brew pub, while hunt trophies set the rustic atmosphere inside the large, two-level log structure. Game and beef play a big role on the menu—bison burgers, venison, farm-raised elk tenderloin with a raspberry demi-glace, and steaks are accompanied by big salads (check out the "Wilderness Salad") and peanut butter or Snickers pie for dessert. Some half dozen brews are available (the wheat beer and Hop Island IPA are the richest), as is good root beer. *See also Chapter 5. 1757 Rock Quarry Rd., Stockbridge, 770/389–8112. Reservations not accepted. AE, D, DC, MC, V. $$*

15 g-6
CABBAGETOWN GRILL

The patio beckons in good weather, and in bad, the big stone-lined bar is a comforting spot. Sunday brunch patrons savor crab cakes Benedict, no foolin' stone-ground grits, crème brûlée French toast with applewood smoked bacon, and excellent Bloody Marys with peppers and olives instead of celery. Lunch focuses on good sandwiches, while dinner is full-blown American fare with southern touches, such as fried green tomatoes. *727 Wylie St., Cabbagetown, 404/525–8818. Reservations not accepted. MC, V. $*

4 g-4
CAREY'S PLACE

This is a really scruffy dive, but if you're passionate about burgers, these monstrous two-handers are such a pleasure you won't care, either. In fact, some Atlantans, whether they're tattooed types or guys and gals in suits, esteem these above all others in town. *1021 Cobb Pkwy., Marietta, 770/422–8042. Reservations not accepted. No credit cards. $*

14 g-3
CRESCENT MOON

Students and rising young professionals alike crowd this slip of a restaurant for big stuffed baked potatoes, great soups, quite good barbecue, excellent chili (the specialty), and house-made desserts. Given the quantity and quality of the fare, a meal here is one of the best deals in town. At press time, the restaurant was planning a move but had not chosen a new location. *254 W. Ponce de Leon Ave., Decatur, 404/377–5623. Reservations not accepted. No dinner. AE, D, DC, MC, V. $*

5 d-7
THE DOWNWIND

You may not think of an airport restaurant as the place to head for a good meal, but the Downwind is an exception. Kids love to view the planes taking off and landing from the outside deck, where grown-ups can relax with a beer. Salads, sandwiches, and specials such as grilled salmon (selections vary daily) are the mainstays of an uncomplicated menu. Greek specials are good, and the monster mushroom-stuffed burger rates high in the city's vegetarian offerings. *2000 Airport Rd., DeKalb-Peachtree Airport, off Clairmont Rd., west of I 85 (exit 99), Chamblee, 770/452–0973. Reservations not accepted. Closed Sun. MC, V. $*

15 g-7
EUREKA!

Sitting on the patio at dusk watching the lights come up and contemplating the peace of Oakland Cemetery may seem a strange way to enjoy a meal, but it works. The menu delves into Mediterranean dishes but gives them a southern touch. Calamari dusted in cornmeal? It works, too, and the good fried chicken holds its own here in Atlanta. Saturday and Sunday brunch patrons pack the patio to partake of brioche French toast with apples, cinnamon cream cheese, and walnuts, so arrive early. *242 Boulevard, Cabbagetown, 404/588–0006. No lunch weekdays. AE, MC, V. $*

5 b-7
FRANK'S FAMOUS FAMILY RESTAURANT

Frank's is attached to a filling station, but don't let the location keep you from enjoying down-home dishes with a slight Mediterranean influence—meat loaf, for example, might come with a touch of red peppers. The prime rib is delicious, and the country-fried steak is fresh and enormous, testifying to the fact that Frank's serves huge portions for fair money. The best dessert is hard to pick, but the tiramisu is a top contender. There is beer and wine only, with decent selections. *1188 Collinsworth Rd., Palmetto (I–85, west off exit 56 [Collinsworth Rd.]), south Fulton County, 770/463–5678. Closed Sun. AE, D, DC, MC, V. $*

14 *b-8*

HEAPING BOWL AND BREW

The funky East Atlanta neighborhood nearly despaired of having any good eateries until this spot came along. Bowls are indeed heaping, whether it's with mashed potatoes, pasta, pierogies, or some other example of the excellent home-style cooking. Saturday and Sunday brunches are very popular. *469 Flat Shoals Ave., East Atlanta Village, 404/523–8030. Reservations not accepted. AE, MC, V. $*

5 *a-4*

HOUCK'S STEAK AND SEAFOOD

Bill Houck and his wife, Judy, and son Chris, 16, are the operative spirits behind this family-focused establishment. The entrance murals depict locals and celebs—including former U.S. House Speaker Newt Gingrich—who have bent elbows here. You may find them in person on a tree-rimmed deck overlooking a small pond or inside the rambling restaurant and bar, where the emphasis is on fresh home cooking: Baked potatoes never see a microwave, black bean tastes of slow cooking with a ham bone, and ribs are oven roasted and then grilled. The deep-fried shrimp, which are lightly battered to order, are very popular. Specials with seafood and fish are offered every night, depending on availability because it's fresh. There is a kids' menu, and the "Kid of the Week" gets a $25 gift certificate. *Paper Mill Village shopping center, 305 Village Pkwy., Marietta, 770/859–0041. Reservations not accepted. No lunch. AE, D, DC, MC, V. $$*

15 *h-3*

JAVA JIVE COFFEE HOUSE AND CAFE

Decorated in 1930s–1950s kitsch, furnished with dinette tables and equipped with period kitchen gear, this is the place to come for breakfast and brunch on weekends. Mark your calendar if you like pumpkin pancakes: Their popular rendition is served every Halloween weekend and on one other occasion each fall, the date chosen at random. The ginger waffles with homemade lemon curd are the weekend special to look for at other times of the year. Come early, or prepare to wait. Closes daily at 2:30 PM. *790 Ponce de Leon Ave., Virginia-Highland, 404/876–6161. No lunch or dinner. MC, V.*

12 *f1*

LANDMARK DINER

This gleaming steel-and-neon 24-hour spot dominates the landscape at its heart-of-Buckhead location. Owner Tom Lambros hails from the Greek Island of Spespes, and Greek specialties include moussaka and pastitsio. Along with meat loaf, broiled fresh fish, shrimp fettuccine, crab-stuffed flounder, and humongous desserts, they are made from scratch. Even the bread is baked on-site. Mammoth breakfasts are served around the clock. *3652 Roswell Rd., Buckhead, 404/816–9090. AE, D, DC, MC, V. $*

13 *a-6*

THE ORIGINAL PANCAKE HOUSE

Apple pancakes, eggs in a blanket, "Dutch babies" (puffed pancakes with powdered sugar and lemon), waffles, all kinds of omelets, and really good sausage pack the weekend breakfast crowd into this chain. The excellent coffee is blended especially for the company, which was founded in Portland, Oregon, in 1953, about three years before IHOP came on the scene. Breakfast starts at 7 AM and goes to 3 PM during the week and to 4 PM on the weekend. *2321 Cheshire Bridge Rd., Northeast, 404/633–5677. No lunch or dinner. AE, D, DC, MC, V. $*

5 *d-7*

4330 Peachtree Rd., Brookhaven, 404/237–4116.

6 *b-5*

3665 Club Dr., Lawrenceville, 770/925–0065.

8 *d-1*

3099 Memorial Dr., Stone Mountain, 404/292–6914.

14 *a-3*

THE RIGHTEOUS ROOM

Pub grub of a healthy sort is the draw here, from quesadillas and excellent sandwiches to onion straws to veggie burgers made from grains, herbs and onions to veggie soup and chili. Omnivores need not worry—they also serve beef burgers. *1051 Ponce de Leon Ave., next to the Plaza Theater, Poncey-Highland, 404/874–0939. MC, V. $*

14 *f-1*

TANNER'S ROTISSERIE GRILL

Founded in Atlanta, Tanner's has nine locations around the metro area that dispense good rotisserie chicken and fresh veggie side dishes. Even your grandmother would approve of the cornbread dressing, to say nothing of the Oreo cookie cake (similar to a cheese cake, with Oreo cookie pieces on top). There's barbecue, too, but the chicken's the deal, and it's wickedly cheap: A quarter-chicken dinner with two sides is just $5.59. Each location has sit-down, but take-out seems to be the popular option. *1371 Clairmont Rd., near N. Decatur Rd., Northeast, 404/634–5500.*

9 *e-4*

Fayette Pavillion shopping center, 94 Pavillion Pkwy., Fayetteville, 770/716–7160.

4 *h-7*

3220 Cobb Pkwy., Northwest, 770/956–8866.

6 *b-1*

525 Peachtree Industrial Blvd., at Lawrenceville-Suwanee Dam Rd., Suwanee, 770/614–1335.

15 *e-3*

THE VARSITY

An Atlanta institution for more than a half century, the Varsity retains its common-man allure, as well as its curb service. Politicians, Bill Clinton among them, have often posed here for campaign gigs. The newer, retro-50s location in Norcross presents an upscale atmosphere, and the less-character-filled Varsity, Jr. in Lindbergh seems more frenzied. But the real McCoy downtown still speaks its special-order lingo: A "naked dog" lacks all condiments, a "naked steak" is a similarly unadorned burger, a "bag o' rags" is a sack of potato chips, and "walk a dog" means a hot dog to go. Whatever terminology you use, you'll savor the chili dogs, the frosted orange drinks, the fruit-filled fried pies, and the onion rings. Curb ser-

vice is available only at Downtown and Norcross. Open daily, and into the wee hours Downtown. *61 North Ave., Downtown, 404/881–1706. No credit cards. $*

13 *a-6*

1085 Lindbergh Dr., at Cheshire Bridge Rd., Dekalb County, 404/261–8843.

5 *g-6*

6045 Dawson Blvd., off Jimmy Carter Blvd., east of I–85 (exit 99), Norcross, 770/840–8519.

14 *a-4*

THE VORTEX

Off the wall decor is the hallmark of these two popular eateries—in fact, an image straight from Edvard Munch's *The Scream* frames the entrance at the Little Five Points location. Burgers, made with black beans, soy beans or turkey, are the specialty, while chicken, fish, and shrimp dishes and deli sandwiches take casual fare to another level. This is a brew-lovers' paradise, with more than 30 beers on tap and more than 210 bottled brands; and for the spirituous, there are 80 single-malt Scotches. It's open very late. *438 Moreland Ave., Little Five Points, 404/688–1828. AE, D, DC, MC, V. $*

15 *e-2*

878 Peachtree St., Midtown, 404/875–1667.

11 *c-2*

WHITE HOUSE

Famous for its American-southern fare, this long-popular spot does good southern-style breakfasts complete with grits and biscuits, and at lunch, the fourth-generation Greek-American owners place southern and Greek dishes (from pastitsio to moussaka and gyros) side-by-side on the steam table. No alcohol is served, and the whole place is no-smoking. *172 Peachtree St., Buckhead, 404/237–7601. No credit cards. No dinner. Reservations not accepted. $*

15 *g-4*

ZESTO DRIVE-INS

Menus and quality vary from location to location, but all the outlets do reliably good milk shakes (banana, butterscotch, and coffee are slam-dunks), hamburgers, foot-long hot dogs, and ice cream desserts. The Ponce de Leon outlet gets the award for the best architecture (it was redesigned in 1991 as a classic 1950s-style diner), as well as for cuisine: Almond chicken salad, grilled tuna sandwiches, and chicken fingers are excellent here. *544 Ponce de Leon Ave., Midtown, 404/607–1118. Reservations not accepted. No credit cards. $*

15 *h-8*

1181 E. Confederate Ave., East Atlanta, 404/622–4254.

8 *b-6*

151 Forest Pkwy., Forest Park, 404/366–0564.

14 *a-5*

377 Moreland Ave., Little Five Points, 404/523–1973.

12 *h-5*

2469 Piedmont Rd., Buckhead, 404/237–8689.

AMERICAN/ CASUAL

12 *f-1*

ARUGULA

Austrian native Fred Schrock cooked his way from home to the Cayman Islands and finally to Atlanta, where he opened a Caribbean restaurant. Now, however, he's transformed the menu with an American slant, although the popular and delicious conch fritters and jerk chicken remain. There are Asian touches, too, in the hoisin-ginger-sauced shrimp and the sesame noodle salad with peanut dressing and grilled chicken. But southern fare clearly has captured this wandering chef's imagination: Fried green tomatoes pair with goat cheese; grilled turkey steak with sweet potatoes and fresh cranberry sauce; fried trout with tartar sauce. The wine list is short but serves these dishes well; there's even a good Riesling to pair with the spicy stuff. *3639 Piedmont Rd., at Roswell Rd., Buckhead, 404/814–0959. No lunch Sat. Closed Sun. AE, MC, V. $$*

3 *h-8*

AQUA TERRA BISTRO

This charming, casual bistro in a tiny town is devoted to inventive eclectic and American fare. Start with the good bread and roasted red pepper hummus, then enjoy hot smoked salmon and West Indian fish 'n' chips with coconut macaroon-battered fish. The kitchen's range goes from these dishes to a very classic

lamb osso buco on white beans and tomato ragù. Pasta with Vodka cream sauce, made pink with red pepper and sun-dried tomatoes, is flecked with fresh basil and studded with asparagus. Very good classic crème brûle is the dessert highlight. *55 E. Main St., Buford, 770/271–3000. Reservations not accepted. No lunch week-ends. Closed Mon. AE, D, DC, MC, V. $$*

15 *e-5*

ATLANTA GRILL

Down-home goes upscale: With its New Orleans-style interior, this restaurant puts its best face on such American staples as macaroni and cheese, stone-ground grits, a rabbit stew, grilled meats and sweet potato corn chowder. Honey pecan pie comes with a little vial of spiced bourbon syrup to be poured over the whole business. The Grill does breakfast, lunch and dinner daily. *Ritz-Carlton Hotel, 181 Peachtree St., at Ellis St., Downtown, 404/659-0400, ext. 6450. AE, D, MC, V. $$$–$$$$*

14 *a-3*

ATKINS PARK

The oldest continuously operating restaurant in the city of Atlanta, founded in 1922, does the classics of fern bar fare a notch above the average. Chicken fingers are fried in a light beer batter and not pulled frozen out of a box, and corned beef hash comes with a pair of poached eggs and a good tarragon-lemon hollandaise sauce. Much of the menu takes its inspiration from Cajun cuisine as well as that of the Southwest: poblano queso blends white cheddar cheese and roasted peppers, while the lagniappe gumbo (the classic Creole soup/stew, with chicken and andouille sausage), the muffaletta (a traditional New Orleans sandwich made with olive salad, deli meats and cheese) and po'boys are worthwhile, too. When it's time for dessert, check out the sweet-potato pecan pie or bananas foster bread pudding. Besides the good wine list, there are numerous brews on tap, including Honey Brown and Caffreys. *794 N. Highland Ave., Virginia-Highland, 404/876–7249. AE, D, DC, MC, V. $–$$*

4 *h-2*

BLUE OLIVE

Blue Olive combines the tones of the Mediterranean with the hues of Provence, and not surprisingly, dishes reflect these regions, too, while wandering occasionally into other lands. A meal might start with Maine lobster ravioli with shiitake mushrooms and soy ginger butter sauce, a soup that is a pleasing blend of leek and potato, or chicken gumbo with andouille or black bean. Main courses are generously portioned, large enough for two to share, and include marinated flank steak, grilled to order and served with Yukon Gold mashed potatoes and balsamic demiglace. For dessert, our choice is the lovely crème brûlée. There's live music in the bar Wednesday–Saturday. *2942 Shallowford Rd., at Sandy Plains Rd., near the Sandy Plains shopping center, Marietta, 770/579–5001. No lunch. AE, D, DC, MC, V. $$*

12 *a-2*
BLUE RIDGE GRILL
Rustic refinement shapes this large restaurant, which takes its architectural cues from north Georgia mountain structures: Rowing sculls hang from the ridge pole; fishing gear forms part of the decor; rich woods take on a warm glow in mellow lighting. The menu changes with the seasons, and the inspiration is American with such dishes as grilled trout, horseradish-crusted grouper, crab and smoked trout cakes, and very good soups that change daily (watch for Carolina-inspired Hoppin' John). *1261 W. Paces Ferry Rd., at U.S. 41 (Northside Dr.), 404/233–5030. AE, D, DC, MC, V. $$$*

3 *h-8*
CALIFORNIA CAFÉ BAR & GRILL
This Marin County, California–based operation has come to Atlanta with a new, stylishly contemporary restaurant where the wide-ranging menu features rotisserie-cooked meats, pizzas cooked in a brick-lined oven, pastas, good salads, and homemade desserts. The company features California products, such as the excellent Laura Chenel goat cheeses and California olive oil. For wines, it's California again, of course, but besides good choices by the glass, there's a good list of half bottles. Sunday brunch runs until 3 PM. *Mall of Georgia, by Barnes & Noble, 3333 Buford Dr., Buford, 770/932–6777. AE, D, DC, MC, V. $$*

15 *e-5*
DAILEY'S
A renovated downtown warehouse with a bustling atmosphere, Dailey's has long been a popular establishment known for its brick walls, brass fixtures, antique carousel horses, and Gaslight-era atmosphere along with its monstrous dessert table. Before you get to that feature, though, check out the crab cakes, steaks, fish, roast chicken, red snapper, and peach barbecued pork tenderloin. Evening wine tastings are often held downstairs is the casual bar and grill, where there's apt to be live music, while the dining room upstairs is for more leisurely dining. There's a good wine list, plus full bar. *17 International Blvd., Downtown, 404/681–3303. Reservations not accepted. AE, D, DC, MC, V. $$*

5 *e-3*
DICK AND HARRY'S
Bringing a new standard of fine dining to the northern suburbs, this popular restaurant changes its menu with the seasons but is known for its crab cakes, veal, and game. The star in the last category is the grilled farm-raised emu with Yukon Gold mashed potatoes and a red wine sauce. The chef salad is a meal in itself, with wood-grilled tenderloin and chicken breast on greens, accompanied by roasted beets and maytag blue cheese dressing. This is a destination for wine aficionados, thanks to the well-selected wine list, which also features a good half-bottle list. *1570 Holcomb Bridge Rd., Roswell, 770/641–8757. Reservations essential at dinner. Closed Sun. No lunch Sat. AE, D, DC, MC, V. $$–$$$*

15 *f-3*
EINSTEIN'S
The front patio of this former Midtown bungalow is wildly popular for Sunday brunch and any day for lunch or dinner, when the fish, pastas, salads and the famous Einstein club sandwich are available. Dishes take their culinary cues from around the world, making American pie out of spiced hummus, calamari with chipotle pepper-spiked tartar sauce, coconut-crusted shrimp and grilled chicken on soba noodles. Brunch dishes range from basic omelets to excellent pancakes. *1077 Juniper St., Midtown, 404/876–2925. Reservations essential. AE, D, DC, MC, V. $*

14 *b-5*
FLYING BISCUIT CAFÉ
This is a most amazing place: It must be, or why else would patrons wait for up to two hours in plastic chairs set

alongside the road or tolerate the absence of parking? Justly famous biscuits are served cold, omelets are packed with all manner of fresh ingredients and excellent goat cheese, the grits are real (which means stone ground), the coffee's good, and the juice is freshly squeezed. The focus is on healthy fare, so don't look for any red meat—turkey's all you'll find, even in the bacon and sausage. *1655 McLendon Ave., Candler Park, 404/687–8888. Reservations not accepted. Closed Mon. AE, DC, MC, V. $*

5 a-5
FOOD 101

New to the neighborhood, Food 101 is graced by a long bar that faces the street. A wall of wood-framed glass can slide entirely open, bringing fresh air and the sounds of the street into the interior on nice days. Beyond the bar and to its left lies a warmly lit casual dining room, with leather-lined banquettes and well-spaced tables. Baby-toting families looking for a decent meal throng. It's a casual place that gives the denizens of this upscale neighborhood such fare as crab and rock shrimp cakes, battered onion rings, pork chops on mashed potatoes and very good sea bass. Desserts, big enough for two, lean toward the familiar, such as a banana split and excellent waffles with toffee crunch ice cream, caramel and chocolate sauces. The wine list is not long but is well selected, and offers many unusual choices by the glass, such as the excellent Fess Parker Viognier. *Belle Isle Square shopping center, 4969 Roswell Rd., Suite 200, Sandy Springs, 404/497–9700. No lunch weekends. AE, D, DC, MC, V. $$$*

14 g-3
THE FOOD BUSINESS

This high-energy establishment provides a friendly place for neighborhood dining and a frequently changing menu that focuses on sandwiches, salads (the best are roasted beet, grilled chicken, and curried tuna), fresh soups, and such local dishes as Georgia lake trout with sesame pumpkin butter. Diners who are more adventurous will find a grilled squid pizza (one of many dishes you can enjoy as an appetizer or small entrée) and grilled sea scallops on a potato pancake with *pico de gallo* (chunky guacamole with flecks of tomato, onion and cilantro) and cilantro

cream sauce (expressing the kitchen's taste for southwestern ingredients). There's a good kids' menu, too, and the extensive wine list, with about 65 choices, includes a cellar selection of fine bottles and a lot of good vintages by the glass. *115 Sycamore St., Decatur, 404/ 371–9121. Reservations not accepted. No lunch Sat. Closed Sun. AE, D, DC, MC, V. $–$$*

15 b-3
FOOD STUDIO

The industrial-style, high-ceilinged space in what once was a plow factory has drawn crowds to an area that no one would have thought suitable for a restaurant. But the King Plow Arts Center, with its theater and offices, has proved to be the perfect venue for this innovative restaurant's clever, witty takes on American regional cuisine. The well-structured wine list offers selections that go well with the food. *887 W. Marietta St., King Plow Arts Center, Downtown, 404/815–6677. No lunch. Reservations essential. AE, MC, V. $$*

6 b-6
GEORGIA DINER

Gwinnett County's reliable 24-hour dining establishment—probably its only one—does delicious meals at any hour, plus breakfast dishes. The omelets are four-square hefty, and the specials are the "best meal deals" with such very well done items as stuffed roasted Cornish hen with mashed potatoes and good veggies. The eye-popping desserts and good coffee make this a good stop at the end of an evening out. *1655 Pleasant Hill Rd., Duluth, 770/806–9880. AE, D, DC, MC, V. $–$$*

6 f-4
HI-LIFE

This lively spot proves that to turn around a seemingly dead restaurant space, all you have to do is provide good food and ambience. Hi-Life has some intriguing features on its menu, notably a wide range of lobster preparations; "Hardwood Grill" selections that focuses on grilled meats, fish, and even veggies; and a four-course tasting menu that changes daily. A publike bar area provides area office workers a good spot to grab a drink after work. The wine list is thoughtfully chosen and offers good selections by the glass; in fact, this is a popular venue for wine events, so be sure to ask about special dinners and tastings. *3380 Holcomb Bridge Rd., Norcross, 770/409–0101. No lunch weekends. AE, D, DC, MC, V. $$$–$$$$*

4 *f-1*
HOPS RESTAURANT & BREWERY
Bringing freshly brewed beers to the northern 'burbs, Hops also does good meat loaf, burritos, sandwiches and salads at lunch, and steaks and other grilled meats, seafood, salads, and pastas at dinner. Four fresh beers, from a light beer to a heavier ale, are brewed on site. *945 Ernest Barrett Pkwy., Kennesaw, 770/919–0434. Reservations not accepted. AE, D, DC, MC, V. $$*

5 *d-4*
HOUSTON'S
This Atlanta-founded chain draws a large lunch crowd, and wait times at peak hours can be frustratingly long. Is the wait worth it? Thai chicken salad, grilled chicken salad with honey-lime vinaigrette, excellent seared ahi tuna dishes may convince you it is. Besides, the bars are nice places to drop in for an after-work drink. *4701 Ashford-Dunwoody Rd., Dunwoody, 770/512–7066. Reservations not accepted. AE, MC, V. $$*

12 *h-2*
3321 Lenox Rd., across from Lenox Square mall, Buckhead, 404/237–7534.

12 *a-2*
3539 Northside Pkwy., Buckhead, 404/262–7130.

12 *d-8*
2166 Peachtree Rd., Brookwood (south Buckhead), 404/351–2442.

4 *h-6*
3050 Windy Hill Rd., Marietta, 770/563–1180.

5 *c-2*
GREENWOODS ON GREEN STREET
A humble former residence serves as the backdrop for what's become a very popular home-style American dining experience. The menu goes regional in such dishes as the outstanding crab cakes, fried chicken with mashed potatoes, duck roasted with plenty of black pepper, and luxuriously deep traditional pies. Come early or prepare to wait a long time. Beer and wine only are available. *1087 Green St., Roswell, 770/992–*

5383. Reservations not accepted. Closed Mon.–Tues. No credit cards. $–$$

15 *f-3*
JOE'S ON JUNIPER
Nostalgia rules the atmosphere at this popular neighborhood bar, where the menu includes burgers, hot dogs, and a standout homemade hash. Count on being able to get breakfast all day long and well into the wee hours, too. The street-side patio is a nice place to dine or relax over a drink. *1049 Juniper St., Midtown, 404/875–6634. Reservations not accepted. AE, DC, MC, V. $*

14 *a-4*
MANUEL'S TAVERN
Now more than a half century old, Manuel's in Poncey-Highland is a gathering spot for neighbors young and old (*see* Chapter 5). They enjoy veggie burgers, steak sandwiches, beer-steamed hot dogs, and chicken wings (which could well be the city's best, served with house-made blue cheese dressing) while they argue politics, watch the Braves, and schmooze owner Manuel Maloof, himself a political leader in DeKalb County. The Stone Mountain location differs markedly in atmosphere, lacking that old pub feeling of the original. *602 N. Highland Ave., Poncey-Highland, 404/525–3447. Reservations not accepted. AE, D, DC, MC, V. $*

8 *f-2*
4877 Memorial Dr., Stone Mountain, 404/296–6919.

15 *e-5*
MAX LAGER'S
The brick walls and industrial atmosphere form an excellent showcase for one of the city's best brew pubs. Ignore the brews if you wish, and savor the house-made root beer or ginger beer. Wine enthusiasts, fear not—the wine list is decent. The fare is casual and features well-made sandwiches, excellent soups, pasta dishes, and salads. This is a handy place to dine before a sports event at the Philips Arena. *See also* Chapter 5. *320 Peachtree St., Downtown, 404/525–4400. Reservations not accepted. AE, D, DC, MC, V. $*

14 *a-2*
MURPHY'S
Tom Murphy's casual spot combines restaurant, bakery, retail wine shop, and

take-out operation all in one comfortable space. Soups change constantly, and all are good, but sweet potato bisque is the one to look for. If it's not available, console yourself with crab cakes, roast chicken, grilled tuna, superior pasta dishes, and the nut tart or another masterful desserts. Outstanding egg dishes, breads, and fresh juices make this a popular spot for Saturday and Sunday brunch. Murphy's also frequently hosts wine-focused events and special wine dinners. *997 Virginia Ave., Virginia-Highland, 404/872–0904. Reservations not accepted. No lunch weekends. AE, D, DC, MC, V. $$*

3 *d-5*

NORMAN'S LANDING

Family-oriented, busy, and a tad noisy, popular Norman's Landing feeds the Cumming area with well-prepared home-cooked fare that's available all day and includes steaks, seafood, and chicken dishes. The crawfish and scallop cake is a tasty retake on crab cakes, and the country-fried steak is made on the premises, a rare thing these days. There's a veranda for waiting, patio tables, and full bar service (but not on Sundays). Work off your meal with a game of Ping Pong; the $1 donation goes to a local charity, with different organizations benefiting from your largess each month. *365 Peachtree Pkwy., Cumming, at GA 400, exit 13 (GA 141), 770/886–0100, fax 770/886–0822 take-out orders. Reservations not accepted. AE, D, DC, MC, V. $$*

15 *e-4*

PLEASANT PEASANT

This restaurant was done on a shoestring—brick walls and a pressed-tin ceiling are what pass for decor, and since its founders could not afford printed menus, specials are scribbled on chalk boards. Crab cakes, pasta dishes, excellent duck and pork, and extravagant desserts have become traditions here. *555 Peachtree St., Midtown, 404/874–3223. No lunch weekends. Reservations not accepted. AE, D, DC, MC, V. $$*

12 *e-8*

R. THOMAS DELUXE GRILL

The covered patio is the only place to dine, and it plays cozy to the street. But that's part of the fun, all the more so because exotic birds frolic in a nearby cage. This popular spot for business

lunches, kids' gatherings, and late-night or early morning feasting serves excellent burgers, stuffed baked potatoes, megasalads, omelets, malteds, and desserts. Service can sometimes be frantic and perfunctory, especially if you're dining solo. *1812 Peachtree Rd., Brookwood (south Buckhead), 404/872–2942. No lunch. AE, D, DC, MC, V. $*

4 *h-6*

RAY'S ON THE RIVER

A more perfect vision of Atlanta dining could not be imagined: Snuggled along the banks of the Chattahoochee River, with a deck for fine patio dining and plenty of window-side seating, Ray's is one of the city's most popular spots, and little wonder. The menu changes frequently, but you can always depend on the grilled pork chops, seared tuna, crab spinach dip, grilled salmon, and crab cakes (these are notable for their nicely balanced flavors and textures). Whatever you have, leave room for key lime pie. Wines range from bottom-rung American choices to first-growth Bordeaux. The Sunday brunch gets raves, a jazz trio plays weekend evenings, and there's happy-hour entertainment (keyboard) weekdays. *6700 Powers Ferry Rd., Marietta, 770/955–1187. No lunch weekends. AE, D, DC, MC, V. $$*

12 *g-3*

ROCK BOTTOM BREWERY

Rock Bottom brews 10 beers on the premises, ranging from seasonal beers to two cask-conditioned beers produced in the traditional British fermentation process. The menu, though, is decidedly American casual, with wood-fired pizzas, sandwiches, pastas, and salads. A warning: Seasonings can be a little hot, so make any aversions you have to spicy fare known when you order. *3242 Peachtree Rd., near Piedmont Rd., Buckhead, 404/264–0253. Reservations not accepted. AE, D, DC, MC, V. $$*

14 *g-3*

SAGE

Remy Kerba, formerly owner of Le Giverny (*see French, below*), recently opened this restaurant in the exposed-brick spaces once occupied by two store fronts. Here he explores the gamut of American fare, including its Italian, French, and southwestern influences. Thus, there's French onion soup and mussels Provençale as well as chicken quesadillas and black bean–yucca cakes with spicy guacamole. For dessert, pray Kerba has made the apricot cheesecake. There's a lengthy wine list, with many by-the-glass choices. *121 Sycamore St., Decatur, 404/373–5574. Reservations not accepted. AE, D, DC, MC, V. $$*

5 *g-2*
SIA'S
Sia Moshk became familiar to Atlantans during his stint as manager of 103 West (*See* Continental, *below*). Here at his own restaurant, Moshk has gone all-out American but fuses influences from around the world, as demonstrated in the lemongrass cured salmon tacos with sake tarragon cream and enoki mush-rooms. But simple dishes work well, too, such as the fried oysters with Creole tartar sauce and arugula salad. Lamb chops come with a touch of cranberry and an apple-bacon spinach strudel. Banana-ginger pound cake supplies a terrific finish. The wine list is very well done. *Shops of St. Ives shopping center, 10305 Medlock Bridge Rd., Duluth, 770/497–9727. Reservations not accepted. No lunch weekends. AE, D, DC, MC, V. $$–$$$*

12 *e-3*
SWAN COACH HOUSE
Very popular with the "ladies who lunch" who often stay for exhibitions at the adjacent art gallery (*see* Atlanta History Center *in* Chapter 4), this tea room also sees duty as a good place for bridal luncheons. Dishes that never change, or so it seems, are the chicken salad, Jell-O salad and zucchini muffins. One trip to this hallowed haunt of Buckhead matrons, and you'll see what it means to grow old graciously, southern style. Don't forget your white gloves. Full bar service is available. *3130 Slaton Dr., on the grounds of the Atlanta History Center, Buckhead, 404/261–0636. No dinner. Closed Sun. AE, MC, V. $*

5 *c-2*
THE SWALLOW AT THE HOLLOW
Paul and Doreen Doster joined forces with Bill Greenwood (of Greenwood's on Green Street; *see* above) to take over a former barbecue joint (pointedly named Georgia Pig) and transform it into a place to celebrate home-style American cooking. Much of the fare is southern style, including the pork barbe-

cue, but broadens to include smoked turkey and, for the Texans among us, beef barbecue. Alongside are macaroni and cheese, baked beans, and a unique (made with chocolate chip cookies) banana pudding. Continuous service weekends from 11 AM to late at night makes this a handy spot to indulge after a round of errands or after church. There's very limited wine service. *1072 Green St., Roswell, 678/352–1975. Reservations not accepted. Closed Mon. No credit cards. $*

8 *e-1*
THE SYCAMORE GRILL
This charming antebellum house with its wide verandas and burnished wood floors saw hospital duty during the Civil War. Today, it's an elegant place to dine well on such signature dishes as blue crab cakes, sweet potato fries, steamed mussels, filet mignon salad, blackberry chicken salad, fresh Georgia mountain trout, fried green tomatoes, crumbed goat cheese salad, angel food pound cake, and deep-dish key lime pie. There's a very good wine list as well. *5329 Mimosa Dr., Stone Mountain, 770/465–6789. Closed Sun.–Mon. AE, D, DC, MC, V. $$*

15 *e-5*
THE TAP ROOM
With an inviting bar and a warmly lit Art Deco dining room, this is a nice spot to relax after work while enjoying popular classics from a multitude of cuisines. The rigatoni Vodka is a delectable vege-tarian dish; chicken satay with a spicy peanut dipping sauce is as good as you'll find in any Thai restaurant; and the crab cakes tap into the food of the South. There's a full bar and an exten-sive wine list, with many good and dif-ferent choices by the glass. *Peachtree Center Mall, 231 Peachtree St., Down-town, 404/577–7860. No lunch weekends. AE, D, DC, MC, V. $$–$$$$*

5 *a-1*
VAN GOGH'S
Brick walls serve as showcases for art by local and regional artists (one of the owners is kin to the owner of Alpha Omega Gallery in Roswell), and these artful surroundings set the stage for a menu that changes monthly but is always enticing: soft-shell crab (sea-sonal), crab cakes, stir fries, a daily risotto, good soups, sautéed sea bass,

grilled Portobello mushroom, grilled vegetable sandwiches, and tiramisu, the house's special dessert. The wine list is very carefully crafted, and a glass of Jepson Brandy after dinner is the perfect finish. The restaurant often hosts wine-focused events, such as winemaker dinners. *70 Crossville Rd., Roswell, 770/993–1156. No lunch Sun. AE, DC, MC, V. $$–$$$*

14 *f3*

WATERSHED

Emily Saliers (of the Indigo Girls) and friends have hit a high note with their casual but excellent take-out and dine-in spot, complete with a store front that sells scented candles, cookbooks, fine bottled salsas, and a superior wine inventory. But the draw is chef Scott Peacock's yummy takes on American-southern classics that include a sharp cheddar pimento cheese sandwich, rich cauliflower soup, and New England salted cod chowder (all soups are off-the-charts wonderful), shrimp salad sandwich or plate made from shrimp that were swimming in the Edisto River only hours before, and desserts to die for, such as (in season) rhubarb cobbler. The dinner menu adds such dishes as potato gnocchi and braised pork on polenta. Yes, sometimes Emily is on hand, dispensing wines at the bar and doing a fine job of it, too. But no crooning, please. *406 W. Ponce de Leon Ave., Decatur, 404/378–4900. Reservations not accepted. Closed Sun. AE, D, DC, MC, V. $–$$*

BARBECUE

15 *f6*

ACE BARBECUE BARN

This basic, no-frills spot supplies take-out for busy Auburn Avenue denizens at lunchtime and provides some tables, too. Eat in or eat out, but get ready for excellent barbecue (sliced pork sandwich, ribs and rib tips), the most delicious baked chicken and pan dressing, and excellent sweet potato pie. It's open very late some nights. *30 Bell St., off Auburn Ave., Sweet Auburn, 404/659–6630. Reservations not accepted. Closed Tues. No credit cards. $*

4 *e-2*

BELL'S

The Yankee kids who wait on you have never heard of a rib sandwich and probably actually think you're going to ingest the bones and all. Oh well. The cue's not bad, the place is so squeaky clean you could bring your mother-in-law here, and the fried pies could give the Varsity (*see* American, *above*) a run for its money (and that's no mean feat). *3815 Cherokee St., Kennesaw, 770/419–2626. AE, MC, V. $*

5 *d-6*

BENNY'S BARBECUE

These tender, smoky ribs taste so good that you won't care if the surroundings are scruffy. The pulled pork piled high on a bun isn't at all shabby, either; maybe the tart vinegar-dressed slaw is

---

an acquired taste, but the crunchy fresh ingredients keep you reaching for more. *2150B Johnson Ferry Rd., Chamblee, 770/454–7810. Reservations not accepted. MC, V. $*

2 *b-8*

BLUE PIG

Here in the suburbs, it's unusual to find good blues and barbecue in the same venue. But the Blue Pig has it all, with great blues Friday and Saturday nights (*see* Chapter 5). The side dishes are excellent, too, including the Brunswick stew and baked beans. The bar's a friendly place, and the seating arrangements make for good listening. *9770 S. Main St., Woodstock, 770/517–2583. Reservations not accepted. MC, V. $*

6 *a-5*

CORKY'S RIBS & BAR-B-Q

If you've got a taste for Memphis-style barbecue, both wet and dry, this franchise of the famous Memphis 'cue joint is about the only place to get some. The dry rub is heavy on the paprika, but the meat is tender. Side dishes include very good Brunswick stew, okay baked beans, and good potato slaw. The chili is good, too, if not distinctive. *1605 Pleasant Hill Rd., Duluth, 770/564–8666. AE, D, DC, MC, V. $*

15 *e-7*

DADDY D'S

A downtown venue for blues and ribs, this joint serves barbecue of variable quality (but when it's good, it's downright good) and consistently good blues (Friday and Saturday nights only). Brunswick stew, macaroni and cheese, baked beans, okra, broccoli casserole, black beans and rice, and collard greens are among the adornments. *264 Memorial Dr., Downtown, 404/222–0206. Reservations not accepted. AE, MC, V. $*

9 *f-1*

DEAN'S

Cooking pigs the hard, traditional way means smoking them slowly all night long and staying up with the critters to make sure the basting's done and the fire stays low. Supremely tender ribs and pulled pork are the reward, as you'll discover at this real hole-in-the-wall barbecue joint with no amenities whatsoever. *9480 S. Main St., Jonesboro, 770/431–0138. Reservations not accepted. No credit cards. $*

9 *d-4*

DU ROC CAFÉ

Another south metro favorite, Du Roc ranks high for slow-smoked ribs and beef. (The "Du Roc" is a breed of pig, so they say.) The pork sandwich may be had Carolina style, with the slaw on top. There's cracklin' cornbread (with sautéed crisped pork fat blended into the batter) and very good barbecue beans. No alcohol is served. *115 Marquis Dr., Fayetteville, off GA 54 toward Peachtree City, 770/719–1744. Reservations not accepted. Closed Sun.–Mon. AE, D, DC, MC, V. $*

13 *c-7*

DUSTY'S

In a simple, rustic wood building perched on a busy corner, Dusty's dishes up North Carolina–style barbecue, the kind that comes with thin vinegar-pepper sauce and with cole slaw on top of the meat. The hot sauce is superior, and so are the vegetable and dessert side dishes. Beer and wine only are available, but not on Sunday. *1815 Briarcliff Rd., at Clifton Rd., Emory area, 404/320–6264. Reservations not accepted. AE, D, DC, MC, V. $*

12 *g-7*

FAT MATT'S RIB SHACK

This shack (and that's what it is) fills quickly with folks who come not only for the barbecue but also for the blues. What they eat while they listen to the sweet sounds is tender ribs and deeply smoky pulled pork sandwiches. The Brunswick stew is so-so, but the beans are good, and there's beer. Barbecued chicken is quite good. Go early if you plan to sit while the music's on, because after it starts, there's standing room only (*see* Chapter 5). *1811 Piedmont Rd., Morningside, 404/607–1622. Reservations not accepted. No credit cards. $*

7 *h-4*

HAROLD'S

This quirky joint in the shadow of the Federal Penitentiary draws suit types, State Patrol officers, and just about everybody else who knows good Brunswick stew. Cracklin' cornbread— cracklin's are pieces of pork fat rendered off until they're crisp–is the standard against which all others are measured. The barbecue itself is some folks' favorite and other folks' least favorite; you'll have to decide for yourself. A second location in Jonesboro offers the same menu, but fanatics swear by the southeast Atlanta spot. *171 McDonough Blvd., southeast Atlanta, 404/627–9268. Reservations not accepted. Closed Sun. No credit cards at McDonough; AE, MC, V at Jonesboro. $*

9 g-2

265 GA 54, Jonesboro, 770/478–5880.

5 f-4
J. R.'S LOGHOUSE
In this log-style rambling structure you'll find some good barbecue that's consistent and reliable, if not stellar. Breakfast, beginning early in the morning, is southern-style, with grits, eggs, sausage, country ham, bacon, good biscuits, and fine coffee. The barbecue omelet is an original and hearty start to the day. *6601 Peachtree Industrial Blvd., Norcross, 770/ 449–6426. Reservations not accepted. AE, D, DC, MC, V. $*

6 d-8
JIMMY'S SMOKEHOUSE
Setting up shop in a mobile unit, Jimmy and Thelma Stokes draw crowds from near and far. What patrons take away with them (there's no place to sit but on the ground or the hood of your car) is tender slow-cooked pork roast, ribs, and beautiful potato casserole. Stokes and family cater private parties most of the week, and feed the public only on Friday and Saturday. *Corner of GA 124 and Everson Rd., Snellville, 770/972–1625. Closed Sun.–Thurs. No credit cards. $*

10 d-4
O. B.'S
Smoke curls enticingly from the chimney of this squeaky-clean rustic cabin, where reliably good, if not stunning, barbecue and sides are served in generous portions. The ribs are your best bet, and the pies are not bad either. *725 Industrial Blvd. (I–75 at exit 218), McDonough, 770/ 954–1234. AE, MC, V. $*

4 g-7
OLD SOUTH
This cabin-style barbecue joint sends out great smells and smoke signals that seem to beckon patrons from far away. One of Cobb County's best, it is famous for its sweet slow-smoked ribs (get the sauce on the side to dip the ribs into), unusual vinegar-dressed cole slaw (no mayonnaise), great Brunswick stew, and

beans. No alcohol is served. *601 Burbank Cir., at Windy Hill Rd., Smyrna, 770/ 435–4215. Reservations not accepted. Closed Mon. MC, V. $*

3 d-5
PAPPY RED'S
A big single-engine plane landing on the roof and plenty of memorabilia provide the atmosphere, while broccoli casserole, ribs, Brunswick stew, pulled pork, baked chicken with barbecue sauce, sweet potato soufflé, and peach-blackberry cobbler provide the nourishment. Beer is available at both locations. *867 Buford Rd., GA 400, exit 14, Cumming, 770/844–9446. Reservations not accepted. AE, D, DC, MC, V. $*

2 e-7

13680 Arnold Mill Rd., Roswell, 770/475– 9910.

12 f3
THE RIB RANCH
Even sophisticated Buckhead gets down-home with these Texas-style barbecue beef ribs. You can get baby-back pork ribs, too, but the deal is the huge beef rib platter ($26.95) that feeds two or three people. Excellent side dishes round out the offerings. The people-watching is a nifty add-on; some real characters dine at the Buckhead location. *25 Irby Ave., off Roswell Road, one block north of W. Paces Ferry Rd., Buckhead, 404/233–7644.*

4 g-3

2063 Canton Rd., near Sandy Plains Rd., Marietta, 770/422–5755. MC, V. $

14 h-1
ROCKIN' ROB'S
This roadhouse-style joint, decorated with plenty of hunting trophies and Marilyn Monroe memorabilia, covers the barbecue range from smoked chicken to beef brisket and sweetly tender, smoky Georgia-style ribs, plus pulled, sliced, and chopped pork sandwiches. The three sauces range from medium-bodied mild with a good vinegar-tomato balance to vinegar and hot pepper and a mustard sauce. Native Atlantan Rob Aldridge plays his extensive collection of classic rock vinyls and brings in live bluegrass music on Saturdays (see Chapter 5). *1479 Scott Blvd., Decatur, 404/378–6041. Reservations not accepted. Closed Sun. MC, V. $*

5 c-2

SLOPE'S

Some Atlantans swear this is the best of the bunch in the barbecue department, especially for ribs. The sauce is a Carolina-style vinegar-pepper sauce, and the Brunswick stew reminds many folks of what their moms used to make. No alcohol is served. *10360 Alpharetta St., Roswell, 770/518–7000. Reservations not accepted. Closed Sun. AE, D, DC, MC, V. $*

2 b-8

10200 GA 92, Woodstock, 770/516–6789.

12 g-7

SMOKEHOUSE RIBS

Midwestern-style 'cue with excellent sides is the style here. Family recipes constitute the sources of some of the recipes; a great-uncle invented the vinegar-based sauce. *1873 Piedmont Rd., near Cheshire Bridge Rd., Buckhead, 404/607–0474. AE, D, DC, MC, V. $*

7 g-8

SPEEDI PIG

Southsiders make tracks for this two-outlet operation for barbecue and all the traditional side dishes. Ribs get the most positive comments, but the sliced pork sandwiches are highly regarded as well. Arguments fly thick and fast as to which location does the better job. It's your call. *8446 GA 85, Riverdale, 770/471–4111. Reservations not accepted Thurs.–Sat. Closed Sun. No credit cards. $*

9 e-4

715 S. Glynn St., Fayetteville, 770/719–2720.

5 h-6

SPICED RIGHT

A major award winner in barbecue competitions with gobs of trophies to show for it, this is an outstanding barbecue joint. In addition to the 'cue, there's a steam table with lots of good side dishes, along with fried chicken and cornbread. But don't pass up the ribs, which are tender and richly smoked. Beer is available, and the iced tea is wonderful. *5364 U.S. 29, Lilburn, 770/564–0355. Reservations not accepted. No dinner Sun.–Wed. AE, D, DC, MC, V. $*

15 f-6

THELMA'S RIB SHACK

This glorious southern fare would please the hardest Yankee heart. Beyond ribs, there's beautifully cooked vegetables, corn bread, barbecued chicken, and homemade cakes. Pack a plate to go and pick at it all the way home. *302 Auburn Ave., Downtown, 404/523–0081. Reservations not accepted. No dinner. Closed Sun. No credit cards. $*

2 e-1

TWO BROTHERS

Even though it is slightly beyond our 10-county area, this down-home joint with sawdust on the floor and classic old-time atmosphere is very popular with residents of the northern suburbs, especially those who live in Cherokee County. You'll enjoy the barbecue, but be forewarned that the Brunswick stew is not as tasty as it is in some other spots. No alcohol is served. *1695 Old Canton Rd., Ball Ground, 770/735–2900. Reservations not accepted. Closed Mon.–Wed. No credit cards. $*

7 b-1

WALLACE BARBECUE

South Cobb County is well served by this emporium, bedecked with antique auto memorabilia that includes an antique gas pump and a '57 Chevy cut into a bench. Enjoy ribs, chopped or sliced pork sandwiches, barbecued chicken, and the side dishes (which, unlike the desserts, are made in house), and then take home a squeeze bottle of the tangy mustard-base sauce that's good on just about anything. *3035 Bankhead Hwy., Austell, 770/739–1686. Reservations not accepted. Closed Sun.–Mon. AE, D, DC, MC, V. $*

5 g-7

WATKINS BBQ PIT

Nothing more than a little stand on a corner, Watkins does everything from breakfast sandwiches to barbecue. "Breakfast in a cup" is a Styrofoam bowl filled with eggs and chopped up country-fried steak, sausage or bacon, and grits. But the 'cue's the thing: pork sandwiches with your choice of mustard-based sauce, tangy vinegar-pepper Carolina style sauce, or tomato-based sauce; beef brisket; and ribs. Grab your choice and go, because there's no place to sit. *3881 Lawrenceville Hwy., Tucker, 770/496–1980. Reservations not accepted. Closed Sun. No credit cards.*

4 g-4

WILLIAMSON BROTHERS

A Cobb County favorite (and popular with local politicians) that also does catering, this rustic-style place is at its best when doing ribs, chopped pork, sliced pork, side dishes, and coconut cream pie (awesome!). Breakfast is served, too. Bottled beer is available. *1425 Roswell Rd., Marietta, 770/971–3201. Reservations not accepted. AE, D, DC, MC, V. $*

BRITISH

15 *f2*

PRINCE OF WALES

Homesick Brits take comfort in this warmly lit authentic-style English pub, which is filled with soccer trophies (*see* Chapter 5). The fare is right down the line authentic, including very good fish-and-chips, shepherd's pie made with beef, and bread pudding. The 10 quaffs on tap include Strongbow Cider, otherwise hard to come by. The Sunday brunch special—a basic English breakfast, here called the "Union Jack," of two eggs, fried bread, Irish bacon and baked beans, grilled tomato, mushrooms, chips, and Scottish bangers—will keep you going all week. *1144 Piedmont Ave., Midtown, 404/876–0227. Reservations not accepted. AE, D, DC, MC, V. $*

15 *d-5*

REGGIE'S BRITISH PUB

Hung with myriad WWII–era photos, Reggie's still serves as headquarters of the "Grand Losers Party" every Fourth of July. In mid-September, the "Battle of Britain Party" celebrates the Allied victory in World War II. Bangers and mash, shepherd's pie, a ploughman's platter, and Scotch eggs attest to the authenticity of the menu. British beers on draught number about 45 and include Bass Ale, Fullers, Guinness, Harp, and Newcastle Nut Brown Ale. *317 CNN Center, Downtown, tel. 404/525–1437. Reservations not accepted. AE, D, MC, V. $*

CAFÉS

15 *e-6*

ATLANTA BREAD COMPANY

There are about 30 locations of this Atlanta-based company in the metro area, with more on the drawing boards, so it's not hard to come by a good breakfast, lunch, or snack. Pastries and cookies are baked on the premises of each shop, as is bread that accompanies soups and salads and is a prime ingredient of excel-

lent sandwiches. *52 Peachtree St., Muses's Bldg. Downtown, 404/614–0170. Reservations not accepted. AE, D, DC, MC, V. $*

5 *b-5*

220 Sandy Springs Cir., Sandy Springs, 404/873–0040.

14 *g-3*

205 E. Ponce de Leon Ave., Decatur, 404/378-6600.

5 *e-1*

1056 North Point Cir., Alpharetta, 770/740–1450.

12 *d-7*

THE BREAD MARKET

Looking for a good sandwich? Try the curry chicken salad with almonds or shiitake mushroom with fresh mozzarella cheese. Want to indulge in a pastry to die for? Try the brownies, cookies, or cheesecake. The espresso is excellent, too; the salad bar is loaded with fresh ingredients; and a breakfast burrito stuffed with scrambled eggs and salsa is a fine way to start a day. No alcohol is served. *1927 Peachtree Rd., Brookwood Village, across from Piedmont Hospital, 404/352–5252. Reservations not accepted. No dinner. AE, DC, MC, V. $*

12 *g-3*

BUCKHEAD BREAD COMPANY & CORNER CAFÉ

Mingling aromas of coffee and freshly baked breads greet patrons, who are likely to be business folks gathering here for breakfast meetings (while enjoying the pancakes and frittatas) and shoppers who stop by for good sandwiches on house-baked bread, salads, and cooked dishes. Such substantial fare as salmon fillet with mashed potatoes and asparagus appears at dinnertime, while house-baked pastries are available throughout the day. Beer and wine available. *3070 Piedmont Rd., Buckhead, 404/240–1978. Reservations not accepted. AE, D, DC, MC, V. $–$$*

7 *g-6*

CAFÉ AT THE CORNER

It's self-service but far better than you might expect it to be. Offerings include homemade pastries, the freshest chicken and goat cheese salads, and numerous daily specials that may well include Cajun French chili. And what a deal this is! A cup of homemade soup and a half sandwich is just $6. No alco-

hol is served. *636 S. Central Ave.,
Hapeville, 404/766–1155, 404/766–2255
menu-specials recording. No dinner.
Closed weekends. No credit cards. $*

12 *d-7*

CAFÉ INTERMEZZO

Although there's a full menu, this Viennese-style café is best for breakfast (this is a great place to read the Sunday paper) or for a late-night, post-performance sweet accompanied by great coffee. The café doesn't make most of its desserts but obtains its sweets from some of the best sources—even if that means ordering from out of town or, for that matter, out of the country. *1845 Peachtree St., Buckhead, 404/355–0411. Reservations not accepted. AE, D, MC, V. $*

5 *d-5*

CAFÉ NORDSTROM

Getting a bite while shopping used to mean having a lunch plate and tea; nowadays expectations have been raised to include Tuscan breads, braised chicken, grilled veggies, pastas, freshly made soups, individual pizzas, and the like, and you will find them all at the café in this Seattle-based store. Not surprisingly, you can order wine by the glass. *Nordstrom at Perimeter Mall, 4390 Ashford-Dunwoody Rd., 770/394–1141, ext. 1610. Reservations not accepted. AE, D, DC, MC, V. $*

14 *d-2*

CAFFÈ ANTICO

If you're paying a visit to the exhibitions at Emory University's Michael C. Carlos Museum (*see* Chapter 4), plan on lunching at this café on the third floor. Soups and chili are homemade, the salads are excellent, and sandwiches are served on whole-grain bread (the hummus on puffed pita bread is excellent, too); leave room for desserts, which, while not made on the premises, are first rate. No alcohol is served. *571 S. Kilgo St., Emory University, Decatur, 404/727–0695. Reservations not accepted. AE, D, MC, V. $*

15 *e-4*

CHURCHILL GROUNDS

The ideal spot for a quick bite before Fox Theatre performances, this café-club (*see* Chapter 5) excels at appetizers (the spinach artichoke dip and hummus are specialties) and sandwiches (the ham and mozzarella cheese with roasted peppers is especially good). Straight-

ahead jazz is featured Tuesday–Sunday, beginning about 9:30 PM; the cover ranges from $5 to $25. Beer, wine, and full bar service are available, and the espresso is notable. *660 Peachtree Rd., Midtown, 404/876–3030. Reservations not accepted. AE, D, MC, V. $*

12 *e-3*

COCA-COLA CAFÉ

A trip to the Atlanta History Center (*see* Chapter 4) simply must include a stop for lunch at this 1950s-style café packed with Coca-Cola memorabilia. Lunch will be a serious treat, all the more so if it includes manager Bernard Douglas's made-on-site chili, best savored on top of a good hot dog. Douglas also turns out superb salads, but with his limited kitchen space, he relies on an outside supplier for soup, which he then tinkers with to make taste as if he'd made it from scratch. Malteds are outstanding, and desserts are sourced from Tuohy's Catering, one of the city's best. If the Hummingbird Cake is one of the offerings, don't resist temptation—it's a classic southern layer cake, not often seen these days. *Atlanta History Center, 130 W. Paces Ferry Rd., Buckhead, 404/ 814–4000. Reservations not accepted. No credit cards. $*

8 *a-1*

CONTINENTAL PARK CAFÉ

A great way to relax on a lazy afternoon is to perch on this outdoor dining terrace above Main Street and watch the trains come and go through the village. While here, sip a fabulous milk shake, savor a salad, or enjoy a sandwich. Then, thus fortified, check out the charming shops up and down the street. No alcohol is served. *941 Main St., Stone Mountain, 770/413–6448. No dinner Sun.–Thurs. MC, V. $*

13 *g-5*

FIVE SISTERS CAFÉ

Such delights as Peg's Veg (with roasted eggplant and tomatoes, mixed greens, goat cheese, and pesto) and Sylvia's Smoked Salmon (an open-face arrangement on toasted bread with horseradish crème fraîche, capers, and cucumbers) elevate sandwiches a level or two above the norm. Three cooked specials are also offered daily and include such welcome dishes as a Senegalese seafood stew, cooked in a light but slightly spicy tomato broth; vegetarians will love the mushroom stroganoff, based on cremini mushrooms. There's a very short, but well-selected, wine list. *Oak Grove Plaza shopping center, 2743 LaVista Rd., Decatur, 404/636–6060. Reservations not accepted. Closed Sun.–Mon. AE, DC, MC, V. $–$$*

14 *b-5*

GATO BIZCO CAFÉ

If you get tired of waiting hungrily for a table across the street at the Flying Biscuit (*see* American/Casual, *above*), here's a satisfying alternative to try. The big biscuits, grits, soy-based sausage, huevos rancheros, and breakfast burrito filled with eggs, potatoes, and cheese would keep anybody going all day, and the Mexican-style lunch fare of the quesadillas-burritos-tacos variety is hefty, too. *1660 McLendon Ave., Candler Park, 404/371–0889. Reservations not accepted. Closed Tues. MC, V. $*

15 *b-2*

MONDO

A newsstand occupies part of this space, so you can catch up on current events while enjoying fresh-baked pastries, cakes and cookies, or a salad or sandwich, all washed down with one of the specialty coffees. Brunch on Saturday is especially popular, with its focus on eggs and home fries, pancakes, and house-made granola. No alcohol is served. *750 Huff Rd., Northwest Atlanta, 404/603–9995. Reservations not accepted. Closed Sun. AE, MC, V. $*

14 *a-2*

SAN FRANCISCO COFFEE ROASTING COMPANY

This long-standing, locally owned outfit roasts its own coffee, makes good pastries (almost all are homemade), and offers live music from time to time. In a restored brick storefront with lots of character and atmosphere, it's a great date spot. Folks often bring along board games for an evening of friendly competition. *1192 N. Highland Ave., Virginia-Highland, 404/876–8816.*

B *c-2*

SKIP'S HOT DOGS

Service is brisk, but this is, after all, a Yankee operation from Chicago. In fact, Chicago-style hot dogs (with all ingredients, right down to the bun, imported from the Windy City) are the draw, and

along with the chili, milk shakes, and fries they pack in a lunchtime crowd from surrounding offices and the nearby Decatur medical center complex. *48 Avondale Rd., Avondale Estates, 404/292–6703. Reservations not accepted. Closed Sun. No credit cards. $*

CAJUN/CREOLE

12 *g-7*

BEST OF CREOLE CAFÉ

This quirky little café spreads out good gumbo, po'boys and similar casual Cajun fare for lunch only. No alcohol is served. *Rock Springs Plaza shopping center, 1877 Piedmont Rd., Morningside, 404/875–6602. Reservations not accepted. Closed Sun.–Mon. No dinner. AE, DC, MC, V. $*

5 *f-4*

CAFÉ LOUISIANE

This comfortable suburban spot does a creditable job of classic Creole dishes, such as jambalaya, shrimp Creole with peppers, celery and onion in a spicy tomato sauce, and crawfish étouffée. One item, though, is off the charts: the crab meat cake with Creole mustard cream sauce. The wine list is a largely unexciting assortment of American wines, but happily it includes the Fetzer Gewurztraminer. *6325 Spalding Dr., at Holcomb Bridge Rd., Norcross, 770/263–0003. Closed Sun. No lunch Sat. AE, D, DC, MC. V. $$*

3 *a-8*

COMEAUX'S LOUISIANA BAR & GRILL

Atlantans flock here for good raw oysters, gumbo, boudin blanc (a pork-and-rice sausage), étouffée, barbecue on Saturday and Sunday, and, in season, boiled crawfish. The bread pudding is worthy of New Orleans, too, and even there you wouldn't find better chicory-laced Creole-style coffee. The strains of jazz from the adjacent bar add a special ambience on Tuesday, Wednesday, Friday and Saturday nights (*see* Chapter 5). Alternate Tuesdays and Thursdays are devoted to the blues. There is no cover charge. *Haynes Bridge Village, 9925 Haynes Bridge Rd., Alpharetta, 770/442–2524. Reservations not accepted. AE, D, DC, MC, V. $–$$*

15 *e-3*

FRENCH QUARTER FOOD SHOP

Atlanta's mecca for Cajun/Creole cuisine strikes some diners as a bit scruffy, although in recent years it's been cleaned up and expanded. (In good weather there's even street-side patio dining). Whether you like the surroundings or not, if you're hungry for the classic New Orleans muffaletta, here's where to find it: The classic New Orleans sandwich, with its layers of deli meats, cheeses and olive salad, is big enough for at least two people. Some rules to follow: Make it a point to have crawfish when they're available in season, be sure to quaff a beer from New Orleans, and order a cup of chicory-laced coffee with your bread pudding (which is awesome). *923 Peachtree St., Midtown, 404/875–2489. Reservations not accepted. Closed Sun. AE, D, DC, MC, V. $$*

5 *d-6*

FRENCH QUARTER, TOO

This bare bones operation doesn't offer much in way of atmosphere, but that makes it all the more authentic. The catfish, gumbo, and bread pudding are indeed authentically Louisiana, and the fried 'gator tail and turtle soup in season are even more so. There's wine, but the beers are better, including New Orleans' Abita Turbodog on draft. *2144 Johnson Ferry Rd., Chamblee, 770/458–2148. Reservations not accepted. Closed Sun. AE, DC, MC, V. $$*

13 *b-4*

FUZZY'S PLACE

Long-time Atlanta restaurateur Joe Dale, now in his eighties, acts as consulting chef and oversees a menu of Creole and Cajun specialties. His "seafood Patsy," a creamy seafood gratin, remains one of the city's favorite dishes, his "carpetbagger steak" is stuffed with shrimp, and his bread pudding is the obvious choice for dessert. A light menu is available until 1 AM, and blues and blues-based rock hum through the often-crowded, usually smoke-filled performance space to the right of the bar. *2015 N. Druid Hills Rd., Northeast, 404/321–6166. Reservations not accepted. AE, D, DC, MC, V. $*

7 *a-2*

GUMBEAUX'S: A CAJUN CAFÉ

LSU and San Francisco 49er football memorabilia decorate the upstairs dining room, where Cajun and Creole fare dominate the menu, with offerings that include seafood gumbo, crawfish or shrimp étouffée, and classic bananas foster and bread pudding. Downstairs there's an oyster bar where the bivalves are served raw, baked and fried. Wine selections are limited, but the Louisiana beers are what you come for anyway. Don't be alarmed by the incessant sound of passing trains—shots are only $1 when a train goes by on the nearby track, so barflies have become adept at faking the telltale noises *6712 E. Broad St., Douglasville, 770/947–8288. Closed Sun.–Mon. AE, D, DC, MC, V. $$*

12 *f-1*

HAL'S

Diners come for the classics of Creole cuisine: the shrimp and crab rémoulade, the trout fillet with crab meat, snapper française, soft-shell crab meunière in season, and bread pudding. Of course, a lively, friendly bar scene is part of the allure at both locations, too. Buckhead's wine list is a bit ho-hum, relying heavily on Chardonnay and Cabernet Sauvignon, but Roswell has a wine cellar with 6,000 bottles. And unlike Buckhead, Roswell is open for lunch weekdays. *30 Old Ivy Rd., Buckhead, 404/261–0025. Closed Sun. AE, D, DC, MC, V. $$$*

5 *c-2*

9835 Old Dogwood Rd., Roswell, 770/645–1998.

12 *d-7*

HUEY'S

Order a plate of beignets—those fabulous New Orleans puffed, deep-fried square doughnuts—and prepare to brush the powdered sugar off your shirt as you indulge yourself. And don't forget a cup of stiff, chicory-laced New Orleans coffee (Community brand) to go with them. Of course, there's more substantial fare to be had here, too: good gumbo, étouffée, jambalaya, red fish from time to time, and Louisiana barbecue. Creole omelets, steak and eggs, and other brunch fare is served Saturday until 3 PM and Sunday until 5 PM. There's wine and beer, including Louisiana beers. *1816 Peachtree Rd., Buckhead,*

404/873–2037. Reservations not accepted. Closed Mon. No dinner Sun. AE, MC, V. $

12 *g-3*

MCKINNON'S LOUISIANE

A lot of patrons stop by Billy McKinnon's long-popular place for a drink (and on Friday and Saturday nights to listen to music), but those in the know stay for dinner, too. They savor superior Cajun popcorn (deep-fried crawfish tails), perfect deep-fried shrimp and oysters, succulent soft-shell crabs, and the famous "Billy's" crab cakes, with corn relish and green onion aïoli. The wine list isn't inspiring, but it does contain lots of reasonably priced and serviceable selections, many of which are available by the glass. *3209 Maple Dr., Buckhead, 404/237–1313. Reservations essential. Closed Sun. No lunch. AE, D, DC, MC, V. $$$*

14 *f-3*

YA YA'S CAJUN CAFÉ

With its color scheme of pink and purple there's something almost mysterious about this casual café. But there's no mystery as to why it's secured a solid reputation for its food. The crawfish, gumbo, 'gator tail, po'boys, jambalaya, and red beans and rice all add up to some good eating, Cajun style. *426 W. Ponce de Leon Ave., Decatur, 404/373–9292. Reservations not accepted. AE, D, DC, MC, V. $–$$*

CARIBBEAN

14 *a-5*

BRIDGETOWN GRILL

At these five rather high-energy metro-area restaurants, there are the conch fritters or a vegetarian black bean soup (topped with Bermuda onion and sour cream) for openers, key lime pie or a delectable mango bread pudding for dessert, and many tempting choices in between. These include good jerk chicken, of course, guava barbecue ribs that are slow-cooked and grilled before the sauce goes on, and mango pork that pairs boneless pork with a house-made mango chutney and tangy habanero-mango coulis. *1156 Euclid Ave., Little Five Points, 404/653–0110. Reservations not accepted. AE, D, DC, MC. V. $–$$*

15 *e-4*

689 Peachtree St., Midtown, 404/873–5363.

4 *h-7*

2997 Cumberland Cir., Smyrna, 770/438–6888.

5 *c-4*

7285 Roswell Rd., Sandy Springs, 770/394–1575.

4 *f-3*

Town Center Esplanade shopping center, 2700 Town Center Blvd., Kennesaw, 678/290–0450.

14 *b-8*

MARTIN'S CARIBBEAN RESTAURANT

This funky, casual spot has been a hit for the past couple of years, so the hard work of Grenadian owners Alice and Susan Alexander is paying off. Their efforts yield such dishes as spicy chicken and veggie patties, curried goat and lamb, oxtails, curried shrimp, and fish that is *escovitched* (made with scotch bonnet pepper and vinegar), all accompanied by rice, peas, and fried plantains. Twelve homemade drinks include, of course, ginger beer. No alcohol is served. *517 Flat Shoals Ave., East Atlanta Village, 404/659–8800. Closed Sun.–Mon. MC, V. $*

CHINESE

5 *e-6*

CANTON HOUSE

This large, bustling emporium is a mecca for Chinese families seeking good dim sum on Saturday and Sunday for breakfast. Selecting shrimp toasts, barbecued pork buns, braised chicken feet, braised Chinese broccoli, and other dishes from carts that are pushed around the room is a cultural experience, and the regular menu has tasty fare as well, including whole steamed or braised fish as well as lobster and crab with ginger-scallion flavors. If you plan to come for dim sum on the weekend, be advised that you won't be able to make a reservation. *4825 Buford Hwy., Chamblee, 770/936–9030. AE, D, DC, MC, V. $–$$*

5 *c-7*

CHOPSTIX

Stylish and sophisticated, with fine Hong Kong cooking as its metier, Chopstix delivers the goods with dumplings, pot stickers, roast duck ravioli, black pepper oysters (superior!) and, in season and not to be missed, soft-shell crab. The wine list sticks with standards and includes just a few choices that actually go well with this food. *Chastain Square, 4279 Roswell Rd., Sandy Springs, 404/255–4868. Reservations essential. No lunch weekends. AE, D, DC, MC, V. $$–$$$*

13 *f-6*

GOLDEN BUDDHA CHINESE RESTAURANT

This big menu, with its comfortable combination plates of well-done Chinese-American fare, has something for everybody. Some dishes, such as spicy Hunan shrimp and braised fish, reach beyond the usual sweet-and-sour drill. Service is friendly and swift. *1905 Clairmont Rd., Decatur, 404/633–5252. Reservations not accepted. AE, D, DC, MC, V. $*

5 *e-7*

HO HO

The name means "very good" in Chinese, and this homey establishment that specializes in Mandarin, Cantonese and Szechuan cuisines really is. Your first move should be to check out the specials scripted on a board on the wall. Do they include oyster pancakes? Pounce on them. Then, move on to the Chinese specialties menu that features such authentic dishes as steamed lion head (Chinese meat balls) and jellyfish salad (must be ordered in advance). Forget the wine list and settle for beer and tea. *3683 Clairmont Rd., Chamblee, 770/451–7240. Reservations not accepted. No lunch weekends. AE, D, DC, MC, V. $–$$*

13 *a-6*

HONG KONG HARBOUR

Patrons flock to this dining room filled with Chinese art for authentic Hong Kong–style cuisine that is exceptionally well prepared and includes pot dishes with bean curd and pork belly and many noodle dishes. Dim sum is served weekdays at lunch, but the best time to come for this traditional meal is Saturday or Sunday morning, when the place fills with families. Other especially tasty morsels to be found on the carts that are wheeled around the room are the chicken feet, which are supremely sweet and tender; the shrimp wrapped in rice noodles, with a dipping sauce of soy and sesame oil; and the crispy fried dumplings stuffed with meat. *2184 Cheshire Bridge Rd., Northeast, 404/325–7630. AE, DC, MC, V. $*

15 *e-5*

HSU'S GOURMET

In this elegant business dining spot, the chopsticks recline on silver rests and fine objets d'art are positioned around the dining room. The Hong Kong–style Chinese cuisine delves expertly into Peking duck and myriad shrimp dishes, including an excellent one with mango and black beans. There's a good wine list, with lots of sparkling wines and champagnes to support the cuisine. *192 Peachtree Center Ave., Downtown, 404/659–2788. No lunch Sun. AE, D, DC, MC, V. $$$*

5 *e-6*

LITTLE SZECHUAN

Starting off business as a hole in the wall in a food court, this star of Atlanta's Chinese restaurant scene has grown and expanded over the years but never lost sight of its purpose. Ask for egg rolls and you'll be politely advised that this is "a real Chinese restaurant." In fact, non-Asian patrons may be invited to peruse the menu first before taking a seat, just in case confrontation with pig tripe soup is off-putting. But the spicy squid, long beans, shrimp with young garlic, and chicken rolls are anything but off-putting. Bring a gang so you can share many dishes. The wine list is limited, but they'll let you bring your own and charge a corkage fee of only $5. *Northwoods Plaza shopping center, 3091C Buford Hwy., Doraville, 770/451–0192. AE, D, MC, V. Closed Tues. $*

5 *d-5*

P. F. CHANG, A CHINESE BISTRO

From Phoenix comes this stylish pair of bistros, complete with sculptures that suggest pieces from the ancient (11th century) city of Xi'an. The art may be elaborate, but the dishes are straightforward and borrowed from various Chinese cuisines, especially that of Canton. Much of the fare, such as moo shu and sweet-and-sour pork, will be familiar, and vegetarians will delight in the number of options available, none boring or pedestrian; in fact, it's easy to compose a vegetarian banquet here, so grab some friends. The wine list includes a few bottles that work well with this food, such as a Riesling and a Gewurztraminer. *500 Ashford-Dunwoody Rd., near Perimeter Mall, Dunwoody, 770/352–*

0500. Reservations not accepted. AE, D, DC, MC, V. $–$$

5 *e-1*

7925 Northpoint Pkwy., near Northpoint Mall, Alpharetta, 770/992–3070.

5 *e-6*

PUNG MIE

Pung Mie continues to cater to Chinese Atlantans from elegant new surroundings. The kitchen delights this clientele with an assortment of steamed, boiled, and fried dumplings; cold dishes that include jellyfish salad; and such authentic specialties as sea cucumber with scallops or pork. *5145 Buford Hwy., Doraville, 770/455–0435. Reservations not accepted. No lunch weekends. AE, DC, MC, V. $*

5 *e-6*

ROYAL CHINA

This cavernous space has a loyal following of Chinese Atlantans, who often hold weddings in the huge private room that adjoins the dining room. The first taste of salt-and-pepper squid or black bean mussels (there may be no better preparation of this dish in town) will explain its popularity. Saturday and Sunday dim sum (served from 10 AM to 3 PM) is excellent and draws the crowds. *3295 Chamblee-Dunwoody Rd., Chamblee, 770/216–9933. Reservations not accepted. AE, DC, MC, V. $*

COLOMBIAN

5 *f-5*

COSTA VERDE

Costa Verde combines the best of Peru and Colombia—from Peru come cold boiled potatoes in a really spicy cream sauce, from Colombian come empanadas with a hotter-than-Hades *ají* dipping sauce. Many of the house specialties (look for them especially on weekends) are seafood dishes. Fish soups, aromatic with cilantro, can come mighty hot, so be warned. Only beer is served. *6200 Buford Hwy., Norcross, 770/582–0060. Reservations not accepted. Closed Mon. MC, V. $*

13 *a-5*

FRUTII VALLE RESTAURANT & BAKERY

A Colombian bakery and restaurant, this well-regarded home-away-from-home for local Colombianos entertains them with

soap operas in Spanish and feeds them such traditional fare as braised chicken with tomato, onions, potatoes and yucca. The food's inexpensive, and you can wash it down with excellent Colombian beer. *Sun Tan shopping center, 2651 Buford Hwy., Northeast, 404/248–1958. Reservations not accepted. MC, V. $*

CONTEMPORARY

15 *b-2*

BACCHANALIA

Chefs Anne Quatrano and Clifford Harrison took Atlanta by storm only a few years ago and instantly challenged the top toques for first place. Atlantans often name this restaurant their favorite in poll after poll. The fixed-price menus change weekly, depending on what the pair finds in the market. Count on something wonderful with foie gras, superior salads with locally grown organic greens, excellent risotto, superb fish, game, American farmstead cheeses, house-made ice creams and sorbets, and desserts that will leave you awestruck. Harrison's personally selected wine list goes way beyond the usual, and the half-bottle list is amazing. *1198 Howell Mill Rd., Northwest Atlanta, 404/365–0410. Reservations essential. Closed Sun.–Mon. No lunch. AE, D, DC, MC, V. $$$$*

4 *h-7*

CANOE

Sit out on the patio by the banks of the Chattahoochee River when the weather is fine, and contemplate what this spot must have looked like 100 years ago when Federal troops forded the river here. Or just contemplate the river while you dine on south Georgia rock shrimp or lunch on a lamb sandwich on focaccia. Chef Gary Minnie knows how to roast a humble chicken, too. This menu changes seasonally, and Minnie does a wicked job on game in the fall. The superior wine list offers unusual varietals, good reserve bottles, and many fine wines by the glass. Sunday brunch is a good time to enjoy the river, especially from the patio in good weather. *4199 Paces Ferry Rd., Vinings, 770/432–2663. Reservations essential. AE, D, DC, MC, V. $$–$$$*

15 *e-6*

CITY GRILL

In the Hurt Building (*see* Chapter 4), one of downtown Atlanta's original skyscrapers, this posh establishment feels like a private club, making it a mecca for business dining at lunch. Dinner guests tend to be conventioneers, but in the absence of a convention, it's easy to get a reservation for a quiet and unrushed meal. The menu changes seasonally but always has certain southern touches, such as quail, barbecue, fried green tomatoes, and crab cakes in some form or other. The cuisine also swings globally, with such dishes as cornmeal-fried veal sweetbreads, onion-crusted sturgeon, shrimp "sausage" on angel hair pasta with saffron cream, and rack of lamb with preserved lemon (a Middle Eastern touch). Vegetarians will love the grilled vegetable roulade. The wine list is huge, with many fine bottles and good choices by the glass. *50 Hurt Plaza, Downtown, 404/524–2489. Reservations essential. Closed Sun. No lunch Sat. AE, D, DC, MC, V. $$$–$$$$*

12 *h-2*

THE DINING ROOM, THE RITZ-CARLTON, BUCKHEAD

The refined, gracious ambience of this prestigious dining room centers on the Asian-influenced cooking of Joel Antunes and one of the city's most fabulous wine lists. Antunes likes to use the products of Georgia within his format, such as Georgia white shrimp in a tomato-olive oil broth—light as a sigh. Dessert and cheeses are extraordinary. The wine list always wins awards, and it's no wonder. There are many by the glass to be savored, and very special bottles at substantial prices. The menu is fixed price, about $70 without wines. You may want to indulge in the tasting menu, a seven-course sybaritic affair paired with sommelier-chosen wines. *3434 Peachtree Rd., Buckhead, 404/237–2700. Reservations essential. AE, D, DC, MC, V. $$$$*

12 *e-3*

SEEGER'S

After taking the structure of this former Buckhead residence down to its beams and joists, designer Bill Johnson gave internationally renowned chef Gunther Seeger a clean, spare, minimally decorated space in which to present his edgy, adventurous cuisine. (Unfortunately, the downstairs space can be noisy, but the upstairs mezzanine is a bit more intimate and quiet.) Seeger believes passionately in using the products of his now home state of Georgia, so he pairs Georgia shrimp with carrot cream and

opal basil as well as Georgia fallow deer with beet and sweet potato gratin. *111 W. Paces Ferry Rd., Buckhead, 404/846–9779. Reservations essential. Jacket. No lunch. Closed Sun. AE, D, DC, MC, V. $$$$*

CONTINENTAL

15 *f-4*

THE ABBEY

Now more than three decades old, the Abbey occupies space that was once a church, creating dining drama. Stained-glass windows capture light beams and play them against walls and tablecloths; in the choir loft, a harpist adds a celestial touch. Equally heavenly are the foie gras, rabbit, fish, duck and lamb that this kitchen turns out, changing its menus with seasonal rhythm. Game also appears from time to time. For vegetarians, there's a mille-feuille of vegetables with carrot-ginger broth. The wine list is a study in older vintages but also includes a good half-bottle selection, many reasonably priced wines by the bottle, and plenty of wines by the glass. *163 Ponce de Leon Ave., Midtown, 404/876–8532. Reservations essential. AE, D, DC, MC, V. $$$$*

12 *g-3*

ANTHONY'S

Here in the antebellum Pope-Walton House (*see* Chapter 4), portraits of 19th-century dowagers haunt the walls of one dining room, while in another, lush romantic landscapes create a pastoral setting. Southern dishes give texture to this otherwise Continental menu, from the lovely she-crab soup to the Georgia venison chop, roasted and served with black truffle spaetzle. For dessert, try the bananas Foster. The good wine list has lots of American and French selections. *3100 Piedmont Rd., just south of Peachtree Rd., Buckhead, 404/262–7379. No lunch. AE, D, DC, MC, V. $$$$*

5 *f-4*

CAFÉ RENAISSANCE

This strip-center restaurant gives the northeast suburbs a taste of good food. The lunchtime steak salad with blue cheese dressing, a special, is the perfect marriage of greens, cheese, and meat and pairs beautifully with a red wine. Osso buco comes with a lemon glaze instead of traditional gremolata, and pork Wellington pairs with a chipotle-scented demi-glace. The restaurant often hosts winemaker dinners and tastings, and accordingly the wine list ranges from the decent but ordinary to the very special. *7050 Jimmy Carter Blvd., Norcross, 770/441–0291. Reservations accepted. No lunch Sat. Closed Sun. $$$*

15 *e-4*

ENCORE AT THE FOX

Most of the diners here are on their way to a performance at the adjacent Fox Theatre (*see* Chapter 4), so the frequently changing menu tends to concentrate on lighter fare. It usually offers small tasty plates such as sweet-and-sour calamari, as well as pastas, salads, and stir fries. Numerous wines by the glass represent good California vintners. *654 Peachtree St., Midtown, 404/881–0223. Reservations essential. No lunch weekends (except on Fox performance days). No dinner Sun. (except on Fox performance days). AE, D, DC, MC, V. $$*

5 *h-2*

KURT'S

The simple white frame structure, once a residence, seems out of place amid the surrounding business buildings. But Suttgart native Kurt Eisele has made his restaurant an important part of the landscape with such dishes as Oyster's 1776, sautéed with apples, herbs, shallots, and white wine and served on toast points under melted cheese; Veal India, with shrimp and curry; snails baked in small potatoes; and Hungarian goulash soup. Son Alexander has joined Kurt in the kitchen and makes superb black bean soup. Strudel is made on the premises, and bananas Foster are made right at tableside. Wines on one list represent numerous varietals and wine-growing regions, and are all priced at $23. *4225 River Green Pkwy., Duluth, 770/623–9413. No lunch. Closed Sun. AE, D, DC, MC, V. $$$*

5 *e-4*

NIKOLAI'S ROOF

One of Atlanta's truly world-class restaurants, Nikolai's, atop the Atlanta Hilton Hotel and Towers (*see* Chapter 5) opened as a pseudo-Russian restaurant, complete with Cossack-garbed waiters. Today, mercifully, that nonsense is gone, except for the presence of piroskis (meat-filled turnovers) on the menu and the flavor-infused vodkas. Chef Johannes Klapdohr concentrates on the classically French-Continental tradition,

but the menu changes frequently. There are two seatings an evening, and the meal is a five-course fixed-price affair. Michel Granier keeps this fine wine list well tuned. *255 Courtland St., at Harris St., Downtown, 404/221–6362. Reservations required. Jacket required. Closed Sun. AE, D, DC, MC, V. $$$$*

12 *f-3*

103 WEST

The opulently decorated interior can seem a bit overswagged, and some of the dishes seem as overfussed as the decor. Stick with simple choices, such as the Dover sole with brown butter, and you'll do just fine. The clientele tends to include conventioneers and folks on expense accounts, who order the house signature deep-fried cold-water lobster tail by the tableful. There's an extensive wine list. *103 W. Paces Ferry Rd., Buckhead, 404/233–5993. Reservations essential. Jacket required. Closed Sun. No lunch. AE, D, DC, MC, V. $$$$*

12 *a-2*

PANO'S & PAUL'S

This Art Deco–inspired space draws large crowds, especially during conventions, who savor the cold lobster tail deep-fried and served with the honey mustard and drawn butter combination. Foie gras and sweetbreads are also on the menu in tasty preparations. If these selections seem rich, turn your attention to the "Trim Cuisine," designed to help achieve dietary goals while enjoying fine fare. The extensive wine list is ably administered by an intelligent sommelier who understands food and wine pairing. *1232 W. Paces Ferry Rd., at Northside Dr., Buckhead, 404/261–3662. Reservations essential. Jacket required. Closed Sun. No lunch. AE, D, DC, MC, V. $$$$*

13 *e-6*

PETITE AUBERGE

This neighborhood restaurant in a busy but not elegant shopping mall has kept the locals well fed for more than a quarter century. Michael Gropp has the good sense to continue the family traditions his German-born parents inspired, so he's changed the menu but not the focus on French bistro fare and German specialties. His menu includes excellent coq au vin, calves' sweetbreads in cognac cream, pork roasted in beer and caraway seed sauce, smoked pork chops, and Wiener schnitzel. Game and other seasonal specials appear, too. *2935 N. Druid Hills, 404/634–6268. Closed Sun. No lunch Sat. AE, D, DC, MC, V. $$–$$$*

12 *f5*

PHILIPPE'S

This narrow slip of space has been totally overhauled, and given a major uplifting, providing Philippe Haddad, also executive chef at The Abbey (*above*), with a venue to launch his eponymous bistro. Haddad is Belgian, so the menu includes mussels, waterzoi (a shellfish stew), braised rabbit, and Belgian beef stew as well as delicious venison loin with ligonberries. The white chocolate bread pudding is the dessert of choice, while the excellent wine list and some Belgian beers make beverage selection delightful. *10 Kings Cir., Peachtree Hills, 404/231–4113.*

5 *f-4*

RESTO NAX

This surprisingly good restaurant in a suburban strip shopping center comes off looking like a fern bar, but the culinary offerings are more serious than the surroundings suggest. Swiss-born owner André Constantin can be cajoled into making special Swiss dishes for gatherings in the private dining room. Unfortunately, they're not on the menu, but good salmon, duck, and pasta dishes are. The mostly California wine list is quite serviceable. *6025 Peachtree Pkwy., Norcross, 770/416–9665. Closed Sun. AE, D, DC, MC, V. $$–$$$*

5 *c-1*

RUSTICA BISTRO

Wolfgang Stoffer's suburban bistro represents his return to the Atlanta culinary scene after a brief absence, and regulars are pleased to be once again enjoying his linzer torte and other specialties, not all of them German. Crab-stuffed ravioli with a rich red pepper-flecked butter sauce tops the appetizers, while specials might include beautifully rare lean lamb loin with orzo. Portions are substantial, too. There's a decent wine list, with good values. *12315 Crabapple Rd., Alpharetta, 770/343–6557. Closed Mon. No lunch. AE, D, DC, MC, V. $$*

7 *d-8*

TEN EAST WASHINGTON

Although it's not in our designated 10-county area, we deem this comfortable, casual establishment about 30 mi from

downtown to be an essential inclusion. It occupies a historic storefront in downtown Newnan, a location that gives it charm and makes a trip here a special excursion. Czech-born George Rasovsky and his New York-born spouse, Carmela, are the affable owners, with George doing the cooking and Carmela doing the greeting. Their Continental cuisine includes crab cakes, lamb, fish, and excellent crème caramel (but ask them to dispense with the whipped cream and other needless garnishes). Beer and wine are available, and the wine list isn't huge but decent. *10 E. Washington St., Newnan, 770/502–9100. Closed Sun. No lunch. AE, MC, V. $$*

CUBAN

12 *h-5*

COCO LOCO

With a firm foothold in the Spanish roots of Cuban cooking, this popular restaurant does a good job with such traditional fare as roast pork, black beans, and paella (which comes in a "big" version for at least two that requires advance notice and a fast version you can order on the spot). Cuban sandwiches, especially the medianoche, are supergood. The wine list focuses on South American and Spanish wines, and the house make its own sangría. *Buckhead Crossing shopping center, 2625 Piedmont Rd., at Sidney Marcus Blvd., 404/364–0212. AE, D, DC, MC, V. $*

4 *h-5*

CRAZY CUBAN

María Arce dishes up her home-style Cuban cooking from a store front in a suburban shopping mall. Croquetas (oblong croquettes made with either ham or chicken and deep-fried) and empanadas make good starters, as do the papas rellenas (potato puffs) filled with seasoned meat and fried. There are black bean soup and Cuban sandwiches for lunch and, at dinner, classics from the Spanish-Cuban kitchen: *ropa vieja* (shredded beef with tomatoes and onions) and *lechón asado* (roast pork, marinated in traditional garlic-flecked mojo sauce), and, for dessert, *tres leches* ("three milks") cake. The house-made sangría is the beverage of choice. *1475 Terrell Mill Rd., Marietta, 770/225–0021. Reservations not accepted. Closed Sun. AE, D, DC, MC, V. $*

5 d-8

HAVANA SANDWICH SHOP

Three generations of the Benedit family, originally from Cuba, run this operation, turning out very good black bean soup, medianoche sandwiches, grilled pork plates, picadillo, flan and rice pudding for dessert—all made on the premises. Some vegetarian plates have been introduced, including empanadas with mushroom, onions, and peppers (but the meat-filled ones are available, too). *2905 Buford Hwy., Northeast, 404/636– 4094. Reservations not accepted. No credit cards.* $

15 f3

LAS PALMERAS

Felipe and Maida Alvarez have been in charge of this spot for the last eight years, and word-of-mouth has made it wildly popular. They see to it that almost everything is authentically Cuban, except, in deference to the American preference for such things, some good quesadillas and burritos. The Cuban-style fried chicken, yucca with mojo, soup, chicken breast in salsa, *boliche* (eye of round) stuffed with chorizo, homemade flan, and rice with milk are all dead-on correct. No alcohol is served, but you may bring your own without paying a corkage fee. *368 5th St., Midtown, 404/872–0846. Reservations not accepted. Closed Sun.–Mon. AE, MC, V.* $

14 a-3

MAMBO

Lucy Alvarez and her husband, Hilton Joseph, natives of Cuba, opened Mambo in 1990. They give their food a salsa flair, with such specials as "firecracker" steak, stuffed with peppers. Paella and black paella are house specialties, and here they are special indeed. The wine list collects Spanish, Chilean, Argentinean and California selections, all available by the glass. *1402 N. Highland Ave., Virginia-Highland, 404/876–2626. No lunch Sat. AE, D, DC, MC, V.* $$

DELICATESSENS

13 e-6

BAGEL PALACE

This popular bagel bakery and delicatessen fills weekends for Saturday and Sunday breakfast, when patrons even can get the *New York Times*. In fact, it's busy every morning of the week, opening at 6:30 for early risers. House-made spreads include superior chopped liver and an assortment of flavored cream cheeses. Snag a square of crumb cake when it's available. *Toco Hills shopping center, 2869 N. Druid Hills Rd., Northeast, 404/315–9016. Reservations not accepted. AE, D, DC, MC, V.* $

5 f-6

BALDINO'S GIANT JERSEY SUBS

Patrons line up daily for the city's best sub sandwiches, made to order on good bread baked on the premises. They really are "giant," so consider getting half a sandwich. For parties, they'll make 'em extralong to cut up into manageable slices. The Marietta location has an all-you-can-eat pasta bar—for only $2.99. Beer and wine only are served. *5697 Buford Hwy., Doraville, 770/455–8570. Reservations not accepted. No credit cards at Doraville; MC, V at Marietta.* $

4 h-5

80 Powers Ferry Rd., Harry's Crossing shopping center, Marietta, 770/321–1177.

5 d-4

E. 48TH STREET ITALIAN MARKET

The dining arrangements include only the shaded patio and a few tables in the store, but the selection of eat-in and take-out fare makes this one of Atlanta's culinary treasure houses. Offerings include outstanding house-made Italian breads, deli meats, such prepared dishes as pasta and eggplant Parmesan, cold mixed greens, superb house-made pastries that include biscotti and cookies, and excellent espresso. There's also a small but well-chosen arrangement of Italian beers and wines. *Williamsburg at Dunwoody shopping center, 2462 Jett Ferry Rd., Dunwoody, 770/392–1499. No credit cards. Closed Sun.* $

5 b-7

GOLDBERG'S

The knishes, brisket, stuffed cabbage, chopped liver, and even the bagels and breads are made in house, and the management of these three outlets has the good sense to import the best from other cities: hot dogs from Chicago, smoked sturgeon and white fish from New York, corned beef and pastrami from New York *and* Chicago. Table seating is limited. *4383 Roswell Rd., Sandy Springs, 404/256–3751. AE, MC, V. $*

5 *d-8*

Georgetown shopping center, 4520 Chamblee-Dunwoody Rd., Dunwoody, 770/455–1119.

12 *a-2*

West Paces Ferry shopping center, 1272 W. Paces Ferry Rd., Buckhead, 404/266–0123.

ECLECTIC

12 *g-3*

ARIA

Passing through a curtain of silver metal beads, you enter a minimalist space done in shades of white. The contemporary room is a perfect setting for the creations that emerge from the kitchen. Dishes hail from every point of the compass and cross culinary cultural lines: seared scallops with lima beans, greens and tomato; seared pepper-crusted ahi tuna with ponzu sauce; rabbit with handmade penne pasta; pork braised in balsamic vinegar until melting tender. Desserts have flair and taste, but change frequently. You might find crème caramel with shaved, toasted fresh coconut curls springing from its gleaming surface. *490 E. Paces Ferry Rd., Buckhead, 404/233–7673. No lunch. Closed Sun. AE, D, DC, MC, V. $$$.*

5 *d-7*

BAJARITO'S

The simple tortilla becomes exotic gourmet fare, with fillings as basic as fish or shrimp or as complex as Thai curry peanut chicken or blackened salmon fillet. Regional flavors include barbecue and jerked chicken. For salad wraps, there's a Greek salad with feta and olives, and the vegetarians will love the black-and-tan beans and grilled Mediterranean veggies. Limited alcohol is served. *Cherokee Plaza, 3877 Peachtree Rd., Brookhaven, 404/239–9727. AE, MC, V. $*

12 *h-2*

BLUEPOINTE

This sophisticated interior depends for its impact on soaring ceilings and ample fenestration, softened by long sheers and panels that suggest soji screens. The menu ranges from impeccable raw oysters to wood-grilled calamari with shiitake mushrooms and pencil asparagus, and grilled rare duck breast with Thai-style red curry. Braised beef short ribs come with a savory/sweet corn mash. The wine list presents a range of mostly American selections, with a fair list by the glass. *Pinnacle Building, 3455 Peachtree Rd., 404/237-9070. No lunch weekends. AE, D, MC, V. $$$$*

12 *g-3*

BUCKHEAD DINER

Crafted by San Francisco diner designer Patrick Kuleto, this gleaming steel-sheathed structure recalls the original diners of the 1940s and 1950s. The menu changes frequently but sometimes includes such local specialties as rock shrimp, served as an appetizer, along with such popular standbys as small pizzas, homemade potato chips, veal meat loaf, and banana cream pie. Wines are definitely not diner stuff, and many are available by the glass. *3073 Piedmont Rd., Buckhead, 404/262–3336. Reservations not accepted. AE, D, DC, MC, V. $$*

12 *f-3*

CAFÉ TU TU TANGO

This is the ideal after-shopping perk-up spot, or the great late-date talk-until-midnight spot. The upper level is configured to resemble an artist's garret and, in fact, hosts ongoing art exhibitions. A good way to dine here is to assemble a gang for a table of tapas, tempting appetizer-size dishes. Kids get to assemble their own pizzas and watch them bake in the wood-fired oven. Good house-made sangría comes both red and white, but there are wines and beers, too. *East Village Square, 220 Pharr Rd., Buckhead, 404/841–6222. AE, D, MC, V. Reservations not accepted. $*

14 *a-3*

DISH

Once upon a time, this brick building on a busy corner housed a gas station. Now it's a popular restaurant with a neighborhood following that prefers to dine on the large, covered street-side patio. The menu goes all over the planet, with Asian touches and Italian concepts nestled side by side: Lobster and shiitake ravioli with pea shoots and ginger sauce claim a place next to molasses-roasted chicken with pappardelle. Sometimes the combinations work and sometimes they don't, but they're never boring. The wine list features interesting selections at very good prices, with many by-the-glass choices among them. *870 N. Highland Ave., Virginia-Highland, 404/897–3463. Reservations not accepted. No lunch. AE, D, DC, MC, V. $$*

13 b-7

FLOATAWAY CAFÉ

Anne Quatrano of the Bacchanalia team (see Contemporary, above) and her partner, Clifford Harrison, staked out new territory in a funky warehouse district that's home to off-beat publications, artists, and sundry small industries. The hard surfaces and high ceilings make for a rather noisy environment, but the food is completely worthwhile. Passionate about quality, Quatrano has sources for organically grown figs, tiny beets, and Georgia white shrimp. The menu responds to the seasons as a result but will always offer pasta and pizza, intriguing salads, fresh fish, farmstead cheeses, and well-crafted desserts. The wine list offers unusual selections, all of which do justice to the food. *1123 Zonolite Rd., near Johnson and Briarcliff Rds., Northeast Atlanta, 404/892–1414. Reservations essential. Closed Sun.–Mon. No lunch. AE, D, MC, V. $$$*

5 b-5

HOLYFIELD'S NEW SOUTH GRILL

Boxer Evander Holyfield, an Atlantan, has lent his name to this sleek operation and signed on Nigerian native John Akhile to craft a diverse menu that takes Italian and Asian flavors and merges them with American, often southern, fare. Catfish fingers are encrusted with blue and yellow cornmeal, fried, and served with cilantro-lime tartar sauce; salmon is wrapped in collard-greens, steamed, and served with honey mustard butter and caviar; and classic Louisiana crawfish show up in ravioli. The wine list offers some by-the-glass choices that serve this food well. *6075 Roswell Rd., Sandy Springs, 404/531–0300. Closed Sun. AE, D, DC, MC, V. $$*

14 a-3

INDIGO COASTAL GRILL

A recent renovation has left Indigo with a sleek new cherrywood bar; fun, bright paintings by Atlanta artist Leigh Catherall; and a menu that clings to coastal cuisines. Dishes tap into myriad cuisines, so you can start with Thai basil spring rolls with shrimp and veggies and move on to Maryland crab cakes. The ever-popular key lime pie, tart and pale, is a legacy from a previous owner, whose mother contributed the recipe. Enjoying Sunday brunch on the patio is a neighborhood ritual. *1307 N. Highland Ave., Virginia-Highland/Morningside, 404/876–0676. No lunch. AE, D, DC, MC, V. $$$*

5 b-6

INSIGNIA

Stylish contemporary decor meets ordinary shopping center with considerable élan. The cuisine draws from every possible corner of the globe and is clearly influenced by an Asian aesthetic, as in the tuna tartare–radish salad with cucumbers and a ginger vinaigrette and the steamed salmon with a spicy peanut vinaigrette. The fish available varies daily with market offerings, and it is pristine fresh. The wine list is nicely organized, with a good section of non-Chardonnay offerings that go with this food. There's a comfortable private room for special events and a singularly nice covered patio for fine-weather dining. *Chastain Square shopping center, 4279 Roswell Rd., Buckhead, 404/256–4040. No lunch weekends. AE, D, MC, V. $$–$$$*

15 e-6

MUMBO JUMBO

With a big bar scene and an upstairs dance floor, these environs can be noisy, but the food is marvelous and full of surprises. For instance, chef Shawn Doty has been known to travel to his native southwest Virginia and come back with ramps, a kind of wild garlicky leek, which he served with soft-shell crab for a unique regional-taste sensation. The famous "Mumbo Gumbo," for which Doty doesn't use the standard roux, is lighter than most but just as flavorful. *89 Park Pl., near Woodruff Park, Downtown, 404/523–0330. Reservations essential. No lunch weekends. AE, D, DC, MC, V. $$–$$$*

15 e-2

PARK 75

In this elegant and somewhat formal hotel dining room, chef Brooke Vosika does a menu that is rooted in exceptional American ingredients, such as small-production cheeses. Presentations can be dramatic but manage not to be silly: For instance, the wait person who delivers the cauliflower bisque will present a dry bowl containing a steamed floret of cauliflower with caviar perched on top, pour the bisque around the floret, then break up the floret with a spoon so it floats in the soup and spreads the caviar around. The result looks pretty and is very, very tasty. Squab, fish, steak, and lamb all are distinctive, as is the Sunday dim sum brunch. The wine list is well assembled, and its final page, Last Chances, showcases unusual selections at good prices. *75 14th St., Four Seasons Atlanta Hotel, Midtown, 404/881–9898. AE, D, DC, MC, V. $$$–$$$$*

15 *d-5*

PRIME MERIDIAN

The Omni's newly refurbished dining room gathers its culinary inspiration from around the world. Thai flavors, with ginger and lime, spike the chicken salad; the veal chop is a taste of Sicily, with creamy cèpes risotto and pancetta; and venison medallions come with a chestnut-chanterelle strudel and pickled Asian plums. For lunch, pizzas emerge from a wood-burning oven, and main-course offerings lean toward stir fries and pastas. The lunch buffet, called a "Chef's Table," is several cuts above your typical self-service. Breakfast also is served and includes southern-style fare with biscuits, red-eye gravy, and grits. *100 CNN Center, Omni Hotel, Downtown, 404/ 659–0000. AE, D, DC, MC, V. $$$$*

14 *f-3*

THE SUPPER CLUB

This dining room is a rather funky space, with gauzy hangings that separate it into intimate areas. Taking advantage of what's available in the markets, the kitchen provides a wide variety of dishes that may range from an excellent oyster bisque to fish tacos; the fresh catch is reliably fresh and beautifully prepared. The wine list isn't long but tilts to thoughtfully selected California and Italian selections. The place is entirely no-smoking until 10 PM. *308 W. Ponce de Leon Ave., Decatur, 404/370– 1207. Reservations essential. Closed Sun.– Mon. AE, MC, V. $$*

14 *a-2*

TIBURON GRILLE

Snuggled behind a post office, this popular neighborhood bistro has hit its stride with excellent food and pleasant surroundings that include a warmly lit dining room where the rough-textured walls are hung with intriguing modern art and a patio hung with baskets of coleus and cooled by slowly twirling fans. Grilled asparagus with a peanut-based dipping sauce and good micro greens makes a perfect first course. Por-

tion sizes are just right, to be followed by such choices as ostrich or veal tenderloin wrapped in Serrano ham. The selection of delectable desserts varies with what the kitchen has made that day. The wine list changes often and has good items by the glass. *1190 N. Highland Ave., at Amsterdam Ave., behind U.S. Post Office, Virginia-Highland, 404/ 892–2393. AE, D, MC, V. Reservations essential. No lunch. Closed Sun. $$*

12 *h-2*

TOMTOM, A BISTRO

Lively, art-filled, and fun, TomTom gathers a collection of Asian and southwestern fare and mingles it with good old-fashioned American cooking. So, you can have sushi, a deep-fried whole catfish with Asian seasonings, a pizza, or roast chicken or roast lamb with mashed potatoes. The wine list has good choices that support this eclectic menu and are reasonably priced. *Lenox Square, 3393 Peachtree Rd., Buckhead, 404/264–1163. Reservations not accepted. AE, D, DC, MC, V. $$*

5 *h-2*

WILDBERRIES, A BISTRO

Todd and Lauren Hogan divide their duties between the kitchen (CIA graduate Todd's domain) and the front of the house, where Lauren rules. Much of the menu is southern in inspiration (Bourbon-glazed pork, for instance), other dishes wander in from Asian sources, and there are pasta and other Italian touches. The wine list is slightly daring; try the Ironstone Symphony with a shrimp cocktail for which Todd perches a cluster of fat shrimp around the edge of a martini glass and tops it with a ginger-laced peach chutney. *Peachtree Hills shopping center, 3455 Peachtree Industrial Blvd., Duluth, 770/476–3733. Reservations essential. No lunch. AE, D, DC, MC, V. $$$*

ETHIOPIAN

13 *c-3*

ETHIOPIAN ABBAY RESTAURANT

This small shopping-center restaurant is dark yet welcoming, and it is a second home to Atlanta's growing Ethiopian community. As you'll soon learn, the custom is to forgo knives and forks and rip off pieces of enjera, the traditional flat bread, to scoop up mouthfuls of lamb, spicy lemon chicken with boiled egg, and vegetarian dishes based on lentils and greens. Beer is the best quaff with this fare. *Northeast Plaza shopping center, 3375 Buford Hwy., Northeast, 404/321–5808. AE, D, DC, MC, V. $*

13 *c-5*

QUEEN OF SHEBA

A full range of Ethiopian classics are served here, beginning with the traditional, lentil-stuffed turnovers called sanbussas and moving on to spicy beef, chicken, lamb, and vegetarian dishes. The staff is happy to guide patrons with gentle palates away from the hottest dishes. There's a full bar, but beer is the best beverage with this fare. *1594 Woodcliff Dr., near the intersection of Briarcliff*

ROMANTIC DINING

Whether you want to pop the question, mark an anniversary, or just get away from the kids for an evening, here are some places to enjoy a private moment.

The Abbey (Continental)
An intimate table in the corner of a former church. A harpist plucking her strings in the choir loft. Ambrosia on the plate. Who wouldn't say "Yes"?

Cosi(Mediterranean)
Casual, warmly lit, fun, and certainly worth the trip for the food, newly opened Cosipromises to be a significant spot for romance. In this lighting, everybody looks especially attractive.

Dining Room, Ritz-Carlton, Buckhead (Contemporary)
The adventurous patron bent on amour can do no better: The sommelier knows just the right wine; the maître d' knows just when to leave a couple alone; and the chef knows just what dishes will set the mood.

Nikolai's Roof (Continental)
The dramatic view alone is enough to make any romance take on a special glow. The dining experience and wine list will enhance it further, and the service is exceptional.

Pano's and Paul's (Continental)
This Art Deco room has probably seen more anniversary action than any other restaurant in town.

---

and N. Druid Hills Rds., Northeast, 404/321–1493. AE, MC, V. $

FRENCH

12 *g-2*

ANIS

Southern France comes to Atlanta in such dishes as fish stews, grilled pork chop with figs, roast chicken with cèpes, mussels, Provençal grilled vegetables, and tuna Niçoise. The list of French wines is excellent, and there's really good espresso. Ironically, Anis pours some of the best iced tea in town. *2974 Grandview Ave., Buckhead, 404/233–9889. No lunch Sun. AE, D, DC, MC, V.$$*

12 *h-3*

BRASSERIE LE COZE

The late Gilbert Le Coze and his sister Maguey, owners of Le Bernardin in New York, launched this casual, Gaslight-era–style bistro in Atlanta and watched it grow and grow in popularity. The French fare is beautifully executed, from the white bean soup laced with truffle oil and glorious mussels to skate wing in brown butter caper sauce and classic crème brûlée for dessert. The wine list is French and American and offers many good choices by the glass. *Lenox Square, 3393 Peachtree Rd., 404/266–1440. Closed Sun. AE, D, MC, V. $$–$$$*

14 *g-3*

CAFÉ ALSACE

Benedicte Cooper and Marceau Verdiere cook the specialties of their native region. Their hearty home-style fare includes the inevitable (but here better than most) quiche Lorraine, but their *tarte à l'oignon* (onion tart) is the tastier choice. The meal may well move on to the very good coq au vin and end with a tart Tatin. Marceau makes yeoman efforts to include well-priced Alsacian wines and beers on the beverage list. *121 E. Ponce de Leon Ave., Decatur, 404/373–5622. Reservations not accepted. Closed Mon. No lunch Sat., no dinner Sun. AE, D, DC, MC, V. $*

14 *a-4*

CAFÉ BOHÈME

Chef Brigitte Barnes, a native of Paris, has crafted a bit of Europe in Atlanta's most bohemian neighborhood. In this slim slip of a restaurant, banquettes slide comfortably along one wall, and the bistro fare runs from lamb stew to savory roast chicken with tarragon, mashed potatoes, and haricots verts. Chocolate mousse and crème brûlée are typical desserts. There's live jazz Sunday and Thursday nights. *453 Moreland Ave., Little Five Points, 404/522–4373. AE, D, DC, MC, V. No lunch. $$*

12 h-7
DEUX PLEX

Contemporary art, photographs, and commissioned murals create an attractive setting, while the menu focuses on small servings to make this an especially good spot for a late-night repast or other light meal. The imaginative offerings include a buttery foie gras perched on a crisp brioche and served with quince, and a small steak that comes with three sauces—peppercorn, béarnaise and blue cheese. You can accompany them with a wide choice of side dishes that include a unique sautée of wild broccoli. *1789 Cheshire Bridge Rd., Northeast, 404/733–5900. Closed Sun.–Mon. $–$$*

8 g-1
FLEUR-DE-LIS

In this cool, bright dining room at the Spa at Château Élan, you can get around fat, sodium, cholesterol, and calories without feeling even slightly deprived. So, you can guiltlessly dine on lobster saffron ravioli with fennel cream sauce, shrimp salad, salmon tournedos, and grilled ostrich fillet with buffalo tenderloin. This is dieting? Château Élan wines are paired with the dishes. Breakfast and lunch also are served. *Spa at Château Élan, 100 Tour de France, Braselton, 770/932–0900. Reservations required. Jacket. No dinner Sun.–Tues. AE, D, DC, MC, V. $$$$*

8 g-1
LE CLOS AT CHÂTEAU ÉLAN

Georgia's largest winery has several dining operations, one of which is this formal dining room in the winery's chateauesque modern main building. Classic Continental and French dishes appear on the ever-changing men, which may include foie gras with Calvados, rack of lamb with Kalamata olive crust, and breast of pheasant wrapped that's wrapped in a cabbage leaf to keep the delicate meat moist and tender. Seven- and eight-course fixed-price dinners are paired with Château Élan wines. *Château Élan, 100 Tour de France, Braselton, 770/932–0900. Reservations required. Jacket required. Closed Sun.–Tues. No lunch. AE, D, DC, MC, V. $$$$*

14 f-1
LE GIVERNY

Rémy and Milena Kerba (*see also* Sage, in Casual, *above*) have endeared themselves to the neighbors so recently expanded their space to accommodate demand. The food maintains the same high standards, from the rich, densely textured country pâté to the freshest fish. The wine list consists of excellent and very affordable bottles. *1355 Clairmont Rd., Decatur, 404/325–7252. Closed Sun.–Mon. AE, D, DC, MC, V. $$*

12 g-7
LE SAINT AMOUR

Occupying a former residence, Le Saint Amour epitomizes luxurious Provençal dining. The colors of the warm rooms are sun-enriched, and a changing menu usually includes such traditional favorites as a terrine of duck, snails, sweetbreads coquilles St. Jacques (always prepared in some kind of unusual way, such as with foie gras), duck, and lamb. Profiterolles, sabayon on fruit, and tart Tatin for two are favorite desserts. The wine list, not too surprisingly, is heavy on French selections. *1620 Piedmont Ave., Morningside, 404/881–0300. Reservations essential. No lunch Sat. AE, MC, V. $$$–$$$$*

4 h-4
PROVENCE

Provence does classic French dishes from the bistro tradition: salad with lardons (here they are crisped duck cracklings), ratatouille, steamed mussels with garlic wine sauce, excellent fish and shellfish, and, occasionally as a special, frogs' legs with mushrooms, garlic, parsley, cream, and Calvados. Homemade chocolate mousse and creme brûlée are the desserts to set your sights on. The wine list is entirely French. *4655 Lower Roswell Rd., Marietta, 770/321–5442. Reservations not accepted for weekend breakfast or Sun. brunch. No lunch Sun. AE, D, DC, MC, V. $$–$$$*

12 g-3
SOLEIL

Soleil packs this former Buckhead residence with patrons eager to enjoy a taste of life in a relaxed, sun-drenched part of the world. The simple *grillade* and bistro dishes are well prepared, from a duck and chicken salad with lavender honey (what could be more Provençal?) to orange glazed duck breast and coq au vin. Roast pork tenderloin with whole grain mustard sauce is singularly tasty. The wine list packs a fair punch, with good bottles under $30 dominating the selection, and lots of them by the glass. *3081 Maple Dr., Buckhead, 404/467–1790. AE, D, DC, MC, V. $$*

13 *e-3*

VIOLETTE

Guy Luc, from Alsace, is a fixture in this northeast neighborhood, and he treats his neighbors to the dishes of his native land. Lunch is on the order of quiche and salad, while the dinner menu includes well-prepared monkfish and salmon and steaks, served au poivre or with Roquefort sauce. The wine list includes many excellent bottles at a good price. *2948 Clairmont Rd., Northeast, 404/633–3363. Closed Sun. No lunch Sat. AE, D, DC, MC, V. $$*

GERMAN

8 *e-1*

BASKET BAKERY & CAFÉ AT THE VILLAGE CORNER

A combination bakery and restaurant, the Basket fills with yeasty aromas that may well tempt you into taking home a loaf of bread and the white-chocolate-chunk macadamia nut cookies. If you stick around for dinner, you can enjoy German specialties that include frikadellen, sausages, schnitzels, sauerbraten, and spaetzle. On the second weekend of the month, local vocalist Lenny Stabile does his rendition of Frank Sinatra standards in the tavern to the rear. *6655 James Rivers Dr., Stone Mountain, 770/498–0329. Closed Mon. AE, D, DC, MC, V. $$*

5 *h-2*

VRENY'S BIERGARTEN

While Vreny Eisele's husband, Kurt, ably runs his eponymous restaurant up front (*see* Continental, *above*), she oversees less formal surroundings and serves old-style German dishes. Her perennially popular standards include sauerbraten, beef rouladen, roast pork

knuckle, spaeztle with black forest ham and mushrooms, sausages, and *maultaschen* (a kind of ravioli). German wines and beers are the beverages of choice. *4225 River Green Pkwy., Duluth, 770/623–9413. Closed Sun. No lunch. AE, D, DC, MC, V. $*

GREEK

14 *f-1*

ATHENS PIZZA HOUSE

Greek-style pizza, with its thicker crust, is the draw at these four outlets, but Greek specialties, such as moussaka and pastitsio, are also available. In fact, the Gwinnett location is called Athens Pizza Kouzzina, which means kitchen, because it offers an expanded menu with a lot more Greek dishes on the menu, such as lamb shank and eggplant with linguine. Wine and beer, including some Greek choices, are served. *1341 Clairmont Rd., Decatur, 404/636–1100. No lunch Sun. at Roswell. AE, D, DC, MC, V. $*

5 *d-6*

Chamblee Plaza shopping center, 5550 Peachtree Industrial Blvd., Chamblee, 770/452–8282.

5 *c-1*

11235 Alpharetta Hwy., Roswell, 770/751–6629.

5 *h-5*

Pleasant Hill Square shopping center, 2205 Pleasant Hill Rd., 770/813–1369.

5 *h-6*

EVELYN'S CAFÉ

Evelyn Barikos started her business more than 20 years ago and has developed a loyal following with her gyros, pastitsio, stuffed grape leaves, blazing cheese with pita bread, and house-made baklava and rice pudding. No alcohol is served, though Barikos is trying to get a license to sell Greek wines. *Beaver Ruin Village shopping center, 4155 Lawrenceville Hwy., Lilburn, 678/380–6155. Reservations not accepted. Closed Sun. AE, D, DC, MC, V. $*

15 *h-2*

GRECIAN GYRO

Nick Loulouris makes it his business to serve good cheap food made in the traditional way, and he succeeds. Patrons go nuts for his potato salad with homemade sauce, served with all gyros, as well as the souvlaki, chicken on pita bread, and other standards—including homemade baklava. No alcohol is served. *855 Virginia Ave., Virginia-Highland, 404/762–1627. Reservations not accepted. Closed weekends. No credit cards. $*

5 *h-7*
KALAMATA GREEK RESTAURANT AND PIZZA
The building looks as though it once held a fast-food operation, but the animated patrons and the excellent cuisine more than compensate for any lack of physical charm. Octopus is seasoned with spices and char-grilled, with marinara sauce on the side, and other Greek specialties include flaming cheese, spinach pie, moussaka, and baked custard with phyllo. The wine list is strongly oriented toward Greek choices. *4075 Lawrenceville Hwy., Lilburn, 770/935–9990. AE, D, MC, V. $–$$*

INDIAN

13 *c-5*
CHAT PATTI
This no-frills, self-service restaurant specializes in Indian vegetarian dishes, and once you discover what assertive seasoning can do for potatoes and chick peas you won't miss meat. Dosai is a crispy rice pancake filled with potatoes, onions and lentils, and the lentil soup is delicious. No alcohol is served. *1594 Woodcliff Dr., intersection of N. Druid Hills and Briarcliff Rds., Northeast, 404/633–5595. Closed Mon. MC, V. $*

15 *e-5*
HAVELI
Many Atlantans know and enjoy the two branches of Haveli, one of the metro area's first Indian restaurants, and they evidently feel very comfortable with such offerings as tandoori meats, curries, and *saag paneer* (sautéed spinach with homemade Indian cheese). Many of these appear on the lunch buffet, which is popular with businesspeople. *Gift Mart, 225 Spring St., Downtown, 404/522–4545. Reservations not accepted. No lunch Sun. AE, D, DC, MC, V. $*

5 *e-6*
HIMALYAS
Still busy after a dozen years at the same location, and filled with draped booths, Indian handicrafts and photographs of long-ago emperors, Himalyas remains a star among the city's Indian restaurants. The onion *bhajee* (crispy deep-fried onion balls) are singularly crisp and sweet tasting here, the tandoori chicken is tender and mildly spicy, and the *chana masala,* a spicy chick pea dish, is unusually long on flavor. There's even a good wine list with Gewurztraminer—the ideal wine for Indian food. *Chamblee Plaza, 5520 Peachtree Industrial Blvd., Chamblee, 770/458–6557. AE, D, DC, MC, V. $$*

5 *f-7*
MAHARAJAH
South Indian cuisine is the specialty here, and that means there are a lot of vegetarian dishes. If you crave meat, try one of the chicken dishes cooked in the tandoori oven. And whatever you have, accompany your meal with one of the delicious breads baked on the premises. Vegetarian and nonvegetarian dinners for two are an especially good bargain. *3900 LaVista Rd., Northlake, 770/414–1010. AE, D, DC, MC, V. $–$$*

14 *h-1*
PALKI
A simple white interior with touches of Indian art here and there evokes India, Pakistan, and Bangladesh, the cuisines of which owner-chef Nur Layla Khanam incorporates into her home-style fare (she even makes her own yogurt for the raita). Shrimp Malaicurry comes in spicy coconut milk, while ground lamb shish kabobs appear sizzling on a bed of onions and are served in the same black cast-iron griddle in which they were cooked. *763 DeKalb Industrial Way, Decatur, 404/294–8989. AE, D, DC, MC, V. $*

6 *a-4*
POONA
This dining room is quiet and serene and decorated with fine Indian art—just the setting in which you can relax and enjoy excellent lamb dishes (the lamb vindaloo is especially tasty), chicken tikka, and vegetarian dishes. The lunch buffet is substantial and very fairly priced. There's a decent wine list. *Wal-Mart shopping center, 1630 Pleasant Hill*

Rd., Duluth, 770/717–1053. AE, D, DC, MC, V. $

12 *e-4*

RAJAH

The last 20 years have seen numerous changes in Buckhead, but one constant has been this tiny bistro-size restaurant. The tandoor (clay oven) is used not only to bake the tender marinated chicken but also to turn out numerous specialty Indian breads. Weekday lunch is wickedly cheap, about $6. Beer and wine are available. *2955 Peachtree Rd., Buckhead, 404/237–2661. No lunch Sun. AE, MC, V. $*

14 *h-1*

UDIPI CAFE

This huge space almost seems like an institutional dining hall, but it is usually filled with Indian families enjoying south Indian vegetarian specialties that range from vegetable samosas to thin rice crepes with vegetables, called *dosai*, to rice specialties, called *pullavs*, that combine lentils and rice. The dinner specials assemble a variety of these dishes to provide newcomers with a tasty introduction to this cuisine. No alcohol is served, and the restaurant is entirely no-smoking. *1850 Lawrenceville Hwy., Decatur, 404/325–1933. Reservations weekdays only. MC, V. $*

14 *h-1*

ZYKA

Cavernous Zyka is short on atmosphere and, with each dish costing $5 or less, very long on value. North Indian *chana masala*, a dish of cooked chick peas and spicy tomatoes, makes a superfast lunch, while goat meat simmered with tomatoes and fennel and tandoori chicken so tender they call it "butter chicken" provide exotic antidotes to snack attacks. Continuous service from noon to late at night (midnight on Friday and Saturday) is available. *1677 Scott Blvd., Decatur, 404/728–4444. Reservations not accepted. Closed Mon. AE, D, DC, MC, V. $*

IRISH

12 *f3*

FADÓ

This dark-paneled pub packs in the Buckhead office crowd for drinks after work (*see* Chapter 5). The kitchen is busy, too, producing good Irish pub grub, from and fish-and-chips to boxty (filled Irish potato pancakes); Irish breakfast, with beans and Irish bacon, is available all day. *3035 Peachtree Rd., Buckhead, 404/841–0066. Reservations not accepted. AE, D, DC, MC, V. $–$$*

8 *g-1*

PADDY'S IRISH PUB

A popular attraction at Château Élan, the pub is a salute to the recently acquired Irish citizenship of Donald Panoz, the pharmaceutical multi-millionaire who owns this lavish hotel-winery-spa complex. Traditional Irish fare includes shepherd's pie and corned beef sandwiches. Irish brews are served on draught, and there's live music on weekends (*see* Chapter 5). *Château Élan, 100 Tour de France, Braselton, 770/932–0900. Reservations not accepted. AE, D, DC, MC, V. $*

ITALIAN

12 *e-6*

ABRUZZI

The setting in a nondescript shopping center will not transport you, but once owner Nico Petrucci and his staff welcome you to the gold- and celery-green-hued dining room, you will realize you have come upon one of the city's best dining experiences. The menu is excellent and focuses on seasonal dishes, including game in season. The excellent wine list is nearly all Italian, but by-the-glass selections are very limited. *Peachtree Battle shopping center, 2355 Peachtree Rd., Buckhead, 404/261–8186. Reservations essential. Jacket required. No lunch Sat. Closed Sun. AE, D, DC, MC, V. $$*

5 *e-2*

ALTOBELI'S ITALIAN RESTAURANT & PIANO BAR

Since 1988, this has been a packed popular spot, serving classic Italian-American fare, with a side of pasta accompanying every main dish unless its already served on pasta. Veal is a major feature of the menu: Veal *a la gourmet* is a sauteed medallion with sun-dried tomatoes, asparagus and mushrooms and served with a brown sauce; veal *a la romana* tops a scallopini with prosciutto and mozzarella, with mushrooms sauteed in white wine. The wine list goes deep into Italian wines, with good Chiantis and Barolos. The piano bar is in full swing Thursday-Saturday. *3000 Old Alabama Rd., Alpharetta, 770/664–8055. No lunch. AE, D, DC, MC, V. $$–$$$*

12 *f3*

AMERIGO

Shoppers love this appealing Buckhead bistro, which has an inviting patio for outdoor dining and stays open throughout the day. Pastas and wood-fired pizzas are the best bets, though the seafood and veal dishes are also good. Late-night dining (to midnight) is available Friday and Saturday. *2694 Peachtree Rd., Buckhead, 404/237–2964. Reservations not accepted. AE, D, DC, MC, V. $$*

12 *g3*

ANTICA POSTA

The taste of Tuscany came to Atlanta in 1999, when Marco Detti arrived from a little town near Florence, took over a modest house, and opened a restaurant very much like the one he ran with his brothers back home. The menu is rigorously authentic, with excellent risotto, gnocchi and fish, and veal dishes, to be followed by the homemade gelato. The steak with balsamic vinegar reduction sauce is outstanding. *519 E. Paces Ferry Rd., Buckhead, 404/262–7112. Reservations essential. No lunch. AE, D, MC, V. $$$*

5 *b-5*

BROOKLYN CAFÉ

Bustling and almost always jammed (arrive early to avoid a wait), this popular Italian-American restaurant serves good food in a friendly environment Start off with crusty, yeasty bread that you can dip in olive oil and grated Parmesan cheese, and then move on to one of the generous pastas and perhaps a fish or shrimp dish. *220 Sandy Springs Cir., Sandy Springs, 404/843–8377. Reservations not accepted. No lunch weekends. AE, D, DC, MC, V. $$*

14 *a-2*

CAMILLE'S

You can dine on the sidewalk patio here even in bad weather (it's covered and heated), and you'll be all the happier if you enjoy one of the excellent pizzas and/or wonderful mussels or calamari with marinara sauce. Whatever you plan on ordering, begin with *aroncini*, deep-fried mozzarella-stuffed rice balls. *1186 N. Highland Ave., Virginia-Highland, 404/872–7203. Reservations not accepted. No lunch. AE, MC, V. $*

4 *h-7*

CARRABBA'S ITALIAN GRILL

These units of a Florida-based corporation are very kid friendly, and the food won't disappoint the grown-ups either. In addition to wood-fired pizzas and pastas, the seafood, veal and beef are excellent, and satisfyingly filling—the *spiedino di mare*, for instance, is a skewer of shrimp and sea scallops that's enough to take home for another meal. The wines are decent and very well priced. *2999 Cumberland Cir., near I–285 and U.S. 41, exits 19/20, Smyrna/Vinings, 770/437–1444. Reservations not accepted. AE, D, DC, MC, V. $$*

4 *f-2*

1160 Ernest W. Barrett Pkwy., Kennesaw, 770/499–0338.

5 *h-4*

3580 Sweetwater Rd., east of I–85, exit 104 (Pleasant Hill), Duluth, 770/935–7600.

0 *c-8*

1887 Mt. Zion Rd., west of I–75, exit 222, Morrow, 770/968–3233.

12 *g-4*

CIAO BELLA

The cooking of the Italian countryside dominates these two Atlanta area trattorias, and that means the emphasis is on hearty pasta dishes: spaghetti with quail or, a little less exotic, lasagna with béchamel sauce and cannelloni with ground veal, spinach and cheese. The Buckhead location is popular for weekend dinners; the Duluth location is closed on Sundays. *309 Pharr Rd., Buckhead, 404/261–6013. Reservations advised. Closed Mon. No lunch weekends. AE, D, MC, V. $$–$$$.*

5 *g-2*

Shops of St. Ives, 10305 Medlock Bridge Rd., Duluth, 770/418–0448.

15 *g-1*

CIPOLLINI

Atlantans have enjoyed John Carver's food at Pricci (*see below*), but a rejuvenated Carver is now in the kitchen of his own establishment, where he turns out heavenly Italian fare as it is prepared in the best kitchens in Italy. Tiny clams "Oregonata style" are sautéed with focaccia crumbs, lemon, and garlic; authentic pastas largely unknown to Americans (such as *strozzapreti*, or "priest stranglers") are made fresh daily; *cipolinni* (tiny flat, sweet onions) infuse their flavor to the roast rack of lamb with mashed sweet potatoes; and a classic osso buco is served as it should be, with gremolata sauce and saffron risotto. This wine list speaks Italian, with many good choices by the glass. *Cross Creek shopping center, 1529 Piedmont Rd., Ansley Park/Morningside, 404/ 875–5001. Reservations not accepted. No lunch weekends. Closed Mon. AE, D, DC, MC, V. $$$*

5 *c-2*

FERRARA'S BISTRO
Owners Michael and Donna Petrucci came south from New York to cook, bringing to Atlanta their own sense of Italian-American cuisine. While they make excellent pizzas, pastas, and veal and fish dishes, they also often veer off into such tasty treats as Thai-style ribs and southern crab cakes. To enjoy some of these creative preparations, check the chalkboard for daily specials. Good wines make dining here a complete experience. *635 Atlanta St., Roswell, 770/ 640–5345. Reservations not accepted. Closed Sun.–Mon. No lunch Sat. AE, D, DC, MC, V. $–$$*

12 *h-7*

FRATELLI DI NAPOLI
Bring a gang of friends or the whole family: You're going to need companions, because Fratelli is not geared to solo dining, unless you plan to take home enough food for the week. The atmosphere in both locations, characterized by rough-textured brick walls and high industrial ceilings, is high-energy. Large platters of salads, good calamari, pastas, excellent fish and chicken dishes, and a good wine list keep guests in their seats for long, leisurely meals. *2101B Tula St., off Peachtree St., next to Brookwood Square, Buckhead, 404/351– 1533. Reservations not accepted. No lunch. AE, D, DC, MC, V. $–$$*

5 *c-2*
928 Canton St., Roswell, 770/642–9917.

5 *d-5*

IL FORNAIO
Gracing the shore of a small lake, this huge (9,000 square feet) restaurant-cum-bakery offers every kind of seating one could want, from patio tables to bar service, plus private dining for small groups (16 or fewer). The cuisine is varied, too: freshly baked breads and pizzas, wood-grilled fish, poultry and game, and homemade pastas. The wine list focuses Italian wines and California Italian varietals, and even features a Chianti Classico from the owner's vineyards in Italy. The bakery opens early weekdays (7 AM) and noon on weekends. *700 Ashwood Pkwy., off Ashford-Dunwoody Rd., north of Perimeter Mall, Dunwoody, 678/ 579–0000. AE, DC, MC, V. $$*

4 *f-1*

IPPOLITO'S FAMILY STYLE ITALIAN RESTAURANT
Casual and catering to the neighborhoods where they're located, the several locations of Ippolito's serve dishes that are straight off the Italian-American shelf, with cheese-filled manicotti baked in tomato sauce, pasta shells stuffed with eggplant and ricotta, and huge, fat calzones. There's sausage and peppers, eggplant Parmigiana, and good sandwiches on hoagie rolls, too. *425 Ernest Barrett Pkwy., Marietta, 770/514–8500. Reservations not accepted. No lunch weekends. AE, D, DC, MC, V. $*

5 *c-2*
1525 Holcomb Bridge Rd., Roswell, 770/ 998–5683.

5 *g-1*
11585 Jones Bridge Rd., Alpharetta, 770/ 663–0050.

5 *b-4*
6623 Roswell Rd., Sandy Springs, 404/ 256–3546.

12 *f3*

LA GROTTA
Classic Italian food. Period. That's what the team of Sergio Favelli and Antonio Abizanda have been doing for more than 20 years, and their elegant, understated dining room at the bottom of a posh condominium is not the place to sample the latest trends. The gnocchi are simply the best anywhere—light as a sigh and simply sauced with Swiss chard, walnuts, and cream. Risotto and pastas are, as the menu says, "like we do them in Italy." Veal, game, and seafood are outstanding, and the mostly Italian wine list, with some by-the-glass selections, reads like a novel. Linger at the bar for an after-dinner Sambuca and

espresso. *2637 Peachtree Rd., Buckhead, 404/231–1368. Reservations essential. Jacket required. No lunch. Closed Sun. AE, D, DC, MC, V.* $$–$$$

5 *d-5*

LA GROTTA AT RAVINIA

Different in feeling from its elder sibling in Buckhead (*see above*), this La Grotta has an open kitchen and magnificent views of the landscaped grounds surrounding the Dunwoody hotel in which it's located. Some of the dishes for which the Favelli and Abizanda team are noted for presenting in Buckhead, such as the excellent gnocchi, appear here, too, but others are unique to this location and include an excellent summer entrée of cold veal in sun-dried tomato sauce. The mostly Italian wine list includes many good offerings by the glass. *Ravinia Crowne Plaza Hotel, 4355 Ashford-Dunwoody Rd., Dunwoody, 770/395–9925. Closed Sun. No lunch Sat. Reservations essential weekends. AE, D, DC, MC, V.* $$–$$$

4 *h-5*

LA STRADA

Residents of east Cobb County swarm all over this family-owned, family-oriented dining establishment, where children 10 and under eat free 5–7 PM (one child per adult patron). Meanwhile, the grown-ups in the group will enjoy good Italian-American food, such as sausage and peppers on polenta, lasagna, linguini with clams, and veal Parmigiana. Finish the meal *with zuppa Inglese* and a shot of the good espresso. *2930 Johnson Ferry Rd., Marietta, 770/640–7008. Reservations not accepted weekends. No lunch at Marietta; no lunch weekends at Dunwoody. AE, D, DC, MC, V.* $

5 *c-3*

8550 Roswell Rd., Sandy Springs, 770/552–1300.

14 *a-2*

LA TAVOLA

This handsome, contemporary bistro offers a wide range of first courses, from superb, fat mussels in vermouth-tomato-herb broth to pappardelle (broad noodles) with duck ragù to pumpkin-stuffed sage ravioli with flavorful red onion confit. Main courses vary daily and often include such substantial fare as spicy sausage, grilled veal chops, and baked lasagna done in the tradi-

tional manner, with Bolognese sauce and ricotta. Your dessert choice is easy: *panna cotta*, that creamy, custardy molded wonder, here served with a blood orange sauce. Dishes such as poached eggs on toasted focaccia under a light cheese sauce are on hand at Sunday brunch. The wines are American and Italian. *992 Virginia Ave., near N. Highland Ave., Virginia-Highland, 404/873–5430. Reservations essential. No lunch. AE, D, MC, V.* $$

12 *g-1*

MAGGIANO'S LITTLE ITALY

The huge, almost cavernous dining room rings with animated conversation, creating a high-energy ambience that attracts families and groups eager to share dishes designed to satisfy at least two healthy appetites. Forgo dishes made with the pallid tomato sauce for the tasty baked clams, supremely moist and tender chicken with vegetables (*giardiniera*), and the veal scallopini prepared piccata style, with lemon and capers. The Corner Bakery, attached to the restaurant, sells fabulous breads and desserts. There are lots of good Italian wines and good California Italian wines to savor with this food. *3368 Peachtree Rd., Buckhead, 404/816–9650. Reservations essential. AE, D, DC, MC, V.* $$

5 *d-5*

MI SPIA

The faux-Tuscan and excellent Italian-inspired fare will transport you to Florence. Begin at the handsome bar, enjoy a drink with the superior fried calamari with spicy marinara sauce and smoked bacon-wrapped grilled shrimp, and then move on to the dining room to enjoy excellent pastas, seafood, and meats. The tiramisu is a must. The extensive wine list features lots of Italian wines. *Park Place shopping center, across from Perimeter Mall, 4505 Ashford-Dunwoody Rd., Dunwoody, 770/393–1333. No lunch weekends. AE, D, DC, MC, V.* $$$

12 *g-2*

NONA'S ITALIAN KITCHEN

The word for "grandmother" in Italian really has two *n*'s in the middle, but don't let the misspelling distract you from enjoying home-style comfort food that includes excellent saltimbocca, sirloin with parsnip potato cake and porcini sauce, and smoked pork loin with garlic mashed potatoes and cider glaze. Pasta dishes include good gnocchi, and the cannoli and flourless chocolate torte are excellent dessert choices. The wine list is Italian and Cal-Ital, with lots of good choices by the glass. *3365 Piedmont Rd., Suite 1025 (upstairs), Buckhead, 404/261–1312. No lunch weekends. AE, D, DC, MC, V. $$*

5 *e-4*

OSCAR'S VILLA CAPRI

Argentine-born Oscar Pereyra has been doing business here for more than 15 years, in a dining room filled with nostalgic art depicting Italian street scenes and the strains of traditional Italian music. Regulars know to rely on Oscar for excellent tiny clams baked with crumbs, herbs, and a bit of prosciutto; good veal dishes; and specials that take advantage of the day's market to include such offerings as a snapper baked with tomatoes, peppers, onions, capers, and herbs on a pasta tricolore (which, like many dishes here, can easily serve two). The wine list offers a range of Italian and American selections. *Orchard Park shopping center, 2090 Dunwoody Club Dr., between Mt. Vernon and Jett Ferry Rds., Dunwoody, 770/392–7950. No lunch. AE, D, DC, MC, V. $$–$$$*

15 *e-3*

PASTA DA PULCINELLA

A tiny spot decorated with gyrating clowns (that's what *pulcinella* means), this popular neighborhood bistro serves what local readers' polls routinely tag "Atlanta's Best Pasta." No wonder. Sweet potato gnocchi and a huge half Caesar salad compose a memorable meal, and ravioli with apples, sausage, and Parmesan cheese topped with brown butter and sage is singularly tasty. *1027 Peachtree St., at 11th St., Midtown, 404/892–6195. Closed Sun. No lunch weekends. MC, V. $*

14 *b-8*

PASTIFICIO CAMELI

This brick-walled trattoria in an up-and-coming neighborhood has much to recommend it, thanks to the Cameli brothers. This pair takes Italian cooking seriously, following fundamental Tuscan models. Their handmade pastas, especially the ravioli with Gorgonzola cheese, are worthy of a much fancier environment; entrées are simply presented, with ample but not overdone

portions; and the nice, if short, wine list does a good by-the-glass job, with many Italian choices. *1263 Glenwood Ave., East Atlanta, 404/622–9926. Reservations not accepted. Closed Mon. No lunch. AE, DC, MC, V. $–$$*

12 *g-3*

PRICCI

Don't come to this contemporary, high-energy dining room to enjoy a quiet, contemplative dinner. But do come to enjoy an exceptional Italian meal that might begin with grilled calamari served with a light tomato sauce, move on to the daily risotto special or a fresh pasta dish, and include one of the grilled meats or the parchment steamed sea bass make outstanding with fresh vegetables. The wine list is heavily Italian and includes many interesting selections. *500 Pharr Rd., at Maple Dr., Buckhead, 404/237–2941. No lunch weekends. AE, D, DC, MC, V. $$–$$$*

5 *d-5*

ROMANO'S MACARONI GRILL

These Dallas-based casual Italian restaurants do a good job of keeping businesspeople content at lunch while feeding families for dinner. The faux-stone walls don't absorb sound, so you'll have to put up with some noise as you enjoy good soups and such standbys as penne with prosciutto in a creamy sauce and grilled chicken. You'll even be immersed in Italiana culture when you visit the rest room, into which the restaurants pipe Italian language lessons. The wine list offers good choices, but pass on the insipid house wine. *4788 Ashford-Dunwoody Rd., north of Perimeter Mall, Dunwoody, 770/394–6676. Reservations not accepted. AE, D, DC, MC, V. $$.*

5 *h-4*

1565 Pleasant Hill Rd., east of I-85, exit 104, Duluth, 770/564–0094.

4 *e-2*

780 Cobb Pl. Blvd., west of Town Center, west of I-75, exit 269, Kennesaw, 770/590–7774.

5 *c-2*

770 Holcomb Bridge Rd., ½ mi east of Alpharetta Hwy., Roswell, 770/993–7115.

5 *g-2*

Medlock Crossing Shopping center, 9700 Medlock Bridge Rd. at State Bridge Rd., Duluth, 770/495–7855.

`15` *h-5*

SOTTO SOTTO

Who would have thought that the entire city would turn out and cram this tiny trattoria for such dishes as spaghetti with sun-dried mullet roe? Chef Riccardo Ullio, born in Italy but reared in Conyers, Georgia, accommodates the crowds nicely and pampers them with huge antipasto misto platters, three special risotto dishes nightly, and such entrées as whole fish roasted on a wood plank. The panna cotta is just plain perfect and is served without needless adornment. The short wine list offers some good, well-priced Italian wines. *313 N. Highland Ave., at Elizabeth St., Inman Park, 404/523–6678. Reservations essential. Closed Sun. AE, MC, V. $*

`15` *e-2*

VENI VIDI VICI

Marcella Hazan, the noted Italian chef and cookbook author, helped plan this menu, and her influence shows in such delectables as little plates of veal meat balls, wood-grilled shrimp with white beans, and octopus potato salad with lemon and olive oil with a salad (a satisfying first course or light luncheon). The house-made pastas are first rate, as are the rotisserie-cooked meats, braised dishes (osso buco), and seafood. The mostly Italian wine list lends superior support to this lovely fare. *41 14th St., between W. Peachtree and Spring Sts., Midtown, 404/875–8424. Reservations essential. No lunch weekends. AE, D, DC, MC, V. $$–$$$*

`5` *d-6*

VILLA CHRISTINA

A ceiling painted with faux clouds to recreate the sky, a floor painted to suggest slate, and contemporary art works on the wall provide the ideal scenario for this beautifully presented, artful Italian food. Happily, chef Darryl Evans prepares food that is not only pretty but tastes good, too. What pastas these! Buffalo ricotta gnocchi are topped with clams oreganata, and local Vidalia onions grace the capellini. Rabbit is always on the menu, sometimes prepared with Italian lentils or maybe white beans. Pastry chef Paul Michael Bodrogi creates dessert that may incorporate a tasty chestnut mousse or roasted pear creme brûlée. The wine list is excellent, and many choices are offered by the glass. *Perimeter Summit, 43 Perimeter Summit Blvd., Chamblee/Dunwoody, 404/303–0133. Closed Sun. No lunch Sat. AE, D, DC, MC, V. $$$$*

`3` *b-8*

VINNY'S ON WINDWARD

This bright, contemporary space glows with light streaming in from large windows. It's a splendid setting for really good Italian food, from the roasted garlic white bean soup to classic tomato-ricotta lasagna with sausage and seared duck with polenta. This menu changes often, but the dishes keep their spirit—Italian to the core. Italian and California Italian wines include wonderful choices that are available by the glass as well as the bottle; heaven should have this many Barbarescos and Barolos. *5355 Windward Pkwy., Alpharetta, 770/772–4644. No lunch weekends. AE, D, DC, MC, V. $$$*

JAPANESE

`12` *g-3*

KAMOGAWA

Atlanta's most elegant Japanese restaurant is a favorite with visiting Japanese businesspeople, who find pristine preparations of sashimi, sushi, and other Japanese classics. The experience is all the richer if you dine in one of the tatami rooms, and very fine sake served chilled is the best beverage to accompany this exquisite fare. *Grand Hyatt Atlanta Hotel, 3300 Peachtree Rd., Buckhead, 404/841–0314. Reservations essential. No lunch weekends. AE, D, DC, MC, V. $$$$*

`12` *g-7*

NAKATO

For years this was the only Japanese restaurant Atlantans knew anything about, and Nakato has continued to build its following since a recent move around the corner into a new, slightly Westernized Asian-style building that resembles a large house. Several dining rooms offer a variety of dining styles; in one, patrons gather at cooking tables to watch while chefs chop and cook steak, fish, chicken, and vegetables. The sushi is dependably good, and there are good traditional dishes such as shabu-shabu, for which beef and vegetables are cooked in a seasoned broth. *1776 Cheshire Bridge Rd., Northeast, 404/873–6582. No lunch. AE, D, DC, MC, V. $$*

13 c-3
SA TSU KI

Sa Tsu Ki is a favorite with the local Japanese community and is as comfortable as a private home. Families with children in tow gather at the sushi bar or enjoy watching excellent shabu-shabu and sukiyaki prepared at tableside. Two dishes not to pass up are the beef *tataki* (seared rare beef with Ponzu dipping sauce) and the deep-fried shrimp heads. *3043 Buford Hwy., north of N. Druid Hills Rd., Northeast, 404/325–5285. Reservations not accepted. No lunch. AE, D, DC, MC, V. $–$$*

12 g-2
SOTO

Sushi master Sotohiro Kosugi learned his art from his father, and in Atlanta his eponymous restaurant is mentioned in the same breath as sushi. The nightly specials feature the best dishes, but they sell out quickly, so you may want to plan on an early supper here. It's worth noting that Soto is not impervious to new influences: The Cajun roll combines curry-flecked soft-shell crawfish, avocado, cucumber, spicy sesame sauce, and a dusting of pretty smelt roe on top. Ginger ice cream, sweet and creamy with chunks of fresh ginger bursting with hot sweetness, is a fine end-of-the-meal palate cleanser. Chilled sake is the beverage of choice, and the restaurant has a good list of them. *Piedmont/Peachtree Crossing shopping center, 3330 Piedmont Rd., Buckhead, 404/233–2005. Closed Sun. No lunch. AE, D, DC, MC, V. $$*

KOREAN

5 e-6
ASIANA GARDEN

As you'll discover here, the combination of Japanese and Korean cuisines works wonderfully. You can enjoy everything from sushi to glass noodle dishes with vegetables and minced seafood to *bulgogi*, Korean barbecue that's grilled at the table (chicken, beef ribs, shrimp, and salmon are prepared this way). It's open until 2 AM daily. *Asian Square shopping center, 5150 Buford Hwy., Doraville, 770/452–1677. AE, DC, MC, V. $*

5 e-5
HAE WOON DAE

You almost have to read Korean to locate this restaurant tucked away in the back of a nondescript strip mall full of Korean signage. But persist, because you'll find yourself in one of the city's best Korean eateries. Sundry nibbles, among them a fine shredded potato salad, appear as soon as you order, and the main course of choice is the excellent Korean barbecue done over wood charcoal. Alcohol is limited to one wine and one Korean beer. It's open very late. *Treasure Village shopping center, 5805 Buford Hwy., Doraville, 770/458–6999. AE, D, DC, MC, V. $*

5 d-5
HANWOORI

There are, literally, two sides to this large, elegant restaurant adorned with gleaming woods. The Japanese side feels almost temple-like and has private tatami rooms; the larger, more gregarious Korean side is filled with tables topped with gas-fired grills for barbecuing eel (so tasty even the kids will want more) and other seafood and meats. Don't be intimidated by the incomprehensible-sounding *Gooksoojuhngol*: it's a tasty dish of noodles, vegetables, and beef cooked in a seasoned broth that's spiced to suit the diner's taste buds. The staff is very friendly and very good with children. *4251 N. Peachtree Rd., Chamblee, 770/458–9191. AE, D, DC, MC, V. $–$$*

5 e-5
SEOUL GARDEN

Frequented chiefly by Koreans, Seoul Garden does a rigorous job of preparing all the traditional favorites, including cold noodle dishes and what must be the best seafood pancake in town. Inexpensive "lunch boxes," available weekdays, contain both Korean and Japanese dishes and are very popular with non-Asian customers. Korean and Japanese beers, sake, and American beers and wines are available. *5938 Buford Hwy., Doraville, 770/452–0123. AE, MC, V. $–$$*

KOSHER

13 c-6
BROADWAY CAFE

This casual restaurant is probably Atlanta's only supervised Kosher dining establishment. Many of the dishes also rank with vegans, as they're made without eggs or dairy products; empanadas and pot stickers are stuffed with tempeh and veggies. Some beer and wine is available. *2166 Briarcliff Rd., Northeast, 404/329–0888. Closed Sat. No lunch Sun. AE, DC, MC, V. $*

LATIN

5 *b-6*

CASA BLANCA

While many of the dishes in this simple restaurant are Mexican, you may want to take advantage of the chance to enjoy the hard-to-find Salvadoran cuisine. The home-style cooking produces *papusas*, corn cakes filled with cheese, meat, or beans, as well as chicken with onions and scrambled eggs with rice, beans, and pico de gallo. *5785 Roswell Rd., Sandy Springs, 404/252–3237. Reservations not accepted. No credit cards. $–$$*

12 *h-4*

ECLIPSE DI LUNA

The twentysomethings seeking other twentysomethings often spill out of the stylish interior onto a patio. Those who take time to notice the cuisine enjoy the small-portioned tapas plates (which include thinly sliced Serrano ham shaved off the leg), then move on to delectable garlic chicken (a recipe from the mother of chef-owner Paul Luna, who's from the Dominican Republic), spicy potatoes, and perfect flan. A wide range of wines is reasonably priced. *764 Miami Cir., Buckhead, 404/846–0449. AE, D, MC, V. Reservations accepted. Closed Sun. $*

13 *c-3*

EL SALVADOR

Mexican and Salvadoran families gather to dine and watch Spanish-language television in a homey, comfortable atmosphere that provides a good family dining experience as well as an introduction to multicultural cuisines. Offerings range from Salvadoran *papusas* (corn cakes) to Mexican tamales, and from *campechana* (a cocktail of shrimp, octopus and oysters) to nachos. *Northeast Plaza, 3375 Buford Hwy., Northeast, 404/325–0482. Reservations not accepted. No lunch weekends. AE, D, DC, MC, V. $*

14 *a-4*

LA FONDA LATINA

These lively restaurants are Latin in atmosphere and in cuisine. There are several kinds of paella (seafood and veg-

etarian, as well as traditional), along with grilled pork chops and chicken, *bocadillos* (Latin sandwiches) with chorizo, and eight kinds of quesadillas. The flan-like baked custard is home-made and delicious. Chilean wines rule. *1150 Euclid Ave., Little Five Points, 404/577–8317. MC, V. $*

14 *d-4*

1639 McLendon Ave., Candler Park, 404/378–5200.

12 *f-4*

2815 Peachtree Rd., Buckhead, 404/816–8311.

5 *b-6*

4427 Roswell Rd., Sandy Springs, 404/303–8201.

14 *a-3*

923 Ponce de Leon Ave., Poncey-Highland, 404/607–0665.

15 *f-3*

LOCA LUNA

Paul Luna of Eclipse di Luna (*see above*) is at it again. Here the food is boldly daring—and yes, the pigs'-feet vinaigrette, fried yucca, and empanadas enclosing beef in a proper lard pastry are indeed daring, and delicious. Naturally, there's a good selection of tapas. *836 Juniper St., at 6th St., Midtown, 404/875–4494. Closed Sun. No lunch weekends. AE, D, DC, MC, V. $*

15 *g-1*

TIERRA

Ticha and Dan Krinsky bring to Atlantans the flavors of Ticha's native South America. The daily soup, *caldo del dia*, is often based on a seafood broth and made rich with fish and shellfish; chipotle peppers infuse the mashed potatoes; and fried plantain and refried beans finish a grilled skirt steak. For dessert, it's "Three Milks Cake," a light but luscious cake enriched with heavy cream, evaporated milk, and condensed milk. *1425B Piedmont Ave., Midtown/Buckhead, 404/874–5951. No lunch. AE, MC, V. $$*

MALAYSIAN

5 *e-6*

PENANG

This attractive, wood-paneled dining room specializes in Malaysian and Thai cuisine. Many of the dishes are spicy, especially the curries, and the offerings include seafood, a wide range of soups, and traditional noodle dishes. The potables include a few beers and wines, and there is a full bar. *Orient Center shopping center, 4897 Buford Hwy., Chamblee, 770/220–0308. AE, D, DC, MC, V. $*

MEDITERRANEAN

15 *h-5*

BABETTE'S CAFÉ

This neighborhood bistro in a small strip shopping center lights up the area with a fun, casual atmosphere and very good food, consistently well prepared. Many of the offerings combine unlikely ingredients with surprising success: steamed mussels with strawberries and serrano peppers; fried oyster biscuits with cucumber sauce; grilled salmon with grapefruit; and, for dessert, a unique espresso flan. At brunch, the best dish is Babette's Benedict, in which poached eggs are perched on a fillet of beef. The coffee is good and strong, and the wine list is excellent and well priced. *471 N. Highland Ave., Poncey-Highland, 404/523–9121. Reservations not accepted. Closed Mon. AE, D, DC, MC, V. $$*

12 *g-2*

BASIL'S
MEDITERRANEAN CAFÉ

Occupying what was once a middle-class residence, the dining rooms here are somewhat small, so in good weather the best place to sit is on the patio in front. In fact, there's no better place to unwind after work or shopping trips. Indoors or out, you'll savor the classics of Mediterranean fare: hummus and stuffed grape leaves; beautifully grilled fresh fish; excellent pasta with light, saffron-scented seafood; and, of course, baklava for dessert. *2985 Grandview Ave., Buckhead, 404/233–9755. No lunch Sun.–Mon. AE, D, DC, MC, V. $$*

4 *h-4*

BASIL'S
NEIGHBORHOOD CAFÉ

Bringing home-style Mediterranean fare to the northern suburbs, this Basil's does a few things differently from its older, successful sibling in Buckhead. The hummus, tabouleh, and baba ghanouj (pureed eggplant with tahini) are as good as anybody's, but the distinguishing dishes include fried calamari with tomato leek sauce and cilantro aioli. Bruschetta topped with olivata, minced tomato, and mozzarella goes especially well with the Gloria Ferrer Blanc de Blancs that's offered by the glass. Homemade pancakes and good turkey sausage top the line-up at Sunday brunch. *Market Plaza, 1255 Johnson Ferry Rd., Marietta, 770/578–0011. No lunch weekends. AE, D, DC, MC, V. $$*

14 *f-3*

CAFÉ LILY

Open in 1999, Café Lily undertook a major renovation of a storefront space, opening its walls with generous windows and giving patrons a fine view of the street. While most dishes are Italian in inspiration, some come from Spain and Portugal. Excellent grilled lamb chops come with a garlic cream sauce and superior skin-on fried potatoes, and Basque eggs with pipérade sauce are a unique brunch dish. Special menus pair food with some intriguing wines. *308B W. Ponce de Leon Ave., Decatur, 404/371–9119. No lunch Sat. AE, D, MC, V. $$*

15 *f-5*

CALITERRA

This gloriously transformed once down-at-the-heels hotel has never seen better days. And within awaits Caliterra, with its adjacent comfortable bar area and a seasonally changing menu that includes calamari appetizer with its three sauces (aioli is best), lamb shank with excellent greens, and a really good tiramisu. This excellent restaurant is handy when you're attending events and performances at the Rialto Theatre or the Tabernacle. *Wyndham Atlanta Hotel, 160 Spring St., Downtown, 678/686–3370. AE, D, DC, MC, V. $$$*

12 *h-4*

CEDARS

From hummus to moussaka, the dishes at this casual restaurant explore the range of Mediterranean food. Excellent lamb kabobs come perfectly pink and tender, and the traditional Middle Eastern *kibbeh*, a mixture of ground sirloin and cracked wheat, is set off by the tang of fine yogurt and grape leaves. Combination platters provide a good way to explore the range of dishes. *Plantation Heights shopping center, 2770 Lenox Rd., 404/261–1826. No dinner weekends. AE, D, DC, MC, V. $$*

14 g-3

COSI

Chef-owner Justin Ward bashed out walls to craft this bisectioned space, with a generous bar in what once was a law office and a dining room that flows into what once was a southern food restaurant. The focus is on Mediterranean fare, from European to Middle Eastern and African sources. The house soup is elephant garlic with *pistou* (a southern French basil-garlic-Parmesan-cheese paste similar to pesto). A very traditional touch, rabbit, appears in the *paella valenciana.* Not even Portuguese cooking is overlooked, with a classic *bacalhau* (refreshed salted cod) and potatoes. This extensive wine list doesn't miss much. The outdoor patio is a particularly attractive place to dine. *129 E. Ponce de Leon Ave., Decatur, 404/373–1049. No lunch weekends. AE, D, DC, MC, V. $$$*

15 e-3

ENO

Jamie Adams, formerly a chef at Veni Vidi Vici (*see* Italian, *above*), and his partner, Doug Strickland, modeled their wine bar in the true style of an Italian enoteca. All wines are available by the taste, glass, and bottle, and the menu is composed of lots of small dishes that come from throughout the Mediterranean world: mussels Cataplana, a Portuguese dish, plops some of the sweetest and fattest of the bivalves into a broth of tomatoes, onions, paprika, prosciutto, and chorizo, then makes them aromatic with fresh cilantro; the hickory-smoked oysters are marvelous, but ask for them just lightly done until the edges crisp; and game hen on couscous is made special with the tang of preserved lemons. Compose your own flights, perhaps to compare styles of Chardonnays or various kinds of red wines; the three rosés on the list ably complement these Mediterranean dishes. *800 Peachtree St., at 5th St., Midtown, 404/685–3191. Closed Sun. No lunch weekends. AE, D, DC, MC, V. $$*

14 a-3

HARVEST

Occupying a former residence, with an inviting front porch, Harvest invites the neighbors in for such Mediterranean-inspired dishes as ample, hearty cassoulet, as well as for Manhattan seafood chowder and maple smoked and grilled pork chops. Creative vegetarian dishes are a house specialty, and Harvest is also known for it Sunday brunch, when low-country grits with shrimp, pork, and biscuits, and Norwegian scramble with smoked salmon appear on the menu. *885 N. Highland Ave., Virginia-Highland, 404/876–8244. No lunch weekends. AE, D, DC, MC, V. $$*

12 d-7

LUNA SÍ

Gauzy fabric suspended from the ceiling divides this tiny space (another creation of chef Paul Luna, Atlanta's culinary wild child; *see* Loca Luna *and* Eclipse de Luna *in* Latin, *above*) into dining alcoves. This menu changes seasonally, and, depending on when you dine here, dishes to watch for are such standouts as salmon with ginger crust, the foie gras (no matter how prepared), and the roasted Cornish hen. *Brookwood Village shopping center, 1931 Peachtree Rd., 404/355–5993. Reservations essential. No lunch. Closed Sun. AE, D, DC, MC, V. $$–$$$*

14 f-3

MOSAIC

Whether its brunch, lunch, or dinner, this tiny bistro is packed with patrons who relish these creatively prepared dishes from around the Mediterranean world: Mussels are steamed with different flavors every day, according to the whim of the chef; the pork tenderloin in grainy mustard sauce comes with roasted fresh pineapple; and trout Andalusa has a citrus caper sauce. Brunch runs to omelets and even a Creole dish, eggs Sardou. This short wine list is intelligently assembled, with many bottles are under $20. *308 W. Ponce de Leon Ave., Decatur, 404/373–9468. Reservations essential. Closed Mon. No lunch Sat. AE, D, DC, MC, V. $$*

13 a-6

SOUTH OF FRANCE

Re-creating the warmth of Provence, this long-popular restaurant is considered by many to be one of the city's most romantic spots. In winter, a warm fire glows in the large hearth; year-round, a chanteuse adds her melodies to the atmosphere (Wed.–Sat.). Little wonder that couples bent on romance come for dishes that include foie gras cooked correctly to the just-pink stage, a house-made terrine, duck à l'orange or with a raspberry hazelnut sauce, and excellent lamb and fresh fish. *Cheshire Square, 2345 Cheshire Bridge Rd., at LaVista Rd., 404/325–6963. Closed Sun. No lunch Sat. AE, D, DC, MC, V. $$$*

14 *a-4*

TERRA COTTA

The menu at this stylish bistro changes often, but whatever turns up will be worth tasting. Many of the dishes reflect American tastes, with a Mediterranean splash thrown in. Jumbo shrimp, for instance, are flavored with tamarind sauce, while pork tenderloin may be adorned with a wild mushroom and sherry cream sauce. Crème brûlée is the dessert of choice. Seeking out interesting wines is a passion for these folks, and wine tastings and wine dinners are frequent. The restaurant is entirely no-smoking. Parking's a pest, with limited spaces to the side and rear. *1044 Greenwood Ave., Virginia-Highland, 404/853–7888. Closed Sun. No lunch. AE, D, DC, MC, V. $$*

12 *e-6*

TOULOUSE

Located at the back of a small strip center, Toulouse started off as a French restaurant (hence the name) and has slowly evolved into an American restaurant with French touches to the dishes. Expect to find goat cheese in your salad and tarragon on your chicken, but you can also get good buffalo meat loaf and a hearty potato soup here. The menu includes wine recommendations for each entrée, and owner George Tice is a passionate teacher who often encourages patrons to experiment with food-wine pairings. The restaurant is entirely no-smoking except for on the outside patio. *2293 Peachtree Rd., Buckhead, 404/351–9533. Reservations essential. No lunch. AE, D, DC, MC, V. $$*

12 *e-4*

VINO!

A tapas and wine bar (*see* Chapter 5) plus full-service restaurant, Vino! has its roots firmly planted in Spanish cuisine. Empanadas (meat-filled turnovers), octopus, olives, and chorizo are good starters, while the better dinner entrées focus on seafood: Grilled salmon with romesco, a Catalan sauce made with peppers, ground nuts, and olive oil, is straight from Barcelona. The very good wine list even has dry (truly dry) sherry by the glass and has moved these aperi-

tif wines off the dessert list into their own category. There's a reserve list of fine Bordeaux as well. *2900 Peachtree Rd., Buckhead, 404/816–0511. Closed Sun. AE, D, MC, V. $$*

MEXICAN

5 *e-7*

DON TACO

Americans are beginning to discover these well-run drive-through operations, long popular with Mexican families in search of authentic home-style cooking. The house-made salsas are fresh and lively tasting, and the burritos, tacos, *tortas* (sandwiches with meat, mayonnaise, onion, jalapeños, lettuce, tomato and avocado), quesadillas, and *huarachas* (a kind of corn patty, topped with meat, beans and cheese) are excellent and inexpensive. Beer and wine are available. *4997 Buford Hwy., Chamblee, 770/458–8735. AE, D, DC, MC, V. Reservations not accepted. $*

5 *d-5*

Perimeter Mall food court, 4400 Ashford-Dunwoody Rd., Dunwoody, 770/ 394–0084.

4 *f-4*

50 S. Cobb Pkwy., Marietta, 770/792–8406.

5 *e-6*

EL PESCADOR

The menu at this simple restaurant advises that it takes 30–45 minutes to prepare the food, so be warned that (1) this is not a fast-food joint and (2) just about anything you order is going to be beautifully prepared. Seviche and seafood soup are excellent starters, and they can be nicely followed with the fish tacos or crabs (*jaivas*), which come either spicy or in garlic sauce (*mojo de ajo*). Fresh shrimp gets peeled for the excellent shrimp salad. A heated patio is a lovely spot for alfresco dining year-round. Good Mexican beers are available. *5768 Buford Hwy., Doraville, 770/ 452–1555. Reservations not accepted. No credit cards. $*

5 *e-6*

EL TACO VELOZ

Metro Atlanta has suddenly become dotted with these simple spots that specialize in totally tasty tacos. Pick up little *tacos de lengua* (tongue), *de barbacoa* (pork), or *de carne asada* (roasted meat), and be sure to specify "*con todo*" (with everything) so you can savor your selection with great salsa verde, minced onions, and cilantro. Oh, and extra jalapeños. Two of the locations (Chamblee and Roswell) use the name Taco Prisa. *5084 Buford Hwy., Doraville, 770/ 936–9094. Reservations not accepted. No credit cards. $*

3 | h-7
2700C Buford Hwy., in Chevron gas station next to Publix, Duluth, 770/622–0138.

5 | d-6
3245 Chamblee-Tucker Rd., Chamblee, 770/458–7779.

5 | b-5
5670 Roswell Rd., Sandy Springs, 404/ 252–5100.

4 | h-6
925 Windy Hill Rd., Smyrna, 770/432– 8800.

5 | c-2
Roswell Village, 10495 Alpharetta Hwy., at Holcomb Bridge Rd., Roswell, 770/993– 2621.

5 | g-3
2077 Beaver Ruin Rd., Norcross, 770/849– 0025.

3 | h-7
950 Jessie Jewel Rd., Gainesville, 770/503– 1100.

5 | e-6
EL CHARRUA
A kiosk-style drive-up stand on the grounds of a shopping center marks the spot where you find excellent tacos and tortas. The burritos, filled meat and beans, are huge and filling. There is one table outside for seating, but if it's occupied, you'll have to eat in your car. *5259 Buford Hwy., Doraville, 770/936–9780. No credit cards. $*

5 | g-5
FONDA SAN CARLOS
Authenticity reigns in this restaurant, which is appended to a fish market and serves the growing Hispanic population of south Gwinnett County. This is the place to savor freshly made pico de gallo; authentic mole, with a sauce that's smokey and deeply seasoned; and perhaps the city's best frozen margaritas. Given the adjoining business, seafood is a major player on the menu.

It's open until 4 AM (at least) on Friday and Saturday. *2077 Beaver Ruin Rd., Norcross, 770/797–2828. AE, D, DC, MC, V. Reservations not accepted. $*

5 | g-6
FRONTERA MEX-MEX GRILL
While all locations of this multi-branch operation serve authentic Mexican specialties (such as *escabeche*, raw fish marinated in citrus juices, and *chilaquiles*, tortillas baked in a casserole), each also offers something a little different. Mexican breakfast (*desuyano*) is served at the Jimmy Carter Boulevard and Stone Mountain locations and features some 15 different dishes, including *carne asada* (roasted meat), *carnitas* (little roasted cubes of pork), and excellent *menudo* (tripe soup). The Norcross location has entertainment Wednesday-Monday, with live mariachi music Sunday and Monday. *4606 Jimmy Carter Blvd., Norcross, 770/493–8341. Reservations not accepted. AE, D, DC, MC, V. $–$$*

5 | e-3
3466 Holcomb Bridge Rd., Norcross, 770/ 411–3488.

8 | e-1
5070 Stone Mountain Hwy. (U.S. 78), Stone Mountain, 770/972–3366.

10 | a-1
3607 GA 138, Stockbridge, 770/474–1540.

10 | h-5
1820 GA 30, Conyers, 770/860–8922.

15 | h-6
GRINGOS'
This former gas station and auto repair garage rolled up its bays a couple of years ago and became a popular neighborhood dining spot. The authentic Mexican dishes include many vegetarian selections, outstanding among them a delicious chile relleno stuffed with farmer's cheese and fresh corn, cooked in cream and *chihuahua* cheese. The Yucatecan specialty *cochinita pibil*, tender pork cooked in banana leaves, is singularly well done here. There's a wine list, but the margaritas are the beverages of choice, while the list of fine tequilas, ranging from the basic *blanco* (silver) to *reposado* (aged 1 year) and *añejo* (aged 3 years), is unequaled in the city. *1238 DeKalb Ave., Inman Park, 404/ 522–8666. Reservations not accepted. Closed Mon. No lunch. AE, MC, V. $*

12 *f3*

OH! . . . MARÍA

Finally, a beautifully atmospheric Mexican restaurant worthy of any gourmet's attention has come to Atlanta, thanks to Lucero Obregón of Zócalo (see below). Step inside and be transported to the land of aromatic spices, lively music, vivid colors, and intriguing textures. The large bar is a popular meeting place, but you'll want to take a seat at a table and begin a sampler platter of three different kinds of quesadillas, garnished with great fresh guacamole and either homemade salsa verde or salsa roja. Steak sabana, a thin rib steak served with black beans and homemade tortillas, is a worthy main course; the flan is superior; and the margaritas are superb. 3167 Peachtree Rd., Buckhead, 404/261–2032. AE, D, DC, MC, V. $–$$

15 *f2*

ZÓCALO

Owner Lucero Obregón learned to cook from her mother and also spent time working with Mexico's queen of cuisine, Patricia Quintana. It's little wonder her dining room and enclosed patio fill quickly, even during the week, and the cuisine lives up to its reputation. Dishes feature the authentic fare of Obregón's native central Mexico, but she wends into other territory when she wishes, doing an excellent sopa de lima (a chicken broth-based soup with lime, pieces of chicken breast and tortilla strips) and cochinita pibil from the Yucatán. Brunch is especially popular, with a menu that includes such satisfying dishes as steak with eggs and tomatillo sauce. 187 10th St., Midtown, 404/249–7576. Reservations not accepted. AE, D, DC, MC, V. $–$$

MIDDLE EASTERN

13 *b-6*

NICOLA'S

For more than a decade, Nicola Ayoub has been introducing Atlantans to the pleasures of the Middle Eastern table. These include his meza, a platter of salads and appetizers, and shawrma, shredded lamb served with lemon, sesame, or spinach-mushroom sauces. If you really want to experience Ayoub's mastery, try kibbey nayee—a delicious dish of raw ground lamb that's available only on Saturday, must be ordered a day in advance, and is prepared for a minimum of three diners. The wine list is very small, but for a corkage fee ($6) you can bring your own bottle. Reservations are essential on weekends, and Ayoub will open any time for special parties of at least 15 people. 1602 LaVista Rd., near Briarcliff Rd., Northeast, 404/325–2524. Closed Mon. No lunch. AE, D, MC, V. $

MOROCCAN

15 *h-5*

CASBAH

This casual, pretty space is draped to look like the tent of a desert shiek, providing an exotic atmosphere in which to enjoy b'stella, in which a Cornish hen is encased in pastry and perfumed with sweet aromatic spices (the dish is traditionally done with pigeon, but the hen is a concession to American tastes). Couscous with vegetables and lamb, tagines (traditional stews), and good baklava are the ideal follow-ups. Belly dancing begins at 8 PM every night. 465 N. Highland Ave., Poncey-Highland, 404/524–5777. Closed Mon. No lunch. AE, MC, V. $$

12 *e-6*

THE IMPERIAL FEZ

Prepare to remove your shoes before stepping into this luxuriously draped and swagged restaurant and taking a seat on one of the cushioned banquettes. You'll wash your hands in water perfumed with scented oils, then dishes from the fixed-price traditional meal will begin to arrive: pastry-baked Cornish hen; assorted salads; lentil soup; your choice of meat, fish, or vegetarian main course; and nut pastries for a conclusion. Traditional (i.e., belly) dancing further enhances the mood. The wine list is quite good and includes some Moroccan wines. Peachtree Battle Condominium, 2282 Peachtree Rd., Buckhead, 404/351–0870. Reservations required. No lunch. $$$$

PAN-ASIAN

12 *g3*

FUSEBOX

This art-filled and usually bustling restaurant (it can be impossibly jammed on Friday and Saturday nights) serves dishes that are Asian in inspiration and often cross culinary lines, such as Maine lobster with Asian seasonings. Meat and fish often go back to American basics, though, along the lines of venison and sweet potatoes. Whatever you order, you'll want to leave room for the crème brûlée—an extravagant presentation in which five different flavors are served in tiny sake cups. This wine list offers both Riesling and Gewurztraminer by the glass to support these dishes. *3085 Piedmont Rd., between Peachtree and E. Paces Ferry Rds., Buckhead, 404/233–3383. Reservations essential weekends. No lunch weekends. AE, D, DC, MC, V. $$$*

12   b-7
MALAYA

There are Chinese, Indonesian, Malaysian, and other southeast Asian dishes to choose from at this simple, family-run operation, and many of them, such as a *goreng* (a stir-fry of spicy string beans and tofu) can be made with or without meat or with seafood. Excellent noodle dishes and soups make fine light lunches, and *rijsttafel*, the traditional Indonesian feast based on rice, is served to a minimum of eight people and must be ordered a couple of days in advance. *857 Collier Rd., Buckhead, 404/609–9991. Reservations not accepted. Closed Sun. No lunch Sat. AE, DC, MC, V. $$*

12   f3
NICKIEMOTO'S

Sitting on a patio at the corner of 10th Street and Piedmont Avenue in Midtown is not a bad way to pass a warm afternoon. When to that scenario you can add the taste of steamed dumplings stuffed with vegetables and chicken, or a coconut broth with black mussels, or a tasty stir-fry, life really is good. At the Buckhead location you can enjoy a wider variety of fare that includes good sushi, cold soba noodles with peanut sauce, deep-fried catfish, and black mussels in coconut broth seasoned with keffir lime. *247 Buckhead Ave., East Village Square, Buckhead, 404/842–0334. Reservations not accepted. No lunch at Buckhead. AE, D, MC, V. $$*

15   f2
990 Piedmont Ave., Midtown, 404/253–2010.

15   f5
PACIFIC RIM

Raymond and Anna Hsu (of Hsu's Gourmet; *see* Chinese, *above*) have crafted a warmly lit, wood-filled interior in which to present the dishes of Asia. Shredded green papayas and tofu moistened with lime juice zing with Thai chilies, while beef dishes offer assertive flavorings that range from Korean hot sauce to the sweet, pungent Hawaiian marinade. The little dishes and sushi work almost like Asian tapas, so it's easy to assemble a light meal. *303 Peachtree Center Ave., Downtown, 404/893–0018. No lunch weekends. AE, D, MC, V. $$*

5   c-5
SAVU

Named for an island off the coast of Indonesia, the restaurant at the hip W Atlanta hotel (*see* Chapter 6) dives coolly and with assurance into a melding of French, Chinese, Japanese, and Thai cuisines, each bringing its distinctive flavors to these dishes. Szechuan lobster pancakes recall the seafood pancakes of China and Korea, while crispy Beijing duck comes with the familiar scallion pancakes and a unique black bean vinaigrette. Dessert returns to Occidental traditions, with Christine's Candy Bar, a layering of dark chocolate, macadamia nut brittle, vanilla, and raspberry. The wine list is extensive, with many bottles that pair well with a wide range of these dishes. Brunch reverts to American (southern) standards, including Georgia pecan waffles and speckle heart grits. *111 Perimeter Center W, Dunwoody, 770/280–0700. AE, D, DC, MC, V. $$$$*

5   d-2
WOK & CHOPS

Out-of-the-ordinary dishes pepper this interesting menu, which gathers a variety of tastes from throughout Asia. The noodle dishes run from Indonesian to Malaysian styles, and you'll find many interestingly spicy seafood dishes, such as mango grouper and coconut curry soft-shell crab. The most exotic combination, though, is frogs' legs with black bean sauce and sweetbreads. *Kings Market shopping center, 1425 Market Blvd., at the intersection of Old Alabama and Holcomb Bridge Rds., Roswell, 770/552–8982. AE, D, MC, V. $*

PERSIAN

5 c-3

MIRAGE

This friendly, bright restaurant serves many good meatless dishes, beginning with appetizers that include an intriguingly tangy combination of herbed feta cheese and yogurt with a sprinkling of shallots, served with flat bread and moving on to such pleasing but simple presentations as vegetable kabob perched on a bed of basmati rice. Meat eaters enjoy excellent lamb and chicken dishes. There's a decent wine list. *6631C Roswell Rd., Abernathy Shopping Center, Sandy Springs, 404/843–8300. AE, D, DC, MC, V. $–$$*

PERUVIAN

13 c-3

MACHU PICCHU

Stuffed toy llamas and a mannequin dressed in traditional costume set the stage for Atlanta's favorite (and just about its only) Peruvian restaurant. Peruvian patrons enjoy authentic *anticuchos* (beef heart kabobs), *chanfainita* (beef heart stew), and *caucau* (tripe stew), while American diners are likely to stick to more accustomed fare such as one of the seviches of marinated seafood or

---

DINING ON THE RUN

Hungry and in a hurry? These spots provide tasty fare served quickly, so you can get back to doing whatever it was you were doing—whether shopping or just scurrying from one point to another.

Bajaritos (Eclectic)
Grab a tray and move down the self-service line, picking up gourmet wraps and fresh salsa. You won't break $10; you'll dine quickly; and you'll enjoy the aesthetics of the vibrant interior.

Don Taco (Mexican)
All shopping-mall food courts should be so lucky as to have food of this caliber—the burritos are especially good.

The Varsity (American)
Nothing ever came faster than a Varsity hot dog with chili, great greasy onion rings, and an orange frosty. A cultural experience besides.

---

mixed seafood soup. Seafood, in fact, is the strong suit here and shows up in everything from omelettes to stews. Beer and wine are served, and the traditional fruit drinks are excellent, especially those with mango. *Northeast Plaza shopping center, 3375 Buford Hwy., Northeast, 404/320–3226. Closed Tues. AE, D, DC, MC, V. $–$$*

PIZZA

12 g-2

CALIFORNIA PIZZA KITCHEN

Lots of glass, wood, and white tile give these designer-pizza specialty restaurants a hip ambience. The pizza tends to be trendy, too, appearing with ingredients from every cuisine imaginable, from Thai to Japanese to Southern. The best, though, stick closer to the pizza's original world, the Mediterranean (the one with goat cheese and roasted peppers is especially good). Sandwiches, salads, and pastas are also available, with the last appearing in such odd international variations as Kung Pao spaghetti. Decent wine and beer are served. *Lenox Square, lower level (near Macy's), 3393 Peachtree Rd., Buckhead, 404/262–9221. Reservations not accepted. AE, D, DC, MC, V. $*

4 f-1

6301 North Point Mall, across from Sears, Alpharetta, 770/664–8246.

5 c-5

4600 Ashford-Dunwoody Rd., just north of Perimeter Mall, Dunwoody, 770/393–0390.

15 h-4

CAMELI'S GOURMET PIZZA JOINT

Cameli's is run by the same two brothers who operate Pastificio Cameli in East Atlanta (*see Italian, above*). Their creations include many tasty "stuffed pizzas," including "half moon" versions that are ideal for solo diners and are filled with ingredients of your choice—the unique combinations include Dante's Delight, with black-olives. *699 Ponce de Leon Ave., Poncey-Highland, 404/249–9020. Reservations not accepted. No lunch Sun. AE, D, DC, MC, V. $*

14 d-2

EVERYBODY'S PIZZA

The pizza with green peppers, mushrooms, and tomatoes is especially popular with Emory students at the Decatur

Road location, but all the pies at both outlets are delicious; so are the pepperoni pizza crisps, especially the one with onions and cheese, and they are a little lower in calories. Huge salads and soups are excellent, too. There's beer and wine only at Decatur Road, full bar at Highland Ave. *1593 N. Decatur Rd., Emory University area, 404/377–7766. Reservations not accepted. AE, D, DC, MC, V. $*

14 *a-2*

1040 N. Highland Ave., Virginia-Highland, 404/873–4545.

13 *c-6*

GRANT CENTRAL PIZZA AND PASTA

This pizza-pasta outlet has operations in both the burgeoning East Atlanta and Grant Park restaurant scenes. What they have in common are excellent pies, but each has its specialties: calzones, salads, and a nightly special, along with table service, at Grant Park, and sandwiches (but counter service only) at East Atlanta. Toppings range from traditional pepperoni to black olive on the pizzas at both locations. Beer and wine are available at both, and the choices are quite decent. *451 Cherokee Ave., Grant Park, 404/523–8900. No lunch Sat. at both locations. Grant Park closed Sun. Reservations not accepted. MC, V. $*

14 *b-8*

1279 Glenwood Ave., East Atlanta, 404/ 627–0007.

5 *d-5*

MELLOW MUSHROOM

Mellow Mushroom has about two dozen franchises around the metro area, so sooner or later anyone in search of good pizza is bound to step into one. Even the most demanding pizza aficionado isn't going to be disappointed, with offerings that include a gourmet white pizza with garlic, olive oil, sun-dried and fresh tomatoes, onions and cheese; pesto pizza with spinach, mushrooms and tomatoes; and steak calzone, a sort of steak-and-cheese sandwich. Beer and wine are available in each store. *Dunwoody Corners shopping center, 9575 Chamblee Dunwoody Rd., Dunwoody, 770/396–1393. AE, MC, V. $*

13 *c-6*

1679 LaVista Rd., Northeast, 404/325–0550.

5 *h-6*

331 Rockbridge Rd., at U.S. 29, Lilburn, 770/921–1612.

5 *f-4*

Marketplace shopping center, 6135 Peachtree Pkwy., Norcross, 770/729–1555.

4 *h-6*

210 Powers Ferry Rd., at Akers Mill Rd., Marietta, 770/955–4311.

4 *f-2*

Town Center Esplanade shopping center, 2700 Town Center Dr., Kennesaw, 770/ 290–2001.

13 *e-3*

MO'S PIZZA

Area high school and college students are among the regulars who flock here for great traditional pizza, which proves they have good taste: The yeasty pizza dough is superior, the tomato sauce is rich, and the mozzarella is rich. Other toppings are available, too, of course, and so are great hot dogs, excellent chicken wings, and sandwiches of all kinds. There's an extensive beer collection, including Haake Beck's nonalcoholic malt, plus wine and wine coolers. *3109 Briarcliff Rd., at Clairmont Rd., Northeast, 404/320–1258. Reservations not accepted. MC, V. $*

9 *a-6*

PARTNERS II PIZZA

Don't look for the same old toppings here—unless you consider potatoes with sour cream, cheddar cheese, green onions, and bacon or buffalo meat, mozzarella cheese, and smoked provolone to be typical toppings. Traditional pasta dishes, including homemade lasagna, and meatball subs get raves, too. Good wine is available. The weekday lunch and Monday-night buffet feature all-you-can eat pizza and salad. *215 Northlake Dr., Peachtree City, 770/487–9393. Reservations not accepted. AE, D, DC, MC, V. $*

12 *d-8*

ROCKY'S BRICK OVEN PIZZA & ITALIAN RESTAURANT

There's a lot more here than just the pizza, including a cioppino (a tomato-based seafood stew) at the Buckhead location that's served in a bowl made out of a hunk of scooped-out bread. But the pizzas are the draw, and they range from basic tomato and cheese to excellent white pies. The Virginia-Highland location adds huge sandwiches to the offerings. Delivery is available from both locations. *1776 Peachtree St., Buckhead, 404/876–9441. Reservations not accepted. AE, D, DC, MC, V. $*

14 *a-3*

1395 N. Highland Ave., Virginia-Highland, 404/876–1111.

15 *d-6*

ROSA'S PIZZA

This unfancy place keeps transplanted New Yorkers and Chicagoans lining up for by-the-slice lunches. Very thin pizza crust with a good yeasty flavor comes topped with a variety of choices, but the best is the classic and simple tomato and cheese. *62 Broad St., Downtown, 404/521–2596. Closed weekends. No credit cards. $*

14 *a-4*

SAVAGE PIZZA

This is a gourmet pizza joint with table service and take-out—along with a funky flair. Mai Pai comes with spicy red pepper sauce and fresh pineapple, while chicken cordon bleu comes off a bit better, with garlic white sauce, roasted chicken, and prosciutto. Small pies, individual slices, salads and calzone are also available. *484 Moreland Ave., Little Five Points, 404/523–0500. Reservations not accepted. AE, MC, V. $*

SEAFOOD

12 *f-4*

ATLANTA FISH MARKET

There's no missing this place, because a huge multistory bronze fish announces its location; the dining room is distinctive, too, divided into sections that resemble railway cars. Despite these decorative excesses, the food stands on its own merit: Gumbo, crab cakes, steamed sea bass Hong Kong style, and the raw oyster selection are all superb. The wine list is worthy and offers good choices by the glass. *265 Pharr Rd., Buckhead, 404/262–3165. Reservations essential. AE, D, DC, MC, V. $$$–$$$$*

12 *g-1*

CHEQUERS SEAFOOD GRILL

Combination pubs and restaurants, these two seafood spots do some things very well and could do some things a lot

better. Stick to basic fare, such as simply prepared fresh fish, and you'll probably be quite happy. Both restaurants are well located for an after-shopping dining bite, and Sunday brunch is popular at both. *3424 Peachtree Rd., across from Phipps Plaza, just behind Ritz-Carlton, Buckhead, 404/842–9997. No lunch weekends. AE, D, DC, MC, V. $$$*

5 *c-5*

236 Perimeter Pkwy., near Perimeter Mall, Dunwoody, 770/391–9383.

5 *e-6*

EL PESCADOR

See Mexican, *above.*

5 *b-5*

EMBERS SEAFOOD GRILL

This seafood grill evokes the shacks you've seen at the shore—wacky, rustic, casual, showing the patina of time. The seafood chowder, fresh grilled fish, blackened amberjack, crab cakes, and key lime pie are as good as any you'd find at a place like that, too. *234 Hildebrand Dr., near Roswell Rd., Sandy Springs, 404/256–0977. Closed Sun. No lunch Sat. or Mon. AE, D, DC, MC, V. $$–$$$*

12 *d-7*

FISHBONE, A PIRANHA BAR

Coconut-battered deep-fried shrimp (crisp and delicious) provide a perfect nibble as you sit at the huge copper-covered bar and prepare you for a wide array of fish and shellfish dishes inspired by cuisines from around the world. Thai-style peppery calamari and wood-grilled Hawaiian wahoo capture the spirit of this inventive food. Don't even bother to try to resist the Barbados rum cake for dessert. *1874 Peachtree Rd., Buckhead, 404/367–4772. Reservations not accepted. No lunch weekends. AE, D, DC, MC, V. $$*

5 *a-5*

FISHMONGER'S

The house soup is the Fishmonger's Stew, based on the lightest possible seafood broth, fragrant with saffron, and containing mussels, clams, fish, and shrimp. Crab and shrimp cakes with a spicy curry mayonnaise make a light but well-seasoned treat. For meat eaters, there's an excellent filet mignon of Argentine beef with chimichurri sauce, a blend of parsley, white vinegar, garlic, and olive oil. Daily specials are based on fresh fish available any given day. The wine list has a number of South African selections, a tribute to the home country of Angelo Laios, one of the two owners whose partner Zimbabwe native Nik Panagopoulos also lived there at length. *Belle Isle shopping center, 4969 Roswell Rd., Suite 160, (lower rear level), 404/459–9003. Reservations essential. No lunch weekends. AE, D, DC, MC, V. $$$*

12 *e-6*

JIM WHITE'S HALF SHELL

The Half Shell is a long-time favorite for Atlantans seeking good seafood. The she-crab soup, a light version of this low-country specialty, is a classic, and this is about the only place in town where you can get scamp, a large-mouth Florida fish that yields a meaty thick fillet. Stone crab claws are a much-awaited seasonal specialty. *2349 Peachtree Rd., Peachtree Battle shopping center, 404/237–9924. No lunch. AE, D, DC, MC, V. $$$–$$$$*

12 *h-7*

MARRA'S SEAFOOD AND STEAKS

Marra's started in a small, unadorned former residence as a simple seafood grill, and as the premises have expanded over the years (they now include a large deck to the rear of the building for alfresco dining in good weather), so has the menu. The kitchen now explores American cuisine from all four corners, with such offerings as swordfish crusted with ancho peppers and served with pineapple-tomatillo salsa and jícama salad, and giant scallops encircled by house-made salmon bacon and are paired with grilled yams and a roasted corn-shallot sauce. *1782 Cheshire Bridge Rd., Northeast, 404/874–7347. Reservations essential. No lunch. AE, D, DC, MC, V. $$$–$$$$*

5 *e-6*

STRINGER'S FISH CAMP

Imagine a fishing camp—you know, slightly scruffy, with worn Formica tables and plastic-covered chairs. That's Stringer's. Seafood may be ordered anyway you wish, but this is the place to spend your fried-fish calories, because the deep-fried catfish, shrimp, scallops, and oysters are perfectly done. The seafood platter will easily feed two persons. *3384 Shallowford Rd., Chamblee, 770/458–7145. AE, D, MC, V. $–$$*

SOUTHERN

15 *g-1*

AGNES & MURIEL'S

Agnes and Muriel are a pair of moms whose children, Glenn Powell and Beth Baskin, jointly own this restaurant where the kitchen puts some interesting twists on the classics of southern home-style cooking—seasoning collard greens with lemon and sesame seeds instead of the usual fatback, for instance. But the turkey meat loaf, salmon patties, and buttermilk fried chicken are right off the list of traditional favorites, and the magnificent chocolate chiffon pie makes a perfect finish to any meal. Beer and very well chosen wines are available, but no liquor. *1514 Monroe Dr., just past Piedmont Ave., near Ansley Park, 404/885–1000. Reservations not accepted. AE, D, DC, MC, V. $$*

15 *d-2*

BOBBY AND JUNE'S KOUNTRY KITCHEN

Hams hang from the rafters and there are rockers on the porch, and both the hard hats and Georgia Tech students who come here for breakfast, lunch, and supper find this rustic cabin–style ambience comfortable. The sliced barbecue pork sandwich is tops in its category, and the biscuits deserve a medal. Some vegetables are frozen but prepared with taste. Breakfast is southern style, with grits (albeit instant ones.) *375 14th St., Home Park, 404/876-3872. Reservations not accepted. MC, V. $*

12 *h-7*

THE COLONNADE

This is southern food as your mother and your aunts made it. Proper biscuits and corn bread, the perfect salmon patty, country ham steak that's not afraid to sport a bone, and excellent southern-style hot and cold vegetables keep the place bustling even on weekdays. There's a separate bar and lounge opposite the dining room. *1879 Cheshire Bridge Rd., Northeast, 404/874–5642. No lunch Sun. No credit cards. $*

4 *f-5*

1848 HOUSE

The name refers to the date this fine Classical Revival plantation house was built. It's said to be haunted (*see* Chapter 4), but its grounds provide the restaurant with a significant buffer from surrounding urban intrusions. Chef Thomas McEachern wanders into Italian dishes, such as a tortelloni with tomatoes, leeks, and wild mushrooms, but in general, it's southern food and the plantation forms of southern cooking all the way, from the excellent she-crab soup to the buttermilk fried quail, fried green tomatoes, trout, and sometimes game, depending on the season. The "Sweet Georgia Brown" dessert tops rhubarb with vanilla bean ice milk, a very southern finale. McEachern can create a vegetarian feast upon request. The good wine list assures a fine dining experience. Sunday brunch is a large buffet from 10:30 to 2 PM, and jazz accompanies the repast. *780 S. Cobb Dr., Marietta, 770/428–1848. Reservations essential. No lunch. AE, D, DC, MC, V. $$$*

14 f1
EVANS FINE FOODS
Decatur's favorite spot for down-home food draws the common man and the elite alike, including former President and Mrs. Carter. The daily specials get raves, and breakfast is a high point, with country ham, grits, eggs, and all the trimmings. For lunch or dinner ("dinner or supper" in southern parlance) the favorites are the fried chicken livers, the meat loaf, the country-fried steak, and the barbecue. At all meals, veggies and everything else are made from scratch. *2125 N. Decatur Rd., Decatur, 404/634–6294. Reservations not accepted. Closed Sun. No credit cards. $*

5 b-6
HORSERADISH GRILL
Occupying a former horse barn, this supremely popular restaurant on the edge of Chastain Park has its concepts firmly rooted in authentic dishes. Chef David Berry's South Carolina barbecue is right out of his dad's recipe book, but the younger Berry piles it onto a corn cake and tops it with cole slaw (the corn cake alludes to the hush puppies that Carolinians enjoy with their 'cue). Low-country shrimp and grits, fantastic fried chicken, quail, rabbit, and traditional southern desserts highlight this constantly changing menu. The extraordinary wine list offers good selections by the glass. *4320 Powers Ferry Rd., Buckhead, 404/255–7277. AE, D, DC, MC, V. $$*

8 c-1
LET'S EAT CAFÉ
There's enough going for this tiny place to make the effort of seeking it out on a side street in an industrial area worth your while. Whiting is dipped in cornmeal, fried, and served with good grits—an outstanding dish in the best of southeast Georgia culinary traditions. The sweet potato pie is flat-out awesome. No alcohol is served. *780 Glendale Rd., Decatur, 404/297–9316. Reservations not accepted. No credit cards. $*

15 f4
MARY MAC'S TEA ROOM
Now in its third generation of ownership, Mary Mac's (which is not a true tea room despite its name) has fed everyone from film stars to old-time Atlantans. When the legislature is in session, politicos hash out their differences over superior fried chicken, country-fried steak, fresh vegetables southern style, and homemade desserts. You sit down, pick up a pencil, and write down your order. Brunch is served Saturday and Sunday. Wine and beer are served. *224 Ponce de Leon Ave., Midtown, 404/876–1800. No dinner Sun. No credit cards. $*

5 g-7
MATTHEWS CAFETERIA
Founded in 1955 and said to be DeKalb County's oldest continuously operating restaurant, this time- and use-worn establishment may look like pure country, but the occasional Rolls-Royce has been known to park outside. No matter what you drive, you line up to claim a tray and select from a steam table containing various specialties, depending on the day of the week, market availability, and the whim of the kitchen. Possibilities include great squash casserole, macaroni and cheese, and grilled Polish sausage with sauerkraut or corned beef and stewed cabbage. Peach cobbler is the dessert to save room for, but then there's the banana pudding, too. The Winder branch does not do breakfast, but otherwise serves the same food. No alcohol is served. *2299 Main St., Tucker, 770/491–9577. No credit cards. $*

18 W. May St., Winder, 770/586–5555.

14 *a-3*

MAJESTIC FOOD SHOPS

This classic diner, open since 1929, is a reliable and safe haven for late-night fare (it's open 24 hours) that includes good breakfast dishes as well as reliable renditions of fried chicken and other offerings. Want a little people-watching with your grilled ham steak and coconut cream pie? The characters who hang out here provide some splendid sightseeing—you could cast a movie. No alcohol is served. *1031 Ponce de Leon Ave., Poncey-Highland, 404/875–0276. Reservations not accepted. No credit cards. $*

7 *f-3*

MRS. BEA'S KITCHEN

Beatrice Heath operates within the confines of Heath's Cascade Grocery, making superb fried chicken, fried pork chops, fresh vegetables, and homemade cakes. Breakfast and all-day lunch to 7:30 are offered. There's take-out only, and no alcohol. *787 Cascade Ave., Cascade Heights, 404/755–0543. Reservations not accepted. No dinner. No credit cards. $*

12 *a-2*

OK CAFÉ

Families love the OK's kid-friendly fare and the casual, 1950s-style atmosphere. The best meal is breakfast, with good grits, omelets, and pancakes; the savory classics of American home-style cooking that show up at other meals include meat loaf, country-fried steak, mashed potatoes and gravy, fried chicken, and pot roast. It's open very early to very late weekends. Take-out is available. *1284 W. Paces Ferry Rd., at I–75, Buckhead, 404/233–2888. Reservations not accepted. AE, D, DC, MC, V. $*

7 *g-6*

ORIGINAL DWARF HOUSE

The menu mounted on a wall of this 1950s-feeling restaurant includes steak and hamburgers and, the real reason to come here, the famous chicken hot brown sandwiches. It closes at 4 AM Sunday morning and reopens 5 AM Monday morning, then is open around the clock until Sunday rolls around again. *461 Central Ave., Hapeville, 404/762–1746. Reservations not accepted. Closed Sun. No credit cards. $*

14 *g-4*

OUR WAY CAFÉ

Home cooking that is wickedly cheap and served on steam tables draws students from nearby Agnes Scott College. Here's the drill: You line up for your tray and select your meat and sides. Choices will vary daily and might include meat loaf, chicken enchiladas, and roast pork and, for veggies, green bean casserole, squash casserole, collard greens, sweet potato soufflé, and macaroni and cheese. You'll get out of here with so much change from a $10 bill that you'll think you stole your lunch, the only meal served. No alcohol is served. *303 E. College Ave., Decatur, 404/373–6665. Reservations not accepted. Closed Sat. No dinner. No credit cards. $*

14 *h-1*

PICCADILLY CLASSIC AMERICAN COOKING

This Baton Rouge, Louisiana–based outfit, founded in 1944, does southern food cafeteria-style at 22 locations around the metro Atlanta area—and maintains a level of quality that is consistently high. Good étouffée and jambalaya are occasional specials, while gumbo is a regular item. Baked chicken, baked and fried fish, fried chicken, salmon patties, good vegetables (only the mashed potatoes are packaged), and desserts are the popular dishes with the budget-conscious diners here, especially families and older folks. It's open until 8:30 PM, with continuous service, and open holidays except Christmas. No alcohol is served, but there's take-out. *Suburban Plaza shopping center, 2595 N. Decatur Rd., Decatur, 404/373–3931. Reservations not accepted. AE, D, DC, MC, V. $*

12 *a-3*

Howell Mill Square shopping center, 1715 Howell Mill Rd., 404/352–1743.

4 *g-7*

2781 S. Cobb Dr., at Windy Hill Rd., Smyrna, 770/435–6707.

12 *g-5*

Lindbergh Plaza shopping center, 2581 Piedmont Rd., Lindbergh Plaza, Buckhead, 404/364–9636.

15 *g-1*

Ansley Mall shopping center, 1452 Piedmont Ave., Suite 403, Ansley Park/Morningside, 404/872–8091.

5 *e-1*

800 Mansell Rd., at Alpharetta Hwy., Roswell, 770/518–8905.

13 *h-5*

QUINNIE'S

This bare-bones, family-run restaurant is short on ambience but is known for preparing vegetables southern style without meat or grease. So, it has the right to designate some dishes "Heart Healthy," but not that everything is. As you move along the steam tables, you'll be justifiably tempted by the Brunswick stew, fried chicken, macaroni and cheese, barbecue, and deep-fried, corn-meal-crusted whole catfish on Fridays. No alcohol is served. *2860 LaVista Rd., Northeast, 404/728–8763. Reservations not accepted. Closed Sun. MC, V. $*

5 *f-5*

ROY'S DINER

A native of Boston owns this classic diner, and a native of Guatemala oversees the kitchen. Nonetheless, the fare is classic southern, with very good grits and eggs for breakfast, and homemade southern specials, which vary daily, but might include stuffed peppers, meat loaf and fried pork chops, and fresh vegetables, plus shakes, malts, and classic floats. There's no alcohol. *600 Buford Hwy., Norcross, 770/242–7211. Reservations not accepted. Closed Sun. No lunch Sat., no dinner. No credit cards. $*

15 *d-2*

SILVER SKILLET

An authentic southern-diner atmosphere abounds in this long-standing establishment, where breakfast and lunch (in the South called "dinner") are the only meals served. Eggs, grits, and country ham breakfasts bring in the locals, and at other meals a mix of blue-collar workers, professionals, and students show up for its the classics of southern home-style fare, including baked chicken and fish, meat loaf, tender grilled pork chops, chicken-fried steak, superb vegetables, and excellent pies. No alcohol is served. *200 14th St., Midtown, 404/874–1388. Reservations not accepted. No lunch weekends, no dinner. AE, D, DC, MC, V. $*

15 *h-5*

SON'S PLACE

The late Deacon Burton need not worry: His reputation is secure in the cooking of his son, Lenn Story (hence the name of this bright, cheery place). The legendary fried chicken, vegetables, pound cake, sweet potato pie, and light, flat cornmeal hoe cakes keep patrons very happy. Great homemade lemonade makes you forget that there's no alcohol served. *100 Hurt St., Inman Park, 404/581–0530. Closed weekends. No dinner. No credit cards. $*

15 *e-2*

SOUTH CITY KITCHEN

This art-filled, bright, high-energy spot stays superbusy every day of the week. Inspired by low-country cooking from the South Carolina and Georgia coasts, the kitchen turns out nifty versions of classic dishes, including a light but rich and tasty she-crab soup, fried green tomatoes, crab hash with poached eggs (a great brunch dish also available at lunch), catfish Reuben sandwich for lunch, and desserts that would bring Scarlett back to life, such as the chocolate pecan pie. This excellent wine list has much to recommend it and is a constant work in progress. *1144 Crescent Ave., between Peachtree and W. Peachtree Sts., Midtown, 404/873–7358. AE, D, DC, MC, V. $*

15 *c-3*

THELMA'S KITCHEN

Though Thelma Grundy was booted out of her longtime Luckie Street location, she soon found a home in this old hotel and remains an Atlanta culinary institution. Her fans have followed her for okra pancakes (a must when they're on the menu), to be accompanied by such favorites as fried catfish, well-seasoned vegetables, macaroni and cheese, "cold" slaw, and pecan pie. No alcohol is served. *768 Marietta St., ground floor of the Roxy Hotel, Downtown, 404/688–5855. No credit cards. Closed weekends. No dinner. $*

8 *a-8*

TRUETT'S GRILL

This authentic 1950s diner is named for Truett Cathy, the grandfatherly motorcycle-riding guy who founded Chick-fil-A in Hapeville. Restored antique cars dot the grounds, a thrill for car buffs, while those in search of good home-style fare will enjoy the famous chicken sandwich, plus fresh vegetables, steaks, and breakfast. *2042 Mt. Zion Rd., Morrow, 770/210–0500. Reservations not accepted. Closed Sun. MC, V. $*

SOUTH AFRICAN

5 *b-6*

10 DEGREES SOUTH

For the substantial South African community in Atlanta, this place is a piece of home. South African cooking borrows from here and there, whether it's Indian curries or native hot peppers, and this geographic diversity shows up in the menu. Chicken livers get the "peri peri" treatment, making them spicy hot and giving them a classic African character, while from Cape Malay come *sosaties*, beef skewers seasoned with spicy curry sauce. Ostrich fillet, a South African classic, is of course on the menu and needs to be savored rare. The wine list is exclusively South African. *4183 Roswell Rd., Sandy Springs, 404/705 8870. No lunch Mon. AE, D, DC, MC, V. $$*

SOUTHWESTERN

8 *a-8*

AZTECA GRILL

Be sure to listen to the specials here, as that's where some of the best examples of the kitchen's inventiveness can be found. In December they've even been known to make *posole*, that great, classic one-pot meal with hominy and pork (traditionally a whole pig's head) of the American Southwest. Menu staples, such as fish tacos, green chili stew, and the chocolate chimichanga for dessert are excellent, too. *1140 Morrow Industrial Blvd., off Jonesboro Rd., near Southlake Mall shopping center, Morrow, 770/968–0907. Reservations not accepted. Closed Sun. AE, D, DC, MC, V. $*

5 *c-5*

CANYON CAFE

This Dallas-based restaurant has recently opened two outlets in Atlanta, and both have been instant hits with their offerings of Tex-Mex fare. Margaritas are generous and not short in the tequila department; South Texas tortilla soup is a good version of this classic, thick with tortillas strips; the paella is respectable; and the chicken-fried steak spills off the sides of the plate. Salad dressings are all made on the premises, including a decent fat-free sun-dried tomato vinaigrette. They have a spinach and Portobello mushroom quesadilla that's out of this world, by the way—you could insert this as a vegetarian option

(though we carnivores love it, too). *118 Perimeter Center W, near Perimeter Mall, Dunwoody, 770/395–6605. AE, D, DC, MC, V. $$*

5 *e-1*

11405 Haynes Bridge Rd., near Northpoint Mall, Alpharetta, 770/346–0996.

12 *e-6*

GEORGIA GRILLE

The "Georgia" part of the name is a reference not to the state but to Georgia O'Keeffe—owner Karen Hilliard is a great admirer of her art, although work by local artist Steve Penley graces the walls of these two popular restaurants. Diners also turn their attention to artful cuisine that includes "hot shots," jalapeños that are stuffed with cotija cheese, breaded in cornmeal and fried, a lobster-stuffed enchilada, and excellent flan. The short wine list is carefully chosen to go with the food, but the margaritas get the raves. *Peachtree Square shopping center, 2290 Peachtree Rd., Buckhead, 404/352–3517. Reservations not accepted. Closed Mon. AE, MC, V. $$*

5 *f-1*

1150 Jones Bridge Rd., Alpharetta, 678/297–0291.

2 *a-8*

LA PAZ

The management of Atlanta-based La Paz could give lessons in how to run a chain dining operation without sacrificing detail, authenticity, and quality. Each restaurant has its own defining architecture and personality: The original location in Sandy Springs evokes a cantina, while the Vinings location resembles a Mexican chapel. All are good spots to stop after work for a drink, and the menu attracts families. Vegetarians will enjoy the spinach enchiladas made with blue corn tortillas. *250 Cinema View, Woodstock, 770/591–1073. Reservations not accepted. No lunch weekends at Sandy Springs. AE, D, DC, MC, V. $-$$*

5 *f-1*

11605 Jones Bridge Rd., Alpharetta, 770/521–0506.

4 *h-6*

2950 New Paces Ferry Rd., Vinings, 770/801–0020.

5 *c-4*

6410 Roswell Rd., Sandy Springs, 404/256–3555.

12 *f3*
NAVA

A collection of fine southwestern art, including exquisite kachina dolls, adorns the several levels of this high-energy restaurant, where traditional fare is enhanced by deft handling of seasonings and sophisticated presentations. Many of the appetizers, including a barbecued rabbit tostada with black beans and arugula salad or a quesadilla with sweet onion and cabrales cheese (a blue cow's-milk cheese), suffice as a light meal. Or, you may want to stay on the lighter side by assembling an assortment of side dishes for a vegetarian platter that could include a tamale stuffed with sweet potato or Portobello mushrooms, white bean enchiladas, and a black bean cake. The B & B Cube (a cube of chocolate with a Brandy & Benedictine-flavored mousse and crushed chocolate chip cookies enfolded within) has won awards—talk about a chocolate attack! The good wine list offers plenty of fine by-the-glass choices. *3060 Peachtree Rd., near W. Paces Ferry Rd., Buckhead, 404/240–1984. Reservations essential. No lunch weekends. AE, D, DC, MC, V. $$$*

14 *a-2*
NOCHE

Tom Catherall, a native of Scotland who owns this bustling, gleaming restaurant, (as well as steak house Prime, above, by the way) has fallen for the flavors of *chipotle, ancho,* and serrano peppers, and they infuse such dishes as tortilla soup with avocado and fresh cheese and grilled shrimp with corn *masa* garlic sauce. The chocolate *tres leches* is served as a latte with chocolate cigarettes— clever, rich and satisfying. There's good wine here, but the margaritas are the draw. *1000 Virginia Ave., Virginia-Highland, 404/815–9155. Reservations not accepted. No lunch weekends. AE, D, DC, MC, V. $$*

4 *h-6*
SOHO

Exploring a wide range of southwestern culinary influences, this menu wanders off into other cuisines as well. The chicken-tortilla soup is a Yucatecan classic, your basic *sopa de lima* with avocado, chili, and lime. Salmon is wrapped in rice paper and served with Thai pesto (a lemon-grass, cilantro, basil, and mint pesto with crushed peanuts and Thai

chilis), ponzu sauce (a citrus soy sauce with rice vinegar) and rice. Meanwhile, a southwestern touch enhances an American classic, the Reuben sandwich, for which a touch of chipotle pepper shows up in the Thousand Island dressing. There are lots of good wines by the glass, and the list is constantly updated and enhanced. *Vinings Jubilee shopping center, 4200 Paces Ferry Rd., Vinings, 770/801–0069. No lunch weekends. AE, D, DC, MC, V. $$*

12 *h-7*
SUNDOWN CAFE

Southwestern fare rarely gets better than this—anywhere: chicken liver salad; roast pork tenderloin rubbed with southwestern spices and served with a tomatillo-infused gravy and ancho mashed potatoes; tangy turnip greens enlivened by zippy chile arbol. The superior dessert is the chocolate chimichanga, a piece of pastry genius. *2165 Cheshire Bridge Rd., Northeast, 404/321–1118. Reservations not accepted. Closed Sun. No lunch Sat. AE, MC, V. $*

15 *h-3*
TORTILLAS

A zippy, hip, long-popular taquerìa, this student hang-out offers some of the best cheap food in town. Burritos and quesadillas are the main attractions that bring in a constant stream of devotees, and the freshly made guacamole and salsas, especially the green tomatillo, are ideal accompaniments. Beer is the best quaff with this fare. *774 Ponce de Leon Ave., Virginia-Highland, 404/892–0193. Reservations not accepted. No credit cards. $*

STEAK

4 *h-7*
BLACKSTONE

The excellent steaks here come from prime Iowa corn-fed beef, and those who want to branch out have plenty of choices, too. A grilled wild game sausage is served with Asiago cheese grits and cranberry onion compote, steak tartare is still on the menu (an increasingly rare sighting these days), and fish and seafood aren't overlooked, either. Some wines are offered by the glass. *Vinings West shopping center, 4835 S. Atlanta Rd., Vinings, 404/794–6100. No lunch. AE, D, DC, MC, V. $$$$*

`12` g-3

BONE'S

In an atmosphere conducive to gathering all the fraternity boys in town, well-established Bone's serves excellent steaks, as well as very fine lamb and veal. The lobster bisque is justifiably well regarded for its silky texture and fulsome lobster flavor, and the huge onion rings are so good they alone have been known to draw in customers. The wine list is a serious piece of work, with fine American, French and Italian wines from which to choose. *3139 Piedmont Rd., Buckhead, 404/237–2663. Reservations essential. No lunch weekends. AE, D, DC, MC, V. $$$$*

`6` a-3

BUGABOO CREEK LODGE & BAR

The rustic, lodge-centered lifestyle of the Canadian Rockies provides the theme for this steak house, which also offers grilled shrimp, salmon, and chicken. Steak is the meal deal, however, and it is offered at very fair prices, too. For lunch, there are a variety of burgers and assorted sandwiches. The wine list is ho-hum, so pick one of the Canadian brews instead. *3505 Satellite Blvd., Duluth, 770/476–1500. Reservations not accepted. AE, D, DC, MC, V.*

`13` a-4

THE CABIN

When you walk into this rustic structure, complete with trophies and antler chandeliers, you will probably feel as though you're entering a very posh, private hunt club. That, of course, is the whole idea, and this is a friendly, casual setting in which to enjoy serious food that includes beef, buffalo steak, wild game dishes, and crab cakes—as well as outrageously good key lime and pecan pies. *2678 Buford Hwy., Northeast, 404/315–7676. Reservations essential. AE, D, DC, MC, V. $$–$$$*

`4` f-3

CHEROKEE CATTLE CO.

Beyond steaks that run the gamut from an applewood-smoked, bacon-wrapped fillet to a 21-ounce porterhouse (many anointed with the house bourbon peppercorn sauce), this roadhouse-style restaurant does such regional classics as chicken-fried steak and house-made chili, straight from the heart of Texas. *2710 Canton Hwy., Marietta, 770/427–*

0490. No lunch weekends. AE, D, DC, MC, V. $$

`12` e-3

CHOPS & THE LOBSTER BAR

The sleek, contemporary clublike interior of the main dining room makes Chops an attractive spot for businessmen (as opposed to businesspeople), which seems to be its principal claim to fame. Steaks and chops are cut with the male appetite in mind, and salads and sandwiches are big, too. The downstairs Lobster Bar, where shellfish and fin critters dominate the menu, is the more appropriate setting for a romantic meal. Raw Blue Points are a grand beginning in either venue, while rum raisin bread pudding with bourbon vanilla sauce is the ideal conclusion. This wine list has a lot to offer, with many good choices by the glass. *70 W. Paces Ferry Rd., Buckhead, 404/262–2675. Reservations essential. No lunch weekends, no lunch at Lobster Bar. AE, D, DC, MC, V. $$$$*

`5` e-1

KILLER CREEK CHOP HOUSE

The building, crafted with Frank Lloyd Wright designs in mind, is a study in natural materials, chiefly stone and wood. Likewise, the steaks, rack of lamb, and Jack Daniels–marinated London broil are prepared naturally, too, grilled over hickory-wood fires. The menu also includes grilled fresh fish and, occasionally, wild boar, venison, and other game, and you can begin a meal with a selection from the raw bar or a pot of mussels. The wine list is extensive and focuses on California wines with a generous number by the glass. Jazz plays every night except Sunday. *1700 Mansell Rd., Alpharetta, 770/649–0064. Reservations not accepted. No lunch. AE, D, DC, MC, V. $$*

`5` b-6

KOBE STEAKS

This Japanese steak house does superior tender beef, chicken, fish, and seafood right before your eyes—with no small amount of flourish, and with extraordinary results. There's a children's menu, so bring the little diners. *The Prado shopping center, 5600 Roswell Rd., Sandy Springs, 404/256–0810. No lunch. AE, D, DC, MC, V. $–$$*

12 *d-7*

LONGHORN STEAKS

It's almost impossible not to come upon one of these Atlanta-based steak houses, since there are 30 of them in the metro area. Families love them for steaks, ribs, chicken, really good salmon and shrimp, and burgers that are legendary. *2151 Peachtree Rd., near Collier Rd., Buckhead, 404/351–6086. Reservations not accepted. AE, D, DC, MC, V. $$*

13 *e-6*

2892 N. Druid Hills Rd., Northeast, 404/636–3817.

7 *b-1*

1355 East-West Connector, Austell, 770/941–4816.

4 *h-6*

Akers Mill Square shopping center, 2973 Cobb Pkwy., Northwest, 770/859–0341.

9 *g-1*

7882 Tara Blvd., near GA 138, Jonesboro, 770/477–5365.

12 *d-6*

MACARTHUR'S CHOP & CRAB HOUSE

If you are looking for a quiet ambience, you may choose to dine on the enclosed front porch of this handsome glass-and-wood building rather than in the noisy dining room. Wherever you choose to dine, you'll enjoy a good deal on seared and slow-roasted prime rib, and you may well want to try the crab meat–stuffed mushrooms, an old favorite worth revisiting here. *2171 Peachtree St., Buckhead, 404/352–3400. No lunch. AE, D, DC, MC, V. $$$*

5 *d-5*

MCKENDRICK'S

This very masculine, very clubby dining room does more than steak. Game, fish dishes (especially the grilled selections), buffalo steaks, and veal chops fare well here, too. The extensive wine list is well selected and varied. *4505 Ashford-Dunwoody Rd., Park Place shopping center, across from Perimeter Mall, Dunwoody, 440/512–8888. Closed Sun. No lunch. AE, D, DC, MC, V. $$$*

15 *e-5*

MORTON'S OF CHICAGO

Atlanta is blessed with two of these Chicago-based steak houses, where you pick your steak from a rolling trolley.

Broccoli with hollandaise and good baked potatoes are ideal companions to these steaks; grilled veal and lamb chops are also available, as are fish and chicken. The American-focused wine list numbers nearly 300 selections. *303 Peachtree St., in Sun Trust Plaza Bldg., 404/577–4366. Reservations essential. No lunch. AE, D, MC, V. $$$$*

12 *g-2*

3379 Peachtree Rd., in the Peachtree Lenox Bldg., Buckhead, 404/816–6535.

5 *b-7*

OUTBACK STEAKHOUSE

This Florida-based operation with the Aussie-theme menu has numerous outlets in Atlanta, all worthwhile for their steaks and other grilled entrées. Besides steaks, there's excellent prime rib, grilled shrimp (order a double appetizer hit for an entrée), and chicken. The wine list is fair enough, with several Australian selections, and there are Australian beers, too, such as Foster's. Outback is popular, so expect to wait in line unless you arrive very early. *3850 Roswell Rd., Buckhead, 404/266–8000. Reservations not accepted. No lunch except Buckhead. AE, D, DC, MC, V. $$*

4 *f-1*

810 Ernest W. Barrett Pkwy., Kennesaw, 770/795–0400.

5 *f-4*

4015 Holcomb Bridge Rd., Norcross, 770/448–6447.

8 *e-1*

1525 E. Park Pl. Blvd., Stone Mountain, 770/498–5400.

13 *e-6*

2145 LaVista Rd., Toco Hills, 404/636–5110.

12 *g-2*

PALM

A branch of the famous New York operation, this classy steak house does justice to its name. It also does good crab cakes, grilled fresh fish, veal chops, steak, and soups, as well as pasta and other Italian dishes. The wine list presents lots of French, Italian, and American wines, with limited by-the-glass selections. *3391 Peachtree Rd., in the Swissôtel, Buckhead, 404/814–1955. AE, D, MC, V. $$$$*

`12` *h-2*

PRIME

Sleek, contemporary, romantic yet suitable for a business meeting, Prime is more than a steak house (a very good one at that), it's also an excellent sushi restaurant. As if these two options weren't enough, Prime also does a magnificent job with veal chops and tuna steak and serves salmon on a bed of grits. The wide-ranging wine list offers a number of fine choices by the glass. *3393 Peachtree Rd., upper level of Lenox Square mall, 404/812–0555. Reservations essential. AE, D, DC, MC, V. $$$$*

`12` *h-3*

RUTH'S CHRIS STEAK HOUSE

Founded in New Orleans, this chain of posh steakhouses has three Atlanta locations. Only hand-cut corn-fed beef is served, and steaks are brought to the table on hot plates so diners may "finish" the steak as desired by cutting pieces and searing them on the plate. Fish, lobster, and lots of good side dishes round out the menu. Excellent wine lists are at all locations. *Atlanta Plaza, 950 E. Paces Ferry Rd., 404/365–0660. No lunch at Sandy Springs, no lunch weekends at Atlanta Plaza. Reservations essential. AE, D, DC, MC, V. $$$*

`5` *b-5*

5788 Roswell Rd., Sandy Springs, 404/255–0035.

`15` *d-5*

Embassy Suites Hotel, 267 Marietta St., at Centennial Park, Downtown, 404/223–6500.

`5` *c-2*

STONEY RIVER

With their huge bars and lively dining rooms, these steak houses fill quickly with hungry diners who enjoy good steaks that could easily feed two. (To avoid a wait, arrive early or grab a seat at the bar and eat there.) In addition to steaks, there are good shrimp, fish, and chicken dishes. The wine list is generous. *10542 Alpharetta Hwy., Roswell, 678/461–7900. Reservations not accepted. No lunch Mon.–Sat. AE, D, DC, MC, V. $$$*

`5` *f-1*

5800 State Bridge Rd., Duluth, 770/476–0102.

TEA

`12` *h-2*

RITZ-CARLTON, BUCKHEAD

High tea is celebrated in the most formal manner, in front of a warm fire in wintertime and including, as it should, a good selection of small sandwiches and pastries as well as, of course, the highest-quality leaves perfectly steeped in warmed pots. There's even an elegant version of peanut butter and jelly for the kids. *3434 Peachtree Rd., Buckhead, 404/237–2700. Reservations essential. AE, D, DC, MC, V. $–$$*

TEX-MEX

`12` *d-7*

CASA GRANDE

This Dallas-based operation serves good fajitas, salsa, and chips, along with the freshest-possible tortillas, made by a gas-fired tortilla press that sits in sight of the dining room. The best bets are the specials, which often include the very good shrimp with papaya pico de gallo. Premium tequilas are a specialty. *1860 Peachtree Rd., near Collier Rd., Buckhead, 404/350–6767. AE, D, DC, MC, V. $$*

`12` *a-8*

NUEVO LAREDO CANTINA

The spirit of the Cadillac Bar in the border town of Nuevo Laredo, Mexico, comes to Atlanta in the form of this casual, family-comfy spot. The food is good, not nearly as homogenized as it is at most other Mexican restaurants, and features freshly made guacamole, refried beans, steak, seafood, and a good flan. Mexican beers and Spanish wines are available, as are terrific margaritas and good sangría. *1495 Chattahoochee Ave., off Howell Mill Rd., 404/352–9009. Closed Sun. AE, D, DC, MC, V. $*

`12` *f-3*

RIO BRAVO CANTINA

Founded in Atlanta—the original location is the Buckhead unit—this chain of 10 metro-area restaurants makes a commitment to fresh food: The kitchen prepares fresh salsa once an hour and makes the tortillas on the premises. The standards of this fare, from chile relleno (a big poblano pepper stuffed with cheese and topped with ranchero sauce) to the fajitas, taste great, and the margaritas are huge. *3172 Roswell Rd., Buck-*

head, 404/262–7431. *Reservations not accepted. AE, D, DC, MC, V. $*

5 a-6
5566 New Northside Dr. at I–285, exit 22, 770/952–3241.

4 f-1
Main Street shopping center, 440 Ernest Barrett Pkwy., Kennesaw, 770/429–0602.

5 h-4
2250 Pleasant Hill Rd., in front of Gwinnett Place, Duluth, 770/623–1096.

5 c-2
Holcomb Woods shopping center, 1570 Holcomb Bridge Rd., Roswell, 770/642–0838.

8 e-1
Perimeter Village shopping center, 4300 U.S. 78, Stone Mountain, 770/736–2900.

5 d-5
4749 Ashford-Dunwoody Rd., Dunwoody, 770/395–6603.

5 e-1
5710 State Bridge Rd., next to Medlock Crossing shopping center, 678/475–0304.

THAI

12 f3
ANNIE'S THAI CASTLE
Lunch at this long-popular restaurant, among the city's best choices for Thai food, is briskly served, even a bit rushed, in deference to limited lunch hours. You may want to come here for a leisurely dinner instead, when you have time to enjoy more of a wide-ranging menu that includes red curry duck, shrimp or chicken Massaman, whole fish dishes, and the ever-popular pad thai. The excellent specials are available only at dinner on weekends. *3195 Roswell Rd., Buckhead, 404/264–9546. Reservations accepted at dinner. No lunch weekends. AE, MC, V. $–$$*

13 a-6
BAI TONG
This pretty restaurant derives much of its charm from the artwork that adorns its walls and the nicely diffused lighting. The fairly standard takes on Thai cuisine are appealing, too. *Larb* (an appetizer of seasoned ground sirloin) is especially tasty here, while the spicy basil lamb will take your taste buds off the planet (ask the kitchen to tone it down if you can't

handle really hot fare). The curries, meanwhile, classically done with coconut milk, are spicy but not searingly so. *2329C Cheshire Bridge Rd., Northeast, 404/728–9040. No lunch weekends. AE, D, DC, MC, V. $*

15 g-1
KING AND I
One of the city's first Thai restaurants, King and I has made pad thai and other noodle dishes as popular as burgers (well, almost). Its other Thai dishes, including the spicy basil chicken and chicken and pork satays, are popular, too, particularly with the lunch crowd. The Brookhaven location is open until early morning. *Ansley Square, 1510F Piedmont Ave., behind Ansley Mall, Ansley Park, 404/892–7743. AE, MC, V. $–$$*

12 a-2
NORTHLAKE THAI CUISINE
A singularly pretty restaurant—with Thai objets d'art on the walls, romantic lighting, and a subdued atmosphere that encourages conversation—this newer restaurant has much to offer that's out of the ordinary. Vegetable cream cheese crisps are a light change-of-pace approach to the egg roll, while giant sea scallops are fried in a light rice batter and served in a garlic–black peppercorn sauce. The wine list isn't much, but the food is so wonderful you won't mind. Free delivery is available up to a radius of 3 mi with a minimum $30 order. *3939 LaVista Rd., Tucker, 770/938–2223. No lunch weekends. AE, D, DC, MC, V. $$*

4 f-8
SUKOTHAI
Pretty Sukothai takes the edge off its location in a pedestrian shopping center space with faux-aged walls and subdued lighting. The standards of Thai cooking are well prepared here, especially the soups, salads, and the coconut milk-based curries. *Windy Hill West shopping center, 1995 Windy Hill Rd., Marietta, 770/434–9276. Closed Sun. No lunch Sat. AE, D, DC, MC, V. $$*

15 e-2
TAMARIND
A contemporary space with a large deck for fine-weather dining, Tamarind has become the Midtown mecca for Thai fare. The menu uses a scale of chiles to guide the unsuspecting palate through the hotness levels, with three chiles

being the hottest most of us can take (the scale does go to four, however!). For those whose hotness tolerance falls on the lower end of the scale, the jumbo prawns in green curry and the panang curries are both mildly spiced and absolutely delicious. Steamed rice-paper basil rolls wrap green veggies, and steamed dumplings with minced pork make a light opener. *80 14th St., Midtown, 404/873–4888. No lunch weekends. AE, D, DC, MC, V. $$$*

13 *c-6*

THAI CHILLI

One of the city's best Thai restaurants is decoratively embellished with fine Thai art. The menu is highly regarded for its authenticity and deals with fairly standard fare, while the chef's specials often include such unusual selections as spicy whole catfish and vegetarian dishes, many based on tofu. *Briarvista shopping center, 2169 Briarcliff Rd., Northeast, 404/315–6750. No lunch weekends. AE, D, DC, MC, V. $*

7 *f-7*

ZAB-E-LEE

This long-established restaurant raises standard Thai dishes to new levels of excellence. Many are vegetarian: *Mee krob* (crispy fried noodles) here is done with tofu, which also appears in one of the coconut milk–based yellow curry dishes. Spicy dishes are clearly marked, and hotness levels can be adjusted up or down. Lunch is a spread of standard Chinese dishes and Thai fare, so dinner is the best time to enjoy the kitchen's full range. Beer and wine are served. *4837 Old National Hwy., College Park, 404/768–2705. Reservations not accepted. Closed Sun. No lunch Sat. AE, DC, MC, V. $*

VEGETARIAN

12 *d-7*

CAFE SUNFLOWER

Atlanta isn't much on vegetarian restaurants, but these two spots have been a hit since the day they opened. Dishes come from around the world: Burritos are filled with beans, moo shu vegetables dip into Chinese culinary tradition, and tofu peanut butter pie is outrageously good. The Brookwood Square location serves beer and wine; Roswell Road does not, and the staff sometimes lecture guests who inquire about it on the evils of alcohol. Both offer good-quality juices, teas, and other nonalcoholic drinks. *Brookwood Square shopping center, 2140 Peachtree Rd., Brookwood, 404/352–8859. Brookwood closed Sun. AE, D, DC, MC, V. $*

5 *b-4*

Hammond Springs shopping center, 5975 Roswell Rd., at Hammond Dr., Sandy Springs, 404/256–1675.

14 *f-1*

RAINBOW GROCERY

Rainbow Grocery is one of Atlanta's longest-established health food stores. At the rear, this casual spot dishes up meatless sandwiches and specials that include excellent soups, veggie chili and lasagna, tofu dishes, walnut loaf, and luscious desserts. No alcohol is served, and smoothies are the drinks of choice. The dinner hour ends at 8 PM. *2118 N. Decatur Rd., Northeast, 404/636–5553. Closed Sun. (except Grocery). No credit cards (MC, V at Grocery). $*

VIETNAMESE

5 *e-6*

BIEN THUY

The clientele consists of local Vietnamese Atlantans and others who savor such authentic traditional dishes as *hu tieu*, a soup of glass noodles with seafood; *banh xeo*, stuffed pancakes; and *cha gio*, Vietnamese spring rolls. This is a good spot for vegetarians. *Northwoods Plaza, 5095F Buford Hwy., Doraville, 770/454–9046. AE, D, MC, V. $*

13 *c-5*

VIETNAMESE CUISINE & THAI PEPPER RESTAURANT

The long list of Vietnamese dishes at this friendly restaurant includes many beef and seafood preparations, often accompanied by noodles and rice. But much of the menu is devoted to Thai fare, from classic light Thai curries to pad thai and basil-flavored dishes that often are spicy hot. There are lots of vegetarian dishes, embellishing non-meat ingredients with the flavors of Thai cuisine; even tofu gets the panang curry treatment. *Northeast Plaza shopping center, 3375 Buford Hwy., Northeast 404/321–1840. AE, D, DC, MC, V. $*

chapter 2

SHOPPING

Like to shop? Got a car? Atlanta's an eastern Los Angeles, with sprawling suburbs that have swallowed up surrounding towns. Within the huge metropolitan area you can find old-fashioned towns that are good places to track down antiques (Marietta, Roswell, Crabapple), old Atlanta shopping neighborhoods with top-of-the-line department stores and one-of-a-kind boutiques (Five Points, Brookwood, Buckhead), and more than a dozen major shopping malls. All these shopping venues are within driving distance (though that means something different to car-culture Atlantans than it does to, say, a New Yorker), and chances are you'll find whatever it is you need in Atlanta along with some genuine southern hospitality, too.

shopping areas

DEPARTMENT STORES

5 *e-1*

DILLARD'S

A long-time favorite of shoppers at North Point Mall, Dillard's has the best Carole Little selection in town, often at great sale prices; a fabulous selection of plus-size lingerie; and an excellent men's clothing department. Don't look for high-end jewelry here, but the costume selection is very good. *North Point Mall, 7000 North Point Cir., Alpharetta, 770/410–9020.*

5 *f-7*

JCPENNY COMPANY

Despite its recent attempts to lure a more upscale market, Penny's remains one of Atlanta's mainstays for pretty good clothing at pretty good prices. The stores are also some of the best places in town for good buys on window treatments and design services here, too. *Northlake Mall, 4840 Briarcliff Rd., Northlake, 770/934–8111.*

6 *a-4*

Gwinnett Place Mall, 2100 Pleasant Hill Rd., Duluth, 770/476–3220.

5 *c-5*

Perimeter Mall, 4400 Ashford-Dunwoody Rd., Dunwoody, 770/394–1220. MARTA: Dunwoody.

5 *e-1*

North Point Mall, 11350 Haynes Bridge Rd., Alpharetta, 770/475–9850.

8 *a-8*

Southlake Mall, 1400 Southlake Mall, Morrow, 770/961–6211.

4 *e-3*

Town Center Mall, 400 Ernest W. Barrett Pkwy., Kennesaw, 770/514–7101.

5 *e-1*

SEARS

Atlantans love their Sears stores: the automobile department, appliances and tools, electronics, and a lot other services and goods, all provided by a staff that tends to be knowledgeable and genuinely helpful. *North Point Mall, 6000 North Point Cir., Alpharetta, 770/667–6700.*

4 *h-7*

Cumberland Mall, 1500 Cumberland Mall, Smyrna, 770/433–7400.

6 *a-4*

Gwinnett Place Mall, 2100 Pleasant Hill Rd., Duluth, 770/476–6600.

5 *f-7*

Northlake Mall, 2201 Henderson Mill Rd., Northlake, 770/493–3210.

8 *a-8*

Southlake Mall, 1300 Southlake Mall, Morrow, 770/961–7110.

4 *e-3*

Town Center Mall, 400 Ernest W Barrett Pkwy., Morrow, 770/429–4155.

12 *h-2*

LORD & TAYLOR

This fashionable establishment originates in New York, so there's plenty of high-quality and fashionable merchandise—and always something on sale. (The best sales are on women's clothing.) Lord & Taylor is especially good for women's career clothing and cocktail party clothes, and these selections are matched by the men's department for career clothing and good suits. Don't look for furniture or appliances here, but there is an excellent selection of linens and small decorative accessories, and they go on sale in January and August.

Phipps Plaza, 3500 Peachtree Rd., Buck-head, 404/266–0600. MARTA: Lenox.

5 e-1
Northpoint Mall, 4000 North Point Cir., Alpharetta, 770/667–0665.

12 h-2
MACY'S
The venerable chain acquired Atlanta's own Davison-Paxon Company in the 1980s, bringing New York sophistication and merchandise to Atlantans. The flagship store at Lenox Square offers excellence in bed and bath, china and crystal, and kitchenware. Also look for the extensive accessory department and a sturdy if somewhat ordinary selection of fine jewelry. The store has good one-day sales and sales after each major—and, if often seems, minor—holiday. The downtown store sports elegant 1920s architecture. Lenox Square, 3393 Peachtree Rd., Buckhead, 404/231–8985. MARTA: Lenox.

15 e-5
180 Peachtree St., Downtown, 404/221–7221. MARTA: Peachtree Center.

4 h-7
Cumberland Mall, 1200 Cumberland Mall, Smyrna, 770/433–3975.

6 a-4
Gwinnett Place Mall, 2100 Pleasant Hill Rd., Duluth, 770/476–6985.

5 c-5
Perimeter Mall, 4400 Ashford-Dunwoody Rd., Dunwoody, 770/399–4985. MARTA: Dunwoody.

8 a-8
Southlake Mall, 1200 Southlake Mall, Morrow, 770/961–3995.

12 h-2
NEIMAN MARCUS
The special aura created by the Dallas-based chain is strong as ever in the Atlanta store, which offers such Neiman trademarks as the consistently high quality of its merchandise, its personal service, and the fabulous "Last Call" storewide sales held twice each year. Lenox Square, 3393 Peachtree Rd., Buckhead, 404/266–8200. MARTA: Lenox.

12 h-2
PARISIAN
It's not from Paris but from Birmingham, Alabama. However, don't let that dissuade you from coming here to find exactly the right outfit for your next occasion. Parisian personnel set the standard for courteous service: they know when to leave you alone, and they know the merchandise from other departments well enough to go get it in your size and favorite color. There are no cheaply made clothes here, and accordingly, the merchandise tends to sell out in a flash. Phipps Plaza, 3500 Peachtree Rd., Buckhead, 404/814–3200. MARTA: Lenox.

2 b-4
North Point Mall, 4500 North Point Cir., Alpharetta, 770/754–3200.

12 h-2
RICH'S
Once owned by a local guy named Rich, this popular emporium is now owned by Federated and wins the award as the behemoth of department stores and allied services in Atlanta. Listing everything takes up nearly two pages of the telephone business directory. You can get alterations, buy eye glasses, have your hair done, and plan a round-the-world tour. Rich's Design Services will redo your home décor, and the store can also service your heating, air and plumbing systems and professionally clean your home, too. There's a great deal of every kind of clothing imaginable (selections of standard lingerie, plus-sizes, and career clothes are especially strong), and if you can't find what you want at one location, it can be shipped to you from another. The glittering flagship store at Lenox Square attracts even teens away from other stores. Lenox Square, 3393 Peachtree Rd., Buckhead, 404/231–2611. MARTA: Lenox.

5 c-5
Perimeter Mall, 4400 Ashford-Dunwoody Rd., Dunwoody, 770/396–2611. MARTA: Dunwoody.

5 e-1
North Point Mall, 5000 North Point Cir., Alpharetta, 770/410–2600.

4 h-7
Cumberland Mall, 1300 Cumberland Mall, Smyrna, 770/434–2611.

5 f-8
North DeKalb Mall, 2144 Lawrenceville Hwy., Decatur, 404/329–2600.

7 c-8
Shannon Mall, 200 Shannon Mall, Union City, 770/969–2600.

MALLS & SHOPPING CENTERS

More than a dozen major malls and hundreds of minimalls dot the 10-county Atlanta landscape and form a large part of Atlanta's central nervous system, each reflecting the character of its surrounding neighborhood.

4 h-7
CUMBERLAND MALL
Located between Atlanta and Marietta, Cumberland reflects the wide demographic mix of the surrounding area with stores that range from Sears to high-end designer boutiques. *I–285 and I–75 at Cobb Pkwy., Smyrna, 770/435–2206.*

4 h-7
GALLERIA SPECIALTY MALL
This mall across from Cumberland is attached to hotel, conference, and convention facilities, so the boutique-type shops cater to visitor and tourist traffic with resort and party wear and expensive souvenirs. There are some excellent restaurants, along with a good cineplex and plenty of parking. *I–285 and I–75 at Cobb Pkwy., Smyrna, 770/955–9100.*

7 e-4
GREENBRIAR MALL
Greenbriar's the "comeback kid" of area malls, due in large part to the aura of Magic Johnson, who chose this site for one of his theater complexes. A recent renovation has brought the visual delights in line with those of other malls, and many of the stores have refurbished their interiors for a better look as well. *I–285 and the Arthur Langford Pkwy. (Hwy. 166), 5 mi west of I–85/I–75 S, Lakewood, 404/344–6611.*

6 a-4
GWINNETT PLACE MALL
One has the impression that this mall *is* Gwinnett County, though we know it's not. But Gwinnett Place and environs take up an impressive amount of acreage (more than any other mall in Atlanta), and it seems as though every small and big chain operates a store here to tap into one of the most rapidly growing areas in the country. The merchandise on hand reflects a taste for the latest trends in attire and an interest in home-oriented projects. *I–85 N at 2100 Pleasant Hill Rd., Duluth, 770/476–5160.*

12 h-2
LENOX SQUARE
The granddaddy of Atlanta malls took root in the late 1950s on a few acres of land. It's been expanded many times since then but continues to thrive on the individuality of its shops (the Waterford-Wedgwood Store, Neiman Marcus, Bally, Cartier, FAO Schwarz, and the Metropolitan Museum of Art Store are here) and the upper incomes of its shoppers. Lenox Square and the even more upscale Phipps Plaza across the street compose one of the largest shopping areas in the city, but parking is a problem only during holidays; Lenox is also on the northern MARTA route, making it one of Atlanta's few shopping centers that are accessible by public transportation. *3393 Peachtree Rd., Buckhead, 404/233–6767. MARTA: Lenox.*

5 e-1
NORTH POINT MALL
With 180 stores and still growing, North Point follows the precedent set by Gwinnett Place. (It's no coincidence that North Point serves an area that is growing at a pace second only to that of the Gwinnett corridor.) North Point reflects the tastes of its higher-income shoppers with one-of-a-kind stores while catering to young visitors with a popular handcrafted carousel. *1000 North Point Cir., exits 8 and 9 from Georgia 400, Alpharetta, 770/740–9273.*

5 c-5
PERIMETER MALL
Surrounded by cow pastures when it was built in the 1960s, Perimeter is now at the center of miles of stores, hospitals, and office and apartment complexes. The mall is not overwhelmingly large, so it won't take all day to find just the boutique or department store you're looking for. The Rich's here has a furniture and interior design center that's very popular with the mid- to upper-income set. *4400 Ashford-Dunwoody Road, off I–285 between Sandy Springs and Chamblee, Dunwoody, 770/394–4270. MARTA: Dunwoody.*

12 h-2
PHIPPS PLAZA
This is one of the prettiest malls in America. Polished dark wood and rosy marbles provide a suitable setting for Saks Fifth Avenue, Lord & Taylor, Tiffany's, and other high-end shops

here, along with a wealth of boutiques and galleries. There is a modest food court on the upper level, and the Pleasant Peasant restaurant is a popular watering hole for lunch. *3500 Peachtree Rd., across from Lenox Square, 404/262–0992. MARTA: Lenox.*

4 *e-3*

TOWN CENTER AT COBB

They don't call it Town Center for nothing: It's the middle of millions of acres of subdivisions that cover much of Marietta and Cobb County, every major chain has a location here, and restaurants, hotels, car dealerships, and services are plentiful, too. *400 Ernest Barrett Pkwy., off I–75 north of Marietta, 770/424–0915.*

15 *e-6*

UNDERGROUND ATLANTA

Underground's claim to fame is its architecture and location. Most of the buildings were constructed during or just after Reconstruction, the streets are cobblestone, and the whole area is truly underground (after the area's Victorian heyday, viaducts and streets were built over it). Today the area throngs with tourists and residents alike who come in search of souvenirs and memorable clothing. Several great bars enliven the atmosphere. History buffs will enjoy coming upon the original railroad marker for Terminus, as Atlanta was originally known, and a small museum. *50 Upper Alabama St., Downtown, 404/523–2311. MARTA: Five Points.*

SHOPPING NEIGHBORHOODS

12 *d-7*

BROOKWOOD

Just south of Buckhead on Peachtree Road, a small complex has grown up in response to Piedmont Hospital across the street and one of the city's loveliest neighborhoods behind it. Brookwood occupies a few blocks of early 20th-century buildings that now house galleries, antiques stores, good restaurants, and cafés. Parking is available behind the complex. *18th and 19th block of Peachtree Rd. across from Piedmont Hospital.*

12 *f-3*

BUCKHEAD

Legend has it this neighborhood is so called because hunters used to string up deer on one of the huge old oaks located at West Paces Ferry and Peachtree Roads. The tree died only a few years ago, and in its place local merchants commissioned a bronze statue of an Indian storyteller with a huge buck's head. Surrounding him sit the forest creatures listening to mythic tales, and beyond them are the Buckhead bar scene, home furnishing and kitchen and bath design stores, and decorative arts and clothing boutiques. For the unique, the expensive, the *avant*, the traditional and trendy, this is the neighborhood to be in, especially if you have your credit cards with you. *Intersection of Roswell Rd. and Peachtree Rd.*

12 *h-7*

CHESHIRE BRIDGE ROAD

An eccentric collection of shops, catering to everyone from aging hippies to upwardly mobile young professionals, is interspersed with gay and lesbian clubs, bars with girlie revues, and some excellent restaurants. *Between Buford Hwy. 23 and Piedmont Rd., Ansley Park.*

15 *d-5*

CNN CENTER

Ted Turner spared no modesty in furnishing the twinkling souvenir shops filled with Braves, Atlanta, and CNN memorabilia. The architecture is a show in itself, and you can take part in the daily *Talk Back Live* show on CNN. *One CNN Center, between International Blvd. and Techwood Dr., Downtown, 404/827–1700. MARTA: Omni/Dome/GWCC.*

2 *g-8*

CRABAPPLE

Once a one-horse whistle stop northwest of Roswell on the Birmingham Highway, this intersection of country roads lies just outside the polished provinces of Atlanta suburbs. A cluster of pre– and post–Civil War buildings houses a fine selection of antiques, with Victoriana holding sway. *Hwy. 372 and Broadwell Rd., 25 mi from the city center in north Fulton County.*

12 *f-3*

EAST ANDREWS DRIVE

This is the place to come if you are in search of the high end of everything and the latest trends, especially in gifts, clothing, and accessories. *Between West Paces Ferry Rd. and Roswell Rd., Buckhead.*

14 a-4
LITTLE FIVE POINTS

If you remember the 1960s with nostalgia and wish you could re-live the cool parts of it, this is a little bit of heaven. Head shops, crystals, beads and bongs, vintage clothing, pottery, inexpensive but well-designed furniture, hippie clothes, candles, incense—it's all here. *Intersection of Euclid and Moreland Aves. and McLendon and Seminole Sts., just east of Downtown.*

4 f-4
MARIETTA SQUARE

This is an old-fashioned kind of place, which is why about 200 antiques dealers fill the Victorian houses surrounding the square with Victorian and 20th-century china, quilts, and other pieces. If you want to stay the night, check into one of the charming B&Bs on the streets that fan out from the square, and be sure to take in a production at Theatre on the Square, one of the area's best. *Marietta, west of I-75 north 35 mins from Downtown, 770/528–4653.*

12 h-4
MIAMI CIRCLE

This former warehouse district in Buckhead, now one of the busiest and most prosperous antiques centers in the Southeast, is where a lot of serious antiques business gets done in Atlanta. Eighty shops carry all you need to furnish a house, everything from Americana to Zumpano tiles. This a big resource for designers located at the Atlanta Decorative Arts Center a few blocks away, so if you see something you want, snap it up. *Off Piedmont Rd., one block north of Sidney Marcus Blvd., Buckhead. MARTA: Lindbergh.*

5 g-5
NORCROSS

The charming train station and many small antiques and crafts shops lining the blocks across from it will satisfy your yearnings for simpler days gone by. *Buford Hwy. 23 and Holcomb Bridge Rd., 20 mins from Downtown, 770/448–2122.*

5 e-1
ROSWELL

Founded in 1836, Roswell survived the Civil War intact because Sherman housed his troops in the town's antebellum mansions and because the railroad lines were farther south. Dozens of these houses (some offer tours) line the streets of old Roswell, and antiques shops now line the main square. Canton Street, about a mile north off Highway 120, is also lined with shops. *Roswell Rd. and Hwy. 120.*

8 f-1
STONE MOUNTAIN VILLAGE

Stone Mountain, once a source for quarried granite, now has more value as a tourist attraction. In addition to the carved diorama and other amusements of Stone Mountain Park are several blocks of shops along Main Street selling antiques, quilts, Victoriana, and other wares. *Hwy. 78 East to Silver Hill Road exit, 30 mins from Downtown.*

13 f-6
TOCO HILLS

In one of Atlanta's major Jewish neighborhoods, you'll find the Bagel Palace, which serves up the best in Atlanta, and Bernie the Baker's, renowned for his high-holiday and everyday offerings; even the local outlet of the Kroger grocery store chain has a kosher section. There's also a college-town atmosphere, provided by nearby Emory University. Students and faculty hang out at area bookshops, coffeehouses, health food stores, and yoga centers. *North Druid Hills and LaVista Rds., 15 mins from Downtown.*

15 h-3 and 14 a-2
VIRGINIA-HIGHLAND

Developed in the 1920s and '30s as a middle-class suburb of large cottages and bungalows, Virginia-Highland still has at its core a village-like collection of groceries, hardware stores, and other practical conveniences. Here, too, are shops selling upscale but funky collectibles. *Highland Ave. between Johnson and Ponce de Leon Rds., 5 mins from Downtown.*

specialist shops

ANTIQUES

antiques centers & flea markets

12 h-7
A FLEA ANTIQUE II
In this collection of little shops you'll find everything from retro metro to 9th-century Korean celadon. *1853 Cheshire Bridge Rd., Midtown, 404/872–4342.*

12 e-6
ATLANTA DECORATIVE ARTS CENTER (ADAC)
It's worthwhile to find an interior designer who can take you through this to-the-trade-only complex. Genuinely fine antiques abound here, often mixed with the best in new design trends. ADAC contains especially good dealers in Oriental rugs, paintings, and furniture. Two or three times a year, there are clearance sales where you can get fabulous stuff for next to nothing. *351 Peachtree Hills Ave., Buckhead, 404/231–1720.*

12 d-7
BENNETT STREET
More than a decade ago, this tired warehouse district near Piedmont Hospital caught the eyes of some artists looking for inexpensive studio space, and today it bustles with galleries and antiques shops (especially those specializing in antiques from England). The street is several blocks long, the variety amazing, and the quantity huge. Interiors Market and the Stalls both have booths stocked by some of Atlanta's savviest designers, where you can acquire wonderful things for your house. *2100 block of Peachtree Rd., Brookwood.*

5 d-6
BROAD STREET ANTIQUES MALL
It seems as though all of the 20th century's, and some of the last's, flotsam and jetsam turn up regularly here. Eugenia's is an especially good place for antique hardware, sconces, and chandeliers. Prices range between silly and way too much. *3550 Broad St., Chamblee, 770/458–6316. MARTA: Chamblee.*

2 g-8
CRABAPPLE
See Shopping Neighborhoods, *above.*

8 c-1
KUDZU ANTIQUES MARKET
Located a couple of blocks west of the famous DeKalb Farmers' Market, Kudzu's collection of dealers finds everything from vintage clothing to *Star Wars* collectibles. It's jumbled, messy, and fun, and when a really fine piece turns up among the clutter, it's gone almost immediately (as the case with a fine Cormandel screen for $250 found among a selection of not-very-good quilts). If you'd like a particular piece, put your name on the list of dealers who like to stock it. Around here, it's the only way to compete. Look beyond the clutter, too. *2874 E. Ponce de Leon Ave., Decatur, 404/373–6498.*

5 b-5
LAKEWOOD ANTIQUES GALLERY
If it's hard for you to get to the Lakewood Antiques Market on the second weekend of each month (*see below*), you can shop here in climate-controlled comfort. The bargain hunting isn't quite up to par with that at the market, but the premises are clean, neat, and well organized and house a delectable assortment of American and European furniture and bric-a-brac. *6336 Roswell Rd., Sandy Springs, 404/459–8994.*

7 h-4
LAKEWOOD ANTIQUES MARKET
The crumbling state fairgrounds, with Art Deco buildings and an attached amphitheater, now house antiques instead of cows and rock stars instead of bake-offs. The second weekend of each month, regardless of the weather, dealers from all over the East and Midwest assemble here with their wares. There's a certain cache to having "found it at Lakewood," which translates to "bargain" even if it wasn't! The best buys are on silver, furniture (especially on Sunday afternoons—they don't want to take it home), china, crystal, exotica, garden furniture and ornaments, architectural oddities, comics, fabrics—well, on just everything! *2000 Lakewood Ave., Lakewood, 404/622–4488. MARTA: Lakewood/Ft. McPherson.*

4 *f-4*

MARIETTA SQUARE
See Shopping Neighborhoods, *above.*

12 *ah-4*

MIAMI CIRCLE
See Shopping Neighborhoods, *above.*

5 *c-1*

**ROSWELL
ANTIQUES GALLERY**
Designer-tiques (meaning new decorative accessories) share space with antiques in an attractive space. The alluring stock includes some good jewelry and silver, lots of great boxes, occasionally some really good furniture, and garden accessories. They may take off a courteous 10% at the desk, but if you're really interested in haggling, ask them to call the dealer in whose stall you found the piece. *10930 Crabapple Rd., Roswell, 770/594-8484.*

7 *h-6*

SCOTT ANTIQUES MARKET
Two buildings house in one weekend (the second weekend of each month) the same amount of merchandise you would have to explore the rest of the Atlanta markets for weeks to find. You'll have to arrive before dawn on Thursday mornings, when the market opens, to find the real bargains that will later turn up on Miami Circle and in other antiques emporiums. But the higher-end antiques and decorative accessories move a little less quickly. *3650 Jonesboro Rd., Forest Park, 404/363-0909.*

12 *e-6*

2300 PEACHTREE
In 1987 Atlanta designer Jane Marsden built a complex based on architecture she'd fallen in love with in France, and her three buildings house some of the area's finest antiques dealers and interior designers. Not surprisingly, this is the place to find incredible French furniture, porcelains, chandeliers, silver and estate jewelry. *2300 Peachtree Rd., at Peachtree Battle Ave., Buckhead, 404/355-1288.*

collectibles

12 *e-6*

**LEVISON
AND CULLEN GALLERY**
Deanne Levison, one of the country's foremost experts in American decorative arts, spent many years of her career at Israel Sack in New York. Her education shows up in her discerning eye for fine American antiques, especially pottery and painted furniture. A visit here will enrich your knowledge and delight your eye. *2300 Peachtree Rd., Buckhead, 404/351-3435.*

8 *c-2*

RAY'S INDIAN ORIGINALS
If you can't find the antiquities you're looking for out West, it's because they're here at Ray's. He sells an astonishing array of Native American collectibles, memorabilia, and antiques. Really good antique Navajo rugs, genuine weaponry, baskets, and pottery seem matched only by the owner's depth of knowledge and willingness to share it. *90 Avondale Rd., Avondale Estates, 404/292-4999.*

12 *g-4*

REGEN-LEIGH
Highly respected, savvy, and well traveled, Bobbie Culbreath locates the crème de la crème of Europe and presents it here in her little shop. *3140 E. Shadownlawn Ave., Buckhead, 404/262-9303.*

furniture

12 *d-7*

BITTERSWEET
The owners love to travel in England and Scotland, where they ferret out their furniture and unique small treasures. Part of the shop is J. B.'s Corner, which specializes in sporting antiques for men—fishing poles, pond boats, golf memorabilia, prints, and oddities. *45 Bennett St., one block north of Piedmont Hospital, Brookwood, 404/351-6594.*

12 *g-5*

FURNITURE EXCHANGE
The stock is an interesting mix of 19th- and 20th-century pieces, and some of them are really very good. Prices for most items are good, too, especially on items such as the red Chinese lacquered furniture. *646 Lindbergh Way, Buckhead, 404/233-2100. MARTA: Lindbergh.*

12 *h-4*

THE GABLES
The owners and managers buy in Europe several times a year, so everything in this interesting mix of French

country and English period furniture, Chinese porcelains, and well-crafted reproduction pieces is handpicked for the shop. The bookcases are especially attractive. With a 9,000-square-ft show-room and 20 years of experience, this shop has become a primary, worldwide source for both designers and collectors. *711 Miami Cir., Buckhead, 404/231-0734. MARTA: Lindbergh.*

12 *e-6*

JACQUELINE ADAMS ANTIQUES AND INTERIORS

The most gorgeous armoires in the city, other country French furniture, and accessories will delight even the most fastidious collector. The owners scour France for their merchandise, and designers from California to Maine come to Atlanta to snap it up. *2300 Peachtree Rd., Buckhead, 404/355-8123.*

12 *h-4*

MAISON DE PROVENCE

This huge inventory of French country pieces is chosen by the owner, who lives in France most of the year, and combines quality and beauty. *764 Miami Cir., Buckhead, 404/364-0205. MARTA: Lindbergh.*

14 *a-2*

20TH CENTURY ANTIQUES

You'll find Heywood Wakefield, Charles and Ray Eames, Knoll, Eero Saarinin, Bauhaus and all the other big names in 20th-century craft and design here. *1044 N. Highland Ave., Virginia-Highland, 404/892-2065.*

quilts

12 *d-7*

GRANNY TAUGHT US HOW

You may want to visit this shop just to feel comfy. Its chock-full of antique quilts in the myriad colors and patterns of yesteryear, and table linens, curtains, dresser runners, and antimacassars fall from period trunks and cover antique tables. The quilted bears from recycled quilts make lovely gifts. *1921 Peachtree Rd., Brookwood, 404/351-2942.*

ART SUPPLIES

12 *g-5*

BINDERS

One of Atlanta's best sources for art supplies is overcrowded and a little dis-organized but has just about anything a graphic or fine artist or craftsperson might need (both these statements are especially true of the Lindbergh Plaza store). The selection of handmade paper section is extraordinary, and Binders also carries clever stationery. *Lindbergh Plaza, 2581 Piedmont Rd., Buckhead, 404/233-5423. MARTA: Lindbergh.*

5 *b-5*

206 Johnson Ferry Rd., Sandy Springs, 404/252-1203.

6 *a-4*

2320 Pleasant Hill Rd., Duluth, 770/497-9919.

5 *c-2*

DICK BLICK

What started out as a half-pet-supplies, half-art-supplies store has blossomed into one of the city's better-stocked sources for art supplies. Crafts supplies share space, too, and there's a catalog if you can't find what you need. Prices tend to be very competitive. *1117 Alpharetta St., Roswell, 770/993-0240.*

4 *f-2*

2615 George Busbee Pkwy., Kennesaw, 770/514-8456.

5 *g-7*

6330 Lawrenceville Hwy., Tucker, 770/939-5719.

12 *h-3*

ICHIYO ART CENTER, INC.

This charming store will infuse you with serenity and excitement at the same time. Shop here for Japanese art sup-plies and art made of paper, or take lessons in calligraphy and other Japa-nese arts. *432 E. Paces Ferry Rd., Buckhead, 404/233-1846.*

5 *b-7*

PEARL ARTIST AND CRAFT SUPPLY

This outlet of the national art-supply department store carries an amazing amount of merchandise and can outfit a whole studio for whatever medium you work in (and in the rare case they don't have what you need, their catalog does).

The crafts section is especially well developed, with lessons and teachers available on and off site. However, while some salespeople are attentive and knowledgeable, others are out to lunch. If one of them doesn't suit you, ask for somebody else. *Powers Ferry Square, 3756 Roswell Rd., between Buckhead and Sandy Springs, 404/233–9400.*

12 c-8

SAM FLAX

Neat, orderly, and precise, this well-designed outlet of the national chain can supply you with presentation materials and portfolios, terrific graphics design furnishings, wonderfully designed contemporary office supplies, and much more—right down to a fine selection of handmade papers. There's a great catalog, too. *1460 Northside Dr., Midtown, 404/352–7400.*

BEAUTY

5 d-5

AVEDA LIFESTYLE STORE

This is the ultimate shopping stop if you're an Aveda products aficionado. They've got it all: perfume, hair care products, body care, even what they call "air care" (candles, etc.). It's the largest store of its kind in Atlanta area. *4400 Ashford-Dunwoody Rd., Dunwoody, 770/522–9972. MARTA: Dunwoody.*

6 d-1

Mall of Georgia, 3333 Buford Dr., Buford, 678/482–6779.

12 f-3

BETH ANN

Owner Beth Ann Taratoot has been a makeup professional for nearly 30 years, as you can tell from her namesake store. The makeup is a private label created especially for the store. *47 Irby Ave., Buckhead, 404/233–4424.*

14 b-8

BUBBLES BATH & CARD SHOP

A store that understands the luxury implicit in a long bath, Bubbles is redolent with hip scents and sumptuous suds. Innumerable reasons never to leave the tub–or never smell anything but sumptuous, for that matter—can be found within these walls. *492 Flat Shoals Ave., East Atlanta, 404/522–5562.*

5 d-5

FIFI MAHONEYS

From glamorous understatement to over-the-top painted lady, you can achieve whatever beauty look you're going for at Fifi Mahoneys. You'll find all the cosmetics a girl could need, plus fun wigs and false eyelashes. *Perimeter Mall, 4400 Ashford-Dunwoody Rd., Dunwoody, 770/522–9972. MARTA: Dunwoody.*

7 f-3

LINSEY COSMETICS

Linsey's cosmetics, foundations, cleansing systems, blushers, lipsticks, and other beauty products are specially created for women of color. You can also indulge in a makeover from a certified staff member. *2140 Martin Luther King Jr. Dr., Lakewood, 404/696–3064. MARTA: Westlake and H.E. Holmes.*

14 a-2

NATURAL BODY'S BLENDING BAR

Yummy scents engulf you when you walk in, a prelude to the creations you can make yourself in this unique boutique. Choose from an array of essential oils to add to basic beauty products like bath wash or body lotion. *1403 N. Highland Ave., Virginia-Highland, 404/876–9380.*

12 h-2

SEPHORA

A French favorite, Sephora's bound to have the elusive lipstick shade you've been looking for: It has more than 300 different colors. The perfume selection is almost as vast. *Lenox Square, 3393 Peachtree Rd., Buckhead, 404/816–0123. MARTA: Lenox.*

6 a-4

Gwinnett Place Mall, 2100 Pleasant Hill Rd., Duluth, 678/473–4719.

5 g-1

UNCOMMON SCENTS

You won't find these bath and body essentials at your corner drug store. This privately owned bath and body shop is patterned after ones in Europe and offers products from around the world. It has an extremely knowledgeable staff and has exclusivity on some of its products. *11550 Jones Bridge Rd., Alpharetta, 770/569–7627.*

BICYCLES

`4` *h-7*

ATLANTA CYCLING
This broad selection of high-end road bikes and mountain bikes includes models by Trek, Schwinn, and Cannondale. Some exercise bikes are available as well. *4335 Cobb Pkwy., Vinings, 770/952–7731.*

`12` *f-3*

3165 Peachtree Rd., Buckhead, 404/237–1188.

`15` *g-1*

1544 Piedmont Rd., Midtown, 404/873–2451.

`4` *e-2*

440 Ernest W. Barrett Pkwy., Kennesaw, 770/427–1980.

`6` *a-4*

3502 Satellite Blvd., Lawrenceville, 770/476–8158.

`12` *f-3*

THE BICYCLE LINK
The spot for Atlanta's road bike enthusiast specializes in Serotta, Ibis, Bianchi, and Trek. The shop provides fitting and repair services and is the starting point for weekly rides. Like many serious shops, it's closed Sunday because everyone's out riding. *210 Pharr Rd., Buckhead, 404/233–4103.*

`5` *b-4*

CYCLEWORKS
These full-service northwest-area shops provide lifetime adjustment service with the purchase of a new bike. They also rent Trek 6500's by day or longer (helmets included). *4880 Lower Roswell Rd., Marietta, 770/509–9494.*

`5` *d-2*

1570 Holcomb Bridge Rd., Alpharetta, 770/993–2626.

`5` *h-3*

3576 Peachtree Industrial Blvd., Duluth, 770/476–4949.

`15` *g-2*

INTOWN BICYCLES
This friendly, neighborhood bike shop for the recreational rider carries a selection of Jamis, Raleigh, and Giant bicycles. The convenient Piedmont Park location makes this a good place to stop in for a quick patch or some needed air in your tires. *1035 Monroe Dr., Midtown, 404/872–1736.*

`6` *a-8*

PEDAL POWER
The largest retail bike shop in the state specializes in tandem bicycles. The staff welcomes inquiries from cyclists looking to become familiar with bicycling in Georgia. *1900 Rockbridge Rd., Centerville, 770/498–2453.*

BOOKS

antiquarian

`14` *a-5*

A CAPPELLA BOOKS
One of the charms of Little Five Points, this cluttered but orderly store will help you in a search for rare books or a not-so-rare classic like *Just So Stories*. One of the best sections focuses on underground and gay and lesbian hard-to-find books. The staff are friendly, know their stuff, and want to share it. *1133 Euclid Ave., Little Five Points, 404/681–5128.*

`12` *h-4*

ANTONIO RAIMO
Antonio looks like a Dickensian scholar, or rather, just Dickensian, and his knowledge and ability to find precisely the book you want in the kind of condition you require are nothing short of encyclopedic. His shop is a fun place to browse among leather and decorative bindings, maps and globes, and thousands of antique prints (custom framing is offered for the prints). *700 Miami Cir., Buckhead, 404/841–0880.*

`12` *h-2*

C. DICKENS
Most people thought anything as esoteric as a rare-book store wouldn't last a minute at a mall, but after 15 years in business C. Dickens proves that Civil War buffs, people who study incunabula, and chefs looking for out-of-print cookbooks also go to malls. *Lenox Square, 3393 Peachtree Rd., Buckhead, 404/231–3825. MARTA: Lenox.*

5 *d-1*

THE NATIONAL LIBRARY BINDERY COMPANY OF GEORGIA

It's not really a shop per se, but it's one of the few places in Atlanta where you can have your family Bible rebound, your masters' thesis immortalized in exotic leather with gold tooled lettering, your family album fashioned into a proper book. *100 Hembree Park Dr., Roswell, 770/442–5490.*

discount

13 *e-1*

BOOK NOOK

Be warned that you may well feel swamped by the books, CDs, paperbacks, comics, magazines, videos, tapes, books on tape—all new or used—that are stacked to the ceilings here. The comic book selection is especially fabulous. If you collect these, here is where you might actually find a *Superman #1*. *3342 Clairmont Rd., Decatur, 404/633–1328.*

6 *a-6*

4664 Hwy. 29, Lilburn, 770/564–9462.

4 *g-4*

595 Roswell St., Marietta, 770/499–9914.

7 *g-7*

6569 Church St., Riverdale, 770/994–3444.

12 *g-8*

CHAPTER 11

"Prices so low, you'd think we were going bankrupt" reads the advertising slogan, and they're right. They deal in high-volume remainders and overstocks, and everything is 11% off the cover price—*New York Times* bestsellers are 30% off. *1544 Piedmont Ave., Midtown, 404/872–7986.*

12 *e-6*

Peachtree Battle Shopping Center, 2345 Peachtree Rd., Buckhead, 404/237–7199.

14 *f-1*

2091 N. Decatur Rd., Decatur, 404/325–1505.

12 *c-2*

3509 Northside Pkwy., Buckhead, 404/841–6338.

5 *b-5*

6237 Roswell Rd., Sandy Springs, 404/256–5518.

6 *d-7*

2280 E. Main St., Snellville, 770/736–0502.

general

15 *e-5*

B. DALTON BOOKSELLER

These are not necessarily stores in which you'll want to do in-depth research on your dissertation, but with this national chain's emphasis on popular titles and ability to snap up prime real estate in handy places, they certainly make it easy to find a good read. *231 Peachtree St., Downtown, 404/577–2555. MARTA: Peachtree Center.*

12 *h-2*

Lenox Square, 3393 Peachtree Rd., Buckhead, 404/231–8516. MARTA: Lenox.

5 *c-5*

Perimeter Mall, 4400 Ashford-Dunwoody Rd., Dunwoody, 770/394–4185. MARTA: Dunwoody.

4 *h-7*

Cumberland Mall, 1317 Cumberland Mall, Smyrna, 770/435–3297.

8 *c-4*

South DeKalb Mall, 2801 Candler Rd., Decatur, 404/244–7705.

5 *f-7*

Northlake Mall, 4800 Briarcliff Rd., Northlake, 770/934–9292.

12 *e-4*

BARNES & NOBLE

Although it seems like they've been here forever, the seven (and the number's going up all the time) clean, well-lighted outlets of this national chain began opening only five years ago, setting up shops that offer 150,000 titles, along with discounts, adjacent coffee shops, and in-house music departments. Architecture books are especially appealing at the discounted prices, and a regular program of visiting authors and comfy chairs adds a touch of the old-bookstore atmosphere. *2900 Peachtree Rd., Buckhead, 404/261–7747.*

5 *c-5*

120 Perimeter Center W, Dunwoody, 770/396–1200. MARTA: Dunwoody.

4 *h-6*

2952 Cobb Pkwy., Smyrna, 770/953–0966.

6 *a-4*

2205 Pleasant Hill Rd., Duluth, 770/495–7200.

4 *f-2*

50 Ernest W. Barrett Pkwy., Kennesaw, 770/422–2261.

8 *a-8*

1939 Mt. Zion Rd., Morrow, 770/471–2227.

12 *h-1*

BORDERS

Books, music and a café work their charms on customers here just as they do at the competition. The difference, though, is that while the volume may not be as hefty as that at B&N, the selection is well edited and you can often find obscure titles mainstreamed on the shelves. Book clubs get hefty discounts for ordering in bulk, and there are standard discounts on best sellers. 3637 Peachtree Rd., Buckhead, 404/237–0707.

5 *d-5*

4745 Ashford-Dunwoody Rd., Dunwoody, 770/396–0004.

6 *a-4*

Gwinnett Place Mall, 3555 Gwinnett Place Dr., Duluth, 770/495–4043.

4 *h-7*

3101 Cobb Pkwy., Marietta, 770/612–0940.

4 *e-7*

1605 East–West Connector, Austell, 770/941–8740.

special-interest

15 *e-5*

ARCHITECTURAL
BOOK CENTER

Atlanta's largest concentration of architecture and related books, more than 10,000 titles, ranges from academic monographs to lavishly illustrated coffee table books. The store also carries gifts with architectural flair. Peachtree Center, 231 Peachtree St., Downtown, 404/222–9920. MARTA: Peachtree Center.

15 *g-1*

BOOKEARS

Audiobooks are big in this car town. These stores carry about 10,000 audio titles, both abridged and unabridged, and will rent, trade and sell. 1579 Monroe Dr., Midtown, 404/815–7475.

13 *b-1*

3944 Peachtree Rd., Brookhaven, 404/816–2665. MARTA: Brookhaven.

5 *c-6*

1100 Hammond Dr., Sandy Springs, 770/671–8273.

5 *d-2*

8465 Holcomb Bridge Rd., Alpharetta, 770/649–8273.

14 *a-5*

CHARIS BOOKS AND MORE

As a center for lesbian-gay literature, music, and networking, Charis has an excellent selection of books on feminism, multicultural children's books, titles on raising children with a same-sex partner, and much more. 1189 Euclid Ave., Little Five Points, 404/524–0304.

5 *f-8*

COKESBURY BOOK STORE

If you're looking for serious theological works, start at this well-stocked and nonsectarian store attached to the Candler School of Theology at Emory University. 2495 Lawrenceville Hwy., Decatur, 404/320–1034.

14 *d-1*

Candler School of Theology, Bishops Hall, Emory University, 404/727–6336.

15 *c-6*

Interdenominational Theology Center, 700 Martin Luther King Dr., 404/525–1414.

15 *f-6*

GEORGIA BOOKSTORE

Georgia State University's (GSU) bookstore offers new and used textbooks (including all authorized textbooks for GSU classes, which come with a generous buy-back policy) and study aids. GSU clothing and school supplies have a place, here, too. It's closed Sundays. 124 Edgewood Ave., Downtown, 404/659–0959. MARTA: Georgia State.

15 *f-2*

OUTWRITE BOOKSTORE
AND COFFEEHOUSE

A popular spot for gays and lesbians living in the Midtown area, this bookstore–coffee shop stocks a good selection of books and periodicals and provides the latest information on AIDS, national and international activist issues, and gay and lesbian services. 991

Piedmont Ave., at 10th St., Midtown, 404/607–0082. MARTA: Midtown.

`15` *e-2*

U.S. GOVERNMENT BOOKSTORE

You can find about 10,000 of the hundreds of thousands of published government documents here, including the ones Al Gore wrote about how to stop wasting government money. *999 Peachtree St., Midtown, 404/347–1900. MARTA: Midtown.*

CLOTHING FOR CHILDREN

`12` *g-3*

ANIMALS

Dubbing its product children's creative clothing, Animals sells its own line of reasonably priced, practical dresses, T-shirts, onesies, and other items for babies and kids that can actually get dirty and not be ruined. *375 Pharr Rd., Buckhead, 404/816–5588.*

`5` *d-4*

CHICKENLIPS

The clothes here are distinctively designed, lean toward casual styles, and fit infants to kids size 6. Handmade items, including personalized artwork for a child's room, are also available. *5484 Chamblee-Dunwoody Rd., Dunwoody, 770/395–1234.*

`12` *f-3*

KANGAROO POUCH

This the place for Buckhead moms to outfit their little darlings. Many of the pieces are handmade, and all of the ware is geared to parents who don't mind that their kid will likely outgrow the outfit before they've gotten their money's worth. *56 E. Andrews Dr., Buckhead, 404/231–1616.*

`12` *f-1*

THROUGH THE LOOKING GLASS

The fine-crafted clothing leans to dressy clothes and includes delicate Isabel Garreton dresses, and vests and dress pants for boys. The staff is knowledgeable about children's wear designers and very helpful. *3802 Roswell Rd., Buckhead, 404/231–4007.*

CLOTHING FOR WOMEN/GENERAL

classic & casual

`5` *d-5*

ANN TAYLOR

The savvy businesswoman (or the aspirant who wants to look her best for an upcoming interview) will find everything she needs here, classic yet chic suits to belts, shoes, and accessories. *Perimeter Mall, 4400 Ashford-Dunwoody Rd., Dunwoody, 770/671–8874.*

`12` *h-2*

Lenox Square, 3393 Peachtree Rd., Buckhead, 404/264–0450.

`10` *c-3*

BECKY YVONNE SHOP

The apparel here includes business and casual wear and runs into cocktail dressing as well. Prices range from moderate to semi-high end. *5900 Jonesboro Rd., McDonough, 770/961–5900.*

`2` *c-4*

BELK'S

The selection here resembles what you would find in a larger department store: active wear, business attire, casual clothing, evening dress, along with accessories and shoes. *1447 River Stone Pkwy., Canton, 770/720–1125.*

`12` *h-2*

BROOKS BROTHERS

See Clothing for Men/General, below.

`5` *c-5*

CHICO'S

All the clothing here is casual, and most is made of cotton. It's great fitting and easy to pack for that upcoming trip. The accessories are fabulous. *4505 Ashford-Dunwoody Rd., Dunwoody, 404/673–0603.*

`12` *f-1*

CP SHADES

This reasonably priced, comfortable clothing, made from all natural fibers, is very stylish. Women of all ages will be able to find something they love in this store. *3106 Roswell Rd., Buckhead, 404/816–0872.*

`12` *f-1*

PEOPLES

This classic clothing is different and suits the upscale southern lifestyle to a tee. *3236 Roswell Rd., Buckhead, 404/816-7292.*

`12` *f-1*

POTPOURRI

There's a fine selection of traditional women's clothing here, including wonderful sportswear, dinner dresses, and accessories. *3718 Roswell Rd., Buckhead, 404/365-0880.*

`12` *f-3*

RASSLE DAZZLE

Almost an Atlanta tradition, this shop specializes in casual clothing, including great sweaters and pants. Some dressier choices are available, too, including evening wear. You'll find a designer label on most of the selections. *49 Irby Ave., Buckhead, 404/233-6940.*

`5` *d-4*

TALBOTS

A leader in sophisticated, tailored clothing, Talbots carries lines that range from casual to career wear. Personal shopping service is available. The chain has multiple locations throughout the metro area. *690 Holcomb Bridge Rd., Dunwoody, 770/642-1852.*

designer

`3` *g-7*

BELLA LUNA

The wonderfully whimsical clothing for women here includes lots of comfortable and unusual outfits in cotton and linen. There's also a nice selection of designer soaps, bath salts, and jewelry. *26 Main St., Buford, 770/832-9878.*

`15` *h-3*

BILL HALLMAN

This talented Atlanta designer creates clothing for the fashion-forward woman and shows his designs in a boutique that is lively and young at heart and design. However, you don't have to be young to wear this clothing, and the store represents other designers as well. *792 N. Highland Ave., Virginia-Highland, 404/876-6055.*

`4` *h-7*

BONNIES BOUTIQUE

The exceptional collections include everything from elegant evening wear to prom and pageant gowns, and the service is exceptionally helpful. *Galleria, 1 Galleria Pkwy., Smyrna, 770/850-0595.*

`12` *g-2*

LUNA

If you've seen top-of-the-line merchandise in the magazines, you'll find it at Luna. Fashions range from designer jeans to gowns and accessories. Incidentally, anything you see here is for sale, right down to the furnishings. *3167 Peachtree Rd., Buckhead, 404/233-5344.*

`15` *g-2*

MINT BEVERLY HILLS

The designer lines here run to the coolest in ethnic print dresses and a good selection of funky, now clothing. *Rio Shopping Center, 595 Piedmont Ave., Midtown, 404/874-4656.*

`15` *h-3*

MITZI & ROMANO

These very cool designer clothes are geared to those who want something different but not awkward. The jewelry and accessories are great, too. *1038 N. Highland Ave., Virginia-Highland, 404/876-7228.*

`12` *h-2*

NEIMAN MARCUS

You know the name and what you can expect to find here—the finest in bridal gowns, shoes, and clothing for any occasion. *Lenox Square, 3393 Peachtree Rd., Buckhead, 404/266-8200.*

`7` *h-2*

RENÉ RENÉ

If you're looking for something to wear to the club scene, you'll find it here, along with accessories. Some of the designs are appropriate for business as well. *1142 Euclid Ave., Downtown, 404/522-7363.*

`5` *c-5*

THE WHITE HOUSE/BLACK MARKET

Most everything here is black and white, from chic business wear to romantic evening dresses. You'll also find accent pieces in contrasting colors, and the inventory extends to accessories and gifts. *4505 Ashford-Dunwoody Rd., Dunwoody, 770/395–7500.*

4 *g-6*

4475 Roswell Rd., Marietta, 770/971–7315.

discount & off-price

5 *e-1*

ALPHARETTA BARGAIN STORE

This store's a secret, at least among the moneyed set who love designer clothing at as much as 70% off. When you see the Benzes, Beamers, Jags, and Lexuses parking in the lot, head in for the new shipment. You may have to pick around the polyester, and some sections may be a bit thin that day, but if you're a regular shopper here, you know what you can come home with—and how often to smile that secret smile when your inquisitive office mate wants to know where you got that blouse. *131 S. Main St., Alpharetta. 770/475–5062.*

13 *d-4*

LOEHMANN'S

To savvy shoppers, this name means, of course, designer closeout merchandise, anything from Donna Karen to Ralph Lauren and Gucci. (As you probably know, you won't see the label because they've been cut out.) There are outstanding buys, too, on jewelry, handbags, and shoes. *2480 Briarcliff Rd., Toco Hills, 404/633–4156.*

5 *c-2*

8610 Roswell Rd., Roswell, 770/998–2095.

4 *g-5*

2460 Cobb Pkwy., Marietta, 770/953–2225.

5 *c-5*

SYMS

The choice of designer clothing runs from business attire straight through evening wear, and its available at a fraction of the cost you'd pay elsewhere. If you don't find what you want, wait a couple of days and come back, because the merchandise changes frequently. *1803 Roswell Rd., Roswell, 770/321–3400.*

5 *g-5*

5775 Jimmy Carter Blvd., Norcross, 770/368–0200.

unsual sizes

5 *b-5*

THE PETITE PLACE

You'll find everything for the petite woman here, including casual, business, and evening wear. In fact, you won't find these designs in a petite section of a department store or anywhere else. *6309 Roswell Rd., Sandy Springs, 404/252–1223.*

4 *h-7*

TALL IS BEAUTIFUL

These elegant fashions for the tall woman come in luxurious fabrics and tasteful designer styles. Coordinating accessories are available, too. *Galleria, 1 Galleria Pkwy., Smyrna, 770/541–6880.*

CLOTHING FOR WOMEN/ SPECIALTIES

1 *e-6*

BOOT VILLAGE AND WESTERN WEAR

You'll find great values on the latest styles in name-brand boots and western wear, along with a selection of belts and accessories. Some of the designs are of alligator and crocodile, when they are available. *1393 Mt. Zion Rd., Morrow, 770/968–0024.*

4 *g-7*

2800 Cumberland Blvd., Smyrna, 770/436–9741.

5 *h-2*

2131 Pleasant Hill Rd., Duluth, 770/476–1555.

7 *a-4*

3221 Highway 5, Douglasville, 770/489–4555.

12 *h-2*

C. C. WHITTIER BRIDAL SALON

This salon has the most beautiful selection of gowns, mother-of-the-bride dresses, shoes, veils, and invitations in Atlanta. *480 E. Paces Ferry Rd., Buckhead, 404/266–1146.*

15 *e-5*

JAGO FASHION ACCESSORIES

Browse here for the newest accessories from Europe, be they scarves, shawls, wraps, hats, belts, or fashion jewelry. *250 Spring St., Downtown, 404/827–9587.*

CLOTHING FOR MEN/GENERAL

classic & casual

`12` h-2

BROOKS BROTHERS

This classic clothier has been a favorite with each new generation of politicians, actors, and businessmen, but it's the ready-to-wear lines that have brought this New York–based store to the masses. Top-of-the-line quality and excellent service may not come cheap, but one of the custom-made suits will make you feel like a million bucks. *Lenox Square, 3393 Peachtree Rd., Buckhead, 404/237–7000. MARTA: Lenox.*

`15` e-5

235 Peachtree St., Downtown, 404/577–4040. MARTA: Peachtree Center.

`5` c-5

Perimeter Mall, 4400 Ashford-Dunwoody Rd., Dunwoody, 770/394–9051. MARTA: Dunwoody.

`15` e-5

H. STOCKTON

Opening his first haberdashery downtown in 1963, Ham Stockton has been an Atlanta staple among discriminating consumers ever since. The shop prides itself in offering the finest products from top-quality manufacturers such as Canali, Zanella, and Bobby Jones, as well as their own custom-made, made-to-measure, and ready-made clothing. *210 Peachtree St., Downtown, 404/523–7741. MARTA: Peachtree Center.*

`12` h-2

Lenox Square, 3393 Peachtree Rd., Buckhead, 404/233–1608. MARTA: Lenox.

`5` d-5

4505 Ashford-Dunwoody Rd., Dunwoody, 770/396–1300. MARTA: Dunwoody.

`4` h-7

Galleria Mall, 1 Galleria Pkwy, Smyrna, 770/984–1111.

`12` h-2

POLO/RALPH LAUREN

Is there a more recognizable logo in men's clothing than this one? A bit of over-indulgence, sure, but this sizable storefront offers a complete men's collection for any dress occasion, including shoes and accessories. *Lenox Square, 3393 Peachtree Rd., 404/261–2663. MARTA: Lenox.*

`12` g-3

THE MEN'S WAREHOUSE

With more than 400 stores in 40 states nationwide and 10 in the metro area, the Men's Warehouse sets the standard for the all-under-one-roof concept in men's clothing. Their large retail spaces allow them to offer a large selection of everything from formal wear to basic business suits to office casual wear, complete with shoes and accessories. A knowledgeable and friendly staff can even help you with all your tailoring needs while you wait. *3255 Peachtree Rd., Buckhead, 404/264–0421.*

`5` f-7

Northlake Mall, 4800 Briarcliff Rd., Northlake, 770/908–1125.

`6` a-4

2131 Pleasant Hill Rd., Duluth, 770/623–6060.

`4` e-3

425 Ernest W. Barrett Pkwy., Kennesaw, 770/429–8955.

`6` a-8

5370 Stone Mountain Hwy., Stone Mountain, 770/498–5871.

`4` h-7

2931 Cobb Pkwy., Smyrna, 770/956–7297.

discount & off-price

`5` e-6

BURLINGTON COAT FACTORY

If you know what you're doing, this is a great place to find name brands at a low price. The selection of men's sports coats is especially large and ranges from shabby to something Rich's would have at twice the price. *4166 Buford Hwy., Doraville, 404/634–5566.*

`5` c-2

608 Holcomb Bridge Rd., Roswell, 770/518–9800.

`7` e-4

Greenbriar Mall, 2841 Greenbriar Pkwy., Lakewood, 404/349–6300.

`8` a-8

1516 Southlake Pkwy., Morrow, 770/960–7555.

6 | *a-4*

3750 Venture Dr., Duluth, 770/497–0033.

6 | *a-4*

K&G MEN'S CENTER

Determined to keep their overhead low, this men's retailer buys in bulk and stocks its selections in stores that resemble warehouses, using basic fixtures and offering little or no ambience for the customer. But if you're looking to get the most for your money, you can't beat the price on the name-brand, first-quality merchandise, much of which is 30%–70% off department store prices. It's open Friday through Sunday only. *3750 Venture Dr., Duluth, 770/623–9895.*

12 | *b-8*

1750 Ellsworth Industrial Blvd., Midtown, 404/350–2927.

4 | *g-2*

2949 Canton Rd., Marietta, 770/428–9660.

8 | *a-8*

1294 Mt. Zion Rd., Morrow, 678/422–2425.

unusual sizes

5 | *f-8*

CASUAL MALE BIG & TALL

This one-stop shop covers all the bases for men whose size limits their selection in other clothing stores. Stocking casual, business, and active wear for men in sizes ranging from 1X to 6X and XLT to 4XLT, Casual Male offers larger-men name-brand apparel at reasonable prices. *3963 LaVista Rd., Tucker, 770/908–2523.*

4 | *h-6*

2778 Cobb Pkwy., Smyrna, 770/984–8050.

6 | *a-8*

5370 Stone Mountain Hwy., Stone Mountain, 770/469–4002.

6 | *a-4*

1950 Pleasant Hill Rd., Duluth, 770/476–8112.

5 | *b-5*

6015 Roswell Rd., Sandy Springs, 404/847–9666.

5 | *d-2*

7681 North Point Pkwy., Alpharetta, 770/642–9700.

CLOTHING FOR MEN/SPECIALTIES

12 | *f-3*

ANDREW

For those of you who prefer your clothes tailored expressly for you, Andrew is a men's boutique catering to the very upscale. Handmade suits made from only the richest fabrics in a European style are designed to make a very fashion-forward statement. The collection also offers a sportswear collection that's every bit in keeping with its sharp dressed man attitude. Adding to the amenities, a recent expansion offers salon hairstyling on Tuesday and Thursday. *56 E. Andrews Dr., Buckhead, 404/869–1881.*

12 | *g-5*

BENNIE'S SHOES

Begun as a repair shop all the way back in 1909, Bennie's is a longtime Atlanta favorite for discount shoes. Footwear runs the gamut from dress to casual to golf—all top name brands. *2851 Piedmont Rd., Buckhead, 404/262–1966. MARTA: Lindbergh.*

5 | *h-5*

5192 Brook Hollow Pkwy., Norcross, 770/447–1577.

4 | *h-6*

2441 Cobb Pkwy, Smyrna, 770/955–1972.

12 | *h-2*

GINGISS FORMALWEAR

A full-service rental and sales outfit, Gingiss offers dozens of sharp styles to suit any individual taste. *Lenox Square, 3393 Peachtree Rd., Buckhead, 404/266–2115. MARTA: Lenox.*

5 | *f-7*

Northlake Mall, 4800 Briarcliff Rd., Northlake, 770/934–0868.

5 | *c-5*

Perimeter Mall, 4400 Ashford-Dunwoody Rd., Dunwoody, 770/394–2860. MARTA: Dunwoody.

4 | *e-3*

Town Center, 400 Ernest W. Barrett Pkwy., Kennesaw, 770/424–0066.

6 | *a-4*

Gwinnett Place Mall, 2100 Pleasant Hill Rd., Duluth, 770/476–2100.

6 | *d-1*

Mall of Georgia, 3333 Buford Dr., Buford, 770/932–0062.

14 *a-5*

STEFAN'S VINTAGE CLOTHING

Atlantans have known for a long time that this is the place to find the fashion styles of generations past, located among the counterculture clothiers in Little Five Points. Stefan's is great for period costumes or for defining that personal sense of style. *1160 Euclid Ave., Little Five Points, 404/688–4929.*

12 *h-2*

VERSACE

Haute couture comes to Atlanta with this world-renowned design house, appropriately situated in the decidedly upscale Phipps Plaza in Buckhead. Here, the fashion elite linger in the spare, uncluttered environment to don the season's latest trend. A good rule of thumb: if you are checking price tags, you probably can't afford it. *Phipps Plaza, 3500 Peachtree Rd., Buckhead, 404/814–0664. MARTA: Lenox.*

COMPUTERS & SOFTWARE

5 *h-4*

COMP USA

Geared toward serving both the savvy user and the novice, this large outlet of the national chain is a key spot for shopping name-brand hardware, but it's the dizzying selection of software titles that makes this an essential stop. *3825 Venture Dr., Norcross, 770/813–8565.*

5 *e-5*

DELTA COMPUTERS

Mid-range prices, good locations, and wide selection make this long-standing local outfit worth looking into. You'll find everything from complete systems down to individual components. *2633 Beacon Dr., Doraville, 770/457–9999.*

5 *d-1*

11240 Alpharetta Hwy., Suite 250, Alpharetta, 770/753–8117.

9 *g-1*

7147 Jonesboro Rd., Jonesboro, 770/968–8822.

4 *g-4*

2100 Roswell Rd., Marietta, 770/579–1212.

5 *g-5*

HIQ COMPUTERS

This is a prime resource for knowledgeable, budget-conscious users who know exactly what they want under the hood. Built-to-order systems can be turned out in 24–48 hours or less. *5600 Oakbrook Pkwy., Suite 260, Norcross, 800/875–2882*

15 *c-3*

LINUX GENERAL STORE

Hard-core, self-professed geeks who believe in a future where this progressive operating system will eventually rule over all can find comfort in this all-things-LINUX shop. Located in the shadow of Georgia Tech, they service individual users and business-to-business concerns. General training classes and specialized services are available. *798 Marietta St., Midtown, 404/881–8090.*

4 *h-5*

MICRO CENTER

For shoppers coming in from the northwest side, this store has many of the perks of a megastore but fewer hassles. Macintosh users are well served here. *1221 Powers Ferry Rd., Marietta, 770/859–1555.*

CRAFTS

12 *d-6*

ART AND SOUL ARTS AND CRAFTS CAFÉ

Make your own pottery but leave the hard part to them. You craft and create, they glaze and fire. Meanwhile, you can sip specialty coffees and nibble pastries in the adjoining café. *2140 Peachtree Rd., Buckhead, 404/352–1222.*

14 *g-3*

BY HAND SOUTH

This quaint, eye-pleasing shop in the heart of cool and quirky downtown Decatur sells original pottery, jewelry, glass, and other handmade items. *112 E. Ponce de Leon Ave., Decatur, 404/378–0118. Closed Sun. MARTA: Decatur.*

5 *h-2*

CARTER HOUSE GALLERY AND FRAMING

Contemporary paintings, other original artworks, collectibles, glass sculpture, and custom framing can be found here.

10820 Abbott's Ridge Rd., Duluth, 770/
495–1998. Closed Sun.

14 b-5

DONNA VAN GOGH'S INTOWN ARTIST MARKET

This charming gallery in the historic
Candler Park neighborhood is a pleasure
to browse. Peruse the eclectic assortment of locally crafted items in a
friendly atmosphere where the motto is
"Art for Y'all." 1165 McClendon Ave., Candler Park, 404/370–1003. MARTA: Edge-
wood/Candler Park.

14 a-2

ECLECTIC ELECTRIC

This funky palace of light carries lamps
of every size and shape, whether candle-
powered or plugged-in. For the most
imaginative in illumination, pick up a
unique original or a reasonably priced
gift item. 1393 N. Highland Ave., Virginia-
Highland, 404/875–2840. Closed Sun.

5 b-4

RAINBLUE

Here you'll discover a trove of functional
as well as decorative pottery and gifts
hand-crafted by American artisans. 1205
Johnson Ferry Rd., Marietta, 770/973–
1091.

5 g-5

REGENCY FINE ART

Look no further for a full range of hand-
pulled lithographs and serigraphs by an
impressive stable of internationally
acclaimed artists. Decorative prints,
framed and unframed, are also available,
and the shop does custom framing. 6458
Dawson Blvd., Norcross, 770/840–7701.

14 a-2

SIDEWALK STUDIO

This inviting enclave of high-end crafts
features the work of more than artists
who specialize in pottery, paintings,
sculptures, and jewelry of the handmade
as well as custom-made variety. 1050 N.
Highland Ave., Virginia-Highland, 404/
872–1047.

8 f-1

STONE MOUNTAIN ARTS AND CRAFTS CENTER

A folksy fantasyland of homespun
mementos, this engaging shop offers
the crafty creations of local and national
artists. You'll find everything from the
inexpensive knickknack to the jaw-dropping showpiece. 943 Main St., Stone
Mountain, 770/469–0329.

12 d-7

VESPERMAN GALLERY

A highly respected showcase of original
glass sculpture, Vesperman offers everything in glass, from one-of-a-kind mas-
terpieces to reasonably priced,
handmade jewelry and gifts. Don't miss
their biannual teapot show, in which
teapots of all shapes and sizes, created
with startling imagination, fill the
gallery. 2140 Peachtree Rd., Brookwood,
404/350–9698.

5 b-6

V. REED GALLERY

It's impossible to walk past this shop's
colorful display of inventive artwork,
jewelry, pottery, and other gewgaws
without venturing a stroll inside. There
you'll find a bright and varied offering of
original pieces at wallet-friendly prices.
4475 Roswell Rd., No. 1000, Marietta,
770/971–0733.

DISCOUNT

14 h-1

BIG LOTS

As the name suggests, they cram huge
amounts of stuff in assortments called
lots. Then they price it cheaply and pack
it in 40 aisles packed with closeouts,
knockoffs, even salvage. If you take the
time to look, you may find just what you
need in home furnishings and household products, tools, hardware, and
sports equipment. 2617 N. Decatur Rd.,
Decatur, 404/378–6187.

4 g-7

3791 S. Cobb Dr. SE, Smyrna, 770/438–
8321.

8 d-1

6011 Memorial Dr., Stone Mountain, 770/
469–7277.

6 d-7

2280 Main St. SW, Snellville, 678/344–
8303.

7 g-7

7055 Highway 85, Riverdale, 770/909–
0824.

4 g-3

2745 Sandy Plains Rd., Marietta, 770/973–
8947.

7 *g-5*

KMART

With celebrities such as Martha Stewart lending cache to its formerly downscale image, Kmart (and its sister component Big Kmart) has remodeled its Atlanta stores and made an effort to attract shoppers with more disposable income. For those without so much of that, it's still the best place to find inexpensive everything. *230 Cleveland Ave. SW, East Point, 404/766–7543.*

2 *b-4*

1750 Marietta Hwy., Canton, 770/479–8757.

8 *d-4*

2395 Wesley Chapel Rd., Decatur, 770/808–0606.

5 *e-6*

5597 Buford Hwy., Doraville, 770/458–9506.

5 *c-2*

606 Holcomb Bridge Rd., Roswell, 770/992–9525.

8 *e-1*

1701 Mountain Industrial Blvd., Stone Mountain, 770/938–0151.

12 *g-5*

MARSHALLS

You can always find discounted perfume such as Anne Klein and Lagerfeld here because most people don't think of shopping here for perfume. The same is true for leather goods such as wallets, for both men and women. There's a good housewares department, and excellent buys on name-brand swim suits, socks, and underwear, especially for men. Get there early, when the shipments first come in. When they go out, they likely won't be restocked. *2625 Piedmont Rd., 404/233–3848. MARTA: Lindbergh.*

13 *e-1*

4166 Buford Hwy., Brookhaven, 404/329–0200.

12 *g-3*

3232 Peachtree Rd., Buckhead, 404/365–8155. MARTA:Buckhead.

6 *a-4*

3675 Satellite Blvd., Duluth, 770/497–1052.

8 *e-1*

6011 Memorial Dr., Stone Mountain, 770/469–4005.

4 *f-3*

425 Ernest W. Barrett Pkwy., Kennesaw, 770/424–2064.

5 *c-5*

STEIN MART

Even though the selection isn't huge, the little housewares department usually yields something really nice. *1155 Mt. Vernon Hwy., Dunwoody, 770/804–9149.*

8 *c-1*

2050 Lawrenceville Hwy., Decatur, 404/329–0927.

5 *b-4*

1309 Johnson Ferry Rd., Marietta, 770/579–0940.

5 *d-2*

Rivermont Plaza, 8560 Holcomb Bridge Rd., Alpharetta, 770/518–4340.

4 *f-3*

50 Ernest W. Barrett Pkwy., Kennesaw, 770/514–8900.

6 *d-7*

1670 Scenic Hwy., Snellville, 770/982–1670.

5 *h-5*

SAM'S CLUB

For the $25 yearly membership fee, you get discounts fit for a king. Discounts are really that substantial. Some people never buy tires and oil anywhere else, and the prices on everything from fine jewelry and watches to appliances, computers, and electronics are really good. Food is always good quality, especially the fresh meat. *3450 Steve Reynolds Blvd., Duluth, 770/497–1165.*

12 *g-6*

515 Garson Dr., Atlanta, 404/266–2005. MARTA: Lindbergh.

5 *g-8*

1940 Mountain Industrial Blvd., Tucker, 770/908–8408.

8 *a-8*

7325 Jonesboro Rd., Morrow, 770/960–8228.

4 *g-4*

150 Cobb Pkwy., Marietta, 770/423–7018.

7 *c-2*

150 Six Flags Dr., Austell, 770/739–0019.

5 b-5
TARGET
With competitors such as Kmart and Wal-Mart beating down the door, you'd think this store would have met its demise a long time ago. But the many Atlanta locations are as popular as ever. *235 Johnson Ferry Rd., Sandy Springs, 404/256–4600.*

12 h-2
3535 Peachtree Rd., Buckhead, 404/237–9494.

13 d-5
2400 N. Druid Hills Rd., 404/325–3211.

5 h-4
2300 Pleasant Hill Rd., Duluth, 770/623–3519.

9 h-1
1940 Mt. Zion Rd., Morrow, 770/472–3355.

4 h-6
2201 South Cobb Pkwy., Smyrna, 770/952–2241.

8 d-4
WAL-MART
These oversize general merchandise stores have invaded Atlanta, offering affordable merchandise that ranges from adhesives to zippers. Most have pharmacies, and the supercenters operate vision centers, car care centers, and one-hour photo divisions. *2496 Wesley Chapel Rd., Decatur, 770/593–3540.*

5 d-5
4725 Ashford-Dunwoody Rd., Dunwoody, 770/395–0199.

4 g-5
1785 Cobb Pkwy. South, Marietta, 770/955–0626.

5 e-3
1580 Holcomb Bridge Rd., Roswell, 770/993–4103.

6 d-7
2135 E. Main St., Snellville, 770/979–2447.

7 d-8
4700 Jonesboro Rd., Union City, 770/964–6921.

ELECTRONICS & AUDIO

12 h-1
BANG & OLUFSEN
Still enjoying its popularity, this high-end chain offers sleek, well-designed products at prices that are not for the faint of heart. *Phipps Plaza, 3500 Peachtree Rd., Buckhead, 404/233–4199.*

5 c-5
BEST BUY
While the megastore competition gets thicker, this chain still wins points for selection and respectable quality across the board. *1201 Hammond Dr., Dunwoody, 770/392–0454.*

6 d-7
HIFI BUYS
For fast service on low, mid-range, or somewhat higher-priced equipment, this chain is a sound performer. Car installations are particularly quick and painless, and warranties are not a hassle. *2059 Scenic Hwy., Suite 101, Snellville, 678/344–0007.*

5 b-6
MUSIC AUDIO
For homeowners looking for custom installations on home theater and other hi-fi solutions, this store carries brands that include NAIM, Arcurus, and Sherwood Newcastle. *4920 Roswell Rd., Marietta, 404/252–5360.*

EYEWEAR

12 g-2
THE EYE GALLERY
Three optometrists began this complete eyewear shop to compete with the major national retailers. Customers can schedule examinations, have prescriptions altered, and shop for frames all under one roof. *3330 Piedmont Rd., Buckhead, 404/231–3772. MARTA: Buckhead.*

5 b-5
5975 Roswell Rd., Sandy Springs, 404/252–4111.

5 e-1
North Point Mall, 1000 North Point Pkwy, Alpharetta, 770/475–6500.

5 c-5

LENS CRAFTERS

This national chain has set up shop in virtually every part of the city to offer full-service eye care known for its speed. *4400 Ashford-Dunwoody Rd., Dunwoody, 770/395–6717. MARTA: Dunwoody.*

12 h-2

Lenox Square, 3393 Peachtree Rd., Buckhead, 404/239–0784. MARTA: Lenox.

7 e-4

Greenbriar Mall, 2841 Greenbriar Pkwy., Lakewood, 404/346–2020.

5 f-7

Northlake Mall, 4800 Briarcliff Rd., Northlake, 770/493–6553.

5 e-1

North Point Mall, 1000 North Point Pkwy., Alpharetta, 770/667–8800.

6 d-1

Mall of Georgia, 3333 Buford Dr., Buford, 678/482–4491.

4 h-6

PEARLE VISION

Possibly the most well known of eye-care specialists, Pearle has more than 20 metro locations offering a complete range of optometry services and a guarantee on the lowest prices for contact lenses. *2778 Cobb Pkwy., Smyrna, 770/859–0444.*

12 h-2

3245 Lenox Rd., Buckhead, 404/816–5532. MARTA: Lenox.

5 g-2

9775 Medlock Bridge Rd., Duluth, 770/022–5300.

6 d-7

1708 Scenic Hwy. SW, Snellville, 770/736–3006.

5 c-2

10775 Alpharetta Hwy., Roswell, 770/998–0331.

2 a-8

9801 Highway 92, Woodstock, 770/592–7100.

12 f-3

PLANET EYEWEAR

An eyeglass boutique whose stock runs from classic to funky, Planet Eyewear is for people who are superserious about their accessories. Dramatically subdued lighting showcases the merchandise, with a selection ample enough that even Elton John could find something to suit his extravagant tastes. Be sure to try one of the select beverages from the organic juice bar. *3167 Peachtree Rd., Buckhead, 404/816–4224. MARTA: Buckhead.*

5 h-5

THE SUNGLASS WAREHOUSE

You'll find a huge selection of sunglasses and accessories—domestics and imports—that are suited to all budgets and tastes. Pick up a pair of shades for as little as $1, but if you're looking for more quality, you'll find many of the finer brands are 5%–15% off what the department stores are charging. *5182 Brook Hollow Pkwy., Norcross, 770/729–1961.*

FABRICS

7 f-6

BUKOM TEXTILES STORE

Bukom is one of the only fabric shops in the city that specialize in African fabrics. Many of the materials are actually imported from Europe, where the manufacturers are located, but are used in the making of traditional African garb. Many customers come in to buy *rials* to create traditional wedding attire. *2680 Godby Rd., College Park, 404/766–0417.*

12 h-4

CURRAN DESIGNER FABRICS & FURNITURE INC.

Tucked away in one of the city's antiques districts, Curran offers more than 5,000 types of fabrics in addition to furniture and home accents at wholesale. *737 Miami Cir., 404/237–4246. MARTA: Lindbergh.*

15 b-2

FORSYTH FABRICS

Serving Atlanta since 1949, Forsyth Fabrics is one of the best-known and most frequented fabric suppliers in the city. Racks and racks of fabrics ranging from feather-light sheers to sumptuous tapestries fill the warehouse space. Plus, they give away free popcorn. *1190 Foster St., Midtown, 404/351–6050.*

15 b-2

1168A Howell Mill Rd., Midtown, 404/607–1064.

15 b-2

LEWIS & SHERON TEXTILE COMPANY

With a whole room devoted just to silks, it's safe to say Lewis & Sheron has an encompassing inventory. The selection is vast, the staff knowledgeable, the reputation long-standing (since 1945). An adjacent furniture store makes for one-stop shopping, if you're so inclined. *912 Huff Road, Midtown, 404/351–4833.*

FLOWERS & PLANTS

12 g-7

ATLANTA WILDFLOWERS

This self-styled European flower market may be a bit out of your way, but it's worth the drive. Thousands of exotic blooms greet customers upon entering the generous space exclusively devoted to flowers, plants, and garden accessories. They also offer six-week floral-design classes throughout the year. *1893 Piedmont Rd., Midtown, 404/873–7300.*

12 f-4

BROOKHAVEN-BUCKHEAD FLOWERS

Family owned and operated, this busy location services most of the local area churches. The shop has developed a reputation for excellent arrangements for any event that won't break the budget and also delivers balloon bouquets, plants, and gift baskets metro-wide. *2905 Peachtree Rd., Buckhead, 404/237–6351.*

4 g-5

CARITHERS

This full-service florist has been serving the local market for 25 years. Messengers cover the metro area twice daily to ensure delivery of the freshest possible arrangements of Holland and Tropical floral designs, along with gourmet and gift baskets for every occasion. Carithers also provides customers with a 24-hour service line. *1708 Powers Ferry Rd., Marietta, 770/980–3000.*

12 h-2

FLOWERS FROM HOLLAND LIMITED

They may be small, but they stock the best. Flowers from Holland eschews the more common bulbs to maximize the space for their top-quality line of exotics.

Lenox Square, 3393 Peachtree Rd., Buckhead, 404/233–0090. MARTA: Lenox.

14 a-3

FOXGLOVES & IVY

Step inside the cobblestone entranceway and take in the lush English garden setting. Given the shop's large variety of the finest tropicals and exotics, you won't find any carnations in the bouquets here. The owners take great pride in their custom-made arrangements and in making sure their employees are trained in the latest design techniques. This is a popular choice for wedding parties and other joyous events. *1060 St. Charles Ave., Midtown, 404/892–7272.*

14 g-3

MAUD BAKER FLORIST

Maud Baker's flowers and gifts are a Decatur landmark. Offering the best from Holland and other exotic locales, arrangements are always custom-tailored. Maud Baker is open most major holidays and, for that last-minute affair, can oftentimes make deliveries within one hour of ordering. *609 Church St., Decatur, 404/373–5791. MARTA: Decatur.*

FOOD & DRINK

A typical Atlantan's shopping list reflects the long-standing influence of outsiders: There's the balsamic vinegar alongside the black-eyed peas. Accordingly, almost any newcomer to Atlanta can find a little taste of home these days in produce markets, gourmet delis, and ethnic food shops. Locating the grits and fried chicken could take a little more effort, but they're still around, too.

breads & pastries

14 a-2

ALON'S

Here's the drill: Early on a summer Saturday, visit this European-style bakery for a bag of fresh pastries and a tall, strong coffee before heading across the street for the Morningside Farmers Market (*see Produce, below*). Or then again, visit anytime. *1394 N. Highland Ave., Virginia-Highland, 404/872–6000.*

15 g-2

BREAD GARDEN

This tiny storefront in a Midtown outlet district sells what are reputed to be the best baked goods in town. The loaves of hot country Italian bread, fresh fruit tarts, and homemade biscotti are heavenly indeed. *549 Amsterdam Ave., Midtown, 404/875–1166.*

12 *g-3*
BUCKHEAD BREAD
A few blocks south of the Ritz-Carlton Buckhead. A stone's throw from a Jaguar dealership. Across the street from the gleaming Buckhead Diner. Get the picture? Amidst the glitz, this large-scale baking operation turns out incredible specialty breads and jewel-like desserts. *3070 Piedmont Rd., Buckhead, 404/240–1978.*

9 *d-4*
CITY CAFE & BAKERY
The German owner focuses on European-style breads—about a dozen kinds each day—in addition to cakes, pies, and pastries. *215 S. Glynn St., Fayetteville, 770/461–6800.*

12 *f-3*
HENRI'S
The French family who founded this Buckhead institution more than 70 years ago has sold, but the new owners continue to turn out superlative cheese straws, Italian cream cake, and chocolate eclairs. *61 Irby Ave., Buckhead, 404/237–0202.*

5 *b-5*
6289 Roswell Road, Sandy Springs, 404/256–7934.

15 *e-4*
KRISPY KREME
These little pillows of sweetness, the southerner's take on a doughnut, have conquered Atlanta's suburbs, which claim several franchises, and the corner grocery, where shoppers can grab a box of glazed to go. But the city's original Krispy Kreme still flashes the red neon when the ovens are on. It's a worthy pit stop. *295 Ponce de Leon Rd., Midtown, 404/876–7307.*

15 *b-2*
MONDO
Located in an industrial area that has been claimed and regentrified by the trendy, this bakery-café is known for original desserts such as the Maker's Mark bourbon fig bars, as well as basics such as carrot cake and Lemon Love Bars. *750 Huff Rd., Midtown, 404/603–9995.*

chocolate & other candy

5 *c-7*
GREENWOOD ICE CREAM CO. OUTLET STORE
The same custom-made, premium ice creams sold in restaurants across Atlanta can be had here by the half-gallon carton or the three-gallon tub. Try the champagne sorbet, the green tea, or just plain vanilla. Flavors vary each day. *4829 Peachtree Rd., Chamblee, 770/455–6166.*

12 *h-2*
KARL BISSINGER FRENCH CONFECTIONS
Visit in May, when the fresh strawberries are dipped in the richest French chocolate. Better yet, wait until July, for the raspberries. Apricots, oranges, and other fruits round out the rest of the year, along with a nice selection of other chocolates and candies. *Phipps Plaza, 3500 Peachtree Road, Buckhead, 404/237–7161.*

5 *e-6*
MAISON ROBERT FINE CHOCOLATES
After a time-out, this European master is again turning out the finest handmade chocolates in town. From his little cottage tucked on a side street in Chamblee, Robert Reeb produces truffles and other chocolates, fruit tarts, assorted quiches and the world's best macaroon. *3708 N. Peachtree Rd., Chamblee, 770/454–6442.*

15 *e-6*
SOUTHERN CANDY CO.
This locally owned confectionery sells pecan pralines, fudge, nut brittles, taffy, candy apples, and other sweets at an aromatic shop in Underground Atlanta. *118 Lower Alabama St., Downtown, 404/577–3697.*

8 *c-1*
SOUTHERN SWEETS
The pecan tart and the Key lime pie should taste familiar at this wholesale baker's outlet store. That's because they're served in some of Atlanta's best restaurants. *186 Rio Cir., Decatur, 404/373–8752.*

8 *e-1*
STONE MOUNTAIN CANDY KITCHEN
The quaint Main Street of Stone Mountain Village is home to this purveyor of

pralines, assorted chocolates, fudge, brittles and gophers, a homemade version of pecan-caramel clusters dipped in chocolate. The owner makes 90% of the goodies on the premises. *977 Main St., Stone Mountain, 770/879–1330.*

coffee & tea

14 *a-4*

AURORA
The locally owned Aurora appeals to the anti-chain coffeehouse set. Coffees by the pound come in a seemingly endless array of roasts, grinds and flavors. *468 Moreland Ave., Little Five Points, 404/523–6856.*

14 *a-2*

922 N. Highland Ave., Virginia-Highland, 404/892–7158.

15 *g-1*

1572 Piedmont Ave., Midtown, 404/607–9994.

5 *c-7*

BARCLAY'S FLOWER & TEA GARDEN
In a charming cottage in an unexpected location amid offices and rental housing you'll find a wide selection of loose teas and tea accessories. Try the formal afternoon tea, served in traditional English style complete with bone china, scones, and finger sandwiches. *285 W. Wieuca Rd., Sandy Springs, 404/705–5900.*

12 *h-2*

ELEPHANT TEA CO.
Whether it's oolong you seek or herbal, this tea-obsessive shop has it. Choose from among 90 kinds of loose teas, tea accessories, and tea by the cup or pot. *Phipps Plaza, 3500 Peachtree Rd., Buckhead, 404/261–3004.*

12 *h-2*

Lenox Square, 2285 Peachtree Rd., Buckhead, 404/495–0760. MARTA: Lenox.

ethnic foods

5 *d-4*

EAST 28TH STREET MARKET
As Italian as it gets in Atlanta. Snap up the authentic crusty Italian bread as soon as it's brought out. There's also a good selection of imported pastas, olive oils, cheeses, and cured meats, including the perfect prosciutto. Top cooks

swear by the canned tomatoes and purees here. *2462 Jett Ferry Rd., Dunwoody, 770/392–1499.*

5 *e-6*

HONG KONG SUPERMARKET
Rice vermicelli, fresh frogs' legs, galangal root— if it's an ingredient in Asian cooking, you'll find it here. This full-service supermarket offers produce, meats, seafood, and all manner of grocery items imported from China, Vietnam, Thailand, Korea, Japan, and elsewhere in Asia. *4166 Buford Hwy., Doraville, 404/325–3999.*

12 *f-7*

LOS AMIGOS TORTILLA MANUFACTURING
Latino markets line the Buford Highway corridor in north Atlanta, but they buy their corn and flour tortillas here, where they're made fresh daily. There's also a limited selection of chips, salsa, jalapeños, and other Mexican specialties. *251 Armour Dr., Midtown, 404/876–8153.*

13 *c-6*

QUALITY KOSHER EMPORIUM
The meats are of the highest quality, and the choices in canned and dry goods are plentiful. Visit the deli for heat-and-eat items. *2153 Briarcliff Rd., Toco Hills, 404/636–1114.*

5 *b-5*

5942 Roswell Rd., Sandy Springs, 404/705–8643.

fish & seafood

12 *f-4*

ATLANTA FISH MARKET
The giant metal fish sculpture created a stir a few years back, but it's a handy landmark for this restaurant-cum-market. Squeeze past the throngs in the restaurant and choose live lobsters, Dungeness crabs, fresh grouper, or whatever else might be among the shop offerings of the day. You can also get to-go orders of most anything from the restaurant menu (*see* Chapter 1). *265 Pharr Rd., Buckhead, 404/240–6664.*

15 *a-2*

INLAND SEAFOOD
This major southeastern wholesaler has no retail storefront and accepts tele-

In case you want to see the world.

At American Express, we're here to make your

journey a smooth one. So we have over 1,700

travel service locations in over 130 countries

ready to help. What else would you expect from

the world's largest travel agency?

In case you want to be welcomed there.

We're here to see that you're always welcomed at

establishments everywhere. That's why millions

of people carry the American Express® Card – for

peace of mind, confidence, and security, around

the world or just around the corner.

do more **AMERICAN EXPRESS**

®

Cards

In case you're running low.

We're here to help with more than 190,000 Express

Cash locations around the world. In order to enroll,

just call American Express at 1 800 CASH-NOW

before you start your vacation.

do more

**Express
Cash**

And in case you'd rather be safe than sorry.

We're here with American Express® Travelers Cheques.

They're the safe way to carry money on your vacation,

because if they're ever lost or stolen you can get a refund,

practically anywhere or anytime. To find the nearest

place to buy Travelers Cheques, call 1 800 495-1153.

Another way we help you do more.

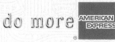

Travelers Cheques

phone orders only. But you're guaranteed a wide selection of fish, crustaceans, bivalves, or any other edible sea creature, flown in fresh daily. *1222 Menlo Dr., Midtown, 404/350–5850.*

gourmet foods

12 *h-2*

EATZI'S MARKET & BAKERY

The Dallas chain strides into Buckhead with wine and flowers, rotisserie chickens, and fresh produce. The heat-and-eat cases are jammed, and the bakery is particularly good. *3221 Peachtree Rd., Buckhead, 404/237–2266.*

15 *b-2*

STAR PROVISIONS

The top purveyor of gourmet products in the Southeast, this 4,000-square-ft store is sister and neighbor to Bacchanalia, one of the city's best restaurants. Offerings range from artisanal cheeses to Kobe beef to Petrossian caviar to 100-year-old balsamic vinegar. Be sure to browse through the selection of unusual kitchen accessories and the library of rare cookbooks. *1198 Howell Mill Rd., Midtown, 404/365–0410.*

13 *a-7*

HAPPY HERMAN'S

Head here for a glimpse of Atlanta's gourmet roots. This upscale grocery store sells fresh produce, wine, ready-to-eat foods, chocolates, and other gourmet items. *2299 Cheshire Bridge Rd., Cheshire Bridge, 404/321–3012.*

5 *d-2*

7921 North Point Pkwy, Alpharetta, 770/993–4770.

5 *b-5*

204 Johnson Ferry Rd., Sandy Springs, 404/256–3354.

8 *b-2*

WATERSHED

This trendy downtown Decatur shop sells the world's best egg salad sandwich, along with a selection of salads, sides, and desserts. *406 W. Ponce de Leon Ave., Decatur, 404/378–4900.*

health food

13 *a-7*

RETURN TO EDEN

The huge vitamin and supplement section is the draw at this totally vegetarian grocery. The produce is all organic and offered only in peak season (so you won't find pink strawberries in December). *2235 Cheshire Bridge Rd., Midtown, 404/320–3336.*

14 *a-4*

SEVANANDA COMMUNITY-OWNED NATURAL FOODS MARKET

From its roots as a food cooperative, this Little Five Points institution has grown into a sophisticated, well-run vegetarian grocery. A membership is $20 a year and provides a 5% discount each Tuesday. *467 Moreland Ave., Little Five Points, 404/681–2831.*

12 *h-2*

UNITY NATURAL FOODS

The location of a health-food store just south of the Buckhead bar district is only coincidental and not meant to be a statement on how the night owls should clean up their acts. Dietary supplements, organic produce, and free-range eggs and poultry round out the offerings. *2955 Peachtree Rd., Buckhead, 404/261–8776.*

13 *c-6*

WHOLE FOODS MARKET

This organic grocery chain has a Southern accent. So, you'll find a variety of vegetarian products, along with free-range chickens and eggs. The produce is superb and some of it from local organic farms. *2111 Briarcliff Rd., Toco Hills, 404/634–7800.*

meat & poultry

12 *f-3*

THE NEW YORKER DELI AND BUTCHER SHOP

Meat or seafood, New Yorker's got it or will find it for you. Call ahead for special orders such as crown roasts or aged prime rib. The deli features heat-and-eat entrées such as filet mignon and grilled salmon, as well as a selection of side dishes. *322 Pharr Rd., Buckhead, 404/240–0260.*

4 c-1

PATAK-BOHEMIA SAUSAGE CHALET

This storybook chalet on a country lane specializes in European processed meats. Cold cuts, bacon, sausages—80 varieties are made right here. The specialty is Eastern European treats such as moskowska and segalli. Also look for high-quality cuts of beef, pork and veal, from roasts to chops. *4107 Ewing Rd., Austell, 770/941–7993.*

11 g-5

SHIELD'S MARKET

An old-timey meat market in the best sense, Shield's is the name in aged beef in the area. *1554 N. Decatur Rd., Decatur, 404/377–0204.*

14 h-2

143 Sycamore St., Decatur, 404/377–0204.

nuts & seeds

8 e-1

STONE MOUNTAIN PECAN CO.

The orchards may be in south Georgia, but the processed pecans are right here, by the pound or the case, along with an assortment of other nuts and candies. *6565 James B. Rivers Dr., Stone Mountain, 770/469–8824.*

pasta & noodles

4 f-4

COSTA'S FRESH PASTA

Call ahead a day if you want something special—fresh tagliatelle, for instance. But Monday through Thursday, the Costas also sell their fresh pastas, including ravioli and tortellini, over the counter. *2045 Attic Pkwy., Kennesaw, 770/514–8814.*

produce

5 d-1

HARRY'S FARMERS MARKET

Don't let the term farmers market fool you. All three locations are clean, well lit, and indoors—basically, they're giant supermarkets. Stop in for great produce, a jar of Indian chutney, a Chianti Classico, or just a gallon of milk. *1180 Upper Hembree Road, Roswell, 770/664–6300.*

5 g-5

2025 Satellite Point, Duluth, 770/416–6900.

4 h-5

70 Powers Ferry Rd., Marietta, 770/578–4400.

12 d-7

HARRY'S IN A HURRY

Designed to appeal to commuters on the run, these stores feature the basics such as wine, flowers and cheese, plus a wide selection of prepared meals-to-go. *1875 Peachtree Rd., Buckhead, 404/352–7800.*

4 h-7

2939 Cobb Pkwy., Marietta, 770/541–9316.

14 a-3

1061 Ponce de Leon Rd., Virginia-Highland, 404/439–1100.

12 f-1

3804 Roswell Rd., Buckhead, 404/266–0800.

9 g-1

5380 Jonesboro Rd., Jonesboro, 404/361–7522.

5 d-4

1418 Dunwoody Village Pkwy., Dunwoody, 770/238–1400.

5 e-6

INTERNATIONAL FARMERS MARKET

You might be able to pick up cooking tips from a Thai restaurant owner as you examine the lemon grass stalks here. This full-scale farmer's market is all indoors and features many ethnic items and draws a large immigrant clientele. *5193 Peachtree Industrial Blvd., Chamblee, 770/455–1777.*

14 a-2

MORNINGSIDE FARMERS MARKET

The local farmers who set up in a Virginia-Highland parking lot each Saturday May through December are certified organic. They sell flowers, herbs, blueberries, heirloom tomatoes, and every other kind of produce that will grow in Georgia. Look for the lady selling heavenly homemade soaps. *1397 N. Highland Ave., Virginia-Highland, 770/788–8707.*

7 h-7

STATE FARMERS MARKET

The old-fashioned farmers' market, with pickup trucks spilling loads of zipper peas, is alive and well. Choose from a full range of produce, plants, and even mysterious southern cure-alls such as yellowroot. *16 Forest Pkwy., Forest Park, 404/675–1782.*

15 *g-6*

SWEET AUBURN CURB MARKET

Sweet Auburn was once the center of a bustling African-American business district. You'll find a taste of this past at this renovated urban bazaar, which offers fresh meats to Caribbean jerk spices to kaolin, the edible white clay. *209 Edgewood Ave., Sweet Auburn, 404/659–1665.*

8 *c-1*

YOUR DEKALB FARMERS MARKET

The dozens of immigrant cultures that inhabit the metro area are well represented in the exotic produce, the aisles of imported dry goods, the tanks of live fish, and on the name tags of the clerks listing all the languages they speak. *3000 E. Ponce de Leon Ave., Decatur, 404/377–6400.*

wines & spirits

2 *h-8*

BEVERAGE WAREHOUSE

For practical, everyday stocking up on beer, ale, wine, and hard liquor, these warehouse-style stores offer common brands at great prices. *11005 Alpharetta Hwy. two blocks north of the Mansell intersection, Roswell, 770/992–0007.*

5 *e-1*

10950 State Bridge Rd., Alpharetta, 770/569–2345.

5 *b-6*

BUCKHEAD FINE WINE

Proprietor Jack Dienier loves a good conversation about wine, and he specializes in designing wine cellars and racking systems then stocking them with the best vintages. If you're thinking about stocking a cellar, or just buying a great bottle of Burgundy or a Bordeaux, this is the place to come. *3906 Roswell Rd., Buckhead, 404/231–8566.*

8 *c-1*

DEKALB FARMERS' MARKET

The emphasis here is on great pricing and a wide range of wines. There's a

good selection of microbrew beers, too. *3000 East Ponce de Leon Ave., Decatur, 404/377–6400.*

5 *e-7*

EMBRY HILLS LIQUOR WAREHOUSE

The women who own this shop know a lot about wine, how to price it, and what's going to taste good with your selection. *3503 Chamblee Tucker Rd., Chamblee, 770/455–8549.*

15 *d-6*

HABERSHAM VINEYARDS AND WINERY

Georgia's own vineyards at Chateau Elan (near Braselton, just off I–85 N) produce wines that even the local connoisseurs are talking about pleasantly. *Underground Atlanta, 50 Upper Alabama St., Downtown, 404/522–9463. MARTA: Five Points.*

13 *a-7*

HAPPY HERMAN'S

Here's the place to find the merlot to put the finishing touch on the dinner you're preparing for your boss. The selection on California, Australian, and French wines is excellent, with many wines from small, exclusive vineyards. Expect to pay for the excellence, service, and variety, but you won't be sorry you did. *2299 Cheshire Bridge Rd., Midtown, 404/321–3012.*

5 *c-2*

7291 North Point Pkwy., Alpharetta, 770/993–4770.

5 *b-5*

204 Johnson Ferry Rd., Sandy Springs, 101/256–3351

12 *h-2*

IL CENTRO

Besides getting a glass of wine, here, you may order wines by the flight, that is, in series of three 2-ounce glasses. You can choose any combination of wines for your flight, or go for one of the three "set flights," with pre-selected wines chosen for comparison purposes, perhaps three chardonnays or three Italian white wines. This small space attracts the upscale shoppers of Phipps Plaza, as well as young couples on dates before or after catching a movie. A tasting menu of simple fare, such as pâté and hummus, changes weekly. You can also order from the coffee bar and nibble on desserts composed by the house pastry chef. *3500 Peachtree Rd., Phipps Plaza, Buckhead, 404/394–9313.*

7 *f-7*

KILROY'S PACKAGE STORE

Folks on the south side of town find that this store has the best prices and largest wine selection in the area. The entire staff is knowledgeable, but ask for Bill, whose in-depth experience will guide you to the perfect choice. *4879 Old National Highway, College Park, 404/768–3159.*

15 *e-3*

MAC'S

Midtowners shop here for its an excellent selection that is especially strong in California and French wines. They offer free wine consultation and will also do special events planning. *929 Spring St., Midtown, 404/872–4897. MARTA: Midtown.*

12 *f-3*

PEARSON'S

Very knowledgeable people shop here, so the staff keeps up on the latest offer-

ings in wines and spirits. The selections of single malt scotches, liqueurs, brandies, and dessert wines is excellent, as is the variety of wines from Europe, Australia, and the United States. There's a decent cigar selection, too. *3072 Early St., Buckhead, 404/231–8752.*

4 *g-4*

SHERLOCK'S BEER AND WINE WAREHOUSE

These two locations have been upgraded and expanded, and there's a fine selection of unusual offerings that include many German and Italian wines. *2156 Roswell Rd., Marietta, 770/971–6333.*

4 *f-3*

135 Ernest W. Barrett Pkwy., Kennesaw, 770/426–6744.

FRAMING

12 *f-3*

BA FRAMER

With more than 700 custom frames for you to choose from, BA Framer has one of the best selections in the city. An experienced staff is on hand to help you with your special framing needs, including shadow boxes and preservation framing. Be sure to check out the ready-framed pictures and mirrors that adorn the walls. *3145 Peachtree Rd., Buckhead, 404/237–3135. MARTA: Buckhead.*

5 *d-5*

4780 Ashford-Dunwoody Rd., Dunwoody, 770/396–1006.

14 *a-1*

1402 N. Highland Ave., Midtown, 404/815–8771.

5 *h-3*

5805 State Bridge Rd., Duluth, 770/497–9850.

4 *h-2*

2960 Shallowford Rd., Marietta, 770/977–8771.

6 *d-7*

1630 W. Scenic Hwy., Snellville, 770/982–1696.

12 *g-5*

FAST FRAME

For simple, practical frames to display your children's artwork or other basic framing needs there is no better place. Good quality at affordable prices. *2615*

ROADSIDE PRODUCE

Toco Hills Shopping Center, La Vista and North Druid Hills Rds., Toco Hills
The freshest produce, including great corn, tomatoes, and peaches, starts arriving in May and keeps coming until September.

Maple Drive, Buckhead
If you're looking for a tomato that really smacks your palate with dusky sweetness and summer twilight, head here.

Merchant's Walk, Hwy. 120 and Johnson Ferry Rd., East Marietta
This outdoor market has more fresh produce than any other place in town, along with fun things like stacks of cane sugar and bales of pine straw. Fabulous pumpkins and Christmas trees in December.

Mt. Vernon Hwy. and Sandy Springs Cir., Sandy Springs
Sweet corn is best when it's only hours old, which is why you should check out this popular truck stand for new shipments regularly.

Piedmont Rd., Buckhead, 404/261–1213.
MARTA: Lindbergh.

5 b-6

4920 Roswell Rd., Sandy Springs, 404/
252–9250.

8 a-1

2205 LaVista Rd., Toco Hills, 404/636–
2787.

5 d-2

1580 Holcomb Bridge Rd., Roswell, 770/
992–5545.

5 d-4

2090 Dunwoody Club Dr., Dunwoody,
770/399–5725.

6 a-4

2180 Pleasant Hill Rd., Duluth, 770/623–
1100.

12 e-6

THE FRAMERS

Specializing in customizing frames for
artwork, the Framers simultaneously
devote a good portion of their retail
space to original artwork. They maintain
a knowledgeable staff with an eye for
complementary framing and friendly
service. 2351 Peachtree Rd., Buckhead,
404/237–2888.

15 d-2

194 14th St., Midtown, 404/892–1271.

12 f-3

THE GREAT FRAME UP

For do-it-yourself framing, the Great
Frame Up allows to be as involved as
you want to be. Select your own frame
and mat, and then move over to the
workbench area to complete the job.
Employees can advise and assist as necessary, or even take the job out of your
hands if you find that you're in over your
head. 3085 Peachtree Rd., Buckhead, 404/
231–9754. MARTA: Buckhead.

15 g-2

985 Monroe Dr., Midtown, 404/892–3212.

5 b-5

220 Sandy Springs Cir., Sandy Springs,
404/255–1400.

14 f-1

2095 N. Decatur Rd., Decatur, 404/325–
5225.

5 f-4

3466 Holcomb Bridge Rd., Norcross, 770/
368–9015.

5 f-7

2138 Henderson Mill Rd., Northlake, 770/
939–7100.

5 d-7

HOUSE OF 10,000 PICTURE FRAMES

If it can be framed, they do it. Family
owned and operated for nearly three
decades, they devote 3,500 square ft of
retail space to their impressive selection
of specialty frames and custom molding. Customers like the prompt service
and attention to detail. 3680 Clairmont
Rd., Chamblee, 770/457–5862.

4 g-5

MARIETTA FRAME & ART

Patrons swear by this place for its excellent selection and customer service.
Employing an expert staff that works
with the customer in determining just
the right form and style for presentation, Marietta Frame & Art puts an
emphasis on customer satisfaction that
is unmatched in the area. 1171 S. Marietta Pkwy., Marietta, 678/355–1445.

GIFTS & SOUVENIRS

14 a-2

BACK TO SQUARE ONE

In a neighborhood consistently abuzz
with hipness, Back to Square One stays
blissfully low key, where handmade picture frames and eclectic birdfeeders
share store space with a cooler stashed
with homemade ice cream. 1054 N.
Highland Ave., Virginia-Highland, 404/
815–9970.

12 f-3

BOXWOODS GARDENS & GIFTS

You can get a little turned around in the
maze of rooms in an endearing cottage
in the heart of Buckhead. Each room is
filled with a different kind of gift—one
with garden-related good and another
with silver tea sets and jewelry boxes.
100 E. Andrews Dr., Buckhead, 404/233–
3400.

10 e-4

THE COUNTRY MOUSE

The Country Mouse fits into its genteel
setting on a classic town square with
folksy home décor items and collectible

figurines. *10 Macon St., McDonough, 770/957–0278.*

8 *e-1*

HOME SWEET HOME GIFTS & COLLECTIBLES

This 1920s-era house on Main Street in Stone Mountain Village is the place to get Georgia souvenirs, toys, and collectibles. *987 Main St., Stone Mountain, 770/413–6200.*

13 *c-6*

JUDAICA CORNER

Don't let its nondescript locale fool you. Judaica Corner is one of the best places in town to get quality-crafted Jewish-related items like handmade menorahs and exquisite seder plates as well as books and music. *2185 Briarcliff Rd., Toco Hills, 404/636–2473.*

14 *a-2*

METROPOLITAN DELUXE

It's deluxe alright. Everything screams primo, from the clever cards and books to the funky picture frames, games and martini-theme bar items. *1034 N. Highland Ave., Virginia-Highland, 404/892–9337.*

5 *h-3*

PARSONS ACE HARDWARE

Parsons has been family owned for all of its 75 years and this heritage is reflected in attentive service and a personally selected range of the utilitarian to the aesthetic, from hardware and gifts to original art. *2780 Buford Hwy., Duluth, 770/623–9976.*

12 *g-3*

PERIDOT DISTINCTIVE GIFTS

For gift givers who don't want to give the usual picture frame (although you'll find those here, too), Peridot tries to suit the against-the-grain aesthete. For the mom-to-be, how about a baby burrito, a blanket with a baby outfit wrapped inside? Home décor and kitchen items are especially appealing. *514 E. Paces Ferry Rd., Buckhead, 404/261–7028.*

5 *b-7*

PHOENIX & DRAGON

This is a great place for anyone interested in metaphysics, the spiritual or the supernatural. Items range from gurgling tabletop fountains to crystals, Buddhas to Wicca books. *5531 Roswell Rd., Sandy Springs, 404/255–5207.*

9 *g-2*

ROAD TO TARA GIFT SHOP

The place to go for *Gone With the Wind* memorabilia—after all, the grandparents of author Margaret Mitchell lived near the Jonesboro location and she spent a good deal of time here as a child. *104 N. Main St., Jonesboro, 770/210–1017.*

15 *f-4*

659 Peachtree St., 404/897–1940. MARTA: North Avenue.

15 *e-6*

50 Upper Alabama St. SW, 404/521–2946. MARTA: Five Points.

14 *g-3*

SEVENTEEN STEPS

The fun array of items runs the gamut from bar utensils to kids' stuff. *205 E. Ponce de Leon Ave., Decatur, 404/377–7564. MARTA: Decatur.*

14 *b-8*

VERDI O

Like the East Atlanta Village where it's located, Verdi O traffics in edgy cool, with unique home accents that break out of the pre-fab mold. *492B Flat Shoals Ave., East Atlanta, 404/880–0708.*

5 *b-5*

VERONICA'S ATTIC

Billing itself as Atlanta's best-kept secret, Veronica's Attic has managed to become anything but. It's a favorite for its selection of unique clothing and jewelry. Look for a variety of beaded items, especially the beaded handbags. *220 Sandy Springs Cir., Sandy Springs, 404/257–1409.*

HOME FURNISHINGS

12 *h-2*

CRATE & BARREL

Remember receiving the catalog in the mail and wishing they had a retail outlet so you could do touch and feel things with the merchandise? Voilà! Here are the answers to your dreams. Don't look for Wedgwood here, but if you need well designed, elegant, and casual things for your table, this is the place. Everything is standard stock, too, so if something breaks, replacing it is easy. *Lenox Square, 3393 Peachtree Rd., Buckhead, 404/239–0008. MARTA: Lenox.*

5 *c-5*
Perimeter Mall, 4400 Ashford-Dunwoody Rd., Dunwoody, 770/671–9797. MARTA: Dunwoody.

12 *h-2*
PIER ONE
Low prices and nice quality tableware and accessories have been spicing up dining rooms, patios and pool areas around Atlanta for years. The seasonal sales are terrific, especially after the December holidays. A cautionary note about purchases such as table mats, however—they shrink. Best to have them dry-cleaned, or wash in cold water and hang to dry. *3435 Lenox Rd., Buckhead, 404/233–1080. MARTA: Lenox.*

5 *g-5*
5795 Jimmy Carter Blvd., Norcross, 770/840–9545.

5 *e-1*
6010 North Point Pkwy., Alpharetta, 770/569–1133.

12 *g-8*
1544 Piedmont Rd., Midtown, 404/881–6549.

12 *e-6*
2298 Peachtree Rd., Brookwood, 404/355–1832.

6 *a-4*
2131 Pleasant Hill Rd., Duluth, 770/497–0513.

architectural artifacts

12 *g-3*
ARCHITECTURAL ACCENTS
The old Sealtest dairy now houses French limestone fireplaces, wonderful doors, massive wrought-iron gates, English judge's paneling, and other European and American artifacts. *2711 Piedmont Rd., Buckhead, 404/266–8700.*

5 *d-7*
METROPOLITAN ARTIFACTS
This 25,000-square-ft wonderland of architectural remnants will astonish you with its variety—paneled rooms in their entirety, acres of wrought and iron, restaurant-hotel decor. *4783 Peachtree Rd., Chamblee, 770/986–0007. MARTA: Chamblee.*

14 *a-5*
THE WRECKING BAR
Since 1969, the components of houses, hotels, and commercial buildings have found their way to this decaying Beaux Arts mansion, where everything is cleaned and restored to operating condition, good as new. Prices may cause some hard swallowing, but old-fashioned quality can be priceless. *292 Moreland Ave., Little Five Points, 404/525–0468.*

bedroom & bath

5 *g-6*
CLASSICAL BRASS AND IRON BEDS ETC.
This outlet store, in business since 1972, carries 450 different styles, and their prices are well below more expensive boutiques. Mattresses and other pieces you might need for the bedroom are available as well. Conveniences include a layaway plan, 90 days of interest-free credit, and seven-days-a-week shopping. *6624 Dawson Blvd., Norcross, 770/441–2529.*

5 *g-6*
THE GREAT FUTON STORE
The exclusive Atlanta distributor of Gold Bond futons offers many other brands of this Japanese bedding solution as well, in a variety of sizes, colors and prices. You can get futon frames here, too, even a Charleston iron rail four-poster. *6576 Dawson Blvd., Norcross, 770/448 9200.*

12 *d-7*
THE HEIRLOOM IRON BED COMPANY
You can choose from a reproduction of a classic antique design or have a bed designed and built to your tastes. Then, you can outfit your choice with the finest linens, including those from Anichini, the Purists, Ygle, Lisa Galimberti, and Ann Gish. Trouble is, when you climb into your masterpiece, you probably won't ever want to get out! *2140 Peachtree Rd., Brookwood, 404/352–3132.*

5 *c-1*
10800 Alpharetta Hwy., Alpharetta, 770/993–7249.

4 f-4

65 Church St., Marietta, 770/514–0556.

4 g-5

ORIGINAL MATTRESS FACTORY

This outlet makes mattresses right on the premises of its seven outlets, saving you money because you're buying direct. Most models are available immediately, and coming up with an odd size never seems to pose a problem. *1335 Capital Cir., Marietta, 770/612–8117.*

5 d-2

1605 Mansell Rd., Alpharetta, 678/461–8755.

6 a-8

5370 Stone Mountain Hwy., Stone Mountain, 770/498–1009.

6 a-4

3360 Satellite Blvd., Duluth, 770/232–0770.

4 e-3

667 Ernest W. Barrett Pkwy., Kennesaw, 770/420–5303.

9 g-1

6735 Jonesboro Rd., Morrow, 678/422–7779.

5 e-6

WALLBEDZZZ

In order to find the hidden bed systems on display in these model rooms you'll have to look behind bi-fold doors, pull-down panels above sofas, swing-out bookcases, and engage in some other sleuthing. In fact, the solutions are so ingenious you may be inspired to create another guest room just about anywhere in your house. *3838 Green Industrial Way, Chamblee, 770/455–7662.*

carpets & rugs

12 f-3

AFGHANISTAN'S NOMADIC RUGS

Come with an open mind and a free afternoon. The proprietor is one of the most knowledgeable dealers around, and he will educate you with tales of the nomadic tribes from whom he buys his colorful wares—and probably send you home with a piece you'll cherish forever. *3219 Cains Hill Pl., Buckhead, 404/261–7259.*

8 d-2

CARPET MILL OUTLET

The largest selection of carpets just about anywhere in the metro area includes broadlooms for less than $5 per yard in hundred of colors, dozens of styles and from many mills. They will give you a list of installers. *3805 Covington Hwy., Decatur, 404/286–5999.*

7 e-4

Winn Dixie Shopping Plaza, 2076 Headland Dr., East Point, 404/763–0776.

7 h-7

7659 Tara Blvd., Jonesboro, 770/472–4545.

12 h-5

THE HOME DEPOT

Atlanta is near the epicenter of U.S. carpet manufacturing, Dalton, Georgia, and it's also near the corporate headquarters of this national chain, in Smyrna, Georgia. Combine these two facts and it's not surprising that the 30-some Atlanta-area home depot outlets are excellent sources for a wide range of carpets in every price range and style, from wool sisal to custom rugs. The sales staff is extremely knowledgeable and will stand behind the recommended installers. *815 Sidney Marcus Blvd., Buckhead, 404/231–1411.*

5 e-5

4343 Tilly Mill Rd., Doraville, 770/452–8858.

5 f-8

2295 Lawrenceville Hwy., Decatur, 404/315–0015.

5 c-1

870 Woodstock Rd., Roswell, 678/461–0155.

6 d-7

1670 Scenic Hwy., Snellville, 770/982–6166.

8 a-8

2034 Mt. Zion Rd., Morrow, 770/478–9990.

12 f-4

SHARIAN

The Sharian family has presented Atlanta with the finest in Oriental rugs since 1931. An expert service department washes and cleans carpets with classic methods used in ancient days and will match yarns and colors to reweave them using centuries-old hand-knotting methods. *Atlanta Decorative Arts Center*

(ADAC), 351 Peachtree Hills Ave., Buckhead, 404/261–2968.

14 f-3
368 W. Ponce de Leon Ave., Decatur, 404/373–2274.

ceramic tiles

5 b-5
COLOR TILE
On hand at four area locations are every kind of tile and flooring alternative you could possibly need, often at very reasonable prices, along with all the attendant material and equipment you need to lay it down with. Though service is uneven, when the sales people are good, they're very good, and they will lead you through the huge selection and instruct you on minute aspects of do-it-yourself installation. 6204 Roswell Rd., Sandy Springs, 404/256–2331.

6 a-4
2131 Pleasant Hill Rd., Duluth, 770/495–1800.

8 d-1
4959 Memorial Dr., Decatur, 404/256–2331.

5 d-2
1475 Holcomb Bridge Rd., Roswell, 770/650–8250.

5 c-5
HOME DEPOT EXPO
The tile and flooring section is especially wonderful at these warehouse-style designer outlets of the popular chain. You can lose yourself in marbles and limestone and easily talk yourself into re-doing that little entry area in a rosy marble. Look for other locations to open soon. 1201 Hammond Dr., across from Perimeter Mall, Dunwoody, 770/913–0111. MARTA: Dunwoody.

12 f-3
TRADITIONS IN TILE
Traditions at these four outlets include providing an excellent product line— tiles, limestone, marble, antique terra cotta, travertine, and mosaics from Italy, Spain, and the United States—along with attentive service, including a free design service and company-backed installation and repair. 3210 Roswell Rd., Buckhead, 404/239–9186.

6 c-2
1256 Oakbrook Dr., Suwanee, 770/448–8133.

5 d-2
11350 Old Roswell Rd., Roswell, 770/343–9104.

4 g-5
4041B Kingston Ct., Marietta, 770/951–1416.

9 e-3
692 N. Glynn St., Fayetteville, 770/461–8141.

5 g-6
ZUMPANO ENTERPRISES
The largest selection of ceramic tile, porcelain, and natural stone in the Southeast attracts designers, architects, and homeowners looking for the best. Appliances and fixtures are available, too, so it's possible to outfit an entire kitchen or bath at the six area stores. 6354 Warren Dr., Norcross, 770/449–3528.

12 h-4
764 Miami Cir., Buckhead, 404/237–6001. MARTA: Lindbergh.

4 g-4
562 Wylie Rd., Marietta, 770/423–0599.

9 g-1
7411 Tara Blvd., Jonesboro, 770/471–0666.

china, glassware, porcelain, pottery, silver

12 f-3
BEVERLY BREMER SILVER SHOP
Nationally acclaimed as a resource for flat and holloware, Bremer's shop contains floor-to-ceiling silver objects. Some of them are exotic, some ordinary, but all are polished (how they remain so is a mystery). If you're missing pieces of your pattern, Beverly Bremer will find them—or convince you to mix and match. The chance to visit with her is alone worth the trip to this shop. 3164 Peachtree Rd., Buckhead, 404/261–4009.

12 h-3
CHARLES WILLIS ATLANTA
Come here for a quiet, hushed atmosphere; individual service; and everything you could possibly want or need in china, crystal, and silver, from Baccarat through Waterford and Wedgwood. Add gracious return policies and a hos-

pitable sales staff, and it's easy to see why Atlanta brides register here first. *465 E. Paces Ferry Rd., Buckhead, 404/233–9487.*

5 *b-5*

FRAGILE

Browse to your heart's content at this warehouse-style store where the selection is huge and great merchandise is to be had at a fair price. Selections of crystal goblet and tumblers, china, and flatware are especially good. There's a section for art glass, too. The store has a bridal registry, gift-wraps for free, and ships anywhere. *175 Mt. Vernon Hwy., Sandy Springs, 404/257–1323.*

12 *e-6*

H. MOOG

If you want to know where a piece of porcelain came from, where it was made, how much it's worth, or where to repair it, the Moogs, in business for more than 30 years, will have the answer. Plus, their selection of Chinese Export, English, and French porcelains will take your breath away. You can rest assured on authenticity and reliability in an increasingly scam-filled market. *2300 Peachtree Rd., Buckhead, 404/351–2200.*

12 *e-6*

JANE J. MARSDEN INTERIORS AND ANTIQUES

Famous for their porcelains, Marsden and her family own and anchor the 2300 Peachtree complex. Mother and daughter are interior designers, too, in case you need more than just an exquisite piece of Rose Medallion. *2300 Peachtree Rd., Buckhead, 404/355–1288.*

12 *h-2*

MACY'S

Watch for the frequent one-day sales in the china-crystal departments at the eight Atlanta branches of this New York–based department store. You're likely to walk away with a great price on the Ralph Lauren crystal tumbler or Waterford flutes you've been craving or, since Macy's carries everything from high-end to low-end merchandise, a set of raspberry-red plastic goblets for the poolside. *Lenox Square, 3393 Peachtree Rd., Buckhead, 404/231–8985. MARTA: Lenox.*

furniture & accessories

12 *e-6*

AXIS TWENTY

Falling somewhere between art gallery and contemporary design studio, Axis Twenty is the city's cutting-edge showcase for artists working in wood and metal furniture and accessories. Established craftspeople as well as emerging designers are represented, and the store provides a full-service interior design service. *200 Peachtree Hills Ave., Buckhead, 404/261–4022.*

5 *b-4*

BABES & KIDS FURNITURE

Some clever merchandiser realized that children grow up, and here's a store filled with furniture designed to be added to, stacked on, and rearranged to meet changing needs and interests. Accessories such as bedding, bookends, student lamps, and computer desks are at hand, too. *Parkaire Landing, 4880 Lower Roswell Rd., at the intersection of Johnson Ferry Rd., Marietta, 770/565–1420.*

5 *c-6*

BELLINI

This furniture for infants, children, and teens is beautifully designed and crafted out of solid wood in the best old-world traditions. Considering the quality, prices are quite reasonable, and you can be guaranteed the high chair or stroller you purchase will be around long enough to become a family heirloom. *5285 Roswell Rd., Sandy Springs, 404/851–1588.*

5 *d-2*

BEVERLY HALL FURNITURE GALLERIES

There's a great deal to be said about furniture that can be handed down to grandchildren, and Beverly Hall has that, and more. Upholstered pieces are endowed with trademarks of old-fashioned quality that include well-tied springs and down cushions. Fine accessories are also available, along with a great interior design service. *740 Holcomb Bridge Rd., Roswell, 770/642–6641.*

12 *d-7*

200 Bennett St., Buckhead, 404/351–7267.

12 *g-4*

2789 Piedmont Rd., Buckhead, 404/261–7580.

`5` g-6

BY DESIGN INTERNATIONAL FURNITURE

Even in traditional Atlanta, this company, which focuses on contemporary design, has managed to do well by virtue of its practical, clean approach to furniture and accessories and its affordable prices. Many of their pieces require assembly, but the store will do it for you. The home-office departments are especially good, and the warehouse in the Norcross location supplies terrific deals on overstocks and damaged pieces—treasure hunts may yield $500 pieces marked down to $5. *6348 Dawson Blvd., Norcross, 770/840–8832.*

`12` h-7

1747 Cheshire Bridge Rd., Midtown, 404/607–9098.

`12` g-7

DOMUS

A group of architects founded Domus in 1972 with the goal of bringing great design at reasonable prices to Atlantans. We've responded very well to the well-crafted, solid wood furniture that's primarily of Italian and European design along postmodern lines, which means it references classical style without imitating it and makes you feel comfortable and *avant* at the same time. *1919 Piedmont Rd., Midtown, 404/872–1050.*

`12` g-3

ETHAN ALLEN

You can furnish every room in the house at this national name in top-of-the-line traditional home furnishings; in fact, a recently expanded sections for kids' furniture gives new status to the young ones' quarters. Sales staff, delivery and return policies, and financing options are all customer friendly; procedures for delivery, returns, and financing are customer friendly; and the store offers an in-house design service. *3221 Peachtree Rd., Buckhead, 404/816–5848.*

`5` e-1

6751 North Point Mall Pkwy., Alpharetta, 770/664–9770.

`6` a-4

1630 Pleasant Hill Rd., Duluth, 770/717–7733.

`4` e-3

1005 Ernest W. Barrett Pkwy., Kennesaw, 770/795–0034.

`4` h-6

2205 Cobb Pkwy., Smyrna, 770/953–3320.

`4` g-5

FLACK'S INTERIORS

Hilda Flack carved a niche for herself by marketing her well-designed traditional furnishings to those who enjoy fine furniture but can't necessarily afford expensive designers. She carries such designers as Ralph Lauren along with her own line of accessories, and she offers 40% off manufacturers' prices. Design services come at no additional charge, and the accommodating staff will happily assist you in choosing an accessory or a whole house full of furniture. *2999 Cobb Pkwy., Smyrna, 770/952–6599.*

`5` d-2

1500 Holcomb Bridge Rd., Roswell, 770/992–7121.

`4` f-3

FURNITURE CRAFTSMEN

Welcome to 40,000 square ft of furniture. Top-of-the-line furniture and bottom-line discounts have kept this business in business for more than five decades. *1700 White Cir., Marietta, 770/427–4205.*

`5` g-6

GEORGIA BABY AND KIDS

If you don't live in Gwinnett County it's well worth the trek out to this huge warehouse filled with Atlanta's largest selection of nursery and children's furniture, including more than 6,000 bedding sets. Many of the beds are designed so they start out as cribs, can be converted into youth beds, then to kid-size couches. *6410 Dawson Blvd., Lilburn, 770/448–2455.*

`4` h-6

HAVERTY'S

This locally owned and operated firm has been in business for more than 115 years, keeping its products affordable and solidly in the middle of the road for design. You can find everything except the kitchen sink and wall coverings at metro stores. At Haverty's you can get every possible kind of furnishing for every room you have, and on-staff designers accessorize it with taste. *2079 Cobb Pkwy., Smyrna, 770/953–2160.*

5 *c-5*

132 Perimeter Center W, Dunwoody, 770/ 352–0901.

5 *e-1*

6731 North Point Pkwy., Alpharetta, 770/ 442–2810.

5 *f-8*

4013 LaVista Rd., Northlake, 770/491– 0536.

6 *a-4*

3380 Satellite Blvd., Duluth, 770/497– 0567.

6 *d-7*

2297 Stone Mountain Hwy., Snellville, 770/972–0564.

12 *g-3*

HORIZON PACIFIC HOME

Exotic, extraordinary furnishings from Pacific Rim countries fill this store's huge showrooms to overflowing, and your cultural horizons will expand just by walking through this collection of Oriental carpets, architectural artifacts, rich leather sofas, chairs and chaises, and beautiful rattan basketry. *3232 Peachtree Rd., Buckhead, 404/352–9990. MARTA: Buckhead.*

5 *g-6*

HOUSE OF DENMARK

The furniture here—which leans toward modular bedroom, dining room, and home-office pieces in teak and rose-wood as well as in glass and medal— shows off the latest innovations in Danish design. Prices, and quality along with them, range from low to high, and much of the stock comes as assemble-it-yourself kits. *6248 Dawson Blvd., Norcross, 770/449–5740.*

12 *g-3*

HUFF FURNITURE

Character rules! Mr. Huff has designed and made his own furniture for more than 30 years, and his designs are dramatic and distinctive, and often wonderfully whimsical and wildly contemporary. The store's worth a visit even if you're not in the market for furnishings. *3178 Peachtree Rd., Buckhead, 404/261–7636. MARTA: Buckhead.*

15 *g-2*

INNOVATIONS

These sofas and chairs are overstuffed and comfy and come in jazzy colors or muted tones; the overall look is elegant yet casual; and the prices affordable. Especially popular are the classic designs from such earlier eras as the 1940s and '50s. *1011 Monroe Dr., Midtown, 404/881–8111.*

5 *g-6*

6218 Dawson Blvd., Norcross, 770/449– 1500.

5 *a-7*

MATTHEWS FURNITURE

The glittering Waterford chandeliers overhead and plush Oriental carpets underfoot transport visitors to worlds far beyond the ordinary shopping center in which this Atlanta landmark happens to reside. The collections reflect an English heritage with some French and Italian influences, and the woods are primarily mahogany and fine fruitwoods. Accessories include exquisite tapestries and paintings. If you're looking for furniture that you will leave to future generations, this is the place to find it. The store offers a complimentary in-home design service as well as free local delivery and installation. *West Paces Ferry Shopping Center, 1240 W. Paces Ferry Rd., 404/237–8271.*

5 *e-1*

RHODES

It's hard to imagine a home in Atlanta without at least something from this multistore chain, which showcases furnishings from such makers as Henredon, Kincaid, Broyhill, Bernhardt, and La-Z-Boy, along with bedding from Sealy and Simmons. This sturdy, good-looking furniture is available in a full range of fabrics and finishes. *6050 North Point Pkwy., Alpharetta, 770/475–1656.*

5 *f-6*

4363 Northeast Expressway Access Rd., Doraville, 770/934–9350.

8 *c-2*

3655 Memorial Dr., Decatur, 404/289– 2136.

5 *d-5*

4175 Ashford-Dunwoody Rd., Dunwoody, 770/395–1812.

4 *h-7*

2540 Cumberland Blvd., Smyrna, 770/ 434–8911.

6 *a-4*

2340 Pleasant Hill Rd., Duluth, 770/476– 1890.

12 h-2

STOREHOUSE

This locally owned and operated franchise has successfully expanded throughout the Southeast for very good reasons: great looks, affordable prices, and varied styles, along with convenient locations and good management. The idea is to buy a plain bookcase or storage unit, then add moldings and accessories to suit your taste. Storehouse operates clearance centers in Buckhead and Norcross, where overstocks, floor samples, and slightly damaged merchandise are piled on top of each other, giving you the opportunity to hunt for treasures. *Lenox Square, 3393 Peachtree Rd., Buckhead, 404/261–3482. MARTA: Lenox.*

5 b-5

6277 Roswell Rd., Sandy Springs, 404/ 256–3844.

5 e-1

North Point Mall, 1100 North Point Cir., Alpharetta, 770/754–5590.

12 f-3

3106 Early St., Buckhead. MARTA: Buckhead.

5 g-6

6368 Northeast Expressway Access Rd., Norcross, 770/446–2646.

12 g-4

STYLUS

If you're hooked on wild color, interesting shapes, and a great look for the year 2050, get on in here. These pieces may have begun with a basic shape, but somewhere along the way, the lines got popped out, curved, imploded, and serpentined. No shape or function goes unexamined or taken for granted. Euro styling and a wealth of interesting fabrics and finishes bring these distinctive pieces from Stylus in line with your existing decor. *3097 Piedmont Rd., Buckhead, 404/231–5888.*

5 g-6

6358 Dawson Blvd., Norcross, 770/409– 3204.

lamps & lighting

15 c-2

THE BIG CHANDELIER

It's the Big Showroom, too, loaded with antique chandeliers and lights. From the street, the myriad twinklings of antique crystal will draw you in, and once you're there, you'll find exactly the right lighting for your home, whether it's old or new. *484 14th St., Midtown, 404/872–3332.*

15 c-2

GEORGIA LIGHTING

If you can imagine it lit, and whether you're talking about atmospheric outdoor illumination or lighting for your art collection, this firm can do the job. Expect to walk around these stores with your neck craned, because there are hundreds of chandeliers and hanging fixtures to examine, often in a multiplicity of colors and finishes. One section in the main showroom of the Midtown store also carries fine European antiques and lighting fixtures to match. *530 14th St., Midtown, 404/875–4754.*

5 c-2

1207 Alpharetta St., Roswell, 770/552– 5438.

9 f-1

735 Hwy. 138, Riverdale, 770/994–0138.

6 d-7

2340 Ronald Reagan Pkwy., north of Hwy 78 outside I–285, Snellville, 770/979– 0146.

12 h-4

HIGHLIGHTERS

If you've been impressed with the incredible things European designers are doing with contemporary lighting, you're in luck. Highlighters can supply you with those sleek, très chic European designs from Artemide, Flos, Leucos, and others and help you create stunning lighting environments. The shop also carries many glass fixtures from Murano, the famous glass-making island in the Venetian lagoon. *690 Miami Cir., Buckhead, 404/264–1599. MARTA: Lindbergh.*

12 h-4

HOUSE OF THEBAUT

For more than 30 years, Hedy Thebaut has led lighting trends in Buckhead and environs. She's mastered the art of making antique Chinese Export porcelain vases into lamps and created new ways to look at old dated lamps by rebuilding and restyling them. She sells antique, custom-built and replica lamps as well as a selection of interesting shades, too. *674 Miami Cir., Buckhead, 404/261–4166. MARTA: Lindbergh.*

15 b-2

LAMP ARTS

Have you lost a couple of crystals off your dining room chandelier? You'll probably find replacements here, along with all the other parts you need to make or repair a lighting fixture or lamp. Ask to see the back room, where they will sell slightly damaged custom shades for $15 to $25. *1199 Howell Mill Rd., Chattahoochee Industrial District, 404/352–5211.*

12 g-3

LIGHT BULBS UNLIMITED

Visit this store for fabulous neon extravaganzas in gorgeous colors, for witty ways to install low-voltage halogen lights, for European lighting and fiber optics. Because they specialize in hard-to-find bulbs, you'll be able to find any odd thing you need for fluorescent, tungsten, aquarium, marine, plant, photo, and health lighting equipment. They'll do neon light repairs, too. *3171 Peachtree Rd., Buckhead, 404/261–3023. MARTA: Buckhead.*

5 e-6

SHARON'S HOUSE OF LAMPS AND SHADES

These locations provide Atlantans easy access to more than 15,000 square ft of lamps, shades, chandeliers, and lighting accessories. Each store has a complete parts and repair center and a courteous staff that knows about proportion and scale when trying to find the right shade for the lamp or vice versa. *5544 Peachtree Industrial Blvd., Chamblee, 770/455–0135.*

5 d-1

10887 Alpharetta Hwy., Roswell, 770/587–4403.

5 b-6

SUNLIGHTING LAMP AND SHADE CENTER

Have you ever thought you could design a better lamp than the ones you see in stores? Here's your chance. The staff here will make lamp bases to your specifications, custom stain or paint them, and add such finishing touches as gold or silver leaf or whatever else suits your fancy. This is a great place to bring a lamp for restyling or a chandelier for retwinkling. *4990 Roswell Rd., Sandy Springs, 404/257–0043.*

paint & wallpaper

5 g-6

JUST WALLPAPER

Although you'll find more than 5,000 patterns from which to choose, this store is blessedly well organized. Just tell the helpful staff members what it is you want—whether it's Grecian columns on faux marble or a cowboy theme—and they will direct you to the right section. Everything on the floor will be in stock; you can make a decision and carry home what you need the same day. *6218 Dawson Blvd., Norcross, 770/409–1992.*

4 h-4

2187 Roswell Rd., Marietta, 770/509–1982.

5 c-5

1155 Mt. Vernon Hwy., Dunwoody, 770/393–4882.

8 a-8

1999 Mt. Zion Rd., Morrow, 770/477–2772.

5 c-2

MARTIN SENOUR PAINTS

This is the only manufacturer of the official authentic Williamsburg paint colors, which are replicas of the colors found inside and on the exterior of the famous buildings in the Virginia town now patiently restored to Colonial glory. They have other colors, too, of course, by the thousands, as well as stains, primers, custom colors, and textures. *1255A Alpharetta St., Roswell, 770/998–2998.*

12 f-3

MYRON DWOSKINS WALLCOVERINGS, INC.

The sales staff in these stores know their merchandise, and they are dedicated to helping you find the right paper in the right quantity. They'll also direct you to their excellent selection of discontinued and overstocked merchandise. *211 Pharr Rd., Buckhead, 404/231–5880.*

6 a-4

3512 Satellite Blvd., Duluth, 770/623–1937.

9 e-4

372 N. Glynn St., Fayetteville, 770/460–0593.

5 b-4

4880 Lower Roswell Rd., Marietta, 770/973–3955.

5 c-2

1211 Alpharetta St., Roswell, 770/587–4711.

5 d-2

1570 Holcomb Bridge Rd., Roswell, 770/641–7818.

5 a-7

SHERWIN WILLIAMS

"Ask Sherwin Williams," suggests the advertising. If you do, they will answer with fine quality, good prices, and the exclusive paint colors coordinating with floor and wallcoverings. 3519 Northside Pkwy., Buckhead, 404/885–5500.

5 f-4

3925 Holcomb Bridge Rd., Norcross, 770/449–7993.

5 d-8

2460 N. Druid Hills Rd., Brookhaven, 404/633–6818.

5 b-5

245 Johnson Ferry Rd., Sandy Springs, 404/257–0514.

5 d-6

5517 Peachtree Industrial Blvd., Chamblee, 770/451–0301.

6 c-3

2017 Lawrenceville-Suwanee Rd., Lawrenceville, 770/962–5294.

rentals

5 f-6

AARON RENTS & SELLS FURNITURE

Aaron can install comfy furnishings in your new digs or office the day after you order them, and make them available on short- or long-term leases. The appliances you need are here, too, along with some electronics. A rent-to-buy policy and great prices on used furniture make Aaron one of the most successful national franchises in the business. 4194B Northeast Expressway Access Rd., Doraville, 770/458–6131.

12 g-6

2173 Piedmont Rd., Buckhead, 404/873–1455.

4 g-6

1710 S. Cobb Pkwy, Marietta, 770/952–7444.

8 a-8

1115 Mt. Zion Rd., Morrow, 770/968–0810.

wicker

5 h-6

PARR'S

Since 1984, Parr's has offered Atlantans competitive prices on a huge selection of wicker, rattan, and outdoor furniture. The store carries some unusual styles and colors, along with sturdy, traditional fare. 3086 Lawrenceville Hwy., Lilburn, 700/923–3153.

3 h-6

3022 Peachtree Industrial Blvd., Buford, 678/482–8008.

2 h-8

512 North Main Street (Hwy. 9), Alpharetta, 770/664–6291.

5 d-1

ROSWELL RATTAN

This tasteful shop arranges its product lines (all of which are top quality and available in a wide range of colors and designs) in home-style settings. So, you can see how the rattan and wicker pieces you like will actually look in the bedroom or on the patio. 11230 Alpharetta Hwy., between Mansell and Upper Hembree Rds., Roswell, 770/442–0237.

HOUSEWARES & HARDWARE

5 c-5

ACE HARDWARE

A few years ago, Ace found itself competing with Home Depot and determined that personal service would provide the leading edge. The strategy worked. Ace personnel know their stock and how to install and use the products they sell. They also have an excellent selection, and since the stock varies quite a bit from location to location, if one Ace doesn't have what you need, another may. 8010 Roswell Rd., Dunwoody, 770/394–5559.

12 g-3

THE CONTAINER STORE

A visit to this store will no doubt convince you that your CDs should be stored more efficiently, that your kid's old toys could live in a sturdy cardboard box until the next tag sale, that your kitchen cupboards could really benefit from a new design system. Designs for most of the products are jazzy, modern, and colorful, and you'll discover storage solutions for things you didn't even know needed storing. Look here for great back-to-school supplies and the best after-Christmas wrapping paper sale in town. *3255 Peachtree Rd., on the south corner of Piedmont Rd., Buckhead, 404/261–4776. MARTA: Buckhead.*

5 *c-5*

120 Perimeter Center W, Sandy Springs, 770/351–0065. MARTA: Dunwoody.

14 *a-2*

HIGHLAND HARDWARE

It's more than a hardware store—it's a legend. People from all over the world buy woodworking tools and other merchandise from the catalog, but visiting this century-old store, with its high molded tin ceilings and wood floors, is an experience in itself. Highland stocks wonderful annuals and perennials, as well as all manner of regular hardware. *1045 N. Highland Ave., Virginia-Highland, 404/872–4466.*

4 *h-7*

LECHTER'S

If you want something for your kitchen, here's the place to find it. These stores are especially good at offering colorful, inexpensive options for spicing up your utilitarian spaces with storage containers and gadgets. *Cumberland Mall, I–285 and I–75 at Cobb Pkwy., Smyrna, 770/801–0810.*

6 *a-4*

Gwinnett Place, 2100 Pleasant Hill Rd., Duluth, 770/623–9892.

5 *f-8*

Market Square, 2050 Lawrenceville Hwy., Decatur, 404/325–0358.

5 *f-7*

Northlake Mall, 4800 Briarcliff Rd., Northlake, 770/938–1055.

5 *e-1*

North Point Mall, 1000 North Point Cir., Alpharetta, 770/475–9404.

4 *e-3*

Town Center, 400 Ernest W. Barrett Pkwy., 770/425–8333.

12 *h-2*

WILLIAMS SONOMA

The catalog becomes real! All the fabulous high-quality kitchenware and other merchandise this California firm loads

into its famous catalog is right here in the store. The oils, vinegars, and other ingredients included in the recipes that appear in the catalog are for sale, too. *Lenox Square,3393 Peachtree Rd., Buckhead, 404/812–1703. MARTA: Lenox.*

5 *c-5*

Perimeter Mall, 4400 Ashford-Dunwoody Rd., Dunwoody, 770/698–8584. MARTA: Dunwoody.

6 *a-4*

Gwinnett Place Mall, 2100 Pleasant Hill Rd., Duluth, 678/473–0766.

5 *a-3*

4475 Roswell Rd., Marietta, 678/560–3660.

JEWELRY

antique & collectible items

7 *h-4*

LAKEWOOD ANTIQUES MARKET

This is the place for collectible costume jewelry and fairly standard fine stuff. If you study the books on costume jewelry of this century, you'll be amazed at what can turn up here for bargain prices. Some dealers, however, will know as much as you do, so don't expect rare pieces to go completely unnoticed. Dealers often spend half the first morning of the show scouring other dealers for deals. You can do it, too, on the second weekend of each month. *2000 Lakewood Ave., 404/622–4488. MARTA: Lakewood/Ft. McPherson.*

12 *e-6*

LAURA PEARCE

Pearce was a buyer at Tiffany's for five years, and she maintains her ties with estate dealers in New York. Her most popular pieces include platinum and diamonds, especially from the 1920s, though she also sells exquisite reproduction pieces. *2300 Peachtree Rd., Buckhead, 404/350–9207.*

12 *f-3*

REED SAVAGE

Reed Savage places esoteric collectibles in museums and private collections often, but for the most part, he likes to carry things that people can wear. He charges by what he has to pay for the piece, not how much the market will bear, and he'll trade, too. *110 E. Andrews Dr., Buckhead, 404/263–3439.*

12 *e-6*

RICHTER'S

Frederick Gray, manager of one of the oldest firms (since 1893) specializing in estate jewelry in the country, favors the "big, powerhouse pieces" for his clientele. These appear to be those with the best stones and that exhibit fine craftsmanship and attention to every detail. *2300 Peachtree Rd., Buckhead, 404/355–4462.*

7 *h-6*

SCOTT'S ANTIQUES MARKET

Jewelry collectors who are hunting bargains on costume and real pieces from the 19th and 20th centuries can have a field day here on the second weekend of every month, when dealers from all over the country set up displays. It's worth your effort to do some comparison shopping (that amethyst necklace might have a less expensive companion on another row) and remember that while many dealers set up here month after month, others are not so reliable. *3650 Jonesboro Rd., Forest Park, 404/363–0909.*

12 *h-2*

SKIPPY MUSKET & CO.

Make a jewelry wish, and it will instantly be granted at this boutique across the way from Tiffany's. Diamonds, rubies, emeralds, and pearls in antique settings find their way here from estates all over the world, and small glamorous accessories, such as tortoise-shell boxes, collectible paperweights, small bronzes, and exquisite watches, command attention, too. *Phipps Plaza, 3500 Peachtree Rd., Buckhead, 404/233–3462. MARTA: Lenox.*

contemporary pieces

12 *h-2*

CARTIER

The House of Cartier, in business for more than 100 years, brings Paris to Atlanta. The surroundings are quiet and tasteful, and the staff handles even the smallest purchase as though it were for the Duchess of Windsor (who wore many of this firm's designs). What's more, Cartier pieces hold their value, and many go up, so any purchase is really an investment. *Lenox Square, 3393 Peachtree Rd., Buckhead, 404/841–0840. MARTA: Lenox.*

12 *h-2*

GEODE

Since 1974, Geode has pioneered the idea that Atlantans will buy fine jewelry in interesting, modern designs. The stock here tends to be geared toward young, affluent buyers who like colored stones and gold and silver jewelry. *Lenox Square, 3393 Peachtree Rd., Buckhead, 404/261–9346. MARTA: Lenox.*

12 *h-2*

ILLUMINA

Once voted by *Atlanta* magazine the best place to buy expensive jewelry that *is* expensive, this jewelry gallery lives up to its reputation. Owned by jeweler Lainey Papageorge, the gallery carries work by master craftspeople such as Kent Raible and Paula Crevoshay as well as the best colored stone jewelry in Atlanta and exotic ambers and pearls. Many pieces are available at prices that those without unlimited resources can afford, and there are sales occasionally. *Phipps Plaza, 3500 Peachtree Rd., Buckhead, 404/233–3010. MARTA: Lenox.*

12 *g-3*

MAIER AND BERKELE

Native Atlantans and newcomers alike will find these stores full of the best in traditional fine jewelry, watches, china, silver, and crystal. There is a small but highly regarded estate jewelry division, and the after-Christmas sales are excellent. Best shopping is at the newly expanded Buckhead store. *3225 Peachtree Rd., Buckhead, 404/261–4911. MARTA: Buckhead.*

12 *h-2*

Lenox Square, 3393 Peachtree Rd., Buckhead, 404/233–8201. MARTA: Lenox.

4 *h-7*

Cumberland Mall, 1331 Cumberland Mall, Smyrna, 770/440–3167.

5 *e-1*

North Point Mall, 1000 North Point Cir., Alpharetta, 770/667–1887.

4 *g-5*

THE SHANE COMPANY

These folks import their diamonds direct from Antwerp and do a fine job on selection, price, and quality. The sales staff know the stock; will educate you on the four C's of clarity, color, cut, and carat; and back their reputation with good guarantees. *2365 Windy Hill Rd., Marietta, 770/984–9900.*

5 *h-5*

3300 Steve Reynolds Blvd., Duluth, 770/ 623–3600.

5 *f-1*

10885 Haynes Bridge Rd., Alpharetta, 678/393–0701.

4 *e-3*

735 Ernest W. Barrett Pkwy., Kennesaw, 678/355–1144.

12 *h-2*

ROSS SIMONS

This is the only outlet of the national chain in Atlanta, and it carries perhaps the widest selection of jewelry in the city. While the designs are not extraordinary, the pieces are solid, well crafted and well priced. Look here for a wide range of earring jackets and studs, and especially good prices in rings, bracelets, and pearls. *Phipps Plaza, 3500 Peachtree Rd., Buckhead, 404/266–9050. MARTA: Lenox.*

12 *h-2*

TIFFANY & CO.

Tiffany's features designers whose names sometimes become household words—Paloma Picasso, for example, who holds sway in the contemporary design area—and who inevitably are the world's top names in jewelry, china, crystal, and silver. While you expect nothing but the best from Tiffany, it's worth noting that prices at the Atlanta store are often less expensive than they are in New York or other cities, because the overhead is lower and the market won't bear bigger-city prices. *Phipps Plaza, 3500 Peachtree Rd., Buckhead, 404/261–0074. MARTA: Lenox.*

costume jewelry

5 *e-1*

DILLARD'S

Because Dillard's doesn't have a fine-jewelry department, the store can concentrate on finding interesting costume pieces. Look here for great fine-jewelry knockoffs and less expensive interpretations of custom designs found in expensive boutiques. For instances, prices are especially good on the standard Monet lines and designer lines such as Anne

Klein. *7000 North Point Cir., Alpharetta, 770/410–9020.*

14 *g-3*

THE FAMILY JEWELS

Probably the city's most comprehensive collection of vintage costume jewelry includes all those things your aunts wore in the 1950s, along with pieces that date as far back as the Roaring '20s and as recently as the hippie era. The shop is great for pins and necklaces, but you will need to adopt the old clip-on earrings for pierced ears. *114 E. Ponce de Leon Ave., Decatur, 404/377–3774.*

12 *h-2*

THE ICING

This store is crammed with every bodily accessory you can think of. The offerings are especially attractive to teenagers, because the jewelry is well priced and designed with the young set in mind. Get great faux body piercing items here, too. *Lenox Square, 3393 Peachtree Rd., Buckhead, 404/869–0800. MARTA: Lenox.*

5 *c-5*

Perimeter Mall, 4400 Ashford-Dunwoody Rd., Dunwoody, 770/677–0313. MARTA: Dunwoody.

8 *a-8*

Southlake Mall, 2413 Southlake Mall, Morrow, 678/422–8395.

12 *h-2*

NEIMAN MARCUS

The "last call" sales here are absolutely the best place to buy the things you've been coveting for a while. The designs range from classic to wacky, and if you're good at spotting next year's design trends, this is the place to pick them up before the rest of the world does. *Lenox Square, 3393 Peachtree Rd., Buckhead, 404/266–8200. MARTA: Lenox.*

KITES

14 *a-5*

IDENIFIED FLYING OBJECTS

Wonderful creations in all shapes and sizes will lure you into the romance of the kite. The selection includes kits and custom-built kites, and the salespeople who will take the time to instruct you how to get your purchase aloft. Look here also for darts, juggling equipment, boomerangs, and other gravity-defying gizmos. *1164 Euclid Ave., Little Five Points, 404/524–4628.*

LEATHER GOODS & LUGGAGE

12 h-2
BENTLEY'S
A national chain, Bentley's guarantees its prices on high-quality day planners and other leather goods are low; carries Samsonite, Hartmann, and Tumi; and takes special orders and gets them to you quickly. Plus, the stores in Sandy Springs, Buckhead, and Decatur provide repair services as well. *Phipps Plaza, 3500 Peachtree Rd., Buckhead 404/841–6247. MARTA: Lenox.*

5 e-5
Perimeter Mall, 4400 Ashford-Dunwoody Rd., Dunwoody, 770/671–1071. MARTA: Dunwoody.

5 f-8
North DeKalb Mall, 2050 Lawrenceville Hwy., Decatur, 404/633–9323.

6 a-4
Gwinnett Place Mall, 2100 Pleasant Hill Rd., Duluth, 770/497–8447.

4 e-3
Town Center, 400 Ernest W. Barrett Pkwy., Kennesaw, 770/422–9406.

6 d-1
Mall of Georgia, 3333 Buford Dr., Buford, 678/482–6404.

12 h-2
CIVILIZED TRAVELER
First-time travelers and veterans alike will love this store for the little things you never think about until you need them. For example, a nearly invisible money-passport belt in flexible cotton can get you through the streets of the world's pickpocket capitals with ease. Maps, electricity adaptors, and savvy travel guides also fill the shelves here. *Phipps Plaza, 3500 Peachtree Rd., Buckhead, 404/264–1252. MARTA: Lenox.*

5 e-5
Perimeter Mall, 4400 Ashford-Dunwoody Rd., Dunwoody, 770/673–0111.

12 h-2
MORI LUGGAGE AND GIFTS
Mori's has been known for quality and price ever since the doors opened in 1971 and prides itself on top-quality leathers, finely crafted desk accessories, collectible pens, and luggage. You'll find lots of good gifts here. The plaza-level shop at Lenox Square has a repair service. *Lenox Square, 3393 Peachtree Rd., Buckhead, 404/231–0074. MARTA: Lenox.*

5 c-5
Perimeter Mall, 4400 Ashford-Dunwoody Rd., Dunwoody, 770/394–3215. MARTA: Dunwoody.

5 f-7
Northlake Mall, 4800 Briarcliff Rd., Northlake, 770/934–8221.

5 e-1
North Point Mall, 1000 North Point Cir., Alpharetta, 770/667–9177.

4 h-7
Cumberland Mall, I–285 and I–75 at Cobb Pkwy., Smyrna, 770/436–6112.

8 a-8
Southlake Mall, 1000 Southlake Mall, Morrow, 770/961–7322.

12 g-3
TUESDAY MORNING
An often overlooked resource for luggage, Tuesday Morning buys overstocks and discontinued items, and there's always plenty of it. In fact, you're sure to find pieces in almost any size and price. *3145 Piedmont Rd., Buckhead, 404/233–6526. MARTA: Buckhead.*

4 h-6
2512 Spring Rd. SE, Smyrna, 770/435–6678.

5 d-5
4502 Chamblee-Dunwoody Rd., Dunwoody, 770/457–3565.

6 d-7
4051 Stone Mountain Hwy., Snellville, 770/978–3573.

5 f-4
6325 Spalding Dr., Norcross, 770/447–4692.

5 b-4
736 Johnson Ferry Rd., Marietta, 770/971–0511.

LINENS

12 *f-3*

IRISH CRYSTAL CO.

This outlet for beautiful Irish products carries linens by the country's major weavers, with damask tablecloths in all sizes, including banquet, a specialty. Oval cloths are always in stock. They can also custom order cloths of any size. They carry linen sheets, mostly by special order, and a large supply of flat weave handkerchiefs and other table linens. *3168 Peachtree Rd., Buckhead, 404/266–3783.*

12 *h-2*

LASSITER'S BATH AND BOUDOIR

Once you've discovered the feel of Egyptian cotton with 500 threads per square inch or a loft-down comforter, a taste for top-of-the-line linens will never leave you. This is the place to indulge those tastes, and, fortunately, you can do so at occasional sales. *Phipps Plaza, 3500 Peachtree Rd., Buckhead, 404/261–0765. MARTA: Lenox.*

5 *e-1*

LINENS & THINGS

These stores carry every mid-range brand of linens for bed, bath, and table, with kitchen wares and window treatments thrown in for good measure. Look here for good, solid utilitarian goods in a wide assortment of colors; you'll find an especially wide variety of bold colors and interesting designs in sheets, comforters, and duvets. *6200 North Point Pkwy., Alpharetta, 770/367–3611.*

6 *a-4*

2340 Pleasant Hill Rd., Duluth, 770/418–1074.

6 *c-8*

5370 Stone Mountain Hwy., Stone Mountain, 770/498–9566.

5 *c-5*

1711 Hammond Dr., Dunwoody, 770/698–0374.

12 *f-4*

2900 Peachtree Rd., Buckhead, 404/816–2700.

6 *d-4*

875 Lawrenceville-Suwanee Rd., 770/995–6413.

MUSIC

8 *e-2*

A TO Z RECORDS

When seeking out specialty R&B, jazz, gospel, reggae and hiphop, this shop is sure to meet your needs. Since the store is keyed into several distribution outlets, the staff can usually track down atypical items in one to three days. *4844 Redan Rd., Lithonia, 404/292–5115.*

5 *e-1*

BEST BUY

It's hard to beat this megachain in terms of the sheer scope of the selection, and it's known for keeping prices at reasonable levels. *975 North Point Dr., Alpharetta, 678/339–1321.*

14 *a-4*

CRIMINAL RECORDS

Located in hip Little Five Points, this shop focuses on new CDs and an array of comic-book titles. There's a premium supply of DVDs and music–pop culture periodicals. *466 Moreland Ave., Little Five Points, 404/215–9511.*

5 *g-6*

EAT MORE RECORDS

The emphasis on the new and used CDs and vinyl here is on U.K. rock and indie imports, but this is an indispensable resource to local collectors of all genres. The knowledgeable staff can help you track down hard-to-find items. *1210 Rockbridge Rd., Lilburn, 770/717–8111.*

12 *f-4*

FANTASYLAND RECORDS

This store is sheer vinyl heaven. Collectors on the hunt will relish in the bin after bin of treasures that stretch across genres and back across the decades. Collections are bought and sold. *2839 Peachtree Rd., Garden Hills, 404/237–3193.*

NEEDLEWORK & KNITTING

4 *h-4*

ABECEDARIUS

Atlanta's most committed cross-stitch shop will make sure you're taught all the techniques correctly and are equipped with all the accessories and framing things you could need. This shop also pays attention to handicap accessibility issues. *2141 Roswell Rd., Marietta, 770/977–3585.*

5 *c-2*

CAST-ON COTTAGE

In one of the old houses along this character-filled streets you'll find a large selection of beautiful woolen yarns. The knitting classes are much in demand, and deservedly so. *1003 Canton St., Roswell, 770/998–3483.*

5 *d-4*

DUNWOODY NEEDLE ACCENT

If you are handy with a needle you will want to seek out this shop for the widest range of materials, and classes. The offerings include hand-painted canvases in one-of-a-kind designs, and limited-edition intricacies from the country's top designers of needlepoint, crewel work, and cross stitch. Mail orders are accepted. *5477 Chamblee-Dunwoody Rd., Dunwoody, 770/393–9322.*

5 *e-4*

JAPANESE EMBROIDERY CENTER

Here, in a serene environment filled with shojii screens, you'll learn Japanese embroidery techniques. Beginners and advanced students can take classes in this world-renown art, taught by Japanese masters and their American colleagues; this is not, however, a discipline for the occasional cross-stitcher. *2727 Spalding Dr., Dunwoody, 770/390–0617.*

13 *c-6*

NEEDLE NOOK

This shop specializes in Judaic designs and has some of the best you can find. There's instruction in cross-stitch, needlepoint, glass beadwork, and other mediums. *2165 Briarcliff Rd., at LaVista Rd., Toco Hills, 404/325–0068.*

4 *h-7*

PINTUCKS AND PINAFORES

This is perhaps the only place in Atlanta where you can learn sewing techniques for flower girl and christening gowns, bar and bat mitzvah clothes, confirmation dresses, and other children's ware. They teach classes in heirloom sewing, smocking, embroidery and needle lace, and you can shop here for all the attendant supplies, too. *Vinings Jubilee Shopping Center, 4200 Paces Ferry Rd., Vinings, 770/384–1216.*

5 *b-6*

STRINGS AND STRANDS

Primarily focused on knitting—with an emphasis on wonderful hand-dyed yarns of every variety and expert instruction—this shop also offers yarns and instruction for crochet aficionados as well. *4632 Wieuca Rd., Sandy Springs, 404/252–9662.*

PHOTO EQUIPMENT

15 *c-2*

CAMERA BUG

This is a one-stop location for both serious hobbyists and everyday picture takers. They're able to track down replacement accessories for standard equipment or your old favorite. *1799 Briarcliff Rd., Toco Hills, 404/873–3925.*

15 *c-2*

PROFESSIONAL PHOTO RESOURCES

This lifeline for working professionals provides repairs, trial rentals on high-end gear, studio resources, and digital editing. *667 11th St., 404/885–1885.*

5 *e-5*

V-PHOTO OF ATLANTA

Convenient to shutterbugs in Northeast, this shop places an emphasis on providing reasonable repair work. The services include free cleanings, check-ups, and estimates. *6950 Peachtree Industrial Blvd., 770/441–1644.*

15 *d-2*

WOLF CAMERA

These are the big retail guys in town for most of your photographic needs, with locations throughout the metro area. This large midtown location also carries used gear, darkroom equipment, and even telescopes. *150 14th St., 404/892–1707.*

RAINWEAR

5 *c-5*

REI

Beyond the province of the mere raincoat, this company has the equipment for the worst blows nature can inflict upon you, from high-tech coats and hats to boots, gloves, and plain old umbrellas. The Clairmont Road location has the largest inventory and best selection. *1165 Perimeter Center W, near Perimeter Mall, Sandy Springs, 770/901–9200.*

13 *e-3*

1800 Northeast Expressway, exit 32 at Clairmont Rd. on the access road next to I–85 S, 404/633–6508.

SPORTING GOODS & CLOTHING

12 *h-2*

NIKETOWN

This place is an event, with huge television screens running sports channels as you try on your shoes or T-shirt. Everything Nike is available here, so if you're swoosh-happy this is the place to shop. *Phipps Plaza, 3500 Peachtree Rd., Buckhead, 404/841–6444. MARTA: Lenox.*

5 *c-7*

PLAY IT AGAIN SPORTS

A few years ago, a Minneapolis entrepreneur had the bright idea that all the sports stuff people got bored with or don't use anymore could be sold in a store instead of in a garage sale. Some of the stock is new and discounted, but much of it has been played with and is deeply discounted. They trade, too, so you may want to wheel in your mountain bike and ride out on a sleek cycle. If a store doesn't have what you're looking for, the staff will call other stores. *4279 Roswell Rd., Buckhead, 404/257–0229.*

5 *f-8*

North DeKalb Mall, 2050 Lawrenceville Hwy., Decatur, 404/329–2005.

6 *d-7*

1630 Scenic Hwy. SW, Snellville, 770/982–1133.

4 *e-3*

800 Ernest W. Barrett Pkwy., Kennesaw, 770/429–8636.

6 *a-4*

3675 Satellite Blvd., Duluth, 678/584–9788.

5 *e-8*

2080 Henderson Mill Rd., 770/493–8299.

5 *e-1*

SPORTS AUTHORITY

If you know what you want, are not interested in frills, and desire a big selection of every sports item under the sun for a reasonable price, this is your store. Serious fitness training equipment, bowling balls, and fishing, tennis, and baseball as well as seasonal equipment have earned these stores a well-deserved reputation for outfitting all people in all sports. There are more than a dozen Atlanta locations. *North Point Mall, 7461 North Point Pkwy., Alpharetta, 770/518–3303.*

12 *g-3*

3221 Peachtree Rd., Buckhead, 404/814–9873. MARTA: Buckhead.

5 *b-5*

6690 Roswell Rd., Sandy Springs, 770/845–0727.

6 *b-8*

4235 Stone Mountain Hwy., Lilburn, 770/979–7020.

4 *h-7*

2963 Cobb Pkwy., Smyrna, 770/955–6662.

4 *g-5*

50 Powers Ferry Rd., Marietta, 770/509–5700.

4 *h-3*

TEAM SPORTS

Team Sports is another place to outfit your team with baseball, football, tennis, and soccer uniforms. Whatever you buy, custom lettering, embroidery, and screen printing are available, and at fast turnaround times. *2250 E. Piedmont Rd., Marietta, 770/973–9991.*

boating

5 *a-3*

GO WITH THE FLOW SPORTS

A dazzling display of canoes and kayaks fill this lovely old building in historic Roswell's shopping district. The staff is committed to providing you with the best you can get for your budget and teaching you how to use it. As a result, if you want to paddle anything, get it here. *4 Elizabeth Way, between Canton St. and Alpharetta Hwy., Roswell, 770/992–3200.*

7 *h-7*

STOVALL MARINE

For more than a quarter century, this superstore has supplied Georgians with boats, yachts, and other water craft. Shop here for Sea Doos and power-boats, large and small yachts, and all the attendant marine accessories. The salespeople are expert, the service and repair services unsurpassed. *5840 South Expressway, Forest Park, 404/363–6910.*

4 *e-3*

2649 N. Cobb Pkwy., Marietta, 770/422–7460.

camping & climbing

5 *c-5*

REI

REI stands for Recreational Equipment, Inc., which describes the offerings neatly. This store is serious about camping, hiking, kayaking, and climbing and, judging from the hip colors and styles of the clothing, believes you can look smashing doing them. *1165 Perimeter Center W, Sandy Springs, 770/901–9200.*

1800 Northeast Expressway, exit 32 at Clairmont Rd. on the access road next to I–85 S, 404/633–6508.

fishing tackle & supplies

12 *f-4*

CLASSIC ANGLER

This hole-in-the-wall carries merchandise as big as all outdoors. The store specializes in fly-fishing and offers some of the most fabulous hand-tied flies you've ever seen. In fact, you'll soon learn that fly fishing is a high art, and you can get every angle on it here. *2817 Peachtree Rd., Buckhead, 404/233–5110.*

12 *f-3*

THE FISH HAWK

Fly-fishing equipment is a specialty here, but this store also offers a high-quality selection of casting and spinning gear for fresh- and saltwater fishing (everything from trout gear to cane poles to big game and IGFA rods and all the accessories you could dream of). You may want to take part in one of the courses or join a guided trip in cold, warm, and saltwater locations. *279 Buckhead Ave., Buckhead, 404/237–3473.*

6 *a-5*

SPORTSMAN'S WAREHOUSE

For fishers living in Gwinnett County, this is the biggest fresh- and saltwater fishing department store around and features a full line of Orvis products. For those unfamiliar with the lure of bass fishing, the 6,000-gallon bass tub is the place to learn how to catch these cagey, finny creatures. *3825 Shackleford Rd., at Steve Reynolds Blvd., on the south side of I–85 N, Duluth, 770/931–1550.*

golf

5 *h-5*

GOLF WAREHOUSE

For almost 20 years, this chain has stocked clubs, shoes, bags, clothes, and accessories for anybody who swings a club, including kids and senior citizens. The prices are low and competitive, and the shops carry name brands and have a complete club repair facility. *5192 Brook Hollow Pkwy., Norcross, 770/447–4653.*

5 *d-2*

King's Market Shopping Center, 1425 Market Blvd., Roswell, 770/643–0061.

4 *h-7*

2697 New Spring Rd., Smyrna, 770/435–1934.

4 *f-3*

390 Ernest W. Barrett Pkwy., Kennesaw, 770/428–8700.

5 *e-6*

5597 Buford Hwy., Doraville, 770/455–8089.

9 *g-1*

6373 Jonesboro Rd., Morrow, 770/960–1992.

6 *a-4*

GOLFSMITH

There is more golfing equipment here than there are greens in the entire world. Plus you can use one of the computerized golf simulators to analyze your swing or learn how to deal with water features. Ways to try out your technique appear on every aisle here. If it's raining so hard outside you can't play, play here all day. *3690 Venture Dr., Duluth, 770/623–6336.*

4 *e-3*

2500 Cobb Place La., Kennesaw, 770/421–0106.

7 g-5

METRO ATLANTA GOLF SHOP

Want some custom clubs? Pro owner Tom "Smitty" Smith can design them for you, sell you some new ones, or for that matter, equip you with used ones for terrific prices. He's been in business for 30 years, keeps his overhead low, and concentrates on the game rather than fancy clothing. *34 Cleveland Ave., near the Brown's Mill Golf Course, East Point, 404/768–9146.*

5 f-6

OLD SPORT GOLF

At this wonderful store there are more than 25,000 used clubs in stock, some from back when golf was a finesse game rather than a power game. There's golf art and memorabilia, antique clubs and new ones, too. The trained professionals on staff will help you choose the clubs that best fit your skills on a buy, sell, rent, or trade basis. *4297 North Access Rd., Northcrest, 770/493–4344.*

3 f-7

4450 Hwy. 20, Sugar Hill, 770/271–0705.

12 g-3

PRO GOLF DISCOUNT OF ATLANTA

Competition drives to a hole in one here. Since 1977, this chain has gone divot to divot with whoever putts a better price. They'll beat any advertised price by 10%, or if you find a lower price within two weeks, they'll refund 120% of the difference. Although their services and products meet and match those of most area stores, they do one thing that no one else lays claim to: they'll deliver clubs to your hotel room—easier than traveling with your favorite clubs. *3141 Piedmont Rd., Buckhead, 404/816–2166. MARTA: Buckhead.*

8 e-1

4961 Memorial Dr., Stone Mountain, 770/ 294–0818.

6 a-4

1645 Pleasant Hill Rd., Duluth, 770/931– 1666.

4 g-5

1581 Cobb Pkwy., Marietta, 770/955– 9500.

5 f-6

5810 Buford Hwy., Doraville, 770/455– 8809.

hunting

12 g-3

ORVIS ATLANTA

This long-established company will gear you up for upland hunting, water-fowling, or sporting clays and supply you with everything from Gokey hunting boots, shoes, and luggage to a custom-made shotgun. Check out the excellent catalog. *3255 Peachtree Rd., Buckhead, 404/841–0093. MARTA: Buckhead.*

riding

2 h-8

ATLANTA SADDLERY

The emphasis here is on showing, so look for the finest in English tack—bridles, strap goods, leg and hoof wear, saddles and pads. The human wear includes boots, breeches, coats, helmets, and outerwear for dressage, show jumping, and pleasure categories. *1670 Hwy. 9, Alpharetta, 770/475–1967.*

4 g-1

HORSE TOWN

You'll find everything you need here for western saddlery, from saddles with pommels to 10-gallon hats and boots made of exotic skins. A full line of English tack is available here as well. *1231 Shallowford Rd., Marietta, 770/926–7346.*

6 d-7

1959 Dogwood Dr. SW, Snellville, 770/ 736–1888.

8 h-5

INTERNATIONAL SADDLERY

When the Olympics came to Atlanta in 1996, this store won the designation "official saddlery." That recommendation, along with a convenient location at the Georgia International Horse Park, makes it a prime place to buy English tack, clothing, and gifts. Barn and stable supplies are available, too. *1960A Centennial Olympic Pkwy., Conyers, 770/929–8832.*

running

12 g-8

PHIDIPPIDES

A requirement of working here is to be a people-oriented runner trained extensively in service. The staff will make you take a little run in front of the store to make sure you are getting the right shoe and that they are fitting you just right.

They also carry some trail running shoes and racing flats and recommend running shoes for all walking because running shoes have all the technology and walking shoes don't, as a general rule. *Ansley Mall, 1544 Piedmont Ave., Midtown, 404/875–4268.*

5 b-5

220 Sandy Springs Cir., Sandy Springs, 404/255–6149.

skating

15 f-2

SKATE ESCAPE

Visitors to Atlanta's Piedmont Park will see some incredible in-line skating, and if you're inspired to join in the fun, this nearby shop can equip you with in-lines, along with skateboards and accessories. The sales staff is dedicated to the sport and will educate beginners and talk the talk with regulars. *1086 Piedmont Ave., Midtown, 404/892–1292.*

5 g-5

SONIC BLADES

For beginners or advanced skaters, this store will sell or rent ice and in-line skates and skateboards. The staff is into these sports, so you can expect great advice. They do repairs, too. *5775 Jimmy Carter Blvd., Norcross, 770/662–5665.*

5 b-4

SPARKLES

The emphasis is definitely below the knee—on in-lines, roller skates, and ice skates. You'll have to go elsewhere for the correct apparel, but you would be hard-pressed to find a better selection of equipment. *4800 Davidson Rd., Marietta, 770/565–8899.*

4 g-7

666 Smyrna Hill Dr., Smyrna, 770/432–6222.

2 c-3

1153 Marietta Hwy., Canton, 770/479–9546.

4 d-2

1000 McCollum Pkwy., Kennesaw, 770/428–3941.

7 g-8

7335 Hwy. 85, Riverdale, 770/997–6363.

6 f-6

1104 Grayson Hwy. 20, Lawrenceville, 770/963–0922.

skiing

5 c-6

ROCKY MOUNTAIN SPORTS SKI SHOP

Atlanta has one of the largest ski clubs in the country, and this store is where most of the members come to buy equipment. That's because the inventory is extensive and the sales staff is dedicated to the sport and knowledgeable about boots, skis, boards, and bindings. It's open from September through March, and on Sundays from November through February. *5232 Roswell Rd., Sandy Springs, 404/252–3157.*

5 b-5

SPORTS EXPRESS

Half the store specializes in ski equipment, half in tennis. That way, you're covered for a whole year of sporting activities. Along with high-tech designer skiwear and tennis wear for everybody in the family, skis, snowboards, racquets, and all the gear and accessories you'll need for either sport are available. Plus, skis can be tuned on a same-day basis. *6681 Roswell Rd., Sandy Springs, 404/252–7963.*

tennis

5 e-1

SERIOUS TENNIS

It's serious in that the stock is geared exclusively and seriously to tennis clothing and equipment. As a result, you can expect to find knowledgeable service and every brand of racket, priced from $90 to $300. Upper-end rackets are stiffer, strong, and can contain metals such as titanium to make them lighter and more durable. With this kind of focus, it's hard to leave without feeling like a serious player. *10800 Alpharetta Hwy., Roswell, 770/641–8321.*

5 a-4

YOUR SERVE TENNIS AND FITNESS

Since 1976, this store has brought Atlantans the newest in clothing and equipment. Its reputation for quality and service is match point to its desire to bring the latest in technology to your game. *1205 Johnson Ferry Rd., Marietta, 770/977–1513.*

5 *f-4*

4015 Holcomb Bridge Rd., Norcross, 770/447–9989.

6 *b-8*

5295 Stone Mountain Hwy., Stone Mountain, 770/469–2791.

STATIONERY & OFFICE SUPPLIES

office supplies

15 *e-5*

IVAN ALLEN

One of the city's most famous mayor's family founded this company in 1900, and it has managed to adapt to the city's constantly changing business environment ever since. The staff her guarantees a wide selection of everything from supplies to furniture and attentive service. *221 Peachtree Center Ave., Downtown, 404/332–3000. MARTA: Peachtree Center.*

12 *g-5*

OFFICE DEPOT

This is the store that ate most of the competition up. The Depot supplies offices with everything from computers and software (a good buy, but the staff doesn't always know the difference between a gig and a byte) to storage boxes. Sometimes the stock is surprisingly extensive, such as the choice of exotic papers for printing your own snazzy newsletters, invitations, and announcements. Atlanta also has many branches of Office Max—same store, same merchandise, just a different name. *2581 Piedmont Rd., Buckhead, 404/261–4111. MARTA: Lindbergh.*

13 *e-2*

14th St. and Techwood, Midtown, 404/724–0584. MARTA: Midtown.

4 *g-4*

119 Cobb Pkwy., Marietta, 770/499–2001.

5 *d-6*

5300 Peachtree Industrial Blvd., Chamblee, 770/452–0187.

8 *e-1*

5064 Memorial Dr., Stone Mountain, 404/297–4841.

5 *g-6*

5495 Jimmy Carter Blvd., Norcross, 770/446–6646.

paperweights

12 *d-7*

VESPERMAN GLASS

Atlanta's premier art glass gallery displays dozens of gorgeous paperweights and also does a healthy business in other kinds of corporate gifts. *2140 Peachtree Rd., Brookwood, 404/359–9698.*

pens & pencils

12 *g-7*

ARTLITE

In this old-fashioned office supply store, people who know fine pens can shop for antique instruments as well as top-of-the-line examples by Waterman, Montblanc, Cross, Sheaffer, and Parker. The fountain pen selection is especially fine, and there are also mechanical pencils and drafting instruments. *1851 Piedmont Rd., Midtown, 404/875–7271.*

12 *h-2*

MONTBLANC

Within the black-and-white polished walls of this store you'll find boxes of fine stationery, handmade papers, leather goods, and, of course, the famous pens, all made by this German company. You can have a $125,000 diamond pen made to order, get one in platinum for $15,500, or settle for the store's most popular item, a black rollerball with gold trim for $175. *Lenox Square, 3393 Peachtree Rd., Buckhead, 404/231–4810. MARTA: Lenox.*

stationery

12 *f-3*

PACES PAPERS INC. BY JACKIE

This is where Buckhead comes for engraved invitations and announcements, along with very fine laid, watermarked, and bonded papers to engrave upon, too. You'll find tasteful, handmade cards here as well, in case you need something fine in a hurry. *Cates Center, 110 E. Andrews Dr., Buckhead, 404/231–1111.*

THEATRICAL ITEMS

13 *c-4*

ATLANTA COSTUME

This outfit supplies many of the area's theaters, motion picture companies, and other commercial concerns with costumes and does custom designs should you not find something to suit you in the huge inventory. Handily, the store extends its hours in October. *2089 Monroe Dr., at I–85 N, 404/874–7511.*

5 *a-2*

A COSTUME BALL

Everybody has a ball here, even if just stopping in to look. Whatever the occasion or the fantasy, whatever your size or age, you'll find just the right costume, along with a good selection of masks, cosmetics, accessories, wigs, hats and mustaches. *3162 Johnson Ferry Rd., Marietta, 770/640–6778.*

4 *f-4*

EDDIE'S TRICK & NOVELTY SHOP

These two shops have an especially fine selection of costumes for Halloween. Throughout the year, too, students of the magical arts find their way through books and props and sit in on the ongoing courses. *70 S. Park Sq., Marietta, 770/428–4314.*

6 *a-4*

3675 Satellite Blvd., Duluth, 770/814–9700.

TOBACCONISTS

12 *f-3*

BUCKHEAD CIGAR FACTORY

Cigars are hand-rolled on site here, with consistently fresh tobacco from the Dominican Republic, (as close as you can get to the legendary Cuban tobacco these days). Owner Boake Moore will help you select the cigar most suited to you and explain the mysteries of rolling a fine cigar. There's a smoking lounge, and occasionally Moore hosts Chivas and Cigar nights. *3061 Peachtree Rd., Buckhead, 404/846–0818.*

12 *g-3*

EDWARD'S PIPE AND TOBACCO SHOPS

This shop has been around for 35 years and traditionally carries an in-depth selection of pipes, cigarettes, cigars, and accessories. Edward's carries thousands of premium handmade cigar brands, along with its own hand-blended tobaccos. *3137 Piedmont Rd., just south of the Peachtree Rd. intersection, Buckhead, 404/233–8082.*

8 *d-1*

444 North Indian Creek Dr., near the Perimeter College Central campus, Clarkston, 404/292–1721.

5 *d-4*

THE CIGAR MERCHANT

These stores offer state-of-the-art walk-in humidors and smoking lounges, along with a wide array of pipes and pipe tobaccos, of course. They'll sell you hand-rolled cigars from Jamaica, Honduras, and the Dominican Republic, encouraging you to test a few before selecting. *2472 Jett Ferry Rd., Dunwoody, 770/671–1777.*

5 *e-2*

9850 Nesbit Ferry Rd., Alpharetta, 770/552–1942.

5 *e-1*

10800 Alpharetta Hwy., Roswell, 770/642–1221.

TOYS & GAMES

collectibles

12 *g-7*

CLASSIC COMICS

Don't be surprised if a Doberman pinscher pops up from behind the counter to wait on you at the Roswell store. Her human will show you hard to find *Star Wars* collectibles, primarily from the latest iterations (since 1995). There's also a good selection of the female action figures that are slowly creeping into a once-all-male domain. *1860 Piedmont Rd., Buckhead, 404/892–4442.*

2 *h-8*

11235 Alpharetta Hwy., between Mansell and Hembree Rds., Roswell, 770/753–9400.

6 *d-4*

GALACTIC QUEST

Here's the largest collection of Star Wars collectibles in Atlanta, both new and old. The action figures are accompanied by new and vintage comics, collectible card games, and animated videos. *155 Gwinnett Dr., Lawrenceville, 770/339–3001.*

3 *g-8*

4300 Buford Hwy., Buford, 770/614–4804.

12 *g-4*

OXFORD COMICS AND GAMES

One of the best selections of comics in town is accompanied by a large section of adult magazines. Great for heavy-metal T-shirts and some action figures. Oxford is also a fine place to find toys targeted for the comic book market. *2855 Piedmont Rd., Buckhead, 404/233–8682.*

new

12 *h-2*

FAO SCHWARZ

This Atlanta outlet of the famous New York store is laid out by age and gender divisions, making it easy to find just the right gift. The staff is unfailingly helpful, too, and knows what each age wants for holiday or birthday. Along with a full line of Steiff products, look for FAO exclusives such as the *Star Wars* Princess Leia/R2D2 combo. *Lenox Square, 3393 Peachtree Rd., Buckhead 404/814–1575. MARTA: Lenox.*

5 *c-5*

LEARNINGSMITH

Thank heaven—this store has cleverly packaged civilization and brought it to kids. Toys and games of every description aim to raise consciousness among kids and their parents as well. Computer programs have been intelligently chosen, and there are many from which to choose. *Perimeter Mall, 4400 Ashford-Dunwoody Rd., Dunwoody, 404/730–8181. MARTA: Dunwoody.*

5 *e-1*

North Point Mall, 1000 North Point Cir., Alpharetta, 770/667–2001.

12 *h-2*

Phipps Plaza, 3500 Peachtree Rd., Buckhead, 404/364–0084. MARTA: Lenox.

4 *e-3*

Town Center, 400 Ernest W. Barrett Pkwy., Kennesaw, 770/425–2097.

6 *a-4*

Gwinnett Place Mall, 2100 Pleasant Hill Rd., Duluth, 770/232–1331.

5 *e-1*

TOYS "R" US

What would we do without this paradise for kids? Well, even if you're not swept away by the vast selection of action figures and Barbie dolls, you'll still have a field day studying what these stores have to tell us about American attitudes toward play, violence, and self-image. *7731 North Point Pkwy., Alpharetta, 770/424–9100.*

12 *g-2*

1 Buckhead Loop, Buckhead, 404/467–8697.

4 *h-7*

2997 Cobb Pkwy., Smyrna, 770/951–8052.

6 *a-4*

2205 Pleasant Hill Rd., Duluth, 770/476–4646.

5 *f-8*

4033 LaVista Rd., Tucker, 770/938–4321.

8 *c-4*

2842 Whites Mill Rd., Decatur, 404/243–4333.

5 *b-5*

ZANY BRAINY

These colorful stores offer a thoughtful approach to play and playing with large selections of books and think-toys. Classes on a wide range of subjects teach kids how to have fun with their imaginations as well as toys. *6285 Roswell Rd., Sandy Springs, 404/252–3280.*

5 *e-1*

6551 North Point Pkwy., Alpharetta, 770/569–0679.

4 *f-3*

50 Ernest W. Barrett Pkwy., Kennesaw, 770/590–0525.

5 *f-4*

3200 Holcomb Bridge Rd., Norcross, 770/447–6222.

6 *d-7*

1905 Scenic Hwy., Snellville, 678/344–8830.

5 *a-3*

1100 Johnson Ferry Rd., Marietta, 770/977–3373.

TROPICAL FISH & AQUARIUMS

12 *f-3*

THE FISH STORE AND MORE

The Fish Store and More includes all the things you need to care for fish, which are the main event here. In fact, you'll find the city's largest quality selection of marine and fresh-water organisms. *3145 Peachtree Rd., Buckhead, 404/231–5111.*

5 *a-3*

MARINE AND TROPICAL FISH

You'll probably relish the experience of watching the incredible colors, shapes, and sizes of the fish swimming around in here. When you're hooked, the experts here will design and maintain your custom aquarium; there's even a fish biologist on staff. *1255 Johnson Ferry Rd., Marietta, 770/321–8404.*

7 *h-8*

PISCES PET

As specialists, the staff here will reveal the secrets of exotic fish, sharks, and eels and supply you with a selection of them as well. They'll also build you a custom aquarium and deliver and install it, or help you build and populate a koi pond. *8013 Tara Blvd., Jonesboro, 770/477–0113.*

VIDEOS

5 *e-7*

BLOCKBUSTER

This huge chain stocks thousands of titles and the list is growing all the time (though even at that it doesn't delve nearly deeply enough into esoterica). The stores also carry every conceivable video game for Sega, Nintendo, and Playstation as well as an increasingly large selection of DVDs. *3550 Chamblee-Tucker Rd., Chamblee, 770/457–1440.*

8 *e-1*

921 N. Hairston Rd., Stone Mountain, 404/299–3500.

4 *g-7*

2900 S. Cobb Dr., Smyrna, 770/431–9700.

15 *g-2*

985 Monroe Dr., Midtown, 404/876–0433.

6 *a-4*

2180 Pleasant Hill Rd., Duluth, 770/497–8189.

5 *f-8*

3934 N. Druid Hills Rd., Decatur, 404/636–0064.

THE MOBILE VIDEO STORE

The selection is not as big as it is at the huge chains, but then again, this place is more about convenience. *770/909–8683 or 404/202–6214.*

14 *a-5*

VIDEO UPDATE

Selections at the 17 Atlanta area locations are pretty much the same, and huge, with more than 10,000 titles in stock at each. Call ahead and a store will reserve a copy of your selection. *299 Moreland Ave., Little Five Points, 404/658–1772.*

12 *g-8*

595 Piedmont Ave., 404/815–9616.

5 *f-4*

3200 Holcomb Bridge Rd., Norcross, 770/449–5454.

5 *a-3*

4400 Roswell Rd., Marietta, 770/321–5300.

6 *d-4*

950 Herrington Rd., Lawrenceville, 770/277–0070.

WATCHES & CLOCKS

antique

12 *b-7*

CLASSIC CLOCKS

Bernie Tekippe and his son have been repairing, restoring, and learning about clocks for more than two decades. In their small shop, find an expanded universe of time. Bernie loves French clocks, which exhibit some of the finest materials and craftsmanship ever found, especially in carriage clocks. He makes his own clocks, often makes his own repair tools, and has an incredible library. They'll quote you fair prices on repair and restoration and do a perfect job. *857 Collier Rd., Midtown, 404/355–5141.*

5 *c-2*

**ROSWELL CLOCK
AND ANTIQUE COMPANY**

The lovely march of swinging pendulums makes itself heard and felt among a good selection of all sorts of antique clocks—mantel clocks, table clocks, grandfather and grandmother clocks, French carriage clocks. *955 Canton St., Roswell, 770/992–5232.*

contemporary

5 *f-4*

CLOCKWORKS

Appropriately enough, you'll find Atlanta's selection of new clocks beneath the clock tower in Gwinnett Walk shopping center. There are two showrooms of grandfather clocks, and a back room where you can find major brand-name clocks at 50%–70% off retail. The offerings also include a few antique clocks on consignment from customers, and the service department restores antique clocks and even makes house calls. *3466 Holcomb Bridge Rd., halfway between GA 400 and I–85, Norcross, 770/446–3553.*

12 *h-2*

IT'S ABOUT TIME

For some people, a clock's a clock and a watch just tells time. This store will probably change that, with its huge selection of clocks and watches in glass, metal, acrylic, leather, and steel. *Lenox Square, 3393 Peachtree Rd., Buckhead, 404/233–0357. MARTA: Lenox.*

5 *c-5*

Perimeter Mall, 4400 Ashford-Dunwoody Rd., Dunwoody, 770/399–6958. MARTA: Dunwoody.

5 *f-7*

Northlake Mall, 4800 Briarcliff Rd., Northlake, 770/493–8404.

4 *h-7*

Cumberland Mall, I–285 and I–75 at Cobb Pkwy., Smyrna, 770/435–8463.

5 *e-1*

North Point Mall, 1000 North Point Cir., Alpharetta, 770/442–9854.

8 *a-8*

Southlake Mall, 1000 Southlake Mall, Morrow, 770/968–1191.

chapter 3

PARKS, GARDENS, & SPORTS

*I*n metropolitan Atlanta's rich variety of parks, preserves, and recreation areas, locals and visitors gather to play, explore, or simply relax. The area's moderate climate invites you to take a hike, enjoy a picnic, play golf or tennis, and enjoy other outdoor activities throughout the year. Area lakes and rivers draw boaters, sailors, and anglers in search of brisk winds, rippling waters, and trophy-size game fish.

Whether in traditional team sports, such as softball and basketball, or newer activities like in-line skating, disc golf, and paintball, Atlantans are competing and having fun. For information on races, tournaments, and other sporting activities, pick up a free copy of the monthly Atlanta Sports and Fitness Magazine, *available at sporting goods stores, fitness centers, bookstores, and newsstands around the city.*

parks

The city of Atlanta and surrounding 10-county metropolitan area offer a tapestry of parks for recreation and relaxation. There are courts and ball fields for organized games, lakes for boating and fishing, pools for sunning and swimming, trails for exploring, and playgrounds and picnic grounds for informal family gatherings. The city alone manages more than 350 parks, recreation centers, and other facilities, from tiny green spaces and gardens to neighborhood and community parks to large multipurpose parks that are major regional destinations. DeKalb County manages 107 parks, many with an Atlanta address even though they are not within Atlanta city limits. The region's rapid growth has created greater demand for green spaces, so counties are expanding their parks systems; Henry County, for instance, opened three new parks in 1999. As a result this listing can include only the most popular of the dozens of parks around Atlanta.

park information

In the descriptions below, a phone number is given for each park that has one. For information on parks that do not

have their own phone number, or to learn more about other parks and park programs in Atlanta and the 10-county area, you can contact the parks departments. For information on particular sports played in the parks, *see also* Sports & Outdoor Activities, *below.*

Atlanta: Department of Parks, Recreation, and Cultural Affairs, 404/817–6744 (city parks) or 404/817–6764 (recreation in city parks). **Cherokee County**: Parks and Recreation Authority, 770/924–7768 (athletic leagues and recreational programs). **Clayton County**: Parks and Recreation Department, 770/477–3766 (athletic leagues and recreational programs). **Cobb County**: Parks and Recreation Department, 770/528–8800. **DeKalb County**: Parks and Recreation Department, 404/371–2631 (leagues and locations). **Douglas County**: Parks and Recreation Department, 770/920–7129. **Fayette County**: Parks and Recreation Department, 770/461–9714. **Forsyth County**: Parks and Recreation Department, 770/781–2215. **Fulton County**: Parks and Recreation Department, 404/704/6300. **Gwinnett County**: Parks and Recreation Department, 770/822–8840. **Henry County**: Parks and Recreation Department, 770/954–2031.

city of atlanta

7 *f-5*

ADAMS PARK

This hilly, wooded park adjacent to the Alfred "Tup" Holmes Golf Course (*see* Golf, *below*) is a favorite destination of southside residents. The multipurpose park features four ball fields, a gymnasium and recreation center, seasonal swimming pool, two tennis courts, and picnic pavilions around a small lake. *1620 DeLowe Dr., north of Campbellton Rd., 404/756–1827.*

8 *a-2*

CANDLER PARK

Situated on land donated to the city by Coca-Cola Company founder Asa Candler, this popular in-town park features a 9-hole golf course that's possibly the least expensive in town and a great course for beginners (*see* Golf, below). There are also a ball field, four tennis courts, basketball court, volleyball court, and picnic area. *1500 McLendon Ave., south of Ponce de Leon Ave., 404/817–6757.*

`15` *d-5*

CENTENNIAL OLYMPIC PARK

Before the 1996 Olympic Games, the neighborhood where this park now stands was filled with decaying warehouses and commercial buildings. Today the park is a lasting legacy of the games and one of the largest urban parks created in the United States. in the last three decades. Everyone, from toddlers to grandparents, loves splashing in the dancing waters of the Rings Fountain, the open spaces for picnicking, and facilities for outdoor concerts and special events. The park also has a casual restaurant. *Techwood Dr. and Marietta St., 404/223–4412. MARTA: Dome/GWCC.*

`5` *b-7*

CHASTAIN PARK

Golf, tennis, and youth team sports are the main attractions at this park (*see Golf and Tennis, below*), but there are other amenities, including a large playground and picnic area, a 3½-mi footpath (watch out for errant golf balls!), an arts-and-crafts center, and an outdoor amphitheater that hosts a popular summer concert program featuring big-name entertainers. *140 W. Wieuca Rd., 404/252–8866.*

`15` *g-8*

GRANT PARK

Best known as the home of the Cyclorama, a monumental circular painting depicting the 1864 Battle of Atlanta, and of Zoo Atlanta (*see Zoos, below*), Grant Park occupies land donated to the city in 1882 by Lemuel P. Grant, the engineer who designed Atlanta's Civil War defenses. The park lends its name to the surrounding area of restored Victorian houses and Craftsman bungalows—one of Atlanta's most ethnically diverse neighborhoods. The rolling, tree-shaded hills were once part of a Civil War battlefield; the hilltop site of a former Confederate artillery battery now offers a splendid view of the city skyline. The park has picnic pavilions, ball fields, tennis courts, a gymnasium, and a swimming pool. On summer weekends, the aroma of grilling chicken, burgers, and barbecue will make your mouth water. *537 Park Ave., south of I–20, 404/624–0697. MARTA: King Center.*

`15` *f-2*

PIEDMONT PARK

Atlanta's most enduringly popular playground, Piedmont Park has been practically loved to death during its century-plus existence. Confederate veterans, football players, presidents, hippies, and road-racers have all put in an appearance here. The first football game played in Georgia (Georgia vs. Auburn) was held here in 1892, as was, three years later, the Cotton States Exposition, a southern version of the Worlds Fair (John Philip Sousa composed his King Cotton March for the occasion). Vestiges of the exposition grounds, designed by landscape architect Frederick Law Olmsted, still remain. In 1969, the park was the scene of a giant hippie love-in that included a free concert by the Allman Brothers; more recently, it has been the site of the finish line for the annual July 4 Peachtree Road Race (*see Hiking, Running & Walking, below*), which with 55,000 runners is the nation's largest 10-K footrace. The passage of years and of millions of feet has taken its toll, but the non-profit Piedmont Park Conservancy works closely with the city in park restoration and preservation efforts. Today, softball and soccer teams play on the three ball fields and tennis buffs chase balls across the public courts (*see Tennis, below*). Picnickers spread their blankets along the shores of Lake Clara Meer, skateboarders and in-line skaters cruise park roads that are closed to automobiles (*see In-Line Skating & Roller-Skating, below*), and children frolic at the unusual playground designed by Japanese artist Isamu Noguchi. On the park's northern boundary are the landscaped grounds of the Atlanta Botanical Garden (*see Botanical Gardens & Nature Preserves, below*). *400 Park Dr., between Piedmont Ave. and Monroe Dr. north of 10th St., 404/817–6757. MARTA: Arts Center and Midtown.*

`7` *h-5*

SOUTHSIDE PARK

This multi-facility park is a major recreational destination for Atlantans who live on the city's south side. Softball and tennis are the main attractions: There are four championship softball fields used for recreational and competitive league play and tournaments (*see Baseball & Softball, below*), plus eight tennis courts for recreational play. *3460 Jonesboro Rd., north of I–285, 404/361–4100.*

15 *e-6*

WOODRUFF MEMORIAL PARK

Watched over by skyscrapers in the heart of the central city, Woodruff Park is the ideal spot for lunchtime people-watching. Street preachers and sidewalk vendors mix with business types in this parcel of green amid a forest of glass and steel. In the spring and summer, the park hosts noontime and after-work events on outdoor stages. *Peachtree St. and Edgewood Ave. at Five Points. MARTA: Five Points.*

cherokee county

2 *c-3*

BOLING PARK

Among the highlights of Cherokee County's park system, this multi-facility park has four lighted tennis courts, four handball-racquetball courts, four soccer fields, 3 softball-baseball fields, a basketball-volleyball court, playground, jogging track, and picnic pavilions. *1279 GA 5, Canton.*

2 *a-8*

HOBGOOD PARK

Conveniently located between Woodstock and Lake Allatoona, Hobgood Park is a very popular recreation destination in southern Cherokee County. The park features four lighted championship softball fields, four lighted tennis courts, a jogging trail, fitness courts, playground, picnic pavilions, and an outdoor amphitheater. *6688 Bells Ferry Rd., Woodstock.*

clayton county

9 *h-1*

CLAYTON COUNTY INTERNATIONAL PARK

On 200 wooded acres, you can go angling in the fishing lake, explore the bike trails, play miniature golf, cool off in the Beer Garden, or simply enjoy a relaxing day in the sun. There's also swimming (*see* Beaches & Water Parks, *below*) and a volleyball complex (*see* Volleyball, *below*). Each summer, the volleyball stadium is transformed into a performance center for an annual concert series (call for event and ticket information); the adjacent meeting space hosts traveling arts and crafts exhibitions. *GA 228, west of I–75 (exit 75), Jonesboro, 770/473–4005.*

9 *f-2*

INDEPENDENCE PARK

One of Clayton County's more popular parks, this green space features a paved walking trail, playground, tennis courts, ball fields, and basketball courts. *8970 Thomas Rd., Jonesboro.*

9 *h-4*

PANHANDLE PARK

This popular park in the southern part of the county features a paved walking path, picnic pavilions, a playground, ball fields, and a basketball court. *10930 Panhandle Rd., Jonesboro.*

8 *c-7*

REX PARK

A popular community gathering place, the park features ball fields, tennis courts, picnic pavilions, and a playground. *3499 Rex Rd., Rex.*

cobb county

4 *e-6*

JIM MILLER PARK

This multi-purpose park is the site of the North Georgia State Fair and Shrine Circus (held annually in September), as well as of rodeo competitions. The park features two 9,000-square-ft exhibition buildings, a lake, equestrian center (*see* Horseback Riding, *below*), cross-country running course, fitness trail, and picnic pavilions. *2245 Callaway Rd., just south of the Al Bishop Softball Complex, Marietta, 770/528–8875.*

4 *f-5*

LARRY BELL PARK

On the grounds of the Cobb County Civic Center, this park has tennis courts, a jogging track, a handicapped-accessible playground, and a fitness trail. It is also home to the 11,600-square-ft Cobb County Gymnastics Center, which offers classes for children 2–18, and of the Cobb Aquatic Center's two heated pools (*see* Swimming, *below*). *592 Fairground St., just southeast of downtown on GA 120 (Marietta Pkwy.), Marietta, 770/528–8450.*

4 *b-5*

LOST MOUNTAIN PARK

This comprehensive recreation center in west Cobb has a tournament softball complex with five fields, football and baseball fields, playgrounds, fitness and jogging trails, ponds, and a senior citizen's center. *4845 Dallas Hwy., Powder Springs, 770/528–8885.*

4 *d-7*

TRAMORE PARK

In addition to an 11-field soccer complex with game and practice facilities, the park has a playground and picnic pavilions. *2150 East-West Connector, south of Hurt Rd. and east of Powder Springs.*

4 *c-7*

WILD HORSE CREEK PARK

This multifaceted park has something for everyone: six softball fields; football, baseball, and soccer fields; tennis courts; playgrounds; fitness trails; picnic pavilions; ponds; a community center; a BMX bicycle course (*see Bicycling, below*); and an equestrian facility (*see Horseback Riding, below*). *3820 Macedonia Rd., Powder Springs, 770/528–8890.*

dekalb county

Note: DeKalb parks with Atlanta addresses are in unincorporated areas of the county.

5 *d-6*

BLACKBURN PARK

The multi-use park in northeastern DeKalb County features soccer fields, softball fields, group picnic areas, walking trails, and a full-service tennis center (*see Tennis, below*). *3493 Ashford-Dunwoody Rd., Dunwoody.*

0 *e-5*

BROWN'S MILL

Youth and adult sports activities are the emphasis at this park, which features baseball, softball, and football fields; tennis courts; a multipurpose recreation center; picnic area; and walking trails. *5101 Brown's Mill Rd., Atlanta, 770/593–5874.*

8 *c-4*

EXCHANGE PARK

A favorite destination of southeastern DeKalb residents, this large park has a variety of facilities and activities. There are baseball-softball fields, a football-soccer field, tennis courts, playgrounds, picnic areas, a fishing lake, foot trails, and a recreation center. *2771 Columbia Dr., Decatur.*

8 *f-1*

GEORGIA'S STONE MOUNTAIN PARK

Standing more than 800 ft high and more than 5 mi in circumference, 300-million-year-old Stone Mountain is the largest piece of exposed granite in the world (geologists believe that less than 1/1000th of the giant rock is above ground). The park's epicenter is the bas-relief sculpture on the north side of the mountain that depicts Confederate leaders, but there's a lot more to see and do in the park (*see Sports & Outdoor Activities, below, and Chapter 4*). Tourist attractions aside, Stone Mountain is a great park. You can swim in the lake, play golf or tennis, ride an old-fashioned steam train or a modern skylift gondola, visit a zoo, or cruise on a riverboat. Biking, running, blading, hiking, and camping are popular activities as well. The park offers a nightly laser show during the summer and a wide array of other events throughout the year. If you plan to use the park several times a year, you can save on admission costs with the Rock, Stock, and Barrel Pass, which allows unlimited admission (excluding golf and tennis) for a year: the pass costs $20 per person or $50 for a family of three. To save on parking fees buy the Classic Rock Parking Permit, which gives you unlimited parking for $30 a year. *U.S. 78, 5 mi outside/east of I–285, Stone Mountain, 770/498–5690, www.stonemountainpark.com. Park open daily 6 AM–midnight; most attractions 10–5 Sept.–May, 10–8 Jun.–Aug. Admission free; attractions $12 for Georgia residents, $15 for non-residents; parking $6.*

0 *b-4*

GRESHAM PARK

Youth sports, such as baseball and football, are the main focus of Gresham Park's facilities, but adults and families enjoy the seasonal swimming pool, playgrounds, picnic areas, fishing lake, trails, and recreation center at this 125-acre southwestern DeKalb County park. *3113 Gresham Rd., Atlanta, 404/244–4890.*

5 *f-7*

HENDERSON PARK

With several fields for play and practice, soccer is the main draw at this large park. In addition to the fields, the park has tennis courts, a playground, trails, picnic areas, and a small lake. *2803 Henderson Rd., Tucker.*

8 b-3

MARK TRAIL PARK

Only a short distance from I–20 in southern DeKalb County, a wide variety of facilities and activities are available in a modest 45-acre park encircled by residential neighborhoods. There are ball fields, basketball and tennis courts, a seasonal swimming pool (*see* Swimming, *below*), playgrounds, picnic areas, a recreation center, and walking trails. *2230 Tilson Rd., Decatur, 404/244–4891.*

5 d-6

MURPHY CANDLER PARK

Best known for its youth baseball, softball, and football programs, this 135-acre park also features a large fishing lake, picnic pavilions, hiking trails, tennis courts, playgrounds, and a seasonal swimming pool (*see* Swimming, *below*). The park is tucked into a pleasant residential area only a short distance south of I–285 in northern DeKalb County. *1551 W. Nancy Creek Rd., Dunwoody.*

8 f-3

REDAN PARK

A favorite destination for disc-golf players (*see* Disc Golf, *below*), Redan Park in eastern DeKalb County also has ball fields, basketball courts, playgrounds, picnic areas, and walking trails. *1745 Phillips Rd., Lithonia.*

8 E-2

WADE-WALKER PARK

In the shadow of Stone Mountain, 177-acre Wade-Walker Park has softball, baseball, and football fields; tennis courts; playgrounds; picnic areas; a swimming pool (*see* Swimming, *below*); a fishing lake; trails; and one of the area's premier street hockey rinks (*see* Hockey, *below*). *5585 Rockbridge Rd., Stone Mountain.*

douglas county

DEER LICK PARK

This multipurpose park offers a rich variety of facilities and activities. In addition to three softball fields and a football field, there is an outdoor amphitheater, a playground, picnic shelters, a 3-acre lake for fishing, a sand volleyball court, a jogging track, and a 9-hole disc-golf course (*see* Disc Golf, *below*). *2105 Mack Rd., Douglasville, a short distance east of I–20 via GA 92 and Mack Rd.*

7 a-2

SWEETWATER CREEK STATE CONSERVATION PARK

Blending scenic beauty and historic heritage, this park protects the swift waters of Sweetwater Creek and preserves the historic ruins of the New Manchester Manufacturing Company, a textile mill burned by Union Army cavalry in 1864. The 2,000-acre park has more than 5 mi of hiking trails, plus picnic areas and 215-acre Sparks Reservoir, a popular site for anglers. Each September a commemoration of Civil War mill days is held, with a reenactment of the encampment, living history demonstrations, and a crafts fair. At park headquarters you can obtain park maps and information as well as fishing licenses, bait, and supplies. *Mount Vernon Rd., south of Blair's Bridge Rd. (Blair's Bridge intersects with Camp Creek Pkwy. just south of I–20 in Lithia Springs), 770/732–5871.*

fayette county

9 d-5

KIWANIS CENTER PARK

This is the county's busiest park, with 10 baseball fields, tennis courts, a playground, picnic areas, and a recreation center. *936 Redwine Rd., Fayetteville, 770/461–9714.*

9 e-4

MCCURRY PARK

In addition to softball fields, McCurry Park has a football complex with a running track, picnic pavilions, and a walking path. You can test your mind and body on the ropes challenge course, on which you navigate rough terrain via a series of ropes. *GA 54 E, at McDonough Rd., east of Fayetteville.*

9 a-5

LAKE KEDRON

County residents enjoy the setting of this small lake just north of Peachtree City. It is a popular local destination for anglers and for boaters with small watercraft. Facilities include a public boat ramp and modest fishing docks. *N. Peachtree Pkwy., off GA 74, north of Peachtree City.*

9 f-7

LAKE HORTON

In the heart of a wooded, rural area of the county, this park has walking trails and a small nature preserve. The 800-acre lake attracts boaters and anglers. *Antioch Rd., east of GA 92, south of Fayetteville.*

forsyth county

`3` *e-4 through h-5*

LAKE SIDNEY LANIER

Named in honor of the famed Georgia poet who wrote *Marshes of Glynn* and *Song of the Chattahoochee*, this 38,000-acre lake (commonly called Lake Lanier) sprawls through the scenic Appalachian foothills of northeastern Georgia. The lake was created in the 1950s when the Army Corps of Engineers built Buford Dam on the Chattahoochee River. Lanier is one of the busiest recreational lakes in the nation, making it very crowded on summer weekends. Along its 540 mi of shoreline, anglers, boaters, campers, water-skiers, and others enjoy all kinds of outdoor pursuits (*see* Beaches & Water Parks; Boating; Fishing; and Sailing, *below*). The vast lakefront features five campgrounds, 42 day-use areas, 10 public parks, 54 boat launches, and 10 commercial marinas. Contact the Resource Manager's Office for detailed information on facilities. *Between GA 400 and I–985 about 35 mi northeast of Atlanta, between Buford and Gainesville, 770/945–9531 office, 770/945–1467 recorded information.*

`3` *d-3*

SAWNEE PARK

With eight youth baseball fields, this park is especially busy during Little League season. But it also has football, softball, and soccer fields; two tennis courts; a playground, picnic pavilion; and a community recreation building. *3995 Watson Rd., off GA 20 and 306, just north of Cumming, 770/886–4085.*

`3` *c-6*

SHARON SPRINGS PARK

Youth and adult team sports are the emphasis at Sharon Springs, Forsyth County's largest and busiest park. There are four youth baseball-softball fields, five adult ball fields (four softball and one baseball), two football-soccer fields, eight tennis courts, a playground, a paved walking-jogging path, a picnic pavilion, and tennis courts. *1950 Sharon Rd., just off GA 141 south of GA 400, near Cumming.*

fulton county

`5` *a-5 through g-3*

CHATTAHOOCHEE RIVER NATIONAL RECREATION AREA

Stretching like a string of pearls through Atlanta's northern suburbs, the several locations of this federal park protect the shoreline and wooded hills along 48 mi of the slow-moving river. The park's 14 units stretch from Bowman's Island just south of Buford Dam to Pace's Mill beneath the concrete of I–75 in northwest Atlanta. Taken together, nine developed park areas contain rich fishing waters (state fishing license required), picnic areas, recreational fields, more than 70 mi of hiking trails, and put-in points for canoes, kayaks, power boats, and seasonal commercial rafting expeditions (*see* Bicycling; Bird-Watching; Canoeing, Kayaking & Rafting; and Hiking, Running & Walking, *below*). The other five units do not yet offer recreational access. Park naturalists offer guided hikes and other activities at various times throughout the year; contact park headquarters at 770/952–4419 for information.

`5` *a-7*

East and West Palisades: Perched on palisades along the east and west banks of the river, these two units flank an area of rapids. Here, just north of Atlanta city limits, you'll find more than 8 mi of trails, a large recreation field, boat ramps, and picnic areas. The take-out point for commercial raft trips is at West Palisades. *West Palisades: U.S. 41 at the river. East Palisades: Indian Trail, off Northside Dr., south of I–285.*

`5` *a-6*

Cochran Shoals/Powers Island: These two units face each other from opposite banks of the river, with Powers Island in between. With its 3.3-mi paved fitness trail, Cochran Shoals is the most popular part of the park. A mountain-biking trail connects the trail with the paths of the Sope Creek Unit. Powers Island's quieter 2-mi Floodplain Trail affords hikers a view of kayakers tackling the Atlanta Whitewater Club's slalom gates. The area also has broad open fields and picnic areas. *Interstate North Pkwy., off I–285 at New Northside Dr., southeast of Marietta.*

5 *a-5*

Sope Creek: The area's 1½-mi Mill Trail winds past mill ruins on the banks of Sope Creek that are rich in Civil War history. Nearby, the 2-mi Fox Creek Loop Trail joins the Scribner Trail, connecting Sope Creek with the trails at Cochran Shoals. These trails are suitable for hikers and mountain bikers. *Paper Mill Rd. off Johnson Ferry Rd., between Marietta and Roswell.*

5 *b-5*

Johnson Ferry: A 2½-mi loop trail follows the river banks and crosses a flood plain. A large boat ramp here serves as the put-in point for seasonal commercial raft trips on the river. You'll also find several large, open fields once used for polo and now for soccer and other activities. *Johnson Ferry Rd. on the north side of the river, between Marietta and Sandy Springs.*

5 *c-3*

Gold Branch: More than 7 mi of trails provide some easy hiking and some difficult routes through thick woods and brush. Trails follow the banks of Bull Sluice Lake, created in 1904 by the construction of nearby Morgan Falls Dam. *Lower Roswell Rd. west of the Chattahoochee Nature Center, between Marietta and Roswell.*

5 *c-3*

Vickery Creek: Six miles of trails meander along wooded ridges and past the dam and ruins of a textile mill (*see box, below*) burned by Union Army cavalry in 1864. *Oxbo Rd. east of Atlanta St. (Roswell Rd.), Roswell.*

5 *c-3*

Island Ford: Massive rock outcrops frame the 3-mi trail that winds along the river and into the surrounding hills. Park headquarters are located in an oversize 1940s log building. *Island Ford Parkway off Roberts Dr. and Northridge Rd., west of GA 400 near Roswell.*

5 *f-3*

Jones Bridge: More than 5½ mi of trails take hikers along quiet river banks and through thick woodlands. Here, the Geosphere Environmental Education Center provides environmental education programs for elementary and high school teachers, scout leaders, and adult educators. It is only open to the public for special events. *Barnwell Rd. off Holcomb Bridge Rd. and GA 400, southeast of Alpharetta.*

5 *g-3*

Medlock Bridge: Three miles of trails, a boat ramp, and several popular fishing spots are the highlights of this part of the recreation area. *Medlock Bridge Rd. off Peachtree Pkwy. (GA 141), west of Duluth.*

5 *c-3*

CHATTAHOOCHEE RIVER PARK

Extending for nearly half a mile along the banks of the Chattahoochee River, this park is a haven for boaters and rafters, picnickers, anglers, and families

---

RIVER OF HISTORY

Deep in the mountains of northern Georgia, the Chattahoochee River—whose name in ancient Cherokee means "river of the painted rocks"—springs cold and clear from the earth. For the Creek and Cherokee the river was a pathway between villages and hunting and fishing grounds. In the 1830s the rushing waters of Vickery Creek, a tributary of the Chattahoochee, brought Roswell King to the area. King established a textile mill on the banks of the creek, and the town of Roswell grew up around the mill. During the Civil War, the Union cavalry raided Roswell, capturing and burning the mill and shipping many of the workers north, never to return. The mill was rebuilt and operated for nearly a century, until the construction of Buford Dam created Lake Sidney Lanier in the 1950s and forced the mills to close for a final time. Over the years the river became a playground for boaters and anglers, and the once remote village of Roswell grew into a thriving Atlanta suburb; the old mill buildings have been converted into office and retail space. By the 1970s, the pace of development in Atlanta threatened to overwhelm the river's scenic but fragile environment. In 1978, Georgia native son President Jimmy Carter created the Chattahoochee River National Recreation Area to protect and preserve vestiges of the river's natural landscape for all to enjoy.

who simply wish to relax and watch the river roll by and feed the many flocks of inquisitive ducks and Canada geese. In addition to a boat ramp, there are picnic tables and two covered pavilions, a playground, a walking trail, and a recreation building. The park is headquarters for the Atlanta Rowing Club (see Canoeing, Kayaking & Rafting, below). *203 Azalea Dr., just west of Roswell Rd. (GA 9), 1 mi south of Roswell, 770/740–2416.*

7 *b-8*

CLARENCE DUNCAN MEMORIAL PARK

This large park in the southern end of the county bustles with activity most of the year. It has lighted baseball-softball-football fields, two tennis courts, two outdoor basketball courts, a playground, hiking trails, picnic pavilions, an indoor-outdoor swimming pool with retractable roof (see Swimming, below), and a small lake. *6000 Rivertown Rd., just west of Fairburn, 770/306–3136.*

1 *c-7*

COCHRAN MILL PARK

This large, heavily wooded park contains several miles of trails for hiking and horseback riding, as well as picnic areas and sites for primitive camping. The park shares trails with the adjacent Cochran Mill Nature Preserve (see Botanical Gardens & Nature Preserves, below). Trails and a challenging ropes course meander through the thick woods to the banks of Bear and Little Bear creeks and past the ruins of 19th-century mill dams. The dams were built by Cheadle Cochran, who received the land as reward for his service in the War of 1812. In 1830 he moved his family to this site deep in the Georgia wilderness, where he farmed and operated a grist mill until his death in 1854. His son and then his grandson continued to work the land until they sold it to Hiram Evans in the 1930s. Evans, Imperial Wizard of the Ku Klux Klan, used the remote location for secret Klan activities. The park and preserve lands were acquired by Fulton County for use as a public park in the late 1970s. *6785 Cochran Mill Rd., just west of South Fulton Pkwy. and Rivertown Rd., near Palmetto, 770/306–0914.*

5 *c-1*

PROVIDENCE OUTDOOR RECREATION CENTER

A forest park and wildlife habitat, the center offers a wide variety of youth and adult education programs covering outdoor skills such as hiking, camping, and map and compass use. Naturalists conduct summer day camps for children here. The park has a lake and an outdoor amphitheater. *13440 Providence Park Dr., off Mayfield Rd., north of Alpharetta, 770/740–2419.*

7 *d-6*

WELCOME ALL PARK

This 37-acre park is jam-packed with recreational facilities, including football and soccer fields, five youth baseball fields, two tennis courts, two picnic shelters, walking trails, and a community center. Gymnastics, aerobics, and swimming (see Swimming, below) take place in the multipurpose fitness center. *4255 Will Lee Rd., just off Welcome All Rd., north of U.S. 29 (Roosevelt Hwy.), College Park, 404/762–4058.*

gwinnett county

5 *g-5*

BEST FRIEND PARK

This 55-acre park has a tennis center, softball-baseball fields, a picnic area, and a community building with a gymnasium and volleyball courts (see Volleyball, below). A swimming pool cools things down in summer. *6224 Jimmy Carter Blvd. (GA 140), north of I-85, Norcross, 770/417–2200.*

3 *h-8*

BOGAN PARK

Variety is the byword at this popular park. Amenities include a year-round aquatic center (see Swimming, below) with both competition and zero-depth wading pools, sand volleyball courts, picnic pavilions, walking-jogging trails, playgrounds, softball-baseball fields, basketball courts with supervised play, and a community building. *2723 North Bogan Rd., west of GA 365/I-985, Buford, 770/614–2060.*

6 *b-2*

GEORGE PIERCE PARK

Forest and wetland are the setting for this multipurpose park, which has softball-baseball fields, walking trails, a small lake, picnic pavilions, a playground, and a five-field soccer complex. *55 Buford Hwy., west of I-85, near Suwanee, 770/614–2060.*

5 *f-3*

JONES BRIDGE PARK

This picturesque 30-acre park sits on the eastern banks of the Chattahoochee River, across from the Jones Bridge unit of the Chattahoochee River National Recreation Area (*above*). Amenities include a large recreation field, playground, community building, and four soccer fields. *4901 E. Jones Bridge Rd., west of Peachtree Pkwy. (GA 141), near Norcross, 770/417–2200.*

6 *d-8*

LENORA PARK

From softball and disc golf to horseback riding, Lenora Park offers a rich blend of recreational opportunities. The 85-acre park has a six-field baseball-softball complex, a gymnasium, a playground, a small fishing lake, a paved walking trail, an equestrian practice ring, and an 18-hole disc golf course (*see Disc Golf, below*). *4514 Lenora Church Rd., south of Centerville–Rosebud Rd., Centerville, 770/237–5626.*

6 *b-7*

MOUNTAIN PARK

One of Gwinnett County's most visited parks, this spot has a seven-field softball-baseball complex, eight tennis courts (*see Tennis, below*), picnic pavilions, a playground, a walking trail, and a year-round aquatics center (*see Swimming, below*). *5050 Five Forks Trickum Rd., east of Lilburn, 770/237–5626.*

5 *h-3*

PINCKNEYVILLE PARK SOCCER COMPLEX

The five-field soccer complex (*see Soccer, below*) is the focal point of this 35-acre park, but there are other amenities, too: playgrounds, a small pond, and picnic pavilions. When the county completes the park's expansion to 108 acres, there will also be a baseball-softball complex, walking trails, a community building, and a roller-hockey rink. *4707 Old Peachtree Rd., Norcross, 770/417–2200.*

6 *e-4*

RHODES JORDAN PARK

The centerpiece of this park is a 22-acre fishing lake. The park also features a seven-field softball-baseball complex, a youth football field, picnic pavilions, playgrounds, two summer swimming pools (*see Swimming, below*), a community

center with gymnasium, and an eight-court tennis facility. *100 E. Crogan St. (U.S. 29), Lawrenceville, 770/237–5626.*

6 *f-6*

TRIBBLE MILL REGIONAL PARK

On 650 wooded acres in rural Gwinnett County is this park with picnic pavilions set around two lakes (a 40-acre fishing lake and a 108-acre boating lake). There are trails for hiking, jogging, and horseback riding; a group camping area; and large recreation fields for impromptu games of touch-football or Frisbee. *2425 Ozora Church Rd., off New Hope Rd., Grayson, 770/978–5270.*

henry county

8 *d-8*

GARDNER PARK

The focal point of this small park is the 12-court tennis facility (*see Tennis, below*). The park also includes a paved walking track, a playground, picnic pavilions, and a community building. *160 East Atlanta Rd., Stockbridge, 770/954–2031.*

8 *d-6*

HIDDEN VALLEY PARK

This large park features four baseball-softball fields, an outdoor basketball court, a nature trail, a ¼-mi paved jogging track, two lighted tennis courts, picnic pavilions, and horseshoe court. *1 Fairview Rd., at Spraggins Memorial Pkwy., Ellenwood.*

10 *h-5*

SANDY RIDGE PARK

A mix of outdoor facilities, including a baseball-softball field, basketball court, tennis courts, a playground, a paved jogging track, and a volleyball court, attracts large numbers of sports enthusiasts to this popular park. *1200 Keys Ferry Rd., McDonough.*

10 *e-4*

SOCCER COMPLEX

This facility has 10 soccer fields (*see Soccer, below*), a playground, picnic shelters, and a jogging trail. It is adjacent to the Red Tail Hawk Nature Preserve (*see Botanical Gardens & Nature Preserves, below*). *143 Henry Pkwy., McDonough.*

10 *d-4*

WINDY HILL PARK
Baseball and soccer fields, an obstacle course, a horseshoe court, a jogging trail, tennis courts, a picnic pavilion, and a playground make this a popular outdoor destination. The park is also home to the Henry County Fairgrounds and Exhibit Area. *100A Windy Hill Rd., McDonough.*

other green spaces

BEACHES & WATER PARKS

Atlanta may be a long drive from the ocean, but Atlantans love to go to the beach and to play in the water. Not surprisingly, the metropolitan area has a number of beaches and waterparks to slake the metro area's thirst for shoreside fun. Thanks to the mild climate, most beaches and waterparks open their doors in late spring and remain busy until mid-September.

9 *h-1*

CLAYTON COUNTY INTERNATIONAL PARK
Enjoy a day at the beach at this multi-purpose park: Swim in a lake bordered by water slides or tag along with the youngsters (under 48" tall) as they frolic in a children's pool complete with its own whimsical water slides. The park has much to offer nonswimmers, too (see Parks, *above*, and Volleyball, *below*). *GA 138 west of I–75, near Jonesboro (exit 75), 770/473–4005. Park daily 8–8; beach and waterpark late May–early Sept., Wed.–Fri. and Sun. 10–6, Sat. 10–8. Beach admission: adults $6.95, children 3–12 and senior citizens 55-plus $4.95, under 3 free; parking $2.*

8 *f-1*

THE BEACH AT GEORGIA'S STONE MOUNTAIN PARK
The Beach at Stone Mountain is a ⅓-mi stretch of white sand along the shores of 363-acre Stone Mountain Lake, where you can sun all afternoon or relax after a day of enjoying the park's other attractions (see Parks, *above*). A large picnic area is shaded by towering pine trees, and twin waterslides offer a thrilling ride suitable for even the youngest of swimmers. Adjacent to the beach there is a concession area and a bath house with rental locker facilities. *U.S 78, 5 mi outside/east of I–285, Stone Mountain, 770/498–5690, www.stonemountainpark.com. Open late May–early Sept., daily 10–7. Beach admission $5, children under 2 free. Parking $6.*

3 *g-5*

LAKE LANIER ISLANDS RESORT BEACH AND WATER PARK
Whether soaking up sun on the mile-long white-sand beach or splashing the day away on a dozen different water slides, the entire family will enjoy a summer day at this popular water playground on the shores of Lake Lanier. Don't miss the Fun Dunker, a multilevel, interactive ride designed to get you wet

---

PICNIC SPOTS

From the bloom of spring's first blossoms until the leaves drop in autumn, Atlanta's parks are a great place for spreading a blanket for a family picnic. These spots are great for enjoying scenery, watching people, or both.

Chattahoochee River Park
This thin ribbon of green along the northern bank of the river offers picnic tables, sheltered pavilions, and playgrounds (see Parks, *above*).

Georgia's Stone Mountain Park
The meadow beneath the giant carving is an ideal spot to enjoy a picnic during a day exploring the park's many attractions (see Parks, *above*).

Grant Park
One of Atlanta's oldest and most historic parks is alive with picnickers on warm-weather weekends. Pack a lunch when you come to explore Zoo Atlanta and the Cyclorama (see Parks, *above*, and Zoos, *below*).

Piedmont Park
Tucked beneath the towering Midtown Atlanta skyline, this is the city's busiest park. Spread a picnic on the grass and watch the people walk, jog, roll, and dance by (see Parks, *above*).

in more than 100 ways. Near the beach is Wild Waves, Georgia's largest wave pool, and Kiddie Lagoon and Wiggle Waves for the youngest swimmers. Also available at the resort are lodging, camping, golf, tennis, biking, horseback riding, sailing, and many other activities (additional charges apply; see Parks, above, and Boating, Fishing, Sailing, below). *6950 Holiday Rd., west of I–985 south of Gainesville, 770/932–7000, www.lakelanierislands.com. Open Memorial Day–Labor Day, Mon.–Thurs. 10–6, Fri–Sun. 10–7; May weekends 10–6. Admission: adults $20, children (under 42") and senior citizens $13.99, children 2 and under free.*

4 *g-4*

WHITE WATER

Test your nerves on the Cliffhanger's 90-ft free-fall, challenge the rapids on the Run-a-Way River, or body-surf in the Atlanta Ocean. When you're ready to relax, soak up some rays on Treehouse Island, and then float on a raft while watching an evening movie with the family. The South's largest waterpark has more than 50 different water attractions to beat the summer heat. Its four sections—Wildwater Lagoon, Slippery Ridge, Pine Valley, and Flash Flood Canyon—offer different combinations of aquatic excitement. Landlubbers can find fun next door at American Adventures (see Miniature Golf, below), where admission to Whitewater gets you in for free. *250 Cobb Pkwy., near I–75 (exit 265), Marietta, 770/424–9283, www.whitewaterpark.com. Open May weekends 10–6; June 1–Labor Day daily 10–6 (until 8 on Fri.). Over 48" $22.99; age 3 to 48" $14.99; up to age 3 $4.99; non-swimmers/riders $9.99.*

BOTANICAL GARDENS & NATURE PRESERVES

botanical gardens

15 *f-2*

ATLANTA BOTANICAL GARDEN

In the northern corner of Piedmont Park (see Parks, above), the Atlanta Botanical Garden is a 30-acre garden lover's delight. Specialty gardens of perennials, herbs, roses, fragrance plants, and veg-

etables, plus a delicate Japanese garden and a serene rock garden, lie outside the shimmering glass of the 16,000-square-ft Dorothy Chapman Fuqua Conservatory, which houses exotic and endangered plant specimens from around the world. Nearby, 15-acre Storza Woods offers shaded foot trails for exploring a vestige of the hardwood forest that once covered much of the Atlanta region. The youngest visitors are enchanted by the whimsical Children's Garden, filled with interactive exhibits, play areas, and an outdoor classroom. Moon Strolls reveal the candlelit garden, and seasonal events highlight plants that are in bloom; the annual Gardens for Connoisseurs Tour is a perennial favorite. Adult plant enthusiasts can also attend educational programs and study in the extensive Sheffield Botanical Library or have their plant-related questions answered by the ABG Hotline. The Botanical Garden offers summer day camps for children, and its Plant-Mobile presents children's programs throughout Atlanta. *1345 Piedmont Ave., Midtown, 404/876–5859, 404/888–4769 ABG hot line, 404/881–5323 Plant-Mobile schedule. Open Apr.–Oct., Tues.–Sun. 9–7; Nov.–Mar., Tues.–Sun. 9–6. Admission: adults $6, senior citizens $5, students $3, children under six free. Free Thurs. 3–closing. MARTA: Arts Center Station.*

12 *e-3*

ATLANTA HISTORY CENTER

Thirty-three acres of gardens around the city's premier historical institution (see Chapter 4) put Atlanta's history into its natural context. There are shaded woodland trails, a quarry garden lined with native plants and shrubs, a rhododendron garden blending into the natural landscape, an Asian-American Garden, an exquisite boxwood garden, terraced lawns, and, alongside a 19th-century farm house, small plots for herbs, vegetables, and medicinal plants. Visitors are invited to relax and stroll through the gardens as they explore the Museum of Atlanta History, the 1840s-era Tullie Smith farm complex, and the elegant 1920s Swan House. *130 W. Paces Ferry Rd., Buckhead, 404/814–4000. Open Mon.–Sat. 10–5:30, Sun. noon–5:30. Admission: adults $7, students (18 and over with valid ID) and senior citizens $5, children 6–17 $4, children 5 and under free; additional $1 for Tullie Smith House, $2 for Swan House.*

6 *f-7*

VINES BOTANICAL GARDEN

Once a private estate, the elegant 18,000-square-ft manor house and its 25 acres of gardens were a gift to Gwinnett County from Charles and Myrna Adams in 1990. Today, visitors are welcome to stroll through lush woodlands, enjoy rich heirloom roses, savor the colors of seasonal plants, admire the elegance of the European Statuary Garden, and chuckle at the yard art in the Whimsical Garden. In a setting overlooking the grounds, the Little Gardens Restaurant features dishes seasoned with herbs from the Culinary Garden. The garden is a popular choice for weddings and special events, and there are a variety of educational programs for children and adults. *3500 Oak Grove Rd., Loganville, 770/466–7532. Open Tues.–Sat. 10–5, Sun. 11–5. Admission free (donations encouraged), educational programs $15.*

nature preserves

5 *g-2*

AUTREY MILL NATURE PRESERVE

Amid several upscale golf-course communities, this 45-acre preserve is the site of wild woodlands and a century-old farm. A 1½-mi nature trail forms a rough figure eight as it meanders along a thickly wooded hillside. A small cabin houses the Tenant Museum, which depicts the rugged life of tenant farmers in the early years of the 20th century. Educational programs are offered in a restored 1880s house and an outdoor classroom. *9770 Autrey Mill Rd., on Old Alabama Rd. east of Peachtree Pkwy. (GA 141), Alpharetta, 770/664–0660. Grounds open daily dawn–dusk, visitor center and museum Thurs.–Sun. 12:30–4:30. Admission free (fee for classes).*

7 *e-4*

CASCADE SPRINGS NATURE PRESERVE

More than a century ago, the pure, bubbling waters of Cascade Springs drew some of the first residents to this western suburb of Atlanta. Cascade Heights became a bustling community that remains vital today. Here, a 120-acre wooded preserve protects the spring waters and a small tract of forest. The preserve is managed by the staff of the Outdoor Activity Center (*see below*), and a network of trails through the preserve is under development. *2852 Cascade Rd.,*

east of I–285, Cascade Heights, 404/752–5385. Hrs vary.

5 *b-3*

CHATTAHOOCHEE NATURE CENTER

A few miles north of Atlanta, more than 2 mi of foot trails crisscross the wooded hillsides and marshes of this 100-acre preserve, which borders the slow-moving waters of the Chattahoochee River. Since its founding in 1976, the center has become a leader in environmental education for children and adults, offering a variety of after-school programs, guided walks, and workshops. Two especially popular activities are the Camp Kingfisher summer camp for kids 5–12 and the summer evening canoe-floats on the Chattahoochee (*see Canoeing, Kayaking & Rafting, below*). In addition to presenting exhibits on river and woodland habitats, the nature center carries on an active wildlife rehabilitation program. Its shop carries a broad selection of field guides, bird houses, feeders, seeds, and hard-to-find gardening and birding accessories. *9135 Willeo Rd., south of GA 120, Roswell, 770/992–2055. Open Mon.–Sat. 9–5, Sun. noon–5. Admission: adults $3, senior citizens and children 3–12 $2, children under 3 and members free (additional fee for camps, classes, and some activities).*

1 *b-5*

CLINTON NATURE PRESERVE

Spread over 200 acres of woods and meadows, Clinton Nature Preserve includes a small lake for fishing, more than 5 mi of marked foot/horse trails, a ½-mi walking track, and an amphitheater for outdoor education programs. Still on its original site is a log cabin built by the Carnes family, pioneer settlers, in 1828. A small museum occupies a three-room farmhouse built by the Carnes family in the early 20th century; it contains period furniture typical of that found on small Georgia farms in first half of the 20th century. The house is also the caretaker's residence. *Ephesus Church Rd., off Post Rd. south of I–20, Douglasville, 770/459–1849. Open Thurs.–Tues. 9 AM–dusk.*

1 *c-7*

COCHRAN MILL NATURE PRESERVE

Trails and a ropes course meander through the thick woods of this preserve at Cochran Mill Park (*see Parks, above*), to the banks of Bear and Little Bear creeks and past the ruins of some 19th-century mill dams. The nature preserve occupies 50 acres along the north side of the park. A visitor center houses natural history exhibits and classrooms; injured wildlife are treated in an adjacent rehabilitation facility. *6875 Cochran Mill Rd., about 5 mi north of Palmetto on GA 154, 770/306–6200 park, 770/306–0914 nature preserve. Park open daily dawn–dusk; preserve Apr.–Oct., Mon.–Sat. 9–5, Sun. 1–5 (call for winter hrs). Admission free (donations welcome; registration fee for ropes courses and educational programs).*

8 g-5
DAVIDSON–ARABIA MOUNTAIN NATURE PRESERVE
Hidden away in a rural part of southeastern DeKalb County, this large preserve is a fascinating mix of forest and open rock. It is home to two endangered primitive plant species and a mix of colorful and unusual native plants and birds (*see Bird-Watching, below*). Park staff conduct guided hikes to the 140-ft-high mountain and offer a variety of outdoor educational programs. *3850 Klondike Rd., south of I–20, Lithonia, 770/484–3060. Open daily 7 AM–dusk.*

14 d-3, d-4
FERNBANK SCIENCE CENTER AND FOREST
During a 1949 visit to this natural treasure just 6 mi east of downtown Atlanta, naturalist Charles Russell of the American Museum of Natural History called it a unique jewel, a showpiece that no other American city can match. Purchased by Col. Zador Harrison in 1881, this piece of virgin forest was zealously protected by his daughter Miss Emily Harrison for more than five decades. She even bought out her siblings' interest in the property to prevent its subdivision. In the 1950s, she enlisted the support of county civic leaders in an effort to preserve the forest in perpetuity, and she lived to see it donated to DeKalb County for use as a science education center. Nearly 40 years later, Fernbank Science Center houses Atlanta's largest planetarium and astronomical observatory (*see Chapter 4*). It offers educational programs for DeKalb County elementary and high school students, as well as adult education programs. The enchanting forest is

accessible by a well-marked 2-mi trail that winds beneath a thick canopy of pines and hardwood trees typical of the woodlands of the southern Piedmont. A portion of the trail has been modified for ease of use by mobility- and visually impaired visitors. *156 Heaton Park Dr., off Ponce de Leon Ave., Druid Hills, 404/370–0960. Forest open Sun.–Fri. 2–5, Sat. 10–5; science center Mon. 8:30–5, Tues.–Fri. 8:30–10, Sat. 10–5, Sun. 1–5. Call for observatory hrs and planetarium show schedule. Admission free (fee for adult education classes and planetarium shows).*

7 e-4
OUTDOOR ACTIVITY CENTER
Called Atlanta's Forest in the City, the Outdoor Activity Center preserves a slice of wilderness on the slopes of Bush Mountain, a few miles southwest of downtown. From a playground adjacent to the visitor center, 2 mi of foot trails trace a loop through 26 acres of mountain ridges and creek valleys, crossing meadows and passing beneath towering hardwoods. There is a fenced playground and teaching area adjacent to the visitor center. Much of the center's environmental education programming reaches out to inner-city children from City of Atlanta schools and nearby neighborhoods. *1442 Richland Rd., just east of Cascade Rd., West End, 404/752–5385. Open Mon.–Sat. 9–4. Admission free (fee for classes).*

8 e-6
PANOLA MOUNTAIN STATE CONSERVATION PARK
More than 600 rolling acres of forest surround the exposed rock of rugged Panola Mountain, a federal Registered Natural Landmark. The mountain is a 125-ft-high outcrop of granite similar to Stone Mountain, its larger neighbor to the north (*above*). But unlike Stone Mountain, Panola Mountain has never been commercially exploited and its fragile environment is carefully protected; several rare plants grow within the park's boundaries. The 3½-mi trail from the visitor center to the top of the mountain is open only for naturalist-guided hikes, but access to three other trails—the ¾-mi Rock Outcrop Trail, the 1¼-mi Watershed Trail, and the 1-mi Fitness Trail—is unrestricted. Exhibits on the geologic history of Panola Mountain are on display at the park interpretive center, where outdoor education

programs are held. Picnic facilities are available adjacent to the parking area. *2600 GA 155 (Snapfinger Rd.), south of 1–20 at Wesley Chapel Rd., near Stockbridge, 770/389-7801. Park open daily 7 AM–dusk; interpretive center Tues.–Fri. 9–5, weekends noon–5. Parking $2.*

10 *e-4*

RED TAIL HAWK NATURE PRESERVE

This heavily wooded park preserves an undisturbed southern mixed forest of pines and hardwoods and is home to wildlife such as white-tail deer, raccoon, and various bird species. The park currently has a nature trail, a wildlife observation area, and a Boy/Girl Scout camp site. At press time, a number of facilities were in the planning stage, including a gazebo for outdoor programs and an open space for model-aircraft flights. *143 Henry Pkwy., McDonough, 770/954–2031 Parks Department. Admission free. Open dawn–dusk.*

8 *a-7*

REYNOLDS NATURE PRESERVE

This 146-acre forest preserve was once the property of hard-working Robert Huie, who purchased the land prior to the Civil War and farmed it for nearly a half-century. The land was acquired by Judge William Reynolds in the 1920s, and he spent many years turning it into a botanical wonderland. Reynolds had a passion for native azaleas, and he traveled throughout the Southeast searching for specimens to plant in his recovering forest. For many years, people came from across Atlanta to see the breathtaking spring colors at Judge Reynolds' farm. Shortly before his death in 1976, Reynolds donated the land to Clayton County as a permanent woodland preserve, where all can stroll along 4 mi of forest trails, picnic by tranquil ponds, and observe white-tail deer, raccoons, beavers, turtles, and land birds and waterfowl in their natural habitat (*see* Bird-Watching, *below*). The preserve offers a wide variety of educational programs. *5665 Reynolds Rd., near GA 54, Morrow, 770/603–4188. Admission free. Preserve open daily 8:30 AM–dusk, interpretive center weekdays 8:30–5:30.*

9 *h-3*

THE NEWMAN WETLANDS CENTER

Operated by the Clayton County Water Authority, this facility preserves a wetlands habitat for public enjoyment and education. The 32-acre park has a ½-mi-long boardwalk over a marsh and an education building with exhibit space, classrooms, and a 50-seat auditorium. Groups may arrange guided tours; the center is a popular gathering place for birding enthusiasts seeking waterfowl and other species on their annual migrations (*see* Bird-Watching *below*). *2755 Freeman Rd., Hampton, 770/603–5606, www.ccwal.com. Admission free. Trail open daily 8:30–5. Exhibit building open Nov.–Feb., weekdays 8:30–5; Mar.–Oct., Mon.–Sat. 8:30–5.*

8 *g-1*

YELLOW RIVER REGIONAL PARK

A short distance east of Georgia's Stone Mountain Park, Yellow River Regional Park is a woodland preserve that follows the meandering course of its namesake river. The 564-acre park contains a rich variety of plant- and wildlife in a mixed forest of pine and hardwood trees. Well-maintained trails are open to hikers, joggers, mountain bikers, and equestrians. *3232 Juhan Rd., off Rockbridge Rd., Stone Mountain, 770/978–5270. Admission free. Open daily dawn–dusk.*

ZOOS

15 *g-8*

ZOO ATLANTA

Like the 1991 Atlanta Braves baseball team, Zoo Atlanta has soared "from worst to first." In the early 1980s, the zoo was a worn-out and neglected complex with aging buildings and diminishing public support. The death of one of the zoo's elephants finally ignited the public's passion to save the zoo. Dr. Terry Maple was brought in to rescue the zoo, and he has done far more than that. Today, Zoo Atlanta is one of the finest zoos in the United States and enjoys tremendous public and corporate support. It is easy to fill an entire day here marveling at the more than 1,000

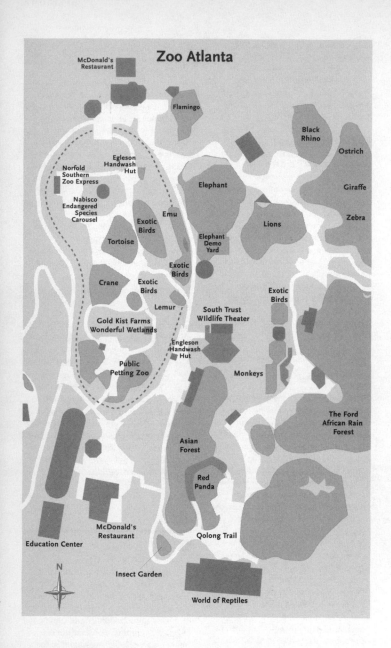

Zoo Atlanta

McDonald's Restaurant

Flamingo

Black Rhino

Ostrich

Giraffe

Norfold Southern Zoo Express

Egleson Handwash Hut

Elephant

Zebra

Nabisco Endangered Species Carousel

Emu

Exotic Birds

Lions

Tortoise

Elephant Demo Yard

Exotic Birds

Crane

Exotic Birds

Exotic Birds

Lemur

South Trust Wildlife Theater

Gold Kist Farms Wonderful Wetlands

Engleson Handwash Hut

Public Petting Zoo

Monkeys

The Ford African Rain Forest

Asian Forest

Red Panda

McDonald's Restaurant

Qolong Trail

Education Center

N

Insect Garden

World of Reptiles

134

animals living in natural settings (*see box, below*). Young visitors can talk to the animals in the Publix Petting Zoo or thrill to rides aboard the Nabisco Carousel and the Norfolk Southern Zoo Train. In addition, the zoo offers a variety of educational programs and children's camps. Zoo Atlanta is in the heart of historic Grant Park (*see Parks, above*) and is adjacent to the Atlanta Cyclorama, a massive circular painting depicting the Civil War Battle of Atlanta (*see Chapter 4*). *800 Cherokee Ave., south of I–20, Grant Park, 404/624–5600, 404/624–5822 educational programs and children's camps, www.zooatlanta.org. Open weekdays 9:30–4:30, weekends 9:30–5:30. Admission: adults $10, senior citizens $8, children 3–11 $6. MARTA: King Contor.*

FROM WORST TO FIRST

Once a deteriorating facility that was both an embarrassment to Atlanta and a threat to the health of the animals confined there, Zoo Atlanta is now among the finest facilities of its kind. This triumphant journey from worst to first has filled the zoo with amazing exhibits:

Ford African Rainforest
This is home for a family group of silverback gorillas including Willie B. Jr., son of the beloved Willie B. (named for then Atlanta mayor, William B. Hartsfield), who came to the zoo in 1961 and lived here until his death in 2000 at the age of 41.

Giant Pandas of Chengdu
When the two Chinese pandas Lun Lun and Yang-Yang, arrived in 1999, they quickly won Atlanta's heart.

Masai Mara
Capturing the feel of the African savanna, Masai Mara is home to lions, rhinos, giraffes, ostriches, and other creatures.

Monkeys of Makoku
Enjoy the antics of drill baboons and mona monkeys as they frolic together.

Orangutans of Ketambe
These captivating primates endear themselves to every visitor.

Sumatran Tiger Forest
Regal Sumatran tigers lounge and play in the shade of the trees.

stadiums

In the metropolitan Atlanta area, there are three major sporting venues that host a wide variety of events, from professional football, baseball, basketball, and ice hockey to track-and-field competitions, circuses, and concerts. Event tickets are available from team box offices, event sponsors, or **Ticketmaster** (404/249–6400 or 800/326–4000). For more information on the teams mentioned here, *see* Sports & Outdoor Activities, *below.*

15 *d-6*

GEORGIA DOME

This 71,500-seat enclosed stadium south of Downtown is home to the National Football League's Atlanta Falcons. The stadium also hosts the Southeastern Conference college football championship and the annual Heritage Bowl (known as the national football championship of the black colleges) and Peach Bowl games. The stadium periodically hosts the NFL Super Bowl and the NCAA's regional and Final Four basketball tournaments. A MARTA station is adjacent to the stadium. *One Georgia Dome Dr., off International Blvd. south of the Georgia World Congress Center, 404/223–9200. Guided tours Tues.–Sat. 10–4, Sun. noon–4 (except game days). MARTA: Vine City and Dome/GWCC.*

15 *d-6*

PHILIPS ARENA

Built on the site of the old OMNI Coliseum, the Philips Arena opened in 1999. It is the home of the National Basketball Association's Atlanta Hawks and the National Hockey League's Atlanta Thrashers. The arena seats 15,179 for hockey, 16,378 for basketball, and up to 17,000 for concerts. Connecting the arena with the adjacent CNN Center is Hawk Walk, an enclosed pedestrian boulevard lined with shops, restaurants, and interactive entertainment venues. The arena is near the Georgia Dome in the heart of downtown. *Techwood Dr. south of Marietta St., 404/827–3865 Hawks, 404/584–7825 Thrashers. MARTA: Dome/GWCC.*

15 *e-8*

TURNER FIELD

Built as an 80,000-seat track-and-field venue for the 1996 Olympics, the facility

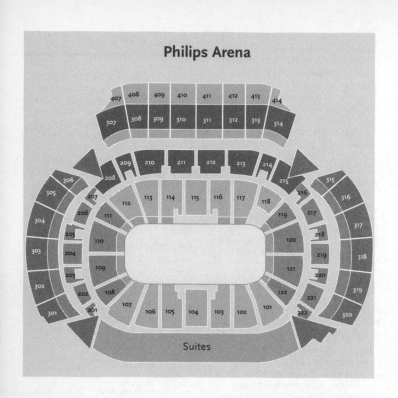

Philips Arena

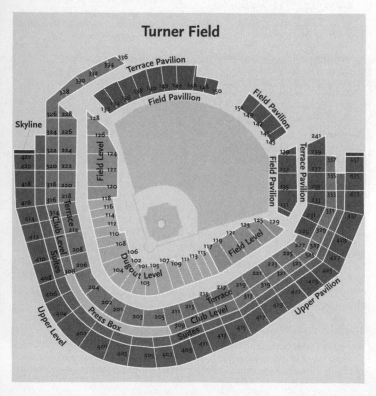

Turner Field

was reconfigured after the games into the present 46,000-seat baseball stadium. The postmodern structure is home to the Atlanta Braves of Major League Baseball's National League and is named for team owner and media mogul Ted Turner (the stadium is nicknamed the Ted). But Turner Field is more than just a ball park, it is an attraction. Fans may test their pitching and hitting skills in Scout's Alley, learn a bit of Braves lore in the Ivan Allen Museum of Braves History (named for the mayor who brought the Braves to Atlanta in 1966) and the Braves Hall of Fame, and enjoy pre- and post-game activities at Braves Plaza behind center field. During ball games, fans flock to Coca-Cola Sky Field (above the left-field stands) hoping to win $1 million by catching the first home run ever to be hit there—since the stadium's opening in 1997, no player has come close to hitting a ball up there. Stadium tours include visits to the locker rooms, press box, and museum. *755 Hank Aaron Dr., adjacent to I–85 and I–20 south of downtown, 404/522–7630 tickets, 404/614–2311 tours.*

Tours Tues.–Sat 9–5 during baseball season, Mon.–Sat. 10–2 off-season. Tours $7 (includes museum admission), museum $3 ($2 with game ticket). MARTA: Georgia State.

sports & outdoor activities

An excellent resource for outdoors-minded Atlantans is *Atlanta Sports and Fitness*, a free monthly magazine with in-depth articles on recreation, listings of all kinds of amateur sports leagues, and a calendar of upcoming events. The magazine is available at sporting goods stores, fitness centers, bookstores, and hundreds of other outlets around the city; you can also call 404/843–2257 or visit its Web site, www.atlantasports-mag.com. The *Atlanta Journal–Constitution* publishes a monthly newspaper insert, "Atlanta at Play," that provides information on local sports activities and events. Copies are available for purchase at 404/526–5668 or 800/756–4197.

Two local outdoor-equipment retailers offer educational programs and guided adventures such as backpacking trips, white-water rafting, and bicycling tours. These are **REI, Inc.** (North Atlanta store 404/633–6508, Perimeter store 770/901–9200) and **High Country, Ltd.** (Buckhead, 404/814–0999). *See* Chapter 2 for store information.

ARCHERY

Local archery clubs host adult and junior competitions at fields around Atlanta. For information on membership, instruction, and competitions, contact the clubs.

JAPANESE ARCHERY ASSOCIATION OF GEORGIA

In Japan, archery is more than recreation or physical exercise: The objective is to achieve total physical and mental concentration in a Zen-like effort to become one with the bow. Membership includes instruction and events. *404/373–0546. Membership: $40 per month.*

KENNESAW ARCHERY CLUB

The club offers target-shooting and bow-hunting instruction ($5–$10) and target

---

WHERE THE PROS PLAY

Atlanta fields competitive teams in nearly all major professional sports:

Atlanta Braves (Baseball)
The perennial National League leaders play their home games at Turner Field.

Atlanta Falcons (Football)
This often-maligned team has put its fans through an emotional roller-coaster ride, cresting with an appearance in the 1999 Super Bowl. The Falcons are at home in the (Georgia) Dome.

Atlanta Hawks (Basketball)
Always competitive, the Hawks light up the scoreboard at Philips Arena.

Atlanta Silverbacks (Soccer)
A small but vocal following cheers the United Soccer League team to victory at DeKalb Memorial Stadium.

Atlanta Thrashers (Hockey)
After a nearly 20-year absence, NHL hockey came back to Atlanta and is now more popular than ever. The Thrashers carve the ice at Philips Arena.

competitions. *770/516–0602. Individual memberships: $25 per year; family memberships: $40. Non-Cobb residents pay an additional $25 per year.*

TRI-COUNTIES ARCHERY CLUB

Juniors and adults can get instruction and participate in target competitions through this club. *770/474–3345.*

BASEBALL & SOFTBALL

teams to watch

THE ATLANTA BRAVES

Since the miraculous "worst-to-first" 1991 season that propelled them to their first World Series since 1958—when they were the Milwaukee Braves—the Braves have become perennial contenders for the National League championship. They have played in five World Series (1991, 1992, 1995, 1996, and 1999), defeating the Cleveland Indians in 1995 to claim Atlanta's first major professional sports championship. The Braves play their home games at Turner Field from April to October. Tickets, available through the stadium box office or Ticketmaster (404/249–6400 or 800/326–4000), cost from $5 to $33; three hours before each game a small number of Skyline seats go on sale for $1. *755 Hank Aaron Dr., adjacent to I–85 and I–20 south of Downtown, 404/522–7630 tickets.*

GEORGIA STATE UNIVERSITY PANTHERS

The GSU Panthers are a NCAA Division I team competing in the Trans-America Athletic Conference. They play their home baseball games at Panthersville Stadium east of downtown Atlanta. Tickets (available by phone or at the GSU Athletic Department at University Plaza) cost $3; the season runs February–May. *2817 Clifton Springs Rd., near Panthersville Rd. (from the Candler Rd. exit/exit 33 off I–20, drive south to Panthersville Rd., turn right on Clifton Springs Rd., and proceed to the stadium, ahead on the left), Panthersville, 404/651–2772 tickets.*

GEORGIA TECH YELLOW JACKETS

A frequent NCAA Division I national championship contender, Tech plays in the power-packed Atlantic Coast Conference. The Yellow Jackets play their home baseball games at cozy 2,500-seat Russ Chandler Stadium in the heart of the Tech campus. The season runs February–May, and games against rivals Florida State, Clemson, and Georgia frequently sell out. Reserved seats cost $5, general admission $4, and children $2; season tickets are available. *Georgia Tech campus, at 5th and Fowler Sts., Midtown, 888/832–4849.*

where to play

ATLANTA MEN'S SENIOR BASEBALL LEAGUE

Guys who still cling to their diamond dreams can play in the Atlanta Men's Senior Baseball League. Teams compete in four age divisions (18–29, 30–39, 40–49, and 50-plus), and tryouts are held to match players of comparable age and ability. The 25-game season is played at local high school and college fields April–September. Team registration is $175–$200; players must furnish their own equipment. *404/851–2861, www.atlantamsbl.com.*

CITY- AND COUNTY-SPONSORED SOFTBALL LEAGUES

There are softball fields at many local parks. The City of Atlanta Department of Parks, Recreation, and Cultural Affairs and county parks departments sponsor organized adult softball leagues in spring and summer. For information on leagues in area parks, call the individual parks departments (*see* Parks, *above*). The following parks offer superior facilities for tournament play:

4 *e-6*

Al Bishop Park: This five-field complex is one of the metro Atlanta area's premier venues for youth and adult softball leagues and tournaments at all skill levels. *1082 Al Bishop Dr., off Powder Springs and Callaway Rds., south of Kennesaw Mountain National Battlefield Park, Kennesaw, 770/528–8860.*

3 *a-8*

Hobgood Park: *See* Parks, *above*. *6688 Bells Ferry Rd., Woodstock, 770/924–7768.*

8 *c-5*

Truelove Softball Complex: *3510 Oakvale Rd., Decatur, 404/371–2631.*

PRIVATE SOFTBALL LEAGUES

Atlanta Club Sport (coed teams). *404/257–3355.*

Atlanta Sport and Social Club (coed teams). *404/262–7655.*

Metro Atlanta Senior Softball League (ages 49-plus). *404/636–9486.*

BASKETBALL

teams to watch

ATLANTA HAWKS

The Hawks compete in the NBA's Central Division, against such traditional rivals as the Indiana Pacers and the Chicago Bulls. In 1999, the Hawks moved into their new home court at Philips Arena (*see* Stadiums, *above*). The NBA season runs from November through April. Tickets ($10–$65) are available from the Hawks box office or from Ticketmaster (404/249–6400 or 800/326–4000). *Techwood Dr. south of Marietta St., 404/827–3865 box office.*

GEORGIA STATE UNIVERSITY PANTHERS

The Panthers' men's and women's teams play in the Trans-America Athletic Conference, in a season that runs November–March. Home games are held in the 5,500-seat GSU Sports Arena downtown. Tickets are $10–$15 for men's games, $3 for women's games, and are available by phone or at the GSU Athletic Department at University Plaza (adjacent to the arena). *Piedmont Ave. at Decatur St., 404/651–2772 tickets.*

GEORGIA TECH YELLOW JACKETS

Tech's men's and women's basketball teams compete in the tough Atlantic Coast Conference, whose season runs November–March. Both the men and the women play at 10,000-seat Alexander Coliseum at MacDonald's Center. Tickets (call the number below) to men's games ($18) frequently sell out, but tickets to women's games ($2–$4) are more readily available. *Georgia Tech campus at 10th and Fowler Sts., off I–75/85, 888/832–4849.*

where to play

You may join basketball leagues that play at many of the county recreation centers; contact county parks departments for information. Pick-up games abound both at public gyms and at numerous outdoor courts across the 10-county area. The following courts are especially popular for both league and pick-up games.

15 *f-4*

BEDFORD–PINE PARK

This inner-city public park is one of Atlanta's truly multi-ethnic playgrounds, where the courts are filled with a mix of white-collar professionals and in-town residents playing pick-up games. Some of the play is highly competitive, but most players will find a group that fits their skills. During warm weather, the courts swarm with pick-up games after business hours and on weekend afternoons. The park also has volleyball courts (*see* Volleyball, *below*). *Bedford Pl. between Angier and Linden Aves., Midtown. Park open daily dawn–dusk. MARTA. North Avenue and Civic Center.*

5 *c-5*

HAMMOND PARK

This Fulton County park hosts league play on indoor courts in a gymnasium and on two lighted outdoor courts. Evenings and weekends, the outdoor courts come to life with highly competitive pick-up games where the "trash–talk" may be a little too strong for children. The park also has volleyball courts (*see* Volleyball, *below*). *705 Hammond Dr., at Glenridge Dr., Sandy Springs, 404/303–6176. Gym open weekdays 11–2, outdoor courts daily 8 AM–10 PM. Free.*

7 *g-4*

RUN N' SHOOT ATHLETIC CENTER

Ranked by *Hoops Nation Tour* as one of the best pick-up basketball courts in the United States, this facility offers open play on seven indoor courts. Most participants take the game very seriously, and you may find yourself lining up against a few current and former NBA players (especially in the summer). *1959 Metropolitan Way, north of Langford Pkwy. (GA 166), south of Downtown, 404/767–1522. Open daily. Admission $6.*

BICYCLING

Atlanta's high volume of automobile traffic and lack of bicycle-lane network means that the city proper is not yet the most bike-friendly of communities. But from mountain biking in the north Georgia hill country to touring on rural back roads, the counties around Atlanta are great places for biking. Official and unofficial bike trails abound; *Atlanta Walks* (Peachtree Publishers, $14.95), a guidebook available in bookstores, has information on biking routes in and near the city. Several biking clubs in the area sponsor bike trips and competitions. A good source for information about local clubs and off- and on-road and track-cycling events is *Atlanta Sports and Fitness Magazine,* available free at health clubs, sporting goods stores, and other outlets around the city.

Many local organizations are dedicated to promoting pedal-powered transportation in Atlanta, such as the advocacy group **Atlanta Bicycle Campaign** (404/522–5525, www.AtlantaBike.org). ABC conducts Effective Cycling classes ($15) to teach bicyclists how to ride safely in the city. It also sponsors a variety of awareness-raising events, including monthly Bike There! rides that celebrate bicycles as transportation and an annual Bike to Work Day, which even has Atlanta's mayor pedaling to City Hall. Several metro-area bicycle-user groups (BUGs) that advocate alternative transportation are affiliated with ABC.

bicycling clubs

Southern Bicycle League. *770/594–8350, www.BikeSBL.org.*

Southern Off-Road Bicycling Association (SORBA). *770/216–9745, www.sorba.org.*

where to ride

Despite heavy traffic on its roadways, Atlanta has a combination of rolling hills, abundant trees, and scenic and historic neighborhoods that make for enjoyable riding. Novices and newcomers are advised to begin their exploration of the city on group rides sponsored by cycling organizations or bike shops. Riders at all levels enjoy several especially popular trails around the metro area.

5 *a-5, a-6*

CHATTAHOOCHEE RIVER NATIONAL RECREATION AREA

Two adjacent units of the national recreation area, Cochran Shoals and Sope Creek (*see* Parks, *above*), are open to bicyclists. The Cochran Shoals Fitness Trail is a 3.1-mi paved loop trail along the banks of the river. It connects with the Fox Creek and Scribner Trails, which ascend through thick woods to Sope Creek. The fitness trail is suitable for road and mountain bikes, but Fox Creek and Scribner are for mountain bikes only. *Cochran Shoals: Interstate North Pkwy. off I–285 at New Northside Dr., between Marietta and Atlanta west of Sandy Springs. Sope Creek: Paper Mill Rd. off Johnson Ferry Rd., between Marietta and Atlanta in East Cobb, 770/952–4419. Daily 7–7 (later in summer). Parking $2 (annual passes available).*

7 *f-5*

DICK LANE VELODROME

Atlanta's only permanent bicycle track, the velodrome in Sumner Park is operated by the Fulton Flyers Cycling Club. In addition to a schedule of local and regional competitions, the club offers track-riding classes and club races here. Call for hours and fees. *1930 Headland-Norman Berry Dr., East Point, 404/767–8041.*

8 *f-1*

GEORGIA'S STONE MOUNTAIN PARK

Miles of lightly traveled roads meander through this 3,200-acre park past the lakes, gardens, historic buildings, and golf courses at the foot of the unique granite mountain (*see* Parks, *above*). Admission is free if you ride your bike into the park; otherwise, you must pay a $6 vehicle daily parking fee. *U.S 78, 5 mi outside/east of I–285, Stone Mountain, 770/498–5690, www.stonemountain-park.com. Daily 6 AM–midnight.*

9 *b-6, b-7*

PEACHTREE CITY

This planned community situated in rolling pine hills about 25 mi southwest of downtown Atlanta is a bicyclist's dream. In fact, practically every house in town has room in the garage for bicycles and a golf cart. The community is best known for its nearly 70 mi of paved recreational paths connecting residential neighborhoods with schools, churches, shopping districts, golf courses, lakes, and numerous parks and recreation areas. Visitors may access the trail system at recreation and shopping areas. *Off GA 74, about 12 mi south of I–85. Information: Peachtree City Information Center, 200 Westpark Dr., 770/487–4726.*

4 *a-4 through f-7*

SILVER COMET TRAIL

For more on this trail, which at press time was complete from Smyrna to Rockmart, *see* Hiking, Running & Walking, *below.*

7 *e-4 through h-2*

STONE MOUNTAIN–ATLANTA GREENWAY TRAIL

For more on this 18-mi trail, which runs from Greenbriar Mall in southwest Atlanta to Stone Mountain Park, *see* Hiking, Running & Walking, *below.*

3 *e-7*

SUGAR HILL BMX FACILITY

This rugged, hilly course on the grounds of E. E. Robinson Park is specially designed for BMX riders. The tight course has enough moguls, banked turns, and obstacles to challenge most riders; competitive events include a race through slalom-style gates. *Sugar Maple Dr. off Level Creek Rd., Sugar Hill, 770/945–6716. Open daily dawn–dusk. Admission free ($3 fee for gate practice; $8 registration fee for participants in Sunday races).*

BILLIARDS

5 *e-5*

BARLEY'S BILLIARDS

Rated one of the nation's best billiard parlors by *Billiard Digest*, Barley's surrounds its more than 20 handcrafted tables with elegant atmosphere. Children must be accompanied by an adult. *6259 Peachtree Industrial Blvd., outside I–285, Doraville, 770/455–1124. Open Mon.–Thurs. 4 PM–12:30 AM, Fri.–Sat. 4 PM–1:30 AM. Tables $6.50–$8.50 per hr.*

12 *f-3*

BUCKHEAD BILLIARDS

In the heart of trendy Buckhead, this 10-table parlor brings out both serious players and bar-hoppers from afternoon until the wee hours of the morning. The parlor offers a full bar with light dining and live bands on weekends. *200 Pharr Rd., Buckhead, 404/237–3705. Call for hrs. Tables $3–$9.50 per hr. MARTA: Buckhead.*

9 *d-4*

CLASSIC CUE

Families are welcome at this parlor with 18 Gandy tables; food and drink are available. During off-peak hours (weekdays 1 PM–6 PM), there is a flat fee of $5 per hour for tables. *200 Glynn St., Fayetteville, 770/461-2496. Sun.–Thurs. 1–1, Fri.–Sat. 1 PM–2 AM. Table rates: $4.75 per hr for one player, $4.25 per person per hr for two, $3.75 per person for three, etc.*

5 *b-6*

CORNER POCKET

With 17 9-ft Gandy tables, a snooker table, and three dart lanes, this parlor is for serious billiard and pool players. Open at 4 PM daily, the parlor has a full bar with food service and presents live music on weekends. Players under 21 years old must be accompanied by a parent. *4920 Roswell Rd., Sandy Springs, 404/255–6002. Call for hrs. Tables $6–$9 per hr.*

5 *h-5*

MR. CUE'S BILLIARDS

One of Atlanta's largest billiard parlors, Mr. Cue's features 30 Gandy tables as well as a snooker and a three-cushion table. *2077 Beaver Ruin Rd., Norcross, 770/840-0750. Mon.–Thurs. 1:30 PM–2 AM, Fri. 11:30 AM–3:30 AM, Sat. 1:30 PM–3:30 AM, Sun. 11 AM–2 AM. Tables $5–$7.50 per hr.*

5 *c-5*

SANDY SPRINGS BILLIARDS

This 5,000-square-ft parlor in Parkside Shopping Center caters to both novice players and experienced competitors. There are 15 billiard tables and one snooker table. Players must be 21 years or older after 6 PM. *5920 Roswell Rd., Sandy Springs, 404/257–0888. Open 11:30 AM–2:30 AM; until 4 AM Fri. and Sat. Tables $6–$9 per hr.*

14 *g-4*

TWAIN'S BILLIARDS AND TAP

A full bar with a broad selection of microbrews is a highlight of this parlor. Twain's has more than 20 Brunswick tables in two rooms (smoking and no-smoking). The parlor is open from afternoon to early morning, and players must be over 21 on Friday and Saturday nights after 7 PM. *See also* Chapter 5. *211 East*

Trinity Pl., Decatur, 404/373–0063. Call for hrs. Tables $2.50–$3.75 per person per hr.

BIRD-WATCHING

The metropolitan Atlanta area is home to more than 100 species of birds, and many more pause here on their annual fall and spring migrations along the Eastern Flyway.

guided walks

ATLANTA AUDUBON SOCIETY

The society offers member-guided field trips and seasonal migration walks at a variety of locations in the 10 counties and beyond. Destinations vary depending on season, bird migrations, nesting activities, sightings, and similar factors. You can find out the times and locations of walks in the Audubon newsletter, *Wingbars*, in local newspapers, and on the club's Web site, www.hitt.com/~jhitt/audubon. *Box 29189, Atlanta 30359, 770/955-4111.*

popular sites

5 *a-7 through g-3*

CHATTAHOOCHEE RIVER NATIONAL RECREATION AREA

See Parks, *above*. Riverside marshes and meadows are ideal habitat for spotting wood ducks, herons, and other waterfowl, as well as many species of land birds, including hawks, owls, and woodpeckers.

8 *g-5*

DAVIDSON–ARABIA MOUNTAIN NATURE PRESERVE

See Botanical Gardens & Nature Preserves, *above*. The park is home to a variety of bird species including bluebirds, goldfinches, screech owls, and pileated woodpeckers.

11 *f-6, g-6*

FERNBANK FOREST

See Botanical Gardens and Nature Preserves, *above*. In-town Atlanta's only stand of virgin forest is home to more than 100 different species of resident and migratory birds, including woodpeckers, thrashers, goldfinches, warblers, and owls.

8 *f-1*

GEORGIA'S STONE MOUNTAIN PARK

See Parks, *above*. Rocky outcrops, woodlands, and open meadows are home to a variety of nesting birds, such as finches, woodpeckers, owls, wrens, and thrashers. The park lakes host both resident and migratory populations of ducks, geese, and other waterfowl.

4 *e-3, e-4, e-5*

KENNESAW MOUNTAIN NATIONAL BATTLEFIELD PARK

See Hiking, Running & Walking, *below*. The excellent bird habitat to be found in open meadows, forested hills, and rugged mountain slopes makes the park one of the best sites in Georgia to see several species of migrating birds in season. Year-round resident species include hawks, owls, woodpeckers, chickadees, thrashers, blue jays, and nuthatches.

9 *h-3*

NEWMAN WETLANDS CENTER

Considered the best birding facilities in the Atlanta area, the Wetlands Center and adjacent E. L. Huie Land Application Facility (a Clayton County sewage and water treatment plant) are home to a rich variety of inland shorebirds, waterfowl, and other resident land birds in season. *2755 Freeman Rd., Hampton, 770/603-5606. Open daily 8:30–5. Free.*

8 *a-7*

REYNOLDS NATURE PRESERVE

See Botanical Gardens & Nature Preserves, *above*. Like the nearby Newman Wetlands Center, the wooded preserve's mix of forest, streams, and ponds sustains a wide variety of resident and migratory land birds and waterfowl.

BOATING

Two excellent power-boating lakes lie not too far from downtown Atlanta. For information on other boating opportunities, *see* Canoeing, Kayaking & Rafting *and* Sailing, *below*.

2 *a-5 and west/northwest*

LAKE ALLATOONA

Lake Allatoona lies about 30 mi northwest of Atlanta, outside the 10-county metro area, but power boaters and sailors head here from the city each weekend. Surrounded by rolling hills, the 12,010-acre lake was created by the Army Corps of Engineers in 1950. It has since become a favorite destination for anglers in search of local game fish such as bream and large-mouth bass. Public facilities include more than 30 public boat ramps, 8 commercial marinas, 19 day-use areas, and 11 campgrounds at various locations between I–75 and I–575. Many visitors access the lake via Red Top Mountain State Park (southeast of Cartersville), which has a lodge, cabins, campgrounds, trails, and a marina. The Lake Allatoona Resource Manager also maintains campsites and day-use areas. *East of I–75 between Acworth and Cartersville, 770/382–4700, 770/386–0549 recorded lake conditions information. Call for camping and commercial marina fees.*

3 *e-4 through h-5*
LAKE SIDNEY LANIER
See Parks, above. With more than 540 mi of shoreline, Lake Lanier offers both wide channels for boating and water skiing, and nearly endless coves for fishing. You can access the lake via several dozen entrances, at commercial marinas, day-use areas, campgrounds, and more than 60 boat-launching areas. Information on specific locations and fees is available by contacting the Lake Resource Manager at 770/945–9531. *Between GA 400 and I–985 about 35 mi northeast of Atlanta, between Buford and Gainesville, 770/945–1467 recorded lake conditions information.*

BOWLING

Like any major metropolitan area, Atlanta has plenty of alleys in which you can try to beat your average. Every alley offers bowling leagues to suit practically every skill level and schedule. Call the alley for leagues information.

city of atlanta
Express Lanes (1936 Piedmont Circle, Midtown, 404/874–5703); **Northeast Plaza Lanes** (3285 Buford Hwy., North Atlanta, 404/636–7548).

cherokee county
Woodstock Lanes (108 Woodpark Blvd., Woodstock, 770/926–2200).

clayton county
Embassy Row Lanes (5885 Old Dixie Rd., Forest Park, 404/363–6110).

cobb county
Azalea Lanes (2750 Austell Rd., Marietta, 770/435–2120); **Cedar Creek Lanes** (2749 Delk Rd., Marietta, 770/988–8813); **Marietta Lanes** (565 Cobb Pkwy., Marietta, 770/427–4696); **U.S. Play** (775 Cobb Place Blvd., Kennesaw, 770/427–7679); **Village Lanes** (2692 Sandy Plains Rd., Marietta, 770/973–2695).

dekalb county
Chamblee Lanes (2175 Savoy Dr., Chamblee, 770/451–8605); **Stone Mountain Lanes** (720 Hambrick Rd., Stone Mountain, 404/296–2400).

fulton county
East Point Triangle Lanes (1471 Cleveland Ave., East Point, 404/761–8831); **Roswell Bowl** (785 Old Roswell Rd., Roswell, 770/998–9437); **Union City Lanes** (5100 Goodson Connector Rd., Union City, 770/969–0100).

gwinnett county
Gwinnett Lanes–AMF (4990 Jimmy Carter Blvd., Norcross, 770/923–5080); **Gwinnett Lanes–Brunswick** (3835 Lawrenceville Hwy., Lawrenceville, 770/925–2000); **Peachtree Lanes** (6345 Spalding Dr., Norcross, 770/840–8200); **Snellville Lanes** (2350 Ronald Reagan Pkwy., Snellville, 770/972–5300).

BOXING

The success of heavyweight champion Evander Holyfield, an Atlanta native, has boosted the popularity of boxing in Atlanta. Several local venues offer boxing instruction and competition.

15 *e-4*
BIGGS MORRISON BOXING
92 Linden Ave., Midtown, 404/872–7049. MARTA: North Avenue.

6 *e-4*
EAGLE BOXING AND KICK-BOXING
133 S. Clayton St., Lawrenceville, 770/682–5046.

7 *g-3*

GEORGIA AMATEUR BOXING ASSOCIATION AND HOLYFIELD ARENA

1000 Beecher St., Atlanta, West End, 404/753–8002. MARTA: West End.

CANOEING, KAYAKING & RAFTING

Atlanta's white-water enthusiasts often head to the rivers of northern Georgia (Chatooga), western North Carolina (Nantahala), and eastern Tennessee (Ocoee), but the metro region's own Chattahoochee River National Recreation Area (*see Parks, above*) has Class I–II rapids. The river is a great place for novice and experienced paddlers alike to hone their skills and for rafters to enjoy a leisurely float down the river. Several outfitters and clubs offer guided trips, equipment, and instruction.

clubs

Several Atlanta clubs offer instruction, outings, competitions, and social gatherings for beginning and experienced paddlers.

ATLANTA ROWING CLUB

Open boats and racing sculls. *770/993–1879.*

ATLANTA WHITEWATER CLUB

Canoes and kayaks. *404/299–3752.*

GEORGIA CANOEING ASSOCIATION

Canoes and kayaks. *770/421–9729, www.gacanoe.home.mindspring.com.*

instruction

ATLANTA CENTER FOR EXCELLENCE

This organization is dedicated to providing training and instruction to people interested in competitive canoeing and kayaking. Membership costs $30 per year and monthly coaching fees run $50–$75. *770/937–5073, www.mindspring.com/~kayaker/.*

LEARN TO ROLL KAYAK SCHOOL

The school offers a four-day beginner's course for $285. *404/634–0065, www.gakayak.com.*

WHITEWATER LEARNING CENTER OF GEORGIA

If you want to learn how to tackle the rapids in an open canoe or how to perform an Eskimo roll in a kayak, the center can give you a hand. *404/231–0042.*

outfitters

High Country Adventures (770/391–9657), **Go with the Flow** (770/664–6785), and **REI** (404/633–6508) offer equipment for rent or sale, as well as scheduled trips to regional destinations. May–September, the **Chattahoochee Outdoor Center** (770/395–6851) rents rafts for floating between units of the Chattahoochee River National Recreation Area.

where to float and paddle

5 *a-7 through g-3*

CHATTAHOOCHEE RIVER

With long, relatively easy stretches for learning basic skills, and Class I–II rapids for a little excitement, the Chattahoochee River is Atlanta's main paddling attraction. Several units of the Chattahoochee River National Recreation Area (*see Parks, above*) have public launching sites, and the park can supply maps. Commercial outfitters (*see above*) offer raft trips between the Johnson Ferry and Paces Mill units of the park, and the Atlanta Whitewater Club (*see above*) maintains slalom gates at the Cochran Shoals–Powers Island unit. The Chattahoochee Nature Center (*see Botanical Gardens & Nature Preserves, above*) schedules evening canoe floats on the river during summer, and the Atlanta Rowing Club (*above*) maintains its boathouse headquarters at Chattahoochee River Park (*see Parks, above*).

CROQUET

There are no public croquet lawns in Atlanta, but if you yearn to play on exquisitely manicured lawns while attired in a crisp white outfit, contact the **Atlanta Mallet Club** (770/242–5955) for membership information.

DISC GOLF

Picture playing a round on the links with a Frisbee, and you've envisioned the game of disc golf. A flying disc is all the equipment you need to take up this fun and increasingly popular sport. For more information about disc golf in the Atlanta area, call the **Atlanta Flying Disc Club** (404/351–0914, www.afdc.com) or stop in at **Identified Flying Objects** (1164 Euclid Ave., Little Five Points, 404/524–4628), operated by disc golf hall-of-famer Patti Kunkle and her husband, John. The store offers a wide assortment of discs and accessories, maps to courses, and club membership information. Just remember—on Metropolitan Atlanta's six disc golf courses there is no "out-of-bounds."

1 b-5
DEER LICK PARK
See Parks, above. 9 holes. 2105 Mack Rd., Douglasville, 770/920–7129.

6 d-8
LENORA PARK
See Parks, above. 18 holes. 4514 Lenora Church Rd., Snellville, 770/978–5260.

4 c-4
OREGON PARK
18 holes. 145 Old Hamilton Rd., Marietta, 770/528–8800 Cobb County Parks and Recreation.

8 f-3
REDAN PARK
18 holes. Phillips Rd. at Deshon Rd., Lithonia, 404/271–2631 DeKalb County Parks and Recreation.

2 c-5
SEQUOYAH PARK.
18 holes. Vaughn Rd. and GA 140, between Alpharetta and Canton, 770/924–7768 Cherokee County Parks and Recreation.

5 c-2
WILLS PARK
See Horseback Riding, below. 18 holes. 525 N. Main St., Alpharetta, 770/410–5780.

FENCING

Would you like to parry or thrust like a nobleman or a swashbuckler? Then contact the **Atlanta Fencing Club** (404/892–0307) to learn more about the finer points of the sport of swordsmanship.

FISHING

The lakes and rivers around Atlanta abound with more than 20 species of game fish, from bass, bream, and crappie to brown and rainbow trout. You can find out where to cast a line at the excellent www.gon.com/fish. To fish in Georgia, people 16 years and older need a state permit. State residents may purchase one-day ($3.50) or annual ($9) licenses; non-residents can buy the one-day license or a weekly ($7) or seasonal ($24) license. Trout anglers pay an additional fee ($5 residents, $13 non-residents) for a trout stamp. Permits are available at sporting goods and fishing supply stores, by calling 888/748–6887, or online at www.permit.com. For information on fishing licenses, call the **Georgia Game and Fish Commission** (770/414–3333).

equipment and outfitters

For the latest fly-fishing ties, fresh- and saltwater accessories, instruction, and tips on local hot spots, Atlanta-area anglers head for **Bass Pro Shops Sportsman's Warehouse** (3825 Shackleford Rd., Norcross, 770/931–1550), the **Classic Angler Fly Fishing Shop** (2817 Peachtree Rd., Buckhead, 404/233–5110, classicangler.com), the **Fish Hawk** (279 Buckhead Ave., Buckhead, 404/237–3473, www.thefishhawk.com), and **Orvis Atlanta** (3255 Peachtree Rd., Buckhead, 404/841–0093, www.orvis.com). A number of local guides offer river and lake trips throughout north Georgia, including **Bill Vanderford's Guide Service** (770/962–1241), the **Bass Bus** (404/296–2923), and **Glenn Morrison's Lake Lanier Guide Service** (770/962–8738).

where to fish

Several county parks and recreation areas have small ponds and lakes that are ideal for family fishing (see Parks, above). Serious anglers focus on three major fishing areas.

5 a-7 through g-3
CHATTAHOOCHEE RIVER
Anglers test their fly-fishing skills in the cold, swift-flowing channels and eddies of the river that courses along Atlanta's northern boundary. The Chattahoochee is habitat to several species of game fish, including brook, brown, and rainbow trout, bream, and catfish. The units of the Chattahoochee River National

Recreation Area (*see* Parks, *above*) offer public access to the river below Lake Lanier. There are public boat launching ramps for small watercraft located at the Johnson Ferry and Paces Mill units of the park and at Chattahoochee River Park (*see* Parks, *above*).

2 *a-5 and west/northwest*

LAKE ALLATOONA

This lake northwest of Atlanta is a popular destination for deep-water anglers searching for trophy-size bass, bream, and trout. When you're in the mood for a day of fishing, you have your pick of any number of boat ramps, marinas, and day-use areas (*see* Boating, *above*).

3 *e-4 through h-5*

LAKE SIDNEY LANIER

On summer weekends, this lake north of Atlanta can become so crowded with water-skiers and power boaters that anglers may find themselves battling boat wakes and tangled lines. For a more relaxing and rewarding experience, find a quiet cove away from the mob, visit on a weekday, or come during the off-season. The lake has several species of game fish, including large- and small-mouth bass, crappie, bream, and catfish. For more on the facilities available to anglers, *see* Boating, *above*.

FLYING

Whether you yearn to pilot your own plane above Atlanta's skyline or seek the thrill of taking to the air in an open-cockpit bi-plane, you can find what you want in metro Atlanta. Several local companies offer instruction or flight-seeing rides.

instruction

4 *e-2*

MARIETTA/COBB AIRPORT (KENNESAW)

Aero Atlanta Flying Club (770/422–2376).

5 *d-7*

PEACHTREE-DEKALB AIRPORT (CHAMBLEE)

Aviation Atlanta (770/458–8034). Epps Aviation (770/455–4203). PDK Flight Academy (770/457–1270). Prestige Helicopters (770/458–6047).

flight-seeing

5 *d-7*

PEACHTREE-DEKALB AIRPORT (CHAMBLEE)

Classic Bi-Plane Rides (770/458–3633).

FOOTBALL

Football—high school, college, and professional—is almost a religion in the South, and Atlanta fans are proud to number themselves among the devout. Their faith has not gone unrewarded: in 1998 Atlanta's NFL team, the Falcons, rewarded long-suffering fans with a string of victories and a trip to their first Super Bowl.

teams to watch

ATLANTA FALCONS

Atlantans finally caught Falcon Fever when the team earned its first-ever Super Bowl berth in 1998. Who cares if they lost to the Denver Broncos—the fans were just happy to be there. Hope for the future is bright and season tickets are hot. The Falcons play their home games at the Georgia Dome (*see* Stadiums, *above*); the NFL season runs from August through December. Game tickets run $25–$41 and are available from the box office or from Ticketmaster (800/249–6400). For Falcon season tickets or team information, call the box office (404/223–8000).

GEORGIA TECH YELLOW JACKETS

The four-time national champions (1917, 1928, 1952, 1990) play Atlantic Coast Conference opponents and other rivals at historic 46,000-seat Bobby Dodd Stadium at Grant Field (North Ave. at Techwood Dr., Midtown), the oldest stadium in NCAA Division I football. Game tickets, available at the Edge Athletic Center (220 Bobby Dodd Way, Midtown) or by calling 888/832–4849, are $20–$28. Home games against the University of Georgia Bulldogs are always sold out, and seats are available only to season-ticket holders.

where to play

You might find a pick-up game of touch football at a local park, but for scheduled play join a local league. For information on adult flag and touch football leagues, contact your county or city

Bobby Dodd Stadium at Grant Field

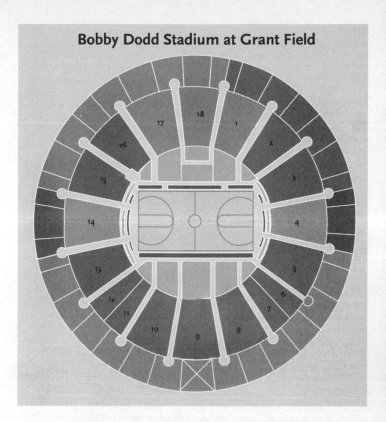

parks department (*see* Parks, *above*) or call **Atlanta Club Sport** (men's and coed teams, 404/257–3355), **Atlanta Metro Flag & Touch Football League** (404/296–2512), or **North Atlanta Flag Football League** (404/223–9800).

GOLF

Maybe it's the climate, which allows year-round play, or the connection with native golf legend Bobby Jones, or the proximity to pro golf's greatest tournament (the Masters in Augusta), but whatever the reason, Atlanta is knee-deep in golf courses. The metro area's links run the gamut from relatively inexpensive (there is no such thing as cheap when it comes to greens fees), daily-fee courses to country clubs with all the amenities. You can get information on more than 60 public courses throughout Atlanta and in north Georgia by visiting **www.AtlantaGolfer.com.** If you want to play today and you have not called ahead for a tee time, check availability at several Atlanta courses by call-

ing **Last Minute Tee Times** (770/664–4653 or 800/671–0750, www.lmtt.com). Last-minute or not, if you love to play, golf keep your clubs handy, for no matter where you are in Atlanta, you are never far from a course.

instruction

Nearly every course has a pro shop staffed by PGA-certified professionals qualified to give individual or group lessons. Check with the pro at your favorite course for rates. Several commercial operations also offer lessons.

5 *c-3*

Eagle Golf Club at Morgan Falls Park (460 Morgan Falls Dr., Dunwoody, 770/390–0424).

5 *f-6*

Great Golf Learning Centers (3545 Northcrest Rd., Doraville, 770/270–8990).

5 *f-4*

Great Golf Learning Centers (6385 Spalding Dr., Norcross, 770/448–6920).

4 *e-8*

Heritage Hills Golf Center (3890 Floyd Rd., Austell, 770/434–6727).

6 *d-4*

Jimmy Mozley Golf Center (292 Oakland Rd., Lawrenceville, 770/962–4918).

4 *g-4*

Marietta Golf Center (1701 Gresham Rd., Marietta, 770/977–1997).

courses

All of the courses listed below are open to the public on a daily-fee basis (memberships are available at many courses), though tee-time reservations are strongly recommended for busy warm-weather weekends. The City of Atlanta and several county parks departments also operate golf courses. The city's courses (Alfred "Tup" Holmes, Bobby Jones, Brown's Mill, and North Fulton) are managed by American Golf Corporation; at any of these you may purchase an annual membership, which gives you a discount on fees. Fee ranges for all courses listed here reflect the cost differences between peak, off-peak, and twilight play.

city of atlanta

7 *f-4*

ALFRED "TUP" HOLMES

Formerly a part of adjacent Adams Park, the course was renamed in 1983 for Alfred Tup Holmes, one of the nation's premier African-American golfers. Holmes was instrumental in integrating Atlanta's public golf courses in the 1950s. This rolling, shaded 18-hole, par-72 course is suitable for both novice and experienced players. *2300 Wilson Dr., off DeLowe Dr., Adams Park, 404/753–6158. Fees $20–$32. MARTA: Oakland City.*

12 *c-6, c-7*

BOBBY JONES

One of Atlanta's busiest courses, the 18-hole, par-71 course is a blend of flat terrain and rugged hillside holes. Jones had a hand in the design of his namesake links in the 1940s. Only 4 mi north of Downtown, the course is especially popular with in-town golfers and those looking to squeeze in a round after work. *384 Woodward Way, off Northside Dr. northeast of I–75, Buckhead, 404/355–1009. Fees $17–$30.*

7 *h-5*

BROWN'S MILL

An easily walkable 18-hole, par-72 course, Brown's Mill is convenient to downtown Atlanta and is a favorite of southside residents. *480 Cleveland Ave., just east of I–75, Lakewood, 404/366–3573. Fees $17–$30.*

14 *b-4*

CANDLER PARK

This open, rolling 9-hole, par-31 course is popular with beginners, neighborhood locals, college students, and casual players interested in getting in a round after work (*see* Parks, *above*). *585 Candler Park Dr., off McLendon Ave., Candler Park, 404/371–1260. Fees $7–$9. MARTA: Edgewood/Candler Park.*

12 *a-5, a-6*

CROSS CREEK

This semi-private 18-hole, par-54 executive course offers a challenging blend of open fairways, water holes, and hilly terrain. Near a popular condominium complex, the course is an enjoyable walk. Facilities include a pro shop and clubhouse restaurant. *1221 Cross Creek Pkwy., off Bohler Rd. south of W. Wesley Rd., Buckhead, 404/352–5612. Fees $11–$15.*

5 *b-7*

NORTH FULTON

In the heart of multipurpose Chastain Park (*see* Parks, *above*), the 18-hole, par-71 links are the city's longest and most challenging. A mix of open and tight fairways and undulating greens, crisscrossed by the meandering waters of Nancy Creek, offers a challenge to even the most experienced golfers. *216 W. Wieuca Rd., north of Roswell Rd. at Powers Ferry Rd., Buckhead, 404/255–0723. Fees $9–$32.*

cherokee county

2 *a-7*

EAGLE WATCH

Arnold Palmer–designed, this 18-hole, par-72 course has been one of Atlanta's favorites since its opening in 1989. In an especially handsome layout of rolling hills, tall trees, and tight fairways, it is a challenging but fair course for players of all skill levels. It has a driving range, practice greens, pro shop, clubhouse, and restaurant. *3055 Eagle Watch Dr., east of Towne Lake Pkwy. off I–575, Woodstock, 770/591–1000. Fees $30–$65.*

2 *a-7*

TOWNE LAKE HILLS

This Arthur Hills–designed 18-hole, par-72 course is one of Atlanta's most scenic, offering views of nearby Kennesaw Mountain. Situated in the Appalachian foothills, the rolling course presents many elevation changes, and an abundance of trees lines the fairways. Facilities include a driving range, practice green, pro shop, and grill. *1003 Towne Lake Hills East, west of I–575 at Town Lake Pkwy., Woodstock, 770/592–9969. Fees $25–$69.*

clayton county

10 *a-2*

LAKE SPIVEY

Spread out along the shores of a lake, this older course has long been one of the most popular courses in Atlanta's southern crescent. It offers 27 challenging holes on three courses (Clubside, par 36; Hillside, par 36; and Lakeside, par 37) for golfers of all abilities and has a driving range, practice green, pro shop, and grill. *8255 Clubhouse Way, off GA 138 west of I–75, Jonesboro, 770/471–4653. Fees $19–$38.*

9 *f-2*

THE LINKS

Equipped to serve golfers with only a few hours to spare, as well as those who have a full day to play, this complex has two courses: an 18-hole, par-72 championship course and a 9-hole, par-31 course suitable for junior golfers and beginners. Facilities include a driving range, practice green, pro shop, and snack bar. *340 Hewell Rd., off Tara Blvd. and GA 54, Jonesboro, 770/461–5100. Fees $17–$32.*

cobb county

Cobb County residents may purchase cards good for discounts at both of the courses (Cobblestone, Legacy) operated by the Cobb County Parks and Recreation Department (*see* Parks, *above*).

4 *f-5*

CITY CLUB OF MARIETTA

On the grounds of the sprawling Marietta Conference Center, this challenging 18-hole, par-71 course was once part of the Marietta Country Club. Minutes from Marietta's historic downtown square, the adjacent conference-center facilities make City Club an ideal venue for group and corporate outings. *510 Powder Springs Rd., south of Marietta Pkwy. (GA 120), 770/528–0555. Fees $39–$49.*

4 *c-2*

COBBLESTONE

Rated by *Golf Digest* as Georgia's number one public golf facility, this 18-hole, par-71 course makes its ruggedly beautiful way through tall pines bordering Lake Acworth. The complex has a practice range, fully equipped pro shop, and a clubhouse with restaurant. *4200 Nance Rd., off U.S. 41 and Acworth Due West Rd., Acworth, 770/917–5151. Fees $17–$59.*

4 *h-6*

FOX CREEK EXECUTIVE COURSE

Next door to Legacy Links (*see below*), this executive course offers 18 holes of par-3 golf in a setting convenient to residents of Cobb and north Fulton counties. The course lies just south of Dobbins Air Force Base; lining up a tough putt while fighter jets scream overhead is a true test of concentration. There is a practice range, pro shop, and snack bar. *1501 Windy Hill Rd., west of U.S. 41 and I–75, Smyrna, 770/435–1000. Fees $18–$32.50*

4 *h-6*

LEGACY GOLF LINKS

This Larry Nelson–designed 18-hole, par-58 executive course evokes the craggy links of Scotland. Tight, tree-lined fairways; sand and grass bunkers; and small, rolling greens challenge players' shot-making skills on even the shortest par-3 hole. The complex also has a driving range, Bogey's Run (an 18-hole grass putting course), and a clubhouse with pro shop and Scottish-inspired pub. *1825 Windy Hill Rd., west of I–75 and U.S. 41, Marietta, 770/434–6331. Fees $12.50–$33.50.*

dekalb county

Challenging play at a reasonable cost can be had at DeKalb's two county-owned golf courses (Mystery Valley, Sugar Creek), and county residents may purchase an annual discount card for reduced fees every time they play.

8 *f-1*
GEORGIA'S STONE MOUNTAIN PARK

Since the park's first course, the Robert Trent Jones–designed, 18-hole, par-72 Stonemont Course, opened in 1969, Stone Mountain's links have been consistently ranked by *Golf Digest* as one of the nation's premier public courses. Two 9-holes, Lakemont, skirting the shores of Stone Mountain Lake, and Woodmont, surrounded by trees and granite outcrops, combine for an especially scenic and technically challenging 18-hole, par-72 round. Superb golf in a magnificent natural setting convenient to Atlanta helps make Stone Mountain Park (*see* Parks, *above*) the most popular golf destination in Georgia. Course facilities include a driving range, practice green, pro shop, and restaurant-lounge. *Stonewall Jackson Dr., off Jefferson Davis Dr. at GA 78, Stone Mountain, 770/498–5715. Fees $32–$45.*

8 *f-4*
METROPOLITAN

Since opening in 1967, this Rees Jones–designed course has delivered championship-caliber golf to the everyday player as well as to PGA professionals competing to join the tour. The course plays long and tight yet remains fair and fun. There is a driving range, practice green, pro shop, and snack bar. *3000 Fairington Pkwy., off Panola Rd. south of I–20, Lithonia, 770/981–5325. Fees $27–$49.*

8 *f-2*
MYSTERY VALLEY

In the shadow of Stone Mountain, this 18-hole, par-72 course of tree-lined fairways and rolling hills has a longstanding reputation for demanding play. Facilities include a driving range, practice green, pro shop, and snack bar. *6100 Shadow Rock Rd., off Stone Mountain–Lithonia Rd., Lithonia, 770/469–6913. Fees $21–$36.*

8 *b-5*
SUGAR CREEK

Extremely popular with south DeKalb golfers, this rolling, open course offers an exciting round without penalizing beginning players. The 18-hole, par-72 course is bisected by I–285, so traffic noise can affect players' concentration on a few holes. Facilities include a pro shop, driving range, practice green, and snack bar. *2706 Bouldercrest Rd. at I–285, southeast of Gresham Park, 404/241–7671. Fees $21–$36.*

douglas county

7 *a-1*
GREYSTONE

This is a favorite of golfers from the Douglasville area and Atlanta's western suburbs. The 18-hole, par-72 layout on tree-shaded hills allows for an enjoyable day's outing at a very reasonable price. Driving range, practice green, pro shop, and grill are all here. *4020 Greystone Dr., north of I–20 via Thornton Rd. and GA 78, Lithia Springs, 770/489–9068. Fees $15.90–$32.*

fayette county

9 *f-5*
RIVER'S EDGE

On the shores of the historic Flint River, this course tests players' skills with a hilly mix of trees and water hazards. Large numbers of southside Atlanta residents golf the 18-hole, par-71 course, especially on weekends. A driving range, practice green, pro shop, and grill are additional draws. *40 Southern Golf Ct., off McDonough and County Line Rds. east of Fayetteville, 770/460–1098. Fees $21–$45.*

9 *d-7*
WHITE WATER

This 18-hole, par-72 course sets a genteel stage for sport in its Old South–style clubhouse and on its manicured greens. Located between golf course–rich Peachtree City and Fayetteville, White Water satisfies players who seek a country-club golfing experience at public-course rates. Facilities include a driving range, practice greens, pro shop, and restaurant-bar. *165 Birkdale Dr., off GA 74, Fayetteville, 770/461–6545. Fees $28–$72.*

fulton county

North Fulton County is the land of country-club communities and upscale semi-private golf courses. With more than 200 golf holes on more than a dozen courses to choose from, players here expect—and receive—high-caliber golf and elegant amenities. Needless to say, the greens fees reflect the quality of the experience.

3 a-6

TROPHY CLUB OF ATLANTA

One of three Champions Club courses in metro Atlanta (see below), this course is highly regarded for its hilly terrain, elevated greens, and tricky water hazards. Players who are proficient with fairway woods and putters can score well here. Facilities include a driving range, practice greens, pro shop, and grill. 15135 Hopewell Rd., off GA 9, Alpharetta, 770/343–9700. Fees $55–$69.

2 g-6

WHITE COLUMNS

This Tom Fazio–designed 18-hole, par-72 course is a perennial award winner: it's been named Atlanta's Best Public Course by the Atlanta Journal–Constitution and one of the nation's top 10 public courses by Golf magazine. The expansive course features large greens and wide fairways lined with an abundance of shade trees. Well suited to the beginning player, it nonetheless offers enough challenges to keep experienced golfers coming back for more. Among its facilities are a driving range, practice greens, pro shop, and clubhouse with restaurant. 300 White Columns Dr., north of Alpharetta, 770/343–9025. Fees $75–$95.

gwinnett county

1 h-2

HAMILTON MILL

This first of the Fred Couples Signature courses has earned recognition from Golf magazine as one of the nation's top public courses, and it has a local reputation for tough but enjoyable play for golfers at all skill levels. Its 18-hole, par-72 layout blends into the picturesque Appalachian foothills of north Georgia. The complex has a large practice facility with driving range and putting-chipping greens, a pro shop, and a clubhouse with a restaurant, bar, and banquet facilities. You can buy a membership that gives you a discount on fees each time you play. 1995 Hamilton Mill Pkwy., north of I–85, Dacula, 770/945–1345. Fees $57–$72.

6 d-2

SPRINGBROOK

A well-maintained, county-operated course on rolling terrain, Springbrook is popular with Lawrenceville and north-metro golfers. In addition to its 18-hole, par-71 course, it has a driving range, practice greens, pro shop, and snack bar. The course is part of the Springbrook Golf, Tennis, and Aquatics Complex (see Swimming and Tennis, below). 585 Camp Perrin Rd., off Collins Hill Rd. north of GA 316, Lawrenceville, 770/822–5400. Fees $21.20–$49.

6 g-3

TROPHY CLUB AT APALACHEE

One of three Champions Clubs in metro Atlanta, this 18-hole, par-71 course features a challenging layout of tight fairways over hills, bunkers, water hazards, and fast greens. The club has a driving range, practice greens, pro shop, and grill. 1008 Dacula Rd., off Cedars and Hurricane Shoals Rds. north of GA 316, Dacula, 770/822–9220. Fees $35–$60.

6 d-8

TROPHY CLUB OF GWINNETT

This 18-hole, par-72 Champions Club course, offers a mix of tight and open fairways, with a healthy dose of hazards to keep even experienced players honest. Facilities include a driving range, practice greens, pro shop, and snack bar. 3254 Clubside View Ct., off GA 124 south of U.S. 78, Snellville, 770/978–7755. Fees $35–$60.

henry county

10 d-5

COTTON FIELDS AND GREEN VALLEY

One of the best and most affordable daily-fee courses on metro Atlanta's south side, this 36-hole spread features the par-71 Cotton Fields and par-72 Green Valley links. Both courses present an open, gently hilly layout that tests the skills of expert players yet does not punish the beginner. There is a driving range, pro shop, grill-bar, and pavilion for groups. 400 Industrial Blvd., between I–75 and GA 155, McDonough, 770/914–1442. Fees $24–$45.

10 e-4

GEORGIA NATIONAL

This superbly maintained Denis Griffeths–designed course lies in a rustic setting near the shores of a picturesque lake. Accuracy off the tee is a must on the 18-hole, par-71 course, which hides large, drive-swallowing bunkers along its wide, inviting fairways. Facilities here are a driving range, practice greens, and a luxurious clubhouse with pro shop and grill. *1715 Lake Dow Rd., between GA 20 and GA 81, east of McDonough, 770/914–9994. Fees $32–$55.*

HANDBALL, RACQUETBALL & SQUASH

Most Atlanta-area racquetball courts are located at YMCAs and private clubs, but a few of them welcome non-member players for a daily guest fee.

13 b-5

ATHLETIC CLUB NORTHEAST

Eight courts for racquetball and handball. *1515 Sheridan Rd., off Briarcliff Rd., North Atlanta, 404/325–2700. Daily guest fee $10.*

5 c-5

CONCOURSE ATHLETIC CLUB

Five courts for racquetball, handball, and squash. *8 Concourse Pkwy., off Peachtree-Dunwoody Rd. north of I–285, Dunwoody, 770/698–2000. Daily guest fee $12.*

5 h-5

SOUTHERN ATHLETIC CLUB

Seven courts for racquetball and handball. *754 Beaver Ruin Rd., east of I–85, Lilburn, 770/923–5400. Daily guest fee $8.*

9 h-1

SOUTHSIDE ATHLETIC CLUB

Eight courts for racquetball and handball, plus leagues and tournaments. *1792 Mt. Zion Rd., west of I–75, Morrow, 770/968–1798. Daily guest fee $10.*

4 h-6

SPORTING CLUB AT WINDY HILL

Five courts for racquetball and 3 courts for squash. *135 Interstate North Pkwy., east of I–75, Marietta, 770/953–1100. Daily guest fee $11.*

5 g-7

TUCKER RACQUET AND FITNESS CENTER

Eight courts for racquetball, handball, and squash. *3281 Tucker–Norcross Rd., Tucker, 770/491–3100. Daily guest fee $5.*

HIKING, RUNNING & WALKING

Atlanta's moderate climate and varied terrain contribute to its growing popularity as a metropolitan area to be explored on foot. The free monthly magazine *Atlanta Sports and Fitness* offers a comprehensive listing of clubs and upcoming running/walking events. It's available in sporting goods stores and many other locations around the metro area.

The **Atlanta Track Club,** with more than 11,000 members, is the nation's second-largest runners' association. Best known for its signature event, the Peachtree Road Race held each Fourth of July, the club also sponsors a number of other annual events, including the Atlanta Marathon (held on Thanksgiving morning) and weekly All-Comers' Meets each summer. You can reach the club at 404/231–9064 or online at www.atlantatrackclub.org. Smaller runners' clubs in the Atlanta area include the **Buckhead Road Runners Club** (404/816–6299), the **Chattahoochee Road Runners** (770/984–0451), the **Greater Gwinnett Road Runners** (770/979–6336), and the **Peachtree City Running Club** (770/460–6349).

Metro Atlanta is also great for walking. The **PATH Foundation** (404/355–6438), a local organization dedicated to developing pedestrian paths in an increasingly automobile-dominated region, continues to develop walking paths and greenways in various parts of the 10 counties. Among its projects are the Stone Mountain–Atlanta Trail and the Silver Comet Trail in Cobb County. If you wish to explore Atlanta on foot, pick up a copy of *Atlanta Walks, A Comprehensive Guide to Walking, Running, and Bicycling the Area's Scenic and Historic Locales* (Peachtree Publishers, $14.95). The guide outlines walking tours of more than 40 neighborhoods, parks, and historic areas around Atlanta. Serious walkers may choose to join one of several local walking clubs, such as the **Georgia Walkers** (770/914–9404), the **McIntosh Trail Walkers in Peachtree City** (770/631–8443), the **Roswell Striders** (770/641–3760), or the **Walking Club of Georgia** (770/593–5817). As members of the American Volksport Association (AVA), a national organization that sanctions non-competitive 10-K walks at hundreds of locations around the United States each year, these clubs host a variety of noncompetitive walks and occasional race-walking events. Club members may

Finally, a travel companion that doesn't snore on the plane or eat all your peanuts.

When traveling, your MCI WorldCom℠ Card is the best way to keep in touch. Our operators speak your language, so they'll be able to connect you back home—no matter where your travels take you. Plus, your MCI WorldCom Card is easy to use, and even earns you frequent flyer miles* every time you use it. When you add in our great rates, you get something even more valuable: peace-of-mind. So go ahead. Travel the world. MCI WorldCom just brought it a whole lot closer.

You can even sign up today at www.mci.com/worldphone or ask your operator to make a collect call to 1-410-314-2938.

EASY TO CALL WORLDWIDE

1 Dial 1-800-888-8000.
2 Dial or give the operator your MCI WorldCom Card number.
3 Dial or give the number you're calling.

EARN FREQUENT FLYER MILES

AmericanAirlines®
A'Advantage®

Continental Airlines
OnePass

▲ Delta Air Lines
SkyMiles·

HAWAIIANMILES
HAWAIIAN AIRLINES

MIDWEST EXPRESS AIRLINES   FREQUENT FLYER
PROGRAM PARTNER

SOUTHWEST AIRLINES®
RAPIDREWARDS
A SYMBOL OF FREEDOM™

☰ MILEAGE PLUS®
United Airlines

☰
US AIRWAYS
DIVIDEND MILES

*You will earn flight credits in the Southwest Airlines Rapid Rewards Program. All airline names and logos are proprietary marks of the respective airlines. All airline program rules and conditions apply.

Fodor's

Distinctive guides packed with up-to-date expert
advice and smart choices for every type of traveler.

Fodor's. For the world of ways you travel.

earn points, badges, and pins for participation in walks.

If you are interested in day-hiking excursions or overnight trips to the mountains or other Georgia destinations, you may wish to contact local outdoor organizations such as the **Georgia Chapter of the Sierra Club** (404/607–1262), the **Georgia Conservancy** (404/876–2900), or the **Georgia Appalachian Trail Club** (404/634–6495). Each group sponsors field trips and other hiking activities.

where to hike, run, or walk

5 *a-7 through g-3*

CHATTAHOOCHEE RIVER NATIONAL RECREATION AREA

More than 70 mi of trails crisscross 10 separate units of the popular recreation area. Most follow wooded ridges and river banks and are best suited for day-hiking. The Cochran Shoals unit has a paved 3.1-mi fitness trail that is a favorite destination for local runners, but be warned: on weekends it is almost impossible to find a parking space. *See* Parks, *above* for details on individual units.

8 *f-1*

GEORGIA'S STONE MOUNTAIN PARK

With more than 15 mi of trails, this park is a walker's and runner's paradise. Walkers may tackle the rugged 1.3-mi Walk-Up Trail, which climbs to the summit of the 800-ft-high granite monadnock, or try the rugged, 5-mi Cherokee Trail, which winds through woods and along mountain flanks. The 5-mi paved sidewalk path that encircles the mountain along Robert E. Lee Boulevard is a favorite of local runners (*see* Parks, *above*). *U.S 78, 5 mi outside/east of I–285, Stone Mountain, 770/498–5690, www.stonemountainpark.com. Open daily 6AM–midnight. Park admission free to pedestrians, parking $6.*

4 *e-3, e-4, e-5*

KENNESAW MOUNTAIN NATIONAL BATTLEFIELD PARK

It's only a foothill in comparison to its Appalachian Mountain cousins farther to the north, but 800-ft-high Kennesaw Mountain lays out nearly 20 mi of park trails in three interconnecting loops that wind through thick woods, open meadows, and across the summits of Kennesaw and Little Kennesaw mountains. The trails are popular with recreational hikers and with Civil War buffs who come to explore the site of a major clash between Union and Confederate soldiers in June 1864 (*see* Chapter 4). There are picnic areas adjacent to the visitor center (*see also* Bird-Watching, *above*). *Old U.S. 41, southwest of I–75 via Barrett Pkwy., Marietta, 770/427–4686, www.nps. gov/kemo. Open daily 8:30–5 daily. Park admission free.*

9 *b-7*

PEACHTREE CITY

This planned community south of Atlanta is known for its 70-plus mi of paved pedestrian and cycling paths that link residential neighborhoods, commercial districts, and recreation areas (*see* Bicycling, *above*). *Off GA 74, about 12 mi south of I 85. Peachtree City Information Center, 200 Westpark Dr., 770/ 487–4726.*

15 *f-2*

PIEDMONT PARK

Atlanta's oldest public park (*see* Parks, *above*) is a favorite destination for in-town runners and walkers. A loop that takes you through the park along its roads and paved paths is about 3½ mi long. The adjacent Atlanta Botanical Garden (*see* Botanical Gardens & Nature Preserves, *above*) and its Storza Woods Preserve are a great place for strolling amidst exotic plants and greenery. *400 Park Dr., between Piedmont Ave. and Monroe Dr. north of 10th St., Midtown, 404/817–6757.*

4 *a-4 through J-7*

SILVER COMET TRAIL

Currently under development by the PATH Foundation, this paved walking-jogging-biking trail will eventually stretch over 60 mi, between western Cobb County and the Alabama state line. At press time, the trail was complete from Smyrna to Rockmart. The eastern trail head is at Concord Road near the East-West Connector in Smyrna, and there are additional access points along the route; the western trail-head moves as the trail is developed. Maps and construction updates are available from the PATH Foundation (404/355–6438).

7 *e-4 through h-2*

STONE MOUNTAIN–ATLANTA GREENWAY TRAIL

Stretching over 18 mi, from Greenbriar Mall in southwest Atlanta to Stone Mountain Village, this popular course of paved pedestrian paths and city sidewalks is open only to walkers, runners, cyclists, and skaters. The trail takes walkers, skaters, and riders past the historic campuses of Atlanta University and Georgia Tech and through Inman Park and Decatur. The Trolley Line Trail, a 7-mi spur, splits from the main trail near Boulevard and reconnects with it near the campus of Agnes Scott College. In downtown Atlanta and some in-town neighborhoods, the trail follows existing sidewalks. At other locations, the trail follows a separate paved path away from the street. The trail was developed by the PATH Foundation (404/355–6438), which can provide information and maps.

HOCKEY

When the NHL's Atlanta Flames took to the ice in 1972, hockey was a sport alien to most native-born southerners. Many skeptics thought that ice and grits would never mix, but the Flames developed a devoted following during their eight years in the city. Their lasting legacy was the introduction of competitive amateur hockey at a growing number of rinks around the city. For two decades following the Atlanta Flames' move to Calgary, local hockey fans had only amateur and minor-league teams to fuel their fervor for this fast-paced game. But the arrival of many newcomers from northern cities (where hockey borders on religion) sparked a rebirth of NHL hockey in Atlanta, and the Thrashers appeared in 1999.

team to watch

ATLANTA THRASHERS

Competing in the Southeastern Division of the NHL's Eastern Conference, the Thrashers play their games at Philips Arena. The NHL season runs from October through April. Game tickets cost $10–$70 and are available from the Thrashers box office or from Ticketmaster (800/249–6400). *Techwood Dr. south of Marietta St., Downtown, 404/584–7825. MARTA: Dome/GWCC.*

where to play

It seems that half the population of Atlanta's suburbs hails from somewhere up north, where hockey is a favorite winter sport. Not surprisingly, the metro area is home to several skating rinks and recreational and competitive hockey leagues for youths and adults. If you want to have a little fun on the ice with others of similar ability, contact the **Atlanta Amateur Hockey League** (AAHL; 770/457–6352), the **Atlanta Coed Hockey League** (ACHL; 770/414–8950), the **Georgia Amateur Hockey Association** (GAHA; 404/816–3303), or the **Southern Ice Hockey Association** (SIHA; 770/812–8807). Skaters interested in participating in roller-hockey leagues should contact the **Metropolitan Atlanta**

A WALK ON THE WILD SIDE

Despite Atlanta's sprawling development, pockets of wilderness remain to explore. Check these out when you need a natural high.

Fernbank Forest
Find virgin wilderness 5 mi from Five Points (see Botanical Gardens & Nature Preserves, above).

Chattahoochee River National Recreation Area
Fortunately, the river is not navigable—otherwise the Atlanta skyline would have banished the millions of trees along its banks (see Parks, above).

Cochran Mill Park and Nature Preserve
Rushing streams flow through this rolling, wooded oasis in the southern metro area (see Parks; Botanical Gardens & Nature Preserves, above).

Davidson–Arabia Mountain Nature Preserve
Winding trails take you through a unique and nearly unspoiled wilderness (see Botanical Gardens & Nature Preserves, above).

Reynolds Nature Preserve
A profusion of wild azaleas and other flowering plants makes this an ideal spot for a springtime walk (see Botanical Gardens & Nature Preserves, above).

Street Hockey Association (MASHA; 770/840–6952).

5 d-1
ALPHARETTA FAMILY SKATE CENTER

Known as the Cooler, this large complex has three full-size rinks for recreational ice skating and competitive youth and adult hockey. The Atlanta Coed Hockey League, the Life University and Georgia State University hockey teams, and teams that compete in AAHL and GAHA competition are based here. There is a fully stocked pro shop, professional hockey and roller-hockey instruction programs, and a restaurant–snack bar. *10800 Davis Dr., off Mansell Rd. at GA 400, Alpharetta, 770/667–2211, www. cooler.com. Recreational skating admission $5–$7, skate rental $3.*

6 b-2
ATLANTA ICE FORUM

The complex, which serves as the training and practice facility for the Atlanta Thrashers, is equipped with two NHL-regulation rinks that host youth and adult teams in AAHL and GAHA league competition. Facilities include a full-service pro shop, instructional programs, and a restaurant–sports bar. *2300 Satellite Blvd., off I–85, Duluth, 770/813–1010, www.iceforum.com. Recreational skating admission $5–$7, skate rental $2 (figure) and $3 (hockey).*

4 e-2
ICE FORUM AT TOWN CENTER

Like its sister facility in Duluth (*see above*), this modern complex with an NHL regulation–size rink offers recreational skating programs, competitive ice hockey leagues for youth and adults, and a comprehensive instructional program. The home of Peach Frost, a national-championship synchronized skating team, Ice Forum has a pro shop and snack bar. *3061 George Busbee Pkwy., off Chastain Rd. and I–75, Marietta, 770/218–1010, www.iceforum.com. Recreational skating admission $5–$7, skate rental $2 (figure) and $3 (hockey).*

5 b-4
PARKAIRE ICE RINK

Atlanta's oldest ice rink is especially popular with Cobb County and northwest Atlanta residents. It has a full-size rink for recreational skating and hockey competition, a fully stocked pro shop, and professional instruction programs. *4880 Lower Roswell Rd., at Johnson Ferry Rd., Marietta, 770/887–4567, www.parkaire.com. Recreational skating admission $4.50–$5, skate rental $2 (figure) and $3 (hockey).*

8 e-2
WADE-WALKER PARK

The Metropolitan Atlanta Street Hockey Association (MASHA) plays league games at an enclosed rink in this large DeKalb County park (*see* Parks, *above*). The rink is for league play only. *Rockbridge Rd. at Stone Mountain–Lithonia Rd., Stone Mountain, 770/840–6952.*

HORSEBACK RIDING

instruction

5 e-4
HAT CREEK STABLES

This suburban farm specializes in riding lessons and offers trail rides on Saturday afternoons. *7010 Nesbit Ferry Rd., Dunwoody, 770/395–9200. Registration $175; lessons $35 (half-hr individual or 1-hr group).*

where to ride

4 e-6
JIM MILLER PARK

This Cobb County park (*see* Parks, *above*) has riding facilities and hosts rodeo competitions sponsored by various organizations. Contact the park for event information. *2245 Callaway Rd., south of the Al Bishop Softball Complex, Marietta, 770/528–8875.*

4 e-1
WILD HORSE CREEK PARK

This large Cobb County park (*see* Parks, *above*) has an equestrian ring and an arena where horse owners can put their mounts through their paces. The park hosts several horse shows during the year. *3280 Macedonia Rd., Powder Springs, 770/528–8890.*

5 e-1
WILLS PARK

Horse owners are welcome to ride their mounts at the park's three public rings, where a wide variety of equestrian events are held throughout the year. *332 Maddox St., Alpharetta, 770/410–5780. Admission $6 (Alpharetta residents $5).*

ICE-SKATING

For information on metro Atlanta facilities that offer recreational skating, figure skating, and instruction, *see* Hockey, *above.*

IN-LINE SKATING & ROLLER-SKATING

Atlanta's hilly terrain and heavy traffic do not dampen the fervor of the city's growing number of in-line skaters. City residents roll through local parks and along side streets, while suburban skaters take to quiet subdivision lanes and commercial rinks. Skaters interested in participating in roller-hockey leagues should contact the **Metropolitan Atlanta Street Hockey Association** (MASHA; 770/840–6952). *See* Hockey, *above,* for information on where to play roller-hockey.

equipment & instruction

15 *g-2*

ASPHALT FLIGHT SCHOOL

Across Monroe Drive from Piedmont Park (*see* Parks, *above*), a favorite spot for skating, you can find a full range of equipment for sale or rent, plus instruction. This is the headquarters of the Peachtree Road Rollers (404/634–9032), who organize group-skate outings at various locations around Atlanta. *1024 Monroe Dr., Midtown, 404/853–5009. Private lessons $30–$60, Sunday afternoon group instruction $15 per person.*

BOHEMIAN SKATE SCHOOL

The school's professional instructors offer group and individual lessons at various Atlanta locations, and its club, Bohemian Skaters, hosts group outings. The school is associated with the Atlanta Peachtree Road Rollers skating club. Lesson packages are available. *404/298–6378. Lessons $30 per hr group, $45 per hr individual.*

15 *f-2*

SKATE ESCAPE

Atlanta's pioneering in-line skating center, across from Piedmont Park (*see*

Parks, *above*), offers equipment for sale or rent. *1086 Piedmont Ave., Midtown, 404/892–1292.*

5 *b-5*

SKATE 2000

This shop sells equipment and gives free lessons. *6309 Roswell Rd., Sandy Springs, 404/303–7633.*

5 *b-4*

SONIC BLADES

Two suburban stores offer the full range of ice skates, in-line skates, and skateboards, as well as lessons on how to stay up on any of them. Group lessons cost $15 per hour per person and individual lessons cost $25 per hour. *736 Johnson Ferry Rd., Marietta, 770/977–0005.*

5 *g-5*

5775 Jimmy Carter Blvd, Norcross, 770/662–5665.

clubs and organizations

Skaters on Atlanta's streets find safety in both numbers and experience through several local clubs that sponsor group-skate outings and social events. For more information, call **Atlanta Skate Patrol** (404/634–9032), **Bohemian Skaters** (404/634–9032), **Cobb County Cruisers** (770/421–1247), **Metropolitan Atlanta Street Hockey Association** (MASHA; 770/840–6952; *see* Hockey, *above*), or **Peachtree Road Rollers** (Box 15482, Atlanta 30333, 404/634–9032).

where to roll

5 *d-1*

ALPHARETTA FAMILY SKATE CENTER

See Hockey, *above.* *10800 Davis Dr., off Mansell Rd. at GA 400, Alpharetta, 770/667–2211, www.cooler.com.*

3 *d-5*

CUMMING SKATE CENTER

With one of the South's largest skating surfaces, this is a favorite destination for recreational and competitive in-line skaters. It is the home rink of national and X-Games racing champion Derek Downey and of the nation's top speed-racing team, the G.T. Speed. In addition to racing, the center sponsors both youth and adult roller-hockey leagues.

863 Buford Hwy., west of GA 400, Cumming, 770/887–5283. Admission $2.50–$3 (Wednesday nights 88¢), rentals 75¢ (roller skates) and $2.50 (in-line skates).

8 f-1

GEORGIA'S STONE MOUNTAIN PARK

The park (see Parks, above) is a popular and scenic spot for skating, with more than 10 mi of streets and lanes. U.S 78, 5 mi outside/east of I–285, Stone Mountain, 770/498–5690, www.stonemountainpark.com. Open daily 6AM–midnight. Park admission free, parking $6.

15 f-2

PIEDMONT PARK

A favorite of in-towners and first-timers (nearby Skate Escape rents skates), the lanes that meander through the city's largest public park (see Parks, above) are closed to automobiles. The people-watching here is as much fun as the skating. 400 Park Dr., between Piedmont Ave. and Monroe Dr. north of 10th St., Midtown, 404/817–6757.

4 a-4 through f-7

SILVER COMET TRAIL

For more on this trail, which at press time was complete from Smyrna to Rockmart, see Hiking, Running & Walking, above.

10 a-1

SPARKLES SKATE CENTER

On a large hardwood floor, this indoor facility on the south side offers open skating to contemporary music. 6766 Mt. Zion Blvd., off I–75, Morrow, 770/565–8899. Admission $4–$6, rentals $1.50–$3.25.

7 e-4 through h-2

STONE MOUNTAIN–ATLANTA GREENWAY TRAIL

For more on this 18-mi trail, see Hiking, Running & Walking, above.

MARTIAL ARTS

With more than 50 martial arts studios in the Atlanta area, it can seem like there is a karate class taking place on nearly every street corner and strip mall. The following are considered some of the best and most authentic martial arts facilities in the 10 counties.

8 b-1

Aikido Center of Atlanta (630 Valley Brook Rd., Decatur, 404/297–7804).

6 f-1

American Karate–Joe Corley Studios (2700 Braselton Hwy., Dacula, 770/614–8788).

6 a-4

American Karate–Joe Corley Studios (2300 Pleasant Hill Rd., Duluth, 770/623–4100).

4 h-5

American Karate–Joe Corley Studios (2500 Delk Rd., Marietta, 770/579–0830; 2900 Delk Rd., Marietta, 770/984–0860).

12 g-8

American Karate–Joe Corley Studios (1837 Piedmont Rd., Midtown, 404/815–7676).

2 a-8

American Karate–Joe Corley Studios (601B Industrial Ct., Woodstock, 770/592 1610).

4 g-3

Chinese Shao-Lin Center (2727 Canton Rd., Marietta, 770/422–9250).

5 e-4

Chinese Shao-Lin Center (3380 Holcomb Bridge Rd., Marietta, 770/446–3529).

5 d-5

Dave Young's World Class Karate and Martial Arts Academy (5400 Chamblee-Dunwoody Rd., Dunwoody, 770/394–5425).

5 b-5

Imperatori Family Karate Center (5920 Roswell Rd., Sandy Springs, 404/252–8200).

MINIATURE GOLF

4 g-4

AMERICAN ADVENTURES

At American Adventures, a theme park for families with children up to age 15, you can dive into the multilevel Foam Factory (filled with 50,000 plastic balls), whiz around the go-cart race track, challenge your friends to a game of laser tag, or play a round of miniature golf. Admission is free when you pay for entry to Whitewater water park next door (*see Beaches & Water Parks, above*). *250 Cobb Pkwy. near I–75 (exit 265), Marietta, 770/424–9283. Open daily 11–8; (outdoor rides open weekends only Labor Day–Memorial Day, except daily during spring break). Fees: Fun Pass (good for all rides): ages 3 and under $4.99; ages 4–17 $13.99; parents $2.99. Foam Factory only: ages 3 and under $4.99; ages 4–17 $7.99; parents $1.99.*

6 *a-4*

PIRATES COVE ADVENTURE GOLF AND VIDEO ARCADE

This multilevel course, with its challenging layout of dips, drops, and nautical-theme obstacles, is popular with kids and adults alike. *3380 Venture Pkwy., Duluth, 770/623–4184.*

PAINTBALL

Paintball crams tag, hide-and-seek, and capture-the-flag into a single fast-paced game. After donning protective gear, two teams arm themselves with air-guns loaded with paint capsules and take to an indoor or outdoor field. Each team's objective is to eliminate opposing players by shooting them with paint, then to capture the opposing team's flag. Half-hour (or longer) sessions offer the adrenaline rush of combat without fear of losing life or limb.

where to play

4 *a-1*

ARKENSTONE PAINTBALL

Twelve playing fields spread across 71 acres feature wooded terrain with creeks, hills, and artificial obstacles. The site also has a speed ball field where you can play a faster version of paintball on a smaller field with fewer obstacles to hide behind. There is a clubhouse and a snack bar. Rates include equipment rental, but you must buy your own paint balls ($7 for 100, $12 for 200). *7257 Cedarcrest Rd., west of I–75, Acworth, 770/974–2535. Open weekends 10–5. Fees: single session (15–20 mins) $12, all-day play $25.*

5 *d-2*

PAINTBALL ATLANTA

Atlanta's first paintball facility has eight outdoor fields on nearly 150 acres, plus two arenas for indoor speed ball, and a

fully stocked pro shop and snack bar. Rates include equipment rental, and paint balls cost $5–$7 for 100. The indoor arenas and one outdoor field are at the Roswell location and the rest of the fields are in Alpharetta. *700 Holcomb Bridge Rd., off GA 400, Roswell, 770/594–0912. Indoor courts open Fri. 4–10, Sat. noon–10, Sun. noon–6. Outdoor courses open Sat. 9–5, Sun. 10–5. Fees: single session $10–$15.*

3 *C-6*

Stoney Point Rd. off McFarland and Shiloh Rds., east of GA 400, Alpharetta, 770/594–0912. Open Sat. 9–5, Sun. 10–5. Fees: single session $10–$15.

ROCK CLIMBING

Traditionally, climbers drove an hour or more to the north Georgia mountains to indulge their passion for scaling sheer rocks. Today, indoor climbing walls, where enthusiasts and novices alike may hone their skills, are all the rage. An increasing number of sporting goods stores are installing walls, and Atlanta has several specialized climbing centers.

12 *a-7*

ATLANTA ROCKS!

With more than 12,000 square ft. of climbing area, Atlanta Rocks! Intown is the largest facility of its type in the Southeast. Introductory climbing classes start at $35. Atlanta Rocks! Perimeter is smaller but has the same climbing challenges. *1019A Collier Rd., Buckhead, 404/351–3009. Hours: Mon., Wed., and Fri. 3–10; Tues. and Thurs. 11–10; Sat. 12C8; Sun. noon–6. Fees: $12.50 per hr weekdays, $14.50 per hr weekends.*

5 *e-5*

4411A Bankers Cir., Doraville, 770/242–30360. Hours: Mon. and Fri. 6 PM–10 PM, Tues.–Thurs. 3–10, Sat. noon–8, Sun. noon–6. Fees: $10.50 per hr weekdays, $12.50 per hr weekends.

14 *c-5*

WALL CRAWLERS ROCK CLUB

More than 6,000 square ft of indoor climbing surfaces here include both a state-of-the-art climbing wall and a 1,700 square ft bouldering cave. Day passes are $12 and memberships are available. *1522 DeKalb Ave., Candler Park, 404/371–8997. Hours: weekdays noon–11, weekends 10–8. Fees: Classes start at $12.*

RUGBY

For many years, rugby has maintained a small but very loyal following in the Atlanta area. If you would like to learn more about this challenging sport or find a team to join, contact one of the local rugby football clubs (RFCs). Among them: **Atlanta Harlequins Women's RFC** (770/705–7317, www.atlantaharlequins.com), **Atlanta Old White RFC** (404/303–5855, www.atlantarugby.com), and **Atlanta Renegades RFC** (770/908–3999).

SAILING

Summer breezes from neighboring mountains bring strong and sometimes tricky breezes to Lakes Allatoona and Sidney Lanier, making both popular with the Atlanta area's inland sailors. The two lakes are the largest bodies of water close to the city and about the only places to enjoy large-craft, open-water sailing. For more information on local lakes, *see* Boating, *above.* If you are looking for rental equipment or instruction, you can find both at Lake Lanier–based **Lanier Sailing Academy** (770/945–8810) and **Windsong Sailing Academy** (404/256–6700).

SOCCER

teams to watch

ATLANTA SILVERBACKS

The Silverbacks compete in the professional United Soccer League's "A" League and are affiliated with Major League Soccer's Dallas Burn. They play their games at DeKalb Memorial Stadium in a season that runs from April to September. Game tickets cost $5–$8. *Outside I–285 off Memorial Drive, near Decatur, 770/645–6655, www.atlantasilverbacks.com.*

where to play

Like the rest of the United States, the Atlanta area has caught soccer fever. More and more kids take up the game each year, and the city's expanding international population has infused adult leagues with talented and devoted players and fans. You can join a soccer club (*see below*), or contact your parks and recreation department (*see* Parks, *above*) for information on their youth and adult leagues. The following municipal facilities have multiple fields and sponsor both league and tournament play.

5 *h-6*
Harmony Grove Soccer Complex (9 Harmony Grove Rd., Lilburn, 770/978–5271).

5 *f-7*
Henderson Park (2803 Henderson Rd., Tucker, 404/371–2631; *see* Parks, *above*).

9 *h-5*
Lovejoy Soccer Complex (1935 McDonough Rd., Hampton, 770/477–3766).

5 *h-4*
Pinckneyville Soccer Complex (4707 Old Peachtree Rd., Norcross, 770/417–2200; *see* Parks, *above*).

10 *e-4*
Soccer Complex (143 Henry Pkwy., McDonough, 770/954–2031; *see* Parks, *above*).

4 *d-7*
Tramore Park (2150 East-West Connector, Marietta, 770/528–8800; *see* Parks, *above*).

soccer clubs and leagues

Metro Atlanta is home to several private soccer teams and leagues suited for both novice and advanced players.

Atlanta Club Sport (coed recreational leagues, 404/257–3355).

Atlanta District Amateur Soccer League (30-team men's league, highly competitive, 770/452–0505).

Greater Atlanta Women's Soccer Association (highly competitive, 404/687–8004).

International Sports Soccer Association (in-town coed recreational league, drop-ins welcome, 770/279–4699).

League Latino Americana (highly competitive men's leagues, 404/873–7629).

Over-35 Masters League (men's league, 770/979–9046).

SWIMMING

instruction

5 g-1
DYNAMO COMMUNITY SWIM CENTERS

The two local Dynamo Centers are well known throughout Atlanta for their excellent instructional programs and their highly competitive youth and adult swim leagues. Lessons begin at $70 for elementary school students and adults, $65 for preschoolers. High school–age swimmers may join competitive swim teams. Contact the centers for information on team fees. *5075 Abbots Bridge Rd., Alpharetta, 770/772–6789.*

5 e-7
3119 Shallowford Rd., Chamblee, 770/451–3272.

6 a-6
SWIM ATLANTA

Swim Atlanta has three pools for instruction and competitive team training and events. Swim lessons begin at $72 for an eight-session program. *324 Holly Ridge Dr., Lilburn, 770/381–7946.*

5 d-2
795 Old Roswell Rd., Roswell, 770/992–1778.

5 h-1
4050 John's Creek Pkwy., Suwanee, 770/622–1735.

15 e-5
YMCA OF METROPOLITAN ATLANTA

Eleven Family YMCAs in the Atlanta area offer aquatics programs and instruction to members and the general public. YMCA members receive discounts. Contact **YMCA of Metropolitan Atlanta** (404/588–9622, www.ymcaatl.org) or the center most convenient to you for program and fee information. *Downtown Branch: 260 Peachtree St., 404/527–7676.*

5 f-1
Alpharetta/E. Isakson Family Branch (3655 Preston Ridge Rd, Alpharetta, 770/664–1220).

5 d-6
Ashford-Dunwoody–Cowart Family Branch (3692 Ashford-Dunwoody Rd., Dunwoody, 770/451–9622).

14 f-2
Decatur-DeKalb Family Branch (1100 Clairmont Rd., Decatur, 404/377–0241).

9 c-7
Fayette Family Branch (14 Eastbrook Bend, Peachtree City, 770/487–2850).

5 f-3
Fowler/Norcross Family Branch (5600 W. Jones Bridge Rd., Norcross, 770/246–9622).

12 a-4
Sanders/Buckhead Family Branch (1160 Moores Mill Rd., Buckhead, 404/350–9292).

8 d-4
South DeKalb Family Branch (2565 Snapfinger Rd., Decatur, 7 70/987–3500).

8 a-3
Southeast Family Branch (1765 Memorial Dr., Decatur, 404/243–9662).

7 f-4
Southwest Family Branch (2200 Campbellton Rd., Adams Park, 404/753–4169).

6 b-4
Tull-Gwinnett Family Branch (2985 Sugarloaf Pkwy., Lawrenceville, 770/963–1313).

where to swim

You can swim in the Y's indoor pools year-round, or you can find a nearby beach in summer (*see* Beaches & Water Parks, *above*). In addition, a number of parks in the 10-county metropolitan area have either seasonal pools (Memorial Day through Labor Day) or year-round aquatics centers. Many of these offer lessons, swim and dive leagues for youth and adults, exercise and hydroaerobics classes, and recreational swimming. Here's where you can find public pools.

CITY OF ATLANTA

The city operates 18 outdoor pools and 3 indoor aquatics centers.

Outdoor Pools: **Adams Park** (*see* Parks, *above*); **Anderson Park** (48 Anderson Ave., Dixie Hills, 404/794–1221); **Candler Park** (*see* Parks, *above*); **Garden Hills Park** (355 Pinetree Dr., Buckhead, 404/848–7220); **Grant Park** (*see* Parks, *above*); **Gun Club Park** (1137 Gun Club

Rd., West Atlanta, 404/799–0314); **John A. White Park** (1053 Cascade Rd., Cascade Heights, 404/817–6757); **Langford (Joyland) Park** (211 Thornton St., Joyland, 404/624–0668); **Maddox Park** (1115 Bankhead Hwy., Grove Park, 404/817–6757); **Mozley Park** (1565 M.L. King Jr. Dr., West End, 404/758–1903); **Oakland City Park** (1305 Oakland Rd., Oakland City, 404/753–0020); **Piedmont Park** (*see* Parks, *above*); **Pittman Park** (950 Garibaldi St., South Atlanta, 404/523–3797); **Rosa L. Burney Park** (477 Windsor St., Mechanicsville, 404/658–7117); **South Bend Park** (1955 Compton Dr., Lakewood, 404/622–4115); **Thomasville Park** (1835 Henry Thomas Dr., Thomasville, 404/627–3413); **Tucson Trail Park** (4610 Tucson Trail, Ben Hill, 404/349–4342).

Aquatics centers: **J. F. Kennedy Park** (225 James P. Brawley Dr., Vine City, 404/524–7111); **M. L. King Natatorium** (70 Boulevard, Sweet Auburn, 404/688–3791); **Southeast Atlanta Park** (365 Cleveland Ave., East Point, 404/624–0772).

CLAYTON COUNTY

The county operates one outdoor pool: **Bonanza Park** (1620 Flicker Rd., Jonesboro, 770/477–3766).

COBB COUNTY

The county operates two outdoor pools and two indoor aquatics centers; a third aquatics center, in Powder Springs, is under construction and scheduled to open in 2001.

Outdoor pools: **Powder Springs Park** (3899 Brownsville Rd., Powder Springs, 770/439–6315); **Sewell Park** (2055 Lower Roswell Rd., Marietta, 770/509–2741).

Aquatic Centers: **East Cobb Aquatic Center** (Gordy Pkwy., Marietta, 770/509–4927); **Larry Bell Park** (*see* Parks, *above*).

DEKALB COUNTY

The county operates 12 outdoor pools: **Briarwood Recreation Center** (2235 Briarwood Way, Ashford Park, 404/579–5911); **Gresham Park Recreation Center** (*see* Parks, *above*); **Kelly C. Cofer Park** (4259 N. Park Dr., Tucker, no phone); **Kittredge Park** (1520 Kittredge Park Rd., North Atlanta, no phone); **Lithonia Park** (2501 Park Dr., Lithonia, no phone); **Lynwood Recreation Center** (3360 Osborne Rd., Lynwood Park, 404/303–2100); **Mark Trail Park Recreation Center** (*see*

Parks, *above*); **Medlock Park** (874 Gaylemont Cir., Decatur, no phone); **Midway Park Recreation Center** (3151 Midway Rd., Decatur, 404/286–3328); **Murphy Candler Park** (*see* Parks, *above*); **Tobie Grant Park Recreation Center** (844 Parkdale Dr., Scottdale, 404/808–7864); **Wade-Walker Park** (*see* Parks, *above*).

FULTON COUNTY

The county operates two indoor aquatics centers: **Clarence Duncan Memorial Park** and **Welcome All Park** (*see* Parks, *above*, for both).

GWINNETT COUNTY

The county operates three outdoor pools and two indoor aquatics centers.

Outdoor pools: **Dacula Park** (205 Dacula Rd., Dacula, 770/822–5410); **Rhodes Jordan Park** (*see* Parks, *above*); **Springbrook Golf, Tennis, and Aquatics Complex** (*see* Golf, *above*).

Aquatics centers: **Bogan Park** and **Mountain Park** (*see* Parks, *above*, for both).

TENNIS

Many county parks in the metro area have free, first-come, first-served tennis courts, and several have full-service tennis centers that offer professional instruction, equipment sales and rentals, and organized competition. You can also join the **Atlanta Lawn Tennis Association** (ALTA; 770/399–5788, www.altatennis.org, membership $20), which is nearly 80,000 members strong. The association organizes singles and doubles competition for players of every skill level and description, with leagues available for men, women, and coed; seniors and youth; wheelchair-bound; and others. ALTA teams play in scores of private and public tennis facilities around the metropolitan area.

where to play

You don't need to buy a membership to play at the following tennis centers in the metropolitan area. Fees listed are per person, per hour.

city of atlanta

12 *c-7*

**BITSY GRANT
TENNIS CENTER**

Twenty-four lighted courts (20 hard, 4 clay). *2125 Northside Dr., Buckhead, 404/609–7193. $2–$4.50.*

5 *b-7*

**CHASTAIN PARK
TENNIS CENTER**

See Parks, *above.* 9 lighted hard courts. *110 W. Wieuca Rd., North Buckhead, 404/255–1993. $2–$2.50.*

7 *g-3*

MCGHEE TENNIS CENTER

Eight lighted hard courts. *820 Beecher St., Cascade Heights, 404/756–1869. $2–$2.50.*

15 *g-2*

**PIEDMONT PARK
TENNIS CENTER**

See Parks, *above.* 12 lighted hard courts. *400 Park Dr., Midtown, 404/872–1507. $2–$4.50.*

15 *a-6*

**WASHINGTON PARK
TENNIS CENTER**

Eight lighted hard courts. *1125 Lena St., Washington Park, 404/658–6229. $2–$2.50.*

cobb county

4 *f-5*

FAIR OAKS PARK

Twelve lighted hard courts. *1460 W. Booth Rd., Marietta, 770/528–8480. $1–$1.50.*

5 *b-2*

HARRISON PARK

Eight lighted hard courts. *2653 Shallowford Rd., Marietta, 770/591–3151. $1–$1.50.*

4 *c-1*

KENNWORTH PARK

Eight lighted hard courts. *4100 GA 293, Acworth, 770/917–5160. $1–$1.50.*

4 *d-8*

SWEETWATER PARK

Eight lighted hard courts. *2447 Clay Rd., Austell, 770/819–3221. $1–$1.50.*

4 *h-5*

TERRELL MILL PARK

Eight lighted hard courts. *480 Terrell Mill Rd., Marietta, 770/644–2771. $1–$1.50.*

dekalb county

5 *d-6*

BLACKBURN PARK

See Parks, *above.* 18 lighted hard courts. *3493 Ashford-Dunwoody Rd., Dunwoody, 770/451–1061. $2–$2.50.*

13 *g-2, f-7*

DEKALB TENNIS CENTER

Seventeen lighted hard courts. *1400 McConnell Dr., Decatur, 404/325–2520. $2–$2.50.*

5 *d-5*

**DUNWOODY
TENNIS CENTER**

Six lighted hard courts. *1850 Cotillion Dr., Dunwoody, 770/551–8578. $8–$12.*

14 *g-2, h-2*

**GLEN LAKE
TENNIS CENTER**

Nine lighted hard courts. *1121 Church St., Decatur, 404/377–7231. $1.50–$2.*

8 *g-1*

**INTERNATIONAL TENNIS
CENTER AT STONE
MOUNTAIN PARK**

Site of the tennis competition at the 1996 Olympic Games and host of many regional and national tournaments, the center has 15 lighted hard courts. *5525 Bermuda Rd., off West Park Pl. east of Stone Mountain Park, Stone Mountain, 770/469–0108. $3.*

8 *b-5*

SUGAR CREEK

Sixteen lighted courts (12 hard, 4 clay). *2706 Bouldercrest Rd., south of Gresham Park, 404/243–7149. $2–$3.*

fayette county

9 *a-6*

**PEACHTREE CITY
TENNIS CENTER**

Eighteen lighted courts (12 hard, 6 clay). *10 Planterra Way, Peachtree City, 770/486–9474. $2.50–$4.50.*

fulton county

7 *e-7*

BURDETT TENNIS CENTER
Eight lighted hard courts. *5975 Old Carriage Dr., College Park, 770/996–3502. $1.50–$2.75.*

5 *c-5*

NORTH FULTON TENNIS CENTER
Twenty-four lighted courts (20 hard, 4 clay). *500 Abernathy Rd., Sandy Springs, 404/303–6182. $2–$3.*

7 *d-7*

SOUTH FULTON TENNIS CENTER
Twenty-four lighted courts (20 hard, 4 clay). *5645 Mason Rd., College Park, 770/ 306–3059. $1.50–$2.75.*

gwinnett county

5 *g-5*

HUDLOW TENNIS CENTER
Sixteen lighted hard courts. *6224 Jimmy Carter Blvd., Norcross, 770/417 2210. $2–$2.50.*

6 *b-7*

MOUNTAIN PARK TENNIS CENTER
See Parks, above. Eight lighted hard courts. *5050 Five Forks Trickum Rd., Lilburn, 770/564–4651. $2–$2.50.*

6 *d-2*

SPRINGBROOK GOLF, TENNIS, AND AQUATICS COMPLEX
See Golf, above. The county-operated center in a 138-acre park has three lighted hard courts. Others come here to play golf or to take a swim in the outdoor pool. *585 Camp Ferrin Rd., Lawrenceville, 770/822–5400. Free.*

henry county

8 *d-8*

GARDNER PARK
See Parks, above. Twelve hard courts (6 lighted). *160 E. Atlanta Rd., Stockbridge. Free.*

VOLLEYBALL

The beach volleyball competition held in Clayton County International Park during the 1996 Olympics sparked a new wave of local interest in volleyball. Today, the number of courts in the Atlanta area is growing, and the Olympic park hosts a variety of regional and national volleyball competitions.

teams to watch

GEORGIA TECH LADY JACKETS
A major presence in the highly competitive Atlantic Coast Conference, the team plays its games at O'Keefe Gymnasium on the Tech campus. During the September November season, tickets cost $3 for adults and $1 for youth, students, and senior citizens. *Techwood Dr. at 6th St., 888/832–4849.*

GEORGIA STATE UNIVERSITY LADY PANTHERS
Runner-up in the 1998 Trans-America Athletic Conference, the Lady Panthers play fast-paced, highly competitive volleyball. Fom September to November, they play at the GSU Sports Arena; admission is free. *Piedmont Ave. and Decatur St., Downtown, 404/651–2772.*

where to play

Many county parks have indoor or outdoor volleyball facilities and organize league play. Check with the local parks departments (*see Parks, above*) for facility and league information. Three independent organizations, including **Atlanta Club Sport** (404/842–0317), sponsor recreational and competitive leagues for both youth and adults. The **North Atlanta Volleyball Club** (770/909–0281, www.northatlantavolleyball.org) and **Volleyball Atlanta** (770/394–7074, www.volleyballatlanta.org) also send teams to compete around the South in tournaments sponsored by the Southern Region Volleyball Association. Listed here are some of the most popular spots around Atlanta to find a pick-up game or join in a league.

BEACH VOLLEYBALL
Clayton County International Park is where Olympic wanna-bes can come pound the sand at the site of the 1996 Olympic Games beach volleyball com-

petition. The heart of the park is the 6,200-seat volleyball stadium and 13-court volleyplex, but there is plenty else to do on a day at "the beach" (*see* Parks *and* Beaches & Water Parks, *above*).

9 *h-1*

GA 138, *west of I–75 near Jonesboro (exit 75), 770/473–4005.*

VOLLEYBALL

15 *f-4*

Bedford—Pine Park (Bedford Pl. between Angier and Linden Aves., Midtown; *see* Basketball, *above*).

5 *g-5*

Best Friend Park (6224 Jimmy Carter Blvd. [GA 140], north of I–85, Norcross, 770/417–2200; *see* Parks, *above*).

14 *g-3*

Decatur Recreation Center (231 Sycamore St., Decatur, 404/377–0494).

14 *b-3*

Druid Hills United Methodist Church (1200 Ponce de Leon Ave., Druid Hills, 404/377–4928).

5 *c-5*

Hammond Park (705 Hammond Dr. at Glenridge Dr., Sandy Springs, 404/303–6176; *see* Parks, *above*).

15 *h-2*

Howell Memorial Park (Virginia Ave. at Barnett Street, Virginia-Highland, no phone).

4 *g-6*

Smyrna Community Center (200 Village Green Cir., Smyrna, 770/431–2842).

5 *d-8*

Salvation Army Gymnasium Fitness Center (2090 N. Druid Hills Rd., North Atlanta, 404/315–7499).

YOGA

In metro Atlanta, several yoga centers and fellowships offer classes, retreats, and other programs.

YOGA CENTERS

13 *e-6*

Metamorphosis Yoga Studio (2931A N. Druid Hills Rd., Toco Hills, 404/633–8484).

12 *f-3*

Peachtree Yoga Center (3130 Peachtree Rd., Buckhead, 404/467–9642).

14 *a-2*

The Pierce Program (1164 N. Highland Ave., Atlanta, Virginia-Highland, 404/875–7110).

15 *f-2*

Stillwater Yoga Studio (270 15th St., Midtown, 404/874–7813).

YOGA FELLOWSHIPS

Yoga fellowships are informal organizations where people may come together to practice yoga or to enjoy social gatherings with like-minded others. You can find out more about local fellowships from **Atlanta Yoga Fellowship** (770/333–9642) and **Southeastern Yoga Association** (404/289–8061).

fitness centers, health clubs & spa services

CLUBS

Atlanta sweats in dozens of health clubs and gyms in storefronts, strip malls, and office buildings. Some of the most popular clubs in the metro area are part of national chains, such as **Australian Body Works** (19 coed clubs and 3 women's centers, 404/848–0222); **Bally Total Fitness** (8 clubs, 800/695–8111); and **Crunch Fitness** (formerly Sportslife, 6 clubs, Buckhead, 404/262—2120; Cobb, 770/952–2120; Gwinnett, 770/497–2120; Roswell, 770/992–2120; Stone Mountain, 770/469–2120; Town Center, 770/428–2120). Local clubs with a loyal following include **Firehouse Fitness** (Riverdale, 770/991–3355), **Lee Haney's Universal Fitness** (Downtown 404/892–6737; Stone Mountain 404/508–8181), and **Planet Fitness** (Brookhaven, 404/325–3351; Sandy Springs, 404/256–4653).

DAY SPAS & MASSAGE THERAPY

An increasing number of Atlantans—men and women alike—are experiencing the physical and mental benefits of a visit to a day spa. There are more than a dozen spas in the metropolitan area, with new ones opening on a regular basis. They offer a full range of services, from therapeutic massage and body treatments to facials and clinical aesthetics consultations. For more information, contact one of the following spas:

5 *d-4*

BEAUTY BY NATURE

Come here for facials, massages, and body treatments. *5544 Chamblee-Dunwoody Rd., Dunwoody, 770/394–3795.*

12 *g-2*

JOLIE THE DAY SPA

Facials and massages will make you feel good all over. *3619 Piedmont Rd., Buckhead, 404/266–0060.*

8 *e-1*

MONARCH DAY SPA

The staff here will pamper you with body wraps, massages, and aromatherapy. *733 Main St., Stone Mountain, 770/465–9034.*

12 *g-2*

NUBELLE

This Buckhead oasis specializes in cosmetic imaging, massage, and skincare. *One Buckhead Loop, Buckhead, 404/233–5575.*

12 *f-4*

SPA SYDEL

This popular local chain provides skin and body care at five locations. *3060 Peachtree Rd., Buckhead, 404/237–2505.*

6 *a-4*

2255 Pleasant Hill Rd., Duluth, 770/622–5580.

5 *c-5*

1165 Perimeter Center West, Dunwoody, 770/551–8999.

5 *b-6*

5064 Roswell Rd., Sandy Springs, 404/255–7727.

4 *h-7*

1259 Cumberland Mall, Smyrna, 770/801–0804.

chapter 4

PLACES TO EXPLORE

galleries, gargoyles, museums & more

Y ou could say Atlanta is like those jars of jalapeño jelly they sell at country fairs on the outskirts of town: topped with homey gingham-covered caps, jars of the stuff stand innocently next to other curiously labeled condiments. The cashier will assure you that the jelly is sweet, "but watch it, honey," she cautions, "because it's got a bite." And without a doubt, Atlanta is sweetly southern with a contemporary bite, and not an unpleasant bite at that.

In 1993 you couldn't get a decent latte in this town. Now, that seems like a century ago. Thanks in part to the 1996 Summer Olympic Games, which put the city at the top of the international menu, Atlanta has become a global business center. In recent years the city and its metro area have swelled like a spiked picnic watermelon as corporate recruits from other parts of the world have poured into its tree-lined neighborhoods. But if it's business opportunity that draws newcomers to Atlanta, then it's southern heritage that gives them a genuine taste for the place. After all, any city worth its salt must preserve its own character even as new, and sometimes exotic, ingredients are added to the mix, and Atlanta's southern flavor remains strong.

This blending of the traditional and the cutting-edge also keeps Atlanta fresh for natives and long-time residents. Historic in-town neighborhoods have been revitalized into thriving cultural hot spots rife with eclectic art galleries, sizzling nightclubs, innovative restaurants, and fashionable boutiques. Alongside epicurean coffeehouses on every corner (where you can get that latte) stand old haunts and neighborhood institutions that anchor the rush of the present in the grace of the past. Cheek-by-jowl with young businesses, Atlanta landmarks have been dusted off to glow in their own right and to lend their patina to their newly pretty environs. As in any world-class city, the shiny new coexists with the quirky old, so that locals can

still feel at home even as they are energized by the excitement of their ever-evolving city. Newcomer or native, you'll find plenty to explore in Atlanta.

where to go

ARCHITECTURE

14 b-8
ABBEY MAUSOLEUM
(Harvey, Hellington and Day, 1943) This architectural oddity is little known because of its location inside antiquated Westview Cemetery (see Graveyards & Cemeteries, below), but don't let that keep you away. Built when legendary Coca-Cola entrepreneur Asa Candler died, the mausoleum holds a jaw-dropping 12,000 entombments, which were needed to alleviate overcrowding at Oakland Cemetery (see Graveyards & Cemeteries, below) in the center of town.The massive structure, final resting place not only of Candler but of writer Joel Chandler Harris and former Atlanta mayor William B. Hartsfield, is built of coarsely cut granite, in the severe style of a medieval monastery—except that the eastern colonnade has a Spanish Revival motif. Westview Cemetery, 1680 Ralph David Abernathy Blvd., West End, 404/755–6611. MARTA: West Lake.

15 e-3
ACADEMY OF MEDICINE
(Philip Trammel Shutze, 1940) This neoclassic meeting place, library, and training center for Atlanta physicians is the work of one of the city's premier architects, who for generations was a local leader in the field. Unfluted Doric columns support the central temple-style facade, and a low, squared tower with large lunette windows distinguishes this Atlanta landmark. Today, the lower level houses offices and the reception rooms and auditorium are used for weddings and special events. 875 W. Peachtree St., Midtown, 404/874–3219. MARTA: Midtown.

14 g-4
AGNES SCOTT HALL
(Bruce and Morgan, 1891) The premiere structure on the grounds of venerable

Agnes Scott College (*see* Historic Structures & Streets, *below*), this steepled landmark is a wonder of Romanesque Revival architecture. Sheathed in ornate brick below a severely angled roof line, the castle-like edifice will take your breath away with its elaborate Victorian accents. Today the building houses dormitories and administrative offices. *Agnes Scott College, 141 E. College Ave., Decatur, 404/638–6000.*

15 *c-6*

ALONZO F. HERNDON HOME

(William Campbell, builder, 1910; restoration Norman D. Atkins, 1982) Alonzo F. Herndon, Atlanta's most successful turn-of-the-20th-century African-American businessman, founded the Atlanta Life Insurance Company, which is still one of the largest black-owned businesses in the nation. His personal residence remains testimony to his success, with 15 rooms, gargantuan yet dignified exterior columns and porches, and elegant balustrades. Today the edifice serves as a museum honoring the Herndon legacy. *587 University Pl., West End, 404/581–9813. MARTA: Vine City.*

15 *e-6*

ATLANTA CITY HALL

(G. Lloyd Preacher, 1930) This dramatic Gothic structure rises 14 stories above the former site of the home that served as General William T. Sherman's headquarters after the conquest of Atlanta. Designed by an Atlantan, the neo-Gothic structure is filled with materials mined, harvested, or manufactured in Georgia. In the stunning main lobby, for instance, are abundant polished marble and a ceiling of gilded wood. A phoenix motif, symbol of Atlanta's rebirth after the Civil War, dominates the architecture of the second story. An addition was completed in 1988 and a complete renovation undertaken in 1989. *68 Mitchell St., Downtown, 404/330–6717. MARTA: Five Points.*

15 *e-5*

ATLANTA–FULTON COUNTY PUBLIC LIBRARY

(Marcel Breuer, Hamilton Smith Associated Architects, with Stevens & Wilkinson, 1969–80) Famed international architect Breuer teamed with Smith of New York and Stevens and Wilkinson of Atlanta to design this structure, which recalls Breuer's Whitney Museum in New York City. The building was commissioned in 1969 and completed in 1980, replacing the stunning Beaux-Arts Carnegie Library (1902). *1 Margaret Mitchell Sq., Downtown, 404/730–1700. MARTA: Peachtree Center.*

15 *d-5*

ATLANTA MARKET CENTER

(Edwards and Portman, 1961; addition by John Portman and Associates, 1986) This wholesale service complex started out as a single building called the Atlanta Merchandise Mart, which was designed by John Portman, one of Atlanta's most noted 20th-century architects. Today, with more than 2 million square ft of showroom floor, the complex is more than triple its original size, encompassing the Atlanta Merchandise Mart, the Atlanta Apparel Mart, the computer and information products Inforum (the only unit open to the public), and the Atlanta Gift Mart on Spring Street, which is perched atop one of Portman's 1960s-era parking garages. The nondescript concrete exterior of the complex belies a stunning interior atrium brightened by skylights and surrounded by cascading balconies. *230, 240 and 250 Peachtree St., and 230 Spring St., Downtown, 404/220–3100. MARTA: Peachtree Center.*

15 *e-4*

BANK OF AMERICA PLAZA

(Kevin Roche, Don Dinkeloo and Associates, 1992) An outstanding feature of Atlanta's modern profile, the Bank of America Plaza (formerly NationsBank Plaza) cuts a majestic outline against the sky. Its stone cladding and striking pyramidal roof with metal spire emulate the architectural accents crowning the Empire State Building in New York City. Also of note are the structure's beveled corners, which soften the edges of the building's horizontal thrust and create eight corner offices on each floor. The building is turned 45 degrees on its lot, so that it faces the surrounding streets at an angle; the result is better views from within and a more dramatic statement from without. *600 Peachtree St., Midtown. MARTA: North Ave.*

15 *e-6*

BANK SOUTH BUILDING

(Wyatt C. Hedrick with Wilner and Milkey, Architects, 1958) The tallest structure in Atlanta when it was built, this office tower presents a plain, unornamented facade of perfectly symmetrical windows. Its simplicity stands in direct contrast to the flashiness of it 1970s-era neighbors. *55 Marietta St. MARTA: Five Points.*

5 *c-2*

BARRINGTON HALL

(Willis Ball, 1842) One of the surviving antebellum gems built by Willis Ball, this temple-shape residence was commissioned by Roswell's manufacturing mogul of old, Barrington King. The pine, poplar, and brick used to construct the home came from King's own mills. *60 Marietta St., Roswell, 770/992–1665.*

15 *f-6*

BIG BETHEL
A.M.E. CHURCH

(Architect unknown, 1891) Atlanta architecture enthusiasts have long bemoaned this church's loss of most of its exquisite Romanesque Revival detailing after a 1923 fire. The loss is especially tragic because it wasn't so much the fault of the flames as it was of the inattentive reconstruction. The church is now known for the illuminated "Jesus Saves" sign on its metal steeple, a favorite downtown landmark easily seen from the ever-busy I–75/I–85 downtown connector. Big Bethel is also of historic interest, because it served as Atlanta's first school for African-American children *(see also Churches & Synagogues, below). 250 Auburn Ave., Sweet Auburn, 404/659–0248. MARTA: Five Points.*

15 *e-3*

BILTMORE HOTEL

(Shultze and Weaver, architects, Leonard Shultze, designer, 1924) In the early 1920s, when the city of Atlanta supported a booming hospitality industry, this hotel was built to accommodate guests with sophisticated tastes. Shultze was the natural choice to design the hotel, since he also designed the venerable Los Angeles Biltmore in California. The Atlanta Biltmore, along with its separate luxury apartment tower, the Biltmore Inn, enclosed an elaborate garden terrace until subsequent additions obliterated the garden. Set in pedimented arches and bookended by paired pilasters, the windows lining the top floor are of particular note, as are the broken-scroll pediments around the other windows and the massive porticoes with Corinthian columns at the main and back entrances. Though the interior was refurbished in the 1960s, urban blight in the neighborhood forced the hotel to close its doors in the early 1980s. In the 1990s, the buildings have been completely renovated to house both commercial and loft residential space. *817 W. Peachtree St., Midtown. MARTA: Midtown.*

5 *c-2*

BULLOCH HALL

(Willis Ball, circa 1840) Uncomplicated yet courtly, Bulloch Hall is a stellar example of antebellum architecture. Built as the home of Major James Stephens Bulloch—Theodore Roosevelt's grandfather—the columned home sits in stately elegance at the end of a wooded cul-de-sac. The building was bought by the city in the 1970s and now serves as a museum *(see History Museums, below). 180 Bulloch Ave., Roswell, 770/992–1665.*

14 *b-3*

CALLANWOLDE
FINE ARTS CENTER

(Henry Hornbostel, 1917–21) This beautiful mansion, built for the son of Coca-Cola mogul Asa Candler, might informally be called "neo-Tudor," but other than that it defies architectural categorization. The house's timberings, accented with a herringbone pattern, are too large for authentic Tudor architecture, and its unevenly stratified elevations also balk tradition. The result, though, is a gorgeous 27,000-square-ft masterpiece with an interior as rich in refreshingly innovative details as its exterior. Today, Callanwolde houses the Fine Arts Center for the DeKalb County Recreation, Parks, and Cultural Affairs Department. *See also Art Museums, below. 980 Briarcliff Rd., Druid Hills, 404/872–5338.*

15 *e-5*

CANDLER BUILDING

(Murphy and Stewart, 1906) One of the most visually interesting structures in downtown Atlanta, this 17-story, triangular neo-Renaissance wonder is named for Coca-Cola tycoon Asa Griggs Candler, who had it built as a testament to his success. State-of-the-art in its day, the building was the tallest and most lavish office building in the city. The exterior, clad in white North Georgia marble, abounds with decorative flourishes, elaborate cornices, and lion-shape brackets in the style of sculptor B.

F. Miles. Medallions in the exterior entrance bays depict the faces of famous men (*see* Statues, Murals & Monuments, *below*). Within, a monumental staircase is adorned with bronze birds and a snarling, winged griffin perched at the end of the marble banister. The frieze adorning the staircase portrays local politicians and other Atlantans of note, including Candler's parents, Samuel and Martha. The edifice still serves as an office building. *127 Peachtree St., Downtown. MARTA: Peachtree Center.*

15 *e-5*

CARNEGIE BUILDING, DOWNTOWN

(G. Lloyd Preacher, 1926) The architect who designed Atlanta's City Hall (*above*) designed this triangular office structure next door to the Winecoff Hotel (*see* Historic Structures & Streets, *below*). Its facade, made of stone on the first floor and brick on the upper floors, is crowned by an ornate stone cornice. The entrance, located at one tip of the triangle, is bookended by rounded porticos. *176 Peachtree St., Downtown, MARTA: Peachtree Center.*

15 *d-3*

CARNEGIE BUILDING, GEORGIA TECH

(Architect unknown, 1907) Situated in the center of the campus' historic district, the Carnegie Building stands next to Georgia Tech's Administration Building. Rather small when compared with its neighbor, the office building has a Beaux Arts–influenced portico. *223 Uncle Heinie Way, Georgia Tech, 404/894–5400. MARTA: North Ave.*

15 *e-2*

THE CASTLE

(Ferdinand McMillan, 1910; renovation and addition, Surber and Barber, 1990) An anomaly among its looming, ultra-modern neighbors in the heart of the Midtown business district, this curiosity is the creation of builder Ferdinand McMillan, who designed it as his own home. McMillan's eccentric take on architecture comes across in the house's montage of mismatched features, including a turret of seeming Chinese influence. Planted atop a foundation of Stone Mountain granite, the Castle was a dilapidated eyesore for decades, until it was saved from demolition by forward-thinking preservation-

ists. *87 15th St., Midtown. MARTA: Arts Center.*

14 *g-4*

CHARLES A. DANA FINE ARTS CENTER

(Edwards and Portman, 1965; renovation Bailey and Associates, 1989) This fine arts complex provides an invigoratingly modern contrast to the Collegiate Gothic structures that define the campus of Agnes Scott College. Only one story tall, it features criss-crossing dormers that provide ample northern sunlight to the arts center's offices. *Agnes Scott College, 141 E. College Ave., Decatur, 404/638–6000.*

15 *f-2*

COLONY SQUARE

(Jova/Daniel/Busby, 1969, 1975) This giant office, retail, and hotel complex was the first multiuse development built in the South. Smack in the center of Atlanta's bustling Midtown business district, it originally had an ice-skating rink at its core, but retail shops and a food court (*see* Chapter 2) replaced the rink in 1978. In addition to the shopping center, the complex includes a 500-room Sheraton (*see* Chapter 6) and two office towers in which many of the floors have no central corridor, so that offices on these floors have views of both the eastern and western panoramas. *1175 and 1201 Peachtree St., Midtown, 404/ 881–6392. MARTA: Arts Center.*

16 *d 6*

COUNSEL HOUSE

(Architect unknown, 1898; addition and renovation, A. Ten Eyck Brown, 1924; restoration, John Steinichen, 1983) Here is the most outstanding example of turn-of-the-20th-century architecture in the West End's historic Terminus District. The brick facade presents a beautiful row of arched windows, terra-cotta accents, and an ornamental cornice. Originally built as a feed-and-grain store, the structure has since housed myriad businesses over the years. *142 Mitchell St., Downtown. MARTA: Garnett St.*

15 *e-4*

FIRE STATION NO. 11

(Morgan and Dillon, 1907) The best-preserved turn-of-the-20th-century fire station in the city, this appealing neighborhood highlight stands just around the corner from the landmark

Fox Theatre (*below*). Still in service as a fire station, the quaint structure sports an exterior of glazed white brick, with two large, arched, and molded entries to the fire-truck bays. *30 North Ave., Midtown. MARTA: North Ave.*

15 *e-6*

FIRST NATIONAL BANK TOWER

(FABRAP with Emory Roth and Sons, architects, Cecil A. Alexander, designer, 1966) The tallest structure in the Southeast at the time of its creation, this tower (currently known as the Wachovia Bank of Georgia Building) is a typical 1960s, International Style skyscraper. Marble columns run the entire height of the 41-story building's facade, in marked contrast to the bronzed aluminum spandrels. *2 Peachtree St., Downtown. MARTA: Five Points.*

15 *e-3*

FIRST UNION PLAZA

(Heery Architects and Engineers, 1987) Though undeniably modern in construction, this tower evokes Art Deco glamour with its recessed silhouette and glittering marble facade. Its most interesting feature is the canopied entrance to the New Visions Gallery on the ground floor, which is considered a beautiful example of deconstructionist design. The 28-story office tower was built as the anchor of the ambitious Peachtree Place development. *999 Peachtree St., Midtown. MARTA: Midtown.*

15 *e-6*

FLATIRON BUILDING

(Bradford Gilbert, 1897; renovation Brisbon, Brook and Benyon, 1977–1987) Eleven stories tall, this is the oldest extant skyscraper in Atlanta—and it predates the famous Flatiron Building (1901) in New York City. Situated on the sliver of a corner formed by Broad and Peachtree streets, the eccentric three-sided structure has a triangular footprint, and a very narrow footprint at that. Nonetheless, it has all the architectural accoutrements of an elegant turn-of-the-20th-century structure, such as bay windows and a colonnaded base. Its designer, New York–based Bradford Gilbert, built that city's Tower Building, America's first skyscraper. Originally called the English-American Building, the Flatiron still functions as an office building and often flies the flag of

Canada, its current owner's homeland. *84 Peachtree St., Downtown. MARTA: Peachtree Center.*

15 *e-4*

FOX THEATRE

(Marye, Alger and Vinour, 1929) Otherworldly and onion-domed, this ornate edifice is one of the most recognized landmarks in Atlanta. Planned as the headquarters for the local Arabic Order of the Nobles of the Mystic Shrine (a.k.a. the Shriners), the building was purchased by movie-house mogul William Fox when the order ran out of construction money. The Fox became a grand movie palace worthy of Hollywood's golden age and has since evolved into a venue for everything from classical recitals to traveling Broadway productions (*see also* Historic Structures & Streets, *below*, and Chapter 5). *660 Peachtree St., Midtown, 404/881–2100. MARTA: North Ave.*

15 *g-6*

FULTON BAG AND COTTON MILL

(Architect unknown, circa 1881; renovation Aderhold Properties, begun 1996, ongoing) A majestic example of exquisite turn-of-the-20th-century industrial architecture, this factory was a dilapidated architectural albatross until it was rescued by a private developer. Restored into a hive of fashionable residential lofts, it is now a major feature of historic, happening Cabbage Town (*see* Historic Structures & Streets, *below*). Especially appealing are the brick arcaded window bays, crowned by terracotta accents, that overlook Boulevard. *170 Boulevard, Cabbagetown, 404/526–9800. MARTA: King Memorial.*

15 *e-6*

FULTON COUNTY GOVERNMENT CENTER

(Rosser Fabrap International with Turner Associates, 1989) Filling an entire downtown city block, this complex encompasses the Fulton County Courthouse, a nine-story edifice built by A. Ten Eyck Brown, with Morgan and Dillon, Architects, in 1914. The postmodern design of the newer structure surrounds an atrium with several 3- to 10-story buildings. As at the City Hall annex (located in a former Ford automobile factory in Poncey Highlands), the halls here are filled with fine art by contemporary artists. Free tours are conducted, but the schedule varies depending on staff availability. *141 Pryor St., Downtown, 404/730–8304. MARTA: Five Points.*

FULTON COUNTY JUDICIAL CENTER

`15` *e-6*

(Rosser Fabrap International, 1993) This dramatic contemporary building houses superior court and state court judges' offices and courtrooms, as well as a law library and the Fulton County sheriff's offices. Contemporary art in the building includes the figurative sculpture *Sardana, Dance of Peace* (1996) by Catalan artist Manuel Alvarez, which was a gift from the city of Barcelona, Spain. Tours of the center may be included with tours of the Fulton County Government Center. *185 Central Ave., Downtown, 404/730–4000. MARTA: Garnett St.*

`12` *d-3*

GEORGIA GOVERNOR'S MANSION

(A. Thomas Bradbury and Associates, 1968) In appearance, the Georgia governor's home has more in common with a plantation house along the Mississippi River delta than with a Georgia-style antebellum mansion. The plain, rectangular residence is sheathed in red brick and has a front porch with a two-story portico of white Doric columns. *391 West Paces Ferry Rd., Buckhead, 404/261–1776.*

`15` *e-5*

GEORGIA-PACIFIC CENTER

(Skidmore, Owings and Merrill, 1982) Opposite Margaret Mitchell Park, this grand 52-story granite skyscraper has a stepped silhouette that is a landmark on the city's skyline. It stands on the site of the Loew's Grand Theater, where *Gone With the Wind* premiered. The theater was demolished after a devastating fire, making way for the forestry company headquarters. *133 Peachtree St., Downtown. MARTA: Peachtree Center.*

`15` *e-5*

GEORGIA RAILWAY AND POWER BUILDING

(Morgan and Dillon, 1907; restoration Stang and Newdow, 1988) Flanked by the modern, flat-fronted Forty-One Marietta and Bank South (*above*) buildings, this brick-and-stone structure stands in stark architectural contrast to its neighbors. Also known as Walton Place, it is a prime example of early 20th-century

architecture. *75 Marietta St., Downtown. MARTA: Five Points.*

`15` *e-7*

GEORGIA STATE CAPITOL

(Erdbrooke and Bernham, 1889) Perhaps the most recognizable element of the state capitol is its bright, golden dome, visible from quite a distance. Restored in 1981, the dome is gilded with gold from Dahlonega, Georgia, the site of the country's first gold rush (in the 1820s). To symbolize Georgia's restored allegiance to the Union after the Civil War, the glorious neoclassical exterior was designed to emulate that of the U.S. Capitol in Washington, D.C. Corinthian columns support a classical pediment four stories above the street, and a portico with large stone piers creates a grand entranceway. The facades are of Indiana limestone, while the interior makes lavish use of Georgia marble. On the surrounding grounds, monuments and statues honor local historical figures (*see* Statues, Murals & Monuments, *below*). *Capitol Square, 206 Washington St., Downtown, 404/656–2844. MARTA: Georgia State.*

`15` *d-5*

GEORGIA WORLD CONGRESS CENTER

(Thompson, Ventulett and Stainback, 1976, 1985) Built in two phases, this convention and trade-fair facility was financed by the state. The second phase more than doubled the original square footage (for a total of 875,000 square ft) and added a dramatic entrance pavilion with a massive glass atrium and pedestrian concourse that opens directly onto International Boulevard. *285 International Blvd., Downtown. MARTA: Omni/Dome/GWCC.*

`15` *e-4*

GEORGIAN TERRACE

(William L. Stoddart, 1911; restoration and addition Smallwood, Reynolds, Stewart, Stewart and Associates, 1991) Touted as the South's answer to Parisian hotels, this was, when it opened, the most lavish hotel in Atlanta. The hotel welcomed Hollywood celebrities during the 1939 world premiere of *Gone With the Wind,* earning it a place in local legend. Almost unbelievably, the palatial building fell into disrepair and was closed in 1981. Frank Howington, a local developer with an eye for elegance, salvaged it in the early 1990s and converted it first to luxury apartments and then back into a hotel. With its cavernous, polished marble lobby and the sweeping, columned terraces for which it is known, the hotel is today one of the most courtly structures in the South (*see also* Chapter 6). *659 Peachtree St., Midtown, 404/897–1991, MARTA: North Ave.*

15 e-2

GLG GRAND

(Rabun Hatch and Associates, 1992) A striking skyscraper 50 stories high, the GLG Grand—with its tripartite construction, exterior terraces, and precast red granite panels accented in bronze—is one of the reasons Midtown Atlanta is known for outstanding development. The building's cascading horizontal silhouette is reminiscent of New York's Chrysler and Empire State buildings. The multiuse facility accommodates a hotel and commercial offices, as well as top-floor luxury apartments. *75 14th St., Midtown, 404/870–4900. MARTA: Arts Center.*

15 e-6

GRANT-PRUDENTIAL BUILDING

(Bruce and Morgan, 1911; restoration and renovation Robert and Company, 1980) Fashioned from limestone and terra cotta, this office building's exterior is considered one of the city's finest examples of neo-Renaissance design. *44 Broad St., Downtown. MARTA: Five Points.*

15 e-6

HEALY BUILDING

(Bruce and Morgan with Walter T. Downing, 1913; renovation Stang and Newdow, 1987) An inarguably beautiful office tower, this building is notable for its Gothic–style facade with terra-cotta ornamentation. Its design typifies the height of early 20th-century architectural fashion, but it departs from the norm in the unique form of its street-level display windows, which project slightly from the facade. Another wonder is the elevator lobby facing Forsyth Street; the expansive rotunda with detailed and ornate molding is awash in sunlight from the many windows above. *47 Forsyth St., Downtown. MARTA: Five Points.*

15 e-2

HIGH MUSEUM OF ART

(Richard Meier, 1983) No survey of Atlanta architecture is complete if it doesn't include the highly acclaimed, award-winning High Museum. The contemporary-style feather in the city's cap sits with a kingly air on Peachtree Street, just north of the heart of the busy Midtown business district. Entirely clad with white panels of enameled steel, this impressively modern building is as much a work of art as the massive collection it encloses. When it was built, it was heralded by the *New York Times* as one of the best American architectural endeavors in a generation, and the American Institute of Architects placed it among the top 10 best-designed American buildings of the 1980s (*see also* Art Museums, *below*). *1280 Peachtree Rd., Midtown, 404/733–4437. MARTA: Arts Center.*

15 e-6

THE HURT BUILDING

(J.E.R. Carpenter, 1913, 1923) Designed to fit on a triangular lot, this building is named for Joel Hurt, the developer behind the Inman Park and Druid Hills neighborhoods (*see* Historic Structures & Streets, *below*). Hurt conceived the original design but brought in J.E.R. Carpenter from New York to finish the project. The stone foundation is supported by pilasters and Corinthian columns, and its front facade is recessed 30 ft to allow for more window space and a better view of the city. Renovated extensively in 1985, the building now houses offices. *50 Hurt Plaza, Downtown. MARTA: Five Points.*

15 e-5

HYATT REGENCY ATLANTA

(Edwards and Portman, 1967; additions John Portman and Associates, 1971, 1982) This blue-topped hotel tower is notable for two firsts: it was the first major hotel built in downtown Atlanta since the 1920s, and it was the prototype for the atrium hotels that the Hyatt chain has since built worldwide. The unassuming entrance gives no indication of the awesome atrium inside, and the dome, which houses a revolving lounge, no longer provides a panoramic view of the city's skyline (taller structures now surround the building). Extensive renovations and additions were completed in 1971 and 1982; a skywalk connects the hotel to Portman's adjacent Peachtree Center Mall (*below*). *265 Peachtree St., Downtown, 404/577–1234. MARTA: Peachtree Center.*

12 *d-3*

JAMES DICKEY HOUSE

(Hentz, Reid and Adler, 1917) One of the first homes that helped make West Paces Ferry Road one of the most opulent thoroughfares in Buckhead, this is an anchor of one of wealthiest neighborhoods in Georgia. The wood-framed plantation-style house is the most massive home designed by Neel Reid; its towering front porch is braced by narrow Tuscan columns that evoke the portico at Mount Vernon, George Washington's Virginia home. It is still a private residence. *456 W. Paces Ferry Rd., Buckhead.*

7 *h-3*

LAKEWOOD FAIRGROUNDS EXHIBITION HALLS

(Edwards and Sayward, 1916) The two main halls in this quadrangle are exquisite examples of Spanish Colonial Revival architecture. Their tile roofs, terra-cotta accents, and mission-style stucco facades recall the buildings of the 1915 Panama-California exhibition in San Diego. *2000 Lakewood Ave., Southwest Atlanta, 404/622–4488.*

15 *e-5*

MACY'S

(Hentz, Adler and Shutze, 1927) This treasured-in-downtown-Atlanta monument takes shoppers back to the days before the malls took over. Ensconced in two-story-high arched moldings, the display windows and store entrances woo customers with a grace rarely found in contemporary department stores. The coarse brick exterior, simple and unadorned except for a heavy cornice, was most likely inspired by the architecture of Italian palazzos (*see also* Chapter 2). *180 Peachtree St., Downtown, 404/221–7221. MARTA: Peachtree Center.*

15 *e-5*

MARRIOTT MARQUIS

(John Portman and Associates, 1985) The biggest convention hotel in the Southeast (1,731 rooms), this tower has a soaring, sunlit atrium that reaches the amazing height of 48 stories. The balconies that overlook the atrium spiral down from the top floor in a cascade that lends the space an almost biomorphic feel. *See also* Chapter 6. *265 Peachtree Center Ave., Downtown, 404/521–0000. MARTA: Peachtree Center.*

14 *g-3*

MARTA DECATUR STATION

(Edwards and Kelsey with Stevens and Wilkinson, Joint Venture Architects, 1978) Like all of MARTA's other rapid rail stations, this one is designed to make a distinctive architectural statement. The entrance to the underground station is encased in a sculptural brick-and-steel structure in the shape of a beamed pyramid. The station's postmodernist presence is a refreshing counterpoint to Decatur's historic courthouse square, which lies just north of the pyramid. *Church St. and Sycamore St., Decatur. MARTA: Decatur.*

15 *e-6*

MARTA FIVE POINTS STATION

(Finch-Heery, Joint Venture, 1979) At the nexus of MARTA's north and south lines, this station pays homage to the building that was demolished to make way for it. Neoclassic arches from the Eiseman Building (Walter T. Downing, 1901), which once stood here, are incorporated into the modern design. *30 Alabama St., Downtown. MARTA: Five Points.*

15 *f-2*

THE MAYFAIR

(Smallwood, Reynolds, Stewart, Stewart and Associates, 1990) Near Midtown's Piedmont Park, this towering residential edifice contains apartments for well-heeled tenants. The eclectic building is crowned with four distinctive turrets and is studded with curious faux balconies. *199 14th St., Midtown, 404/607–9822. MARTA: Arts Center.*

14 *d-1*

MICHAEL C. CARLOS MUSEUM

(Michael Graves, 1993) This museum's architecture is notable not only as pure design but as an excellent example of form that follows function. To house the museum's collection of thousands of ancient artifacts from Greece, Africa, Rome, and Egypt, Graves conceived a space with interior accents themed along classical and pre-classical lines. Located in the middle of the Emory University campus, the 45,000-square-ft is an impressive temple-like edifice of white and rose marble. *See also* Art Museums, *below. 571 S. Kilgo St., Emory University, 404/727–4282.*

15 *e-2 through g-3*

MIDTOWN
RESIDENTIAL DISTRICT

To see Midtown today, it's hard to believe that this well-to-do neighborhood was the epicenter of Atlanta's counterculture three decades ago. But the area originated as an affluent one, its development spearheaded by Richard Peters, a streetcar builder who in 1849 bought a big chunk (405 acres) of choice land and laid out a streetcar network. Prosperous folk moved into the area and built the magnificent Victorian and Craftsman-style homes that now crowd the residential streets. After World War II, however, the rise of the suburbs emptied Midtown of its wealthier denizens. Urban blight set in and the neighborhood's homes fell into disrepair. As a low-rent district, Midtown attracted students, artists, hippies, and hangers-on in the 1960s, and anti-establishment protests often flared in Piedmont Park. But by the mid-1970s, forward-thinking home buyers became interested in this architecturally rich neighborhood close to the city's center. Before long, a new wave of homeowners and entrepreneurs revitalized Midtown, and now street after street is lined with exquisitely renovated turn-of-the-century homes and bustling restaurants and taverns. *North Ave. to 14th St. between Peachtree St. and Monroe Blvd. MARTA: North Ave. and Midtown.*

5 *c-2*

MIMOSA HALL

(Willis Ball, circa 1940) Damaged by a fire soon after its construction, this residence lost its original wood exterior, which was replaced by striated stucco that gives the impression of bricks. Built by Civil War legend Major John Dunwoody, it later became the home of famed Atlanta architect Neel Reid. *127 Bulloch Ave., Roswell, 770/992–1665.*

15 *e-6*

MUSE'S BUILDING

(Philip Trammel Shutze, Hentz, Reid and Adler, 1921) Standing on the former site of a Confederate arsenal, this Italianate building with a limestone base is finished in plain beige brick and topped by a carved frieze. Once occupied by an upscale men's clothing store, it was left vacant in 1992 when the store closed. Today, it has been converted into an apartment building and contains the official residence of the president of Georgia State University. *52 Peachtree St., Downtown, 404/523–7344. MARTA: Five Points.*

15 *f-6*

ODD FELLOWS BUILDING

(William A. Edwards, 1912 and auditorium addition, 1914; tower restoration Stang and Newdow, Architects, 1988; auditorium restoration Perkins and Partners, Architects, 1991) As the headquarters of the Grand United Order of Oddfellows, this was the early-20th-century scene of vital business and social activity in Atlanta's black community. The six-story building, with a turreted roofline and a pleasing facade of weathered brick accented by stone detailing, still retains its turn-of-the-century flavor. Busts of African-Americans adorn the exterior of this Sweet Auburn landmark. *250 Auburn Ave., Sweet Auburn. MARTA: King Memorial.*

15 *e-2*

ONE ATLANTIC CENTER

(John Burgee and Philip Johnson, 1987) This office tower punctuates the Midtown skyline with its unusual roof, on which a foundation of pink granite supports a pyramid of copper. Also known as the IBM Tower (because of its most prominent occupant), it exemplifies revivalist architecture in its evocation of early 20th-century Manhattan skyscrapers. *1201 W. Peachtree St., Midtown, 404/870–2929. MARTA: Arts Center.*

15 *e-4*

ONE GEORGIA CENTER

(Lamberson, Plunkett, Shirley and Woodall, 1968) A monolithic edifice, this 24-story office building is sheathed in an exterior of white marble. As the first major business structure built north of Downtown, it was the cornerstone of commercial expansion into Midtown. *600 W. Peachtree St., Midtown. MARTA: Midtown.*

15 *e-5*

ONE-NINETY-ONE
PEACHTREE TOWER

(John Burgee and Philip Johnson, 1990) Topped with two columned turrets, this modern take on the turn-of-the-20th-century skyscraper slightly resembles New York City's rose-granite, pediment-topped Sony Building (formerly the AT&T Building), which Johnson designed in 1984. The building's granite facade features a recessed central section that runs all the way to the top floor, visually bisecting the structure and creating the effect of two 50-story towers in one. A six-story atrium rises above retail space on the ground floor. *191 Peachtree St., Downtown. MARTA: Peachtree Center.*

`15` *e-5*

ONE PEACHTREE CENTER

(John Portman and Associates, 1992) Designed to be a landmark on the Atlanta skyline, this 60-story office tower lives up to its expectations. Sheathed in varying shades of gray granite, the structure presents a facade whose vertical divisions give it a distinctive beveled appearance. Crowning the tower is a cluster of reflective glass in the shape of a stylized pyramid, making it one of the most identifiable buildings in the city. *303 Peachtree St., Downtown. MARTA: Peachtree Center.*

`15` *e-5*

PEACHTREE CENTER MALL

(John Portman and Associates, 1973; addition 1979; renovation 1986) This retail complex unites four office towers, among them Portman's One Peachtree Center (*above*) via an inviting underground labyrinth of shops and courtyards. The mall (*see* Chapter 2) houses a collection of specialty shops, restaurants, and a food court, which since an extensive 1986 renovation have been virtually invisible from the street level. A system of pedestrian walkways, reminiscent of that in New York City's Rockefeller Center, connect the mall to the surrounding buildings. *231 Peachtree St., Downtown, 404/524-3787. MARTA: Peachtree Center.*

`12` *e-4*

PHILIP MCDUFFIE HOUSE

(Hentz, Reid and Adler, 1922) Developer of the exclusive Garden Hills district in Buckhead, Philip McDuffie built his home on an elevated plot of land overlooking Cherokee Road. Behind a stately facade of stone and red brick is a huge residence that attests to McDuffie's notable taste. Extremely detailed stone accents highlight the red brick exterior, along with four Ionic pilasters that buttress the house's main entrance (which encases a massive stairway). The house is still a private residence. *7 Cherokee Rd., Buckhead.*

`12` *h-2*

PHIPPS PLAZA

(FABRAP, 1969; renovation and addition Thompson, Ventulett, Stainback and Associates, 1992) Once a dowdy throwback overshadowed by the popular Lenox Square mall across the street, Phipps Plaza has, since a miraculous face-lift, become what is arguably the most glamorous shopping center in Atlanta (*see* Chapter 2). *3500 Peachtree Rd., Buckhead, 404/261-7910. MARTA: Lenox or Buckhead.*

`15` *e-4*

PONCE DE LEON APARTMENTS

(William L. Stoddart, 1913) This unusual 11-story structure, fondly known as the Ponce, was the first Atlanta apartment building designed specifically for the wealthy. It is distinguished by a curving facade, an elegant entrance flanked by columns, and an elaborate balustrade atop the cornice. Today the units are privately owned condominiums. *75 Ponce de Leon Ave., Midtown, 404/873-1903. MARTA: North Ave.*

`15` *e-2*

PROMENADE ONE

(Thompson, Ventulett, Stainback and Associates, 1981) This eye-pleasing midrise office complex is constructed of stone slabs. It consists of two sections that are offset from each other to maximize the flow of natural light through the windows. *1200 Peachtree St., Buckhead. MARTA: Arts Center.*

`15` *e-2*

PROMENADE TWO

(Thompson, Ventulett, Stainback and Associates, 1990) A favorite silhouette along Atlanta's skyline, the gorgeous, Art Deco–influenced tower is clad in rose-colored glass all the way from its Adoni granite base to its amazing, cascading-pyramid roof, which is crowned with a stately steel spire. *1230 Peachtree St., 404/607-6700. MARTA: Arts Center.*

`15` *e-1*

REID HOUSE

(Hentz, Adler and Shutze, 1924; remodeling Eugene E. Lowry, 1975) A commanding building constructed in the neo-Georgian style, this edifice presently houses a collection of condominiums and apartments. A characteristic of special note is the Roman-influenced pediment with a medallion-and-bull's-head design. *1325 and 1327 Peachtree St., Midtown, 404/892–7416. MARTA: Arts Center.*

15 *e-1*

RHODES MEMORIAL HALL

(Willis F. Denny, 1904) This odd structure grabs your attention by revealing a new detail every time you drive by on Peachtree Street. Custom-built early in the century as a dream home for the deep-pocketed Amos Giles Rhodes, a prosperous Atlanta furniture dealer, it is made entirely of rough-cut granite quarried at nearby Stone Mountain. Rumor has it that the mansion was modeled after a German castle, and indeed, it sports a tower and a turreted roof. Inside, its magnificent mahogany staircase is lined with exquisite stained-glass windows representing scenes from the Civil War. Today Rhodes Hall houses the Georgia Trust for Historic Preservation (*see* History Museums, *below*). *1516 Peachtree St., Midtown, 404/881–9980. MARTA: Arts Center.*

15 *e-6*

RHODES-HAVERTY BUILDING

(Pringle and Smith, 1929) The tallest structure in Atlanta until the Bank South Building (*above*) dwarfed it in the early 1950s, this office building still calls for admiration. It is a fine example of Art Deco–influenced architecture, with Romanesque and Byzantine touches along the roofline. The interior lobby is worth a look as well for its ornately carved ceilings and beautiful elevator doors. *134 Peachtree St., Downtown. MARTA: Five Points.*

14 *a-3*

STILLWOOD CHASE

(Taylor and Williams, 1988) Unlike most other multifamily developments that sprouted throughout the 10 counties at the end of the 20th century, this one tries to fit in with the surrounding historic neighborhood. The residential complex is laid out in quirky condominium clusters with individualizing details such as clapboard exteriors, ornate latticework, and gazebos. The result is a community within a community, accessed via streets and sidewalks lined with plentiful preserved foliage. *Briarcliff Rd. at the By Way, Druid Hills.*

12 *e-3*

SWAN HOUSE

(Hentz, Adler and Shutze, 1926) One of Atlanta's finest examples of European–style architecture, this manor set on 25 sprawling acres of landscaped grounds is reminiscent of an 18th-century English country home. Its monumental entrance, remarkable horseshoe staircase, and Doric-columned portico create a stunning mix of sophisticated design. The American Institute of Architects considers it the best work by the late, venerable Atlanta architect Philip Shutze. It is now part of the Atlanta History Center (*see* History Museums, *below*). *3101 Andrews Dr., Buckhead, 404/814–4000. MARTA: Buckhead.*

15 *e-4*

TECHWOOD HOMES

(Burge and Stevens, 1935) Born as a federally funded slum-clearance project— the first of its kind in the United States—Techwood Homes is not of much aesthetic value. It has the plain construction, large windows, and flat roof that typified early public housing, but it provided some ground-breaking modern amenities, such as electric stoves, bathtubs, and laundry rooms. The 25-acre complex is now attached to Georgia Tech University, where it houses student dormitories and rental apartments. *Techwood Dr. at North Ave., Georgia Tech. MARTA: North Ave.*

15 *e-1*

THE TEMPLE SYNAGOGUE

(Hentz, Reid and Adler, 1920) A prominent presence on Peachtree Street, this house of worship was commissioned by the Hebrew Benevolent Congregation. The block-shape building is an amalgam of Georgian-style architecture and historical Hebrew accents. Columns support a plain pediment atop the facade, and a wedding cake–like drum of white columns supports the dome of the roof (*see also* Churches & Synagogues, *below*). *1589 Peachtree St., Midtown, 404/873–1731. MARTA: Arts Center.*

12 *g-2*

TOWER PLACE

(Stevens and Wilkinson, Architects, 1975) This visually arresting 29-story building was the first large business development in Buckhead, which has since sprouted an entire mini-downtown of commercial structures. The sharply beveled shape of the exterior affords an unusually high number of corner offices, and the entire structure is sheathed from top to bottom in reflective glass. Today the tower is flanked by a shopping mall, a movie theater, and a hotel. *3340 Peachtree St., Buckhead. MARTA: Buckhead.*

15 *e-4*

THE VARSITY

(Jules Grey, 1940, 1959, 1965) Atlanta's favorite fast-food institution (*see* Chapter 1) popularized drive-in eating nationwide in the 1940s. To everyone's delight it still stands as an almost perfectly preserved example of Streamline Moderne architecture, a more cost-effective offshoot of Art Deco. The piano-shape curve of the southwest facade, the smooth enamel exterior, and the ocean liner–style porthole typify the style. *61 North Ave., Midtown, 404/881–1706. MARTA: North Ave.*

15 *e-5*

WESTIN PEACHTREE PLAZA HOTEL

(John Portman and Associates, 1976; renovation, 1986) At 70 stories, the Westin Peachtree Plaza is the tallest hotel in the United States. Above its tremendous concrete base, the sleek cylinder of a building is completely covered with reflective glass. "Glass" elevators glide up the building's exterior in transparent tubes, taking guests to a revolving cocktail lounge (*see* Chapter 5) provides one of the best cityscape vantages in town. *210 Peachtree St., Downtown, 404/659–1400. MARTA: Peachtree Center.*

15 *g-6*

WIGWAM APARTMENTS

(Vincent Daley, 1940) One of the few examples of Streamline Moderne construction in Atlanta, this structure features flat roofs, stucco facades, cube-shape balconies and wrap-around windows. Located in the historic Old Fourth Ward, the apartments strike an architectural contrast to the shotgun shacks, row houses, and factories that surround them. *587–591 Auburn Ave. and 44–50 Randolph St., Sweet Auburn. MARTA: King Memorial.*

4 *h-5*

WILDWOOD PLAZA

(I. M. Pei and Partners, 1991) Wrapped in smokey granite and reflective glass, these two 15-story office buildings are notable for their exquisite abstract design. Connecting the buildings is a stylized half-pyramid reminiscent of the pyramid Pei created to serve as the entrance to the Louvre museum in Paris. *3200 Windy Ridge Pkwy., Marietta.*

15 *e-6*

WILLIAM-OLIVER BUILDING

(Pringle and Smith, 1930) Developer Thomas G. Healey named this building for his grandsons William and Oliver. Its red granite base is topped by a limestone structure, with corner windows and Art Deco ornamentation on the upper two floors. Originally an office building, it is being converted to residential loft living. *32 Peachtree St., Downtown, 404/658–0047. MARTA: Five Points.*

15 *e-6*

THE WORLD OF COCA-COLA PAVILION

(Thompson, Ventulett, Stainback and Associates, 1990) Though it serves a bubbly purpose as a museum of Coca-Cola memorabilia (*see* History Museums, *below*), the pavilion projects one of the most striking architectural outlines to be found downtown. Its three pyramidal sections are connected with transparent walls and a covered courtyard. Open on two sides, with a ceiling supported by a single giant column, the 4-story-tall entrance pavilion is adorned with a gargantuan, neon Coca-Cola sign. *55 Martin Luther King Jr. Dr., Downtown, 404/676–5151. MARTA: Five Points.*

15 *b-8*

WREN'S NEST

(Architect unknown, circa 1885; restoration W. Lane Greene, 1992) The former family home of Uncle Remus creator Joel Chandler Harris, this majestic home began as a simple, two-room clapboard cottage. Harris added to the structure over the years, creating the cavernous Queen Anne mansion that it is today. Some unusual accents include a funnel-lattice banister and fishtail shingles on the upper exterior. The house is now a museum (*see* Historic Structures & Streets, *below*). *1050 Ralph David Abernathy Blvd., West End, 404/753–7735. MARTA: West End.*

ART EVENTS

For information on performing arts special events, *see* Performing Arts *in* Chapter 5.

february

12 *g-2*

**TRINITY SPOTLIGHT
ON SOUTHERN ARTISTS**
The revered Trinity Gallery (*see* Art Galleries, *below*) hosts this homage to southern artists every year at the ritzy Swissôtel in Buckhead. The gala culminates in a lively art auction, and it's possible to walk away with an original piece at an enviably low price. Auction admission includes a dinner buffet. *404/231–8100 tickets and reservations.*

april

14 *a-5*

INMAN PARK FESTIVAL
Quirky and thoroughly enjoyable, this is among Atlanta's oldest and favorite neighborhood festivals. Along Edgewood and Euclid avenues and the nearby streets, food, crafts, antiques, music, and a hilariously offbeat parade are among the highlights. Also of note is the accompanying Inman Park Tour of Homes, which affords an inside glimpse of the neighborhood's most spectacular Victorian mansions. *770/242–4895.*

may

14 *g-3*

DECATUR ARTS FESTIVAL
Every May, Decatur's charming courthouse square comes vibrantly alive with this family-friendly arts festival. Vendor booths offer a cornucopia of arts, crafts, and charming knick-knacks, while others offer tasty food and drink. *404/371–9583.*

june

14 *c-5*

**CANDLER PARK
& LAKE CLAIRE MUSIC
AND ARTS FESTIVAL**
This breezy, easygoing neighborhood street party along Clifton and McClendon avenues features plenty of art

booths and musical events. Delectable food is central to the fair, especially since it takes place in front of two of Atlanta's favorite breakfast haunts: the Flying Biscuit and the Gato Bizco cafés (*see* Chapter 1). Festivities commence with a 5K run and an in-line skate race. *404/589–8777.*

15 *h-2*

SUMMERFEST
You won't be able to resist the feel-good atmosphere at this cozy Virginia-Highland arts festival. Music, interesting arts, beguiling crafts, handcrafted jewelry, food, and libations abound along Virginia Avenue. *404/222–8244.*

august

5 *g-5*

FOLKFEST
FolkFest founder Steve Slotin's motto is "folk art for all folks," and that's exactly what you'll find at this annual folk-art extravaganza held at the North Atlanta Trade Center in Norcross. The selection is as plentiful and diverse as the genre itself, with more than 80 galleries and dealers showcasing the talent they represent. Past offerings have included works by such southern folk-art stars as Howard Finster, R. A. Miller, Mary Klein, Ab the Flagman, and more. Prices are pleasing to the wallet. *770/932–1000.*

september

4 *f-4*

**ART IN THE PARK,
MARIETTA**
Every year, more than a hundred artists gather in quaint and peaceful Marietta Square to sell their creations out of festive tents and vendor booths. Attractions include silver jewelry, photography, metal sculpture, pottery, inlaid wood, and more. The festival is usually held on Labor Day weekend. *770/429–0832.*

5 *h-3*

**ARTS ON THE
COURTHOUSE SQUARE**
This merry neighborhood festival features a fun mix of arts, crafts, and entertainment in front of Duluth's quaint courthouse. *770/822–5450.*

5 *c-2*

ROSWELL ARTS FESTIVAL

This long-standing annual arts festival is one of the best in metro Atlanta. Held along historic streets lined with beautiful architecture and around lovely Roswell Square, with its cozy collection of storefronts, the festival offers an astounding array of art and handcrafted goods. *770/992–0832.*

october

12 *h-2*

HABITAT FOR HUMANITY BIRDHOUSE ARTFEST

The Atlanta arts scene is all aflutter during this nonprofit art gala showcasing birdhouses built with astounding creativity by top artists nationwide. Also featured are sculptures, quilts, paintings, and folk art with bird-related themes. Held at Phipps Plaza each year, it gives nearly 2,000 artists the opportunity to donate their works. All proceeds go to Habitat for Humanity, a nonprofit organization that builds homes for low-income families. *404/223–5180.*

ART GALLERIES

14 *a-1*

ALIYA GALLERY

This gallery presents recent pieces by regional and national artists working in a variety of media. *1402 N. Highland Ave., Virginia–Highland, 404/892–2835. Open Mon. by appointment only.*

12 *g-7*

ARTIST'S ATELIER OF ATLANTA

This cooperative presents the work of more than 20 artists working in an eclectic mix of media. You can visit individual artists as they work in their studios. *800 Miami Cir., Suite 200, Buckhead, 404/231–5999. Closed Sun. MARTA: Lindbergh.*

3 *g-7*

A. R. WOOD STUDIO

This intriguing gallery on Buford's picturesque town square features an appealing collection of contemporary paintings. *9 E. Main St., Buford, 770/945–1660.*

14 *c-1*

BARBARA ARCHER GALLERY

This gallery is a colorful odyssey of paintings, sculptures, and assemblages by self-taught artists from the American South. *1123 Zonolite Rd., Druid Hills, 404/815–1545. Closed Sun.*

12 *g-3*

CONNELL GALLERY

This visually pleasing space specializes in high-end crafts in an array of mediums—from clay to glass to wood—and carries the lighthearted work of Leo Sewell, "the King of Recycling," who creates playful life-size sculptures from society's castoffs. *333 Buckhead Ave., Buckhead, 404/261–1712. Closed Sun.–Mon. MARTA: Buckhead or Lenox.*

15 *d-6*

EYEDRUM

If you're looking for cutting-edge contemporary art and installations, then head for this gallery, which showcases the raw stylizations of some of Atlanta's most exciting young artists. Art openings coupled with original, atmospheric music installations are a specialty at this gallery. *253 Trinity Ave., Downtown, no phone, www.eyedrum.org. MARTA: Five Points or Garnett St.*

12 *g-3*

FAY GOLD GALLERY

One of the most respected contemporary art galleries in the city, this spot presents an impressive collection of recent paintings, sculpture, photography, and glass. *247 Buckhead Ave., Buckhead, 404/233–3843. Closed Sun. MARTA: Buckhead or Lenox.*

12 *f-2*

GALERIE TIMOTHY TEW

This gallery offers the work of American and European painters who give traditional motifs a bit of a twist. Featured painters include nationally recognized artists such as Leslie Bell, Laura Nothern, and Chuck Bowdish. *309 E. Paces Ferry Rd., Buckhead, 404/869–0511. Closed Sun.–Mon. MARTA: Buckhead or Lenox.*

5 *c-2*

HEAVEN BLUE ROSE GALLERY

A visual delight from the moment you walk through the doors, this artist-owned and -operated collective offers art in two- and three-dimensional media. *934 Canton St., Roswell, 770/642–7380. Closed Sun.–Mon.*

12 g-3

JACKSON FINE ART GALLERY

Here you'll find an incredibly thought-provoking display of 20th-century, vintage, and contemporary photography. *3115 E. Shadowlawn Ave., Buckhead, 404/233–3739. Closed Sun. MARTA: Buckhead or Lenox.*

12 e-6

KIANG GALLERY

This popular gallery offers a varied selection of contemporary works, among them the photographic collages of Lucinda Bunnen and the glazed ceramics of Archie Stapleton. *1923 Peachtree Rd., Buckhead, 404/351–5477. Closed Sun.–Mon. MARTA: Arts Center.*

5 b-6

KNOKE GALLERIES

A stroll through this local institution is an education in itself. Within its walls is one of the most complete collections of 19th- and 20th-century American folk art and pottery to be found anywhere. *5325 Roswell Rd., Sandy Springs, 404/252–0485. Closed Sun.*

15 f-2

LIVING ROOM GALLERY

From her Victorian-era home in Piedmont Park, well-known Atlanta art aficionado Ann Bassarab presents her homage to contemporary African and children's art. Her collection includes an extraordinary display of Kenyan art, as well as the inspiring work of local and international African artists, among them the venerable Ethiopian artist Wosene Kosrof. *305 10th St., Midtown, 404/872–6608. By appointment only. MARTA: Midtown.*

12 d-7

LOWE GALLERY

Buckhead's Bennett Street is lined with shops and galleries, but this one stands out for its spacious loft location and stock of works by some of Atlanta's most talented living and dead artists, including the paintings of an emerging local favorite, Honnie Goode. The gallery is visually impressive in every sense of the phrase. *75 Bennett St., Buckhead, 404/352–8114. Closed Sun.*

12 d-7

MARCIA WOOD GALLERY

Located amid a cluster of galleries in Buckhead, this establishment is highly respected for its distinctive selection of well-seasoned contemporary artwork. Among the featured talent are the well known mixed-media artists Daniel Troppy and Mary Engel. *1831 Peachtree St., Buckhead, 404/885–1808. Closed Sun.–Mon.*

14 a-1

MODERN PRIMITIVE GALLERY

This storefront gallery sits in the heart of Virginia-Highland, one of Atlanta's most inviting neighborhoods, and shows the colorful works of folk, outsider, and visionary artists. *1393 N. Highland Ave., Virginia-Highland, 404/892–0056. Closed Mon.*

12 d-7

OPUS ONE GALLERY

Art-intensive Bennett Street in Buckhead is home to this gallery that represents 30 local and international artists, who create everything from abstract images to landscapes. Among other items, you can find the oil paintings of Deborah Bennett. Opus One is also a stained-glass studio specializing in screens, windows, and custom designs. *75 Bennett St., Buckhead, 404/352–9727. Closed Mon.*

5 c-2

RAIFORD GALLERY

A bright and busy wonderland of original works by local and regional artists, this imaginative gallery—housed in a tremendous, airy cabin built from recycled wood—offers everything from ceramics, fiber art, handmade paper, glass, and even excitingly creative small furniture. *1169 Canton St., Roswell, 770/645–2050. Closed Sun.–Mon.*

12 d-7

RAYMOND LAWRENCE GALLERY

This gallery on Buckhead's happening Bennett Street features contemporary paintings, sculpture, and photography. *75 Bennett St., Buckhead, 404/352–5058. Closed Sun.–Mon.*

14 a-4

RIGHT BRAIN GALLERY

This innovative Virginia-Highland gallery shows original children's book illustrations as well as the painting, ceramics, and sculpture of contemporary artists. Among the highlights are the landscapes of painters Brian Taylor and Jerry Sullivan. *664 N. Highland Ave., Virginia-Highland, 404/872–2696. Closed Sun.–Mon.*

12 *d-7*

ROBERT MATRE GALLERY

With a focus on figurative work, Robert Matre presents powerful contemporary paintings and sculptures by local and international artists. The gallery is pleasingly situated among the other shops and galleries of Buckhead's Bennett Street. *75 Bennett St., Buckhead, 404/ 350–8399. Closed Sun.*

12 *e-7*

SANDLER HUDSEN GALLERY

Here you'll find a selection of art that includes some of the best contemporary work the Southeast has to offer. A recent exhibit, "Portraits: Self and Otherwise," delved into the concept of portraiture in a surprising range of media. *1831A Peachtree Rd., Buckhead, 404/350–8480. Closed Sun.*

14 *g-3*

SHAWN VINSON FINE ART

This cache of sophisticated fine art highlights the work of European and American contemporary artists. *Marlo Building, 119 E. Court Sq., No. 100, Decatur, 404/370–8008. Closed Sun.–Tues. MARTA: Decatur.*

14 *g-5*

SNAPSTONE CENTER FOR THE ARTS

A delightful showcase for ethnic and international artists, this community gallery presents the work of well-known Atlanta artist Cecil Bernard, among others. *2853 Candler Rd., No. 1205, Decatur, 404/241–2453. Closed Sun.*

12 *g-3*

TRINITY GALLERY

One of the most distinguished galleries in the city, Trinity offers an array of original paintings, sculptures, and works on paper, dating from the 17th century to the present. Here you can find the work of David Fraley, well known in Atlanta for his use of bold texture and classical imagery. *315 E. Paces Ferry Rd., Buckhead,* *404/237–0370. Closed Sun.–Mon. MARTA: Buckhead or Lenox.*

12 *g-7*

UPSTAIRS GALLERY

Among other artwork, this gallery carries the massive color monoprints of Richard Gaskin, who creates images up to 8 ft in height using a handmade camera and pinhole optics. *800 Miami Cir., Buckhead, 404/237–2447. Closed Sun.–Mon. MARTA: Lindbergh.*

12 *e-7*

VAKNIN SCHWARTZ

This fine art gallery offers an outstanding array of contemporary work in various media. A recent show, "Self-Evident," celebrated the innovative whimsy of several renowned artists who used themselves as their subject. *1831 Peachtree Rd., Buckhead, 404/351–0035. Closed Sun.–Mon.*

ART MUSEUMS

15 *e-5*

ATLANTA INTERNATIONAL MUSEUM OF ART AND DESIGN

Not your ordinary yawn-fest of dusty relics, this place is all but guaranteed to pique the interest of even the most hardened museum resisters. Founded in 1989, the decisively welcome addition to the local museum scene takes visitors on a trip through time, using exhibits of folk art and design to chart the evolution of world culture. *285 Peachtree Center Ave., Downtown, 404/688–2467. Free. Open Tues.–Sat. 11–5. MARTA: Peachtree Center.*

15 *g-6*

ATLANTA LIFE INSURANCE COMPANY BUILDING

The current headquarters of this enterprise founded by Alonzo Herndon, a former slave, opened in 1980. Its lobby holds an excellent collection of works by black artists from the United States and Africa. *100 Auburn Ave., Sweet Auburn, 404/659–2100. Free. Open weekdays 8:30–5. MARTA: Five Points.*

14 *b-3*

CALLANWOLDE FINE ARTS CENTER

This gorgeous Tudor mansion stands in stately serenity, far back from the street on 12 tree-studded acres. Constructed in 1917 for the oldest son of Coca-Cola mogul Asa Candler, the house was donated to DeKalb County in the early 1970s to house a non-profit fine arts center. The center contains artists' studios, offers classes in painting, drama, dance, pottery, creative writing, and photography, and presents gallery exhibitions. *See also* Architecture, *above*. *980 Briarcliff Rd., Druid Hills, 404/872–5338.*

15 *e-2*

CENTER FOR PUPPETRY ARTS

At this interactive museum, you can see antique and modern puppets from around the world and attend puppet-making workshops. Performances, which include original dramatic works and classics adapted for the museum theater, are presented by professional puppeteers who leave youngsters spell-bound (*see also* Chapter 5). *1404 Spring St., Midtown, 404/873–3391. $5; special exhibits and programs extra. Open Mon.– Sat. 9–5. MARTA: Arts Center.*

15 *g-4*

CITY GALLERY EAST

Don't be put off by its bureaucratic surroundings on the ground floor of Atlanta's City Hall East annex: this gallery consistently offers some of the most sophisticated southern-theme art to be found in the Southeast. Sponsored by the Office of the Mayor, the gallery is known for provocative exhibitions of works by a range or artists, from Atlanta city employees to legendary folk artists such as Thorton Dial. A recent installation, titled "Earth Dance," featured a collaboration between visual artist Jeffrey Coffman and the Beacon Dance Company. *675 Ponce de Leon Ave., Virginia-Highland, 404/817–6815 or 404/ 817–7956. Free. Open weekdays 9–5.*

5 *h-3*

GWINNETT FINE ARTS CENTER

You don't have to hit the mean streets of the city to get your cultural fix. Just head to Duluth to take in the major art shows and exhibits in all media, juried shows, lectures, and art classes offered here. Recent exhibitions have included works by Ferdinand Rosa and Elizabeth Sheppell. The Fine Arts Center is part of the Gwinnett Civic and Cultural Center, which also hosts performing arts events (*see* Chapter 5) and conventions. *6400 Sugarloaf Pkwy., Duluth, 770/623–6002. $5. Open Tues.–Sat. 10–5.*

15 *e-1*

HIGH MUSEUM OF ART

There's no question that the High Museum of Art is one of the proudest examples of architecture the city of Atlanta has to offer (*see* Architecture, *above*). The sleek white structure is awesome outside and in, where a cavernous atrium is surrounded by a cascade of polished ramps. The best way to tackle the High is to take the elevator to the top and work your way downward on foot. Along the way you can admire the 10,000-piece permanent collection of contemporary and classical art from the Americas, Europe, and Africa. The museum also mounts changing exhibits of major works from other collections, such as the recent "Picasso: Masterworks from the Museum of Modern Art" show. Part of the Woodruff Arts Center (*see* Chapter 5), the High Museum is affiliated with the Atlanta College of Art. Founded in 1928, the highly selective ACA has sculpture and photography studios, a large auditorium, darkrooms, and an expansive public art gallery for its student body of about 400. In the basement, the High Cafe with Alon's serves delicious sandwiches, soups, salads, and specialty coffees. *1280 Peachtree Rd., Midtown, 404/733–4437. $6. Open Tues.–Thurs. and Sat. 10–5, Fri. 10–9, Sunday noon–5. MARTA: Arts Center.*

15 *e-5*

HIGH MUSEUM FOLK ART AND PHOTOGRAPHY GALLERY

This extension of the High Museum is a treasure trove of changing folk art and photography exhibits. One notable exhibition, " 'I made this jar'...The Life and Works of the Enslaved African American Potter, Dave," showcased ceramic jugs made by a slave who, unlike most other slaves, signed his work. Many of the haunting pieces were inscribed with Dave's simple yet poignant sayings. *30 John Wesley Dobbs Ave., Downtown, 404/ 577–6940. MARTA: Peachtree Center.*

15 *b-8*

THE HAMMONDS HOUSE GALLERIES AND RESOURCE CENTER

The only museum in Georgia solely dedicated to the preservation of African and African-American fine art and culture occupies an antebellum home in the historic West End district. The stunning collection includes hundreds of works by artists of local, regional, national, and international origin. Those with more than a passing interest in African-American art can attend continuing lecture series and classes here, and scholars are welcome to use the facility's resource center (by appointment). Considered to be one of the oldest homes in the West End, the building once housed a kindergarten that is believed to have been Atlanta's first. *503 Peeples St., West End, 404/752–8730. $2. Open Tues.–Fri. 10–6, Sat. 1–5. MARTA: West End.*

14 *d-1*

MICHAEL C. CARLOS MUSEUM

One of the oldest museums in Georgia, this Emory University institution started out in 1919 as a library containing an odd assortment of curiosities, such as the fingernail of a Chinese Mandarin and a Dead Sea salt crystal that was labeled "part of Lot's wife." Housed in an expansive modern building designed by famed architect Michael Graves (*see* Architecture, *above*), the museum now mounts exhibitions ranging from "So Many Brilliant Talents: Art and Craft in the Age of Rubens" to "Mysteries of the Mummies" to "Uses of Photography in Contemporary Art." The collection still contains plenty of ancient artifacts of exquisite detail and beauty. Many of the artifacts were gathered in the early 1900s, during daring treks across treacherous terrain that was rife with bandits and warring tribes. A 1920 expedition, led by the fabled William Arthur Shelton of Emory's Candler School of Theology (who traveled across Egypt in an armor-plated Rolls-Royce equipped with a machine gun) added about 250 Egyptian, Babylonian, and other Near Eastern antiquities to the collection. *571 S. Kilgo St., Emory University, 404/727–4282. Free ($3 suggested donation). Open Mon.–Sat. 10–5, Sun. noon–5.*

15 *c-4*

NEXUS CONTEMPORARY ART CENTER

Founded in 1973 as an artists' collective with severely limited funding, Nexus can today be counted among the most influential, cutting-edge arts institutions in Atlanta. Gutsy exhibitions, exciting openings, and galas dripping with local celebrities and artists keep the center in the spotlight. In its huge, breathtakingly renovated historic warehouse space just west of the city's center, you will find artists' studios, a gallery with major bimonthly shows, an old-fashioned book press, and the spacious Performance Cafe. *535 Means St., Downtown, 404/688–1970. $3. Open Tues.–Sat. 11–5.*

13 *b-1*

OGLETHORPE UNIVERSITY MUSEUM

This impressive museum provides metro Atlanta with its most comprehensive perspective on the figurative arts, with a focus on historical, mythological, and spiritual content. Founded nine years ago as the Oglethorpe University Art Gallery, it quickly became a cultural contender, with such highly acclaimed early exhibits as "The Family Photographs of Claude Monet in Giverny" and "Portraiture in Holography." Reborn as a museum in 1993, the facility now has two separate galleries. *4484 Peachtree Rd., Oglethorpe University, 404/364–8555. Free. Wed.–Sun. noon–5. MARTA: Brookhaven.*

5 *d-5*

SPRUILL CENTER FOR THE ARTS

Centered on a Victorian farmhouse sleekly restored into a state-of-the-art gallery and house museum, this sprawling arts complex includes the Spruill Center Gallery and the Spruill Education Center. The gallery present a refreshing range of work by emerging as well as established regional artists, often featuring works by students at the education center. In addition to art exhibits, the Spruill Center offers a hefty dose of local heritage. It was established in 1975 by Geraldine Jameson Spruill on land donated by her family, members of the Atlanta aristocracy. Items on display in the house museum include a wall telephone with crank and a carved 1840s cradle, along with historic photographs of the Spruill family and the Dunwoody community. *4681 Ashford-Dunwoody Rd., Dunwoody, 770/394–4019. Wed.–Sat. 11–5.*

ART TOURS

14 *g-3*

BEACON HILL ARTISTS STUDIO TOUR

Every December, arts patrons can get a glimpse of artists at work and look over a truckload of original crafts and artworks just in time for the holidays. On average each year, nine studios with as many as 12 guest artists present a festive collection of pottery, jewelry, paintings, weavings, and woodwork. *404/378–6602.*

14 *a-5*

EUCLID ARTS COLLECTIVE ARTISTS STUDIO TOUR

Nestled at the corner of Austin and Euclid avenues in the heart of Inman Park, the Little Five Points Community Center houses a cluster of artists' studios. The annual tour of the collective usually spans the first two weeks of December and always offers an interesting mix of artists and their creations, such as pottery, woodwork, paintings and jewelry art. *404/221–1530.*

5 *c-2*

ROSWELL ARTISTS STUDIO TOUR

Late each November, one of metro Atlanta's most popular art events leads visitors through a labyrinth of beautiful artists' homes and studios on scenic Willeo Creek, north of historic Roswell Square. Dozens of vendors sell crafts items from booths scattered along the trail, and virtually no aesthetic sensibility is left unsated. *770/993–3980.*

15 *h-4*

TELEPHONE FACTORY STUDIO TOUR

One of Atlanta's most coveted invitations is to this annual shindig that runs from Thanksgiving to Christmas. The highly anticipated event transforms a studio complex into a three-floor arts odyssey, during which the many artists in residence roll out the red carpet, opening their lofts to the public. If you're lucky enough to score an invitation (you can't get in without one), you'll get a look at some incredible original works, as well as a peek into the studios and homes in this converted Art Deco industrial complex. It's a one-stop arts wonderland that's not to be missed. *404/577–0905.*

BRIDGES

5 *e-3*

THE HALF-BRIDGE AT JONES BRIDGE

Within Jones Bridge Recreation Area (*see* Chapter 3) is the babbling Jones Bridge Shoals, famous for its trout fishing. There you'll discover an obscure landmark: a curious, wooden half-bridge that is as scenic as it is interesting. According to tradition, its missing half was stolen in the 1940s. *Jones Bridge Recreation Area, north of Holcomb Bridge Rd. on GA 140.*

4 *e-7*

NICKAJACK CREEK COVERED BRIDGE

About 2 mi northeast of Mableton on Concorde Road, you'll find a very old and very pretty bridge that crosses Nickajack Creek on the way to Smyrna. According to local lore, the covered bridge was built in 1872 because horses sometimes panicked at the sight of the creek's rushing water and refused to traverse an open bridge. Restored for safety late in the 20th century, the bridge is 133 ft long and handles approximately 9,500 vehicles daily. *Concorde Rd. Between Mableton and Smyrna.*

3 *a-2*

POOL'S MILL BRIDGE

Considered the most neglected of Georgia's few surviving covered bridges, this antebellum structure has endured a history of such misfortune and folly that it's a wonder it still stands. First, a flood washed it away in 1901. Then, the local millwright commissioned to rebuild the bridge left his creation riddled with thousands of misdrilled holes and subsequently fled town. The bridge was restored to working order, but by the late 1980s it fell into severe disrepair and finally collapsed into the creek below. Today, thanks to community involvement, Forsyth County officials have again restored the bridge and transformed the surrounding grounds into a park. Most recently, an arsonist tried but failed to torch the structure, inflicting little damage. The bridge's freckling of misplaced auger holes is still visible to this day. *Settendown Creek, near Heardsville in rural Forsyth County.*

8 *f-1*

STONE MOUNTAIN PARK BRIDGE

The bridge on the grounds of Georgia's Stone Mountain Park (*see* History Museums, *below*) was moved here from Athens, Georgia, in 1965. Constructed in 1891, the legendary span was dubbed "Effie's Bridge" in honor of a nearby bordello, which patrons could reach only by crossing the bridge. *U.S. 78, 5 mi outside/east of I–285, Stone Mountain, 770/498–5690.*

CHILDREN'S MUSEUMS

5 *h-3*

CHILDREN'S ARTS MUSEUM
Part of the Gwinnett Civic and Cultural Center, which is also the scene of exhibitions and performances for grown-ups (*see* Chapter 5), the Children's Arts Museum introduces kids to the performing and visual arts. *6400 Sugarloaf Pkwy., Duluth, 770/623–4966.*

14 *c-3*

FERNBANK MUSEUM OF NATURAL HISTORY
This magnificent museum offers a plethora of surprisingly creative exhibits for children to enjoy. Among them are the Fantasy Forest and the Coca-Cola Georgia Adventure, which aim to give kids a hands-on experience of the earth's environment through clever experiments. Another museum feature is storyteller Ruth Manning, who conducts the popular Story Hour on the balconies outside the Discovery Room. Her program has proven remarkably effective at turning kids on to reading. Parents will find plenty to keep them busy while the kids listen to Ruth (*see* Science Museums, *below*). *767 Clifton Rd., Emory, 404/378–0127. Adults $8.95, children 12 and under $6.95. Open Mon.–Sat. 10–5, Sun. noon–5.*

14 *c-3*

FERNBANK SCIENCE CENTER
Kids happily set aside their Nintendo and Game Boys to witness the celestial wonder of the center's planetarium (Atlanta's largest), which comes complete with a real *Apollo* space capsule. Young naturalists enjoy the hiking trail through acres of lush forest (*see* Chapter 3). For more information on the center, *see* Science Museums, *below*. *156 Heaton Park Dr., Emory, 404/378–4311. Free; planetarium show $2. Open Mon. 8:30–5, Tues.–Fri. 8:30 AM–10 PM, Sat. 10–5, Sun. 1–5.*

15 *f-4*

SCITREK SCIENCE AND TECHNOLOGY MUSEUM OF ATLANTA
A favorite destination for kids of all ages, SciTrek is packed with fascinating exhibits that target youthful interests. A host of hands-on science displays introduce children to outer space, natural science, rocket science, chemistry, and more. The museum also presents exceptional seasonal programs such as Holiday Express, which sets a collection of antique toy trains clattering around their tracks. Summer brings day camp as well as the popular overnights that give kids and their guardians an entire night to explore interactive exhibits (*see also* Science Museums, *below*). *395 Piedmont Ave., Downtown, 404/522–5500. Adults $7.50, children $5. Open Mon.–Sat. 10–5, Sun. noon–5. MARTA: Civic Center.*

CHURCHES & SYNAGOGUES

14 *a-3*

ALL SAINTS METROPOLITAN COMMUNITY CHURCH OF ATLANTA
Reverend Ike Parker presides over a congregation that he describes as "progressive and multi-Christian." The church is the offspring of the Universal Fellowship of Metropolitan Community Churches, which was founded in Los Angeles by Rev. Troy Perry with the goal of administering to the gay and lesbian community. Services are held at the Northeast Intown YWCA. *957 N. Highland Ave., Virginia-Highland, 404/296–9822.*

15 *g-6*

BIG BETHEL A.M.E.
Founded by slaves in 1843, this is one of oldest African-American churches in the South. Soon after its inception, the congregation formed the Daughters of Bethel Benevolent Society, whose members tended to the welfare of ailing ex-slaves. In 1880, the church became the nation's first public school for African-American youth (*see also* Architecture, *above*). *220 Auburn Ave., Sweet Auburn, 404/659–0248. MARTA: Five Points.*

5 *c-5*

B'NAI TORAH SYNAGOGUE
A traditional congregation founded by Rabbi Juda Mintz in 1981, this small syn-

agogue is noted for its adherence to daily prayer. Services are offered 365 days a year (366 in leap years). *700 Mt. Vernon Hwy., Sandy Springs, 404/257–0537.*

12 *f-4*

CATHEDRAL OF ST. PHILIP

Luxuriant Buckhead is the perfect setting for this exquisite cathedral, which commands your gaze as you pass by on Peachtree Road. The congregation formed in 1847, making this Atlanta's first Episcopal church, and the cathedral was built in 1933. Though its Gothic home cuts an awesome—even intimidating—figure against the skyline, the congregation inside is known for being warm, diverse and energetic. They participate in several community programs, including delivering meals to homeless shelters and building homes for low-income families through Habitat for Humanity. *2744 Peachtree Rd., Buckhead, 404/365–1000.*

15 *e-6*

CENTRAL PRESBYTERIAN CHURCH

Founded in 1860, this church has a long history of social activism. The original building survived the Battle of Atlanta during the Civil War, but it was replaced by the current structure in 1967. Elegant yet inviting, the Victorian English-style church was designed by English-born Edmund G. Lind, who worked in Atlanta for about a decade. *201 Washington St., Downtown, 404/659–0274. MARTA: Georgia State.*

12 *f-3*

CHRIST THE KING CATHEDRAL

A striking feature of this elegant cathedral is the massive pipe organ, built by the eminent Fratelli Ruffati, who came all the way from Padua, Italy, to install it when construction of the church was finished in 1937. At the time it was built, *Architectural Record* magazine considered this to be the most magnificent building in the city. *2699 Peachtree Rd., Buckhead, 404/872–9557.*

15 *e-3*

CHURCH OF THE REDEEMER

Built in the early 1950s, this Evangelical Lutheran church is an excellent example of the Deco phase of Gothic Revival. From its perch on a hill above Peachtree

Street, it presents a towering exterior of coarsely cut stone bricks, decorated with medieval-style accents. *731 Peachtree St., Midtown, 404/588–1977. MARTA: North Ave.*

15 *e-5*

CHURCH OF THE SACRED HEART OF JESUS

With its two imposing Gothic spires and sculpted tri-arch entry, Sacred Heart is an unmissable presence in the center of the city. Built in 1903, the church housed educational facilities established by the Marist fathers, lauded educators. *335 Peachtree Center Ave., Downtown, 404/522–6800. MARTA: Civic Center.*

14 *c-5*

CLIFTON PRESBYTERIAN CHURCH

Though the congregation here is small in number, its heart is big. The church regularly converts its sanctuary into a shelter for homeless men. *369 Connecticut Ave., Decatur, 404/373–3253. East Lake.*

14 *h-3*

CONGREGATION BET HAVERIM SYNAGOGUE

Billed as "Atlanta's only reconstructionist synagogue," this progressive congregation was founded in 1986 by members of the gay and lesbian community, though today the congregation is thoroughly diverse. Described by its members as open and welcoming, the synagogue is presided over by Rabbi Joshua Lesser. *Services: Atlanta Friends Meeting House, 701 W. Howard Ave., Decatur; mailing address: Box 301, Decatur 30031, 404/607–0054. MARTA: East Lake.*

7 *g-8*

CONGREGATION B'NAI ISRAEL

This reform congregation is the only synagogue on the South Side. Rabbi Julie Schwartz describes her congregation as family-oriented and inviting. *90 Montego Cir., Riverdale, 770/471–3586.*

15 *g-6*

EBENEZER BAPTIST CHURCH

In the heart of the legendary Sweet Auburn district stands a working monument to the memory of Martin Luther King Jr. King, who was born in the neighborhood and later preached at this church regularly before his assassination. *407 Auburn Ave., Sweet Auburn, 404/688–7263. MARTA: King Memorial.*

15 *e-6*
FIRST CONGRESSIONAL CHURCH

Founded in 1867, the First Congressional Church has earned a national reputation for its social activism on behalf of the African-American community. The church itself was built in 1908, with a profusion of archways, whimsical ornamentation, towers, columns, pediments, and stained-glass windows. The effect is eclectic and fanciful, revealing the influence of many architectural styles, including Romanesque, Spanish Mission, and even Victorian. *105 Courtland St., Sweet Auburn, 404/659–6255. MARTA: Georgia State.*

13 *d-6*
FIRST METROPOLITAN COMMUNITY CHURCH OF ATLANTA

This church serves a congregation of predominantly gay and lesbian members. *1379 Tullie Rd., Druid Hills, 404/ 325–4143.*

15 *e-5*
FIRST UNITED METHODIST OF ATLANTA

This is the home of the oldest organized congregation in the city, founded in 1847. The present cathedral, built in 1903 with granite from nearby Stone Mountain, is a prime example of Gothic Revival architecture. *360 Peachtree St., Downtown, 404/524–6614. MARTA: Civic Center.*

14 *n-5*
INMAN PARK METHODIST

Well suited to the charming, easygoing neighborhood in which it resides, this building resembles a simple English parish church. Influenced by Romanesque Revival design, it was built in 1898. *1015 Edgewood Ave., Inman Park, 404/522–9322. MARTA: Inman Park.*

10 *b-1*
KING'S VINEYARD

In addition to ministering to the local community, this church also sends members to Mexico to help build churches in underdeveloped regions. To fund its expeditions, the congregation holds garage sales, car washes, and bake sales. *40 Mays Rd., Stockbridge, 770/389–1211.*

13 *d-4*
OR VE SHALOM SYNAGOGUE

This synagogue was established in 1915 by 12 Sephardic Jews who had come to Atlanta from Turkey and Rhodes. Since then it has thrived, retaining the distinctive Sephardic customs; since the 1960s Rabbi Robert Ichay has served the congregation. The synagogue welcomes Jewish immigrants from all over the world and prides itself on its ethnic and cultural diversity. *1681 N. Druid Hills Rd., Druid Hill, 404/633–1737.*

12 *f-4*
SECOND–PONCE DE LEON BAPTIST CHURCH

Along with Atlanta Community Ministries, this church organizes various community outreach efforts, such as tutoring and neighborhood revitalization. The church makes a point of ministering to everyone. *2715 Peachtree Rd., Buckhead, 404/266-8111.*

7 *g-4*
SHADY GROVE BAPTIST CHURCH

Under the auspices of Rev. Otis B. Burnett Jr., this intown congregation prides itself on its youth programs, and every April they host a weeklong festival titled "Youth and Young Adults Celebration." *1147 Osborne St., 404/755–4332. MARTA: Lakewood/Fort McPherson.*

15 *e-5*
SHRINE OF THE IMMACULATE CONCEPTION

One of the few pre–Civil War structures left standing after the Union Army torched Atlanta (*see also* Historic Structures & Streets, *below*), this mighty French Gothic church incorporates typical Victorian elements, such as two towers of unequal height, each with different ornamentation. The French Gothic influence is apparent in the rose window and the three-part entrance. The use of materials of varying colors is a feature of English High Victorian Gothic architecture. Damaged by fire in 1982, it has been beautifully restored. *48 Martin Luther King Jr. Dr., Downtown, 404/521–1866. MARTA: Five Points.*

15 *e-5*
ST. LUKE'S EPISCOPAL CHURCH

This church is well known for its community outreach program, which includes community kitchen ministries and a soup kitchen. *435 Peachtree St., Downtown, 404/873–7600. MARTA: Civic Center.*

15 *f-3*

ST. MARKS UNITED METHODIST CHURCH

This visually spectacular church is the oldest among the cluster of churches along this stretch of Peachtree Street. Built in 1903, the structure is of neo-Gothic design with touches of the Victorian. Note the enormous, incandescent stained-glass window above the entrance. *781 Peachtree St., Midtown, 404/873–2636. MARTA: North Ave.*

2 *b-8*

ST. MICHAEL THE ARCHANGEL ROMAN CATHOLIC CHURCH

This church opened its doors in 1995, with a congregation of 300 families. The 31,000-square-ft facility has a 700-seat sanctuary, a day chapel, and religious education offices. *1490 Arnold Mill Rd., Woodstock, 770/516–0009.*

4 *h-3*

TEMPLE KOL EMETH

This reform synagogue, presided over by Rabbi Steven Lebow, has become so popular in recent years that it is quickly outgrowing its sanctuary, which was built to accommodate 1,400 people. *1415 Old Canton Rd., Marietta, 770/973–3533.*

15 *e-1*

THE TEMPLE SYNAGOGUE

The Temple, home to a Reform congregation, has a impressive place in local lore: Bombed in 1958, the synagogue inspired the thriller *The Temple Bombing*, by Melissa Fay Green. It also made an appearance in the movie *Driving Miss Daisy* (see also Architecture, *above*). *1589 Peachtree St., Buckhead, 404/873–1731. MARTA: Arts Center.*

15 *g-6*

WHEAT STREET BAPTIST CHURCH

This primarily African-American church stands on the Auburn Avenue, where Martin Luther King Jr. was born and raised. Founded in 1870, it has been one of the most influential institutions of the Civil Rights movement. *359 Auburn Ave., Sweet Auburn, 404/659–4328. MARTA: King Memorial.*

2 *b-8*

WOODSTOCK FIRST BAPTIST CHURCH

As the result of phenomenal residential development in the area, this congregation has grown rapidly in recent years, from 250 members in 1986 to more than 5,000 today. Its shining new facilities now host numerous programs for residents. *777 Neese Rd., Woodstock, 770/591–2646.*

GRAVEYARDS & CEMETERIES

4 *f-5*

MARIETTA CONFEDERATE CEMETERY

Thousands of unfortunate Confederate soldiers who perished in the Civil War have their final resting place in this old cemetery. Founded in 1863, the burial ground is located on a hill overlooking Marietta Square. More than 500 boys and men in gray were buried here immediately following the bloody Battle of Kennesaw Mountain in 1864, and 2,500 more were reinterred here after the Civil War ended, moved from battlefields around Georgia. Each grave marker simply notes the home state of the soldier buried there, and not much more. A distinguished headstone marks the grave of an unknown soldier, who is believed to have fallen in the Battle of Kennesaw. Buried by an artillery shell, his body remained where it fell until 1998, when it was discovered during a construction excavation. Identified as a Confederate infantryman by buttons marked "I" for infantry and by some remnants of a gray uniform, the unknown soldier was laid to rest in a hand-carved coffin. *West Atlanta St. and Cemetery St., Marietta.*

4 *g-4*

MARIETTA NATIONAL CEMETERY

The oldest grave here dates back to 1866, a year after the Civil War ended. In fact, over half of the 18,410 headstones here belong to veterans of the Civil War, all of them Union, as opposed to Confederate, troops. The remainder of the graves belong to veterans of the Spanish-American and Indian wars as well as both World Wars. The cemetery reached full capacity in 1978 and was closed to casket burials; it was closed to cremated remains in 1996. *Cole St. and Washing-*

ton Ave. along Hwy. 120, Marietta, 770/
428–5631.

15 g-7

OAKLAND CEMETERY

Established in 1850—it's the oldest city-
owned cemetery in Atlanta—this is an
88-acre wonderland of weathered headstones and mossy, ornate monuments
to the long-dead. It has met the final
needs of some of the city's most
famous figures, among them author
Margaret Mitchell, who penned the epic
Gone With the Wind. The wooded burial
ground is filled with reminders of the
past, from the unmarked paupers'
graves to the massive tombs of prominent citizens. Some of the thousands of
Confederate soldiers buried here are
said to haunt the site (*see* Haunted
Places, *below*); their memory is honored
by the statue *Lion of Atlanta* (*see* Statues, Murals & Monuments, *below*). *248
Oakland Ave., Downtown, 404/688–2107.
Daily, dawn–dusk. Guided tours Mar.–
Oct., Sat. 10 AM and 2 PM, Sun. 2 PM, $3
adults, $2 seniors, $1 students and children. MARTA: King Memorial.*

14 g-3

OLD DECATUR CEMETERY

Some leading members of old Atlanta
society are buried in this scenic graveyard, whose first burials date back to
1827. Among the graves are those of
Capt. William Towers, who fought with
Andrew Jackson in the Battle of New
Orleans, Capt. John Prather, who, 56
years before his death, fought on this
very site in the 1864 Battle of Decatur,
and Dr. Thomas Chivers, known as "the
lost poet of Atlanta," who was a col-
league of Edgar Allen Poe. *Church St.
near Columbia Dr. and Ponce de Leon Ct.,
Decatur. MARTA: Decatur.*

6 c-4

**OLD LAWRENCEVILLE
CEMETERY**

This atmospheric, worn-at-the-elbows
bone-yard holds the remains of the pio-
neers of Gwinnett County, whose grave-
stones date back to the antebellum era.
Many of the markers are choked with
brush, some of them are weathered by
decades of decay and algae, but the
crumbling wonder of unkempt burial
grounds like this holds definite charm
for more than a few graveyard aficionados. *Bordered by Pike, Crogan, and Corbin
Sts., Lawrenceville.*

5 c-2

OLD ROSWELL CEMETERY

Smack in the heart of bustling downtown Roswell, this enchanting cemetery
was first put into service in 1846, when
its oldest grave was dug for a four-
month-old girl. Though there are plenty
of grand headstones, the most fascinating graves are the earliest, which are
marked by simple fieldstones inscribed
with dates only. *Woodstock Rd. and U.S.
19 (Alpharetta Rd.).*

5 c-2

**ROSWELL FOUNDERS
CEMETERY**

The site of Roswell's earliest recorded
burial, in 1840, tiny Founders Cemetery
counts the grandfather of President
Theodore Roosevelt among its permanent residents. *Sloan St. near Atlanta
St., Roswell.*

5 b-5

SANDY SPRINGS CEMETERY

In 1986, the Alfred Holt Colquit Chapter
of the United Daughters of the Confederacy declared this charming cemetery a
historic site. Though the cemetery has
550 graves, most of them remain
unidentified because their original markers were simple field stones that went
missing over the years, including that of
an unnamed soldier who fought under
Gen. Robert E. Lee. Today, only 195 of
the graves possess identifiable markers.
The cemetery is split in half by Mt. Vernon Hwy. *Mt. Vernon Hwy. and Luke Forest Dr., Sandy Springs.*

7 h-4

SOUTHVIEW CEMETERY

Back in 1886, a group of black Atlantans
founded this graveyard in response to
the overcrowding of Oakland Cemetery
(*above*) downtown and the segregation
practices at Westview Cemetery (*above*)
in the West End. Reflecting the aesthetic
values of the period's Rural Cemetery
Movement, Southview sits on park-like
grounds and contains beautiful examples of Victorian funerary architecture.
Among the graves of prominent black
citizens buried there is that of the Rev.
Martin Luther King Sr. *1990 Jonesboro
Rd., South Side.*

14 *b-8*

WESTVIEW CEMETERY

Established in 1884 to relieve the over-crowding of Oakland Cemetery (*above*), this 600-acre site is home to the massive Abbey Mausoleum (*see* Architecture, *above*), built for Coca-Cola founder Asa Candler. Legendary Atlanta citizens buried here include Joel Chandler Harris, author of the Uncle Remus stories. *1680 Westview Dr., West End, 404/755–6611. MARTA: West Lake.*

HAUNTED PLACES

12 *g-3*

ANTHONY'S

This popular restaurant is housed in the Pope-Walton House (*see* Historic Structures & Streets, *below*), an historic antebellum home that reportedly reveals its history to patrons and employees in strange ways. When you walk past the main staircase, you can supposedly hear children singing and can feel the presence of the house's former mistress. A boy once hanged himself from a big oak tree nearby, and to this day a mysterious light is said to jet occasionally about its branches. To investigate the ghostly rumors, a journalist spent a night in Anthony's in late 1998 and subsequently reported many unearthly occurrences, such as the incessant yet beautiful ringing of high-pitched bells, and the sound of footsteps—accompanied by the sound of rustling skirts—approaching him throughout the night. *3109 Piedmont Rd., Buckhead, 404/261–6009. Dinner only. Closed Sun. MARTA: Buckhead.*

4 *f-6*

1848 HOUSE

A makeshift hospital for wounded soldiers during the Civil War, the 1848 House restaurant in Marietta has a haunted room. In the Scarlet Room, which was the hospital's operating room, guests and employees have reported sightings of a female ghost in a long dress looking in the window. The house also contains a mural depicting antebellum Marietta (*see* Statues, Murals & Monuments, *below*). *780 South Cobb Dr., Marietta, 770/428–1848. Dinner only Tues.–Sat., brunch Sun. Closed Mon.*

4 *e-4*

KENNESAW MOUNTAIN NATIONAL BATTLEFIELD

In the bloody June, 1864, battle at Kennesaw Mountain, more than 3,000 Union and Confederate soldiers were killed. At one point during the fight the Union general had to declare a truce in order to clear the dead and wounded from the slopes of the "Dead Angle." To this day the battlefield is rumored to be haunted. Many ghost sightings have been reported, and photographs taken here show eerie apparitions, including the vague outlines of faces that the photographer did not see until the film was developed. Other apparitions include mysterious clouds of smoke, said to be ghost smoke from cannon fire, that appear in photographs taken on perfectly clear days. *Kennesaw Mountain National Battlefield Park, 905 Kennesaw Mountain Dr., Marietta, 770/427–4686. Free. Daily 8 AM–sundown.*

15 *g-7*

OAKLAND CEMETERY

Nearly 4,000 Confederate soldiers who perished in the Civil War were hastily buried here in mass graves. Ghostly roll calls are said to echo through the night (*see also* Graveyards & Cemeteries, *above*). *248 Oakland Ave., Downtown, 404/688–2107. Daily, dawn–dusk. Guided tours Mar.–Oct., Sat. 10 AM and 2 PM, Sun. 2 PM, $3 adults, $2 seniors, $1 students and children. MARTA: King Memorial.*

8 *e-1*

VILLAGE INN BED & BREAKFAST

This cozy inn (*see* Chapter 6) is housed in a beautifully restored antebellum mansion served as a Confederate hospital during the Civil War. Reportedly, guests are often treated to mysterious specters from the mansion's former life. Mischievous ghosts are said to sing gospel tunes, whistle, walk the halls, and relocate furniture and other items. *992 Ridge Ave., Stone Mountain, 770/469–3459.*

15 *e-1*

WSB STUDIOS

Evidently there's an extra price to pay when you erect a $50 million television and radio station on the site of Confederate trenches used during the Battle of Atlanta. In WSB's case, that price came in the form of a playful ghost dubbed "the General." Staffers have reported hearing furniture rolling across the floor and papers shuffling when they were otherwise alone in the building, and one executive says the ghost teased her by flipping her hair from behind one night. Professional ghost hunters have confirmed, through instrument readings, the presence of a spook, but perhaps most convincing to employees is one of the ghost hunters' snapshots. It shows an empty office, in which the misty outline of a skull wearing a Confederate cap is seen smiling at the camera. *1601 W. Peachtree St., Midtown, 404/897–7000. MARTA: Arts Center.*

HISTORIC STRUCTURES & STREETS

14 *g-4*

AGNES SCOTT COLLEGE

Established in 1889 as a female seminary, Agnes Scott College was named in honor of the mother of George W. Scott, a local benefactor, when it was transformed into a private liberal arts college for women. The 105-acre campus is a beauty to behold, with wooded pathways and Victorian and Romanesque Revival architecture that make it one of the most engaging campuses in the South. The neo-Gothic McCain Library (Edwards and Sayward, 1936) is of special note for its interior reading room, which possesses an artful network of wood framing. *141 E. College Ave., Decatur, 404/ 638–6000. MARTA: Decatur.*

6 *f-3*

ALCOVY ROAD GRISTMILL

Legend has it that this mill's owner outsmarted Union troops during the Civil War by hiding his mules and valuables downstream on the Alcovy River. When the soldiers passed through, the story goes, they didn't deem the miller worthy of pillaging. Built between 1868 and 1879, the three-story, wood-framed gristmill was last used in 1986, but it is still in operating condition today. *Alcovy Rd. between Lawrenceville and Dacula, 770/ 822–5174 (Gwinnett County Historical Society).*

15 *f-1*

ANSLEY PARK

Listed in the National Register of Historic Places, Ansley Park was the first Atlanta suburb built with the automobile, as opposed to the streetcar, in mind. Credited to civil engineer and landscape architect Frederick Law Olmsted, the 1904 neighborhood layout includes advanced (for the turn of the 20th century) features such as "pocket parks." The green spaces and the beautiful homes make the area a favorite place for strolls as well as one of the city's most desirable neighborhoods. *Peachtree St. to Piedmont Rd., between 14th St. and Monroe Ave. MARTA: Arts Center.*

9 *g-1*

ASHLEY OAKS MANSION

This virtual fortress was built with more than a million bricks back in 1879. Understandably, it is one of the best-preserved examples of Greek Revival architecture in metro Atlanta. Tours are conducted Fridays 10–4 and Sundays 1– 5. *144 College St., Jonesboro, 770/478– 8986. Adults $5, children $2.50.*

15 *e-6*

ATLANTA DAILY WORLD BUILDING

This simple two-story brick building, banded with a white frieze of lion's heads, was constructed in the early 1900s; since 1945 it has housed one of the nation's oldest black newspapers. Despite its title, the publication is no longer a daily. Alexis Reeves, now publisher and CEO, is the granddaughter of William A. Scott II, who founded the paper as a weekly in 1928. *145 Auburn Ave., Downtown, 404/659–1110. MARTA: Five Points.*

15 *d-6*

ATLANTA JOURNAL– CONSTITUTION BUILDING

The *Atlanta Journal* and the *Atlanta Constitution*—to this day the two biggest newspapers published in Georgia—were rival publications as far back as 1883, until they were bought by media mogul James Cox in 1950. Since then they have combined to produce daily afternoon and morning editions. Worth a look is the lobby of the headquarters building, which showcases old front-page stories, an exhibit of antique typesetting techniques, and photographs of some more famous staffers, among them Margaret Mitchell of *Gone With the Wind* fame and the venerable late humorist Lewis Grizzard. *72 Marietta St., Downtown, 404/614–2688. MARTA: Omni/ Dome/GWCC.*

15 *e-3*

ATLANTA PRESERVATION CENTER

A favorite sign of spring in these parts is the annual commencement of the Atlanta Preservation Center's schedule of walking tours. What began in 1980 as a grassroots effort to increase public awareness of Atlanta's endangered architectural heritage and historic areas has since become one of the city's strongest forces in protecting its legacy. The walking tours are as popular among locals as they are among tourists, providing as they do an opportunity for leisurely strolls through old neighborhoods, with narration by knowledgeable volunteers. The downtown tours are the favorite among tourists, but locals find the strolls through such neighborhoods as Candler Park, West End, Cabbage Town, Inman Park, and Grant Park a refreshing way to spend a spring day. *156 7th St., Ste. 3, Midtown, 404/876–2041. Free to members, $5 non-member adults, $4 children and seniors. Call for tour schedules. MARTA: Midtown.*

14 *h-3*

AVONDALE ESTATES

The picturesque community of Avondale Estates seems to pop out of the pages of a fairy tale, so beautiful is the area. The town was developed between 1924 and 1941 as part of the "new town" vision of entrepreneur George F. Willis. To this day it retains the charm and warmth of a bygone time. Throughout the wooded berg are homes that reflect a variety of architectural styles, such as Spanish Mission and Dutch Colonial, plus a smattering of Craftsman-style bungalows. *South of Avondale and Covington Rds. between Fairfield and Lakeshore Drs., to Avondale Lake. MARTA: Avondale.*

15 *e-4*

BALTIMORE ROW

You'll think you're in Yankee territory as you stroll this section of Midtown. Atlanta's first row-house development was built in 1886 to the specifications of J. S. Rosenthal, in honor of his Maryland hometown. *5–19 Baltimore Place, Midtown. MARTA: North Ave.*

15 *e-6*

BAPTIST STUDENT UNION AT GEORGIA STATE UNIVERSITY

In 1898, announcing to his shareholders that "it is sufficient for all the needs for all time to come," Asa Griggs Candler built this elegant Victorian structure as the first Coca-Cola bottling plant. Even visionaries, it seems, have their limitations. *125 Edgewood Ave., Downtown, 404/659–8726. MARTA: Five Points or Georgia State.*

4 *g-4*

THE BIG CHICKEN

This 56-ft tall metal chicken was built in 1964 as a roadside oddity to attract customers to the Chick-Chuck-N'-Shake fast-food joint. When that enterprise went belly-up, the bird and its restaurant roost was bought up by a Kentucky Fried Chicken franchise. The Big Chicken came close to extinction in 1993, after severe wind storms plucked it of all but a few of its sheet-metal feathers. KFC was reluctant to fork over the bucks to save the bird, but its plans to demolish the local treasure brought howls of protest. Recognizing a public relations disaster in the making, KFC decided not only to rescue beloved local landmark but to update its look by installing motors to animate its beak and eyes. Today, Marietta residents don't know how to give driving directions without mentioning the Big Chicken. If you can't follow directions from that point on, you can't maneuver around Marietta. *12 N. Cobb Pkwy., Marietta, 770/422–4716.*

15 *g-7*

CABBAGETOWN

This engaging former mill village located just a few miles from the city's center is said to have earned its name when a cabbage cart overturned here. Now it's the site of a renovation rage among urban enthusiasts. The tiny houses, many of them simple shotgun shacks and cottages dating back to 1884, once served as housing for employees of the looming Fulton Bag and Cotton Mill (*see* Architecture, *above*), which has been turned into a hive of upscale loft apartments. The colorful community has many picturesque streets and is on the National Register of Historic Places. *Moreland to DeKalb Aves. between Boulevard and Chester Ave. MARTA: King Memorial.*

14 *a-5, b-5*

CANDLER PARK

Known for its charming collection of varied housing styles dating back to the late 1800s, Candler Park is full of exquisitely restored Eastlake cottages and Craftsman bungalows, with the occasional Victorian mansion thrown into the mix. The portion of Candler Park listed on the National Register of Historic Places is roughly bordered by Moreland, DeKalb, McClendon and Harold avenues, including Mathews Steet and Clifton Terrace. *MARTA: Edgewood/Candler Park.*

15 *e-5*
CAPITOL CITY CLUB
Built in 1911, this stately edifice was designed by architect Donn Barber for an elite private club founded in 1883. Club members have included a Union general, Pennsylvanian John Randolph Lewis (later Atlanta's postmaster), Governor Joseph E. Brown (whose statue stands on the Capitol grounds), Coca-Cola founder Asa Griggs Candler, and unreconstructed rebel Robert Toombs, who was the Confederate Secretary of State. The club remains an exclusive spot, a favorite and lavish lunch setting for the city's leaders. The building's dignified facade includes a columned entrance and twin balconies. *7 Harris St., Downtown, 404/523–8221. MARTA: Peachtree Center.*

15 *d-5*
CENTENNIAL OLYMPIC PARK
This landscaped, 21-acre monument to Atlanta's role as host of the 1996 Olympic Games is rife with interesting sights. Inscriptions mark commemorative bricks purchased by Altantans before the games, artwork dots the grounds (*see* Statues, Murals & Monuments, *below*), and a fountain in the shape of the Olympic Rings is best described as a "water sculpture." *Marietta St. at International Blvd., Downtown. MARTA: Omni/Dome/GWCC.*

2 *c-3*
CHEROKEE COUNTY COURTHOUSE
This well-preserved example of Classic Revival architecture was designed by A. Ten Ecyk Brown, the same architect who designed Atlanta City Hall (*see* Architecture, *above*). *100 North St., Canton.*

15 *d-5*
CNN BUILDING
The bustling core of media king Ted Turner's global broadcasting empire is

much more than an office building. It is a massive complex that includes restaurants, retail shops, the ritzy Omni Hotel, and, of course, a movie theater complex. Tours, offered daily 9–5:30, give visitors the history of CNN and afford a glimpse into the humming newsroom from a glass-enclosed balcony. A VIP tour gets you inside the newsroom and within hand-shaking distance of broadcast personalities. *See also* Architecture, *above.* *1 CNN Center, International Blvd. at Marietta St., Downtown, 404/827–2300. Tours $7, VIP $24.50. MARTA: Omni/Dome/GWCC.*

15 *d-6*
COTTONGIM BUILDING
This classic example of turn-of-the-20th-century mill construction, built in 1890, is in the Terminus District, which was once a busy commercial center. Though somewhat dilapidated, the area has an historic air, since it has changed little since the early 1900s. The Cottongim Building, with wood joists and cast-iron columns, presently awaits restoration. *97 Broad St., Downtown. MARTA: Five Points.*

14 *b-3, c-2*
DRUID HILLS
Developer Joel Hurt (*see* Inman Park, *below*) commissioned Frederick Law Olmsted's firm to lay out Druid Hills. Eventually, Hurt had to sell the property because he was unable to garner financing for its completion, and none other than Coca-Cola mogul Asa Griggs Candler came to the rescue. Druid Hills premiered in 1908 as Atlanta's first effort at suburbia, attracting residents with its sprawling homes and beautiful churches. *N. Decatur Rd. and Ponce de Leon Ave. between Briarcliff and Lullwater Rds.*

9 *e-4*
FAYETTE COUNTY COURTHOUSE
Built in 1825, this is the oldest courthouse in Georgia. Originally constructed as a simple brick building, it later acquired a gray stucco exterior and clock tower. *145 Johnson Ave., on the square in Fayetteville, 770/461–4703.*

15 *e-4*
FOX THEATRE
The Fox is no mere movieplex—it's a dramatic flashback to the times when

ornamental excess was required for a glitzy night on the town. Built in 1929 as the headquarters for Atlanta's Arabic Order of the Nobles of the Mystic Shrine (a.k.a. the Shriners), the awesome conglomeration of curious but beautiful architecture changed hands before its completion. It was purchased by movie-house mogul William Fox, who turned it into the grand movie and performance palace it is today. *See also* Architecture, *above,* and Chapter 5. *660 Peachtree St., Midtown, 404/881–2100. MARTA: North Ave.*

15 *e-6*

GEORGIA RAILROAD FREIGHT DEPOT

Built in 1869, this redbrick, stone-accented depot originally stood three stories tall, but a fire in 1935 reduced it to its present single story. It remains the oldest extant building in downtown Atlanta. Beautifully restored, the Italianate building is used today as a special events and reception space. *65 Martin Luther King Jr. Dr., Downtown, 404/656–3850. MARTA: Five Points.*

15 *e-4*

GEORGIAN TERRACE

Heralded as the time of its construction in 1911 as the most lavish hotel in Atlanta, this is where Hollywood celebrities stayed during the 1939 world premiere of *Gone With the Wind.* The regal building fell into disrepair and was closed in 1981, and a decade later it was converted to luxury apartments. Since then, it has been resurrected as a hotel (*see* Chapter 6). Around a soaring central atrium the interior is awash in polished marble; encircling the atrium are the columned terraces for which the hotel was named. *659 Peachtree St., Midtown, 404/724–0747. MARTA: North Ave.*

10 *e-4*

HENRY COUNTY COURTHOUSE

This little brick courthouse was built in 1897, with arched windows and a clock tower complete with turrets. It was designed to stand out in simpler times, when courtroom trials were the primary source of community entertainment. *1 Courthouse Sq., on the square in McDonough, 770/954–2121.*

14 *a-5*

INMAN PARK

In 1889, developer Joel Hurt (*see* Druid Hills, *above*) began work on Inman Park, which today calls itself "Atlanta's First Suburb." Because of its roller-coaster ride in and out of prosperity over the years, the area encompasses a host of residential styles, from huge Victorian mansions to humble shotgun shacks. As the city expanded, the suburb became an in-town neighborhood. Its charm has made it one of the most popular neighborhoods in the city, home to Mayor Bill Campbell, among others. It is on the National Register of Historic Places. *Between Edgewood, Euclid, and Moreland Aves. MARTA: Inman Park/ Reynoldstown.*

4 *f-4*

KENNESAW HOUSE

In 1993 this exquisite example of late Victorian architecture had a date with the wrecking ball, but citizens with sense of history rallied to save it. The former hotel now houses office and retail space, as well as the Marietta Museum of History (*see* History Museums, *below*) on the second floor. *1 Depot St., Marietta, 770/528–0431.*

15 *f-4*

THE MANSION RESTAURANT

Prepare to lose yourself in another era as you enter this remarkably preserved example of Queen Anne–style architecture. Built in 1885, it was the home of the grandson of Richard Peters, who is credited with developing the Midtown business district. The interior is piled with period antiques. *179 Ponce de Leon Ave., Midtown, 404/876–0727. MARTA: North Ave.*

15 *g-6*

MARTIN LUTHER KING JR. BIRTH HOME

Part of the Martin Luther King Jr. National Historic District (*below*), this modest Queen Anne–style bungalow is where King was born in 1929. On display are photographs and personal effects of he King family. To sign up for National Parks Service-led tours of the house, go to the fire station at 39 Boulevard. *501 Auburn Ave., Sweet Auburn, 404/331–6922. Free. Daily guided ½-hr tours every hr 10–5. MARTA: King Memorial.*

15 *g-6*

MARTIN LUTHER KING JR. NATIONAL HISTORIC DISTRICT

Administered by the National Parks Service, the Martin Luther King Jr. National Historic District occupies several blocks on Auburn Avenue, a few blocks east of Peachtree Street in the traditionally black business and residential community of Sweet Auburn. It includes the birthplace (*above*) of Martin Luther King Jr. Across the street from the Martin Luther King Jr. Center for Nonviolent Social Change (*see* History Museums, *below*), the Parks Service operates a visitor center that contains a multimedia exhibit focused on the civil rights movement and Dr. King's role in it. The Service also leads tours of the district. *450 Auburn Ave., Sweet Auburn, 404/331-5190. Free. Tours daily, 10 AM–5 PM. MARTA: King Memorial station.*

15 *b-7*

MOREHOUSE COLLEGE

The nation's only all-male, primarily African-American liberal arts college has come a long way since its founding in 1867, when it was known as the Augusta Institute. Today, the college has a student body of 3,000 and counts such famous men as Dr. Martin Luther King Jr. and filmmaker Spike Lee among its alumni. *830 Westview Dr., West End, 404/681–2800. MARTA: Ashby St.*

2 *c-4*

OLD ROCK BARN

Picture horse-drawn buggies, harness racing, and small-town gossips, and you'll have a good idea of what Cherokee County's most familiar landmark was like at the turn of the 20th century, when horsebreeder Gus Coggins' barn was the most popular meeting place in the region. But in 1906, the racing stable was burned down by night-riders who opposed Coggins' employment of black ranch hands, and several prized horses were lost in the blaze. Unintimidated, the determined horsebreeder rebuilt the enormous barn in stone and continued to breed champion equines. Today the barn is a Canton city landmark, and plans are underway to convert it to a community convention center. *GA 5 (Marietta Hwy.) Near GA 140, Canton, 770/345–0400.*

12 *g-3*

POPE-WALTON HOUSE

Wiley Woods Pope started building this Classical Revival house in Washington, Georgia (117 mi east of Atlanta) early in the 19th century. After his death, the husband of his granddaughter, Annie Barnett, continued the construction, but while he was away fighting for the Confederacy during the Civil War, Gen. William Sherman's troops invaded Washington and plundered the mansion, even riding through the halls on horseback. In the end, though, they spared the house from their torches because its mistress was caring for a newborn child. In 1967, Anthony's restaurant bought the house and moved it, brick by brick, to its present location in Buckhead. Legend has it that the ghost of Annie Barnett was a stowaway on the journey and that she makes occasional appearances to the restaurant guests and staff (*see* Haunted Places, *above*). The move took three years, but the restoration is intricate and even the attic retains its original lumber and wooden pegs. *3100 Piedmont Rd., just south of Peachtree Rd., Buckhead, 404/262–7379.*

5 *c-2*

ROSWELL MILL

Like most of Atlanta, this cotton mill withstood its dose of fire during the Civil War, but Gen. William Sherman was especially determined to destroy this particular site because it was used to manufacture uniforms for the Confederacy. Reportedly, Sherman deported the mill's 400 female seamstresses to the North, and to this day little is known of what became of them. The structure has been converted into a mall called Roswell Mill, which is full of upscale shops (*see* Chapter 2). *85A Mill St., Roswell, 770/640–3253.*

15 *e-6*

SHRINE OF THE IMMACULATE CONCEPTION

Built in 1848, Atlanta's oldest existing religious structure was one of the few buildings left standing by the Federal troops who burned Atlanta during the Civil War. The story goes that an Irish priest, Father Thomas O'Reilly, persuaded General Sherman that to destroy the building would cause a mutiny among the Union troops, many of whom were Irish Catholic immigrants.

See also Churches & Synagogues, *above.*
48 Martin Luther King Jr. Dr., Downtown,
404/521–1866. MARTA: Five Points.

15 b-7

SPELMAN COLLEGE

Founded as the Atlanta Baptist Female
Seminary in 1881, Spelman Collage is
the oldest surviving institution devoted
to the education of African-American
women. The college is named after Lucy
Henry Spelman, the mother-in-law of
John D. Rockefeller, the school's generous patron. Today, with more than
2,000 students, the college is highly
regarded. Television megastar Oprah
Winfrey donated $1 million to Spelman
in 1997. *350 Spelman La., West End, 404/*
681–3643. MARTA: Vine City or Ashby St.

9 g-1

STATELY OAKS PLANTATION

This sprawling plantation house was
built in 1839 with heart pine, considered
the strongest timber available at the
time. Even so, it's a wonder the mansion survived the torches of the Civil
War. According to reports, Union soldiers camped on the property while its
owner, a Confederate soldier, was away
defending other parts of the South. For
some reason they spared it the torch,
and today the plantation is one of the
few undamaged examples of antebellum
architecture in the South. Tours are
offered Thursday and Friday 11–3. *100*
Carriage Dr., Jonesboro, 770/473–0197.
Adults $3, children $1.

15 e-6

SWEET AUBURN

From the post–Civil War period in the
late 1800s to about 1930, when segregation excluded blacks from the white business and social communities, Sweet
Auburn served as Atlanta's "other" main
street. It was in this thriving hub of black
commerce, and cultural, religious, and
political activity that Dr. Martin Luther
King Jr. was born and raised (*see* Martin
Luther King Jr. National Historic District,
above). King got his start preaching at
the neighborhood's Ebenezer Baptist
Church (*see* Churches & Synagogues,
above). *Decatur St. to Ralph McGill Blvd.*
between Courtland and Randolph Sts.

15 e-6

UNDERGROUND ATLANTA

On this site, Atlanta was born in 1837,
with the original name of Terminus (it

was the last stop on the Western &
Atlantic rail line). Perhaps one of the
most peculiar urban sites in the U.S.,
this was originally an ordinary, street-
level commercial district. The area was
reduced to rubble during the Civil War,
then restored to commercial use by the
1890s. Underground Atlanta was born
in the 1920s, when the city built a system of viaducts to elevate the streets for
automobile traffic. The original street
level went underground, and businesses
set up new entrances on the new street
level. The lower level fell into disuse
until 1968, when it became an entertainment and dining complex, but the development soon fizzled and in 1981 it shut
down altogether. In 1989 the project
reopened, with three levels of upscale
shops and restaurants along the ornamental storefronts along the brick streets. As
a shopping and entertainment complex
Underground Atlanta still struggles, but
it remains a pleasant place to visit and
is dotted with historical markers. *50*
Upper Alabama St., Downtown, 404/523–
2311. MARTA: Five Points.

15 b-8

WEST END

Established in 1835 and incorporated
into the city in 1894, this is Atlanta's
oldest residential neighborhood. It pros-
pered in the early part of the 20th century but entered a decline during World
War II. The area began to turn around
when home buyers discovered that the
neighborhood's huge Victorian and
Craftsman-style homes, though decidedly worn at the elbows, could be
acquired and restored at bargain prices.
Lee to Langhorn Sts. between White Steet
and Westview Drive.

15 e-5

WINECOFF HOTEL

Named for its builder and owner,
William Fleming Winecoff, the hotel was
designed by William L. Stoddart and
built about 1913. It became nationally
famous for a horrendous 1946 fire that
killed 119 people (including Winecoff)
who lived in the hotel. In the wake of the
catastrophe, nationwide reforms in fire
regulations were instituted. Since then,
the building has served as a retirement
home and an office building. The two
upper floors are topped by a sharply
dentiled cornice that stands in stark
contrast to the brick below. *176*
Peachtree St., Downtown. MARTA:
Peachtree Center.

`15` b-8
WREN'S NEST
The fairy-tale look of Wren's Nest befits the former home of beloved children's book author Joel Chandler Harris, who is best known for *Uncle Remus: His Songs and Sayings*. A two-room cabin was built in 1885 and then repeatedly enlarged, so that today it is a veritable mansion. The house got its name when a bird built a nest in Harris' mailbox. Now the property of the Joel Chandler Harris Memorial Association, the house is today a museum. *See also* Architecture, *above*. *1050 Ralph David Abernathy Blvd., Atlanta, 404/753–7735. MARTA: West End.*

HISTORY MUSEUMS

`15` e-6
AFRICAN-AMERICAN PANORAMIC EXPERIENCE (APEX)
Contained within this museum is a stellar testament to black heritage. Start your visit with the introductory film, narrated by African-American celebrities, that chronicles Auburn Avenue's (*see* Sweet Auburn *in* Historic Structures & Streets, *above*) place in the history of black commerce and culture. Among other exhibits, a display of period artifacts accompanies the main lobby display on the history of slavery in the South. *135 Auburn Ave., Sweet Auburn, 404/521–APEX. $3. Tues–Sat. 10–5. MARTA: Five Points.*

`15` g-8
ATLANTA CYCLORAMA AND CIVIL WAR MUSEUM
You'll be mesmerized by the Atlanta Cyclorama, a panoramic painting depicting the 1864 Battle of Atlanta (*see* Statues, Murals & Monuments, *below*), complete with three-dimensional features and audio effects. One of Atlanta's proudest exhibits of its history, it also displays a large collection of Civil War artifacts. *800 Cherokee Ave., Grant Park, 404/624–1071 tickets, 404/658–7625 information. Adults $5, $4 senior citizens, children 6–12 $3. Open Labor Day–May, daily 9:30–4:30; June–Labor Day, daily 9:30–5:30. MARTA: King Memorial.*

`12` e-3
ATLANTA HISTORY CENTER
The Atlanta History Center is a pull-no-punches presentation of the history of this city. The good is presented with the bad, *Gone With the Wind* glamour alongside Ku Klux Klan racism. Right in the pulsing core of Buckhead, the center occupies 32 beautifully landscaped acres. On the grounds are the exquisite Swan House mansion (*see* Architecture, *above*), the Tullie-Smith Plantation, and McElreath Hall, an exhibition space and auditorium that houses the center's research library and archives. Tours are offered. *130 W. Paces Ferry Rd., Buckhead, 404/814–4000. Museum and gardens $7, each house $1. Open Mon.–Sat. 10–5:30, Sun. noon–5:30.*

`5` c-2
BULLOCH HALL
Situated on a sprawling lawn in a forested cul-de-sac is the stately Bulloch Hall, an antebellum mansion that was once the home of President Theodore Roosevelt's grandparents. Today it is the headquarters of the Roswell Historic Preservation Commission, which hosts demonstrations of old-time crafts, such as quilting and basketry, as well as historic reenactments in the magnificent home. *See also* Architecture, *above*. *180 Bulloch Ave., Roswell, 770/992–1951. $5 adults, $3 children 6–16. Open Mon.–Sat. 10–2, Sun. 1–3.*

`15` h-4
CARTER PRESIDENTIAL CENTER LIBRARY
From this hilltop, General Sherman watched the bloody Battle of Atlanta in 1864. Now the site holds an institution dedicated not only to the career and administration of President Jimmy Carter but to the issues of conflict resolution and human rights. The museum and archives are open to the public, but not the center, which sponsors foreign-affairs conferences and projects on such matters as world food supply. Designed in 1986 by Jova/Daniels/Busby with Lawton, Umemura and Yamamoto, the splendid building is set on a landscaped estate with meticulously tended Japanese-style gardens. From here you have a spectacular yet tranquil panorama of the cityscape. *One Copenhill, 441 Freedom Pkwy., Virginia-Highland, 404/331–3942. $6. Open Mon.–Sat. 9–4:45, Sun. noon–4:45.*

`14` g-3
DECATUR HISTORICAL COURTHOUSE
Built in 1823, the Old Courthouse on the Square in Decatur is now home to the

DeKalb Welcome Center. The antique log cabin stands smack in the middle of the city's central square. *101 E. Court Sq., Decatur, 404/373–1088. MARTA: Decatur.*

15 d-5
FEDERAL RESERVE BANK
This bank sits where once was Thrasherville, a settlement that predates the 1837 establishment of Atlanta. An exhibit explains the story of money as a medium of exchange and the history of the U.S. banking system. Items displayed include rare coins, uncut sheets of money, and a gold bar. There's a tour and a video, *Inside the Fed. 104 Marietta St., Downtown, 404/521–8764. Open weekdays 9–4. MARTA: Five Points.*

15 d-7
GEORGIA DEPARTMENT OF ARCHIVES AND HISTORY
A little-known treasure trove of historical information, this agency maintains a plethora of records, photographs, and letters, both official and unofficial, that date back to the Revolutionary War. The windowless fortress encompasses 85,000 cubic ft of public material, including more than 65,000 reels of microfilm. It's a genealogy buff's dream come true. *330 Capitol Ave., Downtown, 404/656–2393. Open weekdays 8–4:45, Sat. 9:30–3:15. MARTA: Garnett St.*

8 f-1
GEORGIA'S STONE MOUNTAIN PARK
One of Georgia's most famous attractions, and certainly its most popular, this 3,200-acre park is best known for the giant Confederate Memorial (*see* Statues, Murals & Monuments, *below*) carved into the side of the mountain. The park also contains a number of regional historical displays, among them the Road to Tara Museum, dedicated to everything and anything *Gone With the Wind.* At the Antebellum Plantation, more than a dozen authentic pre–Civil War buildings moved here from across the state re-create life in the Old South. The park also has three museums: Discovering Stone Mountain, chronicling the geology of the mountain and the story behind the famous carving; Confederate Hall, tracing the course of the Civil War in Georgia; and the Antique Car and Treasure Museum, featuring a selection of vintage autos, jukeboxes, and other interesting artifacts

from Georgia's past. The park offers a nightly laser show during the summer and a wide array of other events throughout the year. There's a ton of other stuff to do here, too, from riding the Stone Mountain Railroad, the Riverboat, or the Skylift to visiting the Wildlife Preserve and Petting Zoo or the Beach and Waterpark, to getting some exercise at Stone Mountain Golf Course or the International Tennis Center (*see* Chapter 3 *for all*). If you plan to visit the park several times a year, you can save on admission by purchasing the Rock, Stock, and Barrel Pass, which gives you unlimited admission (excluding golf and tennis) for a year: the pass costs $20 per person or $50 for a family of three. To save on parking fees buy the $30 Classic Rock Parking Permit for a year's worth of unlimited parking. *U.S. 78, 5 mi outside/east of I–285, Stone Mountain, 770/498–5690, www.stonemountainpark.com. Park open daily 6 AM–midnight; most attractions Sept.–May daily 10–5, Jun.–Aug. daily 10–8. Admission free; attractions $12 for Georgia residents, $15 for non-residents, parking $6.*

6 e-4
GWINNET HISTORIC COURTHOUSE
Built in 1885, this unusual example of Romanesque architecture was last an active courthouse in 1988. Now it houses the Gwinnett County Historical Society. The courthouse itself is hard to miss, occupying an entire block in the Lawrenceville town square. Dotting the property are various monuments, plus tables for picnickers and a gazebo for incurable romantics. *185 Crogin St., Lawrenceville, 770/822–5450.*

4 d-2
KENNESAW CIVIL WAR MUSEUM
Ensconced in a renovated cotton gin, this museum was built as an homage to "The General," an ancient steam locomotive stolen by Union spies during the Civil War with the intent of blasting key bridges throughout the South, and to its conductor, who relentlessly pursued the bandits on foot and by pushcart until the steam engine was recovered and the spies were captured. The adventure was the subject of two Hollywood movies, but nothing beats the real thing. The incident is depicted in a giant mural in the exhibition space (*see* Statues, Murals & Monuments, *below*). The

museum tour includes a display of war artifacts and an interesting slide show. *2829 Cherokee St., Kennesaw, 770/427–2117. Adults $3, senior citizens $2.50, children 7–15 $1.50. Open Mon.–Sat. 9:30–5:30, Sun. noon–5:30.*

15 *e-2*

MARGARET MITCHELL HOUSE & GONE WITH THE WIND MUSEUM

This shrine to Margaret Mitchell, her epic novel *Gone With the Wind,* and the classic movie based upon it, has everything except Tara itself—including the famous portrait of Vivien Leigh as Scarlet O'Hara (which Clark Gable doused with liquor in the movie). The museum documents the making of the movie, its Atlanta premiere, and the movie's impact on society. Adjacent to the museum is the house that Mitchell affectionately nicknamed "The Dump." In this tiny hovel of a habitat, the famous writer penned what is perhaps the most famous epic novel in the world. Though the original structure was all but destroyed by neglect, vandalism, and fire, it was finally restored and painstakingly refurbished with period furniture. On display are Mitchell's Remington portable typewriter as well as the Pulitzer Prize she won for the novel. *990 Peachtree St., Midtown, 404/249–7015. Adults $10, senior citizens and students $9, children 6–11 $7, free for children 5 and under. Open daily 9–5. MARTA: Midtown.*

4 *f-4*

MARIETTA MUSEUM OF HISTORY

Enclosed in a beautiful former hotel (*see* Kennesaw House *in* Historic Structures & Streets, *above*) this relative newcomer was established by volunteers who renovated the space for display. The exhibits, which chronicle the history of Marietta, were donated by long-time residents, and the collection continues to expand as new artifacts arrive. *1 Depot St., Marietta, 770/528–0431. $2. Open Tues.–Sat. 11–4.*

15 *g-6*

MARTIN LUTHER KING JR. CENTER FOR NONVIOLENT SOCIAL CHANGE

A tour of the center is essential if you are seeking to understand the Civil Rights Movement and the impact of the life of Dr. King. His widow, Coretta Scott King, established the center after his assassination in 1968. On display are personal items, such as King's Nobel Peace Prize, Bible, and tape recorder, along with memorabilia and photos chronicling the civil rights movement. The center also includes an auditorium and a gift shop. In the courtyard in front of Freedom Hall is King's white marble tomb (*see* Statues, Murals & Monuments, *below*). The surrounding portion of the Sweet Auburn neighborhood, where King was born and raised, is the Martin Luther King Jr. National Historic District, with the Martin Luther King Jr. Birth Home (*see* Historic Structures & Streets, *above, for both*). *449 Auburn Ave., Sweet Auburn, 404/524–1956. Open daily 9–5. MARTA: King Memorial.*

15 *e-1*

RHODES MEMORIAL HALL

As massive as it is curious, the castle-like mansion (*see* Architecture, *above*) built in 1904 for furniture mogul Amos G. Rhodes is as much a museum piece as the exhibits it now displays. The headquarters of the Georgia Trust for Historic Preservation, Rhodes Hall mounts exhibits on the history of Georgia architecture. Its interior is alight with nine elaborate stained-glass windows depicting scenes from the Civil War. *1516 Peachtree St., Buckhead, 404/881–9980. Adults $5, senior citizens $4, students $3. Open weekdays 11–4. MARTA: Arts Center.*

5 *h-3*

SOUTHEASTERN RAILWAY MUSEUM

A virtual Shangri-La for railway aficionados, this huge collection of period railway curios includes more than 70 vintage locomotives (both steam and diesel), passenger and freight cars, along with thousands of items of railway memorabilia. *3595 Old Peachtree Rd., Duluth, 770/476–2013. Adults $5, senior citizens and children $3. Open Sat. 10–4.*

15 *e-6*

WORLD OF COCA-COLA

It's hard to believe that a simple soft drink could launch such an imposing corporate empire, but it's true, and the World of Coca-Cola is testimony to that fact. Displays in the modern, neon-lit facility (*see* Architecture, *above*) chronicle the soft drink's rise from humble local specialty to the world's most popular refreshment. Guess how many bottles move along the bottling line, sample Coke products, and view a film. Plan on 1 to 2 hours to see everything. There also is an gift shop selling every imaginable item imprinted with the Coca-Cola logo. *55 Martin Luther King Jr. Dr., Downtown, near Underground Atlanta, 404/676–5151. Adults $6, senior citizens $4, children 6–11 $3. Open weekdays 9–5, Sun. noon–6. MARTA: Five Points.*

SCIENCE MUSEUMS

15 *g-1*

DOROTHY CHAPMAN FUQUA CONSERVATORY

Amid the lush landscape of the 30-acre Atlanta Botanical Garden (*see* Chapter 3) stands this 16,000-square-ft shimmering glass home for exotic and endangered plant specimens from around the world. The conservatory's computer-controlled atmosphere is finely tuned for the cultivation of endangered desert and tropical plants. *1345 Piedmont Ave., Midtown, 404/876–5859. Open Apr.–Oct., Tues.–Sun. 9–7; Nov.–Mar., Tues.–Sun. 9–6. Adults $6, senior citizens $5, students and children $3, children under six free. Free Thurs. 3–closing. MARTA: Arts Center.*

14 *c-3*

FERNBANK MUSEUM OF NATURAL HISTORY

Housed in an ultramodern facility, this odyssey of exhibits and galleries details every aspect of Georgia's natural resources and beauty. The center also includes an IMAX theater that for the price of a movie ticket delivers a panoramic thrill ride (*see also* Children's Museums, *above*). *767 Clifton Rd., Emory, 404/370–0960, 404/370–0019 (IMAX). Museum $9.50, IMAX $7.50, combined $14.50. Open Mon.–Sat. 10–5 (Fri. IMAX 10–9), Sun. noon–5.*

14 *e-3*

FERNBANK SCIENCE CENTER

A dream come true for celestial enthusiasts, the Fernbank Science Center proudly houses one of the largest planetariums in the country. On clear nights you can climb to the observatory and peer through its colossal telescope at the zillions of stars shimmering light-years away. An astronomer is on duty to help you identify celestial phenomena (*see also* Children's Museums, *above*). *156 Heaton Park Dr., 404/378–4311. Gen-*

eral admission free. Planetarium show adults $2, students and children $1. Open Mon. 8:30–5, Tues.–Fri. 8:30 AM–10 PM, Sat. 10–5, Sun. 1–5.

15 *e-5*

SCITREK

Packed with 100 creative exhibits, it's no wonder this ranks among the top science museums in the country. The 96,000-square-ft facility is overflowing with innovative, hands-on introductions to all kinds of technology, such as multimedia and the Internet. The interactive excitement makes science anything but dull. *See also* Children's Museums, *above. 395 Piedmont Ave., Downtown, 404/522–5500. Adults $7.50; senior citizens and children $5. Open Mon.–Sat. 10–5, Sun. noon–5. MARTA: Civic Center.*

STATUES, MURALS & MONUMENTS

15 *g-8*

ATLANTA CYCLORAMA

This creation has got to be seen to be believed. A huge, circular panoramic painting—the largest of its kind in the world—forever freezes in vivid color the calamitous 1864 Battle of Atlanta. The oil painting, created in 1885 by a team of German artists, is almost six stories high, 358 ft in circumference, and weighs almost 9,400 pounds. It is enclosed in a colossal, intricately designed exhibit space (*see* History Museums, *above*). *800 Cherokee Ave., Grant Park, 404/624–1071 tickets, 404/658–7625 information. Adults $5, senior citizens $4, children 6–12 $3. Open Labor Day–May, daily 9:30–4:30; June–Labor Day, daily 9:30–5:30. MARTA: King Memorial.*

15 *e-6*

ATLANTA FROM THE ASHES

A stunning civic renovation that injects vitality into a formerly blighted section of Downtown, Robert W. Woodruff Memorial Park is a tiny oasis amid bustling Little Five Points. At the southern entrance stands a blackened-bronze sculpture by Italian artist Gambro Quirino. Liberty, in the form of a woman, frees a captive bird, the mythical phoenix that rose from the ashes of its own destruction and is the symbol of Atlanta's rebirth after the infernos of the Civil War. *Peachtree St. between Edge-*

wood and Auburn Aves., Downtown. MARTA: Five Points.

15 *e-5*

CANDLER BUILDING

The exterior of this 17-story office building built by Coca-Cola founder Asa Candler (*see* Architecture, *above*) is encrusted with bas-relief medallion sculptures of famous men. Buffalo Bill Cody, William Shakespeare, Italian Renaissance painter Raphael, and industrialist Cyrus McCormick are among those depicted. *127 Peachtree St., Downtown. MARTA: Peachtree Center.*

15 *d-5*

CENTENNIAL OLYMPIC PARK

A legacy of the 1996 Olympic Games (*see* Historic Structures & Streets, *above*), this sprawling, urban green space is dotted with commemorative sculptures. The locally famous Rings Fountain sprays water in the shape of the Olympic Rings and is a popular frolicking spot in the summer months. *Marietta St. at International Blvd., Downtown. MARTA: Omni/Dome/GWCC.*

7 *g-6*

CONCOURSE E, HARTSFIELD ATLANTA INTERNATIONAL AIRPORT

In anticipation of the 1996 Olympic Games, a large group of southern artists were commissioned to create permanent works for this airport concourse. The results are spectacular, reflecting whimsy and innovation with a distinctive folk-art flair. *Concourse E, Hartsfield Atlanta International Airport, I–85 at Camp Creek Pkwy. MARTA: Airport.*

8 *f-1*

CONFEDERATE MEMORIAL

Hewn into the side of the promontory that gives Stone Mountain Park (*see* History Museums, *above*) its name, this staggering bas-relief is 90 ft high and 190 ft wide, making it the largest sculpture of its kind on earth. The monument to Confederate leaders depicts Jefferson Davis, Stonewall Jackson, and Robert E. Lee, all on horseback. Work on the carving began in 1912 and was finished 50 years later. To celebrate its unveiling, 20 prominent guests were treated to a formal lunch on General Lee's shoulder. *U.S. 78, 5 mi outside/east of I–285, Stone Mountain, 770/498–5690, www. stonemountainpark.com. Park open daily*

6 AM–midnight; most attractions Sept.– May daily 10–5; June–Aug. daily 10–8. Admission free; attractions $12 for Georgia residents, $15 for non-residents, parking $6.

15 *e-5*

FOLK ART PARK

This formerly prosaic intersection on one of the city's busiest streets is now animated with colorful whirligigs and other sculptures. Part of Atlanta's sprucing-up before the 1996 Centennial Olympic Games, the permanent display incorporates the diverse styles of a dozen American (mostly southern) folk artists. Passersby can enjoy a moment of beauty and whimsy at any time of day; indeed, in some ways nighttime is the best time to view the display, for traffic is not so hectic. *Ralph McGill Blvd. at Courtland St., Baker St., and Piedmont Ave., Downtown. MARTA: Civic Center.*

15 *e-7*

GEORGIA STATE CAPITOL

On the manicured grounds of the Georgia State Capitol (*see* Architecture, *above*), amid lush oak and magnolia trees, is a collection of statues and monuments depicting everyone from Confederate general John B. Gordon (mounted on his horse) to Georgians who fought in the Spanish-American, Korean, and Vietnam wars. Among others honored are Civil War–era Governor Joseph Brown and his wife, Elizabeth; President Jimmy Carter (depicted as a peanut farmer, with his sleeves rolled up); the late senator Richard B. Russell, and the 33 black legislators who were expelled from the State House in 1868. You'll also find the "Statue of Liberty," donated by Boy Scouts in 1951. *206 Washington St., Downtown, 404/656–2844. Free. Open weekdays 8–5, Sat. 10–4, Sun. noon–4. MARTA: Georgia State.*

15 *e-6*

HENRY GRADY STATUE

New York sculptor Alexander Doyle honored this visionary editor of the Atlanta Constitution, who called himself a booster of the post–Civil War New South in this bronze piece that adorns Marietta Street in front of the newspaper's offices. In some ways Grady, a baseball fanatic, was a precursor to Ted Turner. Grady died of pneumonia in 1891 after giving his famous New South speech in Boston. *Corner of Marietta and Forsyth Sts., Downtown. MARTA: Five Points.*

14 b-8

JESSE PARKER WILLIAMS MEMORIAL

This piece of marble funerary art by Daniel Chester French (*see also* Samuel Spence Statue, *below*) represents an angel striding outward, away from the grave. It was erected in the early 20th century on the grave of Williams and his wife, Cora Beth Taylor. *Westview Cemetery, Section 5, Lot 21, 1680 Westview Dr., West End, 404/755–6611. MARTA: West Lake.*

15 g-5

JOHN WESLEY DOBBS PLAZA

Built as part of the effort to improve Atlanta's streets for the 1996 Centennial Olympic Games, the plaza is dominated by a life mask of John Wesley Dobbs, grandfather to Atlanta's first African-American mayor, Maynard Jackson. By looking through the eyes of the mask, visitors get a vision of Auburn Avenue, where Dobbs played a major role in the rise of Atlanta's Black Wall Street. Happily, the plaza has dressed up a formerly scruffy corner near the I–75/85 overpass. *Auburn Ave. adjacent to I–75/85 overpass, Sweet Auburn. MARTA: King Memorial.*

4 e-2

KENNESAW CIVIL WAR MUSEUM

The famous Civil War locomotive "The General" is not the only attraction here (*see* History Museums, *above*). Also of note is the huge mural that covers two entire walls of the large exhibit space. Finished just a few years ago by local artist Terry Buchanan, the panoramic painting depicts a railway station from the Civil War era, with the Union spies who became notorious for stealing the massive locomotive, and the determined conductor who pursued them until "The General" was retrieved and the culprits punished. *2829 Cherokee St., Kennesaw, 770/427–2117. Adults $3, senior citizens $2.50, children 7–15 $1.50. Open Mon.–Sat. 9:30–5:30, Sun. noon–5:30.*

15 g-6

MARTIN LUTHER KING JR. TOMB AND PEACE PAVILION

At the Martin Luther King Jr. Center for Nonviolent Social Change (*see* History Museums, *above*), an eternal flame blazes in the plaza in front of Freedom Hall, before the Meditation Pool. King's tomb rises from the pool on a circular brick pad and bears the inscription FREE

AT LAST! A chapel of all faiths stands at one end of the reflecting pool. Nearby, on the manicured grounds of the Peace Pavilion, King's vision of the future is represented in *Behold*, a statue of a black man raising a child above his head. *449 Auburn Ave., Sweet Auburn, 404/526–8900. Free. Open daily 9–5. MARTA: King Memorial.*

15 g-7

OAKLAND CEMETERY

Among the ornate funerary pieces, headstones, and mausoleums here is the striking *Lion of Atlanta*, a reproduction of the *Lion of Lucerne* memorial in Lucerne, Switzerland, to the soldiers who died there. Carved in 1896 from a single solid slab of marble, this lordly mane-ruffed beast honors the scores of Rebel soldiers who died in the Battle of Atlanta in 1864 and were laid to rest here in minimally marked graves (*see* Graveyards & Cemeteries *and* Haunted Places, *above*). *248 Oakland Ave., Downtown, 404/688–2107. Open daily 8–6 Oct.–Apr., 8–7 Apr.–Oct. MARTA: King Memorial.*

15 e-8

OLYMPIC CAULDRON

Iranian-born American sculptor Cisiah Armajani was chosen to design the cauldron to hold the Olympic Flame for the 1996 Centennial Olympic Games. The sculpture stands close to its original position, near Turner Field. *I–75/85, exit 91 (Fulton St.); I–20 westbound, exit 24 (Capitol Ave.); or I–20 eastbound exit 22 (Windsor St./Spring St.): Fulton St. at Capitol Ave., Downtown, 404/522–7630. MARTA: Georgia State.*

15 e-4

SAMUEL SPENCE STATUE

American sculptor Daniel Chester French (*see also* Jesse Parker Williams Memorial, *above*) created this sculpture just before designing the Lincoln Memorial, and Spence's seated posture echoes the motif of that more famous monument. A gift to the citizens of Atlanta and Georgia, the likeness of the mayor of Atlanta and president of Southern Railroad was commissioned and paid for by company employees. In a peculiar twist of fate, Spence was killed in 1906 in a train wreck on his own railway. The sculpture, dedicated in 1910, sits on its original marble pedestal in the north end of Hardy Ivy Park, illuminated by the original gas lamps, now rewired for electricity. *Porter*

*Pl. at W. Peachtree St., Downtown, 404/
766–9049. MARTA: North Ave.*

4 f-6

SUMMITVIEW MURAL
The mural in Marietta's 1848 House
restaurant (*see* Haunted Places, *above*)
provides patrons a delightful glimpse of
the community as it appeared before the
calamitous destruction of the Civil War.
*780 S. Cobb Dr., Marietta, 770/428–1848.
Tues.–Sat. dinner only, Sun, brunch only,
closed Mon.*

chapter 5

ARTS, ENTERTAINMENT & NIGHTLIFE

Atlantans of all ages and interests can find countless ways to entertain themselves during a night on the town, all over town. Whether you want to relax with a little chamber music or groove to some jazz, take in a ballet or head out for some two-stepping, play the mating game at a cocktail lounge or throw some darts in a pub, metro Atlanta will deliver a good time.

A true New South cultural center, Atlanta has its own opera company and is home to the country's oldest ballet company. The Atlanta Symphony Orchestra, now more than half a century old and with numerous Grammy Awards to its credit, performs at the Woodruff Arts Center. Perhaps because of the long-time influence of the late Robert Shaw, under whom the symphony achieved international acclaim, Atlanta has become famous for its choral groups, including the symphony's own chorale. Area theaters present all kinds of drama, from the classics to new experimental works. You can see a Shakespeare play in a tavern or attend a black-tie premiere of a new Pinter production, and you can take the kids to a puppet show or the in-laws to a musical revival.

Outside the concert hall and theater, metro Atlanta sizzles with even more music and entertainment. This is a music-driven town where blues and jazz rule but rock and other forms of contemporary music abound as well. Nationally recognized musicians like the Indigo Girls live here (in Decatur), and thousands of lesser-known and up-and-coming performers hail from the 10 counties. Others arrive from all over the world, as well as from Georgia towns like Athens and Macon, which rank as musical centers in their own right. Wherever they come from, these crooners and rappers fill Atlanta's clubs with all kinds of music, every day of the week. You can find music in every neighborhood, though Midtown and Buckhead are the hottest spots. Dance clubs and trendy bars keep Midtown and

Buckhead lively into the wee hours, but you don't have to set foot there to find a great place to have a latte or a chardonnay. And if a pint or the game is more your speed, metro Atlanta has no shortage of hangouts to suit your mood.

performing arts

For information on the fine arts, see Art Events, Art Galleries, Art Museums, and Art Tours in Chapter 4.

PERFORMANCE VENUES

15 *f-4*

ATLANTA CIVIC CENTER

Each year, the Atlanta Civic Center hosts myriad arts performances and first-class touring shows, such as Riverdance. Its elegant, 4,600-seat auditorium, beautifully lit with chandeliers, is used by many different Atlanta-area groups for arts-, church-, and education-related events. Although still not all they should be, the acoustics have been improved and upgraded in recent years. 395 Piedmont Ave., Midtown, 404/523–6275, www.atlanta.org/dept/prca/civicctr/civicctr.htm, MARTA: Civic Center.

5 *b-6*

CHASTAIN PARK AMPHITHEATRE

Chastain's unique 7,000-seat facility attracts renowned performers from every musical genre, whether it's Willy Nelson, Al Jarreau, the Beach Boys, or the Atlanta Symphony Orchestra. Enthusiastic audience members frequently indulge in elaborate alfresco meals during shows (except, of course, at some rock concerts). A festive mood takes hold in the amphitheater as music lovers open picnic baskets, set small tables with lacy tablecloths, pour wine or cocktails, and light candles. Some even cook fancy dinners on tabletop grills prior to the show. Unfortunately, some audience members are more interested in their table conversation than in the performance, interfering with the pleasure of those who want to hear the music. Performers complain, too, but they keep signing on. This is a great spot for the 4th of July, when there's a fireworks display and usually a performance by the Atlanta Symphony Orchestra. *135 W. Wieuca Rd., Buckhead, 404/233–2227 (box office), www.atlanta-concerts.com.*

14 b-3

CALLENWOLDE FINE ARTS CENTER

This early 20th-century Tudor-style mansion, with its own built-in organ, was built for Charles Candler, son of Coca-Cola Company founder Asa G. Candler. It serves as a performance venue for DeKalb County, and as such showcases recitals, choral presentations, and opera performances by the Capitol City Opera Company (*see* Opera, *below*). There also is an art gallery (*see* Chapter 4). *980 Briarlcliff Rd., Druid Hills, 404/872–5338, www.callanwolde.org.*

4 f-5

COBB COUNTY CIVIC CENTER

Two buildings house a performing arts theater where the Georgia Ballet, the Cobb Symphony (*both below*), and visiting musical organizations perform. The center also has an exhibition hall that's mostly devoted to trade shows and concerts, but that sometimes hosts pop, rock, and gospel concerts, and other performances for large audiences. The theater seats 606, and the exhibition hall accommodates 3,000. Ticket prices run $15–$30, depending on the performance. *545 S. Marietta Pkwy., Marietta, 770/528–8450. www.co.cobb.ga.us.*

15 e-5

COTTON CLUB

A wide, shallow room with two balconies lets you get close to the stage at this small concert space, where you can hear all kinds of live music—everything short of classical, from Latin, jazz, and alternative to rock, pop, and heavy metal. Major national talent (Johnny Cash, Morphine, Lenny Kravitz), smaller national acts (Luscious Jackson, Lit, The Marvelous Three), and regional and local bands play here, and surprise guests sometimes perform impromptu sets. Four bars and an excellent sound and lighting system keep the party going. Tickets run $5–$15. Some shows require patrons be over 18, and you must present photo ID at all times. Cotton Club occupies the space below The Tabernacle (*below*). *152 Luckie St., Downtown, 404/688–1193.*

14 d-1

EMORY UNIVERSITY

Musical artists from all over the world come to Emory each season to participate in jazz, classical, choral, and theatrical performances, and the university's theater, music, and dance departments mount sophisticated productions. All this activity takes place in several on-campus venues. Glenn Memorial Auditorium (1652 N. Decatur Rd.), in a campus church, is where world-renowned soprano and Mozart specialist Cecilia Bartoli gave her sold-out Atlanta debut in 1995. Cannon Chapel (515 Kilgo Cir.) is a small venue perfect for chamber concerts, and the Performing Arts Studio (1804 N. Decatur Rd.) seats 200–250. The Mary Gray Munroe Theater in Dobbs University Center (605 Asbury Cir.) showcases classical and contemporary theater, as well as dance performances. Film screenings, including those of the Silent Film Society of Atlanta (*see* Film, *below*) take place in White Hall (480 Kilgo Cir.), which is equipped with state-of-the-art equipment. *1380 S. Oxford Rd., Decatur, 404/727–5050 box office, www.emory.edu/ARTS.*

15 f-2

14TH STREET PLAYHOUSE

This three-theater complex, part of the Woodruff Arts Center (*below*), is a locus of diversity and innovation in Atlanta theater. Many respected local performing-arts groups work here, including the theater's resident companies: Art Within (770/585–8804), a dance company; Capitol City Opera Company (*see* Opera, *below*); Jewish Theatre of the South (770/368–7469); Jomandi Productions (*see* Theaters & Theater Companies, *below*); multiShades Atlanta (404/377–8158 or 800/861–4952), a woman-focused multimedia group that blends film and theater; Onstage Atlanta; and Theatre Gael (*see* Theaters & Theater Companies, *below*). The Playhouse also houses the offices of the Atlanta Coalition of Theatres (404/873–1185), Georgia Citizens for the Arts (404/875–1420), and Not Merely Players (404/872–8940), an arts organization for people with disabilities. *173 14th St., Midtown, 404/733–4750 (box office), 404/733–4754 (administrative offices), www.14thstreet.org. MARTA: Arts Center.*

15 *e-4*

FOX THEATRE

The only word for the Fox Theatre is . . . breathtaking. This opulent landmark was originally the Yaarab Temple Shrine Mosque, designed in the late 1920s for the Shriner's organization. Its auditorium has a grand stage that hosts everything from concerts, recitals, and opera to movie premieres and Broadway shows. The splendid Egyptian Ballroom and the Grand Salon are lavishly decorated event facilities equipped for catering and entertaining. The Atlanta Preservation Center conducts tours of the Fox (*see* Chapter 4). *660 Peachtree St., Midtown, 404/881–2100 box office. MARTA: North Avenue.*

9 *b-6*

FREDERICK BROWN JR. AMPHITHEATRE

Seating about 2,000, this bowl nestled in a wooded setting hosts a wide variety of performances, from pops to contemporary music to drum-and-fife concerts. This is south metro's second-most popular and second-largest outdoor performance venue after Lakewood (*below*). Tickets to most events here cost about $21, plus a $3 handling fee. *205 McIntosh Trail, Peachtree City, 770/631–0630.*

6 *b-3*

GWINNETT CIVIC AND CULTURAL CENTER

A quality arts venue in the northeast metro area, the Civic Center hosts trade and commercial exhibitions, while the Performing Arts Center hosts a variety of performing arts events, ranging from the likes of Trisha Yearwood to the Boston Ballet. It's home to the Gwinnett Philharmonic, and the Gwinnett Ballet also performs there. Seating 700, the theater features state-of-the-art equipment including excellent stage lighting and a Wenger orchestra shell. It's located on the same property as the Children's Arts Museum (*see* Chapter 4), devoted to introducing the performing and visual arts to children. The adjacent Fine Arts Center (*see* Chapter 4) features gallery spaces with continuous visual arts programming, two art gift shops, and a large outdoor sculpture garden. These last two nonprofit entities together have been named the Jacqueline Casey Hudgens Center for the Arts (770/623–6002). *6400 Sugarloaf Pkwy., Duluth, 770/623–4966; ext. 3 for box office.*

4 *f-4*

THE HANGER

Built in 1930s, this Art Deco theater-cum-bar has a raised stage, theater seating in the balcony, and some tables and an open dance floor in front of the stage. It's a venue for name bands of local, regional, and national origin. A variety of musical styles are featured, including folk, acoustic, rock, pop, and R&B. Equipped with a full bar, the Hanger has huge audience capacity of 2,200. It's open Wednesday–Saturday; shows begin around 8 PM and run until 1 AM. Cover varies depending on the show, but usually runs around $6. *117 North Park Sq., Marietta, 770/424–9711.*

4 *e-2*

HOWARD LOGAN STILLWELL THEATER

In 1990, Kennesaw State University built this intimate 321-seat theater as a venue for college- and community-based artists as well as visiting stars, such as operatic soprano Marilyn Horne and jazz pianist Marian McPartland. Home to the Cobb Symphony Orchestra (*below*), the theater also hosts Classic Theatreworks, the university's theatrical group. The Kennesaw Jazz Ensemble, composed of students and local musicians, performs here, usually twice a semester. Admission to most music events at the theater is free, but some special events, such as the Premier Series, in which well-known stars from various musical genres perform throughout the academic year, cost $25–$30. Theater events usually cost $10. *3455 Frey Lake Rd., Kennesaw, 770/423–6151.*

7 *h-4*

LAKEWOOD AMPHITHEATRE

Pops, rock, blues, country, and gospel come to this venue, which seats about 20,000. The acoustics are good and the reserved seating is fairly comfortable. Unlike at Chastain Park, food may not be brought in, but you can buy it here, and tailgating is permitted. There's a MARTA stop here, but parking is available on site. *2002 Lakewood Way, south metro, 404/627–5700, MARTA: Lakewood.*

15 *d-6*

RIALTO CENTER FOR THE PERFORMING ARTS

This well-equipped and acoustically superb space is the home stage of the Georgia State University School of Music. In the center, downtown Atlanta

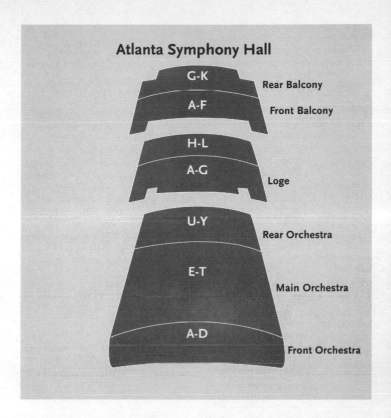

Atlanta Symphony Hall

G-K — Rear Balcony

A-F — Front Balcony

H-L

A-G — Loge

U-Y — Rear Orchestra

E-T — Main Orchestra

A-D — Front Orchestra

has a first-class performance venue for jazz, blues, rock, and classical musicians; local and national dance companies; and theatrical troupes. The 900-seat facility, in the historic Fairlie-Poplar district, was created from the old Rialto movie theater, which in turn was a conversion of a theater built in 1916. *80 Forsyth St., Downtown, 404/651–4727. MARTA: Five Points.*

15 *c-3*

ROBERT FERST CENTER FOR THE ARTS AT GEORGIA TECH

On the Georgia Tech campus is a 1,200-seat performing arts center that brings renowned classical musicians, dancers, and vocalists to Midtown. Named for its benefactor, who was a major contributor to Georgia Tech, the center also houses galleries and a student-run theater. *349 Ferst Dr., Georgia Institute of Technology, Midtown, 404/894–9600.*

15 *e-2*

ROBERT W. WOODRUFF ARTS CENTER

The venue for Atlanta's best theater, music, and art, this is the home of the

Atlanta Symphony Orchestra and the Alliance Theatre Company (*both below*), as well as to the High Museum of Art and the Atlanta College of Art (*see* Chapter 4). Symphony Hall, where performances take place, seats close to 1,800; wheelchair and companion seats are also available. The center also houses ample public rehearsal and studio space, and 34,000 square ft of convention space. Home to nine resident companies, the 14th Street Playhouse (*above*) is also part of Woodruff. *1280 Peachtree St., Midtown, 404/733–5000, www.woodruff-arts.org., MARTA: Arts Center Station.*

5 *c-2*

ROSWELL CULTURAL ARTS CENTER

The Roswell Lyric Opera Company (*see Opera, below*) performs at this intimate suburban theater, which seats 600 in an orchestra-plus-balcony configuration. Another resident company, the Georgia Ensemble Theater (*see* Theaters & Theater Companies, *below*) , is a professional mainstage theater company that offers adult and youth conservatory programs. Orchestra Atlanta, an amateur 63-musician orchestra, also performs here. The community makes extensive use of this facility for high school graduations, dance recitals, and concerts. *950 Forrest St., Roswell, 770/594–6343.*

12 *f-3*

THE ROXY

Buckhead's Roxy, formerly a movie theater, is the scene of rock, pop, blues, jazz, folk, reggae, and other concerts. Audiences in the small, intimate setting have a good view of the stage from any seat in the house. Nearby, you'll find the liveliest nightspots in Buckhead. Elton John, a part-time Atlanta resident, sometimes performs here for the hometown crowd. *3810 Roswell Rd., Buckhead, 404/231–5811.*

8 *b-7*

SPIVEY HALL

With cathedral ceilings and wonderful acoustics (designed by Rein Pirn of Boston), this is an ideal venue for small concerto groups and individual performers. The centerpiece of the elegant 400-seat hall is the Albert Schweitzer Memorial Organ, a 4,413-pipe, three manual, 79-rank wonder with accents of marble and gold leaf. Nationally and internationally renowned artists, primarily small orchestral groups and individual classical music performers, appear here. *N. Lee St., off Clayton State Blvd. (at Clayton State College and University), Morrow, 770/961–3683, www.spiveyhall. org.*

15 *e-5*

TABERNACLE

This huge, five-level hall showcases top local bands as well as national acts. The former church was rehabbed into a performance venue before the 1996 Olympics; the Cotton Club (*above*) is located downstairs. Tabernacle offers everything from Memphis blues to hardcore rock and roll. Acts and show times vary from day to day, so call for information. The club is usually open 7 PM until the music stops, with some snack food available, although a restaurant is being contemplated. Covers vary widely depending on the band; $15–$40 is the usual range. *152 Luckie St., Downtown, 404/659–9022.*

14 *a-5*

VARIETY PLAYHOUSE

Concerts of all kinds, from Cajun and Celtic to jazz, rock, and blues, draw massive crowds to this small theater, so advance planning and early arrival are essential if you want a seat at an event here. A bit worn about the edges, the theater is nonetheless popular with audiences and entertainers alike. Recent shows have featured artists such as pianists Joe Sample and Herbie Hancock, flamenco guitarist Ottmar Liebert, traditional Irish musicians Tommy Makem and the Clancy Brothers, and blues guitarist Tinsley Ellis. You can buy snacks, beer, and wine at the small bar and, if you're lucky, grab one of the tables along the sides of the room. *1099 Euclid Ave., Little Five Points, 404/524–7354.*

CONCERTS IN CHURCHES

12 *e-4*

CATHEDRAL OF ST. PHILIP

The neo-Gothic seat of the Episcopal archdiocese of Atlanta is a frequent setting for concerts associated with religious seasons. An ongoing concert series includes free concerts, such as organ recitals or choral presentations, on Sunday afternoons, followed by an evensong that features the cathedral's Choral Scholars. Other concerts are ticketed and cost $10–$20. Among the artists who have appeared here recently are the Baltimore Consort and the Anonymous Four. *2744 Peachtree Rd., Buckhead, 404/365–1000.*

5 *e-6*

EMBRY HILLS UNITED METHODIST CHURCH

The Sacred and Performing Arts Series here features the church's choir as well as other artists. Acoustics are excellent. Frequent performances are given by the Atlanta Baroque Orchestra (*see Orchestras & Ensembles, below*), sometimes with name guest performers. Ticket prices range from free to about $15. *3404 Henderson Mill Rd., Chamblee, 770/939–6036.*

5 *c-5*

LUTHERAN CHURCH OF THE APOSTLES

At special events and concerts, the Chancel Choir, the New Life Singers, and the Bell Choir perform traditional and inspiring Christian music. Visiting performers, such as Appalachian storytellers and musicians, Harmony—The Atlanta International Youth Choir, the Atlanta Singers, and the National Lutheran Choir have been featured recently. The church also holds an annual Scandinavian musical festival the first Sunday in May. Many church members are professional or semi-professional musicians, and the Members Recital, usually held the last Sunday before Lent, is a fun "Preludes, Pipes and Pizza" evening. Most concerts are free. *6025 Glenridge Dr., Sandy Springs, 404/255–8668.*

5 *c-2*

ROSWELL UNITED METHODIST CHURCH

A variety of musical groups—classical and jazz, from professional and amateur—fill the sanctuary throughout the year. Sounds of the Spirit, the church's resident concert series, presents about a half dozen different concerts annually. Festival of Keyboards (four grand pianos), the Atlanta Wind Symphony (playing sacred and popular traditional music), the church choir (which has performed at Carnegie Hall), and Christian vocalists fill the bill. A donation is requested. *814 Mimosa Blvd., Roswell, 770/594–0412 (music office), www. rumc.com.*

DANCE

companies

5 *b-8*

ATLANTA BALLET

Founded seven decades ago by the extraordinary Dorothy Alexander, this is the oldest continuously operating dance company in the nation. Since taking over as artistic director in November 1994, John McFall has presented four world premieres to Atlanta. An exciting addition to the ballet is the Centre for Dance Education, which instructs youths and adults alike in ballet, jazz, modern, flamenco, hip-hop, yoga, tai chi, and other creative movement. *1400 W. Peachtree St., Midtown, 404/873–5811; Centre for Dance Education, 4279 Roswell Rd., Chastain Square, Sandy Springs, 404/ 892–3303.*

5 *e-3*

ATLANTA DANCE UNLIMITED

The company presents ballet, jazz, and tap at festivals and at venues throughout Atlanta, usually the 14th Street Playhouse in Midtown (*see* Performance Venues, *above*). World-class choreographers from around the United States create arrangements for ADU, which is the performance arm of the Dancer's Studio/Backstage. *8560 Holcomb Bridge Rd., Suite 118, Alpharetta, 770/993–2623.*

7 *f-5*

BALLETHNIC DANCE COMPANY

The Ballethnic blends traditional ballet with ethnic influences, particularly African-American, to create exciting and unique performances. Founded in 1990 by dancers Nena Gibreath and Waverly Lucas of the Dance Theatre of Harlem and Atlanta Ballet, it is Atlanta's first and only professional black ballet company. The company performs at the Rialto Center and the Robert Ferst Center for the Arts (*see* Performance Venues, *above*, for both), and elsewhere. It also offers classes through the Ballethnic Academy. *2587 Cheney St., East Point, 404/762–1416.*

4 *f-4*

GEORGIA BALLET

Founded in Marietta in the 1960s, the company brings together dancers acclaimed at the local, regional, and national levels. Performances are usually held at the Cobb County Civic Center (*see* Performance Venues, *above*). Georgia Ballet's outreach programs aim to expose children of the Atlanta area to the magic of ballet. *31 Atlanta St., 3rd floor, Marietta, 770/425–0258, www. georgiaballet@simplenet.com.*

6 *c-7*

GWINNETT BALLET THEATRE

Artistic Director Lisa Sheppard leads a nonprofit dance troupe and ballet school. Performances are at the Gwinnett Civic and Cultural Center (*see* Performance Venues, *above*). *2204 Fountain Square, Snellville, 770/978–0188.*

15 *h-8*

MOVING IN THE SPIRIT

Operating on the principle that the universal language of dance can break down racial, ethnic, and cultural barriers in order to teach values and life skills, MITS sponsors programs for metro Atlanta youth in schools, public housing, inner-city shelters, and community centers. Its powerful and enlightening performances combine the expertise of professional choreographers and dancers with the hard work and enthusiasm of the young students. MITS presents new work, and sometimes classics, at their own community theater, called the Beam, and at eight other community facilities. Admission to these events is by donation. *750 Glenwood Ave., Grant Park, 404/627–4304.*

15 *f-2*

SEVERAL DANCERS CORE

This professional dance organization performs experimental, contemporary dance, and movement with an innovative and creative approach. Founded in 1980, the group operates in Houston as well as Atlanta. Through special projects, called CORE Initiatives, it collaborates with other arts and social service organizations; the resulting network of shared resources helps the groups to reach a culturally and ethnically diverse audience. Performances are at the 14th Street Playhouse (*see* Performance Venues, *above*). *Box 2045, Decatur 30031, 404/373–4154.*

FILM

*film programs
& theaters of note*

15 *e-6*

CINEFEST

This Georgia State University film society treats fellow students and other Atlanta residents to fascinating documentaries, black-and-white classics, and independent films that they might not be able to view anywhere else in the metro area. A nominal admission is charged for the screenings in the University Center Building. *66 Collins St., at Decatur St., Georgia State University, Downtown, 404/651–2463. MARTA: Georgia State University station.*

15 *f-2*

GOETHE INSTITUTE ATLANTA

The institute presents classic and contemporary German films, sometimes in English, sometimes in German with subtitles. Free for members, screenings are open to the public ($4); the program runs fall–spring in the institute's auditorium. *400 Colony Sq., Midtown, 404/892–2388. MARTA: Arts Center.*

15 *e-2*

HIGH MUSEUM FILM SCREENINGS

Year-round, the museum exhibits films of artistic merit. The program, which includes recent independents, classics, and foreign-language films, is screened in the Rich Auditorium of the Woodruff Arts Center (*see* Performance Venues, *above*). Students and senior citizens receive a discount of $1 off the $5 general admission. *1280 Peachtree St., Woodruff Arts Center, Midtown, 404/733–4570. MARTA: Arts Center.*

12 *d-7*

IMAGE FILM/VIDEO CENTER AT THE TULA ARTS CENTER

IMAGE (Independent Media Artists of Georgia, Etc.) is one of the most respected non-profit media arts centers in the nation. Its mission is to enhance public awareness of film and video as art forms and to promote the cinematic arts by supporting independent media artists in the production and exhibition of films and videos. It thus presents a great deal of offbeat and experimental material that otherwise might not find an audience. Screenings are held at various venues around Atlanta. Tickets generally cost $3–$6. *75 Bennett St., Buckhead, 404/352–4225 or 404/351–3551, www.imagefv.org.*

12 *f-4*

LEFONT GARDEN HILLS CINEMA

Lefont exhibits classic and fine contemporary films, both American and foreign. The consistently high quality of its presentations makes the cinema popular with Atlanta's film buffs. In the small and intimate theater, audiences tend to mind their manners and watch the film, keeping conversation to a minimum. *2835 Peachtree Rd., Buckhead, 404/266–2202.*

14 *a-8*

MEDIAHEAD

MediaHead meets the first Monday of every month to exhibit and discuss out-of-the-ordinary films by local artists and national names. The group is composed of metro-area film and video artists interested in making contact with other members of the media arts community. Open to the general public, screenings are held at the Fountainhead Lounge (see Bars & Lounges, below) at 8:30 PM, and admission is free. *Fountainhead Lounge, 485 Flat Shoals Ave., East Atlanta Village, 404/522–7841.*

5 *c-4*

NORTH SPRINGS CINEMA GRILL

Patrons savor entrées, appetizers, beer, and wine along with second-run films, all at a very reasonable price. Admission is only $2, and dinner entrées are under $10. In addition to good movies, ample leg room and swivel chairs make for a comfortable and entertaining evening. *7270 Roswell Rd., Sandy Springs, 770/ 395–0724.*

THE SILENT FILM SOCIETY OF ATLANTA

The SFSA celebrates the silent years of Hollywood cinema, affording Atlanta audiences the opportunity to see wonderful films that might otherwise be buried and forgotten. The monthly screenings open with an introduction by Bill Eggert, who launched the organization in 1990. The introductions give background not only on the film being shown but on the first 30 years of filmmaking. The society exhibits films at various locations, including Emory University's White Hall (see Performance Venues, above), and hosts an annual festival of silent films. *Box 25435, Atlanta 30322, 404/885–1787.*

festivals & special events

15 *c-6*

AFRICAN FILM FESTIVAL

Clark Atlanta University presents this April homage to African filmmaking, with screenings of such films as Charles Burnett's *To Sleep With Anger* and Haile Gerima's *Sankofa*. Screenings conclude with panel discussions by notable local and international filmmakers. *Clark Atlanta University, 223 James P. Brawley Dr., 404/880–6143.*

THE ATLANTA FILM & VIDEO FESTIVAL

Since 1976 the festival has presented original, innovative works by contemporary independent media makers, with an emphasis on the work of southeastern media artists. More than 150 films are screened each May, over a nine-day period at various venues throughout the metro Atlanta area. Tickets cost $5–$15. *75 Bennett St., Suite N-1, Atlanta, 30309, 404/352–4254, www.imagefv.org.*

15 *e-2*

LATIN AMERICAN FILM FESTIVAL

This much-anticipated annual film festival is produced by the Latin American Art Circle of the High Museum of Art. Film students and other aficionados flock to the screenings, which are often followed by receptions attended by the actors and filmmakers. *404/733–4570.*

12 *d-7*

OUT ON FILM: THE ATLANTA GAY & LESBIAN FILM FESTIVAL

Begun in 1987, the festival brings to the screen films and videos featuring drama and suspense, romance and action. Each October over a four-day period, the festival holds screenings at AMC Phipps Plaza Theaters. Admission ranges from $5 to $10. *75 Bennett St., Suite N-1, Atlanta 30309, 404/352–4254, www. imagefv.org.*

14 *d-1*

SILENT HEAVEN

Named in honor of the silent film *Seventh Heaven* (1927), the festival runs on varying dates from year to year. Co-sponsored by Emory University's film studies department, the festival screens silent classics at White Hall on the Emory University campus (see Performance Venues, above). Admission is free. *Box 25435, Atlanta 30322, 404/885–1787.*

OPERA

opera companies

15 *e-3*

ATLANTA OPERA

The Atlanta Opera really took off after the Metropolitan Opera ceased its customary visits to Atlanta in the 1980s. Today, the company produces four operas a year, usually the classics but occasionally some modern works. All productions are in the Fox Theatre (see Performance Venues, above), where a supertitles screen above the stage translates the libretto. To promote understanding of and appreciation for opera, the Atlanta Opera Studio presents operas and workshops in schools throughout the state. *728 W. Peachtree St., Midtown, 404/881–8801, www.atlantaopera.org.*

CAPITAL CITY OPERA COMPANY

Throughout the year, the company presents modern and traditional operas in a variety of venues, including schools,

---

<table>
<tr><td>CULTURE WITH THE KIDS</td></tr>
</table>

Having fun and exploring the arts need not be mutually exclusive experiences for the younger members of your family. Atlanta is full of exciting activities and events that turn kids on to the arts.

Atlanta Ballet (Dance)
  Who doesn't love Tchaikovsky's Nutcracker during holiday season? And that's not the only children's programming at the Atlanta Ballet, so keep an eye on the schedule.

Atlanta Opera (Opera)
  At holiday time, the AO performs Menotti's interpretation of the familiar story Amahl and the Night Visitors. The one-act production, sung in English and starring a young boy, is an easy introduction to opera.

Capital City Opera (Opera)
  Want a soft introduction to opera for the older kids? Take them out for Italian at San Gennaro restaurant, where they can hear passages from the classics in a casual setting.

Center for Puppetry Arts (Theaters & Theater Companies)
  Puppet plays, a fine exhibition of puppets, and workshops help make boring, rainy Saturday afternoons fun.

Gwinnett Civic and Cultural Center (Performance Venues)
  Here, at the Children's Arts Museum, young audiences have a great time at the workshops, performances, and exhibits that introduce them to the visual and performing arts.

Woodruff Arts Center (Performance Venues)
  Myriad activities at the center are designed to attract young people, from acting lessons to performances by the Atlanta Youth Symphony.

---

around Atlanta. Full-length operas are produced at 14th Street Playhouse and the Callanwolde Fine Arts Center (*see* Performance Venues, *above*). Company members perform pieces from classic operas at prix-fixe dinners on the first and third Tuesday of each month, at South of France and San Gennaro restaurants, respectively. *1266 W. Paces Ferry Rd., Buckhead, 770/592–4197.*

5 *C-2*
ROSWELL LYRIC OPERA COMPANY

Devoted to operas, operettas, and American musical theater, the company stages galas, concerts, and full-length productions. Most performances take place at the Roswell Cultural Arts Center (*see* Performance Venues, *above*). Through its outreach programs, the group also introduces young people in Roswell and the surrounding communities to the art of musical performance. *685 Windwalk Dr., Roswell, 770/619–9171, www.rlopera.org.*

ORCHESTRAS & ENSEMBLES

performing groups

ATLANTA BAROQUE ORCHESTRA

Under the direction of Lyle Nordstrom, this relatively new group (founded 1996) is devoted to performing Baroque music—Bach, Handel, Vivaldi, et al.—on Baroque instruments. The size of the ensemble varies from performance to performance, and internationally renowned soloists, such as Julianne Baird (soprano) and Stanley Ritchie (violinist) are often featured. Plans are afoot to include Baroque dancers in some performances. Spivey Hall and Glenn Memorial Auditorium at Emory University (*see* Performance Venues, *above*) are their favorite stages. Tickets typically cost about $20. *105 Ashwood Ct. North, Stockbridge 30281, 770/507–4666, umbrella@mindspring.com.*

ATLANTA POPS ORCHESTRA

Since the mid-20th century, Paris native Albert Coleman has directed his 55-member orchestra in free concerts throughout the Atlanta area. The group specializes in George Gershwin's compositions, romantic favorites, and the classics, performing in public venues such as Centennial Olympic Park in Downtown. *Box 723172, Atlanta 31139-0172, 770/435–1222.*

15 *e-2*

ATLANTA SYMPHONY ORCHESTRA

Raised to international prominence by the late director Robert Shaw and guided to the end of the 20th century by Yoel Levi, Atlanta's symphony enters the new century under the direction of Robert Spano, music director of the Brooklyn Philharmonic. Partnering with Spano, Donald Runnicles, music director of the San Francisco Opera, will serve as principal guest conductor. ASO has long performed at the Woodruff Arts Center (*see* Performance Venues, *above*), but the push is on to build a new symphony hall. Concerts featuring name artists are frequently sold out well ahead of time, so it is essential to purchase tickets in advance. *Woodruff Arts Center, 1280 Peachtree St., Midtown, 404/733–5000.*

ATLANTA VIRTUOSI

Under the direction of Atlanta Symphony Orchestra violinist Juan Rubín Ramírez, who founded the group in 1977, this chamber ensemble has pursued an active performance schedule. Most of its members also play in the ASO; in this format they appear in local churches, shopping malls, or even private homes. The group sometimes debuts commissioned works; it also sponsors an annual Hispanic Festival of the Arts (*below*). *Box 77047, Atlanta 30357-1047, 770/938-8611, www. atlantavirtuosi.org.*

4 *e-2*

COBB SYMPHONY ORCHESTRA

Performing at Kennesaw State University's Stillwell Theatre (*see* Performance Venues, *above*), this long-established symphony comprises community and professional musicians. The season runs from October through April, although the group does present occasional summer concerts. *3455 Frey Lake Rd., Kennesaw, 770/423–6650 box office.*

6 *b-3*

GWINNETT PHILHARMONIC

The Gwinnett Philharmonic, with 65 principal musicians, was founded in 1995 by conductor and director Monte Nichols, a longtime Gwinnett resident. This fully professional orchestra presents concerts from fall to spring, plus other special events. Performances are at the Gwinnett Civic Center's Performing Arts Center (*see* Performance

Venues, *above*) and tickets run $15–$20. *Box 920159, Norcross 30010, 770/418–1115.*

LANIER TRIO

In 1979 Decaturites Dorothy and Cary Lewis (a cellist and a pianist, respectively) teamed up with violinist William Preucil, former concertmaster of the Atlanta Symphony Orchestra (now with the Cleveland Quartet), to form the Lanier Trio. The company performs works by Dvorak, Mendelssohn, and the like, appearing at venues such as the Rialto (*see* Performance Venues, *above*) around the city and across the country. *School of Music, Georgia State University, Atlanta 30303, 404/636–6265.*

5 *c-2*

ORCHESTRA ATLANTA

This 63-member orchestra performs under the direction of Philip Rice, who directs Chattanooga Choral Arts and is the music director of the Chattanooga Ballet. During its season, from November to May, the orchestra performs classical music in the Roswell Cultural Arts Center (*see* Performance Venues, *above*). Tickets run $20–$30. *1000 Holcomb Woods Pkwy., Suite 112, Roswell, 770/992–2559.*

classical music festivals & special events

15 *e-2*

ATLANTA SYMPHONY ORCHESTRA HOLIDAY CONCERTS

What better way to re-energize after shopping than to take in a relaxing evening of beautiful musical performances? Don't miss the favorite "Gospel Christmas" concerts. *Woodruff Arts Center, 1280 Peachtree St., Midtown, 404/733–5000. MARTA: Arts Center.*

5 *c-2*

CHRISTMAS FESTIVAL CONCERT

Each Christmas season, the Roswell United Methodist Church presents a celebratory program that varies widely from year to year. Processional pageantry, familiar carols, choral and instrumental music, drama and scripture readings make up the event. The show is free, but complimentary tickets, available at the church a month in advance, are strongly recommended as the sanctuary usually fills for this event.

814 Mimosa Blvd., Roswell, 770/594–0412 (music office), www.rumc.com.

5 *e-6*

HISPANIC FESTIVAL OF THE ARTS

Founded in 1990, this festival organized by the Atlanta Virtuosi (*see above*) celebrates Hispanic heritage through traditional and classical music, art exhibitions, folk dance, and lectures about Hispanic culture. Performances take place at the Embry Hills United Methodist Church (*see* Concerts in Churches, *above*). *Box 77047, Atlanta 30357-1047, 770/938-8611, www.atlantavirtuosi.org.*

5 *c-2*

ROSWELL PATRIOTIC CELEBRATION

An annual tradition in Roswell, this "star-spangled spectacular" is presented at the end of June in the Roswell United Methodist Church (*see* Concerts in Churches, *above*). The show consists of narration, ceremony, and traditional patriotic music. Admission is free, but complimentary tickets, available at the church a month ahead, are strongly recommended as the sanctuary usually fills for this event. *814 Mimosa Blvd., Roswell, 770/594–0412 (music office). www.rumc.com.*

THEATERS & THEATER COMPANIES

15 *b-2*

ACTOR'S EXPRESS

This troupe's goal is "to produce plays that sweep us off our feet, fill us with a sense of wonder, and leave us dizzy"— and they certainly accomplish that. Performing both classical and contemporary pieces at King Plow Arts Center, the group is very energetic, very physical, very playful. Actor's Express also runs an acting school and an internship program. *887 W. Marietta St., Suite J-107, King Plow Arts Center, Northwest Atlanta 404/607–7469 box office or 404/875–1606, www.actorsexpress.com.*

15 *e-3*

AGATHA'S—A TASTE OF MYSTERY

Agatha's is the crème de la crème of dinner theater in Atlanta. Delightful and absurd mysteries are staged by professional actors; audience members are enlisted to participate in, and solve, the mysteries. Amid the gasps and laughter, an excellent five-course meal with wine and beverages is served. This is a great experience to share with friends. *693 Peachtree St., Midtown, 404/875–1610.*

15 *e-2*

ALLIANCE THEATRE COMPANY

Without a doubt, this is one of the largest and most revered resident theaters in the South. In its theater at the Woodruff Arts Center (*see* Performance Venues, *above*), it produces the works of renowned regional and local playwrights, reaching an audience of more than 300,000 each season. An integral part of the Atlanta arts community, the Alliance offers training to thespians and runs a delightful children's theater program, which features performances that appeal to both the young and the young at heart. *Woodruff Arts Center, 1280 Peachtree St., Midtown, 404/733–5000, www.alliancetheatre.org. MARTA: Arts Center.*

8 *e-1*

ART STATION

This intimate 100-seat theater hosts professional performances of classic and original plays that reflect the uniqueness of the southern experience. Set in the heart of Stone Mountain Village, the Station also has an art gallery with changing exhibits of local and international artists, plus a learning center, a dance studio, private music rehearsal rooms, and a pottery studio. *534 Manor Dr., Stone Mountain, 770/469–1105.*

15 *e-4*

THE ATLANTA SHAKESPEARE TAVERN

Truly the place to eat, drink, and be merry, this theater-cum-tavern stages lively productions of Shakespeare on a small stage, in the comfortable atmosphere of an old English pub. The tavern also presents works by other classic European dramatists, including Molière and Shaw. A pub fare menu, featuring such items as Cornish pasties and shepherd's pie, is available, and Guinness, Harp, and Bass are offered on tap. *499 Peachtree St., Downtown, 404/874–5299, www.shakespearetavern.com.*

6 *a-3*

AURORA THEATRE

The Aurora is a semi-professional theater company that brings drama, comedy, and musical productions to the North Gwinnett suburbs. Selections largely represent the American classics, including dramas by Tennessee Williams and comedies by Neil Simon. *3087B Main St., Duluth, 770/476–7926, www.auroratheatre.com.*

15 e-1
CENTER FOR PUPPETRY ARTS
Come here for a magical theater experience that offers powerful and thought-provoking entertainment for adults as much as for children. The largest puppetry center in the United States, this institution has three theaters and a museum with interactive displays of antique and modern puppets from all over the world (*see* Chapter 4). *1404 Spring St., Midtown, 404/873–3391 or 404/873–3089, www.puppet.org*

15 h-5
DAD'S GARAGE
One of the city's most innovative young theaters, this operation takes on everything from comedy to musicals. At the comic Theatre Sports shows on Thursday and Saturday nights (10:30), improvisational skits call for audience participation. Friday nights at 10:30, Scandal!, Atlanta's only improvised serial comedy, erupts. Dad's also offers snacks and beverages. Admission is reasonable, running up into the teens at most. *280 Elizabeth St., Suite C101, Inman Park, 404/523–3141, www.dadsgarage.com.*

5 c-2
GEORGIA ENSEMBLE THEATRE
This professional company mounts five productions during its season, which runs roughly September through July. Works from the comedy, drama, and musical genres appeal to a broad spectrum of the community. Performances take place at the Roswell Culural Arts Center (*see* Performance Venues, *above*). The theater also has a children's and adults' conservatory. Ticket prices vary depending on performance. *950 Forrest St., Roswell, 770/641–1260.*

5 c-7
GEORGIA SHAKESPEARE FESTIVAL
The neo-Gothic architecture of Oglethorpe University's campus is the perfect backdrop for Shakespearean productions that pay homage to the Bard's

original intent. In addition to works by Shakespeare, the company produces other classics from time to time. A new permanent theater has replaced the festival's former quarters in a tent, affording style and comfort to actors and audience alike. The group has a rotating repertory schedule. *4484 Peachtree Rd., Oglethorpe University, Brookhaven, 404/264–0020.*

14 a-5
HORIZON THEATRE COMPANY
An intimate 185-seat theater in Little Five Points is the scene of dramas, comedies, and satires produced by this troupe. With a focus on new plays and playwrights, Horizon also sponsors programs such as the Teen Ensemble and the Senior Citizens Ensemble, which are meant to cultivate broader public interest in theater. *1083 Austin Ave., Little Five Points, 404/584–7450.*

15 f-2
JOMANDI PRODUCTIONS
This non-profit group, founded in 1978, is the oldest and largest professional African-American theater company currently producing plays in Georgia. Featuring local and regional talent, particularly black playwrights, the award-winning production company stages challenging works of ethnic significance. The company usually performs at the 14th Street Playhouse (*see* Performance Venues, *above*). *1444 Mayson St., Buckhead, 404/876–6346 or 888/876–1127, www.jomandi.com.*

15 f-2
ONSTAGE ATLANTA
Founded in 1971, this professional company produces an eclectic mix of live theater, including Broadway, off-Broadway, and regional work. The actors like to be close to their audience, so they prefer the intimate stages 2 and 3 at the 14th Street Playhouse (*see* Performance Venues, *above*). Stage 3, for instance, may be configured to seat only 58 patrons. Abracadabra! Children's Theatre, part of Onstage Atlanta, produces classics of children's literature adapted to the stage, such as *Beauty and the Beast, Cinderella,* and *Sleeping Beauty.* Tickets run $7–$10 for the children's theater and $16–$22 for Onstage productions. *Box 54178, Atlanta 30308, 404/897–1802.*

13 *b-7*

PUSHPUSH THEATER

Housed in a warehouse district workshop space, this company develops and premiers new plays and presents productions of everything from contemporary works to Shakespeare to rarely seen plays. PushPush enables playwrights from Atlanta's theater scene to explore new territory and perhaps take risks not always possible at more commercial companies. From time to time, the theater hosts other local groups and presents themed festivals. *The Floataway Building, 1123 Zonolite Rd., off Briarcliff and Johnson Rds., Northeast Atlanta, 404/892–7876.*

14 *a-5*

7 STAGES THEATRE AND PERFORMING ARTS CENTER

This passionately non-conformist theater has brought provocative, modern performance to Atlanta since 1978. Committed to the avant-garde, the company specializes in contemporary twists on old themes, as in a recent reprise of the Faust theme. Other smaller companies perform in the 90-seat black box Backstage theater, located in the rear of the facility. The theater is set in the colorful Little Five Points district. *1355 Euclid Ave., Little Five Points, 404/523–7647, www.7stages.w1.com.*

15 *f-2*

THEATRE GAEL

Founded in 1985, this professional company is dedicated to performing plays, poetry, music, and storytelling from the Celtic tradition. The company's arts education programs target children throughout Georgia, with workshops and programs that deal with issues of human rights and conflict resolution. Theatre Gael from time to time commissions new work. Performances take place at the 14th Street Playhouse (*see* Performance Venues, *above*). *Box 77156, Atlanta 30357, 404/876–1138, www.arthouse.com/gael.*

4 *f-4*

THEATRE IN THE SQUARE

Second only to the Alliance Theatre in the number of people who attend its shows each year, this professional company works in a cotton warehouse that has been converted to 225-seat theater. The group is not afraid to take a few risks, and it strives to produce works that are as stimulating as they are entertaining. *11 Whitlock Ave., Marietta, 770/422–8369.*

5 *c-2*

VILLAGE PLAYHOUSES OF ROSWELL

With two stages and a theater-in-the-round, this 10-year-old community theater comprises the Village Center Playhouse (the main stage), Storybook Theater (the children's theater), and Roswell Village Theater (a proscenium theater). Comedies, uplifting dramas and musicals, and seven children's productions a year are the draws. Tickets usually go for $8–$16. *633 Holcomb Bridge Rd., Roswell, 770/998–3525.*

TICKETS

You can buy tickets to all kinds of metro Atlanta performing arts events by calling **Ticketmaster** (404/279–6400). You must have a charge card., and a service fee will be added to the price of your tickets.

The **Atlanta Coalition of Theatres** offers half-price theater tickets, which are available on the day of the show both through its AtlanTIX Info line (770/772–5572) and its Web site (www.atlantatheaters.org). This organization represents theaters in eight metro Atlanta counties. Its Web site posts the show calendars of all 112 members, with hyperlinks to their Web sites. The telephone information line also has a fax-on-demand service that sends a year-at-a-glance show calendar to callers.

nightlife

BARS & LOUNGES

5 *c-5*

AMERICAN PIE

Boisterous and usually packed, this is a hugely popular gathering spot for young singles. The atmosphere is casual, and the outdoor deck is always open during the summer. In addition to pool tables and dartboards, there's a dance floor with a DJ who spins popular dance music most nights. Saturday afternoons, you can listen to live music on the deck. There are 52 TVs and two wide-screeners, usually tuned to sporting events. The menu favors burgers and salads. *5840 Roswell Rd., Sandy Springs, 404/255–7571.*

14 *b-8*

THE FLATIRON

Shaped just like its name, this classic old building is centered by a u-shaped bar that gathers neighborhood denizens to its chairs. There's a bar menu, with nachos, sandwiches, and similar bar fare, but food is not the focus. Instead, people gather for conversation, drinks, and plain old camaraderie. It's almost nostalgically old-fashioned, but the patrons are young. *520 Flat Shoals Ave., East Atlanta Village, 404/688–8864.*

15 *a-8*

FOUNTAINHEAD LOUNGE

The younger set fills this lively spot, gathering around the bar opposite the entrance or lounging at the tables scattered around the room. Except for the slightly scruffy atmosphere, this might almost qualify as a wine bar, for there's a very impressive wine list, with lots served by the glass—and good glassware to boot. Some appetizers are served, but mostly it's drinks and chatter that bring 'em in. Fountainhead is open into the very late hours (3 AM on weekdays and 4 AM on weekends). *485A Flat Shoals Ave., East Atlanta Village, 404/522–7841.*

15 *e-2*

THE LEOPARD LOUNGE

Live jazz and swing music make this joint jump every Friday and Saturday night. On other nights (except Sunday), recorded (and sometimes live) music of various kinds, from rock to house, bring bodies to the dance floor. The bar serves drinks and light appetizers (shrimp cocktail, jerk chicken, and Portobello flatbread) into the wee hours. After 10 PM Friday–Saturday, the cover is $5 for women, $7 for men. Dress nicely, and leave the sports gear at home. *84 12th St., Midtown, 404/875–7562. MARTA: Midtown.*

12 *f-3*

TONGUE & GROOVE

A chic crowd fills this dance floor or comes to hear occasional live performances. Wednesday is Latin Night, while on other nights, American and European pop and R&B are the draws, with music provided by a DJ. The dress code for this 25–45-year-old crowd prohibits jeans and T-shirts, and the beautiful people here always seem to look their best. Most nights, the club is open

9 PM–4 AM, Saturday until 3 AM. Closed Sunday. *3055 Peachtree Rd., Buckhead, 404/261–2325.*

5 *c-3*

WHISKERS DUNWOODY TAVERN

A real neighborhood bar, Whiskers has pool and TV sports, plus bands five nights a week. Terrific live blues and rock from some of Atlanta's best local groups, including Java Monkey and Cold Chills, begins around 10. Lunch and dinner are served from a menu that focuses on steaks and burgers. There is no cover. *8371 Roswell Rd., Dunwoody, 770/992–7445.*

BILLIARDS

Metro Atlanta has more billiards tables than you can shake a (cue) stick at. In addition to Twain's (*below*), almost any of the hangouts listed under Sports Bars (*below*) are popular spots to shoot some pool. Multiple tables can also be found at places like American Pie (*see* Bars & Lounges, *above*), Churchill Arms (*see* Pubs & Taverns, *below*), Dave & Buster's (*see* Fun, *below*), Scrooges Lounge (*see* Pubs & Taverns, *below*), and The Last Great Watering Hole (*see* Pop/Rock, *below*). For hard-core billiards parlors, *see* Chapter 3.

14 *g-4*

TWAIN'S BILLIARDS & TAP

Test your skill at the 20 billiards tables, half of which are designated no-smoking. The crowd here reflects Decatur demographics, with young couples and middle aged types mixing easily. Upholstered seating—the decor is a bit on the wild and funky side—grouped into four conversation areas, and eight TVs, including a big screen, are often tuned to sports events. Typical bar food is available, including a Reuben sandwich and a veggie burger. Twain's is open to 2 AM during the week and 3 AM on the weekends. *211 E. Trinity Pl., Decatur, 404/373–0063.*

BLUEGRASS

14 *h-1*

ROCKIN' ROB'S

Barbecue has been joined by music at this joint, which rocks to bluegrass on selected Saturday nights, 3–7 PM. When you get hungry, savor the good 'cue and

Brunswick stew (*see* Chapter 1). There is no cover. *1479 Scott Blvd., Decatur, 404/378–6041.*

BLUES

14 *a-3*

BLIND WILLIE'S

This small, nationally renowned club packs a blues wallop with live blues from Chicago, New Orleans, and every-place in between. Local bands—including the house outfit, House Rocker Johnson and the Shadows—as well as national performers are featured. The music starts at 10 but the bar opens at 8, and a limited bar menu is available. Crowds jam the place every night and parking is scarce in this neighborhood, so get here early and come by taxi, or grab the first parking space that catches your eye—don't be fussy. No reservations are accepted, and only those 21 and older are admitted—with ID. The cover charge varies. *828 N. Highland Ave., Virginia-Highland, 404/873–2583.*

2 *b-8*

BLUE PIG

This suburban music and barbecue spot gets down with serious blues on Friday and Saturday nights, beginning at 9. A clean-cut crowd fills the tables and packs the bar to listen to local and regional bands. First-class 'cue with homemade sides, including good baked beans and mac and cheese, is served daily (*see* Chapter 1). There's no cover charge. *9770 S. Main St., Woodstock, 770/517–2583.*

CHIPS BAR & GRILL

Although just outside the 10-county area, this spot's worth the trip if you want to hear important regional performers try out new material. Great blues and rock acts are the draw, with music typically featured on Friday, Saturday, and two Sundays a month. Shows start relatively early (about 9 PM; 4 PM on Sunday), but you can grab a bite from a menu of burgers and barbecue. Cover charges run from $3 for local acts to $25 for nationally known acts, with most shows in the middle of the range. *655 Patrick Mill Rd., Winder, 770/307–2840.*

4 *h-5*

DARWIN'S

Musicians from intown and "outtatown" bring the blues to the northside.

Located 1 mi east of the Big Chicken, a 50-ft-tall Kentucky Fried Chicken that's impossible to miss, Darwin's attracts a blues-knowledgeable crowd. The club changes show times regularly, so call to find out who's playing and when. *1598 Roswell Rd., Marietta, 770/578–6872.*

12 *g-7*

FAT MATT'S RIB SHACK

This little barbecue place (*see* Chapter 1) is a stage for great local blues players, who pack in an early crowd eager to hear some good music. Decent ribs, sandwiches, barbecued chicken, side dishes, and plenty of beer define the menu. Outdoor seating accommodates anyone who'd rather keep the music in the background. No credit cards are accepted. *1811 Piedmont Ave., Midtown, 404/607–1622.*

15 *e-2*

FRONT PAGE NEWS

A journalistic theme prevails in this space, where owner Josh Sagarin decorates the walls with headlines collected from newspapers. On the menu, creole-style food is the order of the day. Musically, there's a little of everything, from zydeco and blues to jazz. Performances by some good artists are usually free. Sunday jazz brunch, served outside when weather permits, is another hit, with some performers showcasing original compositions. *1104 Crescent Ave., Midtown, 404/897–3500.*

13 *b-4*

FUZZY'S PLACE

Fuzzy's is a music venue at one end of its long bar and a restaurant with televised for sports events on the other. The music side fills early as regulars stake out seats, even though the show doesn't start until 10 each night. It's kinda smoky in there, too. Local talents, such as vocalist Francine Reed or Nancy Nagle with Cold Chills, grace the stage. Although the place really comes alive to the blues, the music varies, with rock some nights and a more contemporary sound on others. A full menu of well-prepared creole fare, such as carpetbagger steak stuffed with shrimp, makes this a very popular lunch spot for workers from nearby offices. Later in the evening a limited menu is available until closing (around 2 AM). There's no cover charge, except on New Year's Eve. *2015 N. Druid Hills Rd., northeast Atlanta, 404/321–6166.*

5 *e-4*

LAGNIAPPE ON THE BAYOU

Savor Cajun fare and stick around for classic New Orleans jazz, blues, or swing—and sometimes even R&B. Friday and Saturday are the nights to come, beginning around 9:30. There's no cover. During the week, the restaurant also serves lunch. *1412 Dunwoody Village Pkwy., Dunwoody, 770/671–9777.*

15 *b-2*

NORTHSIDE TAVERN

This full-blooded blues club attracts big-name performing legends every night of the week. The music usually starts at 10, and the tavern closes between 2 and 3 AM. You can order any imaginable drink, but food is served Tuesday–Thursday only, with a few items available on Sunday. Here you can meet die-hard blues fans, as well as some of the best blues players around. *1058 Howell Mill Rd., Collier Hills, 404/874–8745.*

4 *h-5*

POPPER'S

Regional blues acts perform in a casual, low-key atmosphere, surrounded by photos of great blues artists. A full menu, served until late at night, features simple fare like burgers and cheese sticks. Monday is karaoke night, Wednesday is open mike night, and Tuesday and Thursday are set aside for jam sessions. There's a five-buck cover charge (more if a major national band performs) on weekends only. *2555 Delk Rd., Marietta, 770/953–8779.*

BREWPUBS & MICROBREWERIES

10 *b-1*

BUCKHEAD BREWERY & GRILL

A log-finished exterior outlined in lights frames large windows that reveal the gleaming copper brew tanks within. Lots of impressive hunt trophies hang on the walls, and a copper-hooded fire box in the center of the room waits for cold weather. This large brewpub and grill has two levels designed for family dining and a bar that's usually filled with single guys watching sports on TVs. Some half-dozen brews are available at any time, plus a decent root beer—the wheat beer and the Hop Island IPA are the richest tasting. The food is fairly typ-

ical pub grub, such as beer-cheese soup and quite good buffalo shrimp (*see* Chapter 1). It's open daily. *1757 Rock Quarry Rd., Stockbridge, 770/389–8112.*

12 *f-3*

JOHN HARVARD'S BREW HOUSE

Rich woods and gleaming brew tanks, visible just inside the entrance, create a neighborhood pub atmosphere that's more amenable to group gatherings than to romantic dating. The beer's decent, and the food ranges from appetizers like hummus or pepper Jack nachos—served in portions large enough for sharing—to entrées like ale-and-mustard chicken or Cajun salmon. The Stout Mud Slide Pie is made with real stout. *3041 Peachtree Rd., Buckhead, 404/816–2739, www.johnharvards.com.*

5 *d-3*

1564 Holcomb Bridge Rd., Roswell, 770/645–2739.

15 *e-5*

MAX LAGER'S

Busy every day of the week, Downtown's brewpub (*see* Chapter 1) has rough-hewn brick walls inside and seating on an outdoor patio, which offers a view of the urban landscape in nice weather. Order a tasting of the current brews and some of the great gumbo. The veggie pita and grilled chicken are good choices, too. For nondrinkers, the house-made root and ginger beers are refreshing and lively. *320 Peachtree St., Downtown, 404/525–4400.*

15 *g-2*

THE PARK TAVERN AND BREWERY

Overlooking Piedmont Park and the dramatic Midtown skyline, this bar has one of the best views in town. Friendly to park visitors, the staff tolerate patrons who show up wearing in-line skates and lunch guests in sometimes scanty exercise garb. They've even been known to provide water dishes and doggie biscuits for pets. The brewery creates pleasing hand-crafted beers, including a pilsner, a pale ale, an amber, a porter, and usually a couple of specialty items, such as a Scottish ale, with its efficient brewing system. The large patio features live music Thursday through Saturday; inside there are two full bars with a western-lodge look and a cigar humidor. Lounge on giant leather chairs in three "comfy" areas. The Park is open for lunch Friday–Sunday, for brunch on Sunday, and until 2 AM most days. *500 10th St., Midtown, 404/249–0001, www.parktavern.com.*

12 *g-3*
ROCK BOTTOM BREWERY
The latest Buckhead contribution to the brewpub craze feels like a neighborhood pub. There's an extensive menu (*see* Chapter 1) and a good list of well-made suds. Six quite good house-made brews are on tap at all times, plus a couple of specialty brews that vary with the season. With the food running toward the spicy, a brew is almost a required part of a meal here. *3242 Peachtree Rd., at Piedmont Rd., Buckhead, 404/264–0253.*

10 *b-1*
U.S. BORDER BREWERY CANTINA
This Tex-Mex establishment brews fine beers—8 to 10 are on draught at all times—and serves good southwestern fare. From pilsner to stout, amber ale to porter, the selection runs a wide range. Its Sun Salsa is so popular it's sold at local grocery stores. Live acoustic music—folk, pop, rock, contemporary, country, whatever—is offered on Friday and Saturday nights, when the Cantina closes around midnight. From Sunday through Thursday, closing is at 10 PM. *12460 Crabapple Rd., Alpharetta, 770/ 772–4400.*

CAJUN & ZYDECO

13 *a-5*
ATLANTA CAJUN DANCE ASSOCIATION
On select Friday and Saturday evenings (call for the schedule), aficionados of Louisiana culture transform the local Knights of Columbus Hall into a dance club. The musicians come from Cajun country as well as from the local scene; Atlanta Swamp Opera and Hair of the Dog perform when out-of-state groups are, well, out-of-state. Festive evenings open with an hour's lesson in the art of the two-step and other forms of Cajun dance. Class starts at 7 PM, and don't fret if you don't have a partner—everybody mixes. Wear comfortable, loose-fitting clothes and soft-sole shoes. You can grab a bite from the limited menu of Cajun food, and wash it down with beer from the cash bar (wine and the hard stuff are

not available). Depending on who's performing, covers run $10–$15. Parking is horribly tight, so come early or find a spot across the street. *Knights of Columbus Hall, 2620 Buford Hwy., near Lenox Rd., Northeast Atlanta, 770/451–6611.*

CIGAR BARS

12 *g-3*
BELUGA MARTINI BAR
Beluga proffers a vast drink menu—the specialty being wines and martinis— and live piano music in an intimate setting. The place has two humidors and a selection of about a dozen cigars, but does not serve food. Patrons come to smoke, drink, and chill. *3115 Piedmont Rd., Buckhead, 404/869–1090.*

12 *g-3*
GOLDFINGER
This fun martini and cigar bar offers excellent drinks and a humidor full of Montecristos, Cohibas, Macanudos, and other premium cigars. On James Bond (shaken, not stirred) theme nights 007 movies are shown continuously in the Red Room downstairs. It's a good place to kick back and relax, except on Sunday and Monday, when it's closed. *3081 E. Shadowlawn Ave., Buckhead, 404/627–8464.*

15 *e-2*
MARTINI CLUB
This Midtown martini club is decorated Art Deco-style and is locally famous for offering 101 varieties of martini. A fully stocked walk-in humidor holds 30 or so different cigars, including Cohibas, Arturo Fuentes, and Macanudos. On the weekends, the house tobacconist oversees the cigar sales. There's also light menu, with such dishes as a crab-and-spinach dip and chocolate fondue with fresh fruit and pound cake, and all dishes are served in a martini glass. Live jazz is a nightly feature. The bar is closed Sunday and there is no cover or minimum. *1140 Crescent Ave., Midtown, 404/873–0794.*

COFFEEHOUSES

14 *a-4*
CAFÉ DIEM
Espresso and regular coffee are the focus at this full-service restaurant with

a perfectly funky coffeehouse atmosphere. Serving abundant vegetarian fare, salads, and other healthful dishes, it's a favorite with students, academics, artists, and musicians. Conversation and board games, including chess and Trivial Pursuit, pass the time, and there is live entertainment some nights. Monday features a Brazilian musician, and the first Tuesday of each month is poetry night. Sunday evening is reserved for classical guitar on the deck. Amnesty International meets here every Thursday night. *640 N. Highland Ave., Poncey-Highland, 404/607–7008.*

12 *g-2*

JOE MUGGS NEWSSTAND

This coffeehouse-cum-magazine/bookstore is bright and comfortable, with upholstered seating in conversation groups. It's a meeting-place for various local groups, who along with the rest of the customers enjoy Seattle's Best brand coffee and the pastries, which are baked off-site but still delicious. The place opens at 6 AM daily and closes at midnight. *3275 Peachtree Rd., at Piedmont Rd., Buckhead, 404/364–9290.*

14 *a-2*

SAN FRANCISCO COFFEE ROASTING COMPANY

This long-standing, locally owned outfit roasts its own coffee, makes good pastries (almost all are homemade), and offers live music from time to time. In a restored brick storefront with lots of character and atmosphere, it's a great date spot. Folks often bring along board games for an evening of friendly competition. *1192 N. Highland Ave., Virginia-Highland, 404/876–8816.*

STARBUCKS

Myriad outlets around the metro area sponsor Friday Java Jams, with various musicians appearing at certain locations. Some shops also offer music on other nights. A national chain, Starbucks has good coffee and pastries. Check with your neighborhood branch for performance information.

COMEDY

14 *a-8*

GRAVITY PUB

Gravity is a pub, not a comedy club, but every other Thursday it opens the door to hilarity. Comedians, professional and amateur, compete for the crowd's laughs, and the winners leave with some cash. The show begins around 10 and the club is open until the late hours. *1257 Glenwood Ave., Decatur, 404/627–5555.*

5 *b-5*

THE PUNCH LINE

This renowned club draws recognized comics from all over the United States. Local yuckster Jeff Foxworthy made his name here; others of national note who have appeared here include Henry Cho and Paula Poundstone. The menu of finger-food includes chips, dips, sandwiches, and salads, and of course there's a full bar. Reservations are recommended on weeknights and required for weekend shows. Selected shows are no-smoking. *280 Hilderbrand Dr., Sandy Springs, 404/252–5233.*

12 *d-6*

UPTOWN COMEDY CLUB

No reservations are necessary here: just show up and laugh! Local and national standup talent is featured, and on Tuesday night Blacktop Circus Improv Group takes the stage in a show that encourages audience involvement. Noshes are available to accompany the drinks you can order from the full bar. On Sunday's open mike nights, you can enjoy the antics of amateurs or give stand-up a whirl yourself. Appetizers—catfish nuggets and chicken wings—make up the nosh menu. The club is open Tuesday–Sunday and shows start at 9. Tickets are $8 Tuesday–Thursday, and Sunday, $15 Friday–Saturday. *2140 Peachtree Rd., Buckhead, 404/350–6990.*

15 *e-2*

WHOLE WORLD THEATRE

Improvisational comedy flourishes in this intimate 120-seat theater Thursday through Saturday. This is some of the city's most reasonably priced comedy, with admission running $11-$17.50; it's essential to make reservations as shows sell out at least a week in advance. You can, however, see the show for free, via simulcast on a video screen in the building next door. A small bar serves beer and wine, and is an outlet for Rocky's Brick Oven Pizza (*see* Chapter 1). Shows are on Thursday at 8 PM, Friday at 9 PM, and Saturday (at 7 and 10 PM). *1214 Spring St., Midtown, 404/817–0880, www.wholeworldcomedy.com.*

COUNTRY & WESTERN

4 h-6

BUCKBOARD COUNTRY MUSIC SHOWCASE

The theme here is "Nashville comes to Atlanta." As the house band, Peachtree Station, plays country music, boot-scooters Texas-two-step across the dance floor. Famous performers appear from time to time, so it's worth calling for a schedule of upcoming events. A small cover is charged, ranging from $2–$5, depending on day of the week and if you're a guy or a gal. *2080 Cobb Pkwy., Windy Hill Plaza, Smyrna, 770/955–7340.*

3 e-2

CADILLAC RANCH

On the weekends this concert hall and nightclub hosts live local and regional bands of the C&W and southern rock persuasion. On weekdays, DJs spin disks. There's a big dance floor and an all-you-can-eat deli buffet with home-made roast beef, ham, smoked turkey, homemade chili, and soup—and it's included in the $5 cover charge. The club is closed Sunday–Monday. *3885 Brownsbridge Rd., Cumming, 770/844–0304.*

4 e-3

COWBOYS CONCERT HALL

Calling itself "Atlanta's Premier Honky-Tonk," this joint offers live country music nightly and C&W dance lessons on Monday, Wednesday, Saturday, and Sunday evenings. If you think you need exercise after a night of line dancing, you've been doing more watching than dancing. The 44,000-square-ft hall hosts the Cowboy Dance Association on Thursday nights; Wednesday is Ladies' Night, when a balloon drops cash and prizes onto the dance floor. Sunday is family day—no alcohol is served, but there is a free buffet and dance lessons. Most days the club opens at 6:30 and closes between 2 and 3 AM. The cover charge is usually $7, unless the evening's headliner is a major national act. *1750 N. Roberts Rd., Kennesaw, 770/426–5006.*

6 e-3

FLYING MACHINE

At the edge of a runway at Gwinnett County airport, this aviation-theme spot delivers country bands, golden oldies, folk music, and pop/contemporary. The restaurant serves three meals daily, mostly steaks, burgers, sandwiches, and creative specials on the weekend, with entertainment Monday–Saturday beginning at about 7 PM. There is no cover. *510 Briscoe Blvd., South Terminal at Briscoe Field, Lawrenceville, 770/962–2262.*

8 d-2

MAMA'S COUNTRY SHOWCASE

The mammoth Mama's, 32,000 square ft in all, has one of the largest dance floors in Atlanta, a vast 3,000 square ft. A powerful sound system serves not only the dance floor but six full-service bars, a diner (for when the munchies strike), and spaces that hold seven pool tables, a slew of video games, and one mean hydraulic bull. The occasional bikini contest scores large cash prizes for the winners. Thursday evening brings free line-dancing lessons. Open to the late hours from Thursday through Saturday, it's closed the rest of the week. *3952 Covington Hwy., Decatur, 404/288–6262.*

DANCE CLUBS

12 f-3

BELL BOTTOMS

This is disco heaven—a big dance floor, spinning mirrored balls, a light show, a fog machine, a life-size cut-out of John Travolta, and loud music pumping away. Favorite tunes from the 1970s and 1980s keep the crowd grooving; you can request your favorite dance hit by walking upstairs to the DJ booth and asking. There are even a couple of cages that you can dance in. The cover charge is minimal ($5), but you must be 21 (with ID) to enter. *225 Pharr Rd., Buckhead, 404/816–9669.*

12 f-3

THE CHILI PEPPER

This Buckhead dance club offers diversity through the week, with a wide range of music featured on different days. DJs spin throughout the week while patrons dance on a roof-top terrace. An 18-plus crowd is welcomed on Thursday, and Friday's the night to party to Top 40s hits. The club's Skylounge hosts live music, which you can find out about by calling the events line (404/812–0959). *208 Pharr Rd., Buckhead, 404/812–9266.*

8 *c-3*

CLUB MIRAGE

Popular with African-Americans, this club is packed on the weekends, when well-known DJs spin house music for enthusiastic club-goers on the dance floor. Currently, Mirage is keepin' it lively with Greg Street and DJ Dose on the mix. On Ladies' Night each Thursday, the Black Chippendales dance. There's a free buffet 6–8, and a cover charge ($10) that kicks in at either 9 or 10 PM depending on day of the week. The club is open Tuesday–Sunday; nice dress is required. *3843 Glenwood Rd., Decatur, 404/286–1313.*

12 *f-3*

COBALT LOUNGE

High-energy dance and alternative music shake this Buckhead hangout. There are two levels: upstairs, DJs spin heat in the dance club, while lounge lizards inhabit the lower level. You can order from a civilized bar menu (baked Brie, smoked salmon, crab cakes) until 3 or 4 AM. Some private party rooms are available. *265 E. Paces Ferry Rd., at Bolling Way, Buckhead, 404/760–9250.*

15 *e-2*

THE CRESCENT ROOM

At this Midtown club, DJs play house music for those who like to work it on the dance floor. The 25–35 crowd dresses casually but nicely (no scruffy attire allowed). Tuesdays are "Urban Fusion" nights, attracting a young urban professional crowd for soul and hip-hop or blues. Live music (jazz, hip-hop, R&B) from a variety of bands holds forth on Wednesdays. The club is open 9 PM– 2 AM Monday–Thursday, until 4 AM on Friday and 3 AM on Saturday nights; the cover runs $5–$10. *1136 Crescent Ave., Midtown, 404/875–5252.*

7 *g-5*

CRYSTAL PALACE

You need to be a member (and over 21) to gain admission to this private club, but memberships are easily obtained. The Palace spins house Tuesday–Saturday beginning at midnight. Amateur contests of various kinds are held on Friday and Saturday nights. *502 Connell Ave., South Atlanta, 404/762–7241.*

12 *f-3*

HAVE A NICE DAY CAFÉ

This very retro spot across from the Roxy (*see* Performance Venues, *above*) rocks with the music of the 1980s on Thursday nights, which is also Ladies' Night (no cover for the gals). Friday and Saturday are 1970s Dance Party nights, and Wednesday is College Night, when the club opens to everyone age 18 and up. It's closed Monday and Tuesday. *3095 Peachtree Rd., Buckhead, 404/261–8898.*

12 *f-3*

MAKO'S

Dripping with tacky, colorful strings of beads, this club sets out to throw a party as awesome as "Mardi Gras—365 Days a Year." Top 40 hits raise the pulse on the lively dance floor. There's also a cigar and martini lounge and a menu that includes sushi. Mako's is closed Sunday. *3065 Peachtree Rd., Buckhead, 404/846–8096.*

15 *h-4*

THE MASQUERADE

A good place to check out local bands, this club is popular with a college-age crowd. Each of the three floors has its own name and function: Heaven, a rocking concert hall, headlines local bands during the week and on some weekend nights. Hell is where DJs, flashing lights, and lots of sweaty bodies add up to a massive dance party. Purgatory is the game room, where you can chill out with pool and other diversions. Wednesday through Saturday nights feature a theme: Wednesday is Goth Night, Thursday is Old Wave 80s music, Friday is the Playhouse (house music), and Saturday is Foam Party (500 partyers play in foam) during the summer months and during colder months it's high energy dance. Sunday is "Swing Night," and the club opens on Monday–Tuesday only if a national band is booked. The cover runs $5–$8. *695 North Ave., Virginia-Highland, 404/ 577–8178, 404/577–2007 band and ticket info, www.masq.com.*

15 *e-2*

NOMENCLATURE MUSEUM

This funky place is an art parlor . . . but wait—it's a nightclub! Well, it's both, and more. What will you find here? A discotheque where world-renowned DJs spin house music, for one thing. For another, there's a mini avant-garde theater that showcases what the club calls bizarre performance art. Then there's an outdoor patio, the Comatose Den (for chillin' out), and, of course, that art gallery. The Monster Bar serves drinks and little pizzas. Covers vary, $3–$7 depending on performers. *44 12th St., Midtown, 404/874–6344, www.nomenclaturemuseum.com.*

MOVE TO THE MUSIC

If sitting around watching performances is beginning to spread you, well, not so thin, get up and move to the music. Don't know how to dance? Maybe it's time to learn!

Atlanta Cajun Dance Association (Cajun)

For a hopping evening that will set your toes to tapping, there's nothing like an evening of Cajun dancing. Let the good times roll!

Chattahoochee Country Dancers (Bluegrass)

Line up or circle 'round: either way, you'll get a real workout, make some new friends, and hear some fine traditional bluegrass.

City Lights Dance Club (Social & Ballroom Dancing)

Learn to dance with a partner, whether you want to waltz or lambada. That's what it's all about at this smoke- and alcohol-free nightclub.

Cowboys Concert Hall (Country & Western)

There's no way to resist the rhythm of live country music, so you might as well take one of the free line-dancing lessons here. You'll wear yourself a smile at the end of the night.

Hoedown's (Gay and Lesbian Bars & Clubs)

This country-and-western bar teaches line dancing to songs spun by DJs. It's mostly a guy thing, but the place does its best to attract women on Thursday and Sunday nights.

Sanctuary (Latin)

Surrounded by Latin energy and glamour, learn tango, salsa, and merengue.

DINING & DANCING

12 *f-3*

CELEBRITY ROCK CAFE

Don't let the name fool you—this place doesn't tend to draw celebrities, and it's not just a rock-and-roll joint. Instead, a diverse thirtysomething crowd dines from a full menu of bar food such as quesadillas, burgers, and hot wings and dances to live music. Latin rhythms energize Wednesday nights, and a seven-piece house band playing 70s, 80s, and 90s dance music takes over on Thursday, Friday, and Saturday nights. The club is closed Sunday–Tuesday. No cover Thursday, otherwise the cover is $10. *56 E. Andrews Dr., East Andrews Square, Buckhead, 404/262–7625.*

12 *h-7*

DEUX PLEX

A two-story bistro serving simple French fare is upstairs from a dance club at this hot spot. The 7,500-square-ft dance club with a sunken floor can hold about 600 people, who can get comfortable on modern furniture arranged in intimate groupings. World-class DJs work the massive sound system, whether it's Dean Coleman and his Café Society events on Thursday, Carlos Morales on Latin Night (Friday), or the Lord of European House on Saturday. Covers run $5–$10, but may be discounted for patrons who have dined in the bistro. *1789 Cheshire Bridge Rd., northeast Atlanta, 404/733–5900.*

8 *d-1*

HENNESSEY NIGHTCLUB

A wide variety of entertainment graces this recently upscaled club. A comedy show with hostess Wanda Smith takes the stage on Thursday nights. Local radio personalities are featured Friday and Saturday: Joyce Littel hosts Champagne Fridays with live jazz, while Porsche Foxx hosts Saturday nights with a live R&B band 10–11 PM. After that, DJ Chip takes over until 3 AM on Saturday night. Prepare to dress nicely; no sports gear allowed. Cover is $10. *5471 Memorial Dr., Stone Mountain, Atrium Plaza, 404/508–4599.*

5 *b-7*

JOHNNY'S HIDEAWAY

A large, accommodating bar, music from the 1930s through the 1960s, a dance floor for all kinds of dancing, and a full menu featuring steaks, seafood, burgers, and appetizers make this a favorite of the 40-plus crowd, although you'll find younger and older patrons, too. Some folks dress formally and some casually. The Sinatra Room is worth a visit; it houses more than 100 pieces of Frank memorabilia. "King's Corner" is devoted to Elvis memorabilia and photos. The club is open daily. No cover, but there is a two-drink minimum. *3771 Roswell Rd., Buckhead, 404/233–8026.*

15 *e-2*

KAYA BISTRO & NIGHTCLUB

Bistro and nightclub in one, this spot features various types of dance music, from reggae to hip-hop to house. From Wednesday through Sunday, Atlanta's finest DJs spin tunes for dancing, and on Saturday nights Fiesta Latina is the regular program, usually with a live band. The menu is bistro—featuring basic bar food, including wings, mozzarella sticks, sandwiches and salads—the cover charge varies, and ladies enter free before 11 PM. *1068 Peachtree St., Midtown, 404/874–4460.*

5 *f-8*

PREMIER CLUB

This is not your run-of-the-mill dance club. Indian cuisine is the specialty in the kitchen, and Indian pop, Bhangra, and European and American pop are on the play list, mostly thanks to the efforts of a DJ, but sometimes, for special occasions, live Indian music is presented. In addition to the dance floor, there is also karaoke, pool tables, and a full service bar. The club is closed Monday and there is no cover. *2100 Park Lake Dr., Tucker, 770/493–7159.*

2 *h-8*

29 S. MAIN BAR & GRILL AND 1848 WINE LOFT

Here are several operations in one: First, there's a long bar with bar seating and high tables. To one side is a performance space that's basically devoted to rock, while upstairs the 1848 Wine Loft, a fine dining restaurant, presents a jazz schedule, comedy, and sometimes wine-tasting events. Downstairs the menu offers an extensive selection of typical American bar food—burgers, sandwiches, grilled chicken, pasta—and sometimes adds a Peruvian touch. Covers are

charged only occasionally for the music, depending on the band, which sets the rules. The cover for comedy is $10. *29 S. Main St., Alpharetta, 770/751–5954.*

FOLK & ACOUSTIC

12 *f-3*

BUCKHEAD SALOON

This establishment across from the Roxy (*see* Performance Venues, *above*) features live acoustic music, from folk to popular. Casually dressed folks in the 25–30 age group meander in and out of the bar, and much of the time there are performances on the covered deck. There is no cover or drink minimum. *3107 Peachtree Rd., Buckhead, 404/261–7922.*

14 *g-3*

EDDIE'S ATTIC

Dedicated to the performing songwriter, this spot features internationally known musicians as well as struggling locals. Eddie, the proprietor, has helped to give many talented hopefuls, such as the Indigo Girls, their first break. There are regular open mike showdowns, and the space occasionally serves as a gallery for local visual artists. A full and constantly evolving menu of burgers, chicken sandwiches, pasta, and salads, plus bar nibbles such as wings and stuffed mushrooms, is available. Doors open at 4 daily and covers run $3–$10, depending on who's playing. *515B N. McDonough St., Decatur, 404/377–4976, www.eddiesattic.com.*

15 *g-2*

REDLIGHT

At this pioneering cyber café (opened in 1994), you can go on-line for live Internet broadcasts from Wednesday through Sunday from 7 PM. Open to the early morning hours, the café features a variety of live music, including jazz, blues, bluegrass, rock, and acoustic. Wednesday is open mike night, so there's no cover. Thursday is devoted to bluegrass ($3 cover). Friday through Sunday feature local and national acoustic acts, with covers ranging from $5 to $25; jazz is featured occasionally. On Tuesday, patrons bring board games and just hang out. The café offers a simple menu of appetizers (quesadillas, Brie and baguette, garlic cheese bread), salads, sandwiches, pasta and desserts.

Closed Monday. *553 Amsterdam Ave., Virginia-Highland, 404/627–0875, www. redlightcafe.com.*

FOLK DANCING

12 *g-8*

CHATTAHOOCHEE COUNTRY DANCERS

The gym of Morningside Baptist Church was hardly designed as a dance club, but when this group puts on its Friday-night contra dances, you'd never know the difference. The evening starts at 7:30 with an hour of lessons upstairs, where you can learn line and circle dancing. Forget about being a fashion plate—wear comfortable, loose clothing and flat, soft-sole shoes. And you don't have to bring a partner, as mixing's the thing at these friendly bluegrass shindigs. There's a $5 cover, unless a special band is playing. For information, call Atlanta Dance Hotline (404/634–2585). *Morningside Baptist Church, 1700 Piedmont Ave., Morningside.*

14 *e-5*

ENGLISH COUNTRY DANCE ATLANTA

Think of the party scenes in all the Jane Austen movies you've seen, subtract the costumes, and you'll have a picture of English country dancing, whose heyday was from the 16th to the 18th century. A called form of dancing, it is always done to live music. The people here are into truly social dancing, not posing or performing. Wear comfortable, soft-sole shoes. There's a $5 cover; call Atlanta Dance Hotline (404/634–2585) for the schedule. *222 Eastlake Dr., Oakhurst Baptist Church, Decatur.*

ROYAL SCOTTISH COUNTRY DANCE SOCIETY, ATLANTA BRANCH

This international organization is devoted to teaching and preserving the traditional ballroom dancing of Scotland. The graceful, sprightly steps of the form, also known as Scottish country dancing, is the focus of classes and social events. Activities take place at various venues all over town. For schedules, call the Atlanta Dance Hotline (404/634-2585). *Box 33905, Decatur 30033, www.mindspring.com/~atlbrnch.*

FUN

5 *h-5*

DAVE & BUSTER'S

These two adult entertainment complexes are the ultimate hangouts for game players: you can play video games, pinball, virtual reality games, skee-ball, table hockey, and pool. Families get in on the fun, too, often on the midway, where slot machines and other games pay off in tickets that can be exchanged for toy prizes. There is a full-service bar and a restaurant that serves decent American fare. The place is open every day from about 11 AM until late. *2215 D & B Dr., Marietta, 770/951–5554.*

5 *h-4*

4000 Venture Dr., Duluth, 770/497–1152.

12 *f-3*

JELLYROLL'S DUELING PIANOS AND SING-A-LONG

Atlanta's only rock-and-roll dueling piano bar will make you laugh and sing out loud. Four pianists take turns dueling with each other one-on-one while goading the audience into the fray. It's too much fun to ignore. Music is the focus, but the atmosphere can get crazy and wild. The bar is open 7 PM–3 AM, Wednesday–Saturday, and the show begins at 8 (no food is served). You must be 21 to enter; the bar is wheelchair-accessible. The cover is $3 on Thursday, $6 on Friday–Saturday; no cover Wednesday. *295 E. Paces Ferry Rd., Buckhead, 404/261–6866.*

GAY AND LESBIAN BARS & CLUBS

15 *f-4*

ATLANTA EAGLE

Very proudly gay-owned and -operated, this Levis-and-leather bar is a fun, tolerant (women are welcome) place to dance. There are regularly scheduled contests and leather fests, and various organizations meet and hold charity events here. You can get grill/bar food as well as drinks. No cover, but a one-drink minimum applies. *306 Ponce de Leon Ave., Midtown, 404/873–2453, www.atlantaeagle.com.*

15 *e-3*

BACKSTREET

Dance to house, pop, and techno and then catch a fabulous drag show at this

24-hour club, which is probably Atlanta's best known gay space. It welcomes all kinds of people—gay and straight, male and female, the freakier the better—and a veritable crush of folks shows up. Everyone must show ID, no matter your age, to get in. You may use credit cards to pay the cover charge (which varies), but not at the bar to purchase drinks. This is a members-only club, with dues costing $10 per quarter or $35 per year; membership entitles cardholders to free entry from Sunday through Thursday, and $5 admission on Friday and Saturday. Take a taxi if you can, as parking ($5 on the weekends) is a real nuisance and very limited. *845 Peachtree St., Midtown, 404/873–1986, www.cyber-bitch.com. MARTA: Midtown.*

15 *g-1*

BURKHART'S PUB

Dark wood paneling, redbrick floors, and carefully selected artwork generate a warm, friendly, casual atmosphere where gay and straight singles and couples mix and mingle. This is a pub and then some, with pool tables, karaoke on Monday and Wednesday, and Sox with Attitude puppet shows on Tuesday. Imbued with a real spirit of community involvement, the bar prides in being the largest corporate sponsor in Atlanta for HIV/Aids Services. *1924 Piedmont Rd., Ansley Square, Midtown, 404/875 5238, www.burkharts.com.*

15 *g-2*

FUSION ATLANTA

Atlanta's gay men of color come here to dance to house, hip-hop, reggae, and R&B spun by great DJs. Some nights, there are contests or other special events. The club is open from 10:30 PM until whenever, and the cover averages $8. *550C Amsterdam Ave., Midtown Outlet Center, Morningside, 404/872–6411.*

15 *g-3*

HOEDOWN'S

DJs aren't the only ones doing the spinning at this country-music venue. It's a men's bar, but Thursday and Sunday are lesbian nights. Line-dance lessons are offered Tuesday, Wednesday, and Thursday beginning at 8 PM and Sunday at 5 PM. Also on Sunday, there's a free buffet. Hoedown's does not charge a cover except on New Year's Eve, and it's closed Monday. *931 Monroe Dr., Midtown Promenade, 404/876–0001.*

12 *g-7*

THE OTHERSIDE OF ATLANTA

This entertainment complex has it all: dancing to DJs' spins, live music on the patio, ample food and drink choices, live floor shows, female impersonators, a piano lounge, pool tables, and a quiet martini bar. The best of the 1970s and 1980s play on Sunday, Tuesday is martini night, Wednesday features house, hip-hop, and rap music, Thursday night goes country and western, Friday stars female impersonator Lauren LeMasters (10:30 PM) and Heather Scott (1 AM). Saturdays there's a 10:30 PM show by female impersonator Heather Daniels and DJ-driven dance music (top 40s). There's a large covered patio and a game area with pool tables and air hockey. A cover ($6) is charged only on Wednesday, Friday, and Saturday after 9 PM. *1924 Piedmont Rd., Midtown, 404/875–5238, www.otherside–atl.com.*

15 *f-2*

OUTWRITE BOOKSTORE & COFFEEHOUSE

A coffeehouse and bookstore catering to the gay and lesbian community, Outwrite is a casual, comfortable, and civilized spot. Everything printed, and very good coffee with pastries (cakes, brownies and bagels) is the order of the day. Comfortable leather upholstered sofas provide relaxing seating, along with limited bar seating and table seating. Frequent poetry readings are another draw, often with the poets themselves reading original work. Open weekdays 8 AM–11 PM, weekends 8 AM–midnight. *991 Piedmont Ave., Midtown, 404/607–0082.*

14 *g-4*

MY SISTERS' ROOM

Tucked away on a slip of a street near Agnes Scott College, this gathering spot for lesbians of all sorts—especially couples—is a comfortable and safe haven for an evening out. A large patio covered by a domed canvas roof holds table seating; just beyond lies a garden. Within is sofa seating, a bar, and a juke box. From time to time, live entertainment by regional and national lesbian singers draws large crowds. The limited menu mostly sticks to bar food—mozzarella sticks, sandwiches, fries—but also features occasional homemade specials. Curb-side parking is extremely limited. The bar is open late and serves brunch on Sunday. *222 E. Howard Ave., Decatur, 404/370–1990.*

HOTEL BARS

For hotel sports bars, *see* Sports Bars, *below.*

6 *a-4*
BUTTONS LOUNGE

Buttons, in the Gwinnett Marriott, takes its name from Button Gwinnett, who signed the Declaration of Independence. The bar serves a light menu along with good libations. A dance floor beckons in the evening, and a vocalist performs popular tunes on Friday and Saturday. *Gwinnett Marriott Hotel, 1775 Pleasant Hill Rd., Duluth, 770/923–1775.*

15 *e-5*
FANDANGLES

This plush bar in the downtown Sheraton has not quite been discovered by the after-work set, so it's still a mellow place to unwind. Two snuggly curtained-off zones provide an extra bit of privacy. You can nibble on appetizers such as baby back ribs and crab cakes. *Sheraton Atlanta Hotel, 165 Courtland St., Downtown, 404/659–6500.*

12 *g-2*
GRAND HYATT LOBBY LOUNGE

A quiet spot that's just right after a busy business day, this lounge has crystal chandeliers, a waterfall and Japanese garden outside tall windows, and a short bar menu of delectables. It is cigar-friendly, and the specialty of the house is the Grand Martini. Live jazz is offered on weekend evenings until 1 AM. *Grand Hyatt Hotel, 3300 Peachtree Rd., Buckhead, 404/365–8100.*

9 *a-6*
HUNT LOUNGE

A gathering spot for southsiders, this busy hotel bar can get really jammed. Live music on the weekends draws a diverse crowd of people in their 40s and 50s. Music ranges all over the keyboard but usually is loud and louder, so forget conversation. There's a simple bar menu. *Wyndam Peachtree City Conference Center, 2443 GA 54, Peachtree City, 770/487–2000, ext. 7538.*

15 *e-2*
PARK 75 LOUNGE

Cushy upholstered seating, a large bar, and the lilt of piano music make for a genteel and relaxing evening. The atmosphere is pure comfort, whether you prefer to read a book in a corner wing chair or chat with friends around a table. Thursday through Saturday, the piano music is live. Lovely tapas are occasionally served at cocktail hour, and a bar menu with appetizers, soups, salads, pasta, and similar light fare. *Four Seasons Atlanta Hotel, 75 14th St., Midtown, 404/881–9898.*

12 *h-2*
RITZ-CARLTON, BUCKHEAD LOBBY LOUNGE

Besides the inviting bar, this large space has a fireplace and very comfortable seating. Live piano entertainment keeps the room harmonious all day long, and on the weekends there is dancing to light jazz, sometimes with fine vocalists. Afternoon tea is served daily, or order from the appetizer and martini menus. *Ritz-Carlton Buckhead, 3434 Peachtree Rd., Buckhead, 404/237–2700.*

7 *d-2*
RODNEY'S

Take to the Ramada Inn's dance floor to everything from Top 40 to oldies to country and western. Friday and Saturday nights, live bands perform popular rock 'n' roll hits. Bar food is available, or you can order from the adjoining restaurant's full menu. The bar is open daily until the early hours. *Ramada Inn, 4225 Fulton Industrial Blvd., northeast Atlanta, 404/696–2728.*

5 *c-5*
SAVU

Opened in 1999, the lavish W Atlanta@ perimeter center includes a casual yet upscale bar that's as good for after-work gatherings as it is for leisurely unwinding. Plush seating, a cool white-and-gray color scheme, and low lighting create the mood. There's a bar menu for quick noshes. *W Atlanta@perimetercenter, 111 Perimeter Center W, off Ashford-Dunwoody Rd. at I–285, Dunwoody, 770/396–6800.*

15 *e-5*
SUNDIAL RESTAURANT & LOUNGE

High atop the Westin Peachtree Plaza Hotel, revolve your way around the city's skyline while sipping a cocktail. You can hear jazz Thursday through Saturday or piano music the rest of the week. The menu offers appetizers and desserts, and the bartender whips up specialty drinks. *Westin Peachtree Plaza Hotel, 210 Peachtree St., Downtown, 404/589–7506, ext. 7302.*

JAZZ

5 e-2

COMEAUX'S LOUISIANA BAR & GRILL

A Cajun-Creole restaurant (*see* Chapter 1), oyster bar, and jazz-blues club, this is a rock-solid suburban performance venue. The dining room is family-friendly, but couples are comfortable here, too. Live music begins as early as 4 PM, with a second group taking over at 10 PM. There is no cover. *9925 Haynes Bridge Rd., Alpharetta, 770/442–2524.*

12 g-2

DANTE'S DOWN THE HATCH

Hot fondue and cool jazz in a nautical atmosphere are what these sibling bars are all about. The Paul Mitchell Trio entertains regularly, along with visiting guitar players and folk singers. Diners who wish to sit in the jazz area pay a $6 cover; if you want the chocolate fondue, order it when you make your reservations. Open daily. *3380 Peachtree Rd., Buckhead, 404/266–1600.*

15 e-4

CHURCHILL GROUNDS

The menu of light appetizers (*see* Chapter 1) is perfect for the accompanying straight-ahead jazz that performs live from Tuesday through Sunday, beginning about 9:30 PM. Covers run anywhere from $5 to $25, as some of the groups performing are major national and international artists. Pastries and espresso are lovely. This also is a good spot for a quick bite before events at the Fox Theatre, located right next door. *660 Peachtree Rd., Midtown, 404/ 876–3030.*

5 c-5

CAFÉ 290

A favorite place for friends who want to hang out, the café features decently prepared American food and live jazz every night. The talent is often local, but it never fails to be very, very good. Music starts at 9:30 PM and keeps going until 4 AM; on Sunday the crowds thin out. The cover is $5 after 8 PM, and is credited against the cost of your meal. *290 Hilderbrand Dr., Sandy Springs, 404/256–3942.*

5 a-6

RAY'S ON THE RIVER

This restaurant (*see* Chapter 1) overlooking the Chattahoochee features live jazz in the bar on Tuesday through Saturday nights, beginning Tuesday–Thursday at 8 PM and Friday and Saturday 9 PM. The baby grand piano makes good happy hour music Tuesday–Friday from 5:30-7:30 PM, when complimentary hors d'oeuvres are served. The restaurant serves dinner daily, lunch on weekdays, and brunch on Sunday. There is no cover. *6700 Powers Ferry Rd., Marietta, 770/955–1187.*

12 g-3

SAMBUCA JAZZ CAFÉ

After dinner, well-dressed jazz fans queue up to get into this club, so get here early if you want a seat. Hard-core music enthusiasts dive for the center tables so they can sit right in front of the band, while those who like to chat gather around the large bar. You can eat dinner here, although the food's not the greatest, but if you get a good seat the music is worth some mundane munchies. Open daily, the café starts its shows at 7:30 PM. There is no cover, but there is a two-drink minimum at the bar and a $14 per person minimum at dinner (exclusive of alcohol). *3102 Piedmont Rd., Buckhead, 404/237–5299.*

4 h-7

VININGS INN RESTAURANT

This popular, quaint restaurant dishes up a satisfying menu of excellent crab cakes and good barbecue. Wednesday through Saturday, jazz combos play on the early side, followed on Friday and Saturday nights by cover bands that play pop hits. *3011 Paces Mill Rd., Vinings, 770/438–2282.*

15 e-3

YIN YANG MUSIC CAFE

Live music jazzes up Friday and Saturday nights at this café. Wednesday night's Lyricist Lounge is the scene of amateur poetry readings, and other nights bring hip-hop (sometimes with an open mike) to the café. Light dinner fare is served. The café is open Tuesday–Saturday, 9 PM–2:30 AM. *64 3rd St., Midtown, 404/607–0682.*

LATIN

12 f-3
HAVANA CLUB

A club with Latin flair, Havana offers dancing to a variety of live music, from blues and jazz to salsa, until 1 or 2 AM daily. A DJ takes over until closing time (3–4 AM). True to its name, this is also a cigar bar, complete with walk-in humidor. The mixologists specialize in martinis, and a free buffet is served at Salsa Sunday, the weekly Latin disco. A private VIP lounge, complete with private bartender and bar, is available for private events. Open daily, Havana does not charge a cover unless something special is going on. *247 Buckhead Ave., East Village Square, Buckhead, 404/869–8484.*

12 f-3
SANCTUARY LATIN NIGHTCLUB

The dance floor here swings to sizzling Latin rhythms from Thursday through Saturday. The young crowd, which tends to dress sharp, doesn't begin to gather until around 10 PM, and the club stays open way past your bedtime. So, you want to salsa but you don't know a rhumba from a samba? You will if you come here, because they'll show you how. Lessons cost $5, and the cover runs $8–$10, according to the day of the week. *128 E. Andrews Dr., Buckhead, 404/262–1377.*

14 g-3
TANGO/ATLANTA

This group dedicated to Argentine tango teaches classes at Several Dancers Core in downtown Decatur ($56 for an eight-week series). Partners not required. The schedule of social dances varies, but they're usually held on Saturdays in private homes. *519 N. McDonough St., Decatur, 404/378–6985, www.tango-atlanta.com.*

MUSIC FESTIVALS

15 g-8
ATLANTA JAZZ FESTIVAL

Sponsored by the city, this festival celebrates homegrown as well as national and international jazz talent. Concerts are held in Grant Park throughout Memorial Day weekend, with free outdoor "side" concerts elsewhere on the city's streets during the week preceding the event. *404/817–6815.*

MIDTOWN MUSIC FESTIVAL

This May event attracts some of the top performers in the industry, including Santana, the Steve Miller Band, and Howard Jones. Beer and food booths abound. *404/872–1115.*

MONTREAUX ATLANTA INTERNATIONAL MUSIC FESTIVAL

Free music fills the air throughout the week before Labor Day. Internationally renowned ensembles perform public concerts at outdoor venues throughout the city, soaking the atmosphere with the sweet sounds of jazz, blues, and a bit of reggae. *404/817–6815.*

PIANO BARS

5 d-4
ARTURO'S PIANO BAR

This upscale piano bar presents live music from Wednesday through Sunday. Bobby B. handles the keyboard on the baby grand beginning at 7 PM Wednesday and Thursday. On Friday and Saturday beginning at 8 PM, Bill Kahler sings and plays the piano. Sunday is devoted to live jazz by the Dan Coy Trio, beginning at 6 PM. Lots of hardwood and brick create a warm atmosphere at the bar, which is attached to a casual trattoria that serves substantial Italian cuisine. Everything from pizza to pasta, from salad to veal, graces this ample menu. Monthly wine dinners with jazz are a deal for about $45 for a five-course meal. The bar is open daily, but there's no music Monday–Tuesday. *5486 Chamblee-Dunwoody Rd., Shoppes of Dunwoody, Dunwoody, 770/396–0335.*

5 b-7
CARBO'S

For more than 20 years, Carmen and Bob Mazurek have dished out Italian-inspired food in their full-service restaurant. You can start or end your evening in the piano bar, where you can hear live solo piano music nightly beginning at 7:30 PM. Closed Sunday. *3717 Roswell Rd., Buckhead, 404/231–4433.*

12 g-3
MCKINNON'S LOUISIANE

At the back of the bar of this popular Cajun/Creole restaurant (*see* Chapter 1), patrons gather around a piano before or after dinner, on the way home from work. *3209 Maple Dr., Buckhead, 404/237–1313.*

5 *d-5*

PARK PLACE

At one of the city's most comfortable piano bars, pianists perform nightly, beginning in the late afternoon. Located across from Perimeter Mall, it's perfect for an after-shopping chill. Weeknights, a happy-hour buffet starts at 5 PM. The bar is closed Sunday. *4505 Ashford-Dunwoody Rd., Park Place, Dunwoody, 770/ 399–5990.*

POP/ROCK

14 *a-3*

DARK HORSE TAVERN

Local, and sometimes national, bands rock downstairs while diners enjoy a good meal upstairs. You'll have to pay a cover to see the show, which usually begins around 9 PM, Wednesday through Saturday. The bar is open nightly until the very early hours. *816 N. Highland Ave., Virginia-Highland, 404/ 873–3607.*

14 *b-8*

ECHO LOUNGE

Live music every night—primarily contemporary pop and rock—has made this relative newcomer a significant player on Atlanta's music scene. Most shows welcome anyone over 18 (though you must prove you're 21 to drink) and begin at 9 PM. There's a different act every day, so call for the schedule. *551 Flat Shoals Ave., East Atlanta, 404/681–3600.*

5 *g-7*

THE LAST GREAT WATERING HOLE

During the week this totally guy joint draws locals to its seven billiards tables. Tournaments are frequent events. Other games are available as well, including darts. The menu is mostly bar bites— fries, sandwiches, and the like— although substantial steaks at great prices are a major menu draw. On weekends, mostly local rock 'n' roll bands take the fairly large stage. The cover is $3 on weekends. *4341 Hugh Howell Rd., Tucker, 770/270–5571.*

12 *f-3*

METROPOLITAN PIZZA BAR

In addition to terrific pizzas, calzones, and sandwiches, this place serves up rock and roll and R&B until the early

morning hours. Local bands play on Friday and Saturday, but there is never a cover charge. Karaoke rules Tuesday, while DJs take care of Wednesday and Thursday. Metropolitan offers a rare thing: a casual, budget-friendly evening of entertainment in Buckhead. It's closed Sunday–Monday. *3055 Bolling Way, Buckhead, 404/264–0135, www. metropolitanpizza.com.*

12 *g-8*

SMITH'S OLDE BAR

This olde bar is a venue for local and regional musicians. Contemporary electric and alternative music heats the upstairs area, while cool jazz, folk, light rock, and acoustic mellow the downstairs on occasion, usually in the spring on Wednesday nights. Bar food, such as chicken wings, burgers, and Philly

---

NIGHTTIME NOSHES

There's nothing like a tasty bite to eat while you're grooving to some music or sipping a cocktail. Keep yourself fueled up into the wee hours of the morning.

Blue Pig (Blues)
It's hard to decide whether to come for the music or for the ribs. Hmm . . . ribs—now there' an idea! But the music is first-rate, so it's a win-win situation.

Fandangles (Hotel Bars)
When downtown, duck into one of the two private curtained nooks with your sweetie for a quiet after-work rendezvous. Share a drink, and some of the high-end light fare.

Fuzzy's Place (Blues)
So what if it's a bit scruffy? The food's good, the blues are superb, and the atmosphere is neighborhood funky. Better be smoke tolerant, though.

Park 75 Lounge (Hotel Bars)
Settle into a comfy chair with a glass of champagne and savor the delicious small dishes. The piano music, low and mellow, allows conversation with a friend or lover.

Savu (Hotel Bars)
Coolly sophisticated, the bar at the sleek W Atlanta@perimeter center draws its appetizer menu from the hotel restaurant, which prepares elegant Pacific Rim fare.

cheese steak sandwiches, is served in the downstairs restaurant. There's a cover for upstairs shows only; charges depend on the show, generally $5–$10. Smith's is open daily until the very early hours. *1578 Piedmont Ave., Ansley Park/Morningside, 404/875–1522.*

14 *a-4*

THE STAR BAR

This popular bar in the colorful Little Five Points district has funky live music every day of the week. Usually, it's a rock or pop band, but the acts change frequently, so call for details. The kitchen serves sandwiches and the like to go with the wet stuff. *437 Moreland Ave., Little Five Points, 404/681–9018.*

PUBS & TAVERNS

14 *a-4*

BREWHOUSE HOUSE OF BREWS

This lively establishment has a distinctive neighborhood feel to it. In addition to resident locals, the Brits hang out here, so the menu features bangers 'n' mash, fish 'n' chips, and similar pub grub. But the extensive menu holds forth familiar chicken dishes and burgers as well, with full entrees as well as lighter fare. There's patio seating in good weather. Of course, there are beers-a-plenty, with 22 on tap and 24 by the bottle. Brewhoues closes at 3 AM Monday–Saturday, and at 1 AM Sunday. *401 Moreland Ave., Little Five Points, 404/525–7799.*

5 *c-3*

CHAPLINS

This spot has many personalities: It is a restaurant with a full menu of steaks and seafood. It is a sports bar with TVs and a big screen to show the game. It is a casual tavern with a heated outdoor deck where folks can lounge, munch, and converse. And, on Saturday nights, it is a full-tilt karaoke bar with contests and prizes. Chaplins is near the entrance to the Old Southern Mill in Historic Roswell; it's open 7 days. *555 S. Atlanta St., Roswell, 770/552–1147.*

12 *f-3*

CHURCHILL ARMS

Small groups of friends chat around a roaring fireplace, while another bunch warbles around a piano. In the next

room, billiards and darts are the draw. Meanwhile, in the center of it all, an attentive gentleman dispenses drinks at the bar. Come for the camaraderie. *3223 Cains Hill Pl., Buckhead, 404/344–5633.*

4 *f-5*

DIRTY BIRD CAFÉ

While it may seem as though these neighborhood pubs were named for the Atlanta Falcons, known as the "Dirty Birds" after their NFC championship-ending 1998 season, the naming was strictly a coincidence. The burgers are a major draw, and so are the numerous sports-tuned TVs scattered throughout each of several locations across the metro area. Wings are a big thing, with hotness levels ranging from mega mild to searing. Beyond sandwiches and noshes, there's a full menu with everything from meat loaf to steaks and pasta, and more than 100 bottled beers. These are designed as family-friendly operations, so there are pool tables at Powder Springs, and free kids' videos, Nintendo and play stations at Olde Towne. *1750 Powder Springs Rd., at Maclan Rd., Maclan Pointe, Marietta, 770/499–7780.*

5 *b-4*

736 Johnson Ferry Rd., Olde Towne, Marietta, 678/560–1194.

13 *e-6*

2916 N. Druid Hills Rd., Northeast Atlanta, 404/315–8555.

5 *e-1*

1100 North Pointe Dr., Alpharetta, 770/751–1100.

4 *h-5*

1325 Powers Ferry Rd., Marietta, 770/955–1800.

15 *h-3*

DUGAN'S TAVERN

A raft of beers and some singularly odd-sounding drinks complement a good-size menu that's heavy on bar food. The Virginia-Highland tavern seems a bit rowdy, while Stone Mountain has a more sedate atmosphere. Dugan's also serves as a neighborhood sports bar, attracting locals who enjoy sports events on the more than 30 TVs. Stone Mountain has a somewhat more extensive menu. *777 Ponce de Leon Ave., Virginia-Highland, 404/885–1217.*

8 *e-1*

*5922 Memorial Dr., Stone Mountain, 404/
297–8545.*

14 *a-5*

EUCLID AVENUE
YACHT CLUB

This laid-back neighborhood bar has
served good food and every kind of beer
imaginable—including 15 on draft—to
hungry Atlantans for 13 years. It has a
TV, but people don't come here to watch
the tube; they come to hang with friends
and neighbors. The club is open from
noon (12:30 on Sunday) until sometime
after 2:30 AM, depending on the night.
Ask the owners (who do frequent the
place, by the way) the origin of the bar's
name. *1136 Euclid Ave., Little Five Points,
404/688–0163.*

12 *f-3*

FADÓ

Step inside this popular Buckhead after-
work bar, and you'd swear you took a
plane to the Auld Sod itself. Dark-wood
paneling divides the space into intimate
areas, and rough-hewn furnishings,
mostly from Ireland, provide seating.
Friends gather to hoist a pint and watch
delayed-play rugby and Irish football
matches on the large-screen TV. Good
Irish food includes the house-made
soda bread, Poughman's sandwich, and
boxty, the classic Irish potato pancake
filled with various tasty morsels, such as
smoked salmon or corned beef and cabbage (*see* Chapter 1). Selected evenings
feature live performances of traditional
Celtic music. On Sunday, come for the
Irish breakfast. There's brunch on Saturday and Sunday. *3035 Peachtree Rd.,
Buckhead, 404/841–0066.*

5 *g-7*

FLANIGAN'S THERE GOES
THE NEIGHBORHOOD

This neighborhood watering hole with
fair food and very friendly staffers draws
neighbors to watch TV on its numerous
screens, including one big-screener. The
large bar anchors the establishment,
and booth seating lines the opposite
wall. Food ranges from fish 'n' chips
and fried chicken to steaks and crab
legs; check out the specials. But the real
reason to come here is the conviviality.
Live music features Reggae on Wednesday, and a variety on Friday and Saturday, including a live Irish band (The
Charms) at least twice a month. Trivia

contests are slated for Thursday and
Sunday at 8 PM. *4092 Lawrenceville Hwy.,
Tucker, 770/270–0001.*

15 *e-2*

FUBAR

The big draw here is the raw bar, plus
other seafood served in a casual style.
Five beers on draft and another 200 in
the bottle compose an outstanding brew
selection. There's a sidewalk patio, making this a fine fair-weather gathering
place. It's also good singles territory.
*1136 Crescent Ave., Midtown, 404/873–
6307.*

10 *a-1*

GREGORY'S RESTAURANT

On one side is a large full-service, very
family-oriented restaurant. The other
side is a bar, where neighbors greet each
other and lively conversations are the
order of the day. Food is freshly prepared, and it's really more than ordinar-
ily good, with a very fine freshly
crumbed fried shrimp and cobbler
among the best items. *3570 GA 138,
Stockbridge, 770/474–7988.*

5 *b-4*

HOUCK'S STEAK
AND SEAFOOD

Bill Houck's bar and grill is a family-run,
family kind of place (*see* Chapter 1). Parents bring their children, who are especially welcome. Regulars include local
political, arts, and sports celebrities
(some of them depicted in the mural
just inside the entrance) as well as ordinary Joes (whose lesser-known like-
nesses appear on the facing wall).
Outside, a tree-ringed deck overlooks a
small pond. Popular local musicians
Banks & Shane, sometimes joined by
local yuckster Jerry Farber, perform when
they are not busy with corporate engage-
ments. *Paper Mill Village shopping center,
305 Village Pkwy., Marietta, 770/667–
1112.*

15 *f-2*

JOE'S ON JUNIPER

This neighborhood bar's good menu
and fine atmosphere keep it filled with
area denizens, mostly singles. The food
tends toward quality burgers and sandwiches, and breakfast is served all day.
About a dozen good beers are offered
on tap, with many more fine brews
(including micros) sold by the bottle.
The sidewalk patio out front is a good

spot for enjoying supper or a snack or some people-watching in good weather. Joe's stays open late. *1049 Juniper St., Midtown, 404/875–6634.*

14 *a-3*

LIMERICK JUNCTION

Local Celtic bands and singers transport patrons from this pub to the Old Country every night. The traditional Irish music goes well with the clinking of glasses and the hoisting of pints. This is a neighborhood kind of place that draws suburbanites as well as locals with families, so the atmosphere is never rowdy. A small cover is sometimes charged, and the bar stays open until 2 AM on weekends. *822 N. Highland Ave., Virginia-Highland, 404/874–7147.*

14 *a-5*

THE LOCAL

This basic neighborhood spot is popular with youngish upscale locals, although the personnel can be less than friendly. Patrons gather more for conversation than they do for food, which is classic bar fare, including an extensive selection of sandwiches and burgers made fresh on site. Barbecue is house-made Carolina-style, with mustard sauce available, and is even served with hush puppies. If customers are still hanging around, closing isn't until about 4 AM, but sometimes the bar shutters as early as 1:30 AM if it's not busy. *758 Ponce de Leon Ave., Poncey-Highland, 404/873–5002.*

12 *f-3*

MCDUFF'S IRISH PUB

From Wednesday through Saturday, this little pub shakes with lively—and live—folk, pop, and acoustic tunes. Despite the bar's name, Celtic music is featured only occasionally. You can order from a full menu of basic bar fare, such as chicken and buffalo tenders, potato skins and potato soup, nachos, salads, sandwiches, and a house-made chicken curry. Have a drink at the full bar and enjoy some friendly conversation before the show. McDuff's is open daily to the early hours. *56 East Andrews Dr., East Andrews Square, Buckhead, 404/816–8008.*

14 *a-2*

MOE'S & JOE'S BAR & GRILL

Now more than a half century old in Virginia-Highland, Moe's & Joe's draws

neighborhood denizens and Emory students to its personable environment. In July 1999 another opened in Kennesaw, reproducing the long formica-topped bar, booths, and tables that lend such character to the original. The Kennesaw location is more family-focused and has some live acoustic music on Saturday night. Both locations serve beer and wine only. *1033 N. Highland Ave., Virginia-Highland, 404/873–6090.*

4 *d-1*

3900 Legacy Park Blvd., Kennesaw, 770/426–1010.

14 *h-1*

MELTON'S APP & TAPP

Here are two operations, really—a restaurant appended to a classic neighborhood pub. On the pub side, there's a TV for sports devotees, who cluster around the bar. Friendly personnel keep track of patrons, firmly excluding anyone whose behavior doesn't measure up to standards. Ladies can gather at the bar without concern. There are great burgers and buffalo tenders, and fantastic beer cheese soup, when they make it. *2500 N. Decatur Rd., Decatur, 404/634–9112.*

14 *a-4*

MANUEL'S TAVERN

Atlanta's quintessential neighborhood pub, by which locals measure all others, started life more than a half century ago in Poncey-Highland, a booming in-town neighborhood. Politicians (including one former president and his wife), students, and young attorneys and accountants make up the crowd at the original location, while suburbanites flood the newer Stone Mountain location. Large-screen TVs make watching Braves and Falcons games plenty of fun, and the food's quite good, too. The steak sandwich and chicken wings are especially worthy (see Chapter 1). *602 N. Highland Ave., Poncey-Highland, 404/525–3447.*

8 *d-1*

4877 Memorial Dr., Stone Mountain, 404/296–6919.

12 *f-3*

MIKE 'N' ANGELO'S

Buckhead's authentic neighborhood tavern, this place has plenty of regulars, who come throughout the week for the warm atmosphere and friendly service. A standard bar menu is offered, plus a daily special like steak, meat loaf, or stir-fry. There's rock and roll on the speakers and a game room with two pool tables. The bar is open daily until the very early morning hours. *312 E. Paces Ferry Rd., Buckhead, 404/237–0949.*

13 *e-1*
NAUGHTY'S GOOD TIME EMPORIUM

This friendly bar delivers on its name, drawing folks in the Buford-Clairmont area. A game of pool, a few brews, some munchies, and a football game add up to an ideal evening for Emporium customers. It's open daily until after midnight. *3747 Buford Hwy., northeast metro, 404/320–6999.*

5 *g-5*
OLDE PECULIAR PUBLIC HOUSE

What? No TVs? This old-style pub lets patrons relax and talk without the blare of electronic noise. There's a fireplace, a large deck, and lots of beers on tap. More of a British pub, it serves bangers and mash and fish-and-chips—your typical British pub fare. A very warm and fuzzy atmosphere prevails. Traditional Irish music is scheduled on some weekend nights and on the second Wednesday of the month. There's sometimes an acoustic open mike on Tuesdays beginning around 9 PM, when local people perform solo blues, folk, and rock acts. There's no cover. *29 Jones St., Norcross, 678/291–9220, www.oldepeculiar.com.*

PADDY'S IRISH PUB

Oddly enough, this Irish pub just outside the 10 counties stands on the grounds of Château Elan, Georgia's largest winery, snuggled up against the back of its chateauesque main building. The pub's furnishings are imported from Ireland, as are the recipes on the menu (e.g., shepherd's pie; *see* Chapter 1) and the tunes played by live musicians on the weekends. Naturally, instead of the château's wine, you can enjoy good lagers, ales, and stouts. Paddy's is open daily. *100 Tour de France, Braselton, 770/932–0900 or 800/233–9463.*

12 *f-3*
PARK BENCH

Antique wood bars, comfortable booths, and live music make the links in this minichain popular places to relax after work. From Thursday through Saturday, local talent performs live acoustic and popular music; on Wednesday night there is an open mike at Buckhead and Emory. The menu runs to New York–style pizza, burgers, and hot wings. The Buckhead branch is open until 3 AM nightly and is closed Sunday except during football season, when it welcomes patrons looking to enjoy the game and some camaraderie. Dunwoody and Emory, which do lunch, are open daily, Dunwoody until around 11 PM, and Emory until the wee hours. No covers and no drink minimums. *256 E. Paces Ferry Rd., Buckhead, 404/264–1334, www.theparkbench.com.*

5 *d-4*
5592 Chamblee-Dunwoody Rd., Dunwoody Hall, Dunwoody, 770/804–1000.

14 *d-2*
1577 N. Decatur Rd., Emory Village, 404/377–8888.

5 *f-4*
POOR RICHARD'S PUB & PORCH

A sports bar as well as a pub, this neighborhood hangout has 11 TVs, including one big screen. Live music, from blues to rock and roll to jazz, is featured on Friday, and Sunday is open mike night. The food runs to steaks and sandwiches, and there's free happy-hour buffet (with the purchase of a beverage) weekdays 5:30–7. Choose from more than a dozen beers on tap, most of them imports. *3330 Peachtree Corners Cir., Norcross, 770/447–1776.*

15 *f-2*
PRINCE OF WALES

As close to an English pub as you'll get in Atlanta, this place is home-away-from-home for a lot of nostalgic Brits. Among other atmospheric touches, football (i.e. soccer, as Americans call it) trophies won by the amateur league clubs that gather here are scattered about. Dimly lit and paneled in dark wood, the pub is a perfect place to refresh and refuel after a Piedmont Park outing. The food is strictly pub grub, including really good fish-and-chips and bread pudding (*see* Chapter 1). *1144 Piedmont Ave., Midtown, 404/876–0027.*

5 *c-5*
THE PUB AT NORDSTROM'S

A pub in a department store? Yup. So this is where the guys hang out while the girls shop? Nope, the girls are here, too. Smack in the middle of the men's department, the Pub dishes up gumbo, sandwiches (from burgers to grilled Portobello mushroom), fish-and-chips, onion rings, and, of course, beers on draught. Ensconced amid rich, dark-wood paneling, two TVs bring the latest sports to folks seated at the bar. The pub is open during store hours only. *4400 Ashford-Dunwoody Rd., Perimeter Mall, Dunwoody, 770/394–1141, ext. 1620.*

5 *e-5*

SCROOGES LOUNGE

A rustic neighborhood hangout with loyal regulars, Scrooges has four pool tables, two large projection TVs, and a few smaller tubes, which are usually tuned to the game. The joint serves lunch, and offers a full menu with daily specials and weekend buffets. The lemon pepper wings are famous. Daily specials feature Southern and American dishes. You can play pool free on Sunday and Monday nights. The bar is open very late. *4480 Winters Chapel Rd., Doraville, 770/448–8394.*

15 *e-3*

THE STEIN CLUB

Small, and filled with a very local crowd, this has been a Midtown fixture for decades. It's about as unpretentious as a pub can get, and neighborhood regulars are known by name. Nobody cares how anybody dresses. Come not for the food (they don't serve any) or the brews but for the camaraderie. For nearly three decades, the annual Atlanta Open Orthographic Meet has taken place here the last Saturday in January, drawing folks from all over the metro area and even from out of town. *929 Peachtree St., Midtown, 404/876–3707.*

SOCIAL & BALLROOM DANCING

5 *b-6*

ATLANTA BALLROOM DANCE CENTRE

Ballroom, Latin, and swing rule at this popular spot where private lessons and parties devoted to ballroom dancing are held every Thursday from 9:30–11 PM. The place is smoke-free. On Saturday it's open 8:30–11, and the cover is just $10 per couple. *120 Northwood Dr., Sandy Springs, 404/847–0821, www.atlantadancecentre.com.*

5 *f-6*

CITY LIGHTS DANCE CLUB

This smoke- and alcohol-free nightclub has one of the largest open dance floors in the city. The crowd runs from teenagers to seniors, with most folks in the 30s–50s age group. Decor and atmosphere are pretty basic, but that doesn't make it any less fun. Most forms of social dancing are taught here, on a rotating schedule that changes every month: ballroom, country and western, swing, and Latin. Lessons start as early as 6 PM during the week, and run all day Saturday and Sunday. A state-of-the-art sound system adds to the experience. *3539 Chamblee-Tucker Rd., Embry Hills Shopping Center, Embry Hills, 770/451–5461, www.citylightsdanceclub.com.*

12 *f-3*

SWINGERS

Celebrate the revival of swing at this club, which plays music from the big-band era. Dance lessons are offered every night. On Monday and Tuesday, dancers age 18 and up are admitted; on other nights you must be 21 to enter. The cover is $5, and the club is open late Monday through Saturday. *3049 Peachtree Rd., Buckhead, 404/816–9931.*

SPORTS BARS

7 *f-6*

BENTLEY'S LOUNGE

The sports bar at the Airport Marriott has a casual and relaxed atmosphere. You'll find 15 TVs, some video games, and bar food. The lounge is open daily. *Airport Marriott, 4711 Best Rd., College Park, 404/766–7900, ext. 6663.*

15 *e-5*

CASABLANCA BAR

A casual sports bar in the Atlanta Hilton and Towers, this place draws hotel patrons in with its big-screen TV and serves them the usual pub grub: pizzas, quesadillas, and wings. *Atlanta Hilton and Towers, 255 Courtland St., Downtown, 404/659–2000.*

15 *e-5*

CHAMPIONS

Large-screen TVs, pool tables, and video games bring a fun-loving crowd to this bar in the Atlanta Marriott Marquis. The kitchen serves burgers, sandwiches, wings, salads, and the like. Since the hotel is frequented by sports celebrities, you might just bump into one here. The bar is open daily 11:30 AM to 2 AM. *265 Peachtree Center Ave., Atlanta Marriott Marquis, Downtown, 404/586–6017.*

12 *e-6*

CHEYENNE GRILL SPORTS BAR

Buckhead's liveliest sports bar features 27 TVs, including three big screens. The place is famous for its buffalo wing sauce, which they claim comes directly from the Anchor Bar in Buffalo, NY, where the spicy wings were supposedly invented. Tucked onto the grounds of a popular shopping center, the place offers nine beers on draught and tons of bottled brews. There is patio dining in good weather. *2391 Peachtree Rd., Peachtree Battle shopping center, Buckhead, 404/842–1010.*

13 *e-6*

FAMOUS PUB AND SPORTS PALACE

Popular with Emory students, this bar has 30 TVs tuned to sports, 12 pool tables, five dart boards, lots of video games, and dancing to popular recorded tunes. A menu of burgers, wings, and steaks is served with beer, wine, and other libations. *2947 N. Druid Hills Rd., northeast Atlanta, 404/633–3555.*

2 *c-8*

FIREHOUSE GRILL

This sports bar has the usual collection of TVs, pool tables, and video games, but it also features a full menu of bar food, sandwiches, pastas, fish, and steaks. There is a special on draught beer on Tuesday and Thursday, which are also karaoke nights. On weekends, live music attracts crowds. Open daily, the grill offers inexpensive lunch specials Monday through Friday. *12195 GA 92 at Trickum Rd., Woodstock, 770/924–5594.*

5 *b-6*

FRANKIE'S FOOD, SPORTS & SPIRITS

This upscale spot caters to sports fans of all stripes and ages. It also attracts members of Atlanta's pro teams and visiting competitors, who try to blend in with the crowd. Everybody enjoys the 150 TVs and the enclosed outside deck, which also has TVs. Live acoustic music

begins at 6 PM on Friday, but there's no cover. *5600 Roswell Rd., The Prado, Sandy Springs, 404/843–9444.*

15 *d-6*

JOCKS & JILLS

Four satellite dishes and more than 20 TVs anchor the Downtown location of this minichain of sports bars. The branch is a favorite with sports celebrities. Sports mementos decorate the bar, including a pair of Evander Holyfield's boxing gloves and a ball from a Braves no-hitter. A framed Sports Illustrated article about the bar hangs proudly in full view. The Norcross branch is plastered with the pennants of various teams from the last 50 years. At any of the locations, you can order from an all-American menu of hamburgers, salads, seafood, pizza, and similar casual fare. Each of the bars has occasional live music; a DJ spins dance music on Fridays. All the branches are open daily. *1 CNN Center, Downtown, 404/688–4225.*

5 *g-2*

9775 Medlock Bridge Rd., Duluth, 770/ 495–9113.

4 *h-7*

2569 Cobb Pkwy., Galleria Center, 770/ 952–8401.

15 *e-2*

112 10th St., Midtown, 404/873–5405.

5 *c-7*

4046 Peachtree Rd., Sandy Springs, 404/ 816–2801.

10 *a-1*

PENALTY BOX

A huge U-shaped bar adorned with neon beer signs nearly fills this establishment, which was launched just in time for the 2000 Super Bowl at the Georgia Dome. Located in a suburban shopping mall, it's got 37 TVs, including 2 big screeners. This bar substantially enlivens the southside after-hours scene. Very much a neighborhood place, it's open to 2 AM every night but Sunday (when it closes at midnight). Appetizers, pizzas, burgers, sandwiches, and salads constitute the fare. *3570-B GA 138, Stockbridge, 770/389–3551.*

4 *g-4*

ROCCO'S PUB

About 2 mi east of the Big Chicken, in the Town and Country Shopping Center, this sports haven keeps its 20 TVs—including a couple of big screens—tuned to the big events. The kitchen dishes up burgers, sandwiches, salads, and such. The house-made chili is especially popular; in fact, Rocco's is the sponsor of the Georgia State Chili Cook-Off. The pub is open daily. *1393 Roswell Rd., Town and Country Shopping Center, Marietta, 770/971–8806.*

8 *d-6*

SPORTS OASIS

The only sports bar within 10 mi, this is truly a fan's oasis, where everybody knows everybody. Several TVs, video games, a jukebox, and a big-guy menu (steaks, ribs, and other meat) keep the crowd happy. The bar presents live music, from country and western to rock and oldies, usually on Friday and Saturday. Wing Night is Monday and Trivia Night is Tuesday. The Oasis is closed Sunday. *1792 Panola Rd., at Flakes Mill Rd., Five Points Crossing, Ellenwood, 770/593–9505.*

12 *f-4*

THREE DOLLAR CAFÉ

Favored by a younger crowd, this chain of bars features numerous TVs permanently tuned to sports, and some locations have a giant screens. The Buckhead, Marietta, and Sandy Spring branches present live music on the outside decks most weekends during the summer. Best known for its hot wings, the menu also offers steaks, sandwiches, salads, and appetizers. The bars are open 11 AM to midnight from Sunday through Thursday, until 1 AM Friday and Saturday. *3002 Peachtree Rd., at Pharr Rd., Buckhead, 404/266–8667.*

5 *c-3*

8595 Roswell Rd., Dunwoody, 770/992–5011.

4 *f-3*

423 Ernest Barrett Pkwy., Town Center, Kennesaw, 770/426–6566.

4 *g-5*

2580 Windy Hill Rd., at I–75, Marietta, 770/850–0868.

5 *b-5*

5825 Roswell Rd., Sandy Springs, 404/235–2380.

5 *e-3*

TJ'S SPORTS BAR & GRILL

With 54 regular TVs and six big-screen TVs, this place is bound to be showing the game you want to see. While you watch the game, you can chow down on a surprisingly healthful array of eats. In addition to nachos and porterhouse steaks, you can try sandwiches, turkey burgers, a Portobello burger, and chicken grills. TJ's is open daily. *2880 Holcomb Bridge Rd., Holcomb Center, Alpharetta, 770/552–7700.*

WINE BARS

12 *h-4*

ECLIPSE DI LUNA

Tapas for just $2.95 a plate and glasses of wine for just $5.50 a pour keep this place packed with young couples. The wine list is constantly being changed and updated, as management seeks new labels and good values. There are lots of Spanish wines, but also Californian, Australian, Chilean, South African, and the occasional French wine. Chef Paul Luna, a native of the Dominican Republic, launched the restaurant, giving it its Spanish flair, and remains as consulting chef/owner. There's outdoor seating and a high-energy atmosphere. *See also Chapter 1. 764 Miami Cir., Buckhead, 404/846–0449.*

15 *e-3*

ENO

This Mediterranean restaurant (*see* Chapter 1) adds a challenging wine experience to Atlanta's bar scene. With a savory menu of small dishes designed to go with wine, and wine suggestions to match, Eno offers about 100 unusual vintages by the taste size (2-ounce pours) and by the glass, as well as by the bottle. In addition, a fine list of excellent grappas adds depth to the tasting experience. Facing the street with ample windows, the welcoming space has long bar and numerous tables, inviting patrons to drop in for a drink or a quick bite before going on to the Fox Theatre nearby. *800 Peachtree St., at 6th St, Midtown, 404/685–3191.*

12 *h-2*

IL CENTRO

Besides getting a glass of wine, here, you may order wines by the flight, that is, in series of three 2-ounce glasses.

You can choose any combination of wines for your flight, or go for one of the three "set flights," with pre-selected wines chosen for comparison purposes, perhaps three chardonnays or three Italian white wines. This small space attracts the upscale shoppers of Phipps Plaza, as well as young couples on dates before or after catching a movie. A tasting menu of simple fare, such as pâté and hummus, changes weekly. You can also order from the coffee bar and nibble on desserts composed by the house pastry chef. *3500 Peachtree Rd., Phipps Plaza, Buckhead, 404/394–9313.*

12 *f-4*

LO SPUNTINO

This chic Tuscan-inspired wine bar and gourmet food shop is the work of Vicki and Sam Sebastiani of the California wine-producing family. The only wines available are the couple's Viansa line, including Cal-Ital wines and some Italian imports—the 1997 Viansa Arneis is especially good. While sampling wine, you may enjoy small dishes of California-Mediterranean-style fare. Vicki's special recipes, such as a sun-dried tomato aioli, are among the products available in the shop, where you also can buy wine by the bottle. Lo Spuntin is closed Sunday. *3005 Peachtree Rd., at Pharr Rd., Buckhead, 404/237–5724.*

12 *f-4*

VINO!

At this Spanish restaurant (*see* Chapter 1), you can order wines by the flight, which gives you three 2-ounce pours. Try the flight of Spanish wines, or take the Tour de France: a rosé, a white Burgundy, and a Côtes-du-Rhône. The tapas—especially the mussels and octopus—are among the best reasons to come here. *2900 Peachtree Rd., The Peach Shopping Center, Buckhead, 404/816–0511.*

14 *f-3*

WATERSHED

This establishment is primarily a restaurant (*see* Chapter 1), but it also includes a wine bar and a well-stocked wine shop. Carefully selected fine wines, many served by the glass, lend themselves to quiet conversation at the bar, either during cocktail hour or at the end of the evening, with a scrumptious dessert. Part-owner Emily Saliers, of Indigo Girls fame, often does sommelier duty at the bar, pouring wines and discussing them knowledgeably with the wine-savvy patrons. In the restaurant, the varied menu focuses on updated versions of American (mostly southern) home-style fare. *406 W. Ponce de Leon Ave., Decatur, 404/378–4900.*

chapter 6

HOTELS

Going back to 1846, when two hotels were built in the city, Atlanta has always been known for its fine lodgings. The Atlanta Hotel, the city's first brick building, was a soaring two stories high. Washington Hall rose later in the year and was described as being of "an uncertain architecture." After the Civil War—during which most of the city's hotels were burned—new hotels sprang up, beginning in 1866. Then Federal authorities made Atlanta the state's capital in 1868, but the legislators had no place to meet, so Georgia's first postbellum legislative sessions took place in the Kimball Opera House (a hotel, despite its name). Opened in 1869, the grand French Second Empire-style structure glowed in the evenings thanks to its then state-of-the-art gas lighting. Atlanta's hospitality industry continued to prosper, and one of its finest postbellum luxury lodgings, the Hotel Aragon, opened in 1892 to the celebratory sound of booming cannons.

As these granddaddies of Atlanta lodging aged, they were demolished and new hotels took their place, often on virtually the same ground. The city's contemporary reputation for hospitality excellence was secured with the construction, in the 1980s, of two Ritz-Carlton hotels, making Atlanta for a time the only city in the world with more than one of the luxe properties. Since then, the pace of hotel construction in the city has not abated, even since the 1996 Centennial Olympic Games. Recent developments include the refurbishment of old properties and the construction of all-suite hotels that cater to the business traveler. Many of the new properties operate high-end restaurants that showcase some of the world's finest chefs.

In addition to hotels, the metro Atlanta area has gained a number of fine bed-and-breakfast inns, which are especially popular among locals for weekend getaways—they're not too far from the family but just far enough for romance.

These same B&Bs are also popular with business travelers. For both audiences, they combine intimacy and historic charm with convenience and comfort.

price categories

CATEGORY	COST*
Very Expensive Lodgings	over $230
Expensive Lodgings	$170–$230
Moderately Priced Lodgings	$100–$170
Budget Lodgings	under $100

*All prices are for a standard double room, excluding 13% tax and service.

VERY EXPENSIVE LODGINGS

12 g-2

EMBASSY SUITES–BUCKHEAD

This modern high rise in Buckhead is just blocks from the Phipps Plaza and Lenox Square malls. A variety of suites, ranging from deluxe presidential (with wet bar) to more basic bedroom and sitting room combinations, are available. Each suite, with either double or king-size beds, offers a kitchen area, a microwave oven, a small refrigerator, and a coffeemaker with coffee. Living-dining areas have sofa beds, overstuffed chairs, dining tables, and an extra phone. Four suites are designed especially for guests using wheelchairs. Full breakfast is included, and complimentary cocktails are served in the afternoon at the manager's reception. For business purposes, there are meeting rooms and business services available, and some suites are set up to accommodate conferences. A complimentary shuttle travels to points within 1 mi of the property. 3285 Peachtree Rd., 30326, Buckhead, 404/261–7733 or 800/EMBASSY, fax 404/261–6857, www.embassy-suites.com. 316 suites. Restaurant, kitchenettes, indoor pool, outdoor pool, exercise room, in-room data ports, in-room fax, in-room safes, business services, meeting rooms, parking (fee). AE, D, DC, MC, V. MARTA: Buckhead.

15 f-2

FOUR SEASONS HOTEL, ATLANTA

Formerly the Grand Hotel, this property occupies the first 19 floors of a 50-story structure that also contains residences and offices. An elegant entrance leads to a marble-rimmed world that includes a plush bar, an ideal spot to relax and take a breather, perhaps while enjoying afternoon tea. The hotel's restaurant, Park 75 (see Chapter 1), is especially good. Stylish traditional furnishings fill the opulently designed guest rooms; baths and entrance areas are floored in marble. In-room fax machines are available upon request. The hotel has ample space for meetings, conferences, and special occasions. *75 14th St., 30309, Midtown, 404/881–9898 or 800/332–3442, fax 404/ 873–4692. 206 rooms, 18 suites. Restaurant, bar, in-room data ports, in-room safes, minibars, indoor pool, health club, meeting rooms, parking (fee). AE, D, DC, MC, V. MARTA: Arts Center.*

15 *e-3*

GEORGIAN TERRACE

Spend a night where Enrico Caruso and the Metropolitan Opera stars once lodged. This fine old hotel that in its heyday housed the rich and famous stands across the street from the Fox Theatre (see Chapter 5) and is on the National Register of Historic Places (see Chapter 4). Here is where the stars of *Gone With the Wind* stayed when the film debuted in Atlanta in 1939. Since the structure was built as an apartment building, all units are suites with kitchenettes or full kitchens. Now restored, the hotel has an added matching tower. Some suites have minibars. The ground floor offers retail services and a 5,500-square-ft conference center. *659 Peachtree St., 30308, Midtown, 404/897– 1991 or 800/651 2316, fax 404/724 9116. 319 suites. Restaurant, kitchenettes, pool, meeting rooms, parking (fee). AE, D, DC, MC, V. MARTA: North Avenue.*

12 *g-2*

GRAND HYATT ATLANTA

A high-ceilinged lobby facing a courtyard with a Japanese garden and cascading 35-ft waterfall is this towering hotel's opening statement. Muted color schemes, mainly in hues of black, gray, and purple, give the spacious and comfortable rooms a style that's more American than Japanese. Every room has marble baths, irons and ironing boards, and robes. The hotel has two ballrooms, 16 meeting rooms, and three board rooms to accommodate a variety of events; three spacious outdoor terraces are dramatic spaces for special occasions. Japanese and Mediterranean cuisines, respectively, are served in the hotel's two restaurants, Kamogawa (see

Chapter 1) and Cassis. *3300 Peachtree Rd., 30305, Buckhead, 404/365–8100 or 800/233–1234, fax 404/233–5686. 417 rooms, 20 suites. 2 restaurants, bar, in-room data ports, in-room fax, minibars, pool, health club, meeting rooms. AE, D, DC, MC, V. MARTA: Buckhead.*

15 *e-5*

MARRIOTT MARQUIS

Immense and coolly contemporary, the lobby of the Marquis seems to go on forever as you stand under a huge fabric sculpture that appears to float from below the sky-lighted roof 47 stories above. The atrium, a signature element in architect John Portman's hotel design, sweeps up and away from view (see Chapter 4). Glass-enclosed elevators glide noiselessly through this expanse. Each guest room, renovated and redecorated in 1997 with new fabric and colors, opens onto the atrium. For the best view, request a room above the 10th floor; face north to see the city, south to view the airport. *265 Peachtree Center Ave., 30303, Downtown, 404/521– 0000 or 800/MARRIOTT, fax 404/586-6299, www.marriott.com. 1,671 rooms, 60 suites. 5 restaurants, 2 bars, in-room safes, indoor-outdoor pool, health club, parking (fee). AE, D, DC, MC, V. MARTA: Peachtree Center.*

15 *d-5*

OMNI HOTEL AT CNN CENTER

Adjacent to the headquarters of Ted Turner's Cable News Network (see Chapter 4), the Omni welcomes you with a combination of old-world and modern decor. Amid the marble floors, Oriental rugs, and exotic floral and plant arrangements of the lobby are closed-circuit monitors that show unedited CNN film, bloopers and all. Recently updated and redecorated, rooms have large windows and contemporary-style furniture, including a sofa in each room. When you stay here you have access to the CNN health club. In the executive office suite are two small meeting rooms (for four to six people), and the hotel has 15 large meeting rooms and a ballroom with a capacity of 2,000. The hotel is handy to Philips Arena, the Georgia World Congress Center, CNN Center, Centennial Olympic Park, and the Georgia Dome. *100 CNN Center 30335, Downtown, 404/659–0000 or 800/843–6664, fax 404/525–5050. 457 rooms, 13 suites. Restaurant, lobby lounge, business ser-*

vices, meeting rooms, parking (fee). AE, DC, MC, V. MARTA: Omni.

15 e-5
RITZ-CARLTON, ATLANTA

Behind this New Orleans–style facade, amid hunt-theme sculptures and paintings from a simpler age, is a sanctuary from life's hurly-burly. Stroll past the 17th-century Flemish tapestry near the Peachtree Street entrance and take a seat in the intimate, sunken lobby, where you can take a traditional afternoon tea served beneath an 18th-century chandelier. Upstairs, the most luxurious guest rooms are furnished with marble writing tables, plump sofas, four-poster beds, and white marble bathrooms. Atlanta Grill, a contemporary American restaurant, offers excellent casual dining on a veranda overlooking Peachtree

---

FINE HOTEL DINING

Some of the city's best restaurants are in its hotels, where chefs drawn from all over the world hold court in the kitchen. See Chapter 1 for reviews of these stars.

Atlanta Hilton & Towers (expensive)
At Nikolai's Roof, a 30th-floor view of the city's architectural splendor—most dramatic at night—enhances contemporary Continental dining.

Four Seasons Hotel, Atlanta (very expensive)
Inventive and substantial cuisine, excellent American farmstead cheeses, house-baked breads, and a notable wine list add up to fine dining at Park 75.

Grand Hyatt Atlanta (very expensive)
Kamogawa is the most elegant Japanese restaurant in the city, and the restaurant of choice for visiting Japanese when they entertain local guests.

Ritz-Carlton, Buckhead (very expensive)
Exceptional food, service, and ambience are the hallmarks of the Dining Room, where chef Joel Antune earns global recognition for his French-Asian cuisine.

Swissôtel (expensive)
An outpost of the venerable New York steak house, Palm serves up the best in beef to Atlanta's power crowd.

Street. *181 Peachtree St., 30303, Downtown, 404/659–0400 or 800/241–3333, fax 404/688–0400. 403 rooms, 22 suites. Restaurant, bar, minibar, room service, fitness center, concierge, business services, parking (fee). AE, D, DC, MC, V. MARTA: Peachtree Center.*

12 h-2
RITZ-CARLTON, BUCKHEAD

Its public spaces replete with 18th- and 19th-century antiques, this elegant gem bids a discreet welcome to famous and lesser-known guests alike. Film stars, politicos, and performers have been spotted in the lobby here, and shoppers from nearby Lenox Square Mall and Phipps Plaza often revive over afternoon tea or cocktails in the richly paneled Lobby Lounge. Spacious guest rooms are outfitted with reproductions of antique furniture and have decadent white marble baths. In-room fax machines are available upon request. From the hotel's club floors, the view of Buckhead confirms Atlanta's reputation as a city of trees. The Dining Room (*see* Chapter 1) is one of the world's finest restaurants, while the Cafe opens early for breakfast—it's popular for early business rendezvous—and offers lunch and dinner as well. The hotel also provides elegant spaces for special-occasion functions and meetings. *3434 Peachtree Rd., 30326, Buckhead, 404/237–2700 or 800/241–3333, fax 404–239–0078. 524 rooms, 29 suites. 2 restaurants, bar, fitness center, pool, hot tub, concierge, in-room data ports, in-room safes, minibars, business services, meeting rooms, parking (fee). AE, D, DC, MC, V. MARTA: Lenox.*

15 e-5
WESTIN PEACHTREE PLAZA

Sometimes it seems that every photograph of Atlanta's skyline taken since 1990 features this cylindrical glass tower, the tallest hotel in North America (*see* Chapter 4). Designed by John Portman, the hotel has a five-story atrium, and a narrow glass elevator, made famous in the film *Sharkey's Machine*, slithers up the building's exterior. Suites have minibars and rooms on select floors have fax machines and data ports. For great views of Atlanta, have a drink or meal in the revolving, multilevel Sundial Restaurant & Lounge (*see* Chapter 5) atop the hotel. Perfect for casual dining, the street-level Savannah Fish Company is famous for its smoked bluefish dip and fresh fish dishes. Westin also operates a hotel near the airport (*below*). *210 Peachtree St., at International Blvd., 30303, Downtown, 404/659–1400 or 800/228–3000, fax 404/589–7424. 1,020 rooms, 48 suites. 3 restaurants, 3 bars, in-room safes, room service, indoor-outdoor pool, health club, concierge, business services, parking (fee). AE, D, DC, MC, V. MARTA: Peachtree Center.*

EXPENSIVE LODGINGS

15 *e-5*

ATLANTA HILTON & TOWERS

Occupying an entire square block, this is one of the city's largest hotels, with five dining establishments including the world-class Nikolai's Roof (*see* Chapter 1) on the 30th floor. Standard rooms are decorated in restful mauves, greens, and golds, and every room has two 2-line telephones with private voice mail messaging. The Towers provides more luxurious accommodations, plus a third phone, speaker-phone capability, full-size desks, and in-room fax machines. Towers guests enjoy a separate reception area, complimentary evening hors d'oeuvres and daily Continental breakfast. *255 Courtland St., 30303, Downtown, 404/659–2000 or 800/445–8667, fax 404/221–6368. 1224 rooms, 41 suites. 3 restaurants, 4 bars, coffee shop, deli, pool, 4 tennis courts, health club, jogging, concierge, business services, convention center, meeting rooms. AE, D, DC, MC, V. MARTA: Peachtree Center.*

CHÂTEAU ÉLAN

Built in 1982 to fulfill owner Daniel Panoz's dream of operating a winery that produces magnificent vintages, the resort and residential community are centered around a 16th-century-style faux chateaux. The vineyard sweeps up the knoll alongside a driveway that leads to the giant, state-of-the-art winery. The adjacent inn (in the chateau) and 14-room European health spa to the rear house luxurious rooms with splendid views. Complimentary winery tours and tastings, two 18-hole resort golf courses, 25,000 square ft of meeting space, a tennis center, and a variety of restaurants (*see* Chapter 1) keep guests busy. Nature trails invite leisurely strolling or vigorous hiking through well-landscaped grounds. The resort hosts several con-

certs and special events, including monthly horse shows, throughout the year. *100 Tour de France, Braselton 30517, I-85N to exit 126, 770/932–0900 or 800/233–WINE, fax 770/271–6915, www.chateauelan.com. 277 rooms, 20 suites. 7 restaurants, pub, indoor pool, outdoor pools, spa, 2 18-hole golf courses, 6 tennis courts, hiking, equestrian center, meeting rooms. AE, D, DC, MC, V.*

5 *d-5*

CROWNE PLAZA–RAVINIA

Located across the street from Perimeter Mall, this hotel offers a splendid view of lush atrium gardens from its lobby. The lobby bar is an excellent spot for relaxing after shopping. There is a hotel dining room, but the best seat in the house is at La Grotta (*see* Chapter 1), which also has a fine view of the gardens. Its northern Italian cuisine and well-chosen wine list draw food lovers from all over the metro area. The renovated health club, with its hot tub and masseurs, provides the ultimate in self-indulgence. Graceful and expansive banquet space is available for meetings and special events. There is another Crowne Plaza near the airport (*below*). *4355 Ashford-Dunwoody Rd., Dunwoody 30346, 770/395–7700 or 800/2CROWNE, fax 770/392–9503. 462 rooms, 33 suites. 2 restaurants, bar, in-room safes, minibars, indoor pool, massage, sauna, spa, health club, business services, meeting rooms. AE, D, DC, MC, V. MARTA: Dunwoody.*

15 *e-5*

HYATT REGENCY ATLANTA

When it was built, the Hyatt's 23-story lobby inaugurated the chain's atrium look and launched Atlanta architect John Portman's international career (*see* Chapter 4). The hotel stands across from the Merchandise Mart and Peachtree Center (a skywalk connects it to the latter), just a short walk from the Apparel Mart—all of them Portman designs. Easily identified at night by its brightly lighted blue bubble dome over the rooftop Polaris restaurant, this remains one of Atlanta's more unusual-looking hotels. Rooms on the Business Plan floor offer extensive business amenities, including in-room fax machines and data ports and off-hours access to supplies and services. A 1995 expansion created more meeting space, an exhibition facility, and a grand ballroom. *265 Peachtree St., 30303, Down-*

town, 404/577–1234 or 800/233–1234, fax 404/588–4137. 1,206 rooms, 58 suites. 3 restaurants, bar, in-room safes, minibars, pool, health club, business services, meeting rooms, parking (fee). AE, D, DC, MC, V. MARTA: Peachtree Center.

12 *h-2*

JW MARRIOTT

This elegant 25-story hotel connected to Lenox Square Mall sets reproduction antique furniture amid accents of brass and crystal. Irregularly shaped rooms have spacious baths with separate shower stall and tub. Large windows provide expansive views of Buckhead. Nightly jazz plays in Ottley's lounge. Meeting rooms are large and well equipped, and a MARTA stop is right across the street. *3300 Lenox Rd., 30326, Buckhead, 404/262–3344 or 800/228–9290, fax 404/262–8689, www.marriott. com. 371 rooms, 4 suites. Restaurant, bar, minibars, room service, pool, barbershop, beauty salon, health club, baby-sitting, concierge, business services, car rental, meeting rooms, parking (fee). AE, D, DC, MC, V. MARTA: Lenox.*

15 *e-2*

REGENCY SUITES HOTEL

Located in the business and financial district of Atlanta, this small (nine-story) European-style hotel combines personalized hospitality with special amenities such as valet parking to make you feel welcome. All accommodations are suites, some with kitchenette. Continental breakfast buffet is included with the room rate, and there is a mini-convenience store on the premises. Meeting facilities are available for groups up to 40 people. *975 W. Peachtree St., 30309, Midtown, 404/876–5003 or 800/642–3629, fax 404/817–7511, www.regency-suites.com. 99 suites. Minibars, exercise room, baby-sitting, parking (fee). AE, D, DC, MC, V. MARTA: Midtown.*

4 *h-7*

RENAISSANCE WAVERLY–GALLERIA

Perhaps the most luxurious hotel in northwest Atlanta, the Waverly is adjacent to Cobb Galleria Centre and Galleria Mall, and offers easy access to the nearby convention center. Bold contemporary art decorates the public spaces; all rooms include three telephones, a desk area, and nightly turndown service. The top two floors are the club level, where amenities include a club lounge,

complimentary breakfast, and evening hors d'oeuvres. In-house conference facilities include 50,000 square ft of adaptable meeting-banquet space. There are more moderately priced Renaissance properties downtown and near the airport; the chain also operates a resort at Lake Lanier Islands (*all below*). *2450 Galleria Pkwy., 30339, northwest Atlanta, 770/953–4500 or 800/ HOTELS1, fax 770/953–0740, www.renais-sancehotels.com. 497 rooms, 24 suites. 2 restaurants, lounge, bar, in-room data ports, sauna, steam room, health club, indoor pool, outdoor pool, racquetball, concierge, meeting rooms, free parking. AE, D, DC, MC, V.*

15 *e-4*

590 W. Peachtree St., Downtown, 404/ 881–6000, MARTA: North Avenue.

15 *e-5*

SHERATON HOTEL, ATLANTA

In downtown Atlanta, this 12-story hotel greets you with a luxuriously appointed lobby. An atrium pool courtyard is a world of plants and flowers, with a retractable roof that allows for year-round swimming; there's also poolside service. Tower rooms are geared toward the business traveler, and there are a club lounge and executive board room for Tower guests. The health club is open 24 hours, and no-smoking and ADA-accessible rooms are available upon request. You can also find Sheratons at Colony Square and the airport as well as in Buckhead and Dunwoody (*all below*). *165 Courtland St., 30303, Downtown, 404/659–6500 or 800/833–8624, fax 404/681–5306, www.sheraton.com. 734 rooms, 31 suites. 2 restaurants, lounge, in-room fax, in-room data ports, minibars, indoor-outdoor pool, health club, concierge, business services, meeting rooms, car rental, parking (fee). AE, D, DC, MC, V. MARTA: Peachtree Center.*

12 *g-2*

SWISSÔTEL

Sleek and efficient, this stunner boasts a chic glass-and-white tile exterior with curved walls and sophisticated Biedermeier-style interiors. Exquisite modern art fills its halls and public spaces. Handy to Lenox Square mall, a prime location for shopping and dinning, the hotel is a favorite with business travelers. The hotel's restaurant, Palm (*see* Chapter 1), is noted for its steaks, and the new full-service fitness center supplies everything from facials to fitness trainers. *3391 Peachtree Rd., 30326, Buckhead, 404/365–0065 or 800/253–1397, fax 404/365–8787. 349 rooms, 16 suites. Restaurant, bar, in-room fax, in-room data ports, minibars, room service, pool, beauty salon, health club, concierge, business services, parking (fee). AE, D, DC, MC, V. MARTA: Buckhead.*

MODERATELY PRICED LODGINGS

5 *e-2*

AMERISUITES

Comfortable but not luxurious, Amerisuites is designed for the extended-stay traveler. Accommodations at all Atlanta-area properties comprise a living room and separate bedroom, with microwave oven, iron and ironing board, cable TV, and VCR. Each suite is equipped with a desk area that has a two-line phone. Meeting rooms are also available at most locations. Continental breakfast buffet is included with the room rate. *7500 North Point Pkwy., Alpharetta 30022, 770/594–8788 or 800/833–1516, fax 770/594–1977. 126 suites. In-room data ports, refrigerators, pool, business services, exercise room, meeting rooms. AE, D, DC, MC, V.*

12 *g-3*

3242 Peachtree Rd., Buckhead, 404/869–6161, MARTA: Buckhead.

5 *c-5*

1005 Crestline Pkwy., Dunwoody, 770/730–9300.

5 *h-3*

11505 Medlock Bridge Rd., Duluth, 770/622–5858.

6 *a-4*

3390 Venture Pkwy., Duluth, 770/623–6800.

5 *f-4*

5600 Peachtree Pkwy., Norcross, 770/416–7655.

15 *e-1*

BEST WESTERN–GRANADA SUITE HOTEL

Built in 1924 as an apartment building, this three-story Spanish colonial–style hotel was restored in 1986. It is centrally located for business, shopping, and entertainment in the heart of midtown

Atlanta. You have a choice of standard rooms, suites, and apartments. Meeting space for up to 60 is available, and there is a free shuttle service within a 3-mi radius. *1302 W. Peachtree St., 30339, Midtown, 404/876–6100 or 800/528–1234, fax 404/875–0503. 94 rooms. In-room data ports, exercise room, business services, parking (fee). AE, D, DC, MC, V. MARTA: Arts Center.*

5 *c-5*

DOUBLETREE GUEST SUITES HOTEL

This hotel's suite-style accommodations are well equipped for business travelers and those who need temporary housing while relocating to Atlanta. Located just outside I–285 and GA 400 near Perimeter Mall, the Dunwoody property is convenient for shopping as well. Carlini's Italian restaurant is on the premises, as is meeting space and a hot tub. Doubletree also has another metro-area prop-

---

URBAN ESCAPES

Even when it's only a few miles from home, the right hotel can take you far away from your day-to-day life, if only for a day. Try these for relaxation and romance.

Château Élan (expensive)
> *Nature trails, golf, fine food, and frequent concerts make a weekend at the inn or the spa, both set among pine trees and vineyards, a favorite Atlanta getaway.*

Renaissance Pinelsle Resort (moderate)
> *Whisk your honey away for a night of dining, dancing, and relaxing in one of the hot-tub suites, and wake up to a day of golf and water sports.*

Serenbe Bed & Breakfast Inn (moderate)
> *Restore your equanimity with a taste of the country life just beyond the city. Meander through the fields, curl up with a book, or admire the exceptional garden.*

Village Inn at Stone Mountain (moderate)
> *Near historic Stone Mountain Village and Stone Mountain Park is this reasonably priced retreat. Each room has a hot tub to wash away your cares.*

erty, in Smyrna. *6120 Peachtree-Dunwoody Rd., Dunwoody 30328, 770/668–0808 or 800/222–8733, fax 770/668–0008. 224 suites. Restaurant, bar, lounge, indoor-outdoor pool, sauna, exercise room, meeting rooms, business services, free parking. AE, D, DC, MC, V. MARTA: Dunwoody.*

4 h-6

2780 Whitley Rd. NW, Smyrna, 770/980–1900.

5 a-7

EMBASSY SUITES HOTEL–GALLERIA

This luxurious all-suite hotel in northwest Atlanta stands within walking distance of Galleria Convention Centre and Office Complex, minutes away from two major shopping centers and many restaurants. Guest suites, which open onto an enclosed atrium, are divided into separate living and bedroom areas. No-smoking and ADA-accessible rooms are available upon request. There are four other Embassy locations in metro Atlanta (*see also* Very Expensive Lodgings, *above*, for Buckhead Location). *2815 Akers Mill Rd. Marietta 30339, 770/984–9300 or 800/EMBASSY, fax 770/955–4183, www.embassy-suites.com. 261 suites. Restaurant, lounge, exercise room, pool, free parking. AE, D, DC, MC, V.*

7 f-6

4700 South Port Rd., College Park, 404/767–1988.

15 d-5

267 Marietta St., Downtown, 404/223–2300. MARTA: Omni.

5 c-5

1030 Crown Pointe Pkwy., Dunwoody, 770/394–5454.

14 d-1

EMORY CONFERENCE CENTER AND HOTEL

Surrounded by Emory University's tree-filled campus, this is a beautiful setting for conferences, weddings, and other events. Rooms have sitting areas and dual telephone lines. Come to the club room or take a dip in the hot tub for a bit of pampering. If you're feeling more energetic, you can use Emory's Physical Education Center or the hotel's tennis court and basketball court. Hotel facilities include a 230-seat amphitheater, as well as ballroom that can accommodate up to 450 guests or be divided into five

separate rooms. State-of-the-art multimedia technology is available for presentations. *1615 Clifton Rd., Decatur 30329, 404/712–6000, fax 404/712–6235, www.emoryconferencecenter.com. Dining room, in-room data ports, indoor pool, saunas, steam room, exercise room, outdoor lighted tennis court, basketball court, free parking. AE, D, DC, MC, V.*

5 d-5

FOUR POINTS HOTEL BY SHERATON

Located in the Perimeter area, this one of the metro area's three Four Points properties offers easy access to shopping, entertainment, and dining. Rooms feature a desk area with two telephone lines where you can plug in your laptop, and when you're through with work you can settle into a lounge chair with ottoman and sip a cup of coffee that you brew in the room. Or you can order up some room service (available 6 AM–11 PM) and read the complimentary newspaper that's delivered to each room daily. You can request a no-smoking or ADA-accessible room. There is a gift shop in the hotel, as well as ample conference and banquet facilities. *1850 Cotillon Dr., Dunwoody 30338, 770/394–5000 or 800/325–3535, fax 770/394–5114, www.sheraton.com. 393 rooms. Room service, in-room data port, 2 pools, meeting rooms, car rental, free parking. AE, D, DC, MC, V. MARTA: Dunwoody.*

12 h-2

3387 Lenox Rd., Buckhead, 404/261–5500. MARTA: Lenox.

15 e-2

75 14th St., Midtown, 404/881–9898. MARTA: Arts Center.

15 e-5

HAMPTON INN AND SUITES DOWNTOWN

This stunning renovation of an old office building is on the National Register of Historic Places. A lobby atrium reaches up to a skylight, making the subtle, art deco–style space airy. Guest rooms are done in neutral tones with honey-blond, deco-style furnishings; suites include kitchens, good work desks, and sleeper sofas. Complimentary Continental breakfast comes with the room, and you can purchase basic necessities at the gift shop. There is a business center and three meeting rooms for groups of 12–80. The hotel's location is especially convenient if you plan to attend events at any of the marts; Hampton has three other outposts around Atlanta. *161 Spring St., 30303, Downtown, 404/589–1111 or 800/HAMPTON, fax 404/589–8999. 77 rooms, 42 suites. Kitchenettes, in-room data ports, exercise room, coin laundry, dry cleaning, meeting rooms, business services, parking (fee). AE, D, DC, MC, V. MARTA: Peachtree Center.*

3 *a-8*

16785 Morris Rd., Alpharetta, 678/393–0990.

6 *a-5*

1725 Pineland Rd., Duluth, 770/931–9800.

4 *h-5*

1732 Powers Ferry Rd., Marietta, 770/955–1110.

5 *f-4*

HILTON ATLANTA NORTHEAST HOTEL

Located at Technology Park, close to major interstates, this hotel serves Gwinnett County's bustling high-tech industry. A beautiful interior of marble and mahogany, substantial multipurpose meeting space, and a ballroom that can accommodate large conferences and special events are standout features. Each guest is decorated with cherrywood furnishings. Suites are spacious and comfortable and contain full-size work desks, wet bars, and hot tubs. Some rooms have data ports. *5993 Peachtree Industrial Blvd., Norcross 30092, 770/447–4747 or 800/774–1500, fax 770/448–8853, www.hilton.com. 234 rooms, 38 suites. Restaurant, bar, refrigerators, indoor pool, outdoor pool, sauna, golf privileges, exercise room, business services, free parking. AE, D, DC, MC, V.*

14 *g-3*

HOLIDAY INN SELECT ATLANTA–DECATUR HOTEL AND CONFERENCE CENTER

Five miles east of the heart of Atlanta, this striking postmodern lodging offers good value and walking distance to a MARTA stop. Convenient to historic Decatur and its business district, the hotel was spruced up for the 1998 Olympics in clubby shades of dark green, rust, and burgundy. On the top floor—the executive level—all rooms are equipped with coffeemakers. Banquet and meeting rooms here are ideal for small- to medium-size gatherings that don't want to get lost in the crowd.

The metro area also has another Holiday Inn Select, in Chamblee. *130 Clairemont Ave., Decatur 30030, 404/371–0204 or 800/225–6079, fax 404/377–2726. 180 rooms, 4 suites. Restaurant, lounge, in-room data ports, in-room fax, indoor pool, exercise room, business services, meeting rooms, parking (fee). AE, D, DC, MC, V. MARTA: Decatur.*

5 *d-5*

4386 Chamblee-Dunwoody Rd., Chamblee, 770/457–6363.

5 *d-1*

HOMEWOOD SUITES

This newly opened all-suite hotel (one of four Homewoods in the 10 counties), located off GA 400 and Mansell Road, accommodates many different travel needs in comfortable and attractive one- and two-bedroom suites, many with balconies. Suites have separate living rooms and full kitchens. Close to Alpharetta's growing business district and to many company headquarters, shops, and restaurants, the hotel offers a business center, as well as meeting and banquet facilities. Full breakfast is included, and Monday through Thursday there is a social hour with complimentary beer and wine. *10775 Davis Dr., Alpharetta 30004, 770/998–1622 or 800/CALLHOME, fax 770/998–7834, www.homewoodsuites.com. 112 suites. In-room data ports, pool, exercise room, business services, free parking. AE, D, DC, MC, V.*

12 *f-2*

3566 Piedmont Rd., Buckhead, 404/365–0001.

5 *f-4*

450 Technology Pkwy., Norcross, 770/209–4371.

4 *h-7*

3200 Cobb Pkwy., Smyrna, 770/988–9449.

10 *c-2*

THE INN AT EAGLES LANDING

Located 20 minutes south of Atlanta, this European-style inn draws guests looking for a championship golf course and a relaxing atmosphere. A Continental breakfast is served in the living room each morning, as is an innkeeper's reception each afternoon. You have full club privileges at Eagles Landing Country Club, including use of the 18-hole private championship golf course designed by Tom Fazio (greens fees apply), a pool, and a spa. In addition, you can play tennis on the hotel's two hard and four clay surfaces lighted courts. Spacious meeting rooms and catering and business services make this an excellent spot for business gatherings. *590 Country Club Dr., Stockbridge 30281, 770/389–3118 or 887/THEINN, fax 770/389–0928. 53 rooms, 4 suites. Minibars, in-room safes, golf privileges, 6 tennis courts, exercise room, baby-sitting, laundry service, concierge, business services, meeting rooms, free parking. AE, D, DC, MC, V.*

| 4 | *g-4* |

MARIETTA CONFERENCE CENTER AND RESORT

Minutes from Historic Marietta and Kennesaw National Battlefield (*see* Chapter 4) is this resort with rooms decorated in mellow hues of gold, deep red, and rich green and furnished with oversize desks. You can play the 18-hole championship golf course right outside the hotel (greens fees apply) or hit the lighted tennis courts (asphalt surface). These facilities, plus 20,000 square ft of meeting space with 19 dedicated conference rooms, make the center ideal for company outings and group events. A full-service business center and the latest in-house audio-visual technology and support services are available. *500 Powder Springs Rd., Marietta 30064, 770/ 427–2500, fax 770/429–9577, www.mariettaresort.com. 189 rooms, 10 suites. Restaurant, bar, in-room data ports, pool, hot tub, golf privileges, 2 tennis courts, health club, concierge, business services, meeting rooms. AE, D, DC, MC, V.*

| 5 | *e-2* |

LA QUINTA INNS & SUITES

Located near the North Point Mall, minutes from the growing business district of northern Fulton County, this hotel is good for a single night or an extended stay. It reflects the chain's recent redesign of its hotels, with a bright, sunlit lobby and contemporary rooms and suites. As at the Vinings property, large desks, coffeemakers, irons and ironing boards, and extended cable TV are among the amenities. Complimentary Continental breakfast buffet is included. *1350 North Point Dr., Alpharetta 30022, 770/754–7800 or 800/687–6667, fax 770/ 754–9242. 125 rooms, 6 suites. In-room data ports, room service, pool, exercise room. AE, D, DC, MC, V.*

| 4 | *h-7* |
2415 Paces Ferry Rd., Vinings, 770/801– 9002.

| 4 | *f-4* |

MARLOW HOUSE

Among the fine bed-and-breakfast inns in Marietta's historic district is this Queen Anne–style residence, built in 1887, with a pretty courtyard out front. Its three one-bedroom suites are individually decorated with antiques and feature queen beds, pull-out queen sofa beds, full kitchens, private phones, and TVs. Continental breakfast is served. *192 Church St., Marietta 30060, 770/426– 1887. 3 suites. AE, D, MC, V.*

RENAISSANCE PINEISLE RESORT

Set in a majestic, 1,200-acre pine forest in the foothills of the Blue Ridge Mountains, this spectacular lake-front paradise lies just 45 minutes from downtown Atlanta. The resort is a relaxing vacation getaway offering a full complement of recreational facilities, from boat slips and a water park to outdoor and enclosed tennis courts. The hot-tub suites, with king beds, private lanais, hot tubs, and splendid views, are ideal for romance and feature comfortably furnished sitting areas and refreshment centers. Upon request, coffee, tea, or hot chocolate will be deposited outside your door in the morning, along with the day's newspaper. The resort also offers unparalleled facilities for conferences and business meetings, including more than 22,000 square ft of function space and 22 meeting rooms of various size. Take I-985 North to exit 8, near the South Carolina border. If you're looking for a Renaissance closer to the action, you'll find one downtown, in northwest Atlanta (*both above*), and near the airport (*below*). *9000 Holiday Rd., Lake Lanier Islands 30518, 770/945–8921 or 800/HOTELS1, fax 770/945–0351, www.renaissancehotels.com. 222 rooms, 28 suites. 2 restaurants, lounge, in-room data ports, in-room safes, pool, 18-hole golf course, 7 tennis courts, exercise room, sauna, meeting rooms. AE, D, DC, MC, V.*

| 3 | *a-8* |

RESIDENCE INN BY MARRIOTT–ALPHARETTA

This all-suite hotel offers many of the comforts of home, a big draw for anyone planning to stay for an extended period. Each suite's living and work area, bedroom, and full kitchen are separate from each other. No-smoking and ADA-accessible rooms are available upon request. In addition to this property and the airport location (*see* Hotels near the Airport, *below*), there are several other Residence Inns in the metro Atlanta area. *5465 Windward Pkwy. West, Alpharetta 30004, 770/664–0664 or 800/MARRIOTT, fax 770/664–0664, www.residenceinn.com. 103 suites. In-room data ports, pool, exercise room, hot tub. AE, D, DC, MC, V.*

12 *g-3*

2960 Piedmont Rd., Buckhead, 404/239–0677.

15 *e-5*

134 Peachtree St., Downtown, 404/522–0950. MARTA: Peachtree Center.

25 *d-5*

1901 Savoy Dr., Dunwoody, 770/455–4446.

15 *e-2*

1041 W. Peachtree St., Midtown, 404/872–8885. MARTA: Midtown.

4 *h-6*

2771 Hargrove Rd., Smyrna, 770/433–8877.

1 *c-7*

SERENBE BED & BREAKFAST INN

In south Fulton County, this bed-and-breakfast complex has a pastoral setting on a converted farm. The restored farmhouse, where guests take a full breakfast, houses a conference center as well as the owners' residence. Guest rooms are in a barn, a guest house, and a cottage, which has two double rooms, a living room, and a kitchen. The barn is a veritable art gallery, with an excellent collection of American contemporary and folk art, and the garden is painstakingly designed. With a capacity for up to 35 people, the state-of-the-art conference center comes complete with a 125-inch projection screen and computer connections for presentations and teleconferencing. *10950 Hutchinson Ferry Rd., Palmetto 30268, 770/463–2610, fax 770/463–4472, www.serenbe.com. 9 rooms. Meeting rooms. No credit cards.*

15 *f-3*

SHELLMONT BED & BREAKFAST

Named for the shell motif that appears throughout the house, the Shellmont was designed in 1891 by Walter T. Down-

ing for Dr. William Perrin Nicholson. Its classical architectural elements and exquisitely detailed stained-glass windows (most breathtaking is the window in the stairwell) are today complemented by reproductions of the original Victorian stenciling and a delightful garden. Fine American Victorian antiques fill the guest rooms, which receive nightly turndown service with gourmet chocolates. The renovated carriage house has a hot tub for two. A different full gourmet breakfast is served daily. *821 Piedmont Ave., 30306, Midtown, 404/872–9290, fax 404/872–5379, www.shellmont.com. 2 rooms, 2 suites, 1 carriage house. AE, DC, MC, V.*

12 *h-2*

SHERATON BUCKHEAD

Modern and well maintained, this eight-floor hotel places guests right across from Lenox Square, making shopping there a breeze. Rooms have green decor and traditional Chippendale-style furnishings, with a desk and chair in some rooms and sofas in others. Meeting space and a 10,000-square-ft ballroom host gatherings large and small. Complimentary transportation is available around the Buckhead area. If Buckhead's booked, try the Dunwoody property; there are also Sheratons downtown (*above*) and at Colony Square and the airport (*below*). *3405 Lenox Rd., 30326, Buckhead, 404/848–7373 or 800/241–8260, fax 404/848–7391, www.sheraton.com. 230 rooms, 7 suites. Restaurant, bar, in-room data ports, exercise room, parking (fee). AE, D, DC, MC, V. MARTA: Lenox.*

5 *c-5*

111 Perimeter Center West, Dunwoody, 770/396–6800.

15 *f-2*

SHERATON AT COLONY SQUARE

Balconies, piano music, and fresh flowers bring drama and opulence to the dimly lighted lobby of this anchor of the Colony Square office-residential-retail complex (*see* Chapter 2). Rooms are modern and done in muted tones; those on higher floors have nice city views. The hotel is two blocks from the Woodruff Arts Center and the High Museum of Art (*see* Chapter 4). Downtown, Buckhead, and Dunwoody also have Sheratons (*above*), as does the airport (*below*). *188 14th St., 30361, Mid-*

town, 404/892–6000 or 800/325–3535, fax 404/872–9192, www.sheraton.com. 464 rooms, 3 suites. Restaurant, lobby lounge, pool, exercise room, concierge, business services, parking (fee). AE, D, DC, MC, V. MARTA: Arts Center.

5 c-5

SUMMERFIELD SUITES HOTEL

Located 1 mi from Perimeter Mall and the Perimeter business district, this all-suite hotel tailors its many conveniences to the needs of the business traveler. One- and two-bedroom suites are available, with full kitchens and large work areas with PC connections. There's another property in Buckhead. 760 Mount Vernon Hwy., Sandy Springs 30328, 404/250–0110 or 800/833–4353, fax 404/250–9335, www.summerfield-suites.com. In-room data ports, in-room safes, pool, spa, exercise room, meeting rooms, free parking. AE, D, DC, MC, V. MARTA: Dunwoody.

12 g-3

505 Pharr Rd., Buckhead, 404/262–7880.

6 a-4

SUMNER SUITES ATLANTA–GWINNETT

This all-suite hotel in Duluth has easy access to attractions and businesses in Gwinnett County. Designed for extended stays, the suites have separate living and bedroom areas, with refrigerators, microwaves, and desk areas with data ports and voice mail. No-smoking and ADA-accessible rooms are available upon request. Meeting space at this location can accommodate up to 150. Sumner also operates a property in Smyrna and one near the airport (below). 3530 Venture Pkwy., Duluth 30096, 770/622–0444 or 800/747–8483, fax 770/623–4643, www.sumnersuites. com. 125 suites. Lounge, in-room data ports, outdoor pool, exercise room, coin laundry. AE, D, DC, MC, V.

4 h-7

1000 Curtis Dr., Smyrna, 770/384–0060.

6 a-8

THE VILLAGE INN AT STONE MOUNTAIN

Located less than 1 mi from the entrance to Stone Mountain Park, the inn opened in the 1820s and served as a Confederate hospital during the Civil War. It became a private residence in 1868 and opened as a bed-and-breakfast

1995. All rooms have telephones and two-person hot tubs; three rooms have gas fireplaces and two have balconies. A garden, a video library, and in-room coffeemakers are among the amenities. Innkeepers Christy and Earl Collins, who live next door, serve a full southern breakfast. Though the inn is said to be haunted (see Chapter 4), this is a favorite spot for weddings and honeymoons. 992 Ridge Ave., Stone Mountain 30083, 770/469–3459 or 800/214–8385, fax 770/469–1051, www.villageinnbb.com. 5 rooms, 1 suite. In-room data ports, in-room VCRs. AE, D, MC, V.

5 c-5

W ATLANTA @ PERIMETER CENTER

In 1999, after complete renovation of an old hotel, Starwood Hotels opened this link in its popular boutique chain. The contemporary minimalism and cool colors of the lobby suggests Japanese design, and the dining room, Savu (see Chapter 1), serves light Asian-fusion fare. Handy to Perimeter Mall, the hotel weighs in as one of the city's best bargains, with luxury-caliber sheets and comforters, oversize desks, and the latest in-room business amenities (two-line cordless speaker phones, high-speed Internet access). 111 Perimeter Center West, off Ashford-Dunwoody Rd. at I–285, Dunwoody 30346, 770/396–6800 or 877/WHOTELS, fax 770/399–5514. Restaurant, bar, snack bar, minibars, room service, pool, exercise room, concierge, business services, meeting rooms. A, D, DC, MC, V. MARTA: Dunwoody.

4 f-4

THE WHITLOCK INN

This elegant Victorian frame house in Marietta's historic district was in severe decline, slated to be torn down to make way for a parking lot, when Nancy and Sandy Edwards rescued, restored, and turned it into an inn. Now an architectural jewel, the inn has generous spindled verandas, a rooftop porch, pocket doors, hardwood floors, and leaded-glass windows in the reception parlor. Rooms are equipped with cable TV and private phones; breakfast is Continental-plus. An addition provides space for receptions and meetings. Pets are not permitted, and children must be over 12. 57 Whitlock Ave., Marietta 30064, 770/428–1495, fax 770/919–9620, www.whitlockinn.com. 5 rooms. No-smoking rooms, meeting room. AE, D, MC, V.

15 *e-5*

WYNDHAM ATLANTA

A stunning transformation of a down-at-the-heels hotel lit up this star in Downtown's lodging firmament, the most recent addition to the constellation of metro Atlanta Wyndhams (*below*). Business-friendly rooms have large desks, voice mail, coffeemakers, irons and ironing boards, and hair dryers and receive a complimentary newspaper daily. Caliterra, the hotel restaurant (*see* Chapter 1), may well develop as a notable dining destination. The bar, with a good view of the street, frequently hosts live jazz, piano, and vocal entertainment. *160 Spring St., 30303, Downtown, 404/688–8600 or 800/ WYNDHAM, fax 678/686 3327, www.wyndham.com. 286 rooms, 26 suites. Restaurant, in-room data ports, room service, pool, exercise room, parking (fee). AE, D, DC, MC, V. MARTA: Peachtree Center.*

12 *g-2*

WYNDHAM GARDEN HOTEL

Given the excellent location of this hotel, its rates are reasonable, though the adequate service does not compare with that at the luxury establishments in the area. Rooms are decorated with botanical prints and typical chain-hotel furnishings, and guests have access to a local branch of Crunch, a health club. There is complimentary transportation within 2 mi and the hotel is adjacent to a MARTA stop. There's also a Wyndham downtown (*above*) and several others throughout the area (*below*). *3340 Peachtree Rd., 30326, Buckhead, 404/231–1234 or 800/WYNDHAM, fax 404/231–5236, www.wyndham.com. 217 rooms, 4 suites. Restaurant, free parking. AE, D, DC, MC, V. MARTA: Buckhead station.*

9 *a-5*

WYNDHAM PEACHTREE CITY CONFERENCE CENTER

Located 25 minutes from Hartsfield Atlanta International Airport and 35 minutes from downtown Atlanta, this complex offers both the tranquil atmosphere of the countryside and the convenience of a major city. Resort facilities such as a tennis center and a full-service health club offer ample opportunity for relaxation; you also have access to an 18-hole a championship golf course. Guest rooms, each with its own balcony, are attractively decorated and detailed for the business traveler. The Conference Center can host up to 600 people in 33,000 square ft of flexible banquet space with audiovisual equipment, business services, and complete catering services. In addition to the downtown and Buckhead locations (*above*), this is one of a number of metro area Wyndhams. *2443 GA 54, Peachtree City 30269, 770/487–2000 or 800/WYNDHAM, fax 770/487–4428, www.wyndham.com. 244*

BEST FOR BUSINESS

Atlanta is indubitably a grand city of commerce, an international player on the world economic stage. Most of its hotels cater to business travelers, but these stand out.

Atlanta Hilton & Towers (expensive)
With its own convention center, plus meeting rooms and a business center, this giant is ready to meet business needs on every scale. Rooms are equipped with multiple 2-line phones and voice mail; some have fax machines.

Atlanta Marriott Marquis (very expensive)
The latest rooms upgrade brought in ergonomically correct desk chairs and desks that open up into large work surfaces. The phones have data ports, and refrigerators are skillfully concealed in armoires.

Holiday Inn Select Atlanta–Decatur Hotel and Conference Center (moderate)
Handy to the Decatur MARTA station, the hotel offers in-room fax machines and coffeemakers. A conference center with lots of meeting rooms makes this an excellent choice for small gatherings.

Hyatt Regency Atlanta (expensive)
Guests here can get business supplies at off hours, and they have 24-hour access to printers and copiers. One floor contains Business Plan rooms, which have in-room faxes and extralarge desks with high-end desk chairs and ample lighting.

Quality Hotel Downtown (budget)
This small, nicely refurbished hotel is Atlanta's premier value for lodging when you're here to attend events at the nearby Georgia World Congress Center.

rooms, 6 suites. 2 restaurants, bar, pool, massage, sauna, steam room, golf privileges, 3 tennis courts, health club, jogging. AE, D, DC, MC, V.

6 *a-4*

1948 Pleasant Hill Rd., Duluth, 770/476–1211.

15 *e-2*

125 10th St., Midtown, 404/873–4800. MARTA: Midtown.

5 *f-8*

2158 Ranchwood Dr., Northlake, 770/934–6000.

5 *c-5*

800 Hammond Dr., Sandy Springs, 404/252–3344.

BUDGET LODGINGS

15 *e-5*

BEST WESTERN INN AT THE PEACHTREE

This splendid renovation of an old hotel has an excellent location in downtown Atlanta: MARTA stations are within two blocks, and a short walk brings you to numerous restaurants, events facilities, and attractions. When it's time to retreat from the urban mayhem, a courtyard offers restful escape. The hotel is set up for business travelers, with an exercise room, business services, and a guest laundry; king rooms have microwaves and coffeemakers, and suites have full kitchens. A full, hot breakfast is included, and complimentary cocktails are served each evening. The fifth floor is a penthouse suite. Out of town, you'll find a number of Best Westerns in the 10 counties (*below*). *330 W. Peachtree St., 30308, Midtown, 404/577–6970 or 800/242–4642, fax 404/659–3244. 103 rooms, 8 suites. Refrigerators, exercise room, coin laundry, dry cleaning, business services, AE, D, DC, MC, V. MARTA: Civic Center or Peachtree Center.*

6 *b-8*

BEST WESTERN INN—STONE MOUNTAIN

This shiny new property opened in 1999 offers comfortable and economical accommodations minutes from Stone Mountain Park. For the convenience of guests, each room includes an iron and ironing board, a microwave oven, and a coffeemaker. No-smoking rooms are available, as well as rooms that are ADA

accessible. The hotel also has meeting facilities accommodating up to 30 people. There are several Best Westerns throughout metro Atlanta, including Best Western Inn at the Peachtree (*above*). *1595 East Park Pl. Blvd., Stone Mountain 30058, 770/465–1022 or 800/528–1234, fax 770/465–9089. 60 rooms. Restaurant, lounge, in-room data ports, refrigerators, in-room safes, pool, meeting rooms. AE, D, DC, MC, V.*

8 *c-4*

2572 Candler Rd., Decatur, 404/243–6679.

8 *a-8*

6437 Jonesboro Rd., Morrow, 770/961–6300.

5 *g-5*

7035 Jimmy Carter Blvd., Norcross, 770/409–0004.

2 *e-2*

COMFORT INN

A mile from downtown Canton, the hotel is an easy walk from local shopping. Guest rooms are comfortably furnished in contemporary style and feature cable TV, microwave oven, and wet bar. ADA-accessible and no-smoking rooms are available upon request, and Continental breakfast is included. There are also Comfort Inns near the airport, in Doraville (*both below*), and elsewhere throughout the 10 counties, as well as a number of Comfort Suites locations (*below*). *138 Keith Dr., Canton 30114, 770/345–1994 or 800/228–5150, fax 770/345–1994. 47 rooms, 3 suites. In-room data ports, refrigerators, pool, exercise room, business services, meeting room. AE, D, DC, MC, V.*

5 *e-6*

COMFORT INN AND CONFERENCE CENTER

Whether you're in Atlanta for business or pleasure, this place delivers great amenities just 15 minutes from major shopping and business districts. Guest rooms, which open into interior corridors, are decorated in a comfortable contemporary style. The conference facilities can hold 500 people for banquets and meetings. You can also find Comfort in Canton (*above*), near the airport (*below*) and in other Atlanta locations. *2001 Clearview Ave., Doraville 30340, 770/455–1811 or 888/816–0924, fax 770/451–6795. 238 rooms. Restaurant, lounge, pool, meeting rooms, free parking. AE, D, DC, MC, V. MARTA: Doraville.*

12 *g-7*

2115 Piedmont Rd., Buckhead, 404/876–4365.

8 *c-2*

4450 Memorial Dr., Decatur, 404/298–9255.

15 *d-5*

101 International Blvd., Downtown, 404/267–0051. MARTA: Peachtree Center.

1 *c-3*

28 Highway 294, 770/387–1800.

3 *d-5*

COMFORT SUITES

This all-suite hotel is situated close to Lake Lanier, shopping, restaurants, and entertainment. Rooms, decorated in familiar chain style, deliver all the basics; complimentary breakfast is also included. There's another location in Dunwoody, plus a number of Comfort Inns throughout the metro area (*above*). *905 Buford Rd., Cumming 30041, 770/889–4141 or 800/228–5150, fax 770/781–9294. 71 rooms. Microwaves, refrigerators, pool, meeting rooms. AE, D, DC, MC, V.*

5 *c-5*

6110 Peachtree-Dunwoody Rd., Dunwoody, 770/828–0330. MARTA: Dunwoody.

5 *e-2*

COUNTRY INN AND SUITES

Standard rooms at this franchise have ironing boards, coffeemakers, cable TV, and complimentary Continental breakfast; suites also feature king-size bedrooms and separate sitting rooms with microwave ovens, refrigerators, desk areas, and hair dryers. The business center is self-service but is available 24 hours. *2950 Mansell Rd., Alpharetta 30022, 770/552–0006 or 800/456–4000, fax 770/993–3541. 51 rooms, 7 suites. In-room data ports, indoor pool, exercise room, business services, meeting rooms. AE, D, DC, MC, V.*

4 *g-5*

COURTYARD BY MARRIOTT

Designed for the busy business traveler, this property is chock-full of conveniences for those away from home. Spacious rooms feature a comfortable sitting area, large work desk, voice mail, cable TV and in-room coffee. In addition to this property and the airport location (*see below*), there are several other

Courtyards throughout the metro Atlanta area. *2455 Delk Rd., Marietta 30067, 770/956–1188 or 800/321–2211, fax 770/933–0489, www.courtyard.com. 134 rooms, 12 suites. Breakfast room, lounge, in-room data ports, pool, exercise room, coin laundry, dry cleaning, laundry service, meeting rooms. AE, D, DC, MC, V.*

12 *g-2*

3332 Peachtree Rd., Buckhead, 404/869–0818. MARTA: Buckhead.

6 *a-4*

3550 Venture Pkwy., Duluth, 770/476–4666.

15 *e-2*

1132 Techwood Dr., Midtown, 404/607–1112. MARTA: Arts Center.

4 *h-7*

3000 Cumberland Cir., Smyrna, 770/952–2555.

5 *f-8*

4083 LaVista Rd., Tucker, 770/938–1200.

7 *c-2*

DAYS INN AT SIX FLAGS

Located minutes from Six Flags amusement park, this is a convenient, inexpensive place to rest your head after a full day. The basic rooms with double beds offer no surprises—a definite plus in this price range. In addition to this property and the airport location (*below*), there are several other Days Inns throughout the metro Atlanta area. *95 S. Service Rd., Austell 30168, 770/941–1400 or 800/325–2525, fax 770/819–9988. 96 rooms. Pool, free parking. AE, D, DC, MC, V.*

6 *e-5*

2910 Clairmont Rd., 404/633–8411.

6 *a-4*

1920 Pleasant Hill Rd., Duluth, 770/476–8700.

4 *h-6*

2767 Windy Hill Rd., Marietta, 770/952–5038.

15 *e-4*

683 Peachtree St., Midtown, 404/874–9200. MARTA: North Avenue.

5 *b-6*

5750 Roswell Rd., Sandy Springs, 404/252–5782.

7 b-2

FAIRFIELD INN BY MARRIOTT—SIX FLAGS

Located near Six Flags, this budget chain choice is known for accommodations that are comfortable but not extravagant. You can make yourself at home with free local calls, cable TV, in-room movies, and complimentary Continental breakfast. Limited business facilities and no-smoking rooms are available. In addition to this property and the airport location (*see below*), there are several other Fairfield Inns throughout metro Atlanta. *976 West Pointe Ct., Lithia Springs 30057, 770/739–2800 or 800/228–2800, fax 770/739–2800, www.fairfieldinn.com. 81 rooms. Meeting room. AE, D, DC, MC, V.*

12 g-3

3092 Piedmont Rd., Buckhead, 404/846–0900.

15 f-5

175 Piedmont Ave., Downtown, 404/659–7777. MARTA: Peachtree Center.

6 a-4

3500 Venture Pkwy., Duluth, 770/623–9300.

15 e-1

1470 Spring St., Midtown, 404/872–5821. MARTA: Arts Center.

5 f-7

2155 Ranchwood Dr., Northlake, 770/491–7444.

1 b-5

HOLIDAY INN EXPRESS

This chain provides economical rooms for the budget-minded at a number of locations throughout the Atlanta area. Simple, predictable accommodations feature air-conditioning and free local calls. No-smoking rooms are available. *5479 Westmoreland Plaza, Douglasville 30134, 770/949–5730 or 800/465–4329, fax 770/949–2619. 50 rooms. Pool, outdoor hot tub. AE, D, DC, MC, V.*

3 a-8

5455 Windward Pkwy, Alpharetta, 770/664–6661.

5 c-5

765 Hammond Dr., Dunwoody, 404/250–4450. MARTA: Dunwoody.

15 d-4

244 North Ave., Midtown, 404/881–0881. MARTA: North Avenue.

4 h-8

1200 Winchester Pkwy., Smyrna, 770/333–9910.

6 a-8

1790 E. Park Place Blvd., Stone Mountain, 770/465–8847.

5 c-5

QUALITY HOTEL DOWNTOWN

This quiet, older (but renovated) downtown hotel two blocks off Peachtree Street offers modestly proportioned rooms are done in soothing tones of teal and navy blue. A marble lobby, with a sofa and a grand piano that you can play, is an inviting introduction to the property. Because of its proximity to the World Congress Center and the show marts, this spot is very popular for conventions, and prices go up when groups are in town. *89 Luckie St., 30303, Downtown, 404/524–7991 or 800/228–5151, fax 404/524–0672. 70 rooms, 5 suites. AE, D, DC, MC, V.*

4 g-5

RAMADA LIMITED SUITES

Located three blocks west of I–75 and 1 mi from the Marietta business district, this hotel offers typical chain rooms with cable TV and complimentary Continental breakfast and coffee. No-smoking rooms are available. There is also a Ramada in Decatur. *630 Franklin Rd., Marietta 30067, 770/919–7878 or 800/272–6232, fax 770/514–0824. 46 units. In-room data ports, microwaves, refrigerators, pool. AE, D, DC, MC, V.*

8 c-2

3403 Memorial Dr., Decatur, 404/288–8722.

5 c-7

SIERRA SUITES BROOKHAVEN

Cream-and-green color schemes accent the modern, southwestern feel of the rooms here. Opened in 1997, the hotel stands just north of Lenox Square mall and adjacent to a MARTA station, a superior convenience when heading to the airport. As at the other two metro area properties, the small one-bedroom studio suites have fully equipped kitchens, cable TV, and personal voice mail. *3967 Peachtree Rd., 30319, Brookhaven, 404/237–9100 or 800/4–SIERRA, fax 404/237–0055, www.sierra-suites.com. 92 suites. Pool, exercise room,* coin laundry. AE, D, DC, MC, V. MARTA: Brookhaven.

4 *h-5*

2010 Powers Ferry Rd., Smyrna, 770/933–8010.

5 *c-5*

6330 Peachtree-Dunwoody Rd., Dunwoody, 770/379–0111.

4 *f-4*

STANLEY HOUSE

Marietta's historic district surrounds this carefully restored three-story Queen Anne structure that was built as a residence in 1895. Its wrap-around porch and courtyard welcome guests two blocks from Marietta Square, and its five individually decorated guest rooms are filled with antiques. All rooms have private baths. One bedroom has a loft that's appropriate for an older child; another has a four-poster canopy bed and old-fashioned claw-foot tub. Continental breakfast is included. *236 Church St., Marietta 30060, 770/426–1881, fax 770/426–6821. AE, D, MC, V.*

14 *g-3*

SYCAMORE HOUSE BED & BREAKFAST

Built around 1905, this house has large rooms and generous windows that give it a light-filled, airy feeling. Replete with antiques and contemporary furniture and art, the accommodations feature private baths. There is a suite with a queen bedroom and sitting room/library—with wood-burning fireplace—plus two standard rooms. In the secluded garden, whose plantings were chosen for color and fragrance, you'll find a waterfall and a heated pool with hot tub. You can have breakfast whenever you wish, rather than on a set schedule, and any special needs are cheerfully accommodated. A MARTA station, restaurants, galleries, and entertainment are a five-minute walk away. Innkeepers Ren and Judy Manning have dogs and cats, so ask if yours are welcome. The house is a romantic, peaceful getaway in the city, though children are welcome. *624 Sycamore St., Decatur 30030, 404/378–0685, fax 404/373–7123, www.city-directory.com/sycamorehouse. 3 rooms. Pool, hot tub. No credit cards. MARTA: Decatur.*

15 *f-5*

TRAVELODGE–DOWNTOWN

Some staffers have been working at this family-owned hotel since it opened 35 years ago. The downtown location is ideal for conventioneers and business travelers, as are the in-room coffeemakers, irons and ironing boards, and hair dryers. The well-maintained rooms are decorated in burgundy and sea foam; executive rooms are a little more plushly furnished. Two "Sleepy Bear Dens" are designed especially for children, with special decor and an adjoining king-bed room for the grown-ups. Complimentary doughnuts and coffee are provided each morning along with free copies of *USA Today*; local papers are provided in the afternoon. There's another Travelodge out by Hartsfield Atlanta International Airport (*see* Hotels Near the Airport, *below*). *311 Courtland St., 30303, Downtown, 404/659–4545 or 800/578–7878, fax 404/659–5923. 71 rooms. In-room data ports, in-room safes, pool, free parking. AE, D, DC, MC, V. MARTA: Civic Center.*

3 *h-6*

WHITWORTH INN

This spot is popular both with business travelers and with families visiting Lake Lanier. The proprietors wanted to live and work in the same space, so they built their property from scratch. The result is a simple dormered structure, ample but not luxuriously furnished, with wheelchair accessibility. All the rooms are bright and well lit, air-conditioned, and equipped with phones; baths are strictly functional. Breakfast is included and children under 12 stay free. No smoking and no pets are allowed. *6593 McEver Rd., Flowery Branch 30542, 770/967–2386, fax 770/967–2649, www.whitworthinn.com. 10 rooms. AE, MC, V.*

5 *f-4*

WINGATE INN PEACHTREE CORNERS

This small chain of business-oriented inns has several locations in the Atlanta area. The spacious guest rooms have microwave ovens, separate work areas with 900-megahertz cordless phones, and free high-speed Internet access via T1 Ethernet. Suites have hot tubs. In-room entertainment is available in the form of pay-per-view films, Nintendo, and Web TV. Cold buffet Continental breakfast is included. The Norcross location is handy for anyone doing business in metro Atlanta's numerous technology parks and is close to first-class recreational facilities as well. Its meeting rooms can accommodate groups of up to 50 people. Wingate is probably one of the best values around. *5800 Peachtree Industrial Blvd., Norcross 30071, 770/263–2020 or 800/228–1000, fax 770/263–2022, www.wingateinns.com. In-room data ports, in-room safes, refrigerators, exercise room, outdoor lap pool, jacuzzi, coin laundry, laundry service, business services, meeting rooms. AE, D, DC, MC, V.*

LUXE LOUNGES

A good hotel bar is both a convivial spot where you can unwind after a hectic business day and an intimate boîte where you can woo your special someone. See Chapter 5 for more on these standouts.

Four Seasons Hotel, Atlanta (very expensive)
The huge, well-stocked bar beckons irresistibly as you enter the Park 75 Lounge from a plant-filled terrace. Sink into cushy seating grouped around low tables, and let the soft lighting, piano music, and complimentary cocktail buffet work their magic.

Grand Hyatt Atlanta (very expensive)
While you sip your cabernet or cosmopolitan at the Lobby Lounge, set aside your cares and enjoy the sight of the serene, Japanese-style rock garden and the sound of its burbling waterfall.

Ritz-Carlton, Buckhead (very expensive)
The Lobby Lounge attracts imbibers to high tea in the afternoon and to the cocktail hours of the evening, which are sometimes backed by live jazz. The atmosphere is lively, and in winter a fireplace chases away the chill.

Westin Peachtree Plaza (very expensive)
High atop one of Atlanta's most distinctive towers, the slowly spinning Sundial Restaurant & Lounge takes in exquisite views of the city's high-rise architecture.

---

12 *f-2*
3600 Piedmont Rd., Buckhead, 404/869–1100.

13 *e-3*
2920 Clairmont Rd., Northeast, 404/248–1550.

7 *f-6*
2020 Sullivan Rd., College Park, 770/994–3666.

6 *a-4:*
3450 Venture Pkwy., Duluth, 770/622–7277.

HOSTELS

15 *f-4*

HOSTELING INTERNATIONAL ATLANTA

Atlanta's only youth hostel offers dormitory-style rooms with four to six beds each and shared bathrooms with showers. Coffee and doughnuts are served in the morning. A renovation is scheduled to be complete by late 2000 and leave space for about 60 beds; in the meantime the hostel remains open with fewer beds. The hostel office is open from 8 to noon and 5 to midnight; when you check in you will be asked for photo ID. Beds are $18 per night. *223 Ponce de Leon Ave., 30308, Midtown, 404/872–1042, fax 404/870–0042, www.hostel-atlanta.com. Free parking. AE, D, MC, V. MARTA: North Avenue.*

HOTELS NEAR THE AIRPORT

7 *f-6*

THE ABBETT INN

Built in the 1880s, this Queen Anne Victorian was originally the home of H. M. Abbett, secretary and treasurer of the Atlanta and West Point Railroad. Now, it is the scene not only of weekend getaways but of weddings, reunions and even murder mystery parties. The capacious house stands on a large, wooded lot in a quiet neighborhood, yet this inviting, park-like setting is only ten minutes from downtown Atlanta. Innkeepers Donald Taylor-Farmer and John W. Hoard have renovated the house to a contemporary level of comfort, but they've retained all the old bathtubs. Four of the rooms have private baths, and each floor has a kitchen for guests. One convenience offered by the inn is complimentary transportation to and from the airport and the nearby MARTA station. *1746 Virginia Ave., College Park 30337, 404/767–3708, fax 404/767–1626. 6 rooms. In-room fax, in-room data ports, airport shuttle, free parking. AE, D, MC, V. MARTA: College Park. Moderate.*

7 *h-8*

COMFORT INN–AIRPORT

Six miles from Hartsfield Atlanta International Airport and 12 mi from downtown, this hotel offers convenience and comfort for the budget-conscious. All rooms are decorated in straightforward contemporary style and have microwaves; Continental breakfast is included. There are several other Comfort Inn and Comfort Suite properties around the metro Atlanta area (*see* Budget Lodgings, *above*). *6370 Old Dixie Hwy., Jonesboro 30236, 770/961–6336 or 800/228–5150, fax 770/961–0946. 67 rooms. Refrigerators, pool. AE, D, DC, MC, V. Budget.*

7 *f-6*

COURTYARD BY MARRIOTT– AIRPORT SOUTH

Courtyard repeats its successful formula for the busy traveler a mile from the airport and minutes from downtown. Spacious, predictable rooms and express check-in and check-out help your stay to go smoothly, as can the services of the concierge. At the end of the day, relax in the hot tub or over a cocktail. In addition to this property and the Marietta location, there are several other Courtyards in the Atlanta area (*see* Marietta listing, *above*). *2050 Sullivan Rd., College Park 30337, 770/997–2220 or 800/321–2211, fax 770/994–9743, www.courtyard.com. 132 rooms, 12 suites. Restaurant, lounge, in-room data ports, in-room fax, refrigerators, indoor pool, exercise room, airport shuttle. AE, D, DC, MC, V, Moderate.*

7 *g-5*

CROWNE PLAZA– ATLANTA AIRPORT

Business and leisure travelers find a full range of facilities and superb accommodations at this 12-story hotel. From the warm welcome of the bell staff to the personalized attention of the concierge and valet, you will enjoy excellent service. Large guest rooms are equipped

with a well-lit work area, two telephones with voice mail, in-room coffeemaker, iron, hair dryer, and make-up mirror. Public areas include a gift shop and 16,000 square ft of flexible meeting space. The hotel is 1 mi from Hartsfield Atlanta International Airport and six minutes from downtown. There is another Crowne Plaza in Dunwoody (*above*). *1325 Virginia Ave., East Point 30344, 404/768–6660 or 800/2CROWNE, fax 404/766–6121. 378 rooms. Restaurant, lounge, in-room data ports, pool, exercise room, coin laundry, dry cleaning, meeting rooms, airport shuttle. AE, D, DC, MC, V. Moderate.*

7 *f-6*

DAYS INN–ATLANTA AIRPORT

This soundproof six-story hotel is convenient not only to the airport but to the Georgia International Convention and Trade Center. Each room has a coffeemaker and opens onto an interior corridor. The hotel has 1,700 square ft of meeting space. In addition to this property and the Six Flags location, there are several other Days Inns throughout the metro Atlanta area (*see* Budget Lodgings, *above*). *4601 Best Rd., College Park 30339, 404/761–6500 or 800/DAYSINN, fax 404/763–3267. 160 rooms. Restaurant, pool, exercise room, meeting rooms, airport shuttle. AE, D, DC, MC, V. Budget.*

7 *f-7*

FAIRFIELD INN BY MARRIOTT–COLLEGE PARK

At this link in Marriott's affordable chain, each guest room is furnished in familiar motel style and guests have health club privileges. Continental breakfast is complimentary, as is shuttle service (5 AM–midnight) within a 5-mi radius, including to the airport. No-smoking and ADA-accessible rooms are available upon request. The inn is handy to Ft. McPherson, Six Flags, and other points of interest. In addition to this property and the Six Flags location (*above*), there are several other Fairfield Inns throughout metro Atlanta. *2451 Old National Pkwy., College Park 30349, 404/761–8371 or 800/228–2800, fax 404/761–8371, www.fairfieldinn.com. 132 rooms. Pool, airport shuttle, free parking. AE, D, DC, MC, V. Budget.*

7 *f-6*

HILTON ATLANTA AIRPORT AND TOWERS

Atlanta's airport Hilton features plush accommodations with a contemporary flair. If you need to work you'll appreciate the desk area in your room, and if you need to play you'll be glad of the pool table on the property. When you're ready to move on, you can use the on-site Delta ticket desk and the complimentary transportation to the airport. The hotel has extensive, adaptable meeting, banquet, and exhibit space. *1031 Virginia Ave., Hapeville 30354, 404/767–9000 or 800/774–1500, fax 404/768–0185, www.hilton.com. 498 rooms, 5 suites. 3 restaurants, bar, indoor pool, outdoor pool, sauna, tennis court, exercise room, laundry service, concierge, business services, meeting rooms, airport shuttle, free parking. AE, D, DC, MC, V. Moderate.*

7 *f-6*

MARRIOTT– ATLANTA AIRPORT

All guest rooms here offer the familiar Marriott amenities. Among them, 141 are designed specifically to meet the needs of the business traveler. The business center is another plus for professionals on the road, but you can take some time out not only at the health club but at an indoor-outdoor pool and a solarium. The hotel's conference and meeting facilities offer 21,000 square ft of flexible space. *4711 Best Rd., College Park 30337, 404/766–7900 or 800/MARRIOTT, fax 404/209–6808, www.marriott.com. 638 rooms, 10 suites. 2 restaurants, lounge, pool, beauty salon, 2 tennis courts, health club, business services, meeting rooms, airport shuttle. AE, D, DC, MC, V. Moderate.*

7 *f-6*

RENAISSANCE CONCOURSE– ATLANTA AIRPORT

An 11-story atrium heralds the luxury to be found at this state-of-the-art hotel. Each room has an inviting sitting area, spacious bathroom, and executive business amenities, such as direct-dial telephone with message alerts. A club level occupies the hotel's upper floors, which are accessible only to guests staying there; special club-floor concierge service is always ready to meet any need. A multilingual staff and foreign currency exchange make international visitors feel welcome, and all guests have use of the fully equipped business center and its secretarial services. You'll find golf and tennis facilities nearby and the airport five minutes away. There is 34,000 square ft of adaptable meeting space on site. You'll find several other Renaissance locations in the Atlanta area *(above). 1 Hartsfield Centre Pkwy., College Park 30354, 404/209–9999 or 800/HOTELS1, fax 4014/209–7031, www.renaissancehotels.com. 387 rooms. Restaurant, lounge, in-room data ports, minibars, 1 indoor and 1 outdoor pool, massage, sauna, health club, meeting rooms, travel services, airport shuttle, free parking. AE, D, DC, MC, V. Moderate.*

7 *f-6*

RESIDENCE INN BY MARRIOTT– ATLANTA AIRPORT

This all-suite hotel 1½ mi from Hartsfield Atlanta International Airport is designed for extended stays. Each guest room has a full kitchen, separate living and bedroom areas, and a large work space with computer connections. In addition to this property and the Alpharetta inn, there are several other Residence Inns in the Metro Atlanta area *(see Alpharetta listing, above). 3401 International Blvd., Hapeville 30354, 404/761–0511 or 800/MARRIOTT, fax 404/761–0650, www.residenceinn.com. 126 suites. Restaurant, pool, hot tub, exercise room, coin laundry, dry cleaning, free parking. AE, D, DC, MC, V. Moderate.*

7 *f-6*

SHERATON GATEWAY HOTEL–ATLANTA AIRPORT

With easy access to downtown and area attractions, this Sheraton adjoins the Georgia International Convention Center. The hotel has reserved more than half its rooms for nonsmokers and has 10,000 square ft of meeting space. Closer to the city center, you can stay at Sheratons in downtown, Buckhead, and Dunwoody as well as at Colony Square *(all above). 1900 Sullivan Rd., College Park 30337, 770/997–1100 or 800/833–8624, fax 770/991–5906, www.sheraton.com. 396 rooms, 11 suites. Restaurant, 2 lounges, indoor/outdoor pool, jacuzzi, exercise room, meeting rooms, airport shuttle, free parking. AE, D, DC, MC, V. Moderate.*

7 *f-6*

SUMNER SUITES—
ATLANTA AIRPORT

This chain hotel offers suite accommodations at an economic price. You'll have separate living and bedroom areas, plus a computer-ready desk. No-smoking and ADA-accessible rooms are available. There are also Sumners in Duluth and Smyrna (*above*). *1899 Sullivan Rd., College Park 30337, 770/994–2997 or 800/747–8483, fax 770/994–8626, www.sumnersuites.com. 125 rooms. In-room data ports, pool, exercise room, meeting rooms, coin laundry, airport shuttle, free parking. AE, D, DC, MC, V. Moderate.*

7 *f-7*

TRAVELODGE
ATLANTA AIRPORT

Renovated in 1999, this well-situated property is a comfortable and affordable full-service hotel. Each room opens to an interior corridor and features cable TV; no-smoking and ADA-accessible rooms are available upon request. Continental breakfast is included. There's another Travelodge downtown (*see* Budget Lodgings, *above*) *1808 Phoenix Blvd., College Park 30349, 770/991–1099 or 800/578–7878, fax 770/991–1076. 193 rooms. Bar, lounge, in-room data ports, pool, exercise room, airport shuttle. AE, D, DC, MC, V. Budget.*

7 *f-6*

WESTIN HOTEL—
ATLANTA AIRPORT

Located five minutes from Atlanta Hartsfield International Airport and 15 minutes from downtown, this hotel is also near a MARTA line (a complimentary shuttle runs both to the airport and to the station). Rooms in the 10-story glass building surround a central atrium. All feature desks, coffeemakers, in-room movies, and upscale bathrooms, and some also provide speaker phones, basic office supplies, and fax machines with printer and copier functions. Pamper yourself in the hot tub and the tanning bed before heading to the on-site conference facilities. You'll find another Westin downtown (*above*). *4736 Best Rd., College Park 30337, 404/762–7676 or 800/228–3000, fax 404/763–4199. 462 rooms, 33 suites. Restaurant, in-room data ports, indoor-outdoor pool, sauna, health club, basketball, meeting rooms, free parking. AE, D, DC, MC, V. Moderate.*

B&B
RESERVATION
SERVICES

BED & BREAKFAST
ATLANTA

These folks can help you make B&B reservations, arrange home stays, rent corporate apartments, and find other alternative lodging gems. *1608 Briarcliff Rd., Suite 5, 30306, Decatur, 404/875–0525 or 800/967–3224, fax 404/875–8198.*

GEORGIA BED &
BREAKFAST COUNCIL

An affiliate of the Georgia Hospitality and Travel Association, the council publishes a directory that you can request by telephoning or by visiting the Web site. *600 W. Peachtree St., 30308, Downtown, 404/873–4482, www.stay-in-ga.com.*

GREAT INNS OF GEORGIA

This private marketing consortium publishes a brochure listing member inns. For a copy, call and leave your name and address. *404/843–0471 or 404/851–1585.*

chapter 7

CITY SOURCES

getting a handle on the city

basics of city life

BANKS

atms

For the address of the nearest ATM accepting Cirrus cards, call the **Cirrus Cash Machine Locator** (800/307–7309). For help finding an ATM that accepts Plus cards, call the **Plus ATM Locator** (800/843–7587).

major institutions

The following are full-service banks, members FDIC. In addition to those listed here, Atlanta has a plethora of small banks, many with only one or a few locations, that provide service with a small-town feel. But they may not offer all the services the large banks do. Most banks are open 9–4, with exceptions noted at the appropriate listings; the majority of branches have ATMs.

Bank of America Formerly NationsBank until its absorption by Bank of America in 1999, this bank has 46 branches in the Atlanta area, with numerous locations in Kroger grocery stores. Hours weekdays are 10–8 in the Kroger stores and 9–4 in the free-standing banks. Twenty locations are open Saturday (some just drive-through), with hours varying from 9 to noon or 1, while the Kroger locations are open 10–5. *800/299–BANK customer service.*

Citizens Trust Bank With more than 75 years of service to Atlanta's African-American community, CTB has a dozen branches chiefly Downtown and on the south side of Atlanta. Some are open Saturday 9–noon. *404/659–5959 main office.*

Colonial Bank Its 11 branches are principally in the north and west metro area. Those open Saturday chiefly have drive-through service only 9–noon; Dunwoody, Mableton, Wade Green, and Windy Hill offer full-service banking during those hours. *877/502–2265 customer service.*

Fidelity National Bank This Decatur-based bank offers full service banking at 19 branches, with Saturday service 9–noon at all branches. *404/639–6500 main office, 888/248–5466 customer service.*

First Union This large bank resulted from the merger of several well-respected Atlanta area institutions and has branches throughout the metro area. All branches are open Saturday 9–noon. Service is available in Spanish. *800/801–0714, 800/ASKFUNB 24-hour customer service.*

Regions National Bank This small but growing regional bank recently added another branch in the Gwinnett Mall, giving it about 20 branches chiefly located in the north and west metro area, although there also is one in East Point. Selected banks are open Saturday 9–noon. *800–REGIONS customer service, plus 0 for personal attention.*

SouthTrust With more than 140 branches throughout the Atlanta area, it offers Saturday services at about half of its locations 9–noon. *770/956–0634, 800/239–6919 customer service.*

Summit National Bank This small bank, with five branches scattered around the north and west, specializes in the banking needs of the Asian and Latino communities' business owners. The bank's Asian Banking Center (3490 Shallowford Rd., Chamblee, 770/455–1772) has Saturday hours, 9–1. *770/454–0400.*

SunTrust With 79 branches, 50 of them in Publix supermarkets, huge SunTrust was formed by the merger of Trust Company Bank in Atlanta and Sun Bank in Florida in the mid 1980s. SunTrust now is the ninth-largest bank holding company in the country. *404/230–5555 24-hour service, 800/432–4932.*

Tucker Federal Bank This small metro-area bank, serving mostly the north and east sides, touts itself as "Not too big. Not too small. Just right." Tucker Federal has 13 branches around Atlanta, 7 of which are open 9–noon on Saturday. *770/908–6400, 800/277–4075 customer service.*

United Americas Bank N.A. Specializing in the financial needs of the Hispanic community, this young bank has extended Friday hours (9–6) and is open Saturday 9–1. Besides its main branch (3789 Roswell Rd., Buckhead), the bank is planning two new locations (one at the intersection of Buford Hwy. and Chamblee-Tucker Rd., the other in Marietta). *404/240–0101.*

Wachovia Based in Winston-Salem, North Carolina, this large bank has 92 branches all over the metro Atlanta area, including Clayton and Fayette counties. Hours at most locations are Monday–Thursday 9–5, Friday 9–6. However, the Downtown branch does business 8:30–5 only. *800/922–4684 24-hour customer service.*

DRIVING

Like most other modern American cities, Atlanta is difficult to negotiate without an automobile. The city's extensive sprawl forces most residents to rely on major highways to get around, even when it's just to take the kids to soccer practice. Encircling metropolitan Atlanta and cutting through its principle counties (DeKalb, Fulton, Cobb) is I–285. Crossing it are I–75 from the northwest and I–85 from the northeast, the two of which merge into the infamous "Downtown Connector," only to split again and head south to Florida (I–75) or west through the middle of Georgia to Alabama (I–85). Crossing this network from east to west is I–20. Running south from I–285 East is I–675, which provides a shortcut to Henry County and reconnects to I–75 near McDonough.

Atlanta's only toll road is GA 400, a northbound highway that starts near Lenox Square in Buckhead. GA 400 heads toward Roswell and Alpharetta, ending near Dahlonega. If you access or exit the highway near Lenox Square the toll is 50¢, but you can exit or enter at I–285 and not pay the toll. Wisdom dictates avoiding GA 400 at peak rush hours. If you drive GA 400 daily, you may wish to obtain a "Cruise Card" from the **Georgia Department of Transportation** (3525 Piedmont Rd., Bldg. 7, Suite 205, Piedmont Center, Buckhead, 30305, 404/365–7790). Applications may be requested by mail or picked up at the office; renewals may be paid for by a credit card supplied at the time of application. The "Cruise Card" ($40 paid in advance) enables drivers to zip through the toll plaza without stopping to plunk exact change into the basket. Each time you use the cruise lane a scanner reads the electronic device decal mounted on your windshield and 50¢ is automatically deducted from your account. If you use the cruise lane without a "Cruise Card," the fine is $25.50 per occurrence.

The speed limit on interstate highways in the metro Atlanta area is 55 mph. On GA 400 and U.S. 78 (another east–west limited-access highway that goes to Stone Mountain), the speed limit is 65 mph. On I–285 especially, 55 mph is nearly impossible to maintain, as most drivers exceed that substantially. While the local traffic enforcement authorities seem to have thrown their hands up in resignation, occasionally they do crack down and pull over the most flagrant speeders. By and large, they won't bother you until you hit 65 mph. Rule of thumb? Go with the flow, not faster. On secondary streets, posted speed limits average about 35 mph, depending on the number of lanes. In school zones 25 mph is the norm when the blinker light is flashing, and the limit is often vigorously enforced by radar-toting police posted nearby. Right turns on red are permitted following a complete stop.

Except in Downtown and Midtown, Atlanta's streets lack any semblance of an orderly grid pattern. Midtown is the most grid-like zone, with east–west streets bearing numbers running from 4th to 27th. City streets are often one-way, especially in Downtown and Midtown, where narrow roadways make two-way traffic impractical. Street signs are difficult to see, especially at night, and sometimes are missing altogether. On newer, wide streets and major thoroughfares, street signs are often suspended overhead, making them easy to spot well before you need to make a turn. Some streets change names in the mid-course, apparently without any rhyme or reason. For instance, N. Druid Hills Road—which goes nowhere near Druid Hills—becomes Valley Brook Road at Lawrenceville Highway. Downtown's streets are named for notable citizens, so as one leader falls from grace and another comes into favor, the city renames at will. For newcomers, a good street atlas, available at most office supply stores, is essential.

Georgia law requires drivers and front-seat passengers to wear seat belts while the vehicle is in operation, and children four and younger *must* be buckled into appropriate safety seats in the rear. Children 5–12 must sit in the rear seat if the vehicle is equipped with air bags. Georgia law dictates that drivers who fail to use the proper child-safety restraints incur one point on their driving record for the first offense and two points for second and subsequent offenses. Violators also pay a fine of $50 for the first offense and $100 for the second and subsequent offenses.

In Georgia, vehicles, not the individual drivers, must have liability insurance; failure to maintain proper insurance usually results in a six-month license suspension. Most of the 10 counties require an emissions inspection every two years for most newer-model vehicles. If the model year of your vehicle is an odd year you must have it inspected every odd year. Georgia drivers who accumulate 15 points on their license for moving or any other violations within a 24-month period are subject to suspension of their license.

licenses

Georgia requires first-time drivers to pass a written test covering traffic rules and road signs, an eye exam, and a driving test. Drivers with an expired out-of-state license or a Georgia license that expired more than two years ago must pass an eye test and a driving test as well. License renewals may be obtained as much as 150 days in advance of expiration and require an eye exam. New permanent residents of the state must obtain a Georgia driver's license within 30 days of moving here. If you are over 18 and surrender a valid license from another state when applying for a Georgia license, you only need to pass an eye examination. New residents must present their social security cards and evidence of residence (a utility bill, bank statement, or lease or contract of sale), and all drivers under the age of 18 must present proof that they have attended an approved drug and alcohol course. Non-U.S. citizens must present proper INS documentation when they apply for a Georgia driver's license.

The license fee is $15 and the license is good for four years, expiring on the holder's birthday of the renewing year. Veterans and active-duty National Guard members receive their licenses free. You can get your new Georgia driver's license at any of the Georgia State Patrol posts scattered throughout the metro area. If you are renewing, you can also do so at an office in your local Kroger grocery store. When you obtain or renew your driver's license, you may indicate your desire to be an organ donor and you may register to vote. Georgia also

issues non-drivers' photo ID cards at any driver's license examination office at a cost of $10.

If you change your address you must apply for a new license, with your correct address, within 60 days of moving. Be sure to bring evidence of your new address, such as a utility bill or bank statement. If you change your name by marriage or otherwise, you also must obtain a new license, with your correct name, within 60 days. Either change may be made at any of the Kroger locations. A replacement license, valid for the current renewal period, will be issued once in any four-year period, free of charge.

Georgia State Patrol 404/657–9300 information, www.ganet.org\dps.

registration

New, permanent Georgia residents are required to obtain Georgia tags within 30 days of moving to the state. Prior to issuing tags, some jurisdictions require that certain vehicles have emissions inspection certification. You can have your vehicle tested at myriad locations around the metro area for a nominal fee. When you apply for tags, bring your original title documents, previous registration, proof of insurance, and (if required) emissions inspection certification. Note: Motor vehicle registration (rather than voter registration) enters your name into the jury duty pool.

dmv offices

Each county maintains its own motor vehicle division, and satellite offices are usually scattered around each county. For information, call the motor vehicle office of the county in which you reside.

Cherokee County 100 North St., Canton, 770/479–0523; 7545 N. Main St., Woodstock, 770/924–4099.

Clayton County 121 S. McDonough St., Courthouse Annex Three Bldg., Jonesboro, 770/477-3331. Satellite office: Clayton Commons Shopping Center, 5389 Jonesboro Rd., Lake City. Phone calls are not taken at this location.

Cobb County 770/528–4020 24-hour help line, 700 S. Cobb Dr., Marietta. Satellite offices: 4400 Lower Roswell Rd., Government Service Center, Marietta; 2950 Canton Hwy., Market Square Shopping

Center, Marietta; Government Service Center, 4700 Austell Rd., Marietta. Satellite offices closed 11:30 AM–12:30 PM.

DeKalb County 4380 Memorial Dr., Decatur; 1358 Dresden Dr., Atlanta 30319; 1 South DeKalb Mall, I–20 at Candler Rd., Decatur, 404/298–4000.

Douglas County 8700 Hospital Dr., Douglasville, 770/949–2309.

Fayette County 140 W. Stonewall Ave., Suite 109, Fayetteville, 770/461–3611.

Forsyth County 110 E. Main St., Cumming, 770/781–2112.

Fulton County 141 Pryor St., Room 1106, Fulton County Bldg., Downtown; 7741 Roswell Rd., Roswell; 3000 Old Alabama Rd., Kroger grocery store, Haynes Bridge Shopping Center, Alpharetta; 11913 Wills Rd., Alpharetta; 5600 Stonewall Tell Rd., College Park; 2636 Martin Luther King Jr., Dr., Suite 12, Hightower Station Shopping Center, Southwest Atlanta. Two locations are for senior citizens only: 677 Fairburn Rd., south Fulton County also Southwest Atlanta; open only Mon.–Wed. 10–3; 6500 Vernon Woods Dr., Sandy Springs, open only Tues.–Thurs. 9–3. For all Fulton County locations call 404/730–6100).

Gwinnett County 750 S. Perry St., Gwinnett Justice Administration Center, Lawrenceville, 770/822–8818. Satellites: 5030 Georgia Bell Ct., #1030, Norcross; 5270 Peachtree Pkwy., Interlochen Village, Peachtree Corners; 2280 Oak Rd., Snellville. For 24-hour information for all locations, 770/822–8801.

Henry County 345 Phillips Dr., McDonough, 770/954–2471; 130 Berry St., Stockbridge, 770/389–7820; 20 E. Main St. S, Court Council/Police Station, Hampton, Thurs. only, no phone; City Hall, 3644 GA 42, Locust Grove, Tues. only, no phone.

traffic

Traffic jams are becoming as rampant around Atlanta as in any other large city. During rush hours (6 AM–9 AM and 3 PM–7 PM), I–285, the perimeter highway, can be absolutely infuriating as traffic moves at a crawl. Similarly, GA 400, a major conduit from the northern 'burbs to Buckhead, is a solid strip of vehicles during rush hours. If you live in a northern area and have a plane to catch, allow at least one additional hour of travel time to reach Hartsfield Atlanta International Airport during those hours.

Complicating the flow of traffic in metro Atlanta is the apparent failure of every municipality to synchronize traffic lights with speed limits. It was rumored at the time of the 1996 Centennial Olympic Games that a system governing traffic light changes would be established, but the games are long over, and it hasn't happened. You'll often find, as a result, that you'll leave one newly changed-to-green traffic light only to watch the very next one turn red, while the one after that is green, and so forth, creating a string of Christmas lights ahead of you. At some intersections equipped with turn arrows, the interval is curiously brief, so it's important to be ready to go when they change. Making all this worse is the bad habit Atlanta drivers have of not using their turn signals to indicate what they have on their minds. This particularly nefarious habit causes numerous rush-hour accidents.

At any time—including 3 AM—metro Atlanta's highways are likely to become traffic-jammed. When traffic is backed up, it's a good idea to use secondary roads, although lately even these have proven to be clogged at peak hours. Major surface thoroughfares, such as Northside Drive, DeKalb Avenue from Downtown to Decatur, and Roswell Road just south of Roswell, have switch lanes that function as inbound lanes in the morning and outbound lanes in the afternoon. Instructional lighting over these lanes indicates their direction at any given moment. What you see is either a green arrow or a red "X".

Georgia Road Information 404/656–5367.

GAS STATIONS

Georgia has one of the lowest state gasoline taxes in the nation, so filling your tank is relatively inexpensive. Most gas stations in the 10 counties pump fuel and sell groceries, maps, and automotive supplies. Self-service is the norm, although for an extra few cents per gallon you can get full service, which means an attendant pumps your gas and should check your fluids and clean your windshield.

There are some old-fashioned, full-service, 24-hour stations in the metro Atlanta area, but they are few and far between. One is the **BP-Northlake Car Care Center** (4121 LaVista Rd., Tucker, 770/938–1174) at exit 28 of I–285. They don't work on cars at 2 AM, but they will check your coolant and the air in your tires.

GEOGRAPHY

Atlanta was founded on a ridge that now runs the length of Peachtree Street downtown and forms a watershed divide between the Gulf of Mexico and the Atlantic Ocean. The city lies at an elevation of 800 to more than 1,400 ft above sea level, with the lower areas on the south side of town and the higher to the north, toward the Blue Ridge Mountains. Rolling, wooded terrain in the residential north gives way to level land in the south, where Hartsfield Atlanta International Airport now stands.

From its urban center, Atlanta fans out toward the neighborhoods. Encircling Downtown proper are several downtown-style areas with their own high-rise office and apartment buildings. Among these is Midtown, framed by North Avenue to Pershing Point, where Peachtree Rd. intersects with W. Peachtree Street. Peachtree continues north to Buckhead, another cluster of commercial and residential towers. Beyond Buckhead, the outer perimeter is beginning to develop its own set of high-rise clusters, at U.S. 41 and I–285 (known as Galleria) in northwest Atlanta and at Peachtree-Dunwoody Road and I–285 in Dunwoody.

To the east of Downtown/Midtown lie Virginia-Highland, Poncey-Highland, and Inman Park.

To the immediate east of the city of Atlanta, Decatur was founded in 1823 and retains its village-like charm and character. Historic towns like Marietta, Roswell, and Jonesboro, which saw its own Civil War battle, have been integrated into the metroplex while retaining their own traditions and character.

HOLIDAYS

During the following holidays all city and county government offices in metro Atlanta are closed, as are banks and sometimes other businesses. In addition, state offices are closed for Confederate Memorial Day and some businesses also close Christmas Eve.

New Year's Day January 1.

Martin Luther King Jr. Day Third Monday in January.

Presidents' Day Third Monday in February.

Confederate Memorial Day April 26.

Memorial Day Last Monday in May.

Independence Day July 4.

Labor Day First Monday in September.

Columbus Day The Monday closest to October 12.

Thanksgiving Day Fourth Thursday in November.

Christmas Day December 25.

LIQUOR LAWS

Georgia has some quirky alcohol laws that drive newcomers and longtime residents nuts. For instance, folks moving here from out of state are often stunned to learn that it is illegal for their wine clubs to send wine to Georgia residents. In fact, the law makes the shipper a felon on second offense. The courts may soon re-evaluate the legality of this law, but at press time it was still in effect.

Packaged alcohol may be sold until midnight in Georgia jurisdictions that permit its sale, and not all do: The state still has many dry counties and cities. Package stores may sell all alcoholic beverages, and grocery stores may sell beer and wine but not liquor. Neither type of outlet may sell alcohol on Sunday, though restaurants in much of the metropolitan area can serve drinks. However, local jurisdictions are empowered to set their own standards and may prohibit all alcohol sales on Sunday, as is the case in Henry County. To avoid confusion or disappointment, check well in advance of any planned events that may fall on a Sunday. Cities and counties may also prohibit the sale of beverage alcohol on election day, because once upon a corrupt time some politicians bought votes for a shot of whiskey.

You must be at least 21 years of age to buy alcohol in Georgia, and be able to prove it with proper ID. The city of Alpharetta in Fulton County now requires businesses to card anyone who wishes to purchase alcohol, no matter how old he or she may appear. If you do not have a valid driver's license, you should carry a state-issued photo ID card (*see above*) if you plan on buying a cocktail or a six-pack.

NO-SMOKING

Georgia's local jurisdictions regulate smoking in public places via a variety of ordinances. A recent attempt to institute a severe no-smoking policy in Atlanta was defeated. Throughout the 10 counties, smoking is not permitted in most stores and public buildings. Hospitals are no-smoking, and so is most of Hartsfield Atlanta International Airport, which has special spaces set aside for smokers. Restaurants usually designate entire rooms as smoking areas; however, some establishments are too small to do so and instead prohibit smoking entirely. But a number of restaurants do not maintain separate spaces for non-smokers. Bed-and-breakfast inns customarily restrict smoking to common areas such as porches and sitting rooms, although some larger B&Bs and most hotels and motels reserve guest rooms and sometimes entire floors for smoking patrons. If you cannot tolerate tobacco smoke or if you can't enjoy yourself without a cigarette, check with these businesses in advance.

PARKING

Downtown, Midtown, and Buckhead are becoming parking nightmares, and it's very difficult to find parking on the street. Parking in Virginia-Highland and Little Five Points is a veritable horror, and there are only a few lots available to accommodate visitors. Atlanta, Decatur, and other municipalities have metered curb parking, but there is often a limit on how long you may park. Times vary on street meters, and some accept only quarters. In Marietta, Lawrenceville, Tucker, and similar small towns throughout the metropolitan area, municipal street parking is first-come, first served, with no meters.

In the city of Atlanta, valet parking is not allowed during the day, but it is available at night at most of the better restaurants and hotels. Be aware, however, that a few charge for the service. If you're coming into town for an evening's entertainment, you'll find that lots fill early in the evening. In both Downtown and Midtown, parking for events, especially at the Fox Theatre and Woodruff Arts Center, can get expensive—about $6–$7. But just a block or two away from major venues, charges are more reasonable. For sporting events at Turner Field, the Georgia Dome, and Philips Arena, parking costs about $10, depending on the event. Given the high price of parking for sports and entertainment events, consider taking MARTA when you can. It's the best way to get to Woodruff Arts Center, which has Arts Center Station, a connected stop that's accessible via a covered passageway. MARTA is also a great way to get to Philips Arena, where the station (Omni/CNN Center) is practically inside the complex.

rules & enforcement

Metro-area parking regulations vary. Within Atlanta city limits, drivers encounter numerous street signs that forbid parking, limit the length of time for on-street parking, or restrict parking to certain hours. Residential neighborhoods off Peachtree Street have become sensitive to the abuse of street parking in their tree-shaded areas, and many of these streets, such as 17th Street near Peachtree Street, restrict parking. Parking is not allowed along curbs painted yellow, and blue paint restricts those spaces to handicapped vehicles only. White curbs indicate that parking is permitted. For obvious reasons, you may not park in marked fire lanes; violations can result in fines or in some cases towing.

You can pay parking fines by mail, using the envelope left on your windshield by the ticketing officer. Fines for parking violations vary throughout the metro area. In the city of Decatur, for instance, they range from $15 to $50, the latter being the charge levied for parking in a fire lane. In all localities, the fine for parking in a handicap-reserved space can run as high as $500. In most jurisdictions the actual amount is set by a judge, so parking in one of these spaces also means a day in court. The most aggressively enforced parking regulations are at Hartsfield Atlanta International Airport, where foot-patrol officers vigorously—and with alacrity—write tickets for people who leave their vehicle in front of a terminal for any length of time. They do, however, make every effort not to ticket cars' passengers dropping off their luggage at curbside check-in stations.

If your car is towed from the street, you will have to contact the authorities of the jurisdiction that's doing the towing. Fines vary from one jurisdiction to another, and additional charges for storing your vehicle may apply as well. If you've parked on private property, such as in a business parking lot but without doing business at that location, the property owner is the one to contact to locate your vehicle. Businesses in Virginia-Highland guard their spaces with particular zeal and are quick to tow violators.

IMPORTANT ADDRESSES

Department of Police Services, City of Atlanta, Parking Tickets 104 Trinity Ave., Atlanta 30303, 404/658–6935.

City of Decatur 420 W. Trinity Pl., Decatur 30030, 404/377–7911.

parking lots

In major commercial zones there are numerous parking garages where the public may park for a fee, such as at Downtown's Georgia Pacific building and Georgian Terrace Hotel. Parking garages are often attached to banks, hotels, and office buildings. If you are doing business or dining in the connecting establishment, your parking may be complimentary if you get your ticket validated before leaving. Shopping centers and malls have extensive lots and garages where shoppers can park for free; some, such as Lenox Square and Phipps Plaza, offer valet parking for fees of $3–$5.

Downtown and Midtown have a fair number of pay parking lots, which may or may not be attended. In those that are unattended, patrons insert the required amount of cash into a metal box that has numbered slots corresponding to specific parking spaces. Be sure to remember your parking space number so you put your money in the right slot. A cautionary note: Occasionally, scurrilous characters loiter in unattended lots claiming to be attendants, in

order to take your fee. Legitimate parking attendants should be able to give you a receipt, and perhaps also place a ticket on the windshield. Do not pay anyone collecting parking fees in self-park lots without proper ID.

Here are a few convenient places to find parking in the more congested areas of metro Atlanta:

CITY OF ATLANTA

Buckhead Lenox Marketplace, 3535 Peachtree Rd., security: 404/760—1370); Phipps Plaza, 3500 Peachtree Rd., 404/ 261–7910, ext. 63; Sheraton Buckhead Hotel, 3405 Lenox Rd., 404/261–9250, ext. 471; Swissôtel, 3391 Peachtree Rd., 404/ 365–6455; Tower Place, 3340 Peachtree Rd., 404/262–1587.

Downtown 55 Marietta St., at Forsyth St., valet parking only, 404/688–6492; 55 Park Place Bldg., 55 Park Pl., 404/523–3163; the lot behind the building at 42 Auburn Ave. and Peachtree Center Ave., 404/577–1968; 45 John Wesley Dobbs Ave., 404/523– 4661; Georgia Pacific Center, 60 John Wesley Dobbs Ave., 404/524–1909; 160– 174 Piedmont Ave., at Edgewood Ave., near Georgia State University and Grady Memorial Hospital; Peachtree Center, 227 Courtland St., 404/681–0415; Rialto Theatre, lot across the street, 102 Cone St., 404/222–9497; 75 Piedmont Ave., at Auburn Ave., 404/522–2713); 76 Forsyth St., 404/681–2044; 30 Spring St., CNN Center Decks, entrance on Techwood Dr., 404/521–0691; Underground Atlanta, 75 Martin Luther King Jr. Dr., 404/577–2202).

Midtown Bell South Bldg., lot across the street at 662 W. Peachtree St., near Fox Theatre, 404/847–3600); Georgian Terrace Hotel, across from Fox Theatre, 459 Peachtree St., 404/881–6076; Medical Arts Bldg., 384 Peachtree St., 404/522– 2068; Midtown Exchange Bldg., 730 Peachtree St., at 4th St., 404/685–9170; Fox Theatre event parking only, 711 W. Peachtree St., 222 14th St., 404/876–2571.

DECATUR

Holiday Inn Towne Center II, 130 Ponce de Leon Ave., 404/377–9959.

PERSONAL SECURITY

As in any urban area, you should exercise a reasonable level of caution in order to stay safe in metro Atlanta. At night, in particular, know where you're going and how you expect to get there. Downtown Atlanta's reputation as a dangerous neighborhood is somewhat exaggerated, but on the street you should nevertheless be alert to who's around you and what's going on. Most major downtown streets are well lit and patrolled by uniformed police officers, most good bars and music clubs have security, and MARTA employs its own security force as well. In preparation for the 1996 Olympic Games, the city trained "ambassadors" to roam Downtown beats and assist visitors who may be lost or in distress. The program remains in place; ambassadors may be identified by their uniforms and pith helmets. These smiling guys help ward off panhandlers and will happily conduct the lone damsel to her hotel.

PUBLIC TRANSPORTATION

Metro Atlanta's public transportation system, the Metropolitan Atlanta Rapid Transit Authority (MARTA), is limited to the two major metro counties: DeKalb and Fulton. Two other counties, Cobb and Henry, have some public transportation; Cobb's ties into MARTA, but Henry's does not. Cherokee, Clayton, Douglas, Fayette, Forsyth, and Gwinnett counties still have no public transportation.

MARTA comprises two components, bus and rapid rail, which are linked with each other. Riders can transfer between the bus system and the rapid rail system. But if you need to travel crosstown, for instance, from Emory University to Northlake Mall or to Buckhead, you'll have to do a lot of transferring. The fare to ride on MARTA's rapid rail and bus systems is $1.50, paid using tokens purchased from machines at each MARTA rail station. You can also buy tokens at any of the MARTA Ride stores at rapid rail stations; they are located at the Airport (near baggage claim; 404/848—3498, 7 AM–10 PM), in Five Points (30 Alabama St.; 404/848—3205, 7 AM–6 PM), at Lenox Square in Lenox Station, across from Lenox Mall and Marriott; 404/848—3327, 8 AM–4 PM), and in Lindbergh (at Lindbergh Station, across from MARTA headquarters. 2424 Piedmont Rd. 404/848—4100, 8 AM–4 PM).

bus

Cobb Community Transit CCT connects with MARTA at the Arts Center station on 14th Street. Other limited connections operate weekdays between Midtown Atlanta and the Marietta area. Service is generally available from East and South Cobb. The fare on CCT buses is $1.25. A 10-ride pass costs $11.25 and a monthly pass $45. *CCT, 450 N. Cobb Pkwy., Marietta, 770/427–4444 service information, 770/427–2222 paratransit unit for customers with disabilities.*

Henry County Transit This system is designed to serve the elderly and disabled Henry County residents with transportation difficulties. Transportation is available only to points within the county; most riders use it to go to the grocery store and to medical appointments. If you need a ride, call to make arrangements a week in advance. The system does not operate before 9 AM, and return trips should be scheduled for just after lunch. The service is free. *45 Work Camp Rd., McDonough, 770/954–2033.*

MARTA Serving Fulton and DeKalb counties, MARTA's bus system boasts more than 100 routes traversing metropolitan Atlanta. The frequency depends on the day of the week, time of day, and route, and ranges from 8-55 minutes. The fare is $1.50 one way, and transfers between buses and to MARTA rapid rail are free. A weekly pass costs $12 and a monthly $45. *2424 Piedmont Rd., Buckhead, 404/848–4711 general information, 404/848–5389 information for people with disabilities, 404/848 5662 TDD, Spanish language information available.*

rapid rail

MARTA Under constant expansion, the rapid rail system has two lines—one that runs north–south and another that runs east–west. The lines cross at Five Points station in Downtown, and the south line goes directly to Hartsfield Atlanta International Airport. Monday through Friday, trains start running shortly after 4:30 AM from Hartsfield, Dunwoody, Indian Creek, and Hamilton Holmes; the last trains depart around 1:30 AM; weekends: 5 AM–1 AM. Most MARTA rail stations have generous free, short-term parking, but there is no parking at all at the Bankhead, Civic Center, Decatur, and North Avenue stations, and only severely limited parking at the Arts Center station and Midtown stops.

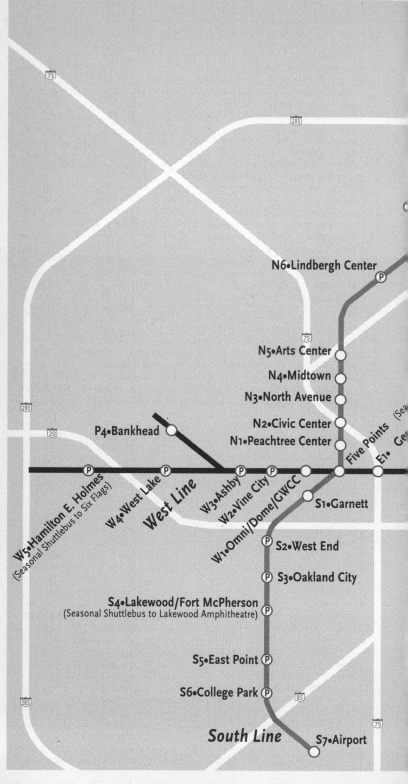

N6•Lindbergh Center

N5•Arts Center

N4•Midtown

N3•North Avenue

N2•Civic Center

N1•Peachtree Center

P4•Bankhead

Five Points

E1•

W5•Hamilton E. Holmes
(Seasonal Shuttlebus to Six Flags)

W4•West Lake

West Line

W3•Ashby

W2•Vine City

W1•Omni/Dome/GWCC

S1•Garnett

S2•West End

S3•Oakland City

S4•Lakewood/Fort McPherson
(Seasonal Shuttlebus to Lakewood Amphitheatre)

S5•East Point

S6•College Park

South Line

S7•Airport

N11•North Springs

North Line

N10•Sandy Springs

Ⓟ N9•Dunwoody

Northeast Line

Ⓟ N8•Medical Center

Ⓟ NE10•Doraville

Ⓟ NE9•Chamblee

N7•Buckhead

Ⓟ NE8•Brookhaven/Oglethorpe University

Ⓟ NE7•Lenox

rts (Seasonal Shuttlebus to ZooAtlanta)

E1• Georgia State

E2•King Memorial

E3•Inman Park/Reynoldstown

E4•Edgewood/Candler Park

E5•East Lake

E6•Decatur

E7•Avondale

East Line

E8•Kensington

E9•Indian Creek

MARTA System

◯ Rail Station

Ⓟ Rail Station with Free Parking

Ⓟ Rail Station with Free and Long-Term Parking

● Rail Station Under Development

Long-term parking in secured areas ($3 per day) is available at the Brookhaven, College Park, Doraville, Dunwoody, Lenox, Lindbergh, and Medical Arts stations. Transfers between trains and to buses are free. The one-way fare is $1.50; a weekly pass costs $12 and a monthly $45. *2424 Piedmont Rd., Buckhead, 404/848–4711 general information, 404/848–5389 handicapped information, 404/848–5662 TDD, Spanish language information available. Office hours 6 AM– 11 PM weekdays, 8 AM–10 PM weekends and holidays.*

taxi

Taxi companies in the metropolitan area have an unfortunate reputation for shabby vehicles and unprofessional, badly dressed drivers. Many seem to have a calculated habit of not carrying change, even for small bills, so if you're taking a taxi, prepare ahead by having small bills on hand. Many drivers are foreign nationals who may not speak good English or know the city as well as they should, although many of these drivers also try very hard to provide good service. It's a question of consistency. One consistently good company is **Buckhead Safety Cab** (2541 E. Paces Ferry Rd., Buckhead, 404/233–1152), but the service area is limited to Buckhead, Midtown, Downtown, and Hartsfield. But with 24 hours' advance notice they will arrange a pick-up anywhere within reasonable distance from Buckhead ($20 limit) to go to the airport.

PUBLICATIONS

Art & Antiques This glossy monthly magazine is devoted to the fine and decorative arts, including graphic arts and homes of collectors. *For subscriptions, 815/734–1162; local telephone, 770/ 955–5656.*

Art Papers This highly regarded tabloid presents in-depth articles on art and prints critiques of local exhibitions. *For information, call 404/588–1837.*

Atlanta Business Chronicle Appearing every Friday, this substantial, business-oriented weekly newspaper is a must-read for anyone interested in the metro area's commercial life. *For subscriptions, 404/249–1010.*

Atlanta Citymag Appearing eight times a year, this glossy publication, formerly

called *Dossier,* focuses on the businesses and lifestyles of entrepreneurial Atlantans. *For subscriptions, 404/231–5433.*

Atlanta Daily World Despite its title, this respected voice of Atlanta's African-American community appears only a few times a week. It's one of the nation's oldest black-owned and -published newspapers. *For information, 404/ 659–1110.*

Atlanta Homes & Lifestyle This glossy monthly publication focuses on area residential design, Atlanta lifestyle, and local personalities. *For subscriptions, 404/252–6670.*

Atlanta Journal–Constitution The city's chief daily newspaper is a combination of two papers that in past decades were published independently. Today, they have separate editorial boards but share news and feature staff. From Monday through Friday, the *Constitution* appears in the morning and the *Journal* in the evening. On weekends and holidays, they combine to publish a single edition. For information on current cultural and special events, see the Friday "Weekend" section, appearing in both papers, and the Saturday "Leisure" section. Other sections concentrate on suburban and neighborhood issues and news. *For subscriptions, 404/522–4141.*

Atlanta Magazine The city's glossy monthly covers everything from politics, education, and the arts to dining, sports, and lifestyle. *For subscriptions, 404/872–3100.*

Atlanta Now This bimonthly magazine is available free through Atlanta Convention and Visitors Bureau centers and at hotels and attractions around the city. *For information, call the ACVB at 404/ 521–6600 or 800/ATLANTA.*

Atlanta Sports & Fitness This monthly magazine, which covers local recreation opportunities, is available free at sporting goods stores and other area locations. *For information, 404/843–2257.*

Atlanta Tribune This well-designed monthly magazine focuses on issues and news of interest to the city's upscale African-American community. *For subscriptions, 770/587–0501.*

Atlanta Wine Report A monthly publication available free at package stores, restaurants, wine shops, and other selected outlets, the report lists tastings and special wine-focused events throughout the metropolitan area. *For information, 678/985–9494.*

Blue Milk A hip quarterly publication devoted to the visual, literary, and performing arts, it also runs an art complex with gallery and studio space, arts services, and exhibitions. *For subscriptions, 404/815–6991.*

Business to Business This monthly magazine addresses issues of interest to the city's Fortune 500 companies. *For subscriptions, 404/888–0555.*

Catalyst This is a bimonthly business magazine for metro Atlanta's young professionals and entrepreneurs. *For subscriptions, 404/888–0555.*

Creative Loafing This popular free weekly paper focuses on entertainment; it is available in boxes at nightclubs, bars, bookstores, and restaurants. *For information, 404/688–5623.*

Dunwoody Crier This free local weekly publication focuses on news and personalities in Dunwoody and the surrounding areas. *For information, 770/451–4147.*

Five Points: A Journal of Literature and Art This national triannual publication, based at Georgia State University's Department of English, focuses on art and literature. *For subscriptions, 404/651–0071, www.webdelsol/five_points.*

Georgia Magazine Published monthly by Oglethorpe Power, this is Georgia's only statewide lifestyle magazine. Residents of the west metro area—in parts of Cobb County, for instance—may receive it gratis if they get their power from an electrical membership cooperative. *For subscriptions, 770/270–7071.*

Georgia Trend This monthly publication surveys business issues around the state but has a decided Atlanta focus. *For information, 770/931–9410.*

Gwinnett Daily Post This suburban daily focuses on Gwinnett County news and lifestyle. *For subscriptions, 770/339–5845.*

The Hudspeth Report This free tabloid publication covers developments in dining and nightlife and lets readers know what's closing and what's opening. *For information, 404/255–3220.*

Jewish Times Atlanta's Jewish community keeps in touch not only with local news but also national and international items of interest through this weekly newspaper. *For subscriptions, 404/252–1600, ext. 205.*

Jezebel Fashion, entertainment, and lifestyle are the topics covered in this glossy monthly magazine about and for upscale Atlantans. *For information, 404/870–0123.*

Knife and Fork A monthly newsletter devoted to reviews of local restaurants—sometimes with tips about out-of-town dining—keeps Atlanta up to date on what's new, what's good, and what's not in the opinion of its French-born publisher, Christiane Lauterbach. *For subscriptions, call 404/387–2775.*

Marietta Daily Journal This daily news paper highlights the goings-on in Marietta and Cobb County, with a focus on the jurisdiction's politics, often to the dismay of its elected officials. *For subscriptions, 770/795–2300.*

Mundo Hispánico A free weekly Spanish-language newspaper in business since 1980, this covers chiefly local events of interest to the Atlanta Hispanic community, with some global news reporting. *For subscriptions, 770/590–0881.*

Museums & Galleries This bimonthly digest-size publication, available free at galleries and other locations, reports the happenings in Atlanta's myriad art galleries. *For information, 770/992–7808.*

The Neighbor Newspapers These weekly publications cover different parts of the city. The North Fulton edition reports on that area only, and the *DeKalb Neighbor* features events in that county. *For subscriptions, 770/428–9411.*

Our Kids This monthly magazine focuses on issues related to children and parenting. *For information, 404/256–4477.*

Presenting the Season This glossy quarterly magazine focuses on the Atlanta social season. *For subscriptions, 770/998–1118.*

Southern Voice The South's most widely read gay and lesbian weekly newspaper offers information on events and topics of special interest to the community. It is available free in boxes at package stores, bookstores, nightclubs, restaurants, and other locations throughout the city. *For information, 404/876–1819.*

Style This bimonthly publication, in partnership with the Woodruff Arts Center, focuses on Atlanta lifestyle and the arts. *For information, 404/252–1600, ext. 206.*

Where Atlanta This monthly publication covers subjects as diverse as shopping and dining, special events and nightclubs, and the arts and entertainment. Available free at selected outlets, mostly hotels, bars, and restaurants that advertise in the publication, it may also be ordered by subscription. Its digest-size semiannual, *Dining Out,* is available free in the same venues. *For information and subscriptions, 404/843–9800.*

RADIO STATIONS

fm
90.1 WABE NPR news, classical and jazz

104.7 WALR Urban rhythm and blues

107.5 WAMJ Rhythm-and-blues oldies

92.1 WBTR Country

102.7 WCKS Adult contemporary

91.9 WCLK Blues and jazz, African-American issues

92.5 WEKS Country

97.1 WFOX Rock-and-Roll oldies

100.7 WGHR Alternative, urban, and electronic

105.7 WGST News and talk, simulcast on 640 AM

97.5 WHTA Urban hip hop and rap

104.1 WJZF Jazz

101.5 WKHX Country and talk

96 WKLS Rock

102.9 WMJE Adult contemporary

100.1 WNSY Oldies

94.9 WPCH Easy listening, contemporary rock

91.1 WREK Contemporary

89.8 WRFG Public radio/folk, Celtic, reggae, jazz, blues

98.5 WSB Adult contemporary

94/94.1 WSTR Contemporary hits

103.3 WVEE Urban rhythm and blues, hip hop

105.5 WYAI Country and news

95.5 WYAP Top 40

106.7 WYAY Country, talk

93 WZGC Classic rock

am
860 WAEC Christian talk

920 WAFS Contemporary Christian music and ministry

1340 WALR Gospel

1380 WAOK Gospel, talk

1330 WBTR News, talk

1290 WCHK News, talk

680 WCNN News

590 WDWD Children's programming

550 WDUN News, talk

1080 WFTD Southern Gospel and ministry

1240 WGGA Music of 1950s and '60s

1190 WGKA Classical, jazz, arts, CNN news

1010 WGUN Christian ministry and information

640 WGST News, talk

1060 WKNG Traditional country, news

1050 WPBS Gospel

610 WPLO Spanish

790 WQXI Sports talk

750 WSB News, talk

1100 WWWE Christian music, ministry, news, and weather in Spanish

1270 WYXC Country, news, sports, weather

1480 WYZE Gospel and ministries

RECYCLING

Most jurisdictions in the 10 counties do not require recycling or separation of cans and bottles from garbage and newspapers. The city of Atlanta offers optional recycling and will supply can-collecting bins to homeowners. BFI, a private trash-garbage collection company, picks up the recyclable material. For information, call the **Recycling Hotline,** manned by BFI, 404/792–1212.

In unincorporated DeKalb County, homeowners must bag lawn clippings separate from other trash in special biodegradable paper bags (sold at grocery stores, hardware stores, and other locations). Alternatively, yard clippings may be placed in a separate garbage can with the lid off. Clippings are collected in designated trucks by the county sanitation department on a schedule that varies from street to street. On the first pick-up day of the week, DeKalb sanitation will pick up aluminum cans bagged in plastic grocery bags; they'll collect newspapers packed in brown grocery bags or stacked and tied on the week's second pick-up day. For information, 404/294–2900.

Some jurisdictions have found creative ways of enticing homeowners into recycling. Believing that an ordinance would be difficult to enforce and too costly to monitor, the City of Decatur gave citizens an economic incentive to recycle. City residents must dispose of trash in 8- to 33-gallon "pay-as-you throw" bags, which cost anywhere from 30¢ to $1 depending on size. The more you throw away, the more you pay. The net effect of this program was to nearly double recycling in Decatur. Ten different retail outfits, city hall, and various stores (Kroger, Publix, Winn-Dixie) sell the bags. For information, call the **City of Decatur, Dept. of Sanitation;** 404/377–5571.

Despite these efforts, most metro-area recycling is done by private individuals and groups. You can find recycling stations at community clubs, grocery stores, and similar locations. Some counties have "Clean and Beautiful" organizations that provide recycling information. Otherwise, you can contact the sanitation department of the city, county, or jurisdiction in which you live. For-profit recycling has also arrived. **Wise Recycling Centers** (404/761–2318 or 800/851–1190) has six recycling centers around the area, with more on the drawing boards.

deposit laws

Georgia does not have a bottle deposit law.

SPORTS INFORMATION

To find out when and where you can see the pros play, contact their ticket offices; *also see* Chapter 3.

Atlanta Braves 404/577–9100.

Atlanta Falcons 404/233–8000.

Atlanta Hawks 404/827–3865.

Atlanta Thrashers 404/827–5300.

Georgia Tech 404/894–5447.

Georgia State University 404/651–3178.

TAXES & TIPPING

sales tax and beyond

Sales tax in the metropolitan Atlanta area is generally 7%, but some jurisdictions are as low as 5% (Cobb). Sales tax in Gwinnett County is 6%. Hotel-motel taxes range from 5% in Henry and Clayton counties to 14% in Fulton County. Cities may charge additional hotel and motel taxes. Ad valorem taxes likewise vary widely, with the more populous Fulton and DeKalb counties charging more than suburban jurisdictions. Property taxes are highest in the city of Atlanta and lower away from the central city core.

tipping

In restaurants, tip 15%–20% depending on the quality of the service, less if service has been inadequate. However, if service was fine but you are disappointed with the food, don't take it out on the wait staff. For large parties (more than six or eight diners) most restaurants automatically add a 20% service charge. If you have brought your own wine and paid a corkage fee, you may add the value of the wine to the total bill and pay the gratuity on that basis, or you may prefer to tip the sommelier directly.

Tip taxi drivers 15% and porters $1–$2 per bag, whether at the airport or at hotels. Valet parking attendants should receive at least $1, depending on the value of your vehicle and how closely they have watched it.

TELEVISION

network
Channel 33 CNN

Channel 5 WAGA (Fox)

Channel 46 WGNX (CBS)

Channel 63 WHSG (TBN)

Channel 30 WPBA (PBS/AT)

Channel 11 WXIA (NBC)

Channel 2 WSB (ABC)

cable channels
64 Food Network

30 MTV

27 Nickelodeon

38 Discovery Channel

39 Learning Channel

40 History Channel

42 American Movie Classics

45 Lifetime Network

49 Cartoon Network

50 Sci-fi Channel

54 Fox News Channel

53 Fox Family Channel

52 Home and Garden Network

VOTER REGISTRATION

U.S. citizens who live in Georgia may register to vote when they obtain their driver's licenses. Otherwise, register at the courthouse of the county in which you live; or, in more populous counties, check with the chief administrator's office, as the county may have auxiliary offices open elsewhere for voter registration. Voter registration lists are no longer the source from which jurors' names are drawn; now you may be called for jury duty if you have registered a motor vehicle.

WEATHER

Atlanta enjoys four distinct seasons. Winter is mercifully short, usually getting really cold only in January and Feb-

ruary. March can go out like a lion, sometimes giving us our most memorable blizzards. Most Atlantans are poorly equipped to deal with the rare snowstorm. We don't have snow tires or chains, our towns don't have snow-removal equipment, and those of us who learned to drive here have no clue about how to handle snow. So when it snows, we stay home.

Spring is undoubtedly the city's most glorious season, when azaleas and dogwoods bloom, filling the city with pinks, whites, and blazing reds along its thoroughfares. But fall is fabulous, too, rivaling spring for color. In between, summer is green with hardwoods and pines. Summer humidity percentages can match the high temperatures, making hot weather seem hotter. Usually, evenings are noticeably cooler.

Annual rainfall in Atlanta is about 48 inches, much of which (or so it seems) falls in wintertime, although August downpours are legendary. Average temperatures range between 52°F (11°C) during the day and 36°F (2°C) at night in January, and 88°F (31°C) daytime and 70°F (21°C) at night in July. Rarely do temperatures drop below 20°F (-6°C) or exceed 100°F (38°C) , and then not for very long.

Time & Temperature 770/455–7141, 770/387–1666.

Weather Channel 770/226–0000.

Weather Channel Connection 900/932–8437, 95¢ per minute from a Touch-Tone phone.

resources for challenges & crises

BABY-SITTING SERVICES

A Friend of the Family You can find a live-in nanny or a Saturday-night baby-sitter through this agency, which serves private, hotel, and convention clients. In business since 1984, the agency charges an initial $75 registration fee and an $11 referral fee per day, each time you use the service to find a sitter; this referral fee is $25 on less than 24 hours notice and $16 for Saturday evenings after 5 PM. The caregiver/sitter charge is $9–$12 per hour for a minimum of four hours. *880 Holcomb Bridge Rd., Roswell, 770/643–3000 permanent help, 770/725–2748 temporary help, www.afriend.com.*

CATERING

In addition to private caterers, many restaurants also cater events. Some of metro Atlanta's larger caterers include the following:

Chef William Neal Prepares gourmet and southern fare for weddings, theme parties, and corporate events. *690 Dalrymple Rd., Sandy Springs, 770/392–0822.*

Jimmy's Smokehouse Bar-B-Q Among the city's busiest caterers, Jimmy Lee Stokes and his wife, Thelma, whip up superior pork barbecue with sauce, potato casserole, and other side dishes. They open to the public Friday and Saturday only, so you can sample their food before hiring them as caterers. *Corner Scenic Hwy./GA 124 and Everson Rd., Snellville, 770/972–1625.*

Linda Easterlin This outfit specializes in private home catering. *3832 W. Nancy Creek Ct., North Atlanta, 404/255–5146.*

Lowcountry Barbecue Catering South Carolina–style barbecue is the focus of this firm, whose preparations include whole pig barbecue, silver queen corn cooked in the husk, low-country shrimp boils, and wild game. Get some to go at Lowcountry Barbecue Catering Express (1281 Collier Rd., Buckhead, 404/352–1121). On-site holiday cooking and corporate events are specialties. *2000 S. Pioneer Dr., Smyrna, 404/799–8049, www.lowcountrybarbecue.com.*

The Preferred Caterer This Kosher caterer specializes in weddings, bar and bat mitzvahs, and other special occasions. *2221 Peachtree Rd., Shops of Buckhead, Buckhead, 404/872–2466.*

Louisiana's Cajun Cookin' Pete Sellers and his family fire up Louisiana-style barbecue, including deep-fried whole turkeys for Thanksgiving and Christmas. Stop by their shopping-center kiosk for a taste. *5025 Winter's Chapel Rd., Doraville, 770/522–8866.*

Proof of the Pudding This long-established caterer handles both private

events and corporate affairs. *2039 Monroe Dr., Buckhead, 404/892–2359.*

Tuohy's Catering Although the company works in various culinary styles and does great desserts, Mediterranean-style fare is the specialty at private parties and corporate events. *442 Armour Cir., Midtown, 404/875–3885.*

CHILD CRISIS

ChildKind Specializes in helping children with AIDS. *828 W. Peachtree St., Suite 201, Midtown, 404/882–8313.*

Children's Healthcare of Atlanta at Egleston This institution is headquartered on the campus of Emory University and operates a number of satellite clinics in metro Atlanta. In 1999 it forged a partnership with Scottish Rite, another children's hospital. *1405 Clifton Rd., Emory University, Atlanta, 404/325–6000, 404/325–6400 24-hour nurse advice line.*

Children's Healthcare of Atlanta at Scottish Rite A premier children's hospital, now in partnership with Emory-based Egleston, this provider has satellite clinics all over the Atlanta area, in addition to its major hospital in Dunwoody. *1001 Johnson Ferry Rd., Dunwoody, 404/256–5252, 404/250–KIDS 24-hour nurse advice line.*

Hughes Spalding Children's Hospital Serving children throughout the metro area, this children's hospital is affiliated with Grady Health Systems and Grady Memorial Hospital. Grady Health Systems also has 10 neighborhood health centers around the metro Atlanta area, which focus on the needs of inner-city children. *35 Butler St., Downtown, 404/616–6600.*

CITY GOVERNMENT

Beyond the city of Atlanta itself, metropolitan Atlanta is split into jurisdictions of all sizes, each with its own ordinances and bureaucracies. The notion of merging all these fragmented governments into a single entity, much discussed in the past, gets less and less air time as the years go by. Thus, residents must identify the local authorities that control their public and legal lives and communicate directly with them. The Bell South White Business Pages list government phone numbers in the blue pages found at the end of the book. Boards of Commissioners control counties, while city councils and mayors or city managers govern municipalities large and small. Sometimes these entities overlap, as in that part of the city of Atlanta that lies in unincorporated areas of DeKalb County. When they do, it can be unclear which entity provides which services.

general information— city government

City of Alpharetta 24-hour Information Line 678/297–6015.

City of Atlanta Mayor's Office 404/330–6100.

City of Decatur City Manager's Office 404/370–4102.

City of Marietta City Manager's Office 770/794–5611.

City of Roswell Mayor's Office 770/641–3727.

general information— county government

Cherokee County Board of Commissioners 770/479–0400.

Clayton County Board of Commissioners 770/477–3208.

Cobb County Board of Commissioners 770/428–3315.

DeKalb County Board of Commissioners 404/371–2886.

Douglas County Board of Commissioners 770/920–7266.

Fayette County Administrator's Office 770/460–5730.

Fulton County Board of Commissioners, Chairman's Office 404/730–8206.

Gwinnett County Commissioners 770/822–7000.

Henry County Board of Commissioners 770/954–2400.

boards of education

Atlanta City Schools 210 Pryor St., Downtown, 404/827–8000.

Cherokee County 110 Academy St., Canton, 770/479–1871.

Clayton County 120 Smith St., Jonesboro, 770/473–2700.

Cobb County 14 Glover St., Marietta, 770/426–3300.

Decatur City Schools 320 N. McDonough St., Decatur, 404/373–8532.

DeKalb County 3770 N. Decatur Rd., Decatur, 404/297–1200.

Douglas County 9030 GA 5, Douglasville, 770/920–4000.

Fayette County 210 Stonewall Ave., Fayetteville, 770/460–3535.

Forsyth County 101 School St., Cumming, 770/887–2461.

Fulton County 786 Cleveland Ave., southwest Atlanta, 404/768–3600.

Henry County 396 Tomlinson St., McDonough, 770/957–6601.

Marietta City School 250 Howard St., Marietta, 770/422–1389.

complaints

City of Atlanta Dead Animal Removal 404/659–6757 weekdays, 404/523–0632 Sat. and holidays.

City of Atlanta Trees Down in the Street 404/817–5813 6 AM–6 PM weekdays; 404/658–6666 nights, weekends, and holidays.

DeKalb County Traffic Signal Malfunction 404/297–2947.

DeKalb Peachtree Airport Noise Abatement 770/936–5442.

Fulton County Airport–Brown Field Noise Hotline 404/699–8900.

Fulton County Rat Control 404/730–1322.

Hartsfield Atlanta International Airport Noise Abatement 404/209–0931.

COAST GUARD

Coast Guard Auxiliary Operations Center The center, at Lake Lanier, is open only during boating season, mid-May to mid-September. 770/967–2322.

CONSUMER PROTECTION

Better Business Bureau of Metropolitan Atlanta 101 Edgewood Ave., Downtown 30303, 404/688–4910.

Governor's Office of Consumer Affairs 2 *Martin Luther King Jr. Dr., Plaza Level East, Suite 356, Sloppy Floyd Bldg., Downtown, 404/651–8600 complaints or 800/869–1123.*

COUNSELING & REFERRALS

aids advice

AIDS Legal Project This is a project of the Atlanta Legal Aid Society, and is staffed Monday–Thursday only. *151 Spring St., Midtown, 404/614–3969.*

Project Open Hand Provides services chiefly within the I–285 perimeter and in Clayton, Gwinnett, and Cobb counties. The project also publishes a booklet of key contacts in the metro Atlanta and throughout the state. *176 Ottley Dr., Midtown, 404/872 6947.*

alcoholism

Alcoholics Anonymous Chapters meet throughout the metropolitan area in churches, community service centers, and social halls, among other locations. *127 Peachtree St., Suite 1310, Downtown, 404/525–3178.*

Charter Treatment Centers The centers specialize in substance abuse treatment and suicide prevention. Outpatient and inpatient care is available for adults, adolescents, children, and seniors. To ascertain which facility has the program you need, call 800/CHARTER. *Decatur: 204 Church St., 404/377–5300; Dunwoody: 2151 Peachford Rd., 770/455–3200; Hartsfield area: 5454 Yorktown Dr., off Riverdale Rd., 770/991–6044; Midtown: 811 Juniper St., 404/881–5800; Virginia-Highland: 934 Briarcliff Rd., 404/888–7860.*

Ridgeview Institute Founded in 1976, this fully accredited private non-profit hospital specializes in inpatient and outpatient chemical dependence and psychiatric treatment services for children, adolescents, and adults. *3995 S. Cobb Dr., Smyrna, 770/434–4567.*

crime victims

Crime Victims Advocacy Council The council sponsors support groups for all kinds of crime victims throughout the metro area. *3101 Paces Mill Rd., Vinings, 770/333–9254.*

drug abuse

Cocaine Anonymous; Cocaine Hotline *404/255–7787.*

DeKalb Addiction Clinic *455 Winn Way, Decatur, 404/508–6430.*

Focus on Recovery This nationwide, 24-hour hot line for drug and alcohol abuse programs is staffed by counselors and recovered addicts. *800/237–0420.*

Narcotics Anonymous Atlanta *404/672–6621 or 404/708–3219.*

Narcotics Anonymous Chamblee *404/672–7647.*

Narcotics Anonymous Douglasville *770/577–0809.*

Narcotics Anonymous Marietta *770/421–8881.*

Narcotics Anonymous North Atlanta *770/451–7373.*

Narcotics Anonymous Smyrna *770/421–8881.*

Narcotics Anonymous South Atlanta *404/362 8484.*

Northside Recovery Center *Northside Hospital, 1100 Johnson Ferry Rd., Suite 190, Dunwoody, 404/851–8961.*

West Paces Medical Center *3200 Howell Mill Rd., Buckhead, 404/350–4450.*

mental health information & referral

Some referral services operate 24 hours a day.

Cherokee County *Georgia Highlands Center, 191 Lamar Haley Pkwy., Canton, 770/704–1600.*

Clayton County *Clayton Response Center, 409A Arrowhead Blvd., Jonesboro, 770/603–8222 Mental Health Intake. Riverwoods, 11 S.W. Upper Riverdale Rd., Riverdale, 770/991–8500 or 770/996–4357.*

Cobb and Douglas Counties *Cobb/Douglas Community Services Boards Access Center 770/422–0202.*

DeKalb County *DeKalb Community Service Board, 404/892–4646.*

Forsyth County *Lakewinds (472 S. Enota Dr., Gainesville, 800/347–5827.*

Fulton County *Department of Mental Health, 404/730–1600.*

Gwinnett County *Mental Health Emergency Line, 770/985–2494.*

Henry County *Mental Health Counseling Center, 770/898–7400.*

Mental Health Association of Georgia *620 Peachtree St., Downtown, 404/875–7081.*

Ridgeview Institute *3995 S. Cobb Dr., Smyrna, 770/434–4567.*

rape victims

Clayton County *770/477–2177.*

Cobb Family Violence Center *770/428–2666.*

DeKalb County *404/377–1428.*

Grady Memorial Hospital Rape Crisis Center *404/616–4861.*

Gwinnett County *770/476–7407.*

DOCTOR & DENTIST REFERRALS

Atlanta Medical Center *303 Parkway Dr., Downtown, 404/265–4000 or 800/541–9637.*

Chiropractic Information Bureau *404/294–4900.*

Fayette Community Hospital *1255 GA 54 W, 770/541–1111.*

Georgia Dental Association *7000 Peachtree-Dunwoody Rd., Dunwoody, 770/668–9093.*

Grady Healthcare System Advice Line *80 Butler St., Downtown, 404/616–0600.*

Greater Atlanta Sports Medicine *3200 Downwood Cir., off W. Paces Ferry Rd., Buckhead, 404/350–0007.*

Henry Medical Center *1133 Eagle's Landing Pkwy., Stockbridge, 770/389–2242.*

Holistic South *4370 Georgetown Sq., Dunwoody, 770/390–0012.*

Medical Association of Atlanta/Academy of Medicine Information & Referral Service *875 W. Peachtree St., Midtown, 404/881–1714.*

North Fulton Regional Hospital *3000 Hospital Blvd., Roswell, 770/751–2600.*

Northlake Regional Medical Center *1455 Montreal Rd., Tucker, 770/270–3330.*

Northside Hospital Doctor Matching *1000 Johnson Ferry Rd., Sandy Springs, 404/851–8817.*

Piedmont Hospital Physician Referral *1968 Peachtree Rd., Buckhead, 404/541–1111.*

St. Joseph's Hospital Physician Referral *5665 Peachtree-Dunwoody Rd., Sandy Springs, 404/851–7312.*

EMERGENCIES

ambulance
Dial 911.

hospital emergency rooms
Metropolitan Atlanta is full of hospital emergency rooms and trauma centers. Here is a partial list of the ones most likely to be of use.

DeKalb Medical Center *2701 N. Decatur Rd., Decatur, 404/501–5350.*

Emory-Adventist Hospital *3949 S. Cobb Dr., Smyrna, 770/434–0710.*

Grady Health System Grady is famous for its burn care and neonatal emergency care units. *35 Butler St., Downtown, 404/616–6200.*

North Fulton Regional Hospital *3200 Hospital Blvd., Roswell, 770/751–2555.*

Northside Hospital *1000 Johnson Ferry Rd., Sandy Springs, 404/851–8937.*

Piedmont Hospital/Promina *1968 Peachtree Rd., Buckhead, 404/605–3297.*

Southern Regional Medical Center *11 Upper Riverdale Rd., Riverdale, 770/991–8188.*

Southwest Hospital & Medical Center *501 Fairburn Rd., southwest Atlanta, 404/505–5680.*

poison control center
Georgia Poison Center *404/616–9000 in metro Atlanta, 800/282–5846, 404/616–9287 TDD.*

suicide prevention
See Mental Health Information & Referral, *above.*

FAMILY PLANNING

Planned Parenthood of Georgia *Downtown:* 100 Edgewood Ave., 404/688–9300; *Cobb Center:* 617 Roswell St., Marietta, 770/424–1477; *Gwinnett Center:* 950 Indian Trail–Lilburn Rd., Lilburn, 770/451–2741.

GAY & LESBIAN CONCERNS

Atlanta Gay & Lesbian Center The center serves as a clearinghouse for information about organizations throughout the metro area. The office is open Monday–Thursday 2–9. There also is a clinic (828 W. Peachtree St.) that's open Monday–Thursday 5:30 PM–9 PM and a library (call for hours). 71 12th St., Midtown, 404/876–5372, 404/892–0661 help line.

HOUSECLEANING HELP AGENCIES

Brittany Maids This agency provides a variety of services on a schedule customized to your needs. 1687 Tullie Cir., Suite 117, northeast Atlanta, 404/633–5152.

INTERIOR DESIGNER & ARCHITECT REFERRALS

American Institute of Architects 231 Peachtree St., Downtown, 404/222–0099.

American Society of Interior Designers 351 Peachtree Hills Ave., Atlanta Decorative Arts Center, Buckhead, 404/321–3938.

American Society of Landscape Architects 605 Tuxworth Cir., Decatur, 404/633–9828.

International Interior Design Association 351 Peachtree Hills Ave., Atlanta Decorative Arts Center, Buckhead, 404/233–4432.

LANDLORD-TENANT ASSISTANCE

Georgia law favors the rights of landlords over tenants, although the courts in each jurisdiction will assist aggrieved tenants. At press time, there was no public entity that advocated for tenants or landlords.

LEGAL SERVICES

American Civil Liberties Union of Georgia Assists in issues of free speech, free press, free assembly, freedom of religion, and due process of law. 142 Mitchell St., Suite 301, Downtown, 404/523–5398.

Atlanta Legal Aid Society Offers assistance with landlord/tenant issues, consumer issues, and divorce. 151 Spring St., between Luckie and Williams Sts., Downtown, 404/524–5811.

Atlanta Legal Aid Society/Clayton, DeKalb, Gwinnett 246 Sycamore St., Suite 120, Decatur, 404/377–0701.

Cobb County Legal Aid Offers a full line of legal services for those citizens below a certain minimum income. 32 Waddell St., near the Square, Marietta, 770/528–2565.

LOST & FOUND

at airlines & airports

Hartsfield Atlanta International Airport 404/530–2100.

on other public transportation

Amtrak 800/USA–RAIL.

MARTA Five Points station, 404/848–3208.

lost credit cards

American Express/Optima 800/327–2177.

AT&T Universal Card 800/423–4343.

Citibank 800/843–0777.

Dillard's 800/643–8276.

Diners Club/Carte Blanche 800/234–6377.

Discover 800/347–2683.

JCB 800/736–8111.

MasterCard 800/307–7309.

Nordstrom 800/964–1800.

Parisian 800/832–2455.

Visa 800/847–2911.

lost traveler's checks

American Express *800/528–4800.*

Citibank *800/645–6556.*

Thomas Cook *800/223–7373.*

NEWCOMER SERVICES

Welcome Wagon *800/464–3856, www.welcomewagon.com.*

PETS

adoptions

Pets can be adopted from area humane societies with ID, proof of address, and a copy of a lease which allows animals if you rent. Fees vary by animal type, age, facility, and range generally from $30–$75.

Atlanta Humane Society *981 Howell Mill Rd., northwest Atlanta, 404/875–5331.*

Cherokee County Humane Society *131 Chattin Dr., Canton, 770/345–7270.*

Clayton County Humane Society *810 N. McDonough St., Jonesboro, 770/471–9436.*

Cobb County Humane Society *8 Fairground St., Marietta, 770/428–5678.*

DeKalb Humane Society *5287 Covington Hwy., Decatur, 770/593–1155.*

Fayette County Humane Society *770/ 487–1073; adoptions at Petsmart, 101 Pavillion Pkwy., Fayetteville, 770/719–4444.*

Forsyth County Humane Society *770/ 889–1365; adoptions at Noah's Ark, Public Shopping Center 580 Atlanta Rd., #220, Cumming, 770/889–7812; Petsmart at Northpoint Mall, 770/343-8511; Wachovia Bank at Lakeland Plaza, 404/ 851–2900.*

Gwinnett County Humane Society *770/ 798–7711; Gwinnett Animal Control Shelter, 632 High Hope Rd., Lawrenceville, 770/339–3200.*

Henry County Animal Shelter *46 Work Camp Rd., off Phillips Dr., McDonough, 770/954–2100.*

Henry County Humane Society Volunteers work out of homes, and adoptions are held at local Petsmart. *770/914–1272, McDonough GA.*

grooming

Petsmart *3221 Peachtree Rd., Buckhead, 404/266–0420; 3803 Venture Dr., Duluth, 770/813—8400; 128 Perimeter Center W, Dunwoody, 770/481–0511; 875 Lawrenceville–Suwanee Rd., Lawrenceville, 770/432–8250; 2540B Hargrove Rd., Smyrna; 2150 Paxton Dr., Snellville, 770/985–0743; 4023 LaVista Rd., Tucker, 770/414–5033).*

lost animals

Most jurisdictions require pet owners to tag their animals (cats and dogs). On the tag, you must indicate the county in which Fido or Fifi is registered and list phone numbers for the county and for the registering agency. The tag must also indicate the year of your pet's most recent rabies vaccination and the year the license was issued. Veterinarians usually dispense rabies tags when they give vaccinations, but it's up to you to register your furry loved one with the county. Registration makes it easier to recover lost pets, because if the information on file is up-do-date, the county will know how to find you.

sitting

Critter Sitters *2266 Ridgemore Rd., Buckhead, 404/377–5475.*

training

Alpha Academy of Dog Training *710 Ponce de Leon Ave., Midtown, 404/874–5224.*

American Dog Training In-home training services are the focus of this company founded in 1970. *770/664–1175.*

Comprehensive Pet Therapy Offers group obedience classes, in-home training and board training, in which your pet lives with the trainer for a designated amount of time. *7274 Roswell Ave., Atlanta 30328, 770/442–0280.*

veterinary hospitals

Cat Clinic of Cobb *2635 Sandy Plains Rd., Marietta, 770/973–6369.*

Fair Oaks Veterinarian Clinic *2142 Austell Rd., Marietta, 770/432–7155.*

For Pet's Sake Mimi Shepherd, DVM, and Ken Slossberg, DVM, only treat reptiles, birds, and other exotic mammals. *3761 N. Druid Hills Rd., Decatur, 404/ 248–8978.*

Lafayette Center Animal Hospital 105 Marquis Dr., Fayetteville, 770/460–0090.

Pharr Road Animal Hospital 553 Pharr Rd., Buckhead, 404/237–4601.

veterinarian referrals

LARGE ANIMAL VETERINARIANS
Hawk's Crest Equine Services Dr. Ron Dawe specializes in chiropractic and acupuncture for horses. 3141 Paddock Rd., Covington, 770/554–0455.

WILDLIFE
AWARE (Atlanta Wild Animal Rescue Effort) This group rescues and rehabilitates injured wildlife found in the metro area. At press time, they were planning to build a new center. 404/373–5163.

PHARMACIES OPEN 24 HOURS

CVS 5446 Peachtree Industrial Blvd., Chamblee, 770/457–4401; 2438 N. Decatur Rd., Decatur, 404/508–2456; 300 Powder Springs Rd., Marietta, 770/422–1413; 5095 Peachtree Pkwy., Norcross, 770/209–9299.

Kroger The supermarket chain has pharmacies in more than a dozen stores in the 10 counties. 404/222–2024.

POLICE

For non-emergencies, call the police department operating in your jurisdiction. Do *not* dial 911. In an emergency, dial 911.

cities
Atlanta Dial this number for information on how to reach your precinct. 675 Ponce de Leon Ave., Midtown, 404/853–3434.

Canton 221 E. Marietta St., 770/479–5316.

Chamblee 3518 Broad St., 770/986–5005.

Cumming 301 Old Buford Rd., 770/781–2000.

Decatur 420 W. Trinity Pl., 404/377–7911.

Douglasville 6730 W. Church St., 770/920–3010.

East Point 2727 E. Point St., 404/761–2177.

Fayetteville 105 Johnson Ave., 770/461–4357.

Jonesboro 1715 Main St., 770/478–7407.

Lawrenceville 405 S. Clayton St., 404/963–2443.

Marietta 150 Haynes St., 770/794–5300.

McDonough 43 Lawrenceville St., 770/957–1218.

Roswell 39 Hill St., 770/640–4100.

Stockbridge 131 Burke St., 770/389–7850.

Woodstock 400 E. Main St., 770/479–3117.

counties
Cherokee Sheriff's Office: 90 North St., Canton, 770/479–3117.

Clayton 7346 N. McDonough St., Jonesboro, 770/477–3747.

Cobb Police: 140 N. Marietta Pkwy., Marietta, 770/499–3911; Sheriff's Office: 185 Roswell St., Marietta, 770/499–4600.

DeKalb Center Precinct: 3630 Camp Cir., Decatur, 404/294–2643; East Precinct: 2484 Bruce St., Lithonia, 770/482–0300; North Precinct: 4453 Ashford-Dunwoody Rd., Perimeter Mall, Dunwoody, 404/294–2375; South Precinct: 1616 Candler Rd., Decatur, 404/286–7911; Sheriff's Office: 4415 Memorial Dr., Decatur, 404/298–8000.

Douglas Sheriff's Department: 6840 W. Church St., 770/942–2121.

Fayette Sheriff's Department: 155 Johnson Ave., Fayetteville, 770/461–6353.

Forsyth Sheriff's Department: 202 Old Buford Rd., Cumming, 770/781–2222.

Fulton Central Precinct: 130 Peachtree St., Downtown, 404/730–5700; Northside Precinct: 7741 Roswell Rd., North Annex, Sandy Springs, 770/551–7600; Southside Precinct: 5600 Stonewall Tell Rd., South Annex, College Park, 770/306–3005; Southwest Precinct: 4121 Cascade Rd., Southwest, 404/505–5780; Sheriff's Office: 185 Central Ave., Northeast 404/730–5100.

Gwinnett Police: 770 High Hope Rd., Lawrenceville, 770/513–5100; Sheriff's Office: 2900 University Pkwy., Lawrenceville, 770/822–3100.

Henry 100-Henry Pkwy., McDonough, 770/754–2900.

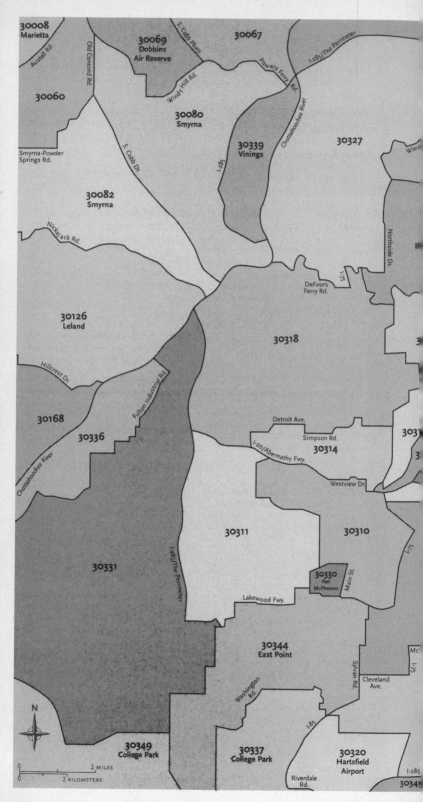

30008
Marietta

Austell Rd.

Old Concord Rd.

30069
Dobbins
Air Reserve

S. Cobb Pkwy.

Windy Hill Rd.

30067

I-285/The Perimeter

Powers Ferry Rd.

30060

30080
Smyrna

I-285

30339
Vinings

Chattahoochee River

30327

Wieu

Smyrna-Powder
Springs Rd.

S. Cobb Dr.

30082
Smyrna

Nickajack Rd.

Northside Dr.

B

DeFoors
Ferry Rd.

I-75

30126
Leland

30318

Hillcrest Dr.

Fulton Industrial Rd.

Detroit Ave.

Simpson Rd.

3

30168

Chattahoochee River

30336

I-20/Abernathy Fwy.

30314

3031

3

Westview Dr.

30311

30310

I-75

I-285/The Perimeter

30330
Fort
McPherson

Main St.

30331

Lakewood Fwy.

30344
East Point

Washington Rd.

Sylvan Rd.

Cleveland
Ave.

I-75

Mc

N

30349
College Park

30337
College Park

I-85

30320
Hartsfield
Airport

I-285

Riverdale
Rd.

3034

0   2 MILES
0   2 KILOMETERS

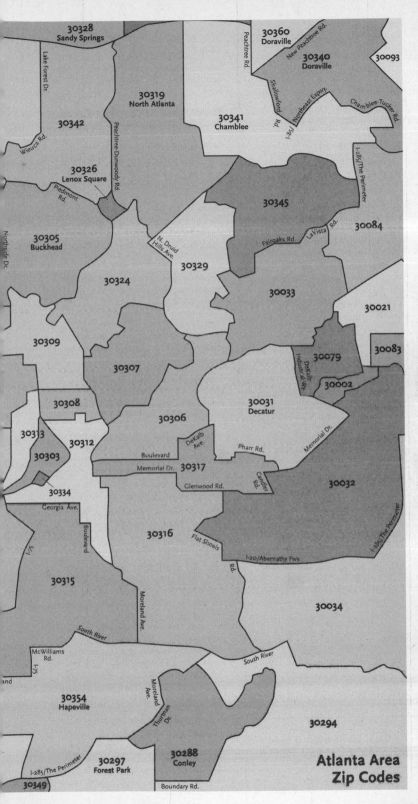

Atlanta Area
Zip Codes

291

POSTAL SERVICES

U.S. Postal Service Take I–75 to Exit 82 or I–285 to Exit I–75 N (Exit 82) to reach this facility, which is open 24 hours 7 days a week, including most holidays. *3900 Crown Rd., Hapeville, 404/765–7518, or 200/275–8777.*

federal express

To find the location closest to you or to schedule pick-ups, call 800/463–3339.

City of Atlanta *3600 Zip Industrial Blvd., 229 Peachtree St., Downtown; 100 Peachtree St., Downtown; 340 Peachtree Rd., Midtown; 1715 Howell Mill Rd.; 49 W. Paces Ferry Rd., Buckhead; 425 Fulton Industrial Blvd. West; 2441 Cheshire Bridge Rd., North Druid Hills; 1201 W. Peachtree St., Midtown; 1255 Executive Park Dr. North Druid Hills; 100 Galleria Pkwy. northwest; 710 Morgan Falls Rd. Sandy Springs.*

Cobb County *1890 N. Cobb Pkwy., Kennesaw; 2049 Franklin Way, Marietta; 3000 Windy Hill Rd., Marietta; 4880 Lower Roswell Rd., Marietta.*

DeKalb County *401 Windsor St., Downtown; 1117 Perimeter Center W, Dunwoody; 5901 Peachtree-Dunwoody Rd., Dunwoody.*

Fayette County *100 N. Peachtree Pkwy., Peachtree City.*

Fulton County *1000 Abernathy Rd., Sandy Springs; 5948 Roswell Rd., Sandy Springs.*

ups

For pick-ups, call 800/PICKUPS. Service centers, which do not have published phone numbers, are generally open weekdays 8:30 AM–7 PM unless otherwise noted.

City of Atlanta *1240 Toffee Terrace, near Hartsfield Atlanta International Airport, open from 4 PM only; Air Service Center, 231 Peachtree St., C-11, Downtown.*

Clayton County *255 Southfield Ct., Forest Park.*

DeKalb County *3930 Pleasantdale Rd., Doraville, open until 8 PM.*

Fulton County *1300 Old Ellis Rd., off Mansell Rd., Roswell; 270 Marvin Miller Dr.*

SENIOR CITIZEN SERVICES

American Association of Retired Persons *999 Peachtree St., Midtown, 404/888–0077.*

Clayton County Aging Programs *877 Battle Creek Rd., Jonesboro, 770/603–4050.*

Cobb Senior Center *1885 Smyrna–Roswell Rd., Smyrna, 770/438–2988.*

Fulton County Council on Aging *236 Forsyth St., Downtown, 404/523–5027.*

Meals on Wheels *1615 Peachtree St., Midtown, 404/873–1345, ext. 26; 1705 Commerce Dr., Midtown, 404/352–9303; 202 Nelson Ferry Rd., Decatur, 404/370–4081.*

Senior Citizen Services of Metropolitan Atlanta *1705 Commerce Dr., Midtown, 404/351–3888.*

Soapstone Center for the Arts Painting, line dancing, and tai chi for senior citizens. *1 S. DeKalb Center, Decatur, 404/241–2453.*

Southeast Arts Center Art classes for senior citizens. *John C. Birdine Neighborhood Center, 215 Lakewood Way, southeast Atlanta, 404/658–6036.*

YMCAs (*see* Swimming *in* Chapter 3) in the metro area offer many special classes for senior citizens, including arthritis therapy classes (chiefly aquatic) and walking clubs. Centennial Place Family YMCA focuses on art.

elder sitting services

A Friend of the Family You can hire temporary and permanent in-home eldercare from this agency. In business since 1984, the agency charges an initial $75 registration fee and an $11 referral fee per day, each time you use the service to find a sitter; this referral fee is $25 on less than 24 hour notice and $16 for Saturday evenings after 5pm. The caregiver/sitter charge is $9–$12 per hour for a minimum of four hours. *880 Holcomb Bridge Rd., Roswell, 770/643–3000 permanent help, 770/725–2748 temporary help.*

Kadan Corporation The firm specializes exclusively in sitting services for older clients with non-medical needs. *2494 Jett Ferry Rd., Suite 201, Dunwoody Club Center, Dunwoody, 770/396–8997.*

SERVICES FOR PEOPLE WITH DISABILITIES

Center for the Visually Impaired Offers in and out-patient services including braille instruction, orientation and mobility, activity and daily living and job placement. *763 Peachtree St., Downtown, 404/875–9011.*

Georgia Interpreting Services Network Provides interpreting services for the deaf in almost any kind of situation for which an interpreter may be needed. *44 Broad St., Suite 503, Downtown, 404/521–9100.*

Shepherd Spinal Center Offers rehabilitation and physical therapy for spinal cord and brain injury patients. By physician referral only. *2020 Peachtree Rd., Buckhead, 404/352–2020.*

TELEVISION–CABLE COMPANIES

Numerous cable companies deliver service in the 10 counties. The identity of your provider will depend on where you live.

BellSouth Service for all of the metropolitan Atlanta area. *770/360–4999.*

InterMedia Serves the south metro area, including south Fulton County, south Atlanta, Peachtree City, and Fayetteville. *482 GA 74 N, Peachtree City, 770/487–5011.*

MediaOne Serves the north metro area and parts of south metro. Customer Service Centers are located at: 2841 Greenbriar Pkwy., Greenbriar Mall, southwest Atlanta (serves the City of Atlanta); 6435 Tara Blvd., Suite 22, Jonesboro (serves Clayton County); 270 Cobb Pkwy., Suite A-5, Marietta Trade Center, Marietta (serves Cobb County); 1824 N.E. Expressway, Atlanta (serves DeKalb County); 5979 Fairburn Rd., Douglas Village Shopping Center, Douglasville (serves Douglas County); 107 S. Glynn St., Fayetteville (Fayette and Clayton Counties); 324 Maxwell Rd., Alpharetta (Fulton County); 1009 Oak Rd., off Five Forks Trickum Rd. at Killian Hill Rd., Lilburn (serves Gwinnett County). *770/559–2000.*

Time Warner Cable Serves Cobb and south Cherokee counties. *770/926–0334.*

UTILITIES

gas & electric

Deregulation of gas services means that residents for all of Atlanta must choose their supplier from among approximately 18 natural gas marketers. If you don't select one, a gas marketer will be chosen for you. Some problems have arisen from this system: The Georgia Public Service Commission is currently investigating the practice of "slamming," in which your gas company is changed without your consent. To obtain a list of certified marketers, call **Atlanta Gas Light Co.** *(770/994–1946).*

Atlanta Gas Light Co. Emergency Service *770/907–4231.*

Austell Natural Gas Serves west and south Cobb County. *2838 Joe Jerkins Blvd., Marietta, 770/948–1841.*

Fairburn Electric Serves City of Fairburn. *56 Malone St., City Hall, Fairburn, 770/964–2244.*

Georgia Power Co. Electric services for state of Georgia and the whole Atlanta Area. *888/660–5890 24-hour customer service, 800/870–3942 in Spanish.*

Georgia Power Co. Lights Out *888/660—5890; 800/870–3942 in Spanish.*

Marietta Power Supplies power within the city limits of Marietta only. *675 N. Marietta Pkwy., Marietta, 770/794–5150.*

Oglethorpe Power Produces electricity and supplies to electricity companies serving west and south Cobb County and part of Fayette County. *2100 Exchange Pl., Tucker, 770/270–1865.*

Palmetto Provides electricity services for only this small south Fulton County town. *509 Toombs St., City Hall, 770/463–3377.*

telephone

BellSouth Provides local and regional service. *404/780–2355 residential service, 404/780–2800 business service.*

Bell South Mobility Provides cellular phone services. *404/847–3600.*

trash & garbage pick-up

Most metropolitan jurisdictions provide waste removal services, which you pay for when you pay your water bill. Some jurisdictions, however, require you to contract with a private service.

All South Robertson Serves Henry County. *500 Industrial Blvd., McDonough, 678/432–1670.*

BFI Waste Systems Serves north Fulton and Cobb counties. *3045 Bankhead Hwy., Northwest Atlanta, 404/792–2660.*

BFI Waste Systems Serves Gwinnett County. *75 Curtis Rd., Lawrenceville, 770/339–9393.*

water

Water, sanitation, and sewer services in the 10 counties are often provided by small municipalities as well as larger municipalities and counties.

Alpharetta Also serves north Fulton County. *141 Pryor St., 404/730–6830.*

Atlanta Water Department Also serves communities, such as Sandy Springs, in unincorporated Fulton County. *68 Mitchell St., Downtown, 404/658–6500.*

Austell Water Department *2716 Broad St., City Hall, Front Desk, 770/944–4300.*

Ball Ground *301 Gilmer Ferry Rd., Ball Ground City Hall, 770/735–2123.*

Canton *687 Marietta Hwy., City Hall, 770/704–1500.*

Cherokee County Water Authority *391 W. Main St., Canton, 770/479–1813.*

Clayton County Water Authority *1600 Battle Creek Rd., Morrow, 770/951–2130.*

Cobb Water Systems *660 S. Cobb Dr., Marietta, 770/423–1000.*

Cumming Water Department *301 Old Buford Rd., City Hall, 770/781–2020.*

DeKalb County Water & Sewer Customer Service *1300 Commerce Annex, Decatur, 404/378–4475.*

Douglasville Water & Sewer Authority Also serves Douglas County. *8763 Hospital Dr., Douglasville, 770/949–7617.*

East Point Water Department *2777 East Point St., City Hall, 404/765–1008.*

Fairburn Water & Sewer *56 Malone St., City Hall, 770/964–2244.*

Fayette County *245 McDonough Rd., Fayetteville, 770/461–1146.*

Forsyth County *110 E. Main St., Cumming, 770/781–2160.*

Fulton County, South *55 Trinity Ave., Government Center, Downtown, 770/306–3133.*

Gwinnett County *75 Langley Dr., Gwinnett Justice Administration Center, Lawrenceville, 770/822–7171.*

Hampton *4 McDonough St., City Hall, 770/946–4306.*

Henry County Water & Sewer Authority *533 Hampton Rd., McDonough, 770/957–6659.*

Kennesaw (City of) Water Department *2529 J.O. Stephenson Ave., Kennesaw, 770/424–8274.*

Lawrenceville *18 S. Clayton St., Lawrenceville Municipal Bldg., 770/963–2414.*

Marietta Water & Sewer *627B N. Marietta Pkwy., Marietta, 770/794–5230.*

McDonough *88 Keys Ferry St., City Hall, 770/957–3915.*

Palmetto *509 Toombs St., City Hall, 770/463–3377.*

Riverdale *6690 Church St., City Hall, 770/997–8989.*

Roswell *38 Hill St., Suite 130, City Hall, 770/641–3754, 770/641–3846, or 770/641–3759.*

Smyrna *2800 King St., City Hall, 770/319–5338.*

Stockbridge Water Department *4545 N. Henry Blvd., Stockbridge, 770/389–7901.*

Woodstock *103 Arnold Mill Rd., City Hall, 770/592–6006.*

VOLUNTEERING

how to

United Way This resource center is open 24 hrs and provides information for volunteer opportunities, such as work in shelters, community clinics, public schools, and senior citizen centers throughout the Atlanta metropolitan area. *100 Edgewood Ave. NE, Downtown, 404/614–1000.*

organizations

Big Brothers Big Sisters of Metropolitan Atlanta Volunteer opportunities include one-on-one mentoring for children ages 6-12 from single-parent households and one-on-one mentoring for specific groups of at-risk teenagers. *100 Edgewood Ave. NE, Suite 710, Downtown, 404/527-7600.*

Friends of the Atlanta Opera Supplies office and production assistance throughout the season. *728 W. Peachtree St., Midtown, 404/881-8801.*

Friends of Zoo Atlanta Offers zoo membership and "Adopt an Animal" programs. *800A Cherokee Ave., Grant Park, 404/624-WILD.*

Habitat for Humanity Atlanta Builds homes for low income families. *1125 Seabord Ave., Reynoldstown, 404/223-5180.*

Hands on Atlanta After participating in a short orientation meeting, residents can become members of this organization and receive a monthly newsletter profiling 250 volunteer opportunities. *1605 Peachtree St., Midtown, 404/872-2252.*

Project Open Hand Meals on Wheels for people with AIDS. Volunteers help cook, package, and deliver meals daily. *176 Ottley Dr., near Briarcliff and Johnson Rds., northeast Atlanta, 404/872-6947.*

ZONING & PLANNING

Atlanta Department of Planning, Development and Neighborhood Conservation *55 Trinity Ave., Government Center, Downtown, 404/330-6070, 404/330-6175 zoning enforcement.*

Cherokee County *130 E. Main St., Suite 202, Canton, 770/479-0504.*

Clayton County Community Development *7994 N. McDonough St., Jonesboro, 770/477-3678.*

Cobb County Community Development *191 Lawrence St., Marietta; 770/528-2199 planning, 770/528-2035 zoning.*

Cumming Planning & Zoning *225 Castleberry Rd., 770/781-2024.*

Decatur *509 N. McDonough St., City Hall, 404/370-4104.*

DeKalb County *1300 Commerce Dr., Suite 400, Decatur, 404/371-2155.*

Douglas County *8700 Hospital Dr., 770/920-7241.*

Fayette County *140 W. Stonewall Ave., Administrative Complex, Fayetteville, 770/460-5730.*

Fayetteville *240 Glenn St. S, City Hall, 770/461-6029.*

Forest Park Planning, Building & Zoning *785 Forest Pkwy., Forest Park, 404/608-2300.*

Forsyth County Planning & Development *100 E. Main St., Suite 100, Administration Bldg., Cumming, 770/781-2115.*

Fulton County Planning & Zoning *141 Pryor St., Suite 2085, Downtown, 404/730-8094 planning, 404/730-7814 zoning.*

Gwinnett County Planning & Development Department *75 Langley Dr., Gwinnett Justice Administration Center, Lawrenceville, 770/822-7500.*

Henry County Planning & Development *100 Windy Hill Rd., Suite C, McDonough, 770/954-2457.*

Marietta Planning & Zoning Department *205 Lawrence St., City Hall, 770/794-5440.*

McDonough Planning & Zoning *88 Keys Ferry St., City Hall, 770/957-3915.*

Peachtree City *101 Willowbend Dr., 770/487-7657.*

learning

acting school

Alliance Theatre Acting Program *1280 Peachtree St., Woodruff Arts Center, Midtown, 404/733-4700.*

basketball

Cherokee Outdoor YMCA *201 E. Bells Ferry Rd., Woodstock, 770/591-8545.*

canoeing

Georgia Canoeing Association *Box 7023, Atlanta 30357, 770/421-9729.*

cheerleading

American Cheerleading Academy 1440 Lucile Ave., Marietta, 770/795–9432.

Cherokee Outdoor YMCA 201 E. Bells Ferry Rd., Woodstock, 770/591–8545.

Gym Elite 5903 Peachtree Industrial Blvd., Norcross, 770/448–1586.

cpr and first aid certification

AMERICAN RED CROSS
DeKalb/Rockdale Service Center 3486 Covington Hwy., Decatur, 404/296–0505.

Fulton Service Center 2581 Piedmont Rd., Lindbergh Plaza, Buckhead, 404/262–7010.

Gwinnett Service Center 550 Hi Hope Rd., off GA 316, Lawrenceville, 770/963–9208.

Northwest Metro Service Center 324 Victory Dr., Marietta, 770/428–2695.

South Metro Service Center 1115 Mount Zion Rd., Suite H, Morrow, 770/961–2552.

driving

Taggart's Driving School 3566 Lawrenceville Hwy., Tucker, 770/934–2144.

Clarkston Driving Academy 4765 Memorial Drive, Decatur, 404/294–9007).

Cool Driving 2453 Coronet Way N.W., Atlanta, 404/327—8760.

equestrian

Reece Center for Handicapped Horsemanship Since 1984 the center has used therapeutic riding to develop muscle tone and physical coordination in children with mental and physical disabilities, including the visually impaired. 4145 Panthersville Rd., Ellenwood, 404/241–4263.

Rock Chapel Outdoor YMCA This Y gives lessons in summer only. 1185 Rock Chapel Rd., Lithonia, 770/484–9622.

Vogt Riding Academy Come here for basic riding lessons, dressage, and some jumping. 1084 Houston Mill Rd., Decatur, 404/321–9506.

YMCA Equestrian Center Programs offered include group lessons, horseback riding day camps, and pony parties for children. 201 E. Bells Ferry Rd., Woodstock, 770/591–5820 or 770/591–8545 for the stables.

flying instruction

American Air Flight Training 2000 Airport Rd., Suite 109, DeKalb Peachtree Airport, Chamblee, 770/455–4203.

Quality Aviation 1951 Airport Rd., Suite 205, DeKalb Peachtree Airport, Chamblee, 770/457–6215.

gardening

Atlanta Botanical Garden Budding green thumbs are nurtured at special Saturday-morning kids' programs in the Children's Garden. 1345 Piedmont Ave., Ansley Park, 404/876–5859.

gymnastics

Gym Elite Starting at age two, your little gymnasts can learn to strut their stuff here. Cheerleading instruction is also available. 5903 Peachtree Industrial Blvd., Norcross, 770/448–1586.

Atlanta School Of Gymnastics This school offers private lessons, group lessons, and team competition to children over three. 3345 Montreal St., Tucker, 770/938–1212.

Buckhead Gymnastics Center Parent child classes offered for children over two. Group and private lessons and team opportunities for older children. 2335 Adams Drive N.W., Buckhead, 404/367–4414.

scuba

YMCA Scuba Program Headquarters This is a resource clearinghouse for finding YMCA scuba instructors throughout the metro area and the national certification headquarters. 5825 Live Oak Pkwy., Suite 2A, Norcross, 770/662–5172.

swimming

Carl Sanders YMCA 1160 Moores Mill Rd., Buckhead, 404/350–9292.

Cherokee Outdoor YMCA Learn to swim in Lake Allatoona (in the summer only). 201 E. Bells Ferry Rd., Woodstock, 770/591–8545.

Cowart Ashford-Dunwoody YMCA 3692 Ashford-Dunwoody Rd., Dunwoody, 770/451–9622.

Decatur–DeKalb YMCA 1100 Clairemont Ave., Decatur, 404/377–0241.

Dynamo Parents' Club *5075 Abbott's Bridge Rd., Suite 1000, Alpharetta, 770/772–6789.*

Dynamo Swim Club *3119 Shallowford Rd., Chamblee, 770/451–3272.*

Ed Isakson/Alpharetta YMCA *3655 Preston Ridge Rd., Alpharetta, 770/664–1220.*

Fayette Family YMCA Summer only. *215 Huiet Rd., Fayetteville, 770/487–2850.*

Fowler Branch YMCA *5600 W. Jones Bridge Rd., Norcross, 770/246–9622.*

M. Tull Branch YMCA *2985 Sugarloaf Pkwy., Lawrenceville, 770/963–1313.*

South DeKalb YMCA *2565 Snapfinger Rd., 770/987–3500.*

Southeast Branch YMCA *1765 Memorial Dr., southeast Atlanta, 404/373–6561.*

Southwest Branch YMCA *2220 Camphellton Rd., Atlanta, 404/753–4169.*

YMCA of Cobb County *1055 E. Piedmont Rd., Marietta, 770/977–5991.*

YMCA of Metro Atlanta The administrative offices here can provide information on the Y's swimming programs. *100 Edgewood Ave., Downtown, 404/588–9622.*

ADULT EDUCATION IN PUBLIC & PRIVATE SCHOOLS

Clayton State College & University Offers day and evening classes in all areas of continuing education from computers, to health care to lawn care. *5900 N. Lee St., Morrow, 770/961–3556.*

Evening at Emory A wide range of courses, from beginning language to home renovation and wine appreciation, are offered. *1560 Clairemont Rd., Emory University, Decatur, 404/727–6000.*

Georgia State University Offers a variety of continuing education classes. *Urban Life Bldg., corner of Piedmont Ave. and Decatur St., University Plaza, Downtown, 404/651–3456).*

Oglethorpe University, University College Offers evening classes in accounting, business administration, humanities, psychology, social sciences, and other departments. *4484 Peachtree Rd., Brookhaven, 404/364–8383.*

Senior University Classes for senior citizens taught by retired professors covering a range of topics including Mozart's Operas, Dante's Divine Comedy, investing, and contemporary Georgian politics. *1560 Clairemont Rd., Evening at Emory, Emory University, Decatur, 404/727–6000.*

Senior University, Mercer University Retired professors teach courses for senior citizens, covering subjects as diverse as the Civil War, health, the Supreme Court, Central Asia, and Neil Simon. *3001 Mercer University Dr., Chamblee, 770/986–3109.*

ART & PHOTOGRAPHY SCHOOLS

American College Offers four-year degrees in fashion, graphic and interior design. *3330 Peachtree Rd., Buckhead, 404/231–9000.*

Art Institute of Atlanta Offers four-year and continuing education programs in all artistic fields. *6600 Peachtree-Dunwoody Rd., Dunwoody, 770/394–8300 or 800/275–4242.*

A R T Station Community arts center which offers basic and intermediate level art classes and runs a community theater program. *5384 Manor Dr., Stone Mountain, 770/469–1105.*

Atlanta College of Art Offers four-year degree and continuing education programs in a variety of artistic pursuits. *1280 Peachtree St., Woodruff Arts Center, Midtown, 404/733–5001.*

Callanwolde Fine Arts Center Offers community classes in painting, music, theater and the meditative arts. *980 Briarcliff Rd., Decatur, 404/872–5338.*

Chastain Arts Center Offers wide variety of art classes including pottery, painting, stained glass, and printmaking for all ages over three. *135 W. Wieuca Rd., Chastain Park, Buckhead, 404/252–2927.*

Creative Circus Here you can receive professional training in advertising, graphic design, photography, and illustration. *812 Lambert Dr., Buckhead, 404/607–8880.*

Georgia State University School of Art and Design Four-year degree programs; non-degree related art classes available only through the continuing education department of Georgia State. *10 Peachtree Center Ave., Art & Humanities Bldg., Room 117, Downtown, 404/651–2257.*

Oglethorpe University Offers a dual-degree with the Atlanta College of Art, and a B.A. in Fine Arts, but no community/non-degree related art classes. *4484 Peachtree Rd., Brookhaven, 404/261–1441.*

Portfolio Center The center offers professional training in photography, graphic design, illustration, and advertising. *125 Bennett St., off Peachtree St., Buckhead, 404/351–5055.*

Soapstone Center for the Arts Senior citizens can take painting lessons here. *1 S. DeKalb Center, Decatur, 404/241–2453.*

Southeast Arts Center Classes in jewelry, pottery, printmaking and black and white photography. Weekend programs for youth. *215 Lakewood Way, John C. Birdine Neighborhood Center, southeast Atlanta, 404/658–6036.*

Spruill Center for the Arts Community arts classes in a variety of areas. *5339 Chamblee-Dunwoody Rd., Dunwoody, 770/394–3447.*

CHILDREN'S EDUCATION PROGRAMS

Centennial Place Family YMCA Offers after-school programs and various drama, sports, and other classes for children. *555 Luckie St., Downtown, 404/724–9622.*

Covington YMCA Offers swimming lessons and other classes, and runs after school programs at some area elementary schools. *2140 Newton Dr., Covington, 770/787–3908.*

Kid Connection The staff here provides transportation between school and after-school programs and supervises field trips and similar activities for private schools. *3260 U.S. 78, Snellville, 770/978–2849.*

Prime Time at Waller Park This program for high-risk, low-income children ages 5–12 runs 2:30–6:30 PM on school days. It features snacks, homework time, and crafts activities. *250 Oak St., Roswell, 770/642–4963; contact Franklin Hamilton, 770/664–1220, ext. 128.*

South DeKalb YMCA Childcare Academy An after school program with snacks and homework time. *2575A Snapfinger Rd., Decatur, 770/987–4666.*

Southeast YMCA Family Place All day daycare for pre-school age children. *3482 Flat Shoals Rd., Decatur, 404/243–9662).*

Southwest YMCA Offers after school programs like karate, swimming, and gymnastic lessons, along with snacks and homework help. *22 Campbellton Rd., off Lakewood Fwy., southwest Atlanta, 404/753–4169.*

COMMUNITY COLLEGES

GEORGIA PERIMETER COLLEGE

Clarkston Campus *550 N. Indian Creek Dr., Clarkston, 404/299–4000.*

Decatur Campus *3251 Panthersville Rd., Decatur, 404/244–5090.*

Dunwoody Campus *2101 Womack Rd., Dunwoody, 770/551–3000.*

Lawrenceville Campus *1201 Atkinson Rd., Lawrenceville, 770/995–2191.*

Rockdale Campus *1115 West Ave., Conyers, 770/785–6970.*

COMPUTER TRAINING

Computer Learning Centers Classes in software engineering, computer programming, and systems analysis. *2359 Windy Hill Rd., Marietta, 770/226–0056; 5678 Jimmy Carter Blvd., Norcross, 678/966–9411.*

Georgia State University Department of Computer Information Systems Degree programs and evening classes in programming, system design and analysis, and related computer science topics. *35 Broad St., Downtown, 404/651–3880.*

Micro Center Computer Education Desktop design, computer programming, and Web site design. *1221 Powers Ferry Rd., Marietta, 800/562–0058.*

COOKING SCHOOLS

Culinary Institute of Atlanta Housed in the Art Institute, degree programs are offered in culinary arts, and has weekend fun workshops for casual cooks. *6600 Peachtree-Dunwoody Rd., Dunwoody, 770/394–8300 or 800/275–4242.*

DANCE

ballet

Atlanta Ballet Centre for Dance Education *1400 W. Peachtree St., Midtown, 404/873–5811; 4279 Roswell Rd., Chastain Square, Buckhead, 404/303–1501.*

Rotaru International Ballet School *6000 Peachtree Industrial Blvd., Norcross, 770/662–0993.*

Ruth Mitchell Dance Studio *81 Church St., Marietta, 770/426–0007.*

Soapstone Center for the Arts Offers ballet instruction for children. *1 S. DeKalb Center, Decatur, 404/241–2453.*

ballroom & latin

Arthur Murray Dance Centers *7256 Roswell Rd., Sandy Springs, 770/396–9444; 2468 Windy Hill Rd., Marietta, 770/951–8811.*

Atlanta Ballroom Dance Centre *120 Northwood Dr., Suite B8, West Terrace Level, Sandy Springs, 404/847–0821.*

Atlanta Dance World *2200 Northlake Pkwy., Suite 270, Tucker, 770/604–9900.*

Dance City Ballroom *2581 Piedmont Rd., Lindbergh Plaza, Buckhead, 404/266–0166.*

Fred Astaire Dance Studios *1170 La Vista Rd., at Cheshire Bridge Rd., Midtown, 404/321–0306.*

Locurto's Ballroom DanceSport Studio *2991D N. Druid Hills Rd., Toco Hills Shopping Center, North Druid Hills, 404/636–7433.*

Tango/Atlanta *133 Sycamore St., Decatur, 404/378–6985.*

folk & social

Atlanta Dance Hotline This number is a general resource for all kinds of recreational and folk dancing, from Cajun to contra. *404/634–2585.*

Chattahoochee Country Dance Association Offers information about contra dance. *1700 Piedmont Ave., Morningside Baptist Church, Morningside, 404/634–2585.*

Soapstone Center for the Arts Senior citizens can participate in in-line dancing here. *1 S. DeKalb Center, Decatur, 404/241–2453.*

Metro Atlanta Square Dance Provides information on addresses and schedules of dozens of Atlanta area and Georgia square dancing clubs. *www.geocities.com/~jgraser.*

LANGUAGE SCHOOLS

esl

Georgia State University The university offers certification in teaching English as a second language, as well as a variety of languages, and traditional academic language programs and classes for non-matriculated auditing students. *Department of ESL and Applied Linguistics, University Plaza, Downtown, 404/651–2265, 404/651–3650 ESL program.*

french

Alliance Française Language instruction classes as well as literature and cultural classes are offered. *1360 Peachtree St., Midtown, 404/875–1211.*

german

Friends of Goethe All types of language and cultural classes are offered. *1197 Peachtree St., Colony Square, Midtown, 404/724–9390.*

japanese

Japan America Society In addition to general language courses, the society offers classes in business Japanese and Japanese culture. *2222 Harris Tower, 233 Peachtree St., Peachtree Center, Downtown, 404/524–7399.*

other

Inlingua Offers private lessons and some group classes in all European languages and many Asian languages including Japanese and Vietnamese. *3355 Lenox Rd., Lenox Center, Buckhead, 404/266—2661.*

LIBRARIES

Auburn Avenue Research Library on African-American Culture and History This is a noncirculating library. *101 Auburn Ave., Downtown, 404/730–4001.*

Cobb County Main Library *266 Roswell St., Marietta, 770/528–2318.*

DeKalb County Main Library *215 Sycamore St., Decatur, 404/370–3070.*

Douglas County *6810 Selman Dr., Douglasville, 770/920–7125; 7100 Junior High Dr., Lithia Springs, 770/944–5931.*

Fayette County *Heritage Park Way, Fayetteville, 770/461–8841.*

Forsyth County *585 Dahlonega Hwy., Cumming, 770/781–9840.*

Gwinnett County Library Headquarters *1001 U.S. 29, Lawrenceville, 770/822–4522.*

Fulton County Main Library *1 Margaret Mitchell Sq., Downtown, 404/730–1700.*

Georgia State Archives *330 Capitol Ave., Downtown, 404/656–2393.*

Jimmy Carter Library This noncirculating research library is part of the Carter Center complex. *1 Copenhill Ave., Poncey-Highland, 404/331–0296.*

National Archives & Records *1557 St. Joseph Ave., East Point, 404/763–7477.*

MUSIC SCHOOLS

Atlanta Music Center Children age three and up can receive Yamaha method instruction in all instruments; instrument rental is available. *5509 Chamblee-Dunwoody Rd., Dunwoody, 770/394–1727; 1205 Johnson Ferry Rd., Marietta, 440/977–0003; 4051 U.S. 78, Lilburn, 770/979–2887.*

Ken Stanton Music Private instruction in percussion, piano, strings, and wind instruments for adults and children. Instrument rental is also available. *777 Roswell St., Marietta, 770/427–2491; 627 Holcomb Bridge Rd., Roswell Village, Roswell, 770/993–8334; 1105 Parkside La., South Pointe Center, Woodstock, 770/516–0805; 1977B Scenic Hwy., Scenic Square Center, Snellville, 770/979–0736).*

Maple Street Guitars Owner George Petsch, a classical guitarist, sells electric and acoustic guitars and gives lessons in classical and rock-styles. *3199 Maple Dr., Buckhead, 404/231–5214.*

Neighborhood Music Schools, Georgia State University School of Music The program provides instruction of many instruments for all ages at numerous Atlanta locations. *Box 55169, Atlanta 30308, 404/651–1111.*

Rotaru International Ballet School Primarily a dance school, Rotaru also gives private piano lessons. *6000 Peachtree Industrial Blvd., Norcross, 770/662–0993.*

Southern Keyboards Voice, piano, guitar, and banjo lessons for children and adults. *1898 Leland Dr., Suite B., Marietta, 770/953–0938, fax 770/955–7553.*

Steinway Piano Galleries Whatever your age, you can take piano lessons here. Piano sales/rental are also available. *2140 Peachtree Rd., Brookwood Square, Brookwood, 404/351–0550 new address: 6650 Roswell Rd., Sandy Springs.*

WINE PROGRAMS

Alliance Française The delights of French wine are taught by Labe Mell. *1360 Peachtree St., Midtown, 404/875–1211.*

Anita L. Laraia's Wine School Designed for both professional and nonprofessional students, the six-week basic diploma course ($240) includes course book and wine tastings. *Box 52723, Atlanta 30355, 770/901–9433.*

Evening at Emory Wine 101 is taught in several sections by faculty associated with the *Atlanta Wine Report*. *1560 Clairemont Rd., Emory University, Decatur, 30322, 404/727–6000.*

Friends of Goethe Don Reddicks, a well-known specialist in German wines, teaches occasional courses in German wine. *1197 Peachtree St., Colony Square, Midtown, 404/724–9390.*

vacation & travel information

AIRPORTS

The only commercial airport in the 10 counties is Hartsfield Atlanta International Airport, located on I-85 on the south side (404/530–6830; Ground Transportation: 404/530–6674; Airport Parking: 404/530–6725; Lost and Found: 404/530–2100; Traffic: 404/635–6800; Weather: 404/486–1133). Metro Atlanta also has several small general aviation airports that serve corporate clients and recreational pilots.

DeKalb Peachtree Airport *2000 Airport Rd., Chamblee, 770/936–5440.*

Fulton County Airport–Brown Field *3952 Aviation Cir., Carol Heights, 404/699–4200.*

Gwinnett County Airport–Briscoe Field *770 Airport Rd., Lawrenceville, 770/822–5196.*

Peachtree City–Falcon Field *7 Falcon Dr., Peachtree City, 770/487–2225.*

McCollum Airport *1723 McCollum Pkwy., Kennesaw, 770/422–4300.*

getting to hartsfield by car

From the north side, take GA 400 to I-285; then drive east to I-85 and take it south to the airport. Airport exits are clearly marked, leaving no doubt as to when you should turn off the highway. Or you can continue east along I-285 and take exit 44 to I-85 north; the airport exit is the first one off I-85. If you live in west metro, take I-285 to I-85 north, then follow the signs to the airport exit. From the southside, take I-85 north to the airport. If you live in the east, travel west on I-20, take I-285 South, then exit 44 to I-85 North, first exit to the airport.

Once you reach Hartsfield you have several parking options, depending on the strength of your legs and the size of your wallet. The hike from the long-term uncovered parking lot ($5 per day in economy) to the terminal is fairly long. It's a bit easier to negotiate if you find an abandoned SMART luggage cart. Less strenuous is the park-and-ride located off the South Terminal, where

uncovered parking costs $6 per day ($1 per hour short-term). From here, you get to the terminals via shuttles that run every few minutes in both directions. Keep your parking stub so you know which shuttle to take back to your parking lot and space. Daily parking in a covered deck costs $12. Hourly short-term parking is available directly across from North and South terminals in covered and uncovered decks. The rate here is $1 for 1–3 hours, $2 for 3–6 hours, $24 for 6–24 hours, and $48 for subsequent days or fractions thereof.

getting to hartsfield by public transportation

Hartsfield Atlanta International Airport lies within the elbow of I-85 and I-285 in the south part of the metropolitan Atlanta area, straddling Fulton and Clayton counties. The amount of luggage you're carrying and whether you're traveling with little ones will likely determine what kind of transportation you take to reach the airport; taxis and shuttles are by far the most expensive.

BUS & TRAIN

The **Metropolitan Atlanta Rapid Trans Authority (MARTA)** provides very easy access to Hartsfield, especially if your luggage is limited; trains go directly into the airport. What's more, at $1.50, this deal cannot be beat. There is a designated luggage space on each MARTA car. The airport sits at the end of the north–south line, so if you board MARTA along the east–west line you will have to change trains at Five Points station. You can park at certain MARTA stations (Brookhaven, Doraville, Chamblee, Lenox Square, Lindbergh, Dunwoody/Medical Center, and College Park) in secured areas for $3 per day. North–south trains run from Doraville and Dunwoody to the airport every 8–10 minutes weekdays, every 15 minutes after 9:30 PM and on Saturday and Sunday. When returning to Doraville or Dunwoody, make sure to get on the destination-designated train, as not all northbound trains go as far as Doraville, and not all deviate to the Dunwoody station. A sign on the front of the train indicates its ultimate destination.

SHUTTLE

Numerous shuttle services operate between suburban points and Hartsfield Atlanta International Airport.

Atlanta Airport Shuttle Licensed by the city of Atlanta, this outfit provides door-to-door service to and from the airport. One-way fares range from $38 from College Park to $65 from Alpharetta. You can save money if you board at the shuttle's Roswell (10930 Crabapple Rd., Roswell, 770/998–1893) or Marietta (200 Interstate North Pkwy., 770/952–1601) terminal. The fare from Roswell is $20 one-way, $32 round-trip, and the fare from Marietta is $15 one-way, $25 round-trip. For door-to-door and terminal service, book your reservation at least 24 hours in advance. *359 Whitehall St., Downtown, 404/768–7600.*

Atlanta Airport Superior Shuttle On the north side, this shuttle picks up from hotels and residences within a 50-mi radius of the airport, although they may travel up to 200 mi. On the south side, only residential pick-up is available. The service requires one week's advance notice for groups and 24 hours' advance notice for individuals. A typical one-way fare is $50 from Alpharetta. *1945 Savoy Dr., Chamblee, 770/457–4794.*

Park 'N Fly From this terminal/parking lot, continuous 24-hour shuttle service runs to the airport every three to five minutes. The lot has 24-hour security; you'll pay $57 per week or $9.50 per day to park your car, but the shuttle is free. *3950 Conley St., College Park, 404/768–8582.*

Park 'N Fly Plus A shuttle leaves for the airport every three to five minutes 24 hours a day. Additional services include baggage check-in and ticketing at the Delta terminal, car wash, and auto detailing. Daily parking rates range from $9.50 (self-park) to $14.25 (covered valet parking), but the shuttle is complimentary. *2525 Camp Creek Pkwy., College Park, 404/761–6220.*

Park 'N Go Park your car in this secured lot and take the shuttle, which leaves every 3–5 minutes 24 hours a day, to Hartsfield. Parking costs $7.75 (uncovered) to $9 (covered) per day. The shuttle ride is free. *3151 Camp Creek Pkwy., East Point, 404/669–9300.*

Park 'N Ticket Uncovered parking at $9 per day is available for this shuttle service to the airport (covered parking is under construction). The shuttle leaves every 7–10 minutes, 24 hours a day and there is no extra charge for the shuttle.

3945 Conley St., College Park, 404/669–3800.

Woodstock Airport Shuttle You must reserve 24 hours in advance for pick-up from residences or offices. The one-way fare from Woodstock is $34.98; round-trip is $62.54. Prices are a little higher from Canton. *1340 Bells Ferry Rd., Marietta, 770/425–4090.*

TAXIS

Taxi service to the airport is costly. From Downtown, the cost is $18 per person; from Buckhead, the cost per person is $28. The farther out you are located, the more expensive the trip. A trip from Sandy Springs to the airport, for instance, costs about $45–$50.

hartsfield lost & found

See Lost & Found *in* Basics of City Life, *above,* for information on retrieving items lost in the airport.

CAR RENTAL

All the big national agencies have concessions at Hartsfield and other locations, but local agencies abound, often providing good rentals at cheaper rates. These may not have access to airport property per se but usually are located nearby. They typically provide pick-up and drop-off service

local agencies

All Star Rent-a-Car *1199 B Roswell Rd., Marietta, 770/429–9999.*

Atlanta Rent-a-Car *3185 Camp Creek Pkwy., East Point, 404/763–1110.*

Payless Car Rental *1931 Roosevelt Hwy., College Park, 404/788–2120.*

Rent-a-Wreck *5222 Old Dixie Rd., Forest Park, 404/363–8720.*

CURRENCY EXCHANGE

All of the currency exchange offices listed here buy and sell travelers' checks and foreign currency, though it's best to call ahead to verify availability, especially if you require special denominations or large amounts of currency. Most banks also can execute currency exchanges with several days' advance notice, sometimes as much as two weeks, depending on the size of the bank's international department.

AMERICAN EXPRESS

General information Both metro Atlanta locations can supply the usual currencies, including travelers' checks in other currencies, on a moment's notice. Exotic currencies require a few days' advance notice. 800/461–8484.

Buckhead 3384 Peachtree Rd., Lenox Plaza, 404/262–7561, weekdays 9:30–6, Sat. 10–5.

Alpharetta 7855 Northpoint Pkwy., 770/625–3900, office hours: weekdays 9–6; financial services: weekdays 10–6, Sat. all services 10–5.

THOMAS COOK

General information All branches are located in Hartsfield Atlanta International Airport. Exotic currencies must be ordered two weeks ahead of time. 800/287–7362.

Concourse E Gate 26, 404/761–6332, 7 AM–9:30 PM.

Customs Branch Downstairs from main office in Concourse E, 404/761–1406, 1:30 PM–9 PM.

EMBASSIES & CONSULATES

Argentina 245 Peachtree Center Ave., Suite 2101, Marriott Marquis Tower I, Downtown, 404/880–0805.

Belgium 235 Peachtree St., Suite 850, North Tower, Peachtree Center, Downtown, 404/659–2150.

Britain 245 Peachtree Center Ave., Suite 2700, Marriott Marquis Tower I, Downtown, 404/836–0301.

Canada 100 Colony Sq., Suite 1700, Midtown, 404/532–2000.

Chile 2876 Sequoyah Dr., Buckhead, 404/350–9030.

Colombia 5780 Peachtree-Dunwoody Rd., Suite 250, Dunwoody, 404/237–1045.

Czech Republic 2110 Powers Ferry Rd., Suite 220, Marietta, 770/859–9402.

Federal Republic of Germany 285 Peachtree Center Ave., Suite 901, Marriott Marquis Tower II, Downtown, 404/659–4760.

Greece 3340 Peachtree Rd., Suite 1670, Tower Place, Buckhead, 404/261–3313.

Iceland 20 Executive Park W, Suite 2023, North Druid Hills, 404/321–0777.

Israel 1100 Spring St., Suite 440, Selig Center, Midtown, 404/487–6500.

Italy 755 Mt. Vernon Hwy., Suite 270, Dunwoody, 404/303–0503.

Japan 100 Colony Sq., Suite 2000, Midtown, 404/892–2700.

Korea 229 Peachtree St., Suite 500, International Tower, Peachtree Center, Downtown, 404/522–1611.

Mexico 2600 Apple Valley Rd., Brookhaven, 404/266–0777.

Netherlands 2015 S. Park Pl., Ronstadt Bldg., Downtown, 770/937–7123.

Panama 229 Peachtree St. NE, International Bldg., Suite 1209, Downtown, 404/522–4114.

Sweden 600 Peachtree St., Bank of America Plaza, Suite 2400, Downtown, 404/815–2250.

Switzerland 1275 Peachtree St. NE, Suite 425, Midtown, 404/870–2000.

Thailand 3333 Riverwood Pkwy., Suite 520, Vinings, 770/988–3304.

Turkey 7155 Brandon Mill Rd., 770/913–0900.

ROUTING SERVICES FOR U.S. TRIPS

AUTO CLUB SOUTH

The local affiliate of the Automobile Association of America (AAA) is Auto Club South, which offers travel agency services and free guidebooks to members. AAA can also map out your trip with customized routing maps called TripTiks®. If you are a member, you can get a TripTik® by visiting or calling one of the club's offices or by visiting the Web site at **www.aaa.com.** Just enter your zip code, click on "Travel," and follow the prompts. There are two local AAA offices:

Norcross World Travel 5450 Peachtree Pkwy., Norcross, 770/448–7024.

Tara Travel 696 Mt. Zion Rd., Jonesboro, 770/961–8085.

SIGHTSEEING INFORMATION

Atlanta Preservation Center *156 7th St., Suite 3, Midtown, 404/876–2041, 404/ 876–2040 tour hot line.*

Gray Line of Atlanta Sightseeing Tours *65 Upper Alabama St., Underground Atlanta, Downtown, in Convention and Visitors Bureau, 404/767–0594.*

TOURIST INFORMATION

for local information

Atlanta Convention & Visitors Bureau *233 Peachtree St., Suite 2000, Downtown, 404/222–6688 or 800/847–4842; 65 Upper Alabama St., Underground Atlanta, Downtown, 404/577–2148.*

DeKalb Convention & Visitors Bureau *750 Commerce Dr., Decatur, 404/378– 2525 or 800/999–6055.*

Clayton County Convention & Visitors Bureau *104 N. Main St., Jonesboro, 770/ 478–4800 or 880/662–STAY.*

Georgia Department of Industry, Trade and Tourism *285 Peachtree Center Ave., Marriott Marquis Tower II, Suite 1000, Downtown, 404/656–3590 or 800/847– 4842.*

Marietta Welcome Center *4 Depot St., Marietta, 770/429–1115 or 800/835–0445.*

Roswell Visitors Center *617 Atlanta St., on the Square, Roswell, 770/640–3253 or 800/776–7935.*

chambers of commerce

Airport Area Chamber of Commerce *600 S. Central Ave., Suite 100, Hapeville, 404/ 209–0910.*

Cherokee County Chamber of Commerce *3605 Marietta Hwy., Canton, 770/ 345–0400.*

Cobb Chamber of Commerce *240 Interstate North Pkwy., Northwest Atlanta, 770/980–2000.*

DeKalb Chamber of Commerce *750 Commerce Dr., Suite 201, Decatur, 404/378– 8000.*

Douglas County Chamber of Commerce *2145 Slater Mill Rd., Douglasville, 770/ 942–5022.*

Fayette County Chamber of Commerce *200 Courthouse Sq., Fayetteville, 770/ 461–9983.*

Forsyth County Chamber of Commerce *110 Old Buford Rd., Suite 120, Forsyth Professional Bldg., Cumming, 770/887–6461.*

North Fulton County Chamber of Commerce *1025 Old Roswell Rd., Roswell, 770/ 993–8806.*

Gwinnett Chamber of Commerce *5110 Sugarloaf Pkwy., Lawrenceville, 770/513– 3000.*

Henry County Chamber of Commerce *1310 GA 20 W, McDonough, 770/957– 5786.*

Metro Atlanta Chamber of Commerce *235 International Blvd., Downtown, near Centennial Olympic Park, 404/880–9000.*

TRAVELER'S AID

TRAVELER'S AID SOCIETY OF METROPOLITAN ATLANTA

Hartsfield Atlanta International Airport *Near baggage claim and general airport information booth, 404/766–4511.*

Marietta *477 Henry Dr., 770/428–1883.*

Midtown *828 W. Peachtree St., 404/817– 7070.*

U.S. CUSTOMS

Port of Atlanta *4341 International Pkwy., Suite 600, Atlanta, across from Hartsfield Atlanta International Airport, 404/675– 1300.*

DIRECTORIES

shops by neighborhood

BUFORD

CANDLER PARK AND INMAN PARK

CANTON

CENTERVILLE

CHAMBLEE

index